Ms. Fright

MEDALLION EDITION • AMERICA READS

LITERATURE and LIFE

MEDALLION EDITION · AMERICA READS

PURPOSE in Literature
Edmund J. Farrell
Ruth S. Cohen
L. Jane Christensen
H. Keith Wright

LITERATURE and LIFE
Helen McDonnell
Ruth S. Cohen
Thomas Gage
Alan L. Madsen

ARRANGEMENT in Literature
Edmund J. Farrell
Ouida H. Clapp
James L. Pierce
Raymond J. Rodrigues

QUESTION and FORM in Literature
James E. Miller, Jr.
Roseann Dueñas Gonzalez
Nancy C. Millett

UNITED STATES in Literature
James E. Miller, Jr.
Carlota Cárdenas de Dwyer
Robert Hayden
Russell J. Hogan
Kerry M. Wood

ENGLAND in Literature
Helen McDonnell
Neil E. Nakadate
John Pfordresher
Thomas E. Shoemate

MEDALLION EDITION • AMERICA READS

LITERATURE and LIFE

Helen McDonnell

Ruth S. Cohen

Thomas Gage

Alan L. Madsen

Scott, Foresman and Company

Editorial Offices: Glenview, Illinois

Regional Sales Offices: Palo Alto, California •
Tucker, Georgia • Glenview, Illinois •
Oakland, New Jersey • Dallas, Texas

HELEN McDONNELL English Supervisor of the Ocean Township Junior and Senior High Schools in Oakhurst, New Jersey. Formerly teacher in Belmar and Asbury Park, New Jersey, and at Monmouth College. Formerly Chairman of the Committee on Comparative and World Literature, National Council of Teachers of English.

RUTH S. COHEN Free-lance writer and editor of books for young people. Author on the *Signal* Program, Scott, Foresman and Company. Editor-Compiler of *Craft of Detection, The Life Force, Present Imperfect, Edges of Reality,* and *The Fractured Image,* collections of shorter long fiction selections.

THOMAS GAGE Associate Professor of English at Humboldt State University in Arcata, California. Formerly Department Chairman at Concord High School and Fremont High School in California. Formerly Director-at-Large for the National Council of Teachers of English. Past President of the Central California Council of Teachers of English.

ALAN L. MADSEN Associate Professor of English Education at the University of Illinois. Formerly teacher of English in high schools in Hillside, Illinois and Iowa City, Iowa. Director, National Council of Teachers of English, 1969–1972. President, Illinois Conference on English Education, 1971–1973.

ISBN: 0-673-12916-0

12345678910-RRW-8584838281807978

Contents

Unit 1

Free Samples

Unit 2

Uncertainties

Unit 3

Poetry

Unit 4

The Well-Told Tale

Unit 5

American Kaleidoscope

Unit 6

Generations

Unit 7

Greek Myths

Unit 8

The Diary of Anne Frank

Handbook
of
Literary
Terms

529

LITERATURE and LIFE

Literature takes many forms.

It is a story, a poem, a play, an essay.

It tells of many things.

It tells a true story of real people.

It tells the fantastic story of characters

who never lived and never will.

Literature does many things.

It makes you think, it makes you feel, it makes you change

To see what it can do, try some **FREE SAMPLES**

1

See **PLOT** Handbook of Literary Terms

"No wonder Aunt Hazel screamed so about my scary stories and my mother flicked off the TV when the monsters came on and Mary was always shushing me. We all had bad hearts."

My Delicate Heart Condition

Toni Cade Bambara

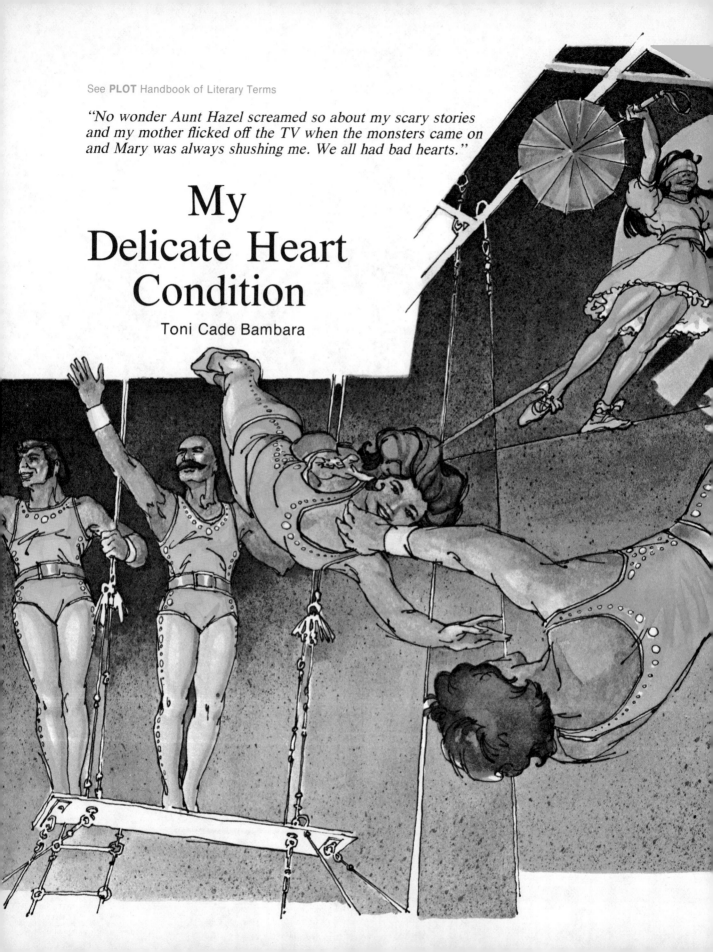

My cousin Joanne has not been allowed to hang out with me for some time because she went and told Aunt Hazel that I scare her to death whenever she sleeps over at our house or I spend the weekend at hers. The truth is I sometimes like to tell stories about blood-thirsty vampires or ugly monsters that lurk in clothes closets or giant beetles that eat their way through the shower curtain, like I used to do at camp to entertain the kids in my bunk. But Joanne always cries and that makes the stories even weirder, like background music her crying. And too—I'm not going to lie about it—I get spookier on purpose until all the little crybabies are stuffing themselves under their pillows and throwing their sneakers at me and making such a racket that Mary the counselor has to come in and shine her flashlight around the bunkhouse. I play like I'm asleep. The rest of them are too busy blubbering and finding their way out from under the blankets to tell Mary that it's me. Besides, once they get a load of her standing against the moonlight in that long white robe of hers looking like a ghost, they just start up again and pretty soon the whole camp is awake. Anyway, that's what I do for fun. So Joanne hasn't been around. And this year I'll have to go to the circus by myself and to camp without her. My mother said on the phone to Aunt Hazel—"Good, keep Jo over there and maybe Harriet'll behave herself if she's got no one to show off to." For all the years my mother's known me, she still doesn't understand that my behaving has got nothing to do with who I hang out with. A private thing between me and me or maybe between me and the Fly family since they were the ones that first got me to sit through monster movies and withstand all the terror I could take.

For four summers now, me and the Fly family have had this thing going. A battle of nerves, you might say. Each year they raise the rope closer and closer to the very top of the tent—I hear they're going to perform outdoors this year and be even higher—and they stretch the rope further across the rings where the clowns and the pony riders perform. Each year they get bolder and more daring with their rope dancing and the swinging by the legs and flinging themselves into empty space making everyone throw up their hands and gasp for air until Mr. Fly at the very last possible second swings out on his bar to catch them up by the tips of their heels. Everyone just dies and clutches at their hearts. Everybody but me. I sit there calmly. I've trained myself. Joanne used to die and duck her head under the benches and stay there till it was all over.

Last summer they really got bold. On the final performance just before the fair closed, and some revival type tent show comes in and all the kids go off to camp, the Fly family performed without a net. I figured they'd be up to something so I made sure my stomach was like steel. I did ten push-ups before breakfast, twenty sit-ups before lunch, skipped dinner altogether. My brother Teddy kidded me all day—"Harriet's trying out for the Olympics." I passed up the icie man on the corner and the pizza and sausage stand by the schoolyard and the cotton candy and jelly apple lady and the pickle and penny candy boy, in fact I passed up all the stands that lead from the street down the little roadway to the fair grounds that used to be a swamp when we first moved from Baltimore to Jamaica, Long Island. It wasn't easy, I'm not going to lie, but I was taking no chances. Between the balloon man and the wheel of fortune was the usual clump of ladies from church who came night after night to try to win the giant punch bowl set on the top shelf above the wheel, but had to settle night after night for a jar of gumdrops or salt and pepper shakers or some other little thing from the bottom shelf. And from the wheel of fortune to the tent was at least a million stands selling B.B. bats and jawbreakers and gingerbread and sweet potato pie and frozen custard and—like I said it wasn't easy. A million ways to tempt you, to unsettle your stomach, and make you lose the battle to the Fly family.

I sat there almost enjoying the silly clowns who came tumbling out of a steamer trunk no bigger than the one we have in the basement where my mother keeps my old report cards and photographs and letters and things. And I almost enjoyed the fire eater and the knife thrower, but I was so close up I could see how there wasn't any real thrill. I almost enjoyed the fat-leg girls who rode the ponies two at a time and standing up, but their costumes weren't very pretty—just an ordinary polo shirt like you get if you run in the PAL meets and short skirts you can wear on either side like the big girls wear at the roller rink. And I almost enjoyed the jugglers except that my Uncle Bubba can juggle the dinner plates better any day of the week so long as Aunt Hazel isn't there to stop him. I was impatient and started yawning. Finally all the clowns hitched up their baggy pants and tumbled over each other out of the ring and into the dark, the jugglers caught all the things that were up in the air and yawning just like me went off to the side. The pony girls brought their horses to a sudden stop that raised a lot of dust, then jumped down into the dirt and bowed. Then the ringmaster stepped into the circle of light and tipped his hat which was a little raggedy from where I was sitting and said—"And now, Ladieeez and Gentlemen, what you've alll been waiting forrr, the Main aTTRACtion, the FLY FAMILEEE." And everyone jumped up to shout like crazy as they came running out on their toes to stand in the light and then climb the ropes. I took a deep breath and folded my arms over my chest and a kid next to me went into hiding, acting like she was going to tie her shoelaces.

There used to be four of them—the father, a big guy with a bald head and a bushy mustache and shoulders and arms like King Kong; a tall lanky mother whom you'd never guess could even climb into a high chair or catch anything heavier than a Ping-Pong ball to look at her; the oldest son who looked like his father except he had hair on his head but none on his face and a big face it was, so that no matter how high up he got you could always tell whether he was smiling or frowning or counting; the younger boy about thirteen, maybe, had a vacant stare like he was a million miles away feeding his turtles or something, anything but walking along a tightrope or flying through the air with his family. I had always liked to watch him because he was as cool as I was. But last summer the little girl got into the act. My grandmother says she's probably a midget cause no self-respecting mother would allow her child to be up there acting like a bird. "Just a baby," she'd say, "Can't be more than six years old. Should be home in bed. Must be a midget." My grandfather would give me a look when she started in and we'd smile at her together.

They almost got to me that last performance, dodging around with new routines and two at a time so that you didn't know which one Mr. Fly was going to save at the last minute. But he'd fly out and catch the little boy and swing over to the opposite stand where the big boy was flying out to catch them both by the wrists and the poor woman would be left kind of dangling there, suspended, then she'd do this double flip which would kill off everyone in the tent except me, of course, and swing out on the very bar she was on in the first place. And then they'd mess around two or three flying at once just to confuse you until the big drum roll started and out steps the little girl in a party dress and a huge blindfold wrapped around her little head and a pink umbrella like they sell down in Chinatown. And I almost—I won't lie about it—I almost let my heart thump me off the bench. I almost thought I too had to tie my shoelaces. But I sat there. Stubborn. And the kid starts bouncing up and down on the rope like she was about to take off and tear through the canvas roof. Then out swings her little brother and before you know it, Fly Jr. like a great eagle with his arms flapping grabs up the kid, her eyeband in his teeth and swoops her off to the bar that's already got Mrs. Mr. and Big Bro on it and surely there's no room for him. And everyone's standing on their feet clutching at their faces. Everyone but me. Cause I know from the getgo that Mr. and Mrs. are going to leave the bar to give Jr. room and fly over to the other side. Which is exactly what they do. The lady in front of me, Mrs. Perez, who does all the sewing in our neighborhood, gets up and starts shaking her hands like ladies do to get the fingernail polish dry and she says to me with her eyes jammed shut "I must go finish the wedding gowns. Tell me later who died." And she scoots through the aisle, falling all over everybody with her eyes still shut and never looks up. And Mrs. Caine taps me on the back and leans over and says, "Some people just can't take it." And I smile at her and at her twins who're sitting there with their mouths open. I fold my arms over my chest and just dare the Fly family to do their very worst.

The minute I got to camp, I ran up to the main house where all the counselors gather to say hello to the parents and talk with the directors. I had to tell Mary the latest doings with the Fly family. But she put a finger to her mouth like she sometimes does to shush me. "Let's not have any scary stuff this summer, Harriet," she said, looking over my shoulder at a new kid. This new kid, Willie, was from my old neighborhood in Baltimore so we got friendly right off. Then he told me that he had a romantic heart so I quite naturally took him under my wing and decided not to give him a heart attack with any ghost tales. Mary said he meant "rheumatic" heart, but I don't see any difference. So I told Mary to move him out of George's tent and give him a nicer counselor who'd respect his romantic heart. George used to be my play boyfriend when I first came to camp as a little kid and didn't know any better. But he's not a nice person. He makes up funny nicknames for people which aren't funny at all. Like calling Eddie Michaels the Watermelon Kid or David Farmer Charcoal Plenty which I really do not appreciate and especially from a counselor. And once he asked Joanne, who was the table monitor, to go fetch a pail of milk from the kitchen. And the minute she got up, he started hatching a plot, trying to get the kids to hide her peanut butter sandwich and put spiders in her soup. I had to remind everyone at the table that Joanne was my first cousin by blood, and I would be forced to waste the first bum that laid a hand on her plate. And ole George says, "Oh don't be a dumbhead, Harriet. Jo's so stupid she won't even notice." And I told

him right then and there that I was not his play girlfriend anymore and would rather marry the wolfman than grow up and be his wife. And just in case he didn't get the message, that night around campfire when we were all playing Little Sally Walker sittin' in a saucer and it was my turn to shake it to the east and to shake it to the west and to shake it to the very one that I loved the best—I shook straight for Mr. Nelson the lifeguard, who was not only the ugliest person in camp but the arch enemy of ole George.

And that very first day of camp last summer when Willie came running up to me to get in line for lunch, here comes George talking some simple stuff about "What a beautiful head you have, Willie. A long, smooth, streamlined head. A sure sign of superior gifts. Definitely genius proportions." And poor Willie went for it, grinning and carrying on and touching his head, which if you want to know the truth is a bullet head and that's all there is to it. And he's turning to me every which way, like he's modeling his head in a fashion show. And the minute his back is turned, ole George makes a face about Willie's head and all the kids in the line bust out laughing. So I had to beat up a few right then and there and finish off the rest later in the shower for being so stupid, laughing at a kid with a romantic heart.

One night in the last week of August when the big campfire party is held, it was very dark and the moon was all smoky, and I just couldn't help myself and started in with a story about the great caterpillar who was going to prowl through the tents and nibble off everybody's toes. And Willie started this whimpering in the back of his throat so I had to switch the story real quick to something cheerful. But before I could do that, ole George picked up my story and added a wicked witch who put spells on city kids who come to camp, and a hunchback dwarf that chopped up tents and bunk beds, and a one-eyed phantom giant who gobbled up the hearts of underprivileged kids. And every time he got to the part where the phantom ripped out a heart, poor Willie would get louder and louder until finally he started rolling around in the grass and screaming and all the kids went crazy and scattered behind the rocks almost kicking the fire completely out as they dashed off into the darkness yelling bloody murder. And the counselors could hardly round us all up—me, too, I'm not going to lie about it. Their little circles of flashlight bobbing in and out

"I wasn't picking on him, I was just trying to tell a story——"

"All that talk about hearts, gobblin' up hearts, and underpriv——"

"Yeh, you were directing it all at the little kid. You should be——"

"I wasn't talking about him. They're all underprivileged kids, after all. I mean all the kids are underprivileged."

I huddled back into the shadows and almost banged into Willie's iron bed. I was hoping he'd open his eyes and wink at me and tell me he was just fooling. That it wasn't so bad to have an underprivileged heart. But he just slept. "I'm an underprivileged kid too," I thought to myself. I knew it was a special camp, but I'd never realized. No wonder Aunt Hazel screamed so about

of the bushes along the patches of pine, bumping into each other as they scrambled for us kids. And poor Willie rolling around something awful, so they took him to the infirmary.

I was sneaking some ginger snaps in to him later that night when I heard Mary and another senior counselor fussing at ole George in the hallway.

"You've been picking on that kid ever since he got here, George. But tonight was the limit——"

my scary stories and my mother flicked off the TV when the monsters came on and Mary was always shushing me. We all had bad hearts. I crawled into the supply cabinet to wait for Willie to wake up so I could ask him about it all. I ate all the ginger snaps but I didn't feel any better. You have a romantic heart, I whispered to myself settling down among the bandages. You will have to be very careful.

It didn't make any difference to Aunt Hazel that I had changed, that I no longer told scary stories or dragged my school-mates to the latest creature movie, or raced my friends to the edge of the roof, or held my breath, or ran under the train rail when the train was already in sight. As far as she was concerned, I was still the same ole spooky kid I'd always been. So Joanne was kept at home. My mother noticed the difference, but she said over the phone to my grandmother, "She's acting very ladylike these days, growing up." I didn't tell her about my secret, that I knew about my heart. And I was kind of glad Joanne wasn't around 'cause I would have blabbed it all to her and scared her to death. When school starts again, I decided, I'll ask my teacher how to outgrow my underprivileged heart. I'll train myself, just like I did with the Fly family.

"Well, I guess you'll want some change to go to the fair again, hunh?" my mother said coming into my room dumping things in her pocketbook.

"No," I said. "I'm too grown up for circuses."

She put the money on the dresser anyway. I was lying, of course. I was thinking what a terrible strain it would be for Mrs. Perez and everybody else if while sitting there, with the Fly family zooming around in the open air a million miles above the ground, little Harriet Watkins should drop dead with a fatal heart attack behind them.

"I lost," I said out loud.

"Lost what?"

"The battle with the Fly family."

She just stood there a long time looking at me, trying to figure me out, the way mothers are always doing but should know better. Then she kissed me goodbye and left for work. □□

Discussion

1. Do you think the "discovery" that Harriet makes at camp will affect the rest of her life? Explain.

2. The first major part of the story deals with the Fly family of aerialists. (a) What is the challenge that the Fly family represents to Harriet? (b) How does Harriet prepare for this challenge?

3. Each summer, after the circus, Harriet goes to camp. (a) What sort of counselor is George? (b) What does Harriet think are her responsibilities to the children at camp? (c) What is physically wrong with Willie? (d) How does George react to this? (e) How does Harriet react? (f) What makes Harriet think she too has a "romantic heart"?

4. (a) How has Harriet's belief that she has a "romantic heart" changed her behavior? (b) What is Harriet's mother's reaction? (c) What does Harriet mean when she says she lost the battle with the Fly family?

5. In plotting this story, the author has focused on two seemingly separate parts of Harriet's life: circus and camp. (a) How does each part relate to the main conflict of the story? (b) What would be the effect if the order of events were reversed: if the author had started her story with the camp episode? (c) Would you say that Harriet's conflict is internal or external? Why?

Toni Cade Bambara 1939 •

Much of what Toni Bambara writes is a reflection of her own experiences. A native New Yorker, she continued her academic education in both New York and Paris. However, her interest in dancing led her to study at various schools of dance and at the Studio Museum of Harlem Film Institute. She has been a contributor to such works as *The Black Woman* and *Tales and Stories for Black Folks*.

Superman

John Updike

Discussion

1. Would you say that the Superman of the poem is an individual or one of the crowd? Explain.

2. The speaker calls his world one of "supercolossality." Give a few examples from the poem that prove his world is "super" and "colossal."

3. Is the author criticizing America? poking fun at America? having fun with the American language? doing other than these? Explain.

John Updike 1932 •

Born and raised in a small town in Pennsylvania, John Updike has used the scenes of his boyhood to form the background for much of his writing. Updike, who established himself as a writer while still in his early twenties, writes with a verbal dexterity almost unmatched by his contemporaries. He is interested in all fields of writing, and has published a number of widely acclaimed novels as well as short stories and poems.

I drive my car to supermarket,
    The way I take is superhigh,
A superlot is where I park it,
    And Super Suds are what I buy.

5 Supersalesmen sell me tonic—
    Super-Tone-O, for Relief.
The planes I ride are supersonic.
    In trains, I like the Super Chief.

Supercilious men and women
10   Call me superficial—*me,*
Who so superbly learned to swim in
    Supercolossality.

Superphosphate-fed foods feed me;
    Superservice keeps me new.
15 Who would dare to supersede me,
    Super-super-superwho?

See **INFERENCE** Handbook of Literary Terms

*Charles was certainly a
bad influence. But just who was he?*

Charles

Shirley Jackson

From *The Lottery* by Shirley Jackson, copyright 1948, 1949 by Shirley Jackson, copyright renewed 1976 by Laurence Hyman, Barry Hyman, Mrs. Sarah Webster, and Mrs. Joanne Schnurer. Reprinted with the permission of Farrar, Straus & Giroux, Inc. and Brandt & Brandt.

The day my son Laurie started kindergarten he renounced corduroy overalls with bibs and began wearing blue jeans with a belt. I watched him go off the first morning with the older girl next door, seeing clearly that an era of my life was ended, my sweet-voiced nursery-school tot replaced by a long-trousered, swaggering character who forgot to stop at the corner and wave good-bye to me.

He came home the same way, the front door slamming open, his hat on the floor, and the voice suddenly become raucous shouting, "Isn't anybody *here?*"

At lunch he spoke insolently to his father, spilled his baby sister's milk, and remarked that his teacher said we were not to take the name of the Lord in vain.

"How *was* school today?" I asked, elaborately casual.

"All right," he said.

"Did you learn anything?" his father asked.

Laurie regarded his father coldly. "I didn't learn nothing," he said.

"Anything," I said. "Didn't learn anything."

"The teacher spanked a boy, though," Laurie said, addressing his bread and butter. "For being fresh," he added, with his mouth full.

"What did he do?" I asked. "Who was it?"

Laurie thought. "It was Charles," he said. "He was fresh. The teacher spanked him and made him stand in a corner. He was awfully fresh."

"What did he do?" I asked again, but Laurie slid off his chair, took a cookie, and left, while his father was still saying, "See here, young man."

The next day Laurie remarked at lunch,

as soon as he sat down, "Well, Charles was bad again today." He grinned enormously and said, "Today Charles hit the teacher."

"Good heavens," I said, mindful of the Lord's name. "I suppose he got spanked again?"

"He sure did," Laurie said. "Look up," he said to his father.

"What?" his father said, looking up.

"Look down," Laurie said. "Look at my thumb. Gee, you're dumb." He began to laugh insanely.

"Why did Charles hit the teacher?" I asked quickly.

"Because she tried to make him color with red crayons," Laurie said. "Charles wanted to color with green crayons so he hit the teacher and she spanked him and said nobody play with Charles but everybody did."

The third day—it was Wednesday of the first week—Charles bounced a see-saw on the head of a little girl and made her bleed, and the teacher made him stay inside all during recess. Thursday Charles had to stand in a corner during story-time because he kept pounding his feet on the floor. Friday Charles was deprived of blackboard privileges because he threw chalk.

On Saturday I remarked to my husband, "Do you think kindergarten is too unsettling for Laurie? All this toughness and bad grammar, and this Charles boy sounds like such a bad influence."

"It'll be all right," my husband said reassuringly. "Bound to be people like Charles in the world. Might as well meet them now as later."

On Monday Laurie came home late, full of news. "Charles," he shouted as he came up the hill; I was waiting anxiously on the front steps. "Charles," Laurie yelled all the way up the hill, "Charles was bad again."

"Come right in," I said, as soon as he came close enough. "Lunch is waiting."

"You know what Charles did?" he demanded, following me through the door. "Charles yelled so in school they sent a boy in from first grade to tell the teacher she had to make Charles keep quiet, and so Charles had to stay after school. And so all the children stayed to watch him."

"What did he do?" I asked.

"He just sat there," Laurie said, climbing into his chair at the table. "Hi, Pop, y'old dust mop."

"Charles had to stay after school today," I told my husband. "Everyone stayed with him."

"What does this Charles look like?" my husband asked Laurie. "What's his other name?"

"He's bigger than me," Laurie said. "And he doesn't have any rubbers and he doesn't ever wear a jacket."

Monday night was the first Parent-Teachers meeting, and only the fact that the baby had a cold kept me from going; I wanted passionately to meet Charles's mother. On Tuesday Laurie remarked suddenly, "Our teacher had a friend come to see her in school today."

"Charles's mother?" my husband and I asked simultaneously.

"Naaah," Laurie said scornfully. "It was a man who came and made us do exercises, we had to touch our toes. Look." He climbed down from his chair and squatted down and touched his toes. "Like this," he said. He got solemnly back into his chair and said, picking up his fork, "Charles didn't even *do* exercises."

"That's fine," I said heartily. "Didn't Charles want to do the exercises?"

"Naaah," Laurie said. "Charles was so fresh to the teacher's friend he wasn't *let* do exercises."

"Fresh again," I said.

"He kicked the teacher's friend," Laurie said. "The teacher's friend told Charles to touch his toes like I just did and Charles kicked him."

"What are they going to do about Charles, do you suppose?" Laurie's father asked him.

Laurie shrugged elaborately. "Throw him out of school, I guess," he said.

Wednesday and Thursday were routine; Charles yelled during story hour and hit a boy in the stomach and made him cry. On Friday Charles stayed after school again and so did all the other children.

With the third week of kindergarten Charles was an institution in our family; the baby was being a Charles when he filled his wagon full of mud and pulled it through the kitchen; even my husband, when he caught his elbow in the telephone cord and pulled telephone, ashtray, and a bowl of flowers off the table, said, after the first minute, "Looks like Charles."

During the third and fourth weeks it looked like a reformation in Charles; Laurie reported grimly at lunch on Thursday of the third week, "Charles was so good today the teacher gave him an apple."

"What?" I said, and my husband added warily, "You mean Charles?"

"Charles," Laurie said. "He gave the crayons around and he picked up the books afterward and the teacher said he was her helper."

"What happened?" I asked incredulously.

"He was her helper, that's all," Laurie said, and shrugged.

"Can this be true, about Charles?" I asked my husband that night. "Can something like this happen?"

"Wait and see," my husband said cynically. "When you've got a Charles to deal with, this may mean he's only plotting."

He seemed to be wrong. For over a week Charles was the teacher's helper; each day he handed things out and he picked things up; no one had to stay after school.

"The PTA meeting's next week again," I told my husband one evening. "I'm going to find Charles's mother there."

"Ask her what happened to Charles," my husband said. "I'd like to know."

"I'd like to know myself," I said.

On Friday of that week things were back to normal. "You know what Charles did today?" Laurie demanded at the lunch table, in a voice slightly awed. "He told a little girl to say a word and she said it and the teacher washed her mouth out with soap and Charles laughed."

"What word?" his father asked unwisely, and Laurie said, "I'll have to whisper it to you, it's so bad." He got down off his chair and went around to his father. His father bent his head down and Laurie whispered joyfully. His father's eyes widened.

"Did Charles tell the little girl to say *that?*" he asked respectfully.

"She said it *twice,*" Laurie said. "Charles told her to say it *twice.*"

"What happened to Charles?" my husband asked.

"Nothing," Laurie said. "He was passing out the crayons."

Monday morning Charles abandoned the little girl and said the evil word himself three or four times, getting his mouth washed out with soap each time. He also threw chalk.

My husband came to the door with me that evening as I set out for the PTA meeting. "Invite her over for a cup of tea after the meeting," he said. "I want to get a look at her."

"If only she's there," I said prayerfully.

"She'll be there," my husband said. "I don't see how they could hold a PTA meeting without Charles's mother."

At the meeting I sat restlessly, scanning each comfortable matronly face, trying to determine which one hid the secret of Charles. None of them looked to me haggard enough. No one stood up in the meeting and apologized for the way her son had been acting. No one mentioned Charles.

After the meeting I identified and sought out Laurie's kindergarten teacher. She had a plate with a cup of tea and a piece of chocolate cake; I had a plate with a cup of tea and a piece of marshmallow cake. We maneuvered up to one another cautiously, and smiled.

"I've been so anxious to meet you," I said. "I'm Laurie's mother."

"We're all so interested in Laurie," she said.

"Well, he certainly likes kindergarten," I said. "He talks about it all the time."

"We had a little trouble adjusting, the first week or so," she said primly, "but now he's a fine little helper. With occasional lapses, of course."

"Laurie usually adjusts very quickly," I said. "I suppose this time it's Charles's influence."

"Charles?"

"Yes, " I said, laughing, "you must have your hands full in that kindergarten, with Charles."

"Charles?" she said. "We don't have any Charles in the kindergarten." ☐ ☐

Discussion

1. Were you surprised to find there was no Charles in Laurie's kindergarten class? Why or why not?

2. (a) How does Laurie treat his father after his first morning at school? (b) Does Laurie's behavior toward his parents improve as time goes on? (c) Do you think Laurie's parents should have acted differently? Explain.

3. (a) Why might Laurie first have invented Charles? (b) Laurie describes Charles in these words: "He's bigger than me. And he doesn't have any rubbers, and he doesn't ever wear a jacket." What inferences about Laurie can you make from this description?

4. (a) This is a story that builds suspense which is released in a surprise ending. Discuss why you believe the ending is or is not a good one. (b) Do you think Laurie's mother ever told his teacher the story of Charles? Explain.

Vocabulary • Context

These aids can help you understand words you don't know:
CONTEXT: the setting the word appears in; that is, other words or ideas in the

sentence, paragraph, or selection.

STRUCTURE: the arrangement and meaning of parts of words (root words and affixes).

PRONUNCIATION: use the dictionary when you need help with pronunciation.

DICTIONARY: if the meaning can't be determined by using context or structure clues, consult the dictionary.

Often the context in which a word appears will give you enough of a clue that you can figure out the word's meaning. For instance, many times writers use two different words or phrases to express the same meaning. The phrase "tired and worn out" in the example below provides an obvious clue to the meaning of *haggard:*

Tina noticed her brother's *haggard* expression right away. "Ed," she said, "you'd better get some rest. I've never seen you look so tired and worn out."

Sometimes you can learn a word's meaning through the examples the writer uses. In this paragraph the last three sentences all contain examples that clarify the meaning of *deprived:*

Generally speaking, the prisoners were *deprived* of all bodily comforts. They slept on rock-hard beds. They wore thin uniforms that provided no protection against the cold. They were given meat only on Sundays.

Knowing that words like *but, although,* and *however* often signal that things are different or opposite can also help you figure out word meanings. What words in this example are the opposite of *raucous?*

Although Tony usually speaks in a soft, gentle tone of voice, get him near a football game and he immediately becomes *raucous.*

Use context clues to figure out the meanings of the italicized words in these sentences. Write the letters of the correct answers on your paper.

1. He talks back to his teacher, ignores his father, and makes fun of his mother—have you ever seen such an *insolent* child? (a) clever; (b) loud; (c) insulting; (d) friendly.

2. Though Mother generally believes me, she was *incredulous* when I said I'd never be late again. (a) thankful; (b) doubtful; (c) trustful; (d) angry.

3. Claiming that he didn't need money to be happy, Ted *renounced* his entire inheritance. (a) announced; (b) saved; (c) spent; (d) gave up.

4. Treat an unfamiliar dog *warily* until it gets to know you. (a) cautiously; (b) fairly; (c) kindly; (d) firmly.

5. If you all speak *simultaneously,* how can I understand what any one person is saying? (a) too loudly; (b) too softly; (c) discourteously; (d) at the same time.

Extension • Speaking

Based upon what you know of the story, put on an impromptu skit of Laurie's mother's meeting with his teacher, or of Laurie's mother telling his father about the PTA meeting.

Shirley Jackson
1919 • 1965

Laurie, the child in "Charles," is indeed modeled on a real person—Shirley Jackson's first child. The story appears, among other places, in a collection of Jackson's stories, *Life Among the Savages,* which she once called "a disrespectful memoir of my children."

Born in San Francisco, Jackson spent most of her married life in Bennington, Vermont. She wrote another collection of stories of her domestic life, *Raising Demons.* Jackson was equally at home writing spine-chilling Gothic thrillers with a frightening vein of psychological realism, the most famous of which, "The Lottery," has been made into a play and a film.

When asked why she wrote, Jackson once said, "It's the only chance I get to sit down."

Boarding House

Ted Kooser

Discussion

1. (a) Do you think the blind man leaves his light on accidentally? Explain. **(b)** What is the effect of the light on the deaf man?

2. (a) What is noteworthy about the deaf man's shoes? **(b)** How is their effect on the blind man similar to the effect of the light on the deaf man?

3. This poem can be looked at in two different ways. On one level, it is simply about two handicappped men who are dependent on each other. On another level, the way the two men deal with each other might suggest a more general message that can be applied to all people. What might this message be?

Ted Kooser 1939 •

Born and raised in Iowa, currently living in Nebraska, and a confirmed Midwesterner, Kooser says of himself: "I am a poet, artist, and film-maker. . . . Most of my work reflects my interest in my surroundings here on the Great Plains."

The blind man draws his curtains for the night
and goes to bed, leaving a burning light

above the bathroom mirror. Through the wall,
he hears the deaf man walking down the hall

5 in his squeaky shoes to see if there's a light
under the blind man's door, and all is right.

George Gardner

The season is Spring, in 1876. The place is the Great Plains, homeland of the Lakota, whom white men call Sioux (sü). The day is one that will change forever the lives of Whirlwind and her grandson, Shoots.

How Whirlwind Saved Her Cub

Dorothy Johnson

Whirlwind was a widow now. Her hair, hacked off in mourning for White Thunder, had grown out long enough to make short, ragged braids, but she no longer cared very much how she looked. The cuts made when she had gashed her arms and her legs had healed to scars. She no longer had a lodge of her own. When White Thunder died of a wasting sickness—not in battle, as he had wished—she abandoned the lodge as was proper and let other people take away everything in it.

But she had a good home with her son, Morning Rider. She was Grandmother Whirlwind, the old-woman-who-sits-by-the-door. She worked hard and took pride in her work. She was the one who told small children the old stories about the White Buffalo Maiden and the other sacred spirits just as those stories had been told to her by Grandmother Earth Medicine when she was very small. . . .

All over the huge encampment there was singing and drumming, and all over people were busy. There was much to be done, because they would move again very soon. The pony herds needed new grazing.

There was plenty of work to be done in the lodge of Morning Rider, but there were

From *Buffalo Woman* by Dorothy M. Johnson. Copyright © 1977 by Dorothy M. Johnson. Adapted and reprinted by permission of Dodd, Mead & Company, Inc. and McIntosh and Otis, Inc.

plenty of women there to do it, so Whirlwind left on a project of her own.

"I'm going to dig roots," she explained to Round Cloud Woman. "Shall I take the baby for company?"

"He has just been fed, so take him if you like," her daughter-in-law agreed. His ears had not yet been pierced,[1] so he did not have a boy name yet; his baby name was Jumps.

Whirlwind slung her baby grandson's cradleboard onto her back with the ease of long practice and went walking at a brisk pace, answering the baby when he made small sounds. She had two things hidden under her dress: her digging stick and a soft leather bag for carrying roots. She thought she knew where biscuit root would be

growing—desert parsley. The roots were good to eat raw, or she might dry and grind them to make big flat cakes. The biscuit root made good mush with a wild onion cooked in it.

As a rule she liked company when she worked, but there was no point in inviting some other busy woman to come along to dig something that might not be there.

She did tell her destination to one person, her grandson Shoots, thirteen years old. She met him when he was returning on foot from his turn at guarding part of the vast pony herd.

---

1. *His ears . . . been pierced.* With this ceremony, a Lakota baby officially became a member of the tribe.

"Your little brother is going to help me dig biscuit root over there," she said. "Don't tell anybody where we are. Let the other women be sharp-eyed and find their own roots."

Shoots smiled and promised. He patted his baby brother's cheek and said, "Ho, warrior, old man chief. Take care of Grandmother." The baby jumped in his buckskin wrappings and cooed.

The biscuit root was plentiful on flat ground under a cutbank, just out of sight of the lodges. Whirlwind carefully propped the baby's cradleboard against a rock so the sun wouldn't shine in the child's face. Then, talking to him quietly, she began to dig skillfully, filling her buckskin bag, stooping and kneeling and rising again like a young woman. She was not young, she had lived through fifty-six winters, but she was strong and happy and healthy.

Her back was toward the baby when she heard him shriek with glee. She turned instantly—and saw a dreadful thing. Between her and the baby was another kind of baby, an awkward little bear cub, the cub of the frightfully dangerous grizzly bear. The cub itself was harmless, but the old-woman bear, its mother, must be near, and she would protect her child.

Whirlwind did not even think of danger to herself. She ran to save *her* cub. She snatched up the baby on his cradleboard and threw him, with all her strength, above her head toward the level top of the cutbank.

At that moment the old-woman bear appeared. She snarled and came running, a shambling, awkward-looking run but very fast.

Whirlwind saw with horror the cradleboard with its precious burden sliding back down the cutbank. She had been too close when she threw the baby upward. The baby was screaming. Grandmother Whirlwind ran, picked up the cradleboard, ran back a few steps, and then threw hard again. This time the bundle stayed up there.

Whirlwind ran again toward the cutbank and climbed as fast as she could, digging into the dirt frantically with clutching fingers and digging toes.

The upper part of her body was on the flat ground and she was gripping a small tree as she tried to pull up her legs. Just then the old-woman grizzly reached up and tore at the legs with curved claws as long as a big man's middle finger.

Whirlwind thought, I am dead—but my cub is safe if the sow bear does not come up here. No, I am not dead yet. I have something more to do. She screamed as hard as she could.

And her scream was heard.

Shoots was an untried boy. He had never even asked to go along with a war party to do errands for men of proved courage, to watch how a man should act. He had only thought of going on the hill to starve and thirst and lament to the Powers, praying for a powerful spirit helper.[2] He had not yet done this thing. He believed his heart was strong. That day he found out.

He was only playing when he heard the she-bear snarl. He was practicing a stealthy approach, intending to startle Grandmother Whirlwind. He was creeping quietly through thin brush, pretending that she was an enemy. He did not really expect to surprise her; she was usually very alert. She would scold when she discovered what he was up to, and then she would laugh at him because she had caught him.

---

2. *going on the hill . . . spirit helper.* A Lakota youth had to go through this ritual before he could be regarded as a man and warrior.

He saw a bundle fly through the air and slide down the cutbank. It happened too fast for him to see that it was the cradleboard with his baby brother. He heard fast movement in the weeds as Whirlwind ran back and threw the cradleboard again. He stood up, mouth open, just as she scrambled up the bank. With horror he saw the old-woman bear's claws rake her struggling legs.

With his heart in his mouth he did the best thing he could think of. He dropped his bow and grabbed the cub with both hands, so that it squalled with fear and pain. Then he threw it hard—past its mother.

Hearing her child cry, the woman bear whirled away from the cutbank to protect her cub. Shoots snatched up his bow; it was a good one, as strong as he could pull, and in a quiver on his shoulder he had six hunting arrows tipped with sharpened iron. At his waist he had a good steel knife.

But his enemy was better armed, with twenty immensely long, curved, sharp, death-dealing claws and a mouthful of long, sharp teeth, and she weighed more than five times as much as he did. She was protected by thick fur. Shoots was almost naked.

He stood his ground and fired his arrows at her, fast but very carefully. Few grizzlies had ever been killed by one man alone; there were true tales of some bears killing men even after they should have been dead themselves. The woman bear yelled in pain and fury. She batted at the arrows deep in her flesh. She bit at them. But she kept coming.

Then Shoots did the last thing he could do, because it was too late to run. While the grizzly fought at the arrows, especially one that had gone into her left eye, he leaped on her back. With all his strength he sank his good steel knife into her throat, through the heavy fur and hide.

Then, as Grandmother Whirlwind had

done, he clambered up the cutbank while the bear groped and swiped at him. He wondered why he could not see very well. He wondered who was screaming. He wondered if this was the day he was going to die.

Whirlwind, lying helpless with the calf of one leg torn away, screamed louder when she saw him with blood running down his face, but he did not even know blood was there.

She cried, "Take the baby and run!" in so commanding a voice that he never thought of doing otherwise. With the cradled baby under one arm, he ran toward camp, howling for help, but stumbling.

His yells were heard. Two men on horseback lashed their ponies and met him. One seized the squalling baby. The other pulled Shoots up behind him on the pony. They rode fast toward where Whirlwind lay.

They leaped off—the one with the baby hung the cradleboard on a tree branch—and Shoots tumbled off. He had just realized that there was something he ought to do to prove his valor. He did something that his people talked about for many years afterward. While the men knelt by Whirlwind, he slid down the cutbank, picked up his bow, and struck the bear with it. She was coughing and dying. He shouted, as warriors do, "I, Shoots, have killed her! I count the first coup!"

Whirlwind and the men above heard him say it. They shouted in wonder and admiration. For a man to kill a grizzly without help was a very great thing indeed, and he had actually gone back into danger to count coup and claim the credit that was due him. He had counted coup against an armed enemy, after he was wounded, although he had never gone to war before that day. Now he was entitled to wear an eagle feather upright in his hair for first coup, a feather tipped with red paint because he had been wounded in battle.

He was the one who rode toward camp for more help while the two men stayed with Whirlwind and did what they could to make her comfortable. A crowd of people came hurrying after he delivered his message. There were women on horseback with poles and hides to make a pony drag for Whirlwind, because a great chunk of the muscles in the calf of one leg had been torn out by the she-bear's claws. There were men riding and boys riding, leading horses. More women brought supplies to help the wounded, and a medicine woman came with them, carrying her bundle of magic things. Round Cloud Woman came riding, crying, and Morning Rider came at a hard gallop to see about his mother and his infant son.

Whirlwind fought them off, so keyed up and triumphant that she did not yet feel much pain. "Let me carry my grandchild!" she ordered when Round Cloud tried to take him away.

"I saved your cub," Whirlwind kept boasting, laughing and proud. "And Shoots saved us both. He is not a cub any more. He is a warrior!" She tried to make a victory trill in his honor, but as they lifted her gently onto the pony drag she fainted.

Morning Rider himself attended to the wound of his son Shoots, who did not even remember when the old-woman bear had slashed his forehead. The boy was able to laugh as he said, "She tried to scalp me!"

Morning Rider covered the wound with clotted blood from the bear and tied the flap of skin down with a strip of buckskin around the boy's head. He remarked fondly, "You will have a big scar there. The girls will keep asking you to tell how you got it. I am very proud of you."

Now maybe Grandmother Whirlwind would stop treating him like a little boy, to be ordered around.

He heard her shouting, laughing: "Behold Shoots—he is a warrior. He fought a grizzly bear and killed her."

Shoots shouted back, "Behold Whirlwind! She is a warrior. She was wounded in battle."

He began to sing a praise song for her, although he was feeling weak all of a sudden.

She laughed hysterically. "I am a warrior who was wounded while running away! Take the hide of the enemy—it belongs to Shoots."

Women were skinning out the dead, bloody bear and fighting with a horse that reared, not wanting to carry the hide on its back. The medicine woman filled a big dish with bear blood. She washed the great wound on Whirlwind's leg with water, chanting prayers. She covered the wound with the bear's thickening blood and then cut a big piece of the bear's hide, covering the wound and the blood with the raw side of the fresh hide.

She said with pity, "My friend, I think you will have trouble walking—always, as long as you live. But nobody will ever forget how you saved your son's cub today."

They killed the great bear's cub and cut off its claws to make a necklace for the baby when he grew older. They cut off the immense claws of the woman bear; these were for Shoots. Not long afterward, when he went out to lament for a vision, his dream was a powerful one and when he made up his protective medicine bag, one of the claws was in it. The others he wore for a necklace when he dressed up.

That night the people had a victorious kill dance over the bloody hides of the great bear and the little one. Morning Rider rode

around the camp circle leading a fine horse to give away, with Shoots riding beside him. Morning Rider sang:

> "A bear killed a woman long ago.
> A bear killed a mother long ago.
> Now the woman's son has avenged her.
> The warrior son has avenged his mother!"

Morning Rider gave the fine horse to a very brave old warrior, who gave Shoots a new name. The warrior shouted, "The boy Shoots counted first coup on a grizzly bear and killed her to save two people. So I give him an honorable name. Kills Grizzly is his name!"

Grandmother Whirlwind lay on her bed, smiling as she listened to the singing and the triumphant drumming of the kill dance in honor of Shoots—no, now she must remember to call him Kills Grizzly. Her daughter was with her, and the medicine woman, who used all her spells and prayers and medicines to try to ease the pain. No matter how Whirlwind lay, with her foot propped up, the pain was very great, but her pride was greater.

"It does not hurt," she said. "It is nothing." She pretended to sleep.

Brings Horses stayed, and Morning Rider's wives came back with their sleepy children. They spoke softly but were full of talk that Whirlwind wanted to hear: about how everyone was honoring Shoots for his courage and talking about how brave Whirlwind herself was.

"Everybody wants to see you," one of them remarked, smiling, "but we refused them all—all except one, who will come soon."

They were hurrying around, Whirlwind noticed, to tidy up the lodge—her work, but she could not do it now. It must be an important visitor or the women would not be so careful to have everything neat and nice this late at night, with the baby and the little girl, Reaches Far, asleep.

Men's voices came nearer, two men. One was Morning Rider; his mother did not recognize the other one. Morning Rider entered and ushered in his companion. He said, "This is Whirlwind Woman, my mother. She saved my baby son."

The other man stood looking down at her. He smiled a little and said, "I am Crazy Horse."

Whirlwind gasped. For once in her life, she had nothing to say. This was the great man, the quiet one, whose very presence made the hearts of his people big.

Morning Rider told her, "I have asked Crazy Horse to name the baby, and he agrees. When the boy is old enough, we will have the ear-piercing ceremony. But today Crazy Horse will give my youngest son a name."

Round Cloud Woman brought the sleeping infant. She was shaking with excitement.

Crazy Horse looked long at the sleeping little face. Then he touched the child's forehead and said, "I give you a name that you can make great in honor of your grandmother, who saved you, and your brother, who counted first coup on the bear. I name the child She Throws Him."

A murmur of delight went up among Morning Rider's family: "Thank you, friend, thank you!"

Round Cloud Woman said to her child, "Wake up, She Throws Him, so that sometime you can say you looked on the face of Crazy Horse the day he gave you your name." The baby opened his eyes, yawned, and went to sleep again.

Now Whirlwind thought of something to say: "My son has forgotten his manners. I did not raise him right. He has not asked our visitor to sit down in the place of honor beside him."

The two men chuckled, and Morning Rider explained, "I asked him before we came, but he thought he would not stay long enough. Will the visitor sit down and smoke?"

Crazy Horse would. Morning Rider filled and lighted the sacred pipe and smoked it to the Powers of the six directions. Then he passed it to Crazy Horse, who did the same and gave back the sacred pipe.

"I wish also to speak to the warrior woman," he said. "Grandmother, how is it with you in your pain?" He used the term "grandmother" in the sense of great respect.

"Not so bad," she replied stoutly, as a warrior should.

Crazy Horse stood up, then knelt beside her and looked into her face. "I give you a name, too, Grandmother. Your name is Saved Her Cub."

Then he nodded and left the lodge, leaving Whirlwind speechless for the second time that day.

When she got her wits back, she complained happily, "But I am too old to remember another name for myself!"

Morning Rider replied, "Others will remember." ☐ ☐

Discussion

1. Who do you think has the more important role in this episode, Whirlwind or Shoots? Explain.

2. (a) What changes have occurred in Whirlwind's life since the death of her husband? (b) How does she make herself useful in her son's lodge?

3. (a) Why does the grizzly bear attack Whirlwind? (b) How does Whirlwind react? (c) What does Shoots do as soon as he realizes what is happening?

4. (a) What honors does Shoots receive for his bravery? (b) How is Whirlwind honored? (c) If a woman and a boy performed similar life-saving actions in our own time, how might they be honored or rewarded?

5. After reading this story, one student commented, "I don't know who was braver, Whirlwind or Shoots, but they were brave in different ways." Do you agree or disagree? Explain.

Extension • Reading

"How Whirlwind Saved Her Cub" is an excerpt from Dorothy Johnson's novel *Buffalo Woman* (Dodd, Mead, 1977). In portraying the personal story of Whirlwind from infancy to old age, Johnson tells the larger story of the life and times, the glory and the tragedy of the Lakota people during the years 1820 to 1877.

Dorothy Johnson 1905 •

A resident of Montana, Dorothy Johnson has written many novels and stories about the American frontier. She has been honored in many ways for the quality and authenticity of her writing. Among the more unusual honors: she is honorary police chief of Whitefish, Montana, where she grew up, and is an adopted member of the Blackfeet tribe, with the name "Kills Both Places."

Many television productions and several motion pictures have been based on her stories, including "The Man Who Shot Liberty Valence" and "A Man Called Horse."

Lakota Names

In "How Whirlwind Saved Her Cub" an infant, a youth, and a grandmother each receives a name which celebrates a great deed. Lakota names were frequently earned in this manner; other names might be taken from natural phenomena (Whirlwind, White Thunder), or from respected animals (Brave Bear, Grey Bull); still others might stress a personal trait or characteristic. The name Wooden Leg speaks for itself, and we might guess that a man named Touch the Clouds stood seven feet tall.

Girls usually kept their original names throughout their lives; they did not change their names when they married.

Boys were usually given a new name when they reached manhood.

Name giving was a serious proceeding, for names themselves were regarded as valuable property, possessing magical qualities. Names could be sold, given away, even pawned.

Many Indian names may strike us as long, awkward, sometimes unflattering—a result of the difficulties of translation. Several English words were usually needed to express one or two Indian words—and often those English words were badly chosen. One warrior took pride in a name which proclaimed that he was so active on the warpath he had no time to clean his equipment. That idea was lost in the English version of his name: Stinking Saddle Blanket. Young Man Afraid of His Horses may seem to us a strangely timid name for a Lakota chief, but the correct meaning of the name was quite different: Young Man Whose Very Horses Are Feared.

Young Man Afraid of His Horses

Photo by G. Trager,
Nebraska State Historical
Society

Crazy Horse, the greatest war chief of the Lakota, had an interesting history of names. He was the son and grandson of medicine men who had been named Crazy Horse. As a youth he had the name His Horse Looking, but he was also called Strange One and Curly because of his brown, curly hair, rare among the Lakota. For outstanding bravery in his first battle, his father gave him his own name, Crazy Horse. (The father then took a new name, Worm, for himself.) Among the Lakota and other tribes, "Crazy" did not mean "insane"; rather, it had the much-valued meaning of "enchanted" or "controlled by the spirits."

Lakota or Sioux?

The Lakota are commonly known as *Sioux*, a term first used by the French, who learned it from their Chippewa allies. In Chippewa, the word *Sioux* means "snakes" or "enemies"; the Chippewa were bitter enemies of the Lakota.

The name Lakota (or Dakota or Nakota, depending on the dialect) means "friends" or "allies." The names most Indian peoples had for themselves have similiar meanings: "the people," "human beings," "the first ones."

See **THEME** Handbook of Literary Terms

some dreams

Lucille Clifton

Discussion

1. Does the speaker sound as though most of her dreams came true? Explain.

2. (a) What characteristics do the dreams have in common with smoke? **(b)** When would these dreams make you cry?

3. Which of the following might best express the theme of this poem? **(a)** smoke can irritate your eyes and be harmful to your clothes; **(b)** dreams can persist and affect us even after hope is gone; **(c)** dreams are like smoke; **(d)** you shouldn't dream too much.

Lucille Clifton   1936 •

Born in New York State and educated at Howard University and Fredonia State Teachers College, Lucille Clifton now lives in Baltimore, Maryland, where since 1971 she has been poet-in-residence at Coppin State College. She is also a member of the Maryland State Committee for Black Art and Culture.

some dreams hang in the air
like smoke. some dreams
get all in your clothes and
be wearing them more than you do and
5 you be half the time trying to
hold them and half the time
trying to wave them away.
their smell be all over you and
they get to your eyes and
10 you cry. the fire be gone
and the wood but some dreams
hang in the air like smoke
touching everything.

See **IMAGERY** Handbook of Literary Terms

He was only seven; she was sixty-something.
They were distant cousins who had only each other.
Now grown, Buddy recalls Christmas and his unusual friend.

A Christmas Memory

Truman Capote

Imagine a morning in late November. A coming of winter morning more than twenty years ago. Consider the kitchen of a spreading old house in a country town. A great black stove is its main feature; but there is also a big round table and a fireplace with two rocking chairs placed in front of it. Just today the fireplace commenced its seasonal roar.

A woman with shorn white hair is standing at the kitchen window. She is wearing tennis shoes and a shapeless gray sweater over a summery calico dress. She is small and sprightly, like a bantam hen; but, due to a long youthful illness, her shoulders are pitifully hunched. Her face is remarkable— not unlike Lincoln's, craggy like that, and tinted by sun and wind; but it is delicate too, finely boned, and her eyes are sherry-colored and timid. "Oh my," she exclaims, her breath smoking the windowpane, "it's fruitcake weather!"

The person to whom she is speaking is myself. I am seven; she is sixty-something. We are cousins, very distant ones, and we have lived together—well, as long as I can remember. Other people inhabit the house, relatives; and though they have power over us, and frequently make us cry, we are not,

on the whole, too much aware of them. We are each other's best friend. She calls me Buddy, in memory of a boy who was formerly her best friend. The other Buddy died in the 1880's, when she was still a child. She is still a child.

"I knew it before I got out of bed," she says, turning away from the window with a purposeful excitement in her eyes. "The courthouse bell sounded so cold and clear. And there were no birds singing; they've gone to warmer country, yes indeed. Oh, Buddy, stop stuffing biscuit and fetch our buggy. Help me find my hat. We've thirty cakes to bake."

It's always the same: a morning arrives in November, and my friend, as though officially inaugurating the Christmas time of year that exhilarates her imagination and fuels the blaze of her heart, announces: "It's fruitcake weather! Fetch our buggy. Help me find my hat."

The hat is found, a straw cartwheel corsaged with velvet roses out-of-doors has faded: it once belonged to a more fashionable relative. Together, we guide our buggy,

a dilapidated baby carriage, out to the garden and into a grove of pecan trees. The buggy is mine; that is, it was bought for me when I was born. It is made of wicker, rather unraveled, and the wheels wobble like a drunkard's legs. But it is a faithful object; springtimes, we take it to the woods and fill it with flowers, herbs, wild fern for our porch pots; in the summer, we pile it with picnic paraphernalia and sugar-cane fishing poles and roll it down to the edge of a creek; it has its winter uses, too: as a truck for hauling firewood from the yard to the kitchen, as a warm bed for Queenie, our tough little orange and white rat terrier who has survived distemper and two rattlesnake bites. Queenie is trotting beside it now.

Three hours later we are back in the kitchen hulling a heaping buggyload of windfall pecans. Our backs hurt from gathering them: how hard they were to find (the main crop having been shaken off the trees and sold by the orchard's owners, who are not us) among the concealing leaves, the frosted, deceiving grass. Caarackle! A cheery crunch, scraps of miniature thunder sound as the shells collapse and the golden mound of sweet oily ivory meat mounts in the milk-glass bowl. Queenie begs to taste, and now and again my friend sneaks her a mite, though insisting we deprive ourselves. "We mustn't, Buddy. If we start, we won't stop. And there's scarcely enough as there is. For thirty cakes." The kitchen is growing dark. Dusk turns the window into a mirror: our reflections mingle with the rising moon as we work by the fireside in the firelight. At last, when the moon is quite high, we toss the final hull into the fire and, with joined sighs, watch it catch flame. The buggy is empty, the bowl is brimful.

We eat our supper (cold biscuits, bacon, blackberry jam) and discuss tomorrow. Tomorrow the kind of work I like best begins: buying. Cherries and citron, ginger and vanilla and canned Hawaiian pineapple, rinds and raisins and walnuts and whiskey and oh, so much flour, butter, so many eggs, spices, flavorings: why, we'll need a pony to pull the buggy home.

But before these purchases can be made, there is the question of money. Neither of us has any. Except for skinflint sums persons in the house occasionally provide (a dime is considered very big money); or what we earn ourselves from various activities: holding rummage sales, selling buckets of hand-picked blackberries, jars of homemade jam and apple jelly and peach preserves, rounding up flowers for funerals and weddings. Once we won seventy-ninth prize, five dollars, in a national football contest. Not that we know a fool thing about football. It's just that we enter any contest we hear about: at the moment our hopes are centered on the fifty-thousand-dollar Grand Prize being offered to name a new brand of coffee (we suggested "A.M."; and, after some hesitation, for my friend thought it perhaps sacrilegious, the slogan "A.M.! Amen!"). To tell the truth, our only *really* profitable enterprise was the Fun and Freak Museum we conducted in a back-yard woodshed two summers ago. The Fun was a stereopticon with slide views of Washington and New York lent us by a relative who had been to those places (she was furious when she discovered why we'd borrowed it); the Freak was a three-legged biddy chicken hatched by one of our own hens. Everybody hereabouts wanted to see that biddy: we charged grownups a nickel, kids two cents. And took in a good twenty dollars before the museum shut down due to the decease of the main attraction.

But one way and another we do each

year accumulate Christmas savings, a Fruit-cake Fund. These moneys we keep hidden in an ancient bead purse under a loose board under the floor under a chamber pot under my friend's bed. The purse is seldom removed from this safe location except to make a deposit, or, as happens every Saturday, a withdrawal; for on Saturdays I am allowed ten cents to go to the picture show. My friend has never been to a picture show, nor does she intend to: "I'd rather hear you tell the story, Buddy. That way I can imagine it more. Besides, a person my age shouldn't squander their eyes. When the Lord comes, let me see him clear." In addition to never having seen a movie, she has never: eaten in a restaurant, traveled more than five miles from home, received or sent a telegram, read anything except funny papers and the Bible, worn cosmetics, cursed, wished someone harm, told a lie on purpose, let a hungry dog go hungry. Here are a few things she has done, does do: killed with a hoe the biggest rattlesnake ever seen in this county (sixteen rattles), dip snuff (secretly), tame hummingbirds (just try it) till they balance on her finger, tell ghost stories (we both believe in ghosts) so tingling they chill you in July, talk to herself, take walks in the rain, grow the prettiest japonicas in town, know the recipe for every sort of old-time Indian cure, including a magical wart-remover.

Now, with supper finished, we retire to the room in a faraway part of the house where my friend sleeps in a scrap-quilt-covered iron bed painted rose pink, her favorite color. Silently, wallowing in the pleasures of conspiracy, we take the bead purse from its secret place and spill its contents on the scrap quilt. Dollar bills, tightly rolled and green as May buds. Somber fifty-cent pieces, heavy enough to weight a dead man's eyes: Lovely dimes, the liveli-est coin, the one that really jingles. Nickels and quarters, worn smooth as creek pebbles. But mostly a hateful heap of bitter-odored pennies. Last summer others in the house contracted to pay us a penny for every twenty-five flies we killed. Oh, the carnage of August: the flies that flew to heaven! Yet it was not work in which we took pride. And, as we sit counting pennies, it is as though we were back tabulating dead flies. Neither of us has a head for figures; we count slowly, lose track, start again. According to her calculations, we have $12.73. According to mine, exactly $13. "I do hope you're wrong, Buddy. We can't mess around with thirteen. The cakes will fall. Or put somebody in the cemetery. Why, I wouldn't dream of getting out of bed on the thirteenth." This is true: she always spends thirteenths in bed. So, to be on the safe side, we subtract a penny and toss it out the window.

Of the ingredients that go into our fruit-cakes, whiskey is the most expensive, as well as the hardest to obtain: state laws forbid its sale. But everybody knows you can buy a bottle from Mr. Haha Jones. And the next day, having completed our more prosaic shopping, we set out for Mr. Haha's business address, a "sinful" (to quote public opinion) fish-fry and dancing café down by the river. We've been there before, and on the same errand; but in previous years our dealings have been with Haha's wife, an iodine-dark Indian woman with brassy peroxided hair and a dead-tired disposition. Actually, we've never laid eyes on her husband, though we've heard that he's an Indian too. A giant with razor scars across his cheeks. They call him Haha because he's so gloomy, a man who never laughs. As we approach his café (a large log cabin festooned inside and out with chains of garish-gay naked lightbulbs and standing by the river's muddy edge under the shade of river trees where moss drifts through the branches like gray mist) our steps slow down. Even Queenie stops prancing and sticks close by. People have been murdered in Haha's café. Cut to pieces. Hit on the head. There's a case coming up in court next month. Naturally these goings-on happen at night when the colored lights cast crazy patterns and the Victrola wails. In the daytime Haha's is shabby and deserted. I knock at the door, Queenie barks, my friend calls: "Mrs. Haha, ma'am? Anyone to home?"

Footsteps. The door opens. Our hearts overturn. It's Mr. Haha Jones himself! And he *is* a giant; he *does* have scars; he *doesn't* smile. No, he glowers at us through Satan-tilted eyes and demands to know: "What you want with Haha?"

For a moment we are too paralyzed to tell. Presently my friend half-finds her voice, a whispery voice at best: "If you please, Mr. Haha, we'd like a quart of your finest whiskey."

His eyes tilt more. Would you believe it? Haha is smiling! Laughing, too. "Which one of you is a drinkin' man?"

"It's for making fruitcakes, Mr. Haha. Cooking."

This sobers him. He frowns. "That's no way to waste good whiskey." Nevertheless, he retreats into the shadowed cafe and seconds later appears carrying a bottle of daisy yellow unlabeled liquor. He demonstrates its sparkle in the sunlight and says: "Two dollars."

We pay him with nickels and dimes and pennies. Suddenly, jangling the coins in his hand like a fistful of dice, his face softens. "Tell you what," he proposes, pouring the money back into our bead purse, "just send me one of them fruitcakes instead."

"Well," my friend remarks on our way home, "there's a lovely man. We'll put an extra cup of raisins in *his* cake."

The black stove, stoked with coal and firewood, glows like a lighted pumpkin. Eggbeaters whirl, spoons spin round in bowls of butter and sugar, vanilla sweetens the air, ginger spices it; melting, nose-tingling odors saturate the kitchen, suffuse the house, drift out to the world on puffs of chimney smoke. In four days our work is done. Thirty-one cakes, dampened with whiskey, bask on window sills and shelves.

Who are they for?

Friends. Not necessarily neighbor friends: indeed, the larger share are intended for persons we've met maybe once, perhaps not at all. People who've struck our fancy. Like President Roosevelt. Like the Reverend and Mrs. J. C. Lucey, Baptist missionaries to Borneo who lectured here last winter. Or the little knife grinder who comes through town twice a year. Or Abner Packer, the driver of the six o'clock bus from Mobile, who exchanges waves with us every day as he passes in a dust-cloud whoosh. Or the young Wistons, a California couple whose car one afternoon broke down outside the house and who spent a pleasant hour chatting with us on the porch (young Mr. Wiston snapped our picture, the only one we've ever had taken). Is it because my friend is shy with everyone *except* strangers that these strangers, and merest acquaintances, seem to us our truest friends? I think yes. Also, the scrapbooks we keep of thank-you's on White House stationery, time-to-time communications from California and Borneo, the knife grinder's penny post cards, make us feel connected to eventful worlds beyond the kitchen with its view of a sky that stops.

Now a nude December fig branch grates against the window. The kitchen is empty, the cakes are gone; yesterday we carted the last of them to the post office, where the cost of stamps turned our purse inside out. We're broke. That rather depresses me, but my friend insists on celebrating—with two inches of whiskey left in Haha's bottle. Queenie has a spoonful in a bowl of coffee (she likes her coffee chicory-flavored and strong). The rest we divide between a pair of jelly glasses. We're both quite awed at the prospect of drinking straight whiskey; the taste of it brings screwed-up expressions and sour shudders. But by and by we begin to sing, the two of us singing different songs simultaneously. I don't know the words to mine, just: *Come on along, come on along, to the dark-town strutters' ball.* But I can dance: that's what I mean to be, a tap dancer in the movies. My dancing shadow rollicks on the walls; our voices rock the chinaware; we giggle: as if unseen hands were tickling us. Queenie rolls on her back, her paws plow the air, something like a grin stretches her black lips. Inside myself, I feel warm and sparky as those crumbling logs, carefree as the wind in the chimney. My friend waltzes round the stove, the hem of her poor calico skirt pinched between her fingers as though it were a party dress: *Show me the way to go home,* she sings, her tennis shoes squeaking on the floor. *Show me the way to go home.*

Enter: two relatives. Very angry. Potent with eyes that scold, tongues that scald. Listen to what they have to say, the words tumbling together into a wrathful tune: "A child of seven! whiskey on his breath! are you out of your mind? feeding a child of seven! must be loony! road to ruination! remember Cousin Kate? Uncle Charlie? Uncle Charlie's brother-in-law? shame! scandal! humiliation! kneel, pray, beg the Lord!"

Queenie sneaks under the stove. My friend gazes at her shoes, her chin quivers, she lifts her skirt and blows her nose and runs to her room. Long after the town has gone to sleep and the house is silent except for the chimings of clocks and the sputter of fading fires, she is weeping into a pillow already as wet as a widow's handkerchief.

"Don't cry," I say, sitting at the bottom of her bed and shivering despite my flannel nightgown that smells of last winter's cough syrup, "don't cry," I beg, teasing her toes, tickling her feet, "you're too old for that."

"It's because," she hiccups, "I *am* too old. Old and funny."

"Not funny. Fun. More fun than anybody. Listen. If you don't stop crying you'll be so tired tomorrow we can't go cut a tree."

She straightens up. Queenie jumps on the bed (where Queenie is not allowed) to lick her cheeks. "I know where we'll find pretty trees, Buddy. And holly, too. With berries big as your eyes. It's way off in the woods. Farther than we've ever been. Papa used to bring us Christmas trees from there: carry them on his shoulder. That's fifty years ago. Well, now: I can't wait for morning."

Morning. Frozen rime lusters the grass; the sun, round as an orange and orange as hot-weather moons, balances on the horizon, burnishes the silvered winter woods. A wild turkey calls. A renegade hog grunts in the undergrowth. Soon, by the edge of knee-deep, rapid-running water, we have to abandon the buggy. Queenie wades the stream first, paddles across barking complaints at the swiftness of the current, the pneumonia-making coldness of it. We follow, holding our shoes and equipment (a hatchet, a burlap sack) above our heads. A mile more: of chastising thorns, burs and briers that catch at our clothes; of rusty pine needles brilliant with gaudy fungus and molted feathers. Here, there, a flash, a flutter, an ecstasy of shrillings reminds us that not all the birds have flown south. Always, the path unwinds through lemony sun pools and pitch vine tunnels. Another creek to cross: a disturbed armada of speckled trout froths the water round us, and frogs the size of plates practice belly flops; beaver workmen are building a dam. On the farther shore, Queenie shakes herself and trembles. My friend shivers, too: not with cold but enthusiasm. One of her hat's ragged roses sheds a petal as she lifts her head and inhales the pine-heavy air. "We're almost there; can you smell it, Buddy?" she says, as though we were approaching an ocean.

And, indeed, it is a kind of ocean. Scented acres of holiday trees, prickly-leafed holly. Red berries shiny as Chinese bells: black crows swoop upon them screaming. Having stuffed our burlap sacks with enough greenery and crimson to garland a dozen windows, we set about choosing a tree. "It should be," muses my friend, "twice as tall as a boy. So a boy can't steal the star." The one we pick is twice as tall as me. A brave handsome brute that survives thirty hatchet strokes before it keels with a creaking, rending cry. Lugging it like a kill, we commence the long trek out. Every few yards we abandon the struggle, sit down and pant. But we have the strength of triumphant huntsmen; that and the tree's virile, icy perfume revive us, goad us on. Many compliments accompany our sunset return along the red clay road to town; but my friend is sly and noncommittal when passers-by praise the treasure perched on our buggy: what a fine tree and where did it come from? "Yonderways," she murmurs vaguely. Once a car stops and the rich mill owner's lazy wife leans out and whines: "Give ya two-bits cash for that ol' tree." Ordinarily my friend is afraid of saying no; but on this occasion she

promptly shakes her head: "We wouldn't take a dollar." The mill owner's wife persists. "A dollar, my foot! Fifty cents. That's my last offer. Goodness, woman, you can get another one." In answer, my friend gently reflects: "I doubt it. There's never two of anything."

Home: Queenie slumps by the fire and sleeps till tomorrow, snoring loud as a human.

A trunk in the attic contains: a shoebox of ermine tails (off the opera cape of a curious lady who once rented a room in the house), coils of frazzled tinsel gone gold with age, one silver star, a brief rope of dilapidated, undoubtedly dangerous candy-like light bulbs. Excellent decorations, as far as they go, which isn't far enough: my friend wants our tree to blaze "like a Baptist window," droop with weighty snows of ornament. But we can't afford the made-in-Japan splendors at the five-and-dime. So we do what we've always done: sit for days at the kitchen table with scissors and crayons and stacks of colored paper. I make sketches and my friend cuts them out: lots of cats, fish too (because they're easy to draw), some apples, some watermelons, a few winged angels devised from saved-up sheets of Hershey-bar tin foil. We use safety pins to attach these creations to the tree; as a final touch, we sprinkle the branches with shredded cotton (picked in August for this purpose). My friend, surveying the effect, clasps her hands together. "Now honest, Buddy. Doesn't it look good enough to eat?" Queenie tries to eat an angel.

After weaving and ribboning holly wreaths for all the front windows, our next project is the fashioning of family gifts. Tie-dye scarves for the ladies, for the men a home-brewed lemon and licorice and aspirin syrup to be taken "at the first Symptoms of a

Cold and after Hunting." But when it comes time for making each other's gifts, my friend and I separate to work secretly. I would like to buy her a pearl-handled knife, a radio, a whole pound of chocolate-covered cherries (we tasted some once, and she always swears: "I could live on them, Buddy, Lord yes I could—and that's not taking His name in vain"). Instead, I am building her a kite. She would like to give me a bicycle (she's said so on several million occasions: "If only I could, Buddy. It's bad enough in life to do without something *you* want; but confound it, what gets my goat is not being able to give somebody something you want *them* to have. Only one of these days I will, Buddy. Locate you a bike. Don't ask how. Steal it, maybe"). Instead, I'm fairly certain that she is building me a kite—the same as last year, and the year before: the year before that we exchanged slingshots. All of which is fine by me. For we are champion kite-fliers who study the wind like sailors; my friend, more accomplished than I, can get a kite aloft when there isn't enough breeze to carry clouds.

Christmas Eve afternoon we scrape together a nickel and go to the butcher's to buy Queenie's traditional gift, a good gnawable beef bone. The bone, wrapped in funny paper, is placed high in the tree near the silver star. Queenie knows it's there. She squats at the foot of the tree staring up in a trance of greed: when bedtime arrives she refuses to budge. Her excitement is equaled by my own. I kick the covers and turn my pillow as though it were a scorching summer's night. Somewhere a rooster crows: falsely, for the sun is still on the other side of the world.

"Buddy, are you awake?" It is my friend, calling from her room, which is next to mine;

and an instant later she is sitting on my bed holding a candle. "Well, I can't sleep a hoot," she declares. "My mind's jumping like a jack rabbit. Buddy, do you think Mrs. Roosevelt will serve our cake at dinner?" We huddle in the bed, and she squeezes my hand I-love-you. "Seems like your hand used to be so much smaller. I guess I hate to see you grow up. When you're grown up, will we still be friends?" I say always. "But I feel so bad, Buddy. I wanted so bad to give you a bike. I tried to sell my cameo Papa gave me. Buddy"—she hesitates, as though embarrassed—"I made you another kite." Then I confess that I made her one, too; and we laugh. The candle burns too short to hold. Out it goes, exposing the starlight, the stars spinning at the window like a visible caroling that slowly, slowly daybreak silences. Possibly we doze; but the beginnings of dawn splash us like cold water: we're up, wide-eyed and wandering while we wait for others to waken. Quite deliberately my friend drops a kettle on the kitchen floor. I tap-dance in front of closed doors. One by one the household emerges, looking as though they'd like to kill us both; but it's Christmas, so they can't. First, a gorgeous breakfast: just everything you can imagine—from flapjacks and fried squirrel to hominy grits and honey-in-the-comb. Which puts everyone in a good humor except my friend and I. Frankly, we're so impatient to get at the presents we can't eat a mouthful.

Well, I'm disappointed. Who wouldn't be? With socks, a Sunday school shirt, some handkerchiefs, a hand-me-down sweater and a year's subscription to a religious magazine for children. *The Little Shepherd.* It makes me boil. It really does.

My friend has a better haul. A sack of

Satsumas,[1] that's her best present. She is proudest, however, of a white wool shawl knitted by her married sister. But she *says* her favorite gift is the kite I built her. And it *is* very beautiful; though not as beautiful as the one she made me, which is blue and scattered with gold and green Good Conduct stars; moreover, my name is painted on it, "Buddy."

"Buddy, the wind is blowing."

The wind is blowing, and nothing will do till we've run to a pasture below the house where Queenie has scooted to bury her bone (and where, a winter hence, Queenie will be buried, too). There, plunging through the healthy waist-high grass, we unreel our kites, feel them twitching at the string like sky fish as they swim into the wind. Satisfied, sunwarmed, we sprawl in the grass and peel Satsumas and watch our kites cavort. Soon I forget the socks and hand-me-down sweater. I'm as happy as if we'd already won the fifty-thousand-dollar Grand Prize in that coffee-naming contest.

"My, how foolish I am!" my friend cries, suddenly alert, like a woman remembering too late she has biscuits in the oven. "You know what I've always thought?" she asks in a tone of discovery, and not smiling at me but a point beyond. "I've always thought a body would have to be sick and dying before they saw the Lord. And I imagined that when He came it would be like looking at the Baptist window: pretty as colored glass with the sun pouring through, such a shine you don't know it's getting dark. And it's been a comfort: to think of that shine taking away all the spooky feeling. But I'll wager it never happens. I'll wager at the very end a body realizes the Lord has already shown Himself. That things as they are"—her hand circles in a gesture that gathers clouds and

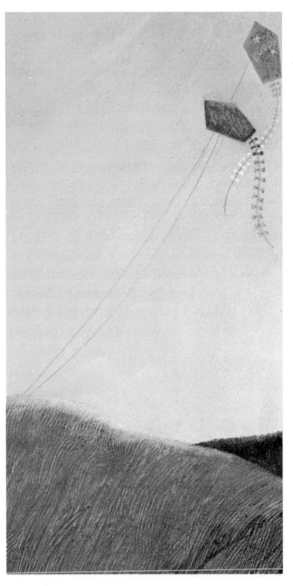

kites and grass and Queenie pawing earth over her bone—"just what they've always seen, was seeing Him. As for me, I could leave the world with today in my eyes."

This is our last Christmas together.

Life separates us. Those who Know Best decide that I belong in a military school. And so follows a miserable succession of bugle-blowing prisons, grim reveille-ridden sum-

---

1. *Satsumas,* a type of orange.

mer camps. I have a new home too. But it doesn't count. Home is where my friend is, and there I never go.

And there she remains, puttering around the kitchen. Alone with Queenie. Then alone. ("Buddy dear," she writes in her wild hard-to-read script, "yesterday Jim Macy's horse kicked Queenie bad. Be thankful she didn't feel much. I wrapped her in a Fine Linen sheet and rode her in the buggy down to Simpson's pasture where she can be with all her Bones. . . . ") For a few Novembers she continues to bake her fruitcakes single-handed; not as many, but some: and, of course, she always sends me "the best of the batch." Also, in every letter she encloses a dime wadded in toilet paper: "See a picture show and write me the story." But gradually in her letters she tends to confuse me with her other friend, the Buddy who died in the 1880's; more and more thirteenths are not the only days she stays in bed: a morning arrives in November, a leafless birdless coming of winter morning, when she cannot rouse herself to exclaim: "Oh my, it's fruitcake weather!"

And when that happens, I know it. A message saying so merely confirms a piece of news some secret vein had already received, severing from me an irreplaceable part of myself, letting it loose like a kite on a broken string. That is why, walking across a school campus on this particular December morning, I keep searching the sky. As if I expected to see, rather like hearts, a lost pair of kites hurrying toward heaven. ☐ ☐

Discussion

1. (a) When and where does this story take place? (b) Who is telling this story?

2. (a) How do Buddy and the old woman feel toward one another? (b) How are they different from the rest of the household? (c) Point out passages which you think are particularly effective in showing their friendship.

3. (a) Review the passage in which Buddy lists the things his friend has and has not done (29a). What is unusual about this list? (b) What characteristics does his friend display? (c) How do you feel toward her?

4. The first sentence of "A Christmas Memory" asks you to "imagine a morning in late November," and throughout the selection Truman Capote uses vivid sensory imagery. Pick one scene in which you think the images are particularly good. (a) Point out the senses to which they appeal. (b) Explain how they help you to become involved in the scene.

5. This story deals with a series of rather unimportant events. (a) Why did they make such a lasting impression on the child? (b) Recall similar incidents in your own life that seemed trivial but that were not.

Truman Capote 1924 •

He began writing when still a child; in fact, in school nothing *but* writing interested Capote. After publishing many stories in local newspapers, he wrote his first major prize-winning story at the age of nineteen. Since then he has written numerous stories and novels ranging in scope from nightmarish tragedy to light comedy. Much of his writing reflects his Southern background.

Capote is recognized as a very particular writer, one who spends an unusual amount of time rewriting in order to say something in exactly the right way. Among his best-known works are *Other Voices, Other Rooms; The Grass Harp; The Muses Are Heard; Breakfast at Tiffany's;* and *In Cold Blood*, a factual account of a Kansas murder case.

Ode to a Violin

Luis Omar Salinas

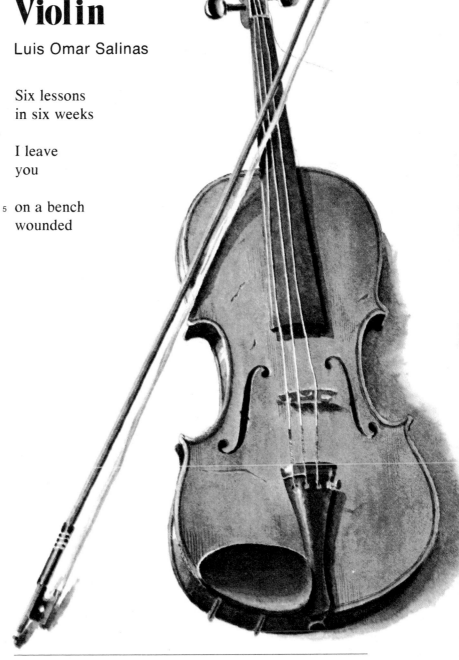

Discussion

1. (a) How well might a person be expected to play a violin after six lessons? (b) Why does the speaker refer to the violin as "wounded"?

2. Do you think the violin lessons will be continued? Explain.

3. An ode is usually a formal poem on a serious subject. (a) Is this poem formal and serious? (b) Why might the speaker call this poem "Ode to a Violin"?

4. What is the tone of this poem—sad, humorous, disgusted, sympathetic, resigned, ironic, or what?

Six lessons
in six weeks

I leave
you

5 on a bench
wounded

Luis Omar Salinas (lü ēs′ ô′mär sä lē′näs)

*In this mixed-up royal court there's a Prince
who isn't dashing and a Princess with not one, but two
fairy godmothers. In this most unlikely kingdom things aren't
quite what you'd expect. . . .*

The Ugly Duckling

A. A. Milne

CHARACTERS

THE KING
THE QUEEN
THE PRINCESS CAMILLA
THE CHANCELLOR
DULCIBELLA
THE PRINCE SIMON
CARLO

SCENE: *The Throne Room of the Palace; a
room of many doors, or, if preferred,
curtain-openings: simply furnished with
three thrones for Their Majesties and Her
Royal Highness the* PRINCESS CAMILLA—*in
other words, with three handsome chairs. At
each side is a long seat: reserved, as it might
be, for His Majesty's Council (if any), but
useful, as today, for other purposes. The*
KING *is asleep on his throne with a handkerchief over his face. He is a king of any
country from any story-book, in whatever
costume you please. But he should be wearing his crown.*

A VOICE *(announcing).* His Excellency, the
Chancellor! *(The* CHANCELLOR, *an elderly
man in horn-rimmed spectacles, enters,
bowing. The* KING *wakes up with a start
and removes the handkerchief from his
face.)*

KING *(with simple dignity).* I was thinking.

CHANCELLOR *(bowing).* Never, Your
Majesty, was greater need for thought
than now.

KING. That's what I was thinking. *(He
struggles into a more dignified position.)*
Well, what is it? More trouble?

"The Ugly Duckling" by A. A. Milne. Reprinted by permission of
Curtis Brown Ltd.

CHANCELLOR. What we might call the old trouble, Your Majesty.

KING. It's what I was saying last night to the Queen. "Uneasy lies the head that wears a crown,"[1] was how I put it.

CHANCELLOR. A profound and original thought, which may well go down to posterity.

KING. You mean it may go down well with posterity. I hope so. Remind me to tell you some time of another little thing I said to Her Majesty: something about a fierce light beating on a throne.[2] Posterity would like that, too. Well, what is it?

CHANCELLOR. It is in the matter of Her Royal Highness's wedding.

KING. Oh . . . yes.

CHANCELLOR. As Your Majesty is aware, the young Prince Simon arrives today to seek Her Royal Highness's hand in marriage. He has been travelling in distant lands and, as I understand, has not—er—has not—

KING. You mean he hasn't heard anything.

CHANCELLOR. It is a little difficult to put this tactfully, Your Majesty.

KING. Do your best, and I will tell you afterwards how you got on.

CHANCELLOR. Let me put it this way. The Prince Simon will naturally assume that Her Royal Highness has the customary—so customary as to be in my own poor opinion, slightly monotonous—has what one might call the inevitable—so inevitable as to be, in my opinion again, almost mechanical—will assume, that she has the,

---

1. *"Uneasy . . . crown"*, a line from Shakespeare's play, *Henry IV, Part II*.
2. *fierce . . . throne*, a reference to a line from a poem about King Arthur by Alfred, Lord Tennyson (1809–1892).

as *I* think of it, faultily faultless, icily regular, splendidly—

KING. What you are trying to say in the fewest words possible is that my daughter is not beautiful.

CHANCELLOR. Her beauty is certainly elusive, Your Majesty.

KING. It is. It has eluded you, it has eluded me, it has eluded everybody who has seen her. It even eluded the Court Painter. His last words were, "Well, I did my best." His successor is now painting the view across the water-meadows from the West Turret. He says his doctor has advised him to keep to landscape.

CHANCELLOR. It is unfortunate, Your Majesty, but there it is. One just cannot understand how it can have occurred.

KING. You don't think she takes after *me*, at all? You don't detect a likeness?

CHANCELLOR. Most certainly not, Your Majesty.

KING. Good. Your predecessor did.

CHANCELLOR. I have often wondered what happened to my predecessor.

KING. Well, now you know. *(There is a short silence.)*

CHANCELLOR. Looking at the bright side, although Her Royal Highness is not, strictly speaking, beautiful—

KING. Not, truthfully speaking, beautiful—

CHANCELLOR. Yet she has great beauty of character.

KING. My dear Chancellor, we are not considering Her Royal Highness's character, but her chances of getting married. You observe that there is a distinction.

CHANCELLOR. Yes, Your Majesty.

KING. Look at it from the suitor's point of view. If a girl is beautiful, it is easy to assume that she has, tucked away inside her, an equally beautiful character. But it is impossible to assume that an unattrac-tive girl, however elevated in character, has, tucked away inside her, an equally beautiful face. That is, so to speak, not where you want it—tucked away.

CHANCELLOR. Quite so, Your Majesty.

KING. This doesn't, of course, alter the fact that the Princess Camilla is quite the nic-est person in the Kingdom.

CHANCELLOR *(enthusiastically)*. She is in-deed, Your Majesty. *(hurriedly)* With the exception, I need hardly say, of Your Majesty—and Her Majesty.

KING. Your exceptions are tolerated for their loyalty and condemned for their ex-treme fatuity.

CHANCELLOR. Thank you, Your Majesty.

KING. As an adjective for your King, the word "nice" is ill-chosen. As an adjective for Her Majesty, it is—ill-chosen. *(At which moment* HER MAJESTY *comes in. The* KING *rises. The* CHANCELLOR *puts himself at right angles.)*

QUEEN *(briskly)*. Ah. Talking about Camil-la? *(She sits down.)*

KING *(returning to his throne)*. As always, my dear, you are right.

QUEEN *(to the* CHANCELLOR*)*. This fellow, Simon— What's he like?

CHANCELLOR. Nobody has seen him, Your Majesty.

QUEEN. How old is he?

CHANCELLOR. Five-and-twenty, I under-stand.

QUEEN. In twenty-five years he must have been seen by somebody.

KING *(to the* CHANCELLOR*)*. Just a fleeting glimpse.

CHANCELLOR. I meant, Your Majesty, that no detailed report of him has reached this country, save that he has the usual personal advantages and qualities expect-ed of a Prince, and has been traveling in distant and dangerous lands.

QUEEN. Ah! Nothing gone wrong with his eyes? Sunstroke or anything?

CHANCELLOR. Not that I am aware of, Your Majesty. At the same time, as I was venturing to say to His Majesty, Her Royal Highness's character and disposition are so outstandingly—

QUEEN. Stuff and nonsense. You remember what happened when we had the Tournament of Love last year.

CHANCELLOR. I was not myself present, Your Majesty. I had not then the honour of— I was abroad, and never heard the full story.

QUEEN. No; it was the other fool. They all rode up to Camilla to pay their homage—it was the first time they had seen her. The heralds blew their trumpets, and announced that she would marry whichever Prince was left master of the field when all but one had been unhorsed. The trumpets were blown again, they charged enthusiastically into the fight, and— (The KING looks nonchalantly at the ceiling and whistles a few bars.)—don't do that.

KING. I'm sorry, my dear.

QUEEN (to the CHANCELLOR). And what happened? They all simultaneously fell off their horses and assumed a posture of defeat.

KING. One of them was not quite so quick as the others. I was very quick. I proclaimed him the victor.

QUEEN. At the Feast of Betrothal held that night—

KING. We were all very quick.

QUEEN. The Chancellor announced that by the laws of the country the successful suitor had to pass a further test. He had to give the correct answer to a riddle.

CHANCELLOR. Such undoubtedly is the fact, Your Majesty.

KING. There are times for announcing facts, and times for looking at things in a broad-minded way. Please remember that, Chancellor.

CHANCELLOR. Yes, Your Majesty.

QUEEN. I invented the riddle myself. Quite an easy one. What is it which has four legs and barks like a dog? The answer is, "A dog."

KING (to the CHANCELLOR). See that?

CHANCELLOR. Yes, Your Majesty.

KING. It isn't difficult.

QUEEN. He, however, seemed to find it so. He said an eagle. Then he said a serpent; a very high mountain with slippery sides; two peacocks; a moonlight night; the day after tomorrow—

KING. Nobody could accuse him of not trying.

QUEEN. *I* did.

KING. I *should* have said that nobody could fail to recognize in his attitude an appearance of doggedness.

QUEEN. Finally he said "Death." I nudged the King—

KING. Accepting the word "nudge" for the moment, I rubbed my ankle with one hand, clapped him on the shoulder with the other, and congratulated him on the correct answer. He disappeared under the table, and, personally, I never saw him again.

QUEEN. His body was found in the moat next morning.

CHANCELLOR. But what was he doing in the moat, Your Majesty?

KING. Bobbing about. Try not to ask needless questions.

CHANCELLOR. It all seems so strange.

QUEEN. What does?

CHANCELLOR. That Her Royal Highness, alone of all the Princesses one has ever heard of, should lack that invariable attribute of Royalty, supreme beauty.

QUEEN (*to the* KING). That was your Great-Aunt Malkin. She came to the christening. You know what she said.

KING. It was cryptic. Great-Aunt Malkin's besetting weakness. She came to *my* christening—she was one hundred and one then, and that was fifty-one years ago. (*to the* CHANCELLOR) How old would that make her?

CHANCELLOR. One hundred and fifty-two, Your Majesty.

KING (*after thought*). About that, yes. She promised me that when I grew up I should have all the happiness which my wife deserved. It struck me at the time—well, when I say "at the time," I was only a week old—but it did strike me as soon as anything could strike me—I mean of that nature—well, work it out for yourself, Chancellor. It opens up a most interesting field of speculation. Though naturally I have not liked to go into it at all deeply with Her Majesty.

QUEEN. I never heard anything less cryptic. She was wishing you extreme happiness.

KING. I don't think she was *wishing* me anything. However.

CHANCELLOR (*to the* QUEEN). But what, Your Majesty, did she wish Her Royal Highness?

QUEEN. Her other godmother—on my side—had promised her the dazzling beauty for which all the women in my family are famous—(*She pauses, and the* KING *snaps his fingers surreptitiously in the direction of the* CHANCELLOR.)

CHANCELLOR (*hurriedly*). Indeed, yes, Your Majesty. (*The* KING *relaxes.*)

QUEEN. And Great-Aunt Malkin said— (*to the* KING) —what were the words?

KING.

> I give you with this kiss
> A wedding day surprise.

> *Where ignorance is bliss*
> *'Tis folly to be wise.*[3]

I thought the last two lines rather neat. But what it *meant*—

QUEEN. We can all see what it meant. She was given beauty—and where is it? Great-Aunt Malkin took it away from her. The wedding day surprise is that there will never be a wedding day.

KING. Young men being what they are, my dear, it would be much more surprising if there *were* a wedding day. So how— (*The* PRINCESS *comes in. She is young, happy, healthy, but not beautiful. Or let us say that by some trick of make-up or arrangement of hair she seems plain to us: unlike the princess of the story-books.*)

PRINCESS (*to the* KING). Hello, darling! (*seeing the others*) Oh, I say! Affairs of state? Sorry.

KING (*holding out his hand*). Don't go, Camilla. (*She takes his hand.*)

CHANCELLOR. Shall I withdraw, Your Majesty?

QUEEN. You are aware, Camilla, that Prince Simon arrives today?

PRINCESS. He has arrived. They're just letting down the drawbridge.

KING (*jumping up*). Arrived! I must—

PRINCESS. Darling, you know what the drawbridge is like. It takes at *least* half an hour to let it down.

KING (*sitting down*). It wants oil. (*to the* CHANCELLOR) Have *you* been grudging it oil?

PRINCESS. It wants a new drawbridge, darling.

CHANCELLOR. Have I your Majesty's permission—

---

3. *Where ignorance . . . be wise,* from "On a Distant Prospect of Eton College," by Thomas Gray (1716–1771).

KING. Yes, yes. *(The* CHANCELLOR *bows and goes out.)*

QUEEN. You've told him, of course? It's the only chance.

KING. Er—no. I was just going to, when—

QUEEN. Then I'd better. *(She goes to the door.)* You can explain to the girl; I'll have her sent to you. You've told Camilla?

KING. Er—no. I was just going to, when—

QUEEN. Then you'd better tell her now.

KING. My dear, are you sure—

QUEEN. It's the only chance left. *(dramatically to heaven)* My daughter! *(She goes out. There is a little silence when she is gone.)*

KING. Camilla, I want to talk seriously to you about marriage.

PRINCESS. Yes, father.

KING. It is time that you learnt some of the facts of life.

PRINCESS. Yes, father.

KING. Now the great fact about marriage is that once you're married you live happy ever after. All our history books affirm this.

PRINCESS. And your own experience too, darling.

KING *(with dignity).* Let us confine ourselves to history for the moment.

PRINCESS. Yes, father.

KING. Of course, there *may* be an exception here and there, which, as it were, proves the rule; just as—oh, well, never mind.

PRINCESS *(smiling).* Go on, darling. You were going to say that an exception here and there proves the rule that all princesses are beautiful.

KING. Well—leave that for the moment. The point is that it doesn't matter *how* you marry, or *who* you marry, as long as you *get* married. Because you'll be happy ever after in any case. Do you follow me so far?

PRINCESS. Yes, father.

KING. Well, your mother and I have a little plan—

PRINCESS. Was that it, going out of the door just now?

KING. Er—yes. It concerns your waiting-maid.

PRINCESS. Darling, I have several.

KING. Only one that leaps to the eye, so to speak. The one with the—well, with everything.

PRINCESS. Dulcibella?

KING. That's the one. It is our little plan that at the first meeting she should pass herself off as the Princess—a harmless ruse, of which you will find frequent record in the history books—and allure Prince Simon to his—that is to say, bring him up to the—in other words, the wedding will take place immediately afterwards, and as quietly as possible—well, naturally in view of the fact that your Aunt Malkin is one hundred and fifty-two; and since you will be wearing the family bridal veil—which is no doubt how the custom arose—the surprise after the ceremony will be his. Are you following me at all? Your attention seems to be wandering.

PRINCESS. I was wondering why you needed to tell me.

KING. Just a precautionary measure, in case you happened to meet the Prince or his attendant before the ceremony; in which case, of course, you would pass yourself off as the maid—

PRINCESS. A harmless ruse, of which, also, you will find frequent record in the history books.

KING. Exactly. But the occasion need not arise.

A VOICE *(announcing).* The woman Dulcibella!

KING. Ah! *(to the* PRINCESS*)* Now, Camilla,

if you just retire to your own apartments, I will come to you there when we are ready for the actual ceremony. *(He leads her out as he is talking, and as he returns calls out:)* Come in, my dear! *(DULCIBELLA comes in. She is beautiful, but dumb.)* Now don't be frightened, there is nothing to be frightened about. Has Her Majesty told you what you have to do?

DULCIBELLA. Y-yes, Your Majesty.

KING. Well now, let's see how well you can do it. You are sitting here, we will say. *(He leads her to a seat.)* Now imagine that I am Prince Simon. *(He curls his moustache and puts his stomach in. She giggles.)* You are the beautiful Princess Camilla whom he has never seen. *(She giggles again.)* This is a serious moment in your life, and you will find that a giggle will not be helpful. *(He goes to the door.)* I am announced: "His Royal Highness Prince Simon!" That's me being announced. Remember what I said about giggling. You should have a faraway look upon the face. *(She does her best.)* Farther away than that. *(She tries again.)* No, that's too far. You are sitting there, thinking beautiful thoughts—in maiden meditation, fancy-free,[4] as I remember saying to Her Majesty once . . . speaking of somebody else . . . fancy-free, but with the mouth definitely shut—that's better. I advance and fall upon one knee. *(He does so.)* You extend your hand graciously—*graciously;* you're not trying to push him in the face—that's better, and I raise it to my lips—so—and I kiss it— *(He kisses it warmly.)* —no, perhaps not so ardently as that, more like this *(He kisses it again.)* and I say, "Your Royal Highness, this is the most—er—Your Royal Highness, I shall ever be—no—Your Royal Highness, it is the proudest—" Well, the point is that

he will say it, and it will be something complimentary, and then he will take your hand in both of his, and press it to his heart. *(He does so.)* And then—what do *you* say?

DULCIBELLA. Coo![5]

KING. No, *not* Coo.

DULCIBELLA. Never had anyone do *that* to me before.

KING. That also strikes the wrong note. What you want to say is, "Oh, Prince Simon!" . . . Say it.

DULCIBELLA *(loudly).* Oh, Prince Simon!

KING. No, no. You don't need to shout until he has said "What?" two or three times. Always consider the possibility that he *isn't* deaf. Softly, and giving the words a dying fall, letting them play around his head like a flight of doves.

DULCIBELLA *(still a little over-loud).* O-o-o-o-h, Prinsimon!

KING. Keep the idea in your mind of a flight of *doves* rather than a flight of panic-stricken elephants, and you will be all right. Now I'm going to get up, and you must, as it were, *waft* me into a seat by your side. *(She starts wafting.)* *Not* rescuing a drowning man, that's another idea altogether, useful at times, but at the moment inappropriate. Wafting. Prince Simon will put the necessary muscles into play—all you require to do is to indicate by a gracious movement of the hand the seat you require him to take. Now! *(He gets up, a little stiffly, and sits next to her.)* That was better. Well, here we are. Now, I think you give me a look: something, let us say, halfway between the breathless adoration of a nun[6] and the voluptuous aban-

---

4. *in . . . fancy-free,* a line from Shakespeare's play, *A Midsummer Night's Dream.*
5. *Coo,* a British slang expression of delight.
6. *breathless . . . nun,* a paraphrase of a line from "It is a Beauteous Evening," a poem by William Wordsworth (1770–1850).

donment of a woman of the world; with an undertone of regal dignity, touched, as it were, with good comradeship. Now try that. *(She gives him a vacant look of bewilderment.)* Frankly, that didn't quite get it. There was just a little something missing. An absence, as it were, of all the qualities I asked for, and in their place an odd resemblance to an unsatisfied fish. Let us try to get it another way. Dulcibella, have you a young man of your own?

DULCIBELLA *(eagerly, seizing his hand).* Oo, yes, he's ever so smart, he's an archer, well not as you might say a real archer, he works in the armoury, but old Bottlenose, *you* know who I mean, the Captain of the Guard, says the very next man they ever has to shoot, my Eg shall take his place, knowing Father and how it is with Eg and me, and me being maid to Her Royal Highness and can't marry me till he's a real soldier, but ever so loving, and funny like, the things he says. I said to him once, "Eg," I said—

KING *(getting up).* I rather fancy, Dulcibella, that if you think of Eg all the time, *say* as little as possible, and, when thinking of Eg, see that the mouth is not more than partially open, you will do very well. I will show you where you are to sit and wait for His Royal Highness. *(He leads her out. On the way he is saying:)* Now remember—*waft—waft*—not *hoick.*[7] *(PRINCE SIMON wanders in from the back unannounced. He is a very ordinary-looking young man in rather dusty clothes. He gives a deep sigh of relief as he sinks into the king's throne.* CAMILLA, *a new and strangely beautiful* CAMILLA, *comes in.)*

PRINCESS *(surprised).* Well!

PRINCE. Oh, hello!

PRINCESS. Ought you?

PRINCE *(getting up).* Do sit down, won't you?

PRINCESS. Who are you, and how did you get here?

PRINCE. Well, that's rather a long story. Couldn't we sit down? You could sit here if you liked, but it isn't very comfortable.

PRINCESS. That is the King's Throne.

PRINCE. Oh, is that what it is?

PRINCESS. Thrones are not meant to be comfortable.

PRINCE. Well, I don't know if they're meant to be, but they certainly aren't.

PRINCESS. Why were you sitting on the King's Throne, and who are you?

PRINCE. My name is Carlo.

PRINCESS. Mine is Dulcibella.

PRINCE. Good. And now couldn't we sit down?

PRINCESS *(sitting down on the long seat to the left of the throne, and, as it were, wafting him to a place next to her).* You may sit here, if you like. Why are you so tired? *(He sits down.)*

PRINCE. I've been taking very strenuous exercise.

PRINCESS. Is that part of the long story?

PRINCE. It is.

PRINCESS *(settling herself).* I love stories.

PRINCE. This isn't a story really. You see, I'm attendant on Prince Simon, who is visiting here.

PRINCESS. Oh? I'm attendant on Her Royal Highness.

PRINCE. Then you know what he's here for.

PRINCESS. Yes.

PRINCE. She's very beautiful, I hear.

PRINCESS. Did you hear that? Where have you been lately?

PRINCE. Traveling in distant lands—with Prince Simon.

PRINCESS. Ah! All the same, I don't understand. Is Prince Simon in the Palace now? The drawbridge *can't* be down yet!

PRINCE. I don't suppose it is. *And* what noise it makes coming down!

PRINCESS. Isn't it terrible?

PRINCE. I couldn't stand it any more. I just had to get away. That's why I'm here.

PRINCESS. But how?

PRINCE. Well, there's only one way, isn't there? That beech tree, and then a swing and a grab for the battlements, and don't ask me to remember it all— *(He shudders.)*

PRINCESS. You mean you came across the moat by that beech tree?

PRINCE. Yes. I got so tired of hanging about.

PRINCESS. But it's terribly dangerous!

PRINCE. That's why I'm so exhausted. Nervous shock. *(He lies back.)*

PRINCESS. Of course, it's different for *me.*

PRINCE *(sitting up).* Say that again. I must have got it wrong.

PRINCESS. It's different for me, because I'm used to it. Besides, I'm so much lighter.

PRINCE. You don't mean that *you—*

---

7. *hoick,* jerk or yank.

PRINCESS. Oh yes, often.

PRINCE. And I thought I was a brave man! At least, I didn't until five minutes ago, and now I don't again.

PRINCESS. Oh, but you are! And I think it's wonderful to do it straight off the first time.

PRINCE. Well, *you* did.

PRINCESS. Oh no, not the first time. When I was a child.

PRINCE. You mean that you crashed?

PRINCESS. Well, you only fall into the moat.

PRINCE. Only! Can you *swim?*

PRINCESS. Of course.

PRINCE. So you swam to the castle walls, and yelled for help, and they fished you out and walloped you. And next day you tried again. Well, if *that* isn't pluck—

PRINCESS. Of course I didn't. I swam back, and did it at once; I mean I tried again at once. It wasn't until the third time that I actually did it. You see, I was afraid I might lose my nerve.

PRINCE. Afraid she might lose her nerve!

PRINCESS. There's a way of getting over from this side, too; a tree grows out from the wall and you jump into another tree—I don't think it's quite so easy.

PRINCE. Not quite so easy. Good. You must show me.

PRINCESS. Oh, I will.

PRINCE. Perhaps it might be as well if you taught me how to swim first. I've often heard about swimming, but never—

PRINCESS. You can't swim?

PRINCE. No. Don't look so surprised. There are a lot of other things which I can't do. I'll tell you about them as soon as you have a couple of years to spare.

PRINCESS. You can't swim and yet you crossed by the beech tree! And you're *ever* so much heavier than I am! Now who's brave?

PRINCE *(getting up).* You keep talking about how light you are. I must see if there's anything in it. Stand up! *(She stands obediently and he picks her up.)* You're right, Dulcibella. I could hold you here forever. *(looking at her)* You're very lovely. Do you know how lovely you are?

PRINCESS. Yes. *(She laughs suddenly and happily.)*

PRINCE. Why do you laugh?

PRINCESS. Aren't you tired of holding me?

PRINCE. Frankly, yes. I exaggerated when I said I could hold you for ever. When you've been hanging by the arms for ten minutes over a very deep moat, wondering if it's too late to learn how to swim— *(He puts her down.)* —What I meant was that I should *like* to hold you forever. Why did you laugh?

PRINCESS. Oh, well, it was a little private joke of mine.

PRINCE. If it comes to that, I've got a private joke too. Let's exchange them.

PRINCESS. Mine's very private. One other woman in the whole world knows, and that's all.

PRINCE. Mine's just as private. One other man knows, and that's all.

PRINCESS. What fun. I love secrets. . . . Well, here's mine. When I was born, one of my godmothers promised that I should be very beautiful.

PRINCE. How right she was.

PRINCESS. But the other one said this:
I give you with this kiss
A wedding day surprise.
Where ignorance is bliss
'Tis folly to be wise.
And nobody knew what it meant. And I grew up very plain. And then, when I was

about ten, I met my godmother in the forest one day. It was my tenth birthday. Nobody knows this—except you.

PRINCE. Except us.

PRINCESS. Except us. And she told me what her gift meant. It meant that I *was* beautiful—but everybody else was to go on being ignorant, and thinking me plain, until my wedding day. Because, she said, she didn't want me to grow up spoilt and wilful and vain, as I should have done if everybody had always been saying how beautiful I was; and the best thing in the world, she said, was to be quite sure of yourself, but not to expect admiration from other people. So ever since then my mirror has told me I'm beautiful, and everybody else thinks me ugly, and I get a lot of fun out of it.

PRINCE. Well, seeing that Dulcibella is the result, I can only say that your godmother was very, very wise.

PRINCESS. And now tell me *your* secret.

PRINCE. It isn't such a pretty one. You see, Prince Simon was going to woo Princess Camilla, and he'd heard that she was beautiful and haughty and imperious—all *you* would have been if your godmother hadn't been so wise. And being a very ordinary-looking fellow himself, he was afraid she wouldn't think much of him, so he suggested to one of his attendants, a man called Carlo, of extremely attractive appearance, that *he* should pretend to be the Prince, and win the Princess's hand; and then at the last moment they would change places—

PRINCESS. How would they do that?

PRINCE. The Prince was going to have been married in full armour—with his visor down.

PRINCESS *(laughing happily)*. Oh, what fun!

PRINCE. Neat, isn't it?

PRINCESS *(laughing)*. Oh, very . . . very . . . very.

PRINCE. Neat, but not so terribly *funny*. Why do you keep laughing?

PRINCESS. Well, that's another secret.

PRINCE. If it comes to that, *I've* got another one up my sleeve. Shall we exchange again?

PRINCESS. All right. You go first this time.

PRINCE. Very well. I am not Carlo. *(Standing up and speaking dramatically.)* I am Simon!—ow! *(He sits down and rubs his leg violently.)*

PRINCESS *(alarmed)*. What is it?

PRINCE. Cramp. *(in a mild voice, still rubbing)* I was saying that I was Prince Simon.

PRINCESS. Shall I rub it for you? *(She rubs.)*

PRINCE *(still hopefully)*. I am Simon.

PRINCESS. Is that better?

PRINCE *(despairingly)*. I am Simon.

PRINCESS. I know.

PRINCE. How did you know?

PRINCESS. Well, you told me.

PRINCE. But oughtn't you to swoon or something?

PRINCESS. Why? History records many similar ruses.

PRINCE *(amazed)*. Is that so? I've never read history. I thought I was being profoundly original.

PRINCESS. Oh, no! Now I'll tell you *my* secret. For reasons very much like your own the Princess Camilla, who is held to be extremely plain, feared to meet Prince Simon. Is the draw-bridge down yet?

PRINCE. Do your people give a faint, surprised cheer every time it gets down?

PRINCESS. Naturally.

PRINCE. Then it came down about three minutes ago.

PRINCESS. Ah! Then at this very moment your man Carlo is declaring his passionate love for my maid, Dulcibella. That, I think, is funny. *(So does the* PRINCE. *He laughs heartily.)* Dulcibella, by the way, is in love with a man she calls Eg, so I hope Carlo isn't getting carried away.

PRINCE. Carlo is married to a girl he calls "the little woman," so Eg has nothing to fear.

PRINCESS. By the way, I don't know if you heard, but I said, or as good as said, that I am the Princess Camilla.

PRINCE. I wasn't surprised. History, of which I read a great deal, records many similar ruses.

PRINCESS *(laughing).* Simon!

PRINCE *(laughing).* Camilla! *(He stands up.)* May I try holding you again? *(She nods. He takes her in his arms and kisses her.)* Sweetheart!

PRINCESS. You see, when you lifted me up before, you said, "You're very lovely," and my godmother said that the first person to whom I would seem lovely was the man I should marry; so I knew then that you were Simon and I should marry you.

PRINCE. I knew directly when I saw you that I should marry you, even if you were Dulcibella. By the way, which of you *am* I marrying?

PRINCESS. When she lifts her veil, it will be Camilla. *(Voices are heard outside.)* Until then it will be Dulcibella.

PRINCE *(in a whisper).* Then goodbye, Camilla, until you lift your veil.

PRINCESS. Goodbye, Simon, until you raise your visor. *(The* KING *and* QUEEN *come in arm-in-arm, followed by* CARLO *and* DULCIBELLA, *also arm-in-arm. The* CHANCELLOR *precedes them, walking backwards, at a loyal angle.)*

PRINCE *(supporting the* CHANCELLOR *as an accident seems inevitable).* Careful! *(The* CHANCELLOR *turns indignantly round.)*

KING. Who and what is this? More accurately, who and what are all these?

CARLO. My attendant, Carlo, Your Majesty. He will, with Your Majesty's permission, prepare me for the ceremony. *(The* PRINCE *bows.)*

KING. Of course, of course!

QUEEN *(to* DULCIBELLA*).* Your maid, Dulcibella, is it not, my love? *(*DULCIBELLA *nods violently.)* I thought so. *(to* CARLO*) She* will prepare Her Royal Highness. *(The* PRINCESS *curtsies.)*

KING. Ah, yes. Yes. *Most* important.

PRINCESS *(curtsying).* I beg pardon, Your Majesty, if I've done wrong, but I found the gentleman wandering—

KING *(crossing to her).* Quite right, my dear, quite right. *(He pinches her cheek, and takes advantage of this kingly gesture to say in a loud whisper:)* We've pulled it off! *(They sit down; the* KING *and* QUEEN *on their thrones,* DULCIBELLA *on the princess's throne.* CARLO *stands behind* DULCIBELLA, *the* CHANCELLOR *on the right of the* QUEEN, *and the* PRINCE *and* PRINCESS *behind the long seat on the left.)*

CHANCELLOR *(consulting documents).* H'r'm! Have I Your Majesty's authority to put the final test to His Royal Highness?

QUEEN *(whispering to the* KING*).* Is this safe?

KING *(whispering).* Perfectly, my dear. I told him the answer a minute ago. *(over his shoulder to* CARLO*)* Don't forget. *Dog.* *(aloud)* Proceed, Your Excellency. It is my desire that the affairs of my country should ever be conducted in a strictly constitutional manner.

CHANCELLOR *(oratorically).* By the constitution of the country, a suitor to Her Royal Highness's hand cannot be deemed successful until he has given the correct answer to a riddle. *(conversationally)* The last suitor answered incorrectly, and thus failed to win his bride.

KING. By a coincidence he fell into the moat.

CHANCELLOR *(to* CARLO*)*. I have now to ask Your Royal Highness if you are prepared for the ordeal?

CARLO *(cheerfully)*. Absolutely.

CHANCELLOR. I may mention, as a matter, possibly, of some slight historical interest to our visitor, that by the constitution of the country the same riddle is not allowed to be asked on two successive occasions.

KING *(startled)*. What's that?

CHANCELLOR. This one, it is interesting to recall, was propounded exactly a century ago, and we must take it as a fortunate omen that it was well and truly solved.

KING *(to the* QUEEN*)*. I may want my sword directly.

CHANCELLOR. The riddle is this. What is it which has four legs and mews like a cat?

CARLO *(promptly)*. A dog.

KING *(still more promptly)*. Bravo, bravo! *(He claps loudly and nudges the* QUEEN, *who claps too.)*

CHANCELLOR *(peering at his documents)*. According to the records of the occasion to which I referred, the correct answer would seem to be—

PRINCESS *(to the* PRINCE*)*. Say something, quick!

CHANCELLOR. —not dog, but—

PRINCE. Your Majesty, have I permission to speak? Naturally His Royal Highness could not think of justifying himself on such an occasion, but I think that with Your Majesty's gracious permission, I could—

KING. Certainly, certainly.

PRINCE. In our country, we have an animal to which we have given the name "dog," or, in the local dialect of the more mountainous districts, "doggie." It sits by the fireside and purrs.

CARLO. That's right. It purrs like anything.

PRINCE. When it needs milk, which is its staple food, it mews.

CARLO *(enthusiastically)*. Mews like nobody's business.

PRINCE. It also has four legs.

CARLO. One at each corner.

PRINCE. In some countries, I understand, this animal is called a "cat." In one distant country to which His Royal Highness and I penetrated it was called by the very curious name of "hippopotamus."

CARLO. That's right. *(to the* PRINCE*)* Do you remember that ginger-coloured hippopotamus which used to climb onto my shoulder and lick my ear?

PRINCE. I shall never forget it, sir. *(to the* KING*)* So you see, Your Majesty—

KING. Thank you. I think that makes it perfectly clear. *(firmly to the* CHANCELLOR*)* You are about to agree?

CHANCELLOR. Undoubtedly, Your Majesty. May I be the first to congratulate His Royal Highness on solving the riddle so accurately?

KING. You may be the first to see that all is in order for an immediate wedding.

CHANCELLOR. Thank you, Your Majesty. *(He bows and withdraws. The* KING *rises, as do the* QUEEN *and* DULCIBELLA.*)*

KING *(to* CARLO*)*. Doubtless, Prince Simon, you will wish to retire and prepare yourself for the ceremony.

CARLO. Thank you, sir.

PRINCE. Have I Your Majesty's permission to attend His Royal Highness? It is the custom of his country for Princes of the

royal blood to be married in full armour, a matter which requires a certain adjustment—

KING. Of course, of course. *(CARLO bows to the KING and QUEEN and goes out. As the PRINCE is about to follow, the KING stops him.)* Young man, you have a quality of quickness which I admire. It is my pleasure to reward it in any way which commends itself to you.

PRINCE. Your Majesty is ever gracious. May I ask for my reward *after* the ceremony? *(He catches the eye of the PRINCESS, and they give each other a secret smile.)*

KING. Certainly. *(The PRINCE bows and goes out. To DULCIBELLA.)* Now, young woman, make yourself scarce. You've done your work excellently, and we will see that you and your—what was his name?

DULCIBELLA. Eg, Your Majesty.

KING. —that you and your Eg are not forgotten.

DULCIBELLA. Coo! *(She curtsies and goes out.)*

PRINCESS *(calling)*. Wait for me, Dulcibella!

KING *(to the QUEEN)*. Well, my dear, we may congratulate ourselves. As I remember saying to somebody once, "You have not lost a daughter, you have gained a son." How does he strike you?

QUEEN. Stupid.

KING. They made a very handsome pair, I thought, he and Dulcibella.

QUEEN. Both stupid.

KING. I said nothing about stupidity. What I *said* was that they were both extremely handsome. That is the important thing. *(struck by a sudden idea)* Or isn't it?

QUEEN. What do *you* think of Prince Simon, Camilla?

PRINCESS. I adore him. We shall be so happy together.

KING. Well, of course you will. I told you so. Happy ever after.

QUEEN. Run along now and get ready.

PRINCESS. Yes, mother. *(She throws a kiss to them and goes out.)*

KING *(anxiously)*. My dear, have we been wrong about Camilla all this time? It seemed to me that she wasn't looking *quite* so plain as usual just now. Did *you* notice anything?

QUEEN *(carelessly)*. Just the excitement of the marriage.

KING *(relieved)*. Ah, yes, that would account for it.

CURTAIN

Discussion

1. The title of this play comes from a fairy tale about an ugly duckling that grew up to be a beautiful swan. How does Princess Camilla's story parallel that of the ugly duckling?

2. What details in the opening description (38a, 1) suggest that what follows will *not* be a straight dramatization of a fairy tale?

3. (a) As the play opens, why are the King and the Chancellor concerned about Princess Camilla? (b) What had happened the previous year at the Tournament of Love? (c) How do the King, Queen, and Chancellor set about making certain this does not happen again?

4. (a) Do you think Princess Camilla was right not to tell anyone about her godmother Malkin's gift? Explain. (b) How did Malkin's gift benefit Princess Camilla?

5. (a) In what ways is Prince

Simon unlike the traditional fairy-tale prince? **(b)** Do you like him more or less for these differences? Explain. **(c)** In what other ways is the play unlike the usual fairy tale or fantasy? **(d)** In what respects, if any, does the play uphold the traditions of the fairy tale?

6. Many of the passages of the play contain incidental or ironic humor. What is the underlying humor of each of the following? **(a)** Queen to Chancellor about Prince: "Nothing gone wrong with his eyes? Sunstroke or anything?" (41a, 1). **(b)** Queen to Chancellor: "No, it was the other fool" (41a, 5). **(c)** King to Queen after Chancellor has announced that a *different* riddle must be solved by Prince Simon: "I may want my sword directly" (50a, 7).

Vocabulary • Structure

Recognizing the meaningful parts, or the structure, of a word may help you understand the meaning of the whole word. Many words are made up of a root word plus one or more affixes (that is, one or more prefixes or suffixes).

prefix	root	suffix
in	appropriate	
	compliment	ary
un	doubt	ed, ly

The root is the main part of the word and carries the word's basic meaning. If you recognized the roots of *in*appropri*ate,* **compliment***ary,* and *un*doubt*edly* when you came

across these words in your reading, you would have had a good start toward figuring out the meaning of each word.

A prefix is usually placed before a root to change the meaning of the root in some way; *in*appropriate, for example, means "not" appropriate. Other common prefixes are *dis-, un-, non-* (all meaning "not"), *pre-* ("before"), *re-* ("again"), and *trans-* ("across").

Usually a suffix placed after a root word changes the way the word is used in a sentence: He paid me a *compliment.* He made a *compliment*ary remark to me. But sometimes a suffix will also change the meaning of a root word.

Look closely at the structure of the italicized words in the following questions. Then answer the questions on a separate sheet of paper.

1. What is the root word of *precautionary?* Based on its structure, do you think *precautionary* means "having advance notice," "not being careful," or "taking care beforehand"?

2. To form the word *invariable,* the **y** in *vary* is changed to an **i**. If a person is known for her *invariable* cheerfulness, is she cheerful some of the time, most of the time, or all of the time?

3. An *orator* is a person known for skill and power in public speaking. In which of the following situations would you most likely expect to hear someone speaking

oratorically—at an awards dinner, on a TV variety show, or on a five-minute radio news report?

4. The word *monotonous* is made up of the prefix *mono-,* the root word *ton(e),* and the suffix *-ous. Mono-* comes from a Greek word meaning "one; single." Do you think you would enjoy listening to someone who had a *monotonous* voice? Why or why not?

Extension • Speaking

As a class project, prepare a tape recording of this play. In addition to the characters themselves, you will need a director, a sound effects expert, a technician in charge of the tape recording, and possibly assistants for each.

A. A. Milne 1882 • 1956

He wanted to be remembered for such serious writing as *Peace with Honor,* a book condemning war. Yet A. A. Milne is known all over the world for something far different—warm, light-hearted stories featuring Winnie the Pooh, a character whose adventures have signaled bedtime for thousands of children. One of Winnie the Pooh's friends, Christopher Robin, was named for Milne's own son.

See **FIGURATIVE LANGUAGE**
Handbook of Literary Terms

dandelions

Deborah Austin

under cover of night and rain
the troops took over.
waking to total war in beleaguered houses
over breakfast we faced the batteries
5 marshalled by wall and stone, deployed
with a master strategy no one had suspected
and now all
firing

pow

10 all day, all yesterday
and all today
the barrage continued
deafening sight.
reeling now, eyes ringing from noise, from
    walking
15 gingerly over the mined lawns
exploded at every second
rocked back by the starshellfire
concussion of gold on green
bringing battle-fatigue

From *The Paradise of the World* by Deborah Austin. Published by The Pennsylvania State University Press. Copyright © 1964 by The Pennsylvania State University. Reprinted by permission.

Discussion

1. (a) At which phase of a dandelion's growth does it become active in the battle? **(b)** How long does the battle continue? **(c)** What finally stops the siege? **(d)** To what does "smoke" in line 24 refer? **(e)** What are "guerrilla snipers" (line 36)?

2. (a) Explain the comparison on which the first stanza is based. **(b)** Is this comparison consistent throughout the poem?

Maurice B. Cook

20 pow by lionface firefur pow by
goldburst shellshock pow by
whoosh   splat   splinteryellow   pow   by
pow   by   pow
tomorrow smoke drifts up
25 from the wrecked battalions,
all the ammunition, firegold fury, gone.
smoke
drifts
thistle-blown
30 over the war-zone, only

here and there, in the shade by the
peartree
pow   in the crack by the
curbstone   pow   and back of the
35 ashcan, lonely
guerrilla snipers, hoarding
their fire shrewdly
never

pow

40 surrender

3. In line 13, "deafening sight" is a figurative expression that suggests an effect on the eyes similar to that of an explosion on the ears. What other figurative expressions can you find that have a similar effect?

4. Since the poem doesn't rhyme, the poet must achieve her effects through other means, such as the physical arrangement of the lines. What effect does this arrangement have on the pace of the poem?

5. Which of the following words best describes the poem: grim, fanciful, or happy?

"I want to walk again among the ghost birches. . . . I want to hear the drums; I want to hear the drums and feel the blue whispering winds."

Blue Winds Dancing

Thomas S. Whitecloud

There is a moon out tonight. Moon and stars and clouds tipped with moonlight. And there is a fall wind blowing in my heart. Ever since this evening, when against a fading sky I saw geese wedge southward. They were going home. . . . Now I try to study, but against the pages I see them again, driving southward. Going home.

Across the valley there are heavy mountains holding up the night sky, and beyond the mountains there is home. Home, and peace, and the beat of drums, and blue winds dancing over snow fields. The Indian lodge will fill with my people, and our gods will come and sit among them. I should be there then. I should be at home.

But home is beyond the mountains, and I am here. Here where fall hides in the valleys and winter never comes down from the mountains. Here where all the trees grow in rows; the palms stand stiffly by the roadsides, and in the groves the orange trees line in military rows and endlessly bear fruit. Beautiful, yes; there is always beauty in order, in rows of growing things! But it is the beauty of captivity. A pine fighting for existence on a windy knoll is much more beautiful.

In my Wisconsin, the leaves change before the snows come. In the air there is the smell of wild rice and venison cooking; and when the winds come whispering through the forests, they carry the smell of rotting leaves. In the evenings, the loon calls, lonely; and birds sing their last songs before leaving. Bears dig roots and eat late fall berries, fattening for their long winter sleep. Later, when the first snows fall, one awakens in the morning to find the world white

"Blue Winds Dancing" by Thomas S. Whitecloud. First appeared in *Scribner's Magazine*, February 1939. Reprinted by permission.

and beautiful and clean. Then one can look back over his trail and see the tracks following. In the woods there are tracks of deer and snowshoe rabbits and long streaks where partridges slide to alight. Chipmunks make tiny footprints on the limbs; and one can hear squirrels busy in hollow trees, sorting acorns. Soft lake waves wash the shores, and sunsets burst each evening over the lakes and make them look as if they were afire.

That land which is my home! Beautiful, calm—where there is no hurry to get anywhere, no driving to keep up in a race that knows no ending and no goal. No classes where men talk and talk, and then stop now and then to hear their own words come back to them from the students. No constant peering into the maelstrom[1] of one's mind; no worries about grades and honors; no hysterical preparing for life until that life is half over; no anxiety about one's place in the thing they call Society.

I hear again the ring of axes in deep woods, the crunch of snow beneath my feet. I feel again the smooth velvet of ghost-birch bark. I hear the rhythm of the drums. . . . I am tired. I am weary of trying to keep up this bluff of being civilized. Being civilized means trying to do everything you don't want to, never doing anything you want to. It means dancing to the strings of custom and tradition; it means living in houses and never knowing or caring who is next door. These civilized white men want us to be like them—always dissatisfied, getting a hill and wanting a mountain.

Then again, maybe I am not tired. Maybe I'm licked. Maybe I am just not smart enough to grasp these things that go to make up civilization. Maybe I am just too lazy to think hard enough to keep up.

Still, I know my people have many things that civilization has taken from the whites. They know how to give, how to tear one's piece of meat in two and share it with one's brother. They know how to sing—how to make each man his own songs and sing them; for their music they do not have to listen to other men singing over a radio. They know how to make things with their hands, how to shape beads into design and make a thing of beauty from a piece of birch bark.

But we are inferior. It is terrible to have to feel inferior, to have to read reports of intelligence tests and learn that one's race is behind. It is terrible to sit in classes and hear men tell you that your people worship sticks of wood—that your gods are all false, that the Manitou[2] forgot your people and did not write them a book.

I am tired. I want to walk again among the ghost-birches. I want to see the leaves turn in autumn, the smoke rise from the lodgehouses, and to feel the blue winds. I want to hear the drums; I want to hear the drums and feel the blue whispering winds.

There is a train wailing into the night. The trains go across the mountains. It would be easy to catch a freight. They will say he has gone back to the blanket; I don't care. The dance at Christmas. . . .

A bunch of bums warming at a tiny fire talk politics and women and joke about the Relief and the WPA[3] and smoke cigarettes. These men in caps and overcoats and dirty overalls living on the outskirts of civilization are free, but they pay the price of being

---

1. **maelstrom** (māl′strəm), literally, a whirlpool. A violent confusion of thoughts and feelings.
2. **Manitou,** great spirit; often identified as a supernatural force of nature.
3. **Relief . . . WPA.** During the Depression, the Work Projects Administration was organized by the federal government to create jobs and reduce unemployment.

free in civilization. They are outcasts. I remember a sociology professor lecturing on adjustment to society; hobos and prostitutes and criminals are individuals who never adjusted, he said. He could learn a lot if he came and listened to a bunch of bums talk. He would learn that work and a woman and a place to hang his hat are all the ordinary man wants. These are all he wants, but other men are not content to let him want only these. He must be taught to want radios and automobiles and a new suit every spring. Progress would stop if he did not want these things. I listen to hear if there is any talk of communism or socialism in the hobo jungles. There is none. At best there is a sort of disgusted philosophy about life. They seem to think there should be a better distribution of wealth, or more work, or something. But they are not rabid about it. The radicals live in the cities.

I find a fellow headed for Albuquerque, and talk road-talk with him. "It is hard to ride fruit cars. Bums break in. Better to wait for a cattle car going back to the Middle West, and ride that." We catch the next east-bound and walk the tops until we find a cattle car. Inside, we crouch near the forward wall, huddle, and try to sleep. I feel peaceful and content at last. I am going home. The cattle car rocks. I sleep.

Morning and the desert. Noon and the Salton Sea, lying more lifeless than a mirage under a somber sun in a pale sky. Skeleton mountains rearing on the skyline, thrusting out of the desert floor, all rock and shadow and edges. Desert. Good country for an Indian reservation. . . .

Yuma and the muddy Colorado. Night again, and I wait shivering for the dawn.

Phoenix. Pima country.[4] Mountains that look like cardboard sets on a forgotten stage. Tucson. Papago country. Giant cacti that look like petrified hitchhikers along the highways. Apache country. At El Paso my road-buddy decides to go on to Houston. I leave him and head north to the mesa country. Las Cruces and the terrible Organ Mountains, jagged peaks that instill fear and wondering. Albuquerque. Pueblos along the Rio Grande. On the boardwalk there are some Indian women in colored sashes selling bits of pottery. The stone age offering its art to the twentieth century. They hold up a piece and fix the tourists with black eyes until, embarrassed, he buys or turns away. I feel suddenly angry that my people should have to do such things for a living. . . .

Sante Fe trains are fast, and they keep them pretty clean of bums. I decide to hurry and ride passenger coal tenders. Hide in the dark, judge the speed of the train as it leaves, and then dash out, and catch it. I hug the cold steel wall of the tender and think of the roaring fire in the engine ahead and of the passengers back in the dining car reading their papers over hot coffee. Beneath me there is a blur of rails. Death would come quick if my hands should freeze and I fall. Up over the Sangre De Cristo range, around cliffs and through canyons to Denver. Bitter cold here, and I must watch out for Denver Bob. He is a railroad bull who has thrown bums from fast freights. I miss him. It is too cold, I suppose. On north to the Sioux country.

Small towns lit for the coming Christmas. On the streets of one I see a beam-shouldered young farmer gazing into a window filled with shining silver toasters. He is tall and wears a blue shirt, buttoned, with no tie. His young wife by his side looks at him hopefully. He wants decorations for his

---

4. *Pima,* an Indian people of the American Southwest. The *Papago* (pä′pä gō), mentioned later, are closely related to the Pima.

place to hang his hat to please his woman. . . .

Northward again. Minnesota, and great white fields of snow; frozen lakes and dawn running into dusk without noon. Long forests wearing white. Bitter cold, and one night the northern lights. I am nearing home.

I reach Woodruff at midnight. Suddenly I am afraid, now that I am but twenty miles from home. Afraid of what my father will say, afraid of being looked on as a stranger by my own people. I sit by a fire and think about myself and all other young Indians. We just don't seem to fit in anywhere—certainly not among the whites, and not among the older people. I think again about the learned sociology professor and his professing. So many things seem to be clear now that I am away from school and do not have to worry about some man's opinion of my ideas. It is easy to think while looking at dancing flames.

Morning. I spend the day cleaning up and buying some presents for my family with what is left of my money. Nothing much, but a gift is a gift, if a man buys it with his last quarter. I wait until evening, then start up the track toward home.

Christmas Eve comes in on a north wind. Snow clouds hang over the pines, and the night comes early. Walking along the railroad bed, I feel the calm peace of snowbound forests on either side of me. I take my time; I am back in a world where time does not mean so much now. I am alone; alone but not nearly so lonely as I was back on the campus at school. Those are never lonely who love the snow and the pines, never lonely when the pines are wearing white shawls and snow crunches coldly underfoot. In the woods I know there are the tracks of deer and rabbit; I know that if I leave the rails and go into the woods, I shall find them.

I walk along feeling glad because my legs are light and my feet seem to know that they are home. A deer comes out of the woods just ahead of me and stands silhouetted on the rails. The North, I feel, has welcomed me home. I watch him and am glad that I do not wish for a gun. He goes into the woods quietly, leaving only the design of his tracks in the snow. I walk on. Now and then I pass a field, white under the night sky, with houses at the far end. Smoke comes from the chimneys of the houses, and I try to tell what sort of wood each is burning by the smoke; some burn pine, others aspen, others tamarack. There is one from which comes black coal smoke that rises lazily and drifts out over the tops of the trees. I like to watch houses and try to imagine what might be happening in them.

Just as a light snow begins to fall, I cross the reservation boundary; somehow it seems as though I have stepped into another world. Deep woods in a white-and-black winter night. A faint trail leading to the village.

The railroad on which I stand comes from a city sprawled by a lake—a city with a million people who walk around without seeing one another; a city sucking the life from all the country around; a city with stores and police and intellectuals and criminals and movies and apartment houses; a city with its politics and libraries and zoos.

Laughing, I go into the woods. As I cross a frozen lake, I begin to hear the drums. Soft in the night the drums beat. It is like the pulse beat of the world. The white line of the lake ends at a black forest, and above the trees the blue winds are dancing.

I come to the outlying houses of the village. Simple box houses, etched black in the night. From one or two windows soft lamplight falls on the snow. Christmas here, too, but it does not mean much; not much in the way of parties and presents. Joe Sky will get drunk. Alex Bodidash will buy his children red mittens and a new sled. Alex is a Carlisle man[5] and tries to keep his home up to white standards. White standards. Funny that my people should be ever falling farther behind. The more they try to imitate whites, the more tragic the result. Yet they want us to be imitation white men. About all we imitate well are their vices.

The village is not a sight to instill pride, yet I am not ashamed; one can never be ashamed of his own people when he knows they have dreams as beautiful as white snow on a tall pine.

Father and my brother and sister are seated around the table as I walk in. Father stares at me for a moment; then I am in his arms, crying on his shoulder. I give them the presents I have brought, and my throat tightens as I watch my sister save carefully bits of red string from the packages. I hide my feelings by wrestling with my brother when he strikes my shoulder in token of affection. Father looks at me, and I know he has many questions, but he seems to know why I have come. He tells me to go on alone to the lodge, and he will follow.

I walk along the trail to the lodge, watching the northern lights forming in the heavens. White waving ribbons that seem to pulsate with the rhythm of the drums. Clean snow creaks beneath my feet, and a soft wind sighs through the trees, singing to me. Everything seems to say, "Be happy! You are home now—you are free. You are among friends—we are your friends; we, the trees, and the snow, and the lights." I follow the trail to the lodge. My feet are light, my heart seems to sing to the music, and I hold my head high. Across white snow fields blue winds are dancing.

Before the lodge door I stop, afraid. I wonder if my people will remember me. I wonder— "Am I Indian, or am I white?" I stand before the door a long time. I hear the ice groan on the lake, and remember the story of the old woman who is under the ice, trying to get out, so she can punish some runaway lovers. I think to myself, "If I am white, I will not believe that story; if I am Indian, I will know that there is an old woman under the ice." I listen for a while, and I know that there is an old woman under the ice. I look again at the lights and go in.

Inside the lodge there are many Indians. Some sit on benches around the walls; others dance in the center of the floor around a drum. Nobody seems to notice me. It seems as though I were among a people I have never seen before. Heavy women with long black hair. Women with children on their knees—small children that watch with intent black eyes the movements of the dancers, whose small faces are solemn and serene. The faces of the old people are serene, too, and their eyes are merry and bright. I look at the old men. Straight, dressed in dark trousers and beaded velvet vests, wearing soft moccasins. Dark, lined faces intent on the music. I wonder if I am at all like them. They dance on, lifting their feet to the rhythm of the drums, swaying lightly, looking upward. I look at their eyes and am startled at the rapt attention to the rhythm of the music.

The dance stops. The men walk back to the walls and talk in low tones or with their hands. There is little conversation, yet everyone seems to be sharing some secret. A woman looks at a small boy wandering away, and he comes back to her.

Strange, I think, and then remember. These people are not sharing words—they are sharing a mood. Everyone is happy. I am

5. **Carlisle man**, a graduate of Carlisle School in Pennsylvania, the first reservation school to be established.

so used to white people that it seems strange so many people could be together without someone talking. These Indians are happy because they are together, and because the night is beautiful outside, and the music is beautiful. I try hard to forget school and white people, and be one of these—my people. I try to forget everything but the night, and it is a part of me; that I am one with my people and we are all a part of something universal. I watch eyes and see now that the old people are speaking to me. They nod slightly, imperceptibly, and their eyes laugh into mine. I look around the room. All the eyes are friendly; they all laugh. No one questions my being here. The drums begin to beat again, and I catch the invitation in the eyes of the old men. My feet begin to lift to the rhythm, and I look out beyond the walls into the night and see the lights. I am happy. It is beautiful. I am home. □□

Discussion

1. (a) What triggers White-cloud's homesickness? (b) What does he appear to miss most? (c) Might the season of the year be in any way responsible? Explain.

2. Many of Whitecloud's comments and images provide insight into his ways and feelings as a Chippewa. What is conveyed in each of the following? (a) ". . . there is always beauty in order, in rows of growing things! But it is the beauty of captivity. A pine fighting for existence on a windy knoll is much more beautiful" (56b, 3). (b) "Being civilized means trying to do everything you don't want to, never doing anything you want to" (57a, 2). (c) ". . . my throat tightens as I watch my sister save carefully bits of red string from the packages" (60a, 2). (d) What do these various thoughts tell you about the character of Whitecloud himself?

3. "Culture shock" is a phrase that describes what occurs when a person is suddenly transferred from a familiar environment to an alien one. Discuss the effects of culture shock on Whitecloud.

4. There are many descriptive passages in this essay. Which is your favorite? Why?

5. Much of this selection contrasts the ways of modern society with the traditions of the Indian. (a) List several of the ways in which Whitecloud feels Indian customs and beliefs are superior. (b) Do you agree with Whitecloud? Explain.

Vocabulary
Pronunciation, Dictionary

Would you know what *tamarack* means if you read it in the following sentence?

I just saw a *tamarack.*

Unless you were already familiar with the word *tamarack,* it would be impossible to figure out its meaning from this sentence. There is very little context to help you, no way to analyze the structure of the word. When neither context nor structure gives you clues to meaning, you will need to consult a dictionary.

Besides definitions and pronunciations, dictionaries also provide information on such things as the origins of words (etymologies), various spellings of words, common abbreviations, biographical information on well-known people, geographical facts, and information on language usage.

Use your Glossary to answer the following questions. Be sure you know the meaning of each word you look up.

1. A *tamarack* is (a) an aspen; (b) a rock formation; (c) a steep hill; (d) a tree.

2. What is the meaning of *tender* in this sentence from the selection (58b, 1): "I hugged

the cold steel wall of the *tender*"?

3. What is another correct spelling of *somber?*

4. Is the **i** in *Pima* pronounced like the **i** in *lime,* the **i** in *wind,* or the **ea** in *team*? In what river valleys do the Pima live?

5. What is the origin of the word *hobo?*

6. What language does the word *pueblo* come from?

7. Read all the definitions of *rabid.* What disease is *rabid* sometimes used to describe?

8. The last syllable of *mirage* sounds like the last syllable of which of these words: *outrage, garage?*

Extension • Writing

Whitecloud says of himself and the other young Indians, "We just don't seem to fit anywhere." His, of course, was an extreme case, but all of us have experienced feelings of alienation, of not belonging, at one time or another. Write a·paragraph or two in which you describe a personal experience with alienation. Remember that your reaction to the experience, the way you felt, is very important in this composition.

Thomas S. Whitecloud
1914 • 1972

Whitecloud crowded a great deal of living into his lifetime. He was raised on the Lac du Flambeau Chippewa Reservation in Wisconsin, of which he writes in "Blue Winds Dancing."

After being expelled from several Indian schools, he decided to become a doctor to serve his people. Studying first at the University of New Mexico, he later graduated from the University of Redlands in California and Tulane University Medical School.

Whitecloud practiced medicine first with the Indian service, then as the only doctor in an entire Texas county, and later as a ship's surgeon. He also maintained a writing career and founded the Three Feathers Society, an Indian correspondence group.

"Blue Winds Dancing," which Whitecloud wrote when he was a college student, received first prize in a Phi Beta Kappa essay contest.

1: Free Samples

CONTENT REVIEW

1. This unit is called "Free Samples" because it provides a taste of the units that follow. Which one of the selections in the unit made you most eager to read more like it? Why?

2. A number of these selections give us deeper insights into people or into cultures different from ours. Which selection do you think was most successful in this respect? Why?

3. Conflict is an important element in most short stories and dramas, and in some nonfiction and poetry as well. List those selections in which you can detect a conflict and explain its nature in each.

4. This unit includes five poems, each very different from the others. Which is your favorite, and why?

5. Select any one of the following ideas, which two or more selections in this unit have in common, and discuss its use in those selections. You will have to review the unit briefly to decide which selections develop that idea. **(a)** An individual's responsibility to others; **(b)** dreams that are realized; **(c)** disappointment, and various reactions to it; **(d)** misjudging someone or something.

6. Assume that you could meet and talk to one of the characters in these selections. Who would it be, and why?

Unit 1, Test I
INTERPRETATION: NEW MATERIAL

Read carefully the short story reprinted below. Then on a separate sheet of paper write your answers to the questions that follow the story. Do not write in your book.

The Drummer Boy of Shiloh
Ray Bradbury

In the April night, more than once, blossoms fell from the orchard trees and lighted with rustling taps on the drumhead. At midnight a peach stone left miraculously on a branch through winter, flicked by a bird, fell swift and unseen; it struck once, like panic, and jerked the boy upright. In silence he listened to his own heart ruffle away, away—at last gone from his ears and back in his chest again.

After that he turned the drum on its side, where its great lunar face peered at him whenever he opened his eyes.

His face, alert or at rest, was solemn. It was a solemn time and a solemn night for a boy just turned fourteen in the peach orchard near Owl Creek not far from the church at Shiloh.

". . . thirty-one . . . thirty-two . . . thirty-three." Unable to see, he stopped counting.

Beyond the thirty-three familiar shadows forty thousand men, exhausted by nervous expectation and unable to sleep for romantic dreams of battles yet unfought, lay crazily askew in their uniforms. A mile farther on, another army was strewn helter-skelter, turning slowly, basting themselves with the thought of what they would do when the time came—a leap, a yell, a blind plunge their strategy, raw youth their protection and benediction.

Now and again the boy heard a vast wind come up that gently stirred the air. But he knew what it was—the army here, the army there, whispering to itself in the dark. Some men talking to others, others murmuring to themselves, and all so quiet it was like a natural element arisen from South or North with the motion of the earth toward dawn.

What the men whispered the boy could only guess and he guessed that it was "Me, I'm the one, I'm the one of all the rest who won't die. I'll live through it. I'll go home. The band will play. And I'll be there to hear it."

Yes, thought the boy, *that's all very well for them, they can give as good as they get!*

For with the careless bones of the young men, harvested by night and bindled around campfires, were the similarly strewn steel bones of their rifles with bayonets fixed like eternal lightning lost in the orchard grass.

Me, thought the boy, *I got only a drum, two sticks to beat it, and no shield.*

There wasn't a man-boy on this ground tonight who did not have a shield he cast, riveted, or carved himself on his way to his first attack, compounded of remote but nonetheless firm and fiery family devotion, flag-blown patriotism, and cocksure immortality strengthened by the touchstone of very real gunpowder, ramrod, Minié ball,[1] and flint. But without these last, the boy felt his family move yet farther off in the dark, as if one of those great prairie-burning trains had chanted them away, never to return—leaving him with this drum which was worse than a toy in the game to be played tomorrow or someday much too soon.

The boy turned on his side. A moth brushed his face, but it was peach blossom. A peach blossom flicked him, but it was a moth. Nothing stayed put. Nothing had a name. Nothing was as it once was.

If he stayed very still, when the dawn came up and the soldiers put on their bravery with their caps, perhaps they might go away,

---

1. **Minié ball** (min/ē), a cone-shaped bullet that expanded when fired.

the war with them, and not notice him living small here, no more than a toy himself.

"Well, by thunder now," said a voice. The boy shut his eyes to hide inside himself, but it was too late. Someone, walking by in the night, stood over him. "Well," said the voice quietly, "here's a soldier crying *before* the fight. Good. Get it over. Won't be time once it all starts."

And the voice was about to move on when the boy, startled, touched the drum at his elbow. The man above, hearing this, stopped. The boy could feel his eyes, sense him slowly bending near. A hand must have come down out of the night, for there was a little *rat-tat* as the fingernails brushed and the man's breath fanned the boy's face.

"Why, it's the drummer boy, isn't it?"

The boy nodded, not knowing if his nod was seen. "Sir, is that you?" he said.

"I assume it is." The man's knees cracked as he bent still closer. He smelled as all fathers should smell, of salt-sweat, tobacco, horse and boot leather, and the earth he walked upon. He had many eyes. No, not eyes, brass buttons that watched the boy.

He could only be, and was, the general. "What's your name, boy?" he asked.

"Joby, sir," whispered the boy, starting to sit up.

"All right, Joby, don't stir." A hand pressed his chest gently, and the boy relaxed. "How long you been with us, Joby?"

"Three weeks, sir."

"Run off from home or join legitimate, boy?"

Silence.

"Fool question," said the general. "Do you shave yet, boy? Even more of a fool. There's your cheek, fell right off the tree overhead. And the others here, not much older. Raw, raw, the lot of you. You ready for tomorrow or the next day, Joby?"

"I think so, sir."

"You want to cry some more, go on ahead. I did the same last night."

"You, sir?"

"It's the truth. Thinking of everything ahead. Both sides figuring the other side will just give up, and soon, and the war done in weeks and us all home. Well, that's not how it's going to be. And maybe that's why I cried."

"Yes, sir," said Joby.

The general must have taken out a cigar now, for the dark was suddenly filled with the Indian smell of tobacco unlighted yet, but chewed as the man thought what next to say.

"It's going to be a crazy time," said the general. "Counting both sides, there's a hundred thousand men—give or take a few thousand—out there tonight, not one as can spit a sparrow off a tree, or knows a horse clod from a Minié ball. Stand up, bare the breast, ask to be a target, thank them and sit down, that's us, that's them. We should turn tail and train four months, they should do the same. But here we are, taken with spring fever and thinking it blood lust, taking our sulphur with cannons instead of with molasses, as it should be—going to be a hero, going to live forever. And I can see all them over there nodding agreement, save the other way around. It's wrong, boy, it's wrong as a head put on hindside front and a man marching backward through life. Sometime this week more innocents will get shot out of pure Cherokee enthusiasm than ever got shot before. Owl Creek was full of boys splashing around in the noonday sun just a few hours ago. I fear it will be full of boys again, just floating, at sundown tomorrow, not caring where the current takes them."

The general stopped and made a little pile of winter leaves and twigs in the dark as if he might at any moment strike fire to them to see his way through the coming days when the sun might not show its face because of what was happening here and just beyond.

The boy watched the hand stirring the leaves and opened his lips to say something, but did not say it. The general heard the boy's breath and spoke himself.

"Why am I telling you this? That's what you wanted to ask, eh? Well, when you got a bunch of wild horses on a loose rein somewhere, somehow you got to bring order, rein them in. These lads, fresh out of the milkshed, don't know what I know; and I can't tell them—men actually die in war. So each is his own army. I got to make one army of them. And for that, boy, I need you."

"Me!" The boy's lips barely twitched.

"You, boy," said the general quietly. "You are the heart of the army. Think about that. You are the heart of the army. Listen to me, now."

Library of Congress

And lying there, Joby listened. And the general spoke. If he, Joby, beat slow tomorrow, the heart would beat slow in the men. They would lag by the wayside. They would drowse in the fields on their muskets. They would sleep forever after that—in those same fields, their hearts slowed by a drummer boy and stopped by enemy lead.

But if he beat a sure, steady, ever faster rhythm, then, then, their knees would come up in a long line down over that hill, one knee after the other, like a wave on the ocean shore. Had he seen the ocean ever? Seen the waves rolling in like a well-ordered cavalry charge to the sane? Well, that was it, that's what he wanted, that's what was needed. Joby was his right hand and his left. He gave the orders, but Joby set the pace.

So bring the right knee up and the right foot out and the left knee up and the left foot out, one following the other in good time, in brisk time. Move the blood up the body and make the head proud and the spine stiff and the jaw resolute. Focus the eye and set the teeth, flare the nostril and tighten the hands, put steel armor all over the men, for blood moving fast in them does indeed make men feel as if they'd put on steel. He must keep at it, at it! Long and steady, steady and long! Then, even though shot or torn, those wounds got in hot blood—in blood he'd helped stir—would feel less pain. If their blood was cold, it would be more than slaughter, it would be murderous nightmare and pain best not told and no one to guess.

The general spoke and stopped, letting his breath slack off. Then, after a moment, he said, "So there you are, that's it. Will you do that, boy? Do you know now you're general of the army when the general's left behind?"

The boy nodded mutely.

"You'll run them through for me then, boy?"

"Yes, sir."

"Good. And, maybe, many nights from tonight, many years from now, when you're as old or far much older than me, when they ask you what you did in this awful time, you will tell them—one part humble and one part proud—I was the drummer boy at the battle of Owl Creek or the Tennessee River, or maybe they'll just name it after the church there. I was the drummer boy at Shiloh. Good grief, that has a beat and sound to it fitting for Mr. Longfellow. 'I was the drummer boy at Shiloh.' Who will ever hear those words and not know you, boy, or what you thought this night, or what you'll think tomorrow or the next day when we must get up on our legs and move."

The general stood up. "Well, then. God bless you, boy. Good night."

"Good night, sir." And tobacco, brass, boot polish, salt-sweat, and leather, the man moved away through the grass.

Joby lay for a moment staring, but unable to see where the man had gone. He swallowed. He wiped his eyes. He cleared his throat. He settled himself. Then, at last, very slowly and firmly he turned the drum so it faced up toward the sky.

He lay next to it, his arm around it, feeling the tremor, the touch, the muted thunder as all the rest of the April night in the year 1862, near the Tennessee River, not far from the Owl Creek, very close to the church named Shiloh, the peach blossoms fell on the drum. □□

1. In what season does "The Drummer Boy of Shiloh" take place?

2. The Battle of Shiloh is named after a (a) river; (b) creek; (c) church; (d) mountain.

3. In order to fall asleep, the boy counts (a) trees; (b) sheep; (c) soldiers; (d) blossoms.

4. The "vast wind" that the boy sometimes hears (page 65, 2) is (a) a sign that a storm is approaching; (b) the rustle of the peach trees; (c) the sound of the enemy's cannon; (d) the whispering of other soldiers.

5. Why does the boy believe that the other soldiers must feel less afraid of the coming battle than he does?

6. Joby (a) joined the army legitimately; (b) was forced by his family to join the army; (c) was drafted into the army; (d) ran away from home to join the army.

7. When the general tells Joby, "There's your cheek, fell right off the tree overhead" (page 66, 12), what is he comparing Joby's cheek to?

8. The general is upset because he realizes that (a) the enemy's army is better trained than his army; (b) neither army is well trained; (c) Joby is a coward; (d) Joby is very young.

9. The general says that Owl Creek was "full of boys" earlier in the day and that he fears "it will be full of boys again . . . tomorrow" (page 67, 1). What frightening difference does he expect "tomorrow"?

10. The general says that he wants Joby (a) to give spirit to the soldiers; (b) to learn how to use a weapon; (c) to be his orderly; (d) to go back home.

11. Which word best describes Joby's feelings after his talk with the general? (a) frightened; (b) bitter; (c) reassured; (d) happy.

12. In describing the general, the author emphasizes the imagery of (a) sound; (b) sight; (c) smell; (d) touch.

13. When the general asks Joby if he has ever "seen the waves rolling in like a well ordered cavalry charge" (page 67, 8), is he using a simile or a metaphor?

14. The personalities of Joby and the general are revealed mainly through (a) the setting of the story; (b) speech and behavior; (c) descriptions of their physical traits; (d) the opinions of other characters.

15. The main conflict in the story is between (a) Joby and the general; (b) Joby and his fears; (c) Joby and the other soldiers; (d) the general and his raw recruits.

Unit 1, Test II
COMPOSITION

Choose one of the following assignments to write about. Unless you are told otherwise, assume that you are writing for your classmates.

1. Imagine that you are the drummer boy of Shiloh, and write a letter to a friend describing your conversation with the general. Make the situation seem real to your friend by explaining the way you were feeling earlier that evening, how the general happened to stop to talk to you, some of the things he said to you, and what your feelings were after he left.

2. "One who deceives will always find those who allow themselves to be deceived." Are Laurie's parents in "Charles" people who allow themselves to be deceived? Should they have been able to see that Laurie's stories were really about himself? Write a composition explaining why you think they should or should not have known. Use examples from the story to back up your opinion.

3. Sometimes young people learn values because their elders tell them how to behave; more often, however, they learn because their elders give them good examples to follow. Choose one of the characters listed below, and write a composition discussing some of the specific values and attitudes about life that an older person in his family teaches him through example.

a. Buddy ("A Christmas Memory")

b. Shoots ("How Whirlwind Saved Her Cub")

4. Very often the setting of a story contributes a great deal to its overall mood or feeling. Discuss at least two specific places mentioned in "Blue Winds Dancing" that cause the narrator to react emotionally.

To see something happening—but not to be able to act;

to be forced to choose—with your life at stake;

to have to let go—when you've just learned to hang on;

to be near—and yet far . . .

These are the problems, the predicaments,

the choices that fill one's life

with UNCERTAINTIES

See **CHARACTERIZATION** Handbook of Literary Terms

Charlie Gordon had the unique opportunity of living in two worlds.
In which was he happier? If he had been given a choice, which would he have chosen?

Flowers for Algernon

Daniel Keyes

progris riport 1—martch 5

Dr. Strauss says I shud rite down what I think and every thing that happins to me from now on. I dont know why but he says its importint so they will see if they will use me. I hope they use me. Miss Kinnian says maybe they can make me smart. I want to be smart. My name is Charlie Gordon. I am 37 years old. I have nuthing more to rite now so I will close for today.

progris riport 2—martch 6

I had a test today. I think I faled it. And I think maybe now they wont use me. What happind is a nice young man was in the room and he had some white cards and ink spillled all over them. He sed Charlie what do yo see on this card. I was very skared even tho I had my rabits foot in my pockit because when I was a kid I always faled tests in school and I spillled ink to.

I told him I saw a inkblot. He said yes and it made me feel good. I thot that was all but when I got up to go he said Charlie we are not thru yet. Then I dont remember so good but he wantid me to say what was in the ink. I dint see nuthing in the ink but he said there was picturs there other pepul saw some picturs. I couldnt see any picturs. I reely tryed. I held the card close up and then far away. Then I said if I had my glases I coud see better I usally only ware my glases in the movies or TV but I said they are in the closit in the hall. I got them. Then I said let me see that card agen I bet Ill find it now.

I tryed hard but I only saw the ink. I told him maybe I need new glases. He rote something down on a paper and I got skared of faling the test. I told him it was a very nice inkblot with littel points all around the edges. He looked very sad so that wasnt it. I said please let me try agen. Ill get it in a few minits becaus Im not so fast somtimes. Im a slow reeder too in Miss Kinnians class for slow adults but I'm trying very hard.

He gave me a chance with another card that had 2 kinds of ink spilled on it red and blue.

He was very nice and talked slow like Miss Kinnian does and he explaned it to me that it was a *raw shok.*[1] He said pepul see things in the ink. I said show me where. He said think. I told him I think a inkblot but that wasn't rite eather. He said what does it remind you—pretend something. I closed my eyes for a long time to pretend. I told him I pretend a fowntan pen with ink leeking all over a table cloth.

I dont think I passed the *raw shok* test

progris riport 3—martch 7

Dr Strauss and Dr Nemur say it dont matter about the inkblots. They said that maybe they will still use me. I said Miss Kinnian never gave me tests like that one only spelling and reading. They said Miss Kinnian told that I was her bestist pupil in the adult nite school because I tryed the hardist and I reely wantid to lern. They said how come you went to the adult nite scool all by yourself Charlie. How did you find it. I said I asked pepul and sumbody told me where I shud go to lern to read and spell good. They said why did you want to. I told them becaus all my life I wantid to be smart and not dumb. But its very hard to be smart. They said you know it will probly be tempirery. I said yes. Miss Kinnian told me. I dont care if it herts.

Later I had more crazy tests today. The

"Flowers for Algernon" by Daniel Keyes. Copyright 1959 by Mercury Press, Inc.; originally appeared in the *Magazine of Fantasy and Science Fiction;* reprinted by permission of the author and his agent, Robert P. Mills.

1. *raw shok,* Rorschach (rôr/shäk) test, a psychological test used to measure personality traits and general intelligence.

nice lady who gave it to me told me the name and I asked her how do you spellit so I can rite it my progris riport. THEMATIC AP-PERCEPTION TEST.[2] I dont know the frist 2 words but I know what *test* means. You got to pass it or you get bad marks. This test lookd easy becaus I coud see the picturs. Only this time she dint want me to tell her the picturs. That mixd me up. She said make up storys about the pepul in the picturs.

I told her how can you tell storys about pepul you never met. I said why shud I make up lies. I never tell lies any more becaus I always get caut.

She told me this test and the other one the raw-shok was for getting personality. I laffed so hard. I said how can you get that thing from inkblots and fotos. She got sore and put her picturs away. I don't care. It was sily. I gess I faled that test too.

Later some men in white coats took me to a difernt part of the hospitil and gave me a game to play. It was like a race with a white mouse. They called the mouse Algernon. Algernon was in a box with a lot of twists and turns like all kinds of walls and they gave me a pencil and paper with lines and lots of boxes. On one side it said START and on the other end it said FINISH. They said it was *amazed*[3] and that Algernon and me had the same *amazed* to do. I dint see how we could have the same *amazed* if Algernon had a box and I had a paper but I dint say nothing. Anyway there wasnt time because the race started.

One of the men had a watch he was trying to hide so I wouldnt see it so I tryed not to look and that made me nervus.

Anyway that test made me feel worser than all the others because they did it over 10 times with different *amazeds* and Alger-non won everytime. I dint know that mice were so smart. Maybe thats because Alger-non is a white mouse. Maybe white mice are smarter than other mice.

progris riport 4—Mar 8

Their going to use me! Im so exited I can hardly write. Dr Nemur and Dr Strauss had a argament about it first. Dr Nemur was in the office when Dr Strauss brot me in. Dr Nemur was worryed about using me but Dr Strauss told him Miss Kinnian rekemmended me the best from all the people who she was teach-ing. I like Miss Kinnian becaus shes a very smart teacher. And she said Charlie your going to have a second chance. If you volen-teer for this experament you mite get smart. They dont know if it will be perminint but theirs a chance. Thats why I said ok even when I was scared because she said it was an operashun. She said dont be scared Charlie you done so much with so little I think you deserv it most of all.

So I got scaird when Dr. Nemur and Dr. Strauss argud about it. Dr. Strauss said I had something that was very good. He said I had a good *motorvation.* I never even knew I had that. I felt proud when he said that not every body with an eye-q of 68[4] had that thing. I dont know what it is or where I got it but he said Algernon had it too. Algernons *motor-vation* is the cheese they put in his box. But it cant be that because I didn't eat any cheese this week.

Then he told Dr Nemur something I dint understand so while they were talking I wrote down some of the words.

He said Dr. Nemur I know Charlie is not what you had in mind as the first of your new brede of intelek** (coudnt get the word)

---

2. *Thematic Apperception Test,* another psychological test.
3. *amazed,* a maze, a network of paths through which one must find one's way.
4. *eye-q of 68.* An average I.Q. is 100.

superman. But most people of his low ment** are host** and uncoop** they are usually dull apath** and hard to reach. He has a good natcher hes intristed and eager to please.

Dr Nemur said remember he will be the first human beeng ever to have his intellijence tripled by surgicle meens.

Dr. Strauss said exakly. Look at how well hes lerned to read and write for his low mentel age its as grate an acheve** as you and I lerning einstines therey of **vity without help. That shows the inteness motorvation. Its comparat** a tremen** achev** I say we use Charlie.

I dint get all the words but it sounded like Dr Strauss was on my side and like the other one wasnt.

Then Dr Nemur nodded he said all right maybe your right. We will use Charlie. When he said that I got so exited I jumped up and shook his hand for being so good to me. I told him thank you doc you wont be sorry for giving me a second chance. And I mean it like I told him. After the operashun Im gonna try to be smart. Im gonna try awful hard.

progris riport 5—Mar 10

Im skared. Lots of the nurses and the people who gave me the tests came to bring me candy and wish me luck. I hope I have luck. I got my rabits foot and my lucky penny. Only a black cat crossed me when I was comming to the hospitil. Dr Strauss says dont be supersitis Charlie this is science. Anyway Im keeping my rabits foot with me.

I asked Dr Strauss if Ill beat Algernon in the race after the operashun and he said maybe. If the operashun works Ill show that mouse I can be as smart as he is. Maybe smarter. Then Ill be abel to read better and spell the words good and know lots of things

and be like other people. I want to be smart like other people. If it works perminint they will make everybody smart all over the wurld.

They dint give me anything to eat this morning. I dont know what that eating has to do with getting smart. Im very hungry and Dr. Nemur took away my box of candy. That Dr Nemur is a grouch. Dr Strauss says I can have it back after the operashun. You cant eat befor a operashun. . . .

progress report 6—Mar 15

The operashun dint hurt. He did it while I was sleeping. They took off the bandijis from my head today so I can make a PROGRESS REPORT. Dr. Nemur who looked at some of my other ones says I spell PROGRESS wrong and told me how to spell it and REPORT too. I got to try and remember that.

I have a very bad memary for spelling. Dr. Strauss says its ok to tell about all the things that happin to me but he says I should tell more about what I feel and what I think. When I told him I dont know how to think he said try. All the time when the bandijis were on my eyes I tryed to think. Nothing happened. I dont know what to think about. Maybe if I ask him he will tell me how I can think now that Im suppose to get smart. What do smart people think about. Fancy things I suppose. I wish I knew some fancy things alredy.

progress report 7—Mar 19

Nothing is happining. I had lots of tests and different kinds of races with Algernon. I hate that mouse. He always beats me. Dr. Strauss said I got to play those games. And he said some time I got to take those tests over again. Those inkblots are stupid. And those pictures are stupid too. I like to draw a picture of a man and a woman but I wont make up lies about people.

I got a headache from trying to think so much. I thot Dr Strauss was my frend but he dont help me. He dont tell me what to think or when Ill get smart. Miss Kinnian dint come to see me. I think writing these progress reports are stupid too.

progress report 8—Mar 23

Im going back to work at the factory. They said it was better I shud go back to work but I cant tell anyone what the operashun was for and I have to come to the hospitil for an hour evry night after work. They are gonna pay me mony every month for learning to be smart.

Im glad Im going back to work because I miss my job and all my frends and all the fun we have there.

Dr Strauss says I shud keep writing things down but I dont have to do it every day just when I think of something or something speshul happins. He says dont get discoridged because it takes time and it happins slow. He says it took a long time with Algernon before he got 3 times smarter than he was before. Thats why Algernon beats me all the time because he had that operashun too. That makes me feel better. I coud probly do that *amazed* faster than a reglar mouse. Maybe some day Ill beat him. That would be something. So far Algernon looks smart perminent.

Mar 25 (I dont have to write PROGRESS REPORT on top any more just when I hand it in once a week for Dr Nemur. I just have to put the date on. That saves time)

We had a lot of fun at the factery today. Joe Carp said hey look where Charlie had his operashun what did they do Charlie put some brains in. I was going to tell him but I remembered Dr Strauss said no. Then Frank Reilly said what did you do Charlie forget your key and open your door the hard way. That made me laff. Their really my friends and they like me.

Sometimes somebody will say hey look at Joe or Frank or George he really pulled a Charlie Gordon. I dont know why they say that but they always laff. This morning Amos Borg who is the 4 man at Donnegans used my name when he shouted at Ernie the office boy. Ernie lost a packige. He said Ernie what are you trying to be a Charlie Gordon. I dont understand why he said that.

Mar 28. Dr. Strauss came to my room tonight to see why I dint come in like I was suppose to. I told him I dont like to race with Algernon any more. He said I dont have to for a while but I shud come in. He had a present for me. I thot it was a little television but it wasnt. He said I got to turn it on when I go to sleep. I said your kidding why shud I turn it on when Im going to sleep. Who ever herd of a thing like that. But he said if I want to get smart I got to do what he says. I told him I dint think I was going to get smart and he puts his hand on my sholder and said Charlie you dont know it yet but your getting smarter all the time. You wont notice for a while. I think he was just being nice to make me feel good because I dont look any smarter.

Oh yes I almost forgot. I asked him when I can go back to the class at Miss Kinnians school. He said I wont go their. He said that soon Miss Kinnian will come to the hospitil to start and teach me speshul.

Mar 29 That crazy TV kept up all night. How can I sleep with something yelling

crazy things all night in my ears. And the nutty pictures. Wow. I don't know what it says when Im up so how am I going to know when Im sleeping.

Dr Strauss says its ok. He says my brains are lerning when I sleep and that will help me when Miss Kinnian starts my lessons in the hospitl (only I found out it isn't a hospitil its a labatory.) I think its all crazy. If you can get smart when your sleeping why do people go to school. That thing I don't think will work. I use to watch the late show and the late late show on TV all the time and it never made me smart. Maybe you have to sleep while you watch it.

progress report 9—April 3

Dr Strauss showed me how to keep the TV turned low so now I can sleep. I don't hear a thing. And I still dont understand what it says. A few times I play it over in the morning to find out what I lerned when I was sleeping and I don't think so. Miss Kinnian says Maybe its another langwidge. But most times it sounds american. It talks faster than even Miss Gold who was my teacher in 6 grade.

I told Dr. Strauss what good is it to get smart in my sleep. I want to be smart when Im awake. He says its the same thing and I have two minds. Theres the *subconscious* and the *conscious* (thats how you spell it). And one dont tell the other one what its doing. They dont even talk to each other. Thats why I dream. And boy have I been having crazy dreams. Wow. Ever since that night TV. The late late late show. I forgot to ask him if it was only me or if everybody had those two minds.

(I just looked up the word in the dictionary Dr. Strauss gave me. The word is *subconscious. adj. Of the nature of mental operations not yet present in consciousness; as,*

subconscious conflict of desires.) There's more but I still dont know what it means. This isnt a very good dictionary for dumb people like me.

Anyway the headache is from the party. My friends from the factery Joe Carp and Frank Reilly invited me to go to Muggsys Saloon for some drinks. I don't like to drink but they said we will have lots of fun. I had a good time.

Joe Carp said I shoud show the girls how I mop out the toilet in the factory and he got me a mop. I showed them and everyone laffed when I told that Mr. Donnegan said I was the best janiter he ever had because I like my job and do it good and never miss a day except for my operashun.

I said Miss Kinnian always said Charlie be proud of your job because you do it good.

Everybody laffed and we had a good time and they gave me lots of drinks and Joe said Charlie is a card when hes potted. I dont know what that means but everybody likes me and we have fun. I cant wait to be smart like my best friends Joe Carp and Frank Reilly.

I dont remember how the party was over but I think I went out to buy a newspaper and coffe for Joe and Frank and when I came back there was no one their. I looked for them all over till late. Then I dont remember so good but I think I got sleepy or sick. A nice cop brot me back home Thats what my landlady Mrs Flynn says.

But I got a headache and a big lump on my head. I think maybe I fell but Joe Carp says it was the cop they beat up drunks some times. I don't think so. Miss Kinnian says cops are to help people. Anyway I got a bad headache and Im sick and hurt all over. I dont think Ill drink anymore.

April 6 I beat Algernon! I dint even know

I beat him until Burt the tester told me. Then the second time I lost because I got so exited I fell off the chair before I finished. But after that I beat him 8 more times. I must be getting smart to beat a smart mouse like Algernon. But I don't *feel* smarter.

I wanted to race Algernon some more but Burt said thats enough for one day. They let me hold him for a minit. Hes not so bad. Hes soft like a ball of cotton. He blinks and when he opens his eyes their black and pink on the eges.

I said can I feed him because I felt bad to beat him and I wanted to be nice and make friends. Burt said no Algernon is a very specshul mouse with an operashun like mine, and he was the first of all the animals to stay smart so long. He told me Algernon is so smart that every day he has to solve a test to get his food. Its a thing like a lock on a door that changes every time Algernon goes in to eat so he has to lern something new to get his food. That made me sad because if he couldn't lern he would be hungry.

I don't think its right to make you pass a test to eat. How would Dr Nemur like it to have to pass a test every time he wants to eat. I think Ill be friends with Algernon.

April 9 Tonight after work Miss Kinnian was at the laboratory. She looked like she was glad to see me but scared. I told her dont worry Miss Kinnian Im not smart yet and she laffed. She said I have confidence in you Charlie the way you struggled so hard to read and right better than all the others. At werst you will have it for a littel wile and your doing somthing for science.

We are reading a very hard book. Its called *Robinson Crusoe* about a man who gets merooned on a dessert Iland. Hes smart and figers out all kinds of things so he can have a house and food and hes a good swimmer. Only I feel sorry because hes all alone and has no frends. But I think their must be somebody else on the iland because theres a picture with his funny umbrella looking at footprints. I hope he gets a frend and not be lonly.

April 10 Miss Kinnian teaches me to spell better. She says look at a word and close your eyes and say it over and over until you remember. I have lots of truble with *through* that you say *threw* and *enough* and *tough* that you dont say *enew* and *tew*. You got to say *enuff* and *tuff*. Thats how I use to write it before I started to get smart. Im confused but Miss Kinnian says theres no reason in spelling.

Apr 14 Finished *Robinson Crusoe.* I want to find out more about what happens to him but Miss Kinnian says thats all there is. *Why.*

Apr 15 Miss Kinnian says Im lerning fast. She read some of the Progress Reports and she looked at me kind of funny. She says Im a fine person and Ill show them all. I asked her why. She said never mind but I shouldnt feel bad if I find out everybody isnt nice like I think. She said for a person who god gave so little to you done more then a lot of people with brains they never even used. I said all my friends are smart people but there good. They like me and they never did anything that wasnt nice. Then she got something in her eye and she had to run out to the ladys room.

Apr 16 Today, I lerned, the *comma,* this is a comma (,) a period, with a tail, Miss Kinnian, says its important, because, it makes writing, better, she said, somebody, coud lose, a lot of money, if a comma, isnt, in the, right place, I dont have, any money, and I dont see, how a comma, keeps you, from losing it,

Apr 17 I used the comma wrong. Its punctuation. Miss Kinnian told me to look up long words in the dictionary to lern to spell them. I said whats the difference if you can read it anyway. She said its part of your education so now on Ill look up all the words Im not sure how to spell. It takes a long time to write that way but I only have to look up once and after that I get it right.

You got to mix them up, she showed? me" how. to mix! them (and now; I can! mix up all kinds" of punctuation, in! my writing? There, are lots! of rules? to lern; but Im gettin'g them in my head.

One thing I like about, Dear Miss Kinnian: (thats the way it goes in a business letter if I ever go into business) is she, always gives me' a reason" when—I ask. She's a gen'ius! I wish I cou'd be smart" like, her;

(Puncuation, is; fun!)

April 18 What a dope I am! I didn't even understand what she was talking about. I read the grammar book last night and it explanes the whole thing. Then I saw it was the same way as Miss Kinnian was trying to tell me, but I didn't get it.

Miss Kinnian said that the TV working in my sleep helped out. She and I reached a plateau. Thats a flat hill.

After I figured out how punctuation worked, I read over all my old Progress Reports from the beginning. Boy, did I have crazy spelling and punctuation! I told Miss Kinnian I ought to go over the pages and fix all the mistakes but she said, "No, Charlie, Dr. Nemur wants them just as they are. That's why he let you keep them after they were photostated, to see your own progress. You're coming along fast, Charlie."

That made me feel good. After the lesson I went down and played with Algernon. We don't race any more.

April 20 I feel sick inside. Not sick like for a doctor, but inside my chest it feels empty like getting punched and a heartburn at the same time. I wasn't going to write about it, but I guess I got to, because its important. Today was the first time I ever stayed home from work.

Last night Joe Carp and Frank Reilly invited me to a party. There were lots of girls and some men from the factory. I remembered how sick I got last time I drank too much, so I told Joe I didn't want anything to drink. He gave me a plain coke instead.

We had a lot of fun for a while. Joe said I should dance with Ellen and she would teach me the steps. I fell a few times and I couldn't understand why because no one else was dancing besides Ellen and me. And all the time I was tripping because somebody's foot was always sticking out.

Then when I got up I saw the look on Joe's face and it gave me a funny feeling in my stomach. "He's a scream," one of the girls said. Everybody was laughing.

"Look at him. He's blushing. Charlie is blushing."

"Hey, Ellen, what'd you do to Charlie? I never saw him act like that before."

I didn't know what to do or where to turn. Everyone was looking at me and laughing and I felt naked. I wanted to hide. I ran outside and I threw up. Then I walked home. It's a funny thing I never knew that Joe and Frank and the others liked to have me around all the time to make fun of me.

Now I know what it means when they say "to pull a Charlie Gordon."

I'm ashamed.

progress report 11

April 21 Still didn't go into the factory. I told Mrs. Flynn my landlady to call and tell Mr. Donnegan I was sick. Mrs. Flynn looks at me very funny lately like she's scared.

I think it's a good thing about finding out how everybody laughs at me. I thought about it a lot. It's because I'm so dumb and I don't even know when I'm doing something dumb. People think it's funny when a dumb person can't do things the same way they can.

Anyway, now I know I'm getting smarter every day. I know punctuation and I can spell good. I like to look up all the hard words in the dictionary and I remember them. I'm reading a lot now, and Miss Kinnian says I read very fast. Sometimes I even understand what I'm reading about, and it stays in my mind. There are times when I can close my eyes and think of a page and it all comes back like a picture.

Besides history, geography, and arithmetic, Miss Kinnian said I should start to learn foreign languages. Dr. Strauss gave me some more tapes to play while I sleep. I still don't understand how that conscious and unconscious mind works, but Dr. Strauss says not to worry yet. He asked me to promise that when I start learning college subjects next week I wouldn't read any books on psychology—that is, until he gives me permission.

I feel a lot better today, but I guess I'm still a little angry that all the time people were laughing and making fun of me because I wasn't so smart. When I become intelligent like Dr. Strauss says, with three times my I.Q. of 68, then maybe I'll be like everyone else and people will like me.

I'm not sure what an I.Q. is. Dr. Nemur said it was something that measured how intelligent you were—like a scale in the drugstore weighs pounds. But Dr. Strauss had a big argument with him and said an I.Q. didn't weigh intelligence at all. He said an I.Q. showed how much intelligence you could get, like the numbers on the outside of a measuring cup. You still had to fill the cup up with stuff.

Then when I asked Burt, who gives me my intelligence tests and works with Algernon, he said that both of them were wrong (only I had to promise not to tell them he said so). Burt says that the I.Q. measures a lot of different things including some of the things you learned already, and it really isn't any good at all.

So I still don't know what I.Q. is except that mine is going to be over 200 soon. I didn't want to say anything, but I don't see how if they don't know *what* it is, or *where* it is—I don't see how they know *how much* of it you've got.

Dr. Nemur says I have to take a *Rorschach Test* tomorrow. I wonder what *that* is.

April 22 I found out what a Rorschach is. It's the test I took before the operation—the one with the inkblots on the pieces of cardboard.

I was scared to death of those inkblots. I knew the man was going to ask me to find the pictures and I knew I couldn't. I was thinking to myself, if only there was some way of knowing what kind of pictures were hidden there. Maybe there weren't any pictures at all. Maybe it was just a trick to see if I was dumb enough to look for something that wasn't there. Just thinking about that made me sore at him.

"All right, Charlie," he said, "you've seen these cards before, remember?"

"Of course I remember."

The way I said it, he knew I was angry, and he looked surprised. "Yes, of course. Now I want you to look at this. What might this be? What do you see on this card? People see all sorts of things in these ink-blots. Tell me what it might be for you—what it makes you think of."

I was shocked. That wasn't what I had expected him to say. "You mean there are no pictures hidden in those inkblots?"

He frowned and took off his glasses. "What?"

"Pictures. Hidden in the inkblots. Last time you told me everyone could see them and you wanted me to find them too."

He explained to me that the last time he had used almost the exact same words he was using now. I didn't believe it, and I still have the suspicion that he misled me at the time just for the fun of it. Unless—I don't know any more—could I have been *that* feeble-minded?

We went through the cards slowly. One looked like a pair of bats tugging at some-thing. Another one looked like two men fencing with swords. I imagined all sorts of things. I guess I got carried away. But I didn't trust him any more, and I kept turning them around, even looking on the back to see if there was anything there I was sup-posed to catch. While he was making his notes, I peeked out of the corner of my eye to read it. But it was all in code that looked like this:

WF+A   DdF−Ad orig.   WF−A
SF+obj

The test still doesn't make sense to me. It seems to me that anyone could make up lies about things that they didn't really imagine? Maybe I'll understand it when Dr. Strauss lets me read up on psychology.

April 25 I figured out a new way to line up the machines in the factory, and Mr. Donnegan says it will save him ten thousand dollars a year in labor and increased produc-tion. He gave me a $25 bonus.

I wanted to take Joe Carp and Frank Reilly out to lunch to celebrate, but Joe said he had to buy some things for his wife, and Frank said he was meeting his cousin for lunch. I guess it'll take a little time for them to get used to the changes in me. Everybody seems to be frightened of me. When I went over to Amos Borg and tapped him, he jumped up in the air.

People don't talk to me much any more or kid around the way they used to. It makes the job kind of lonely.

April 27 I got up the nerve today to ask Miss Kinnian to have dinner with me tomor-row night to celebrate my bonus.

At first she wasn't sure it was right, but I asked Dr. Strauss and he said it was okay. Dr. Strauss and Dr. Nemur don't seem to be getting along so well. They're arguing all the time. This evening I heard them shouting. Dr. Nemur was saying that it was *his* experi-ment and *his* research, and Dr. Strauss shouted back that he contributed just as much, because he found me through Miss Kinnian and he performed the operation. Dr. Strauss said that someday thousands of neu-rosurgeons might be using his technique all over the world.

Dr. Nemur wanted to publish the results of the experiment at the end of this month. Dr. Strauss wanted to wait a while to be sure. Dr. Strauss said Dr. Nemur was more interested in the Chair of Psychology at

Princeton[5] than he was in the experiment. Dr. Nemur said Dr. Strauss was nothing but an opportunist trying to ride to glory on *his* coattails.

When I left afterwards, I found myself trembling. I don't know why for sure, but it was as if I'd seen both men clearly for the first time. I remember hearing Burt say Dr. Nemur had a shrew of a wife who was pushing him all the time to get things published so he could become famous. Burt said that the dream of her life was to have a big-shot husband.

April 28 I don't understand why I never noticed how beautiful Miss Kinnian really is. She has brown eyes and feathery brown hair that comes to the top of her neck. She's only thirty-four! I think from the beginning I had the feeling that she was an unreachable genius—and very, very old. Now, every time I see her she grows younger and more lovely.

We had dinner and a long talk. When she said I was coming along so fast I'd be leaving her behind, I laughed.

"It's true, Charlie. You're already a better reader than I am. You can read a whole page at a glance while I can take in only a few lines at a time. And you remember every single thing you read. I'm lucky if I can recall the main thoughts and the general meaning."

"I don't feel intelligent. There are so many things I don't understand."

She took out a cigarette and I lit it for her. "You've got to be a *little* patient. You're accomplishing in days and weeks what it takes normal people to do in a lifetime. That's what makes it so amazing. You're like a giant sponge now, soaking things in. Facts, figures, general knowledge. And soon you'll begin to connect them, too. You'll see how different branches of learning are related. There are many levels, Charlie, like steps on a giant ladder that take you up higher and higher to see more and more of the world around you.

"I can see only a little bit of that, Charlie, and I won't go much higher than I am now, but you'll keep climbing up and up, and see more and more, and each step will open new worlds that you never even knew existed." She frowned. "I hope . . . I just hope——"

"What?"

"Never mind, Charles. I just hope I wasn't wrong to advise you to go into this in the first place."

I laughed. "How could that be? It worked, didn't it? Even Algernon is still smart."

We sat there silently for a while and I knew what she was thinking about as she watched me toying with the chain of my rabbit's foot and my keys. I didn't want to think of that possibility any more than elderly people want to think of death. I *knew* that this was only the beginning. I knew what she meant about levels because I'd seen some of them already. The thought of leaving her behind made me sad.

I'm in love with Miss Kinnian.

progress report 12

April 30 I've quit my job with Donnegan's Plastic Box Company. Mr. Donnegan insisted it would be better for all concerned if I left. What did I do to make them hate me so?

The first I knew of it was when Mr. Donnegan showed me the petition. Eight hundred names, everyone in the factory, except Fanny Girden. Scanning the list

---

5. *Chair of Psychology at Princeton,* an appointment as professor of psychology at Princeton University.

quickly, I saw at once that hers was the only missing name. All the rest demanded that I be fired.

Joe Carp and Frank Reilly wouldn't talk to me about it. No one else would either, except Fanny. She was one of the few people I'd known who set her mind to something and believed it no matter what the rest of the world proved, said or did—and Fanny did not believe that I should have been fired. She had been against the petition on principle and despite the pressure and threats she'd held out.

"Which don't mean to say," she remarked, "that I don't think there's something mighty strange about you, Charlie. Them changes. I don't know. You used to be a good, dependable, ordinary man—not too bright maybe, but honest. Who knows what you done to yourself to get so smart all of a sudden. Like everybody around here's been saying, Charlie, it's not right."

"But how can you say that, Fanny? What's wrong with a man becoming intelligent and wanting to acquire knowledge and understanding of the world around him?"

She stared down at her work and I turned to leave. Without looking at me, she said: "It was evil when Eve listened to the snake and ate from the tree of knowledge. It was evil when she saw that she was naked. If not for that none of us would ever have to grow old and sick, and die."[6]

Once again, now, I have the feeling of shame burning inside me. This intelligence has driven a wedge between me and all the people I once knew and loved. Before, they laughed at me and despised me for my ignorance and dullness; now, they hate me for my knowledge and understanding. What do they want of me?

They've driven me out of the factory. Now I'm more alone than ever before. . . .

May 15 Dr. Strauss is very angry at me for not having written any progress reports in two weeks. He's justified because the lab is now paying me a regular salary. I told him I was too busy thinking and reading. When I pointed out that writing was such a slow process that it made me impatient with my poor handwriting, he suggested I learn to type. It's much easier to write now because I can type seventy-five words a minute. Dr. Strauss continually reminds me of the need to speak and write simply so people will be able to understand me.

I'll try to review all the things that happened to me during the last two weeks. Algernon and I were presented to the *American Psychological Association* sitting in convention with the *World Psychological Association.* We created quite a sensation. Dr. Nemur and Dr. Strauss were proud of us.

I suspect that Dr. Nemur, who is sixty—ten years older than Dr. Strauss—finds it necessary to see tangible results of his work. Undoubtedly the result of pressure by Mrs. Nemur.

Contrary to my earlier impressions of him, I realize that Dr. Nemur is not at all a genius. He has a very good mind, but it struggles under the spectre of self-doubt. He wants people to take him for a genius. Therefore it is important for him to feel that his work is accepted by the world. I believe that Dr. Nemur was afraid of further delay because he worried that someone else might make a discovery along these lines and take the credit from him.

Dr. Strauss on the other hand might be called a genius, although I feel his areas of knowledge are too limited. He was educated

---

6. *"It was evil . . . die."* Fanny is referring to the biblical story of the fall of Adam and Eve and their expulsion by God from the Garden of Eden. [Genesis 2]

in the tradition of narrow specialization; the broader aspects of background were neglected far more than necessary—even for a neurosurgeon.

I was shocked to learn the only ancient languages he could read were Latin, Greek, and Hebrew, and that he knows almost nothing of mathematics beyond the elementary levels of the calculus of variations. When he admitted this to me, I found myself almost annoyed. It was as if he'd hidden this part of himself in order to deceive me, pretending—as do many people I've discovered—to be what he is not. No one I've ever known is what he appears to be on the surface.

Dr. Nemur appears to be uncomfortable around me. Sometimes when I try to talk to him, he just looks at me strangely and turns away. I was angry at first when Dr. Strauss told me I was giving Dr. Nemur an inferiority complex. I thought he was mocking me and I'm oversensitive at being made fun of.

How was I to know that a highly respected psycho-experimentalist like Nemur was unacquainted with Hindustani and Chinese? It's absurd when you consider the work that is being done in India and China today in the very field of his study.

I asked Dr. Strauss how Nemur could refute Rahajamati's attacks on his method if Nemur couldn't even read them in the first place. That strange look on Strauss's face can mean only one of two things. Either he doesn't want to tell Nemur what they're saying in India, or else—and this worries me—Dr. Strauss doesn't know either. I must be careful to speak and write clearly and simply so people won't laugh.

May 18 I am very disturbed. I saw Miss Kinnian last night for the first time in over a week. I tried to avoid all discussions of intellectual concepts and to keep the conversation on a simple, everyday level, but she just stared at me blankly and asked me what I meant about the mathematical variance equivalent in Dorbermann's *Fifth Concerto*.

When I tried to explain she stopped me and laughed. I guess I got angry, but I suspect I'm approaching her on the wrong level. No matter what I try to discuss with her, I am unable to communicate. I must review Vrostadt's equations on *Levels of Semantic Progression*. I find I don't communicate with people much any more. Thank God for books and music and things I can think about. I am alone at Mrs. Flynn's boarding house most of the time and seldom speak to anyone.

May 20 I would not have noticed the new dishwasher, a boy of about sixteen, at the corner diner where I take my evening meals if not for the incident of the broken dishes.

They crashed to the floor, sending bits of white china under the tables. The boy stood there, dazed and frightened, holding the empty tray in his hand. The catcalls from the customers (the cries of "hey, there go the profits!" . . . *"Mazeltov!"*[7] . . . and "well, *he* didn't work here very long . . ." which invariably seem to follow the breaking of glass or dishware in a public restaurant) all seemed to confuse him.

When the owner came to see what the excitement was about, the boy cowered as if he expected to be struck. "All right! All right, you dope," shouted the owner, "don't just stand there! Get the broom and sweep that mess up. A broom . . . a broom, you idiot! It's in the kitchen!"

The boy saw he was not going to be punished. His frightened expression disap-

---

7. **Mazeltov!**, a Yiddish expression meaning, in this case, "May you have better luck in the future."

peared and he smiled as he came back with the broom to sweep the floor. A few of the rowdier customers kept up the remarks, amusing themselves at his expense.

"Here, sonny, over here there's a nice piece behind you . . . "

"He's not so dumb. It's easier to break 'em than wash 'em!"

As his vacant eyes moved across the crowd of onlookers, he slowly mirrored their smiles and finally broke into an uncertain grin at the joke he obviously did not understand.

I felt sick inside as I looked at his dull, vacuous smile, the wide, bright eyes of a child, uncertain but eager to please. They were laughing at him because he was mentally retarded.

And I had been laughing at him too.

Suddenly I was furious at myself and all those who were smirking at him. I jumped up and shouted, "Shut up! Leave him alone! It's not his fault he can't understand! He can't help what he is! But he's still a human being!"

The room grew silent. I cursed myself for losing control. I tried not to look at the boy as I walked out without touching my food. I felt ashamed for both of us.

How strange that people of honest feelings and sensibility, who would not take advantage of a man born without arms or eyes—how such people think nothing of abusing a man born with low intelligence. It infuriated me to think that not too long ago I had foolishly played the clown.

And I had almost forgotten.

I'd hidden the picture of the old Charlie Gordon from myself because now that I was intelligent it was something that had to be pushed out of my mind. But today in looking at that boy, for the first time I saw what I had been. *I was just like him!*

Only a short time ago, I learned that people laughed at me. Now I can see that unknowingly I joined with them in laughing at myself. That hurts most of all.

I have often reread my progress reports and seen the illiteracy, the childish naïveté, the mind of low intelligence peering from a dark room through the keyhole at the dazzling light outside. I see that even in my dullness I knew I was inferior, and that other people had something I lacked—something denied me. In my mental blindness, I thought it was somehow connected with the ability to read and write, and I was sure that if I could get those skills I would automatically have intelligence too.

Even a feeble-minded man wants to be like other men.

A child may not know how to feed itself, or what to eat, yet it knows of hunger.

This then is what I was like. I never knew. Even with my gift of intellectual awareness, I never really knew.

This day was good for me. Seeing the past more clearly, I've decided to use my knowledge and skills to work in the field of increasing human intelligence levels. Who is better equipped for this work? Who else has lived in both worlds? These are my people. Let me use my gift to do something for them.

Tomorrow, I will discuss with Dr. Strauss how I can work in this area. I may be able to help him work out the problems of widespread use of the technique which was used on me. I have several good ideas of my own.

There is so much that might be done with this technique. If I could be made into a genius, what about thousands of others like myself? What fantastic levels might be achieved by using this technique on normal people? On *geniuses*?

There are so many doors to open. I am impatient to begin.

progress report 13

May 23 It happened today. Algernon bit me. I visited the lab to see him as I do occasionally, and when I took him out of his cage, he snapped at my hand. I put him back and watched him for a while. He was unusually disturbed and vicious.

May 24 Burt, who is in charge of the experimental animals, tells me that Algernon is changing. He is less cooperative; he refuses to run the maze any more; general motivation has decreased. And he hasn't been eating. Everyone is upset about what this may mean.

May 25 They've been feeding Algernon, who now refuses to work the shifting-lock problem. Everyone identifies me with Algernon. In a way we're both the first of our kind. They're all pretending that Algernon's behavior is not necessarily significant for me. But it's hard to hide the fact that some of the other animals who were used in this experiment are showing strange behavior.

Dr. Strauss and Dr. Nemur have asked me not to come to the lab any more. I know what they're thinking but I can't accept it. I am going ahead with my plans to carry their research forward. With all due respect to both these fine scientists, I am well aware of their limitations. If there is an answer, I'll have to find it out for myself. Suddenly, time has become very important to me.

May 29 I have been given a lab of my own and permission to go ahead with the research. I'm on to something. Working day and night. I've had a cot moved into the lab. Most of my writing time is spent on the notes which I keep in a separate folder, but from time to time I feel it necessary to put down my moods and thoughts from sheer habit.

I find the *calculus of intelligence* to be a fascinating study. Here is the place for the application of all the knowledge I have acquired.

May 31 Dr. Strauss thinks I'm working too hard. Dr. Nemur says I'm trying to cram a lifetime of research and thought into a few weeks. I know I should rest, but I'm driven on by something inside that won't let me stop. I've got to find the reason for the sharp regression in Algernon. I've got to know *if* and *when* it will happen to me.

June 4
LETTER TO DR. STRAUSS *(copy)*
Dear Dr. Strauss:

Under separate cover I am sending you a copy of my report entitled, "The Algernon-Gordon Effect: A Study of Structure and Function of Increased Intelligence," which I would like to have published.

As you see, my experiments are completed. I have included in my report all of my formulae, as well as mathematical analysis in the appendix. Of course, these should be verified.

Because of its importance to both you and Dr. Nemur (and need I say to myself, too?) I have checked and rechecked my results a dozen times in the hope of finding an error. I am sorry to say the results must stand. Yet for the sake of science, I am grateful for the little bit that I here add to the knowledge of the function of the human mind and of the laws governing the artificial increase of human intelligence.

I recall your once saying to me that an

experimental *failure* or the *disproving* of a theory was as important to the advancement of learning as a success would be. I know now that this is true. I am sorry, however, that my own contribution to the field must rest upon the ashes of the work of two men I regard so highly.

Yours truly,
Charles Gordon

June 5 I must not become emotional. The facts and the results of my experiments are clear, and the more sensational aspects of my own rapid climb cannot obscure the fact that the tripling of intelligence by the surgical technique developed by Drs. Strauss and Nemur must be viewed as having little or no practical applicability (at the present time) to the increase of human intelligence.

As I review the records and data on Algernon, I see that although he is still in his physical infancy, he has regressed mentally. Motor activity is impaired; there is a general reduction of glandular activity; there is an accelerated loss of coordination.

There are also strong indications of progressive amnesia.

As will be seen by my report, these and other physical and mental deterioration syndromes can be predicted with significant results by the application of my formula.

The surgical stimulus to which we were both subjected has resulted in an intensification and acceleration of all mental processes. The unforeseen development, which I have taken the liberty of calling the *Algernon-Gordon Effect,* is the logical extension of the entire intelligence speed-up. The hypothesis here proven may be described simply in the following terms: Artificially increased intelligence deteriorates at a rate of time directly proportional to the quantity of the increase.

I feel that this, in itself, is an important discovery.

As long as I am able to write, I will continue to record my thoughts in these progress reports. It is one of my few pleasures. However, by all indications, my own mental deterioration will be very rapid.

I have already begun to notice signs of emotional instability and forgetfulness, the first symptoms of the burnout.

June 10 Deterioration progressing. I have become absent-minded. Algernon died two days ago. Dissection shows my predictions were right. His brain had decreased in weight and there was a general smoothing out of cerebral convolutions, as well as a deepening and broadening of brain fissures.[8]

I guess the same thing is or will soon be happening to me. Now that it's definite, I don't want it to happen.

I put Algernon's body in a cheese box and buried him in the back yard. I cried.

June 15 Dr. Strauss came to see me again. I wouldn't open the door and I told him to go away. I want to be left to myself. I am touchy and irritable. I feel the darkness closing in. It's hard to throw off thoughts of suicide. I keep telling myself how important this journal will be.

It's a strange sensation to pick up a book you enjoyed just a few months ago and discover you don't remember it. I remembered how great I thought John Milton was, but when I picked up *Paradise Lost* I couldn't understand it at all. I got so angry I threw the book across the room.

I've got to try to hold on to some of it.

---

8. *His brain . . . fissures.* There seems to be a direct relationship between intelligence and brain size, and between intelligence and the number of cerebral convolutions (folds or ridges on the surface of the brain).

Some of the things I've learned. Oh, God, please don't take it all away.

June 19 Sometimes, at night, I go out for a walk. Last night, I couldn't remember where I lived. A policeman took me home. I have the strange feeling that this has all happened to me before—a long time ago. I keep telling myself I'm the only person in the world who can describe what's happening to me.

June 21 Why can't I remember? I've got to fight. I lie in bed for days and I don't know who or where I am. Then it all comes back to me in a flash. Fugues of amnesia. Symptoms of senility—second childhood. I can watch them coming on. It's so cruelly logical. I learned so much and so fast. Now my mind is deteriorating rapidly. I won't let it happen. I'll fight it. I can't help thinking of the boy in the restaurant, the blank expression, the silly smile, the people laughing at him. No— please—not that again. . . .

June 22 I'm forgetting things that I learned recently. It seems to be following the classic pattern—the last things learned are the first things forgotten. Or is that the pattern? I'd better look it up again. . . .

I reread my paper on the *Algernon-Gordon Effect* and I get the strange feeling that it was written by someone else. There are parts I don't even understand.

Motor activity impaired. I keep tripping over things, and it becomes increasingly difficult to type.

June 23 I've given up using the typewriter. My coordination is bad. I feel I'm moving slower and slower. Had a terrible shock today. I picked up a copy of an article I used

in my research, Krueger's *Uber psychische Ganzheit,* to see if it would help me understand what I had done. First I thought there was something wrong with my eyes. Then I realized I could no longer read German. I tested myself in other languages. All gone.

June 30 A week since I dared to write again. It's slipping away like sand through my fingers. Most of the books I have are too hard for me now. I get angry with them because I know that I read and understood them just a few weeks ago.

I keep telling myself I must keep writing these reports so that somebody will know what is happening to me. But it gets harder to form the words and remember spellings. I have to look up even simple words in the dictionary now and it makes me impatient with myself.

Dr. Strauss comes around almost every day, but I told him I wouldn't see or speak to anybody. He feels guilty. They all do. But I don't blame anyone. I knew what might happen. But how it hurts.

July 7 I don't know where the week went. Todays Sunday I know because I can see through my window people going to church. I think I stayed in bed all week but I remember Mrs. Flynn bringing food to me a few times. I keep saying over and over I've got to do something but then I forget or maybe its just easier not to do what I say I'm going to do.

I think of my mother and father a lot these days. I found a picture of them with me taken at a beach. My father has a big ball under his arm and my mother is holding me by the hand. I dont remember them the way they are in the picture. All I remember is my father drunk most of the time and arguing with mom about money.

He never shaved much and he used to scratch my face when he hugged me. My Mother said he died but Cousin Miltie said he heard his dad say that my father ran away with another woman. When I asked my mother she slapped me and said my father was dead. I dont think I ever found out the truth but I dont care much. (He said he was going to take me to see cows on a farm once but he never did. He never kept his promises. . . .)

July 10 My landlady Mrs. Flynn is very worried about me. She says the way I lay around all day and dont do anything I remind her of her son before she threw him out of the house. She said she doesn't like loafers. If Im sick its one thing, but if Im a loafer thats another thing and she won't have it. I told her I think Im sick.

I try to read a little bit every day, mostly stories, but sometimes I have to read the same thing over and over again because I don't know what it means. And its hard to write. I know I should look up all the words in the dictionary but its so hard and Im so tired all the time.

Then I got the idea that I would only use the easy words instead of the long hard ones. That saves time. I put flowers on Algernons grave about once a week. Mrs. Flynn thinks Im crazy to put flowers on a mouses grave but I told her that Algernon was special.

July 14 Its sunday again. I dont have anything to do to keep me busy now because my television set is broke and I dont have any money to get it fixed. (I think I lost this months check from the lab. I don't remember)

I get awful headaches and asperin doesnt help me much. Mrs. Flynn knows Im really sick and she feels very sorry for me. Shes a wonderful woman whenever someone is sick.

July 22 Mrs. Flynn called a strange doctor to see me. She was afraid I was going to die. I told the doctor I wasnt too sick and I only forget sometimes. He asked me did I have any friends or relatives and I said no I dont have any. I told him I had a friend called Algernon once but he was a mouse and we used to run races together. He looked at me kind of funny like he thought I was crazy. He smiled when I told him I used to be a genius. He talked to me like I was a baby and he winked at Mrs. Flynn. I got mad and chased him out because he was making fun of me the way they all used to.

July 24 I have no more money and Mrs. Flynn says I got to go to work somewhere and pay the rent because I havent paid for two months. I dont know any work but the job I used to have at Donnegans Box Company. I dont want to go back because they all knew me when I was smart and maybe they'll laugh at me. But I dont know what else to do to get money.

July 25 I was looking at some of my old progress reports and its very funny but I cant read what I wrote. I can make out some of the words but they dont make sense.

Miss Kinnian came to the door but I said go away I don't want to see you. She cried and I cried too but I wouldnt let her in because I didn't want her to laugh at me. I told her I didnt like her any more. I told her I didnt want to be smart any more. That's not true. I still love her and I still want to be smart but I had to say that so shed go away. She gave Mrs. Flynn money to pay the rent. I dont want that. I got to get a job.

Please . . . please let me not forget how to read and write. . . .

July 27 Mr. Donnegan was very nice when I came back and asked him for my old job of janitor. First he was very suspicious but I told him what happened to me and he looked very sad and put his hand on my shoulder and said Charlie Gordon you got guts.

Everybody looked at me when I came downstairs and started working in the toilet sweeping it out like I used to. I told myself Charlie if they make fun of you dont get sore because you remember their not so smart as you once thot they were. And besides they were once your friends and if they laughted at you that doesnt meant anything because they liked you too.

One of the new men who came to work there after I went away made a nasty crack he said hey Charlie I hear your a very smart fella a real quiz kid. Say something intelligent. I felt bad but Joe Carp came over and grabbed him by the shirt and said leave him alone you lousy cracker or I'll break your neck. I didnt expect Joe to take my part so I guess hes really my friend.

Later Frank Reilly came over and said Charlie if anybody bothers you or trys to take advantage you call me or Joe and we will set em straight. I said thanks Frank and I got choked up so I had to turn around and go into the supply room so he wouldnt see me cry. Its good to have friends.

July 28 I did a dumb thing today I forgot I wasn't in Miss Kinnians class at the adult center any more like I use to be. I went in and sat down in my old seat in the back of the room and she looked at me funny and she said Charles. I dint remember she ever called me that before only Charlie so I said hello Miss Kinnian Im redy for my lesin today only I lost my reader that we was using. She startid to cry and run out of the room and everybody looked at me and I saw they wasnt the same pepul who use to be in my class.

Then all of a suddin I remembered some things about the operashun and me getting smart and I said holy smoke I reely pulled a Charlie Gordon that time. I went away before she come back to the room.

Thats why Im going away from New York for good. I dont want to do nothing like that agen. I dont want Miss Kinnian to feel sorry for me. Evry body feels sorry at the factery and I dont want that eather so Im going someplace where nobody knows that Charlie Gordon was once a genus and now he cant even reed a book or rite good.

Im taking a cuple of books along and even if I cant reed them Ill practise hard and maybe I wont forget every thing I lerned. If I try reel hard maybe Ill be a littel bit smarter then I was before the operashun. I got my rabits foot and my luky penny and maybe they will help me.

If you ever reed this Miss Kinnian dont be sorry for me Im glad I got a second chanse to be smart becaus I lerned a lot of things that I never even new were in this world and Im grateful that I saw it all for a littel bit. I dont know why Im dumb agen or what I did wrong maybe its because I dint try hard enuff. But if I try and practis very hard maybe Ill get a littl smarter and know what all the words are. I remember a littel bit how nice I had a feeling with the blue book that has the torn cover when I red it. Thats why Im gonna keep trying to get smart so I can have that feeling agen. Its a good feeling to know things and be smart. I wish I had it rite now if I did I would sit down and reed all the time. Anyway I bet Im the first dumb person in the world who ever found out somthing importent for science. I remember I did somthing but I dont remember what. So I gess its like I did it for all the dumb pepul like me.

Goodbye Miss Kinnian and Dr. Strauss and evreybody. And P.S. please tell Dr Nemur not to be such a grouch when pepul laff at him and he would have more frends. Its easy to make frends if you let pepul laff at you. Im going to have lots of frends where I go.

P.P.S. Please if you get a chanse put some flowrs on Algernons grave in the bak yard. . . . ☐ ☐

Discussion

1. If you were asked to write a continuation of this story, what would you have happen to Charlie? Why?

2. What are some of Charlie's outstanding characteristics?

3. (a) How does Charlie feel immediately after the opera- tion? (b) What first gives him hope of becoming smart? (c) How does this incident change his attitude toward Algernon?

4. Miss Kinnian, Charlie's landlady, and the factory work- ers all have different attitudes toward Charlie at different times in the story. Explain how each feels about Charlie (a) be- fore his operation; (b) as his intelligence increases; and (c) as he regresses.

5. (a) As a result of his in- creased ability to think, how does Charlie's view of others change? Point out specific ex- amples. (b) What effect does this new knowledge of people have on Charlie? (c) Charlie

uses his gift to do something for retarded people. Is this in keeping with the character he has displayed throughout the story? Explain.

6. (a) At what point in the story do you first know that Charlie is going to lose his new-found mental ability? (b) How do his reactions to Algernon's deterioration differ from his reactions to his own deterioration? (c) Why does he decide to leave town?

7. (a) Is Charlie happier with an I.Q. of 68 or with one of 200+? Explain. (b) If he had been given a choice, which I.Q. do you think he would have chosen? Why?

8. The author has written this story in the form of a journal kept by Charlie. What particular method or methods of characterization are emphasized by this technique of telling a story?

9. (a) To what does the title of the story refer? (b) Why might the author have chosen this title?

Vocabulary · Context

Read the following sentences. Figure out the meaning of each italicized word from the context and write the letter of the correct meaning on your paper. Be sure you know how to pronounce each italicized word.

1. Her vision was *impaired* by that accident; now she can't see any object more than six feet away from her. (a) made worse; (b) made better; (c) barely affected; (d) destroyed.

2. I caught him staring dully, with a *vacuous* expression on his face. (a) showing great concentration; (b) showing no thought or intelligence; (c) pleased; (d) concerned.

3. We need *tangible* evidence, not just rumors and foolish theories. (a) simple; (b) definite; (c) additional; (d) complex.

4. The unhappy child was so used to being slapped that she *cowered* whenever anyone came near her. (a) smiled shyly; (b) offered to shake hands; (c) shouted angrily; (d) crouched in fear.

5. If lying about his co-workers would help his own career, an *opportunist* like Benchley wouldn't hesitate to stoop to it. (a) person who is very confident about his own ability; (b) person who works better alone than with others; (c) person who uses every opportunity, right or wrong, to his own advantage; (d) person who is afraid of success.

6. Henry's belief in everything he hears or reads can be blamed on his *naïveté.* (a) lack of sophistication; (b) lack of money; (c) bad temper; (d) forgetfulness.

Extension · Writing

Imagine an event or experience that does not appear in this story and write a progress report as if you were Charlie Gordon sometime *after* the operation has taken place. Remember that Charlie does not become "smart" right away. He gradually acquires his new intelligence and then he gradually loses it. Let your language reflect the feelings and understanding that Charlie has (1) immediately after the operation, or (2) when he has an I.Q. of 200, or (3) when he is aware that he is losing his acquired intelligence.

Here are some samples of events you might write about as Charlie:

1. a television program that you have just seen
2. a visit with your family
3. buying a typewriter in a department store
4. a telephone conversation with a newspaper reporter who is interviewing you
5. taking a test for a driver's license
6. deciding to buy a mouse to keep at home.

After you have written your progress report, your teacher may ask you to let classmates read your report to see if they can discover at what point after the operation you are presenting Charlie's ideas and feelings.

Fifteen

William Stafford

South of the Bridge on Seventeenth
I found back of the willows one summer
day a motorcycle with engine running
as it lay on its side, ticking over
5 slowly in the high grass. I was fifteen.

I admired all that pulsing gleam, the
shiny flanks, the demure headlights
fringed where it lay; I led it gently
to the road and stood with that
10 companion, ready and friendly. I was fifteen.

We could find the end of a road, meet
the sky on out Seventeenth. I thought about
hills, and patting the handle got back a
confident opinion. On the bridge we indulged
15 a forward feeling, a tremble. I was fifteen.

Thinking, back farther in the grass I found
the owner, just coming to, where he had flipped
over the rail. He had blood on his hand, was pale—
I helped him walk to his machine. He ran his hand
20 over it, called me good man, roared away.

I stood there, fifteen.

From *The Rescued Year* by William Stafford. Copyright © 1964 by William E. Stafford. Reprinted by permission of Harper & Row, Publishers, Inc.

Discussion

1. Summarize what the speaker does in each stanza of the poem.

2. Why do you think the line "I was fifteen" is repeated so many times in the poem?

3. (a) If you had been the one to find the motorcycle, would you have been tempted to take it for a ride? Why or why not? (b) Can you think of an occasion when you, like the speaker in the poem, were inclined to follow a dream but did not? Explain.

Mama, is it time to go?"

I hadn't planned to cry, but the tears came suddenly, and I wiped them away with the back of my hand. I didn't want my older sister to see me crying.

"It's almost time, Ruri," my mother said gently. Her face was filled with a kind of sadness I had never seen before.

I looked around at my empty room. The clothes that Mama always told me to hang up in the closet, the junk piled on my dresser, the old rag doll I could never bear to part with; they were all gone. There was nothing left in my room, and there was nothing left in the rest of the house. The rugs and furniture were gone, the pictures and drapes were down, and the closets and cupboards were empty. The house was like a gift box after the nice thing inside was gone; just a lot of nothingness.

It was almost time to leave our home, but we weren't moving to a nicer house or to a new town. It was April 21, 1942. The United States and Japan were at war, and every Japanese person on the West Coast was being evacuated by the government to a concentration camp. Mama, my sister Keiko, and I were being sent from our home, and out of Berkeley, and eventually, out of California.

The doorbell rang, and I ran to answer it before my sister could. I thought maybe by some miracle, a messenger from the government might be standing there, tall and proper and buttoned into a uniform, come to tell us it was all a terrible mistake; that we wouldn't have to leave after all. Or maybe the messenger would have a telegram from Papa, who was interned in a prisoner-of-war camp in Montana because he had worked for a Japanese business firm.

The FBI had come to pick up Papa and hundreds of other Japanese community

See **SYMBOL** Handbook of Literary Terms

The United States and Japan were at war. Ruri, like almost every other Japanese-American on the West Coast, was being sent to an internment camp.

The Bracelet

Yoshiko Uchida

leaders on the very day that Japanese planes had bombed Pearl Harbor. The government thought they were dangerous enemy aliens. If it weren't so sad, it would have been funny. Papa could no more be dangerous than the mayor of our city, and he was every bit as loyal to the United States. He had lived here since 1917.

When I opened the door, it wasn't a messenger from anywhere. It was my best friend, Laurie Madison, from next door. She was holding a package wrapped up like a birthday present, but she wasn't wearing her party dress, and her face drooped like a wilted tulip.

"Hi," she said. "I came to say good-bye."

She thrust the present at me and told me it was something to take to camp. "It's a bracelet," she said before I could open the package. "Put it on so you won't have to pack it." She knew I didn't have one inch of space left in my suitcase. We had been instructed to take only what we could carry into camp, and Mama had told us that we could each take only two suitcases.

"Then how are we ever going to pack the dishes and blankets and sheets they've told us to bring with us?" Keiko worried.

"I don't really know," Mama said, and she simply began packing those big impossible things into an enormous duffel bag—along with umbrellas, boots, a kettle, hot plate, and flashlight.

"Who's going to carry that huge sack?" I asked.

But Mama didn't worry about things like that. "Someone will help us," she said. "Don't worry." So I didn't.

Laurie wanted me to open her package and put on the bracelet before she left. It was a thin gold chain with a heart dangling on it. She helped me put it on, and I told her I'd never take it off, ever.

"Well, good-bye then," Laurie said awkwardly. "Come home soon."

"I will," I said, although I didn't know if I would ever get back to Berkeley again.

I watched Laurie go down the block, her long blond pigtails bouncing as she walked. I wondered who would be sitting in my desk at Lincoln Junior High now that I was gone. Laurie kept turning and waving, even walking backwards for a while, until she got to the corner. I didn't want to watch anymore, and I slammed the door shut.

The next time the doorbell rang, it was Mrs. Simpson, our other neighbor. She was going to drive us to the Congregational church, which was the Civil Control Station where all the Japanese of Berkeley were supposed to report.

It was time to go. "Come on, Ruri. Get your things," my sister called to me.

It was a warm day, but I put on a sweater and my coat so I wouldn't have to carry them, and I picked up my two suitcases. Each one had a tag with my name and our family number on it. Every Japanese family had to register and get a number. We were Family Number 13453.

Mama was taking one last look around our house. She was going from room to room, as though she were trying to take a mental picture of the house she had lived in for fifteen years, so she would never forget it.

I saw her take a long last look at the garden that Papa loved. The irises beside the fish pond were just beginning to bloom. If Papa had been home, he would have cut the first iris blossom and brought it inside to Mama. "This one is for you," he would have said. And Mama would have smiled and said, "Thank you, Papa San," and put it in her favorite cut-glass vase.

But the garden looked shabby and forsaken now that Papa was gone and Mama was too busy to take care of it. It looked the way I felt, sort of empty and lonely and abandoned.

When Mrs. Simpson took us to the Civil Control Station, I felt even worse. I was scared, and for a minute I thought I was going to lose my breakfast right in front of everybody. There must have been over a thousand Japanese people gathered at the church. Some were old and some were young. Some were talking and laughing, and some were crying. I guess everybody else was scared too. No one knew exactly what was going to happen to us. We just knew we were being taken to the Tanforan Racetracks, which the army had turned into a camp for the Japanese. There were fourteen other camps like ours along the West Coast.

What scared me most were the soldiers standing at the doorway of the church hall. They were carrying guns with mounted bayonets. I wondered if they thought we would try to run away, and whether they'd shoot us or come after us with their bayonets if we did.

A long line of buses waited to take us to camp. There were trucks, too, for our baggage. And Mama was right; some men were there to help us load our duffel bag. When it was time to board the buses, I sat with Keiko and Mama sat behind us. The bus went down Grove Street and passed the small Japanese food store where Mama used to order her bean-curd cakes and pickled radish. The windows were all boarded up, but there was a sign still hanging on the door that read, "We are loyal Americans."

The crazy thing about the whole evacuation was that we were all loyal Americans. Most of us were citizens because we had been born here. But our parents, who had come from Japan, couldn't become citizens because there was a law that prevented any Asian from becoming a citizen. Now everybody with a Japanese face was being shipped off to concentration camps.

"It's stupid," Keiko muttered as we saw the racetrack looming up beside the highway. "If there were any Japanese spies around, they'd have gone back to Japan long ago."

"I'll say," I agreed. My sister was in high school and she ought to know, I thought.

When the bus turned into Tanforan, there were more armed guards at the gate, and I saw barbed wire strung around the entire grounds. I felt as though I were going into a prison, but I hadn't done anything wrong.

We streamed off the buses and poured into a huge room, where doctors looked down our throats and peeled back our eyelids to see if we had any diseases. Then we were given our housing assignments. The man in charge gave Mama a slip of paper. We were in Barrack 16, Apartment 40.

"Mama!" I said. "We're going to live in an apartment!" The only apartment I had ever seen was the one my piano teacher lived in. It was in an enormous building in San Francisco with an elevator and thick carpeted hallways. I thought how wonderful it would be to have our own elevator. A house was all right, but an apartment seemed elegant and special.

We walked down the racetrack looking for Barrack 16. Mr. Noma, a friend of Papa's, helped us carry our bags. I was so busy looking around, I slipped and almost fell on the muddy track. Army barracks had been built everywhere, all around the race-track and even in the center oval.

Mr. Noma pointed beyond the track toward the horse stables. "I think your barrack is out there."

He was right. We came to a long stable that had once housed the horses of Tanforan, and we climbed up the wide ramp. Each stall had a number painted on it, and when we got to 40, Mr. Noma pushed open the door.

"Well, here it is," he said, "Apartment 40."

The stall was narrow and empty and dark. There were two small windows on each side of the door. Three folded army cots were on the dust-covered floor and one light bulb dangled from the ceiling. That was all. This was our apartment, and it still smelled of horses.

Mama looked at my sister and then at me. "It won't be so bad when we fix it up," she began. "I'll ask Mrs. Simpson to send me some material for curtains. I could make some cushions too, and . . . well . . . ." She stopped. She couldn't think of anything more to say.

Mr. Noma said he'd go get some mattresses for us. "I'd better hurry before they're all gone." He rushed off. I think he wanted to leave so that he wouldn't have to see Mama cry. But he needn't have run off, because Mama didn't cry. She just went out to borrow a broom and began sweeping out the dust and dirt. "Will you girls set up the cots?" she asked.

It was only after we'd put up the last cot that I noticed my bracelet was gone. "I've lost Laurie's bracelet!" I screamed. "My bracelet's gone!"

We looked all over the stall and even down the ramp. I wanted to run back down the track and go over every inch of ground

FSA photo by Russell Lee, courtesy of the Library of Congress

National Archives

Wide World Photos

we'd walked on, but it was getting dark and Mama wouldn't let me.

I thought of what I'd promised Laurie. I wasn't ever going to take the bracelet off, not even when I went to take a shower. And now I had lost it on my very first day in camp. I wanted to cry.

I kept looking for it all the time we were in Tanforan. I didn't stop looking until the day we were sent to another camp, called Topaz, in the middle of a desert in Utah. And then I gave up.

But Mama told me never mind. She said I didn't need a bracelet to remember Laurie, just as I didn't need anything to remember Papa or our home in Berkeley or all the people and things we loved and had left behind.

"Those are things we can carry in our hearts and take with us no matter where we are sent," she said.

And I guess she was right. I've never forgotten Laurie, even now. ☐☐

Discussion

1. Suppose Ruri and her friend Laurie met again later, after they had both graduated from high school. What do you think they would say to each other? Do you think Ruri would reveal that she lost the bracelet?

2. (a) Describe the bracelet that Laurie gives to Ruri. (b) What does the bracelet symbolize to Ruri? (c) How does she react to the loss of the bracelet?

3. What details in the story help suggest the sense of emptiness, loneliness, and abandonment experienced by Ruri and her family?

4. In spite of humiliation and mistreatment, Ruri's mother remains calm, dignified, and courageous. In what specific ways does she show these qualities?

Extension • Writing

Do one of the following:

1. Suppose that after two years Ruri has returned to Berkeley and enrolled in the same high school that Laurie is attending. On her first day of classes, before the school day actually begins, Ruri sees Laurie standing in the corridor by one of the classrooms. Ruri walks over to Laurie and says . . .

Write a dialogue between Ruri and Laurie showing what you think they would say to each other at their first meeting. Arrange the dialogue in "script" form as shown in the next column. Allow each person at least five speaking turns, though you may allow more speaking turns than that if you need to. If you wish, you may use the beginning lines that follow.

RURI. Laurie . . . Laurie, is that you? I am so glad I found you. I wasn't sure we would ever see each other again!
LAURIE. Ruri! I was looking for you. Keiko told me you were coming. How was it . . . in the camp, I mean?

2. Imagine that you are Ruri writing your first letter to Laurie after you have finally reached Topaz, your final destination in the middle of the Utah desert. Will you tell her about the bracelet? the trip to the internment camp? your mother? your sister Keiko? the new school? your new home? what you are frightened of, what you worry about? Your letter should be at least two paragraphs long. You may wish to read the article on the following page to get some ideas of what actually happened to the Japanese-Americans who were interned.

The Story Behind the Story

The author of "The Bracelet," Yoshiko Uchida, knows first hand about a harsh chapter of American history. Of her childhood she says: "There was a lot of discrimination. Japanese people would never go into certain stores and restaurants because we were made to feel so uncomfortable. I remember when I was going to get my first haircut, I was so afraid of being rejected that I called first to make sure they would take me. Once, my Girl Reserves group was having its picture taken for the newspaper. The photographer carefully eased me out, and I knew why.

"I was tremendously hurt by these incidents—they color a child's outlook on life enormously. One never forgets."

Her most traumatic experience happened at the end of her studies at the University of California. Uchida was graduated with honors, but wasn't allowed to attend the ceremonies. It was May, 1942. Her family, along with thousands of Japanese on the West Coast, were forced to leave their homes and move to "relocation centers." She explains, "My family was first put in a horse stall at Tanforan Race Track. It was there I received my diploma, delivered in a cardboard tube."

The horse stall was bad enough, but Topaz, the next camp the family was sent to, was worse. Uchida lived in this dusty, desolate place in the Utah desert for a year. Deciding to make the best of the situation, she volunteered to teach in the camp school. She refused to become embittered.

"That your own country would put you behind barbed wire without any trial, simply because of race, is a real tragedy. I know many young Japanese-Americans today blame us for having acquiesced, as they see it. But the world was a different place. Our thought was to show that we were loyal Americans. We believed we could prove this by doing what the government asked.

"Most Japanese responded with a great deal of dignity. Yes, we were angry, but I think we should distinguish between anger and bitterness. I always feel that when you're bitter, you're only destroying yourself. This is something I hope to convey in my writing."

Uchida was allowed to leave Topaz in 1943, when she received a scholarship to study at Smith College. In the years since, she has followed interests in folk scholarship, writing, crafts, and art. An accomplished artist, she has illustrated two of her own books.

Breaking and Entering

Joyce Carol Oates

One of us touched the door and it swung open.

Slowly, we went inside,
Knowing better, we went inside.

The kitchen was darkened,
5 the light we'd left on in the hallway was out.
Downstairs, no sign of disorder.
Knowing better, we went upstairs.
If I had tried to caution you, you would have pulled away,
eager, anxious, needing to see——
10 and there in the bedroom
the acted-out drama, there
bureau drawers yanked out, overturned, thrown,
a skid mark on one wall——
our clothes tumbled together——
15 twisted, kicked, someone's fury run to earth.
On the doorframe there is a smear of blood.

Later, we will discover the smashed window in the basement;
the drops of a stranger's blood.
He must have been very small, the police said,
20 *to crawl through there.*
Later, slowly, as if shy of knowledge,
we discover things missing:
my wristwatch, a small typewriter,
a tarnished silver vase.
25 We are slowed-down, stupefied.
We want none of our possessions back,
we don't care what else has been stolen,
yet we talk about it constantly:
the mess! the surprise!

30 Later, we will transform it into an anecdote.
We will say, *One of us touched the door and it swung open. . . .*
knowing no way to explain the stupor, the despair,
the premonition of theft to come.

Discussion

1. What are some of the early signs that things are not as they should be in the house, even though the house is not in disorder downstairs?

2. It is possible to make several inferences about the thief. **(a)** For example, how did he enter the house? **(b)** What was his probable emotional state? **(c)** How big was he? **(d)** What did he take? **(e)** How did he get out of the house? **(f)** Does his robbery appear to have cost him anything?

3. How has the robbery affected the speaker?

4. Do you think you would have reacted the way the speaker did if you had discovered your home in a similar condition? Explain.

Joyce Carol Oates   1938 •

At the age of twenty-five, Joyce Carol Oates published her first collection of short stories, though she had been writing poems and stories since childhood. "Before I could write," she says, "I drew pictures to tell my stories."

Oates teaches English at the University of Windsor, in Ontario, Canada. Her poems, stories, and novels have earned her several honors, including a National Book Award in 1970.

See **IRONY** Handbook of Literary Terms

She loved the young man, but she could not have him. Now she had a choice. Would she give him to . . .

The Lady, or the Tiger?

Frank R. Stockton

In the very olden time, there lived a semi-barbaric king, whose ideas, though somewhat polished and sharpened by the progressiveness of distant Latin neighbors,[1] were still large, florid, and untrammeled, as became the half of him which was barbaric. He was a man of exuberant fancy, and, withal, of an authority so irresistible that, at his will, he turned his varied fancies into facts. He was greatly given to self-communing; and, when he and himself agreed upon anything, the thing was done. When every member of his domestic and political systems moved smoothly in its appointed course, his nature was bland and genial; but whenever there was a little hitch, and some of his orbs got out of their orbits, he was blander and more genial still, for nothing pleased him so much as to make the crooked straight, and crush down uneven places.

Among the borrowed notions by which his barbarism had become semifixed was that of the public arena, in which, by exhibitions of manly and beastly valor, the minds of his subjects were refined and cultured.

But even here the exuberant and barbaric fancy asserted itself. The arena of the king was built, not to give the people an opportunity of hearing the rhapsodies of dying gladiators, nor to enable them to view the inevitable conclusion of a conflict between religious opinions and hungry jaws, but for purposes far better adapted to widen and develop the mental energies of the people. This vast amphitheater, with its encircling galleries, its mysterious vaults, and its unseen passages, was an agent of poetic justice, in which crime was punished, or virtue rewarded, by the decrees of an impartial and incorruptible chance.

From *The Lady, or the Tiger and Other Stories* by Frank R. Stockton (Charles Scribner's Sons, 1884).
1. Latin neighbors, peoples of the ancient Roman empire.

When a subject was accused of a crime of sufficient importance to interest the king, public notice was given that on an appointed day the fate of the accused person would be decided in the king's arena, a structure which well deserved its name; for, although its form and plan were borrowed from afar, its purpose emanated solely from the brain of this man, who, every barleycorn a king,[2] knew no tradition to which he owed more allegiance than pleased his fancy, and who ingrafted on every adopted form of human thought and action the rich growth of his barbaric idealism.

When all the people had assembled in the galleries, and the king, surrounded by his court, sat high up on his throne of royal state on one side of the arena, he gave a signal, a door beneath him opened, and the accused subject stepped out into the amphitheater. Directly opposite him, on the other side of the enclosed space, were two doors, exactly alike and side by side. It was the duty and the privilege of the person on trial to walk directly to these doors and open one of them. He could open either door he pleased; he was subject to no guidance or influence but that of the aforementioned impartial and incorruptible chance. If he opened the one, there came out of it a hungry tiger, the fiercest and most cruel that could be procured, which immediately sprang upon him and tore him to pieces, as a punishment for his guilt. The moment that the case of the criminal was thus decided, doleful iron bells were clanged, great wails went up from the hired mourners posted on the outer rim of the arena, and the vast audience, with bowed heads and downcast hearts, wended slowly their homeward way, mourning greatly that one so young and fair, or so old and respected, should have merited so dire a fate.

But if the accused person opened the other door, there came forth from it a lady, the most suitable to his years and station that his majesty could select among his fair subjects; and to this lady he was immediately married, as a reward for his innocence. It mattered not that he might already possess a wife and family or that his affections might be engaged upon an object of his own selection; the king allowed no such subordinate arrangements to interfere with his great scheme of retribution and reward. The exercises, as in the other instance, took place immediately, and in the arena. Another door opened beneath the king, and a priest, followed by a band of choristers and dancing maidens blowing joyous airs on golden horns and treading an epithalamic measure, advanced to where the pair stood, side by side, and the wedding was promptly and cheerily solemnized. Then the gay brass bells rang forth their merry peals, the people shouted glad hurrahs, and the innocent man, preceded by children strewing flowers on his path, led his bride to his home.

This was the king's semibarbaric method of administering justice. Its perfect fairness is obvious. The criminal could not know out of which door would come the lady; he opened either he pleased, without having the slightest idea whether, in the next instant, he was to be devoured or married. On some occasions the tiger came out of one door, and on some out of the other. The decisions of this tribunal were not only fair, they were positively determinate; the accused person was instantly punished if he found himself guilty, and, if innocent, he was rewarded on

---

2. ***every barleycorn a king.*** A barleycorn is a measure equal to one-third of an inch. However, the term John Barleycorn is a humorous personification of barley as the source of liquor. The author is combining the usual phrase "every inch a king" with the concept of John Barleycorn to create a humorous effect.

the spot, whether he liked it or not. There was no escape from the judgments of the king's arena.

The institution was a very popular one. When the people gathered together on one of the great trial days, they never knew whether they were to witness a bloody slaughter or a hilarious wedding. This element of uncertainty lent an interest to the occasion which it could not otherwise have attained. Thus, the masses were entertained and pleased, and the thinking part of the community could bring no charge of unfairness against this plan; for did not the accused person have the whole matter in his own hands?

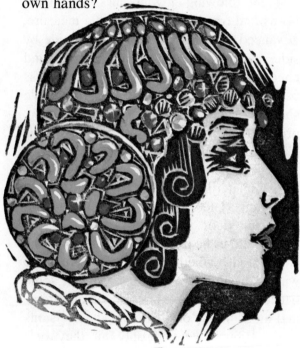

This semibarbaric king had a daughter as blooming as his most florid fancies and with a soul as fervent and imperious as his own. As is usual in such cases, she was the apple of his eye and was loved by him above all humanity. Among his courtiers was a young man of that fineness of blood and lowness of station common to the conventional heroes of romance who love royal maidens. This royal maiden was well satisfied with her lover, for he was handsome and brave to a degree unsurpassed in all this kingdom, and she loved him with an ardor that had enough of barbarism in it to make it exceedingly warm and strong. This love affair moved on happily for many months, until one day the king happened to discover its existence. He did not hesitate nor waver in regard to his duty in the premises. The youth was immediately cast into prison, and a day was appointed for his trial in the king's arena. This, of course, was an especially important occasion, and his majesty, as well as all the people, was greatly interested in the workings and development of this trial. Never before had such a case occurred; never before had a subject dared to love the daughter of a king. In after-years such things became commonplace enough, but then they were, in no slight degree, novel and startling.

The tiger cages of the kingdom were searched for the most savage and relentless beasts, from which the fiercest monster might be selected for the arena, and the ranks of maiden youth and beauty throughout the land were carefully surveyed by competent judges, in order that the young man might have a fitting bride in case fate did not determine for him a different destiny. Of course, everybody knew that the deed with which the accused was charged had been done. He had loved the princess, and neither he, she, nor anyone else thought of denying the fact, but the king would not think of allowing any fact of this kind to interfere with the workings of the tribunal, in which he took such great delight and satisfaction. No matter how the affair turned out, the youth would be disposed of, and the king would take an aesthetic pleasure in watching the course of events, which would determine whether or not the young man had done wrong in allowing himself to love the princess.

The appointed day arrived. From far and near the people gathered and thronged the great galleries of the arena, and crowds, unable to gain admittance, massed themselves against its outside walls. The king and his court were in their places opposite the twin doors—those fateful portals so terrible in their similarity.

All was ready. The signal was given. A door beneath the royal party opened, and the lover of the princess walked into the arena. Tall, beautiful, fair, his appearance was greeted with a low hum of admiration and anxiety. Half the audience had not known so grand a youth had lived among them. No wonder the princess loved him! What a terrible thing for him to be there!

As the youth advanced into the arena, he turned, as the custom was, to bow to the king, but he did not think at all of that royal personage; his eyes were fixed upon the princess who sat to the right of her father. Had it not been for the moiety of barbarism in her nature, it is probable that lady would not have been there, but her intense and fervid soul would not allow her to be absent on an occasion in which she was so terribly interested.

From the moment that the decree had gone forth, that her lover should decide his fate in the king's arena, she had thought of nothing, night or day, but this great event and the various subjects connected with it. Possessed of more power, influence, and force of character than anyone who had ever before been interested in such a case, she had done what no other person had done— she had possessed herself of the secret of the doors. She knew in which of the two rooms that lay behind those doors stood the cage of the tiger, with its open front, and in

which waited the lady. Through these thick doors, heavily curtained with skins on the inside, it was impossible that any noise or suggestion should come from within to the person who should approach to raise the latch of one of them, but gold and the power of a woman's will had brought the secret to the princess.

And not only did she know in which room stood the lady ready to emerge, all blushing and radiant, should her door be opened, but she knew who the lady was. It was one of the fairest and loveliest of the damsels of the court who had been selected as the reward of the accused youth should he be proved innocent of the crime of aspir-

ing to one so far above him, and the princess hated her. Often had she seen, or imagined that she had seen, this fair creature throwing glances of admiration upon the person of her lover, and sometimes she thought these glances were perceived and even returned. Now and then she had seen them talking together; it was but for a moment or two, but much can be said in a brief space; it may have been on most unimportant topics, but how could she know that? The girl was lovely, but she had dared to raise her eyes to the loved one of the princess, and, with all the intensity of the savage blood transmitted to her through long lines of wholly barbaric ancestors, she hated the woman who blushed and trembled behind that silent door.

When her lover turned and looked at her, and his eye met hers as she sat there paler and whiter than anyone in the vast ocean of anxious faces about her, he saw, by that power of quick perception which is given to those whose souls are one, that she knew behind which door crouched the tiger and behind which stood the lady. He had expected her to know it. He understood her nature, and his soul was assured that she would never rest until she had made plain to herself this thing, hidden to all other lookers-on, even to the king. The only hope for the youth in which there was any element of certainty was based upon the success of the princess in discovering this mystery, and the moment he looked upon her, he saw she had succeeded, as in his soul he knew she would succeed.

Then it was that his quick and anxious glance asked the question: "Which?" It was as plain to her as if he shouted it from where he stood. There was not an instant to be lost. The question was asked in a flash; it must be answered in another.

Her right arm lay on the cushioned parapet before her. She raised her hand, and made a slight, quick movement toward the right. No one but her lover saw her. Every eye but his was fixed on the man in the arena.

He turned, and with a firm and rapid step he walked across the empty space. Every heart stopped beating, every breath was held, every eye was fixed immovably upon that man. Without the slightest hesitation, he went to the door on the right and opened it.

Now, the point of the story is this: Did the tiger come out of that door, or did the lady?

The more we reflect upon this question, the harder it is to answer. It involves a study of the human heart which leads us through devious mazes of passion, out of which it is difficult to find our way. Think of it, fair reader, not as if the decision of the question depended upon yourself, but upon that hot-blooded, semibarbaric princess, her soul at a white heat beneath the combined fires of despair and jealousy. She had lost him, but who should have him?

How often, in her waking hours and in her dreams, had she started in wild horror and covered her face with her hands as she thought of her lover opening the door on the other side of which waited the cruel fangs of the tiger!

But how much oftener had she seen him at the other door! How in her grievous reveries had she gnashed her teeth and torn her hair, when she saw his start of rapturous delight as he opened the door of the lady! How her soul had burned in agony when she had seen him rush to meet that woman, with her flushing cheek and sparkling eye of triumph; when she had seen him lead her forth, his whole frame kindled with the joy of recovered life; when she had heard the glad shouts from the multitude, and the wild ringing of the happy bells; when she had seen the priest, with his joyous followers, advance to the couple and make them man and wife before her very eyes; and when she had seen them walk away together upon their path of flowers, followed by the tremendous shouts of the hilarious multitude, in which her one despairing shriek was lost and drowned!

Would it not be better for him to die at once, and go to wait for her in the blessed regions of semibarbaric futurity?

And yet, that awful tiger, those shrieks, that blood!

Her decision had been indicated in an instant, but it had been made after days and nights of anguished deliberation. She had known she would be asked, she had decided what she would answer, and without the slightest hesitation, she had moved her hand to the right.

The question of her decision is one not to be lightly considered, and it is not for me to presume to set myself up as the one person able to answer it. And so I leave it with all of you: Which came out of the opened door— the lady, or the tiger? ☐ ☐

Discussion

1. What do you think the princess decides? Give reasons for your views.

2. (a) Describe the king's method for achieving justice. (b) The author says of this method, "Its perfect fairness is obvious." Is the author using verbal irony, dramatic irony, or irony of situation? (c) Find at least one other example of such irony in the story.

3. (a) Describe the character of the princess. (b) What is her attitude toward the young lady selected to be the young man's bride? (c) How does this attitude complicate her position?

4. Some readers of this story have felt cheated because the author does not say for certain what was behind the door that the princess chose for the young man. (a) Did you feel "cheated" by the ending? Why or why not? (b) Do you think that an author has an obligation to eliminate all uncertainty for readers? Explain.

Vocabulary
Pronunciation, Dictionary

When most dictionaries give pronunciations, they show which syllable of a word receives the most stress by marking it with a heavy, or primary, accent mark. If another syllable in the word also receives some stress, it is marked with a lighter, or secondary, accent.

Use your Glossary to divide the following words into syllables. Then underline the syllable that has the *primary* stress. [Example: parapet   par a pet] Be sure you know the meanings of all the words.

1. fervid
2. reverie
3. impartial
4. emanate
5. retribution
6. unsurpassed
7. incorruptible
8. exuberant

Extension • Writing

We have a saying for having to choose between two equally unpleasant alternatives: "Being on the horns of a dilemma." Another colorful expression meaning the same thing is "Being caught between a rock and a hard place."

Write a paragraph in which you describe a dilemma of your own, when you were "caught" between two equally tempting or equally unpleasant choices. Which did you finally choose? Why? Did you regret the choice you made?

Frank R. Stockton
1834 • 1902

"The Lady, or the Tiger?" first appeared in *Century Magazine* in 1882 and was an immediate success. In it Stockton continued to use the absurd situations and qualities of fantasy which had characterized the stories he had written for children. Before he began writing for adults in 1879, he served for several years as an editor of *St. Nicholas Magazine,* a popular periodical for children.

War Between the Eagle and the Crows

Mei-mei Berssenbrugge

The crows dive-bomb eagle
carrying his big fish home
from the bay;
zoom down on him
5 like fighter planes or gnats.

Eagle hunches his head down
into his shoulders and flaps on,
his eyeless fish so heavy
he must circle his tree
10 around and around to gain height.

The crows crackle like smoke around him,
like a pack of hounds.
Eagle takes a swipe at one of them.
The fish thuds on the forest floor.

15 All swoop down for a bite.

Discussion

1. Whose side are you on, crows or eagle? Why?

2. (a) The poet uses figurative language in describing the actions of the crows. List at least three things to which the crows are compared. (b) Explain why you think these comparisons are appropriate or inappropriate.

3. How does the eagle react to the crows' attack?

Not Poor, Just Broke

Dick Gregory

I never learned hate at home, or shame. I had to go to school for that. I was about seven years old when I got my first big lesson. I was in love with a little girl named Helene Tucker, a light-complected little girl with pigtails and nice manners. She was always clean and she was smart in school. I think I went to school then mostly to look at her. I brushed my hair and even got me a little old handkerchief. It was a lady's handkerchief, but I didn't want Helene to see me wipe my nose on my hand. The pipes were frozen again, there was no water in the house, but I washed my socks and shirt every night. I'd get a pot, and go over to Mister Ben's grocery store, and stick my pot down into his soda machine. Scoop out some chopped ice. By evening the ice melted to water for washing. I got sick a lot that winter because the fire would go out at night before the clothes were dry. In the morning I'd put them on, wet or dry, because they were the only clothes I had.

Everybody's got a Helene Tucker, a symbol of everything you want. I loved her for her goodness, her cleanness, her popularity. She'd walk down my street and my brothers and sisters would yell, "Here comes Helene," and I'd rub my tennis sneakers on the back of my pants and wish my hair wasn't so nappy and the white folks' shirt fit me better. I'd run out on the street. If

I knew my place and didn't come too close, she'd wink at me and say hello. That was a good feeling. Sometimes I'd follow her all the way home, and shovel the snow off her walk and try to make friends with her Momma and her aunts. I'd drop money on her stoop late at night on my way back from shining shoes in the taverns. And she had a Daddy, and he had a good job. He was a paper hanger.

I guess I would have gotten over Helene by summertime, but something happened in that classroom that made her face hang in front of me for the next twenty-two years. When I played the drums in high school it was for Helene and when I broke track records in college it was for Helene and when I started standing behind microphones and heard applause I wished Helene could hear it, too. It wasn't until I was twenty-nine years old and married and making money that I finally got her out of my system. Helene was sitting in that classroom when I learned to be ashamed of myself.

It was on a Thursday. I was sitting in the back of the room, in a seat with a chalk circle drawn around it. The idiot's seat, the troublemaker's seat.

The teacher thought I was stupid. Couldn't spell, couldn't read, couldn't do arithmetic. Just stupid. Teachers were never interested in finding out that you couldn't concentrate because you were so hungry, because you hadn't had any breakfast. All you could think about was noontime, would it ever come? Maybe you could sneak into the cloakroom and steal a bite of some kid's lunch out of a coat pocket. A bite of something. Paste. You can't really make a meal of paste, or put it on bread for a sandwich, but sometimes I'd scoop a few spoonfuls out of the paste jar in the back of the room. Pregnant people get strange tastes. I was preg-nant with poverty. Pregnant with dirt and pregnant with smells that made people turn away, pregnant with cold and pregnant with shoes that were never bought for me, preg-nant with five other people in my bed and no Daddy in the next room, and pregnant with hunger. Paste doesn't taste too bad when you're hungry.

The teacher thought I was a trouble-maker. All she saw from the front of the room was a little black boy who squirmed in his idiot's seat and made noises and poked the kids around him. I guess she couldn't see a kid who made noises because he wanted someone to know he was there.

It was on a Thursday, the day before the Negro payday. The eagle always flew on Friday. The teacher was asking each student how much his father would give to the Community Chest. On Friday night, each kid would get the money from his father, and on Monday he would bring it to the school. I decided I was going to buy me a Daddy right then. I had money in my pocket from shining shoes and selling papers, and whatever Helene Tucker pledged for her Daddy I was going to top it. And I'd hand the money right in. I wasn't going to wait until Monday to buy me a Daddy.

I was shaking, scared to death. The teacher opened her book and started calling out names alphabetically.

"Helene Tucker?"

"My Daddy said he'd give two dollars and fifty cents."

"That's very nice, Helene. Very, very nice indeed."

That made me feel pretty good. It would-n't take too much to top that. I had almost three dollars in dimes and quarters in my pocket. I stuck my hand in my pocket and held onto the money, waiting for her to call my name. But the teacher closed her book

after she called everybody else in the class.

I stood up and raised my hand.

"What is it now?"

"You forgot me."

She turned toward the blackboard. "I don't have time to be playing with you, Richard."

"My Daddy said he'd . . ."

"Sit down, Richard, you're disturbing the class."

"My Daddy said he'd give . . . fifteen dollars."

She turned around and looked mad. "We are collecting this money for you and your kind, Richard Gregory. If your Daddy can give fifteen dollars you have no business being on relief."

"I got it right now, I got it right now, my Daddy gave it to me to turn in today, my Daddy said . . ."

"And furthermore," she said, looking right at me, her nostrils getting big and her lips getting thin and her eyes opening wide, "we know you don't have a Daddy."

Helene Tucker turned around, her eyes full of tears. She felt sorry for me. Then I couldn't see her too well because I was crying, too.

"Sit down, Richard."

And I always thought the teacher kind of liked me. She always picked me to wash the blackboard on Friday, after school. That was a big thrill, it made me feel important. If I didn't wash it, come Monday the school might not function right.

"Where are you going, Richard?"

I walked out of school that day, and for a long time I didn't go back very often. There was shame there.

Now there was shame everywhere. It seemed like the whole world had been inside that classroom, everyone had heard what the teacher had said, everyone had turned around and felt sorry for me. There was shame in going to the Worthy Boys' Annual Christmas Dinner for you and your kind, because everybody knew what a worthy boy was. Why couldn't they just call it the Boys' Annual Dinner, why'd they have to give it a name? There was shame in wearing the brown and orange and white plaid mackinaw the welfare gave to three thousand boys. Why'd it have to be the same for everybody so when you walked down the street the people could see you were on relief? It was a nice warm mackinaw and it had a hood, and my Momma beat me and called me a little rat when she found out I stuffed it in the bottom of a pail full of garbage way over on Cottage Street. There was shame in running over to Mister Ben's at the end of the day and asking for his rotten peaches, there was shame in asking Mrs. Simmons for a spoonful of sugar, there was shame in running out to meet the relief truck. I hated that truck, full of food for you and your kind. I ran into the house and hid when it came. And then I started to sneak through alleys, to take the long way home so the people going into White's Eat Shop wouldn't see me. Yeah, the whole world heard the teacher that day, we all know you don't have a Daddy. □□

Discussion

1. **(a)** Why do you think Richard claimed that his Daddy would donate fifteen dollars to the Community Chest? **(b)** If you had been the teacher, how would you have reacted when he said this?

2. Richard had conflicting, or differing, feelings about his teacher before he made up the story about the money. What evidence is there in the story that he feels his teacher also had two different feelings about him?

3. **(a)** List at least three things which are shameful to Richard. **(b)** Which of these seems to affect Richard most?

4. The author suggests that this classroom incident had a long-range influence on his life. How does he feel the incident affected his self-respect and the respect he wanted others to have for him?

Dick Gregory 1932 •

Though first known as a co-median, Dick Gregory has since won national attention as a writer, civil rights leader, and political activist. He frequently publicizes his concerns not only through his writing (he is author of more than a half-dozen books), but by fasting and long-distance running. In his books and in performance, Gregory combines an urgent sense of social justice with a sharp sense of humor.

See **ALLITERATION** Handbook of Literary Terms

The Beetle in the Country Bathtub

John Hall Wheelock

After one more grandiloquent effort he slips back—
Slumping? Oh no, he may be down but he's never out
(Probably wishes he were); now, pondering a fresh attack,
He wheels his slender, simonized bulk about,

5 Fumbles at the slippery surface until he has come to grips,
Mounts, very slowly, with ever-increasing hope, and then
Mounts, more slowly, with ever-increasing hope—and slips
All the way down to the bottom of the tub again;

Lies there, motionless, pretty discouraged perhaps? not he—
10 It's dogged as does it, keep your chin up, don't take
No for an answer, etc.—he plots a new strategy,
The oblique approach. This too turns out to be a mistake.

The enamelled surface of his predicament
Resembles those pockets in time and space that hold
15 Sick minds in torture, his struggle is a long argument
With a fact that refuses to be persuaded or cajoled.

Midnight finds him still confident. I slink to bed,
Worn out with watching. The suave heavens turn
Blandly upon their axis, overhead
20 The constellations glitter their polite unconcern.

Toward morning, hounded by anxiety, slumberless,
I post to the scene. Where is he? The enamelled slopes below,
Vacant—the uplands, vacant—a bathtub full of emptiness,
The insoluble problem solved! But how? Something no
        one of us, perhaps, will ever know.

25 Unless he went down the drain?

Discussion

1. What do you think happened to the beetle at the end of the poem? Why?

2. Reread stanzas one, two, and three. What words or phrases in the stanzas show how the beetle faces its predicament?

3. The poet uses many words which begin or end with the letter *s* in stanzas one and two. Find some of these and read them aloud. What do you think the poet is trying to emphasize by means of this alliteration?

4. Why do you think the speaker did not assist the beetle?

John Hall Wheelock
1886 • 1978

As an author and publisher of poetry for more than sixty years, John Hall Wheelock learned that poetry *reading* may in some ways be as difficult as poetry writing. "Some poems take a long time for the meaning to develop in them. . . . A really good poem . . . takes a good deal of rereading, an almost living yourself into it, I think, to understand it."

*"The mountain, to all of us, was no longer a mere giant of ice:
it had become a living thing, an enemy,
watching us, waiting for us, hostile, relentless."*

Top Man

James Ramsey Ullman

The gorge bent. The walls fell suddenly away and we came out on the edge of a bleak, boulder-strewn valley. And there it was.

Osborn saw it first. He had been leading the column, threading his way slowly among the huge rock masses of the gorge's mouth. Then he came to the first flat, bare place and stopped. He neither pointed nor cried out, but every man behind him knew instantly what it was. The long file sprang taut, like a jerked rope. As swiftly as we could, but in complete silence, we came out into the open ground where Osborn stood, and raised our eyes with his. In the records of the Indian Topographical Survey it says:

Kalpurtha: a mountain in the Himalayas, altitude 28,900 ft. The highest peak in British India and fourth highest in the world. Also known as K3. A Tertiary formation of sedimentary limestone——

There were men among us who had spent months of their lives—in some cases, years—reading, thinking, planning about what now lay before us, but at that moment statistics and geology, knowledge, thought and plans, were as remote and forgotten as the faraway western cities from which we had come. We were men bereft of everything but eyes, everything but the single, electric perception: There it was!

Before us the valley stretched away into miles of rocky desolation. To right and left it was bounded by low ridges which, as the eye followed them, slowly mounted and drew closer together until the valley was no longer a valley at all, but a narrowing, rising corridor between the cliffs. What happened then I can describe only as a single, stupendous crash of music. At the end of the corridor and above it—so far above it that it shut out half the sky—hung the blinding white mass of K3.

It was like the many pictures I had seen, and at the same time utterly unlike them. The shape was there, and the familiar distinguishing features—the sweeping skirt of glaciers; the monstrous vertical precipices of the face and the jagged ice line of the east ridge; finally the symmetrical summit pyra-

mid that transfixed the sky. But whereas in the pictures the mountain had always seemed unreal—a dream image of cloud, snow and crystal—it was now no longer an image at all. It was a mass, solid, imminent, appalling. We were still too far away to see the windy whipping of its snow plumes or to hear the cannonading of its avalanches, but in that sudden silent moment every man of us was for the first time aware of it, not as a picture in his mind but as a thing, an antagonist. For all its twenty-eight thousand feet of lofty grandeur, it seemed, somehow, less to tower than to crouch—a white-hooded giant, secret and remote, but living. Living and on guard.

I turned my eyes from the dazzling glare and looked at my companions. Osborn still stood a little in front of the others. He was absolutely motionless, his young face tense and shining, his eyes devouring the mountain as a lover's might devour the face of his beloved. One could feel in the very set of his body the overwhelming desire that swelled in him to act, to come to grips, to conquer. A little behind him were ranged the other men of the expedition: Randolph, our leader, Wittmer and Johns, Doctor Schlapp and Bixler. All were still, their eyes cast upward. Off to one side a little stood Nace, the Englishman, the only one among us who was not staring at K3 for the first time. He had been the last to come up out of the gorge and stood now with arms folded on his chest, squinting at the great peak he had known so long and fought so tirelessly and fiercely. His lean British face, under its mask of stubble and windburn, was expressionless. His lips were a colorless line, and his eyes seemed almost shut. Behind the sahibs ranged the porters, bent over their staffs, their brown, seamed faces straining upward from beneath their loads.

For a long while no one spoke or moved. The only sounds between earth and sky were the soft hiss of our breathing and the pounding of our hearts.

Through the long afternoon we wound slowly between the great boulders of the valley and at sundown pitched camp in the bed of a dried-up stream. The porters ate their rations in silence, wrapped themselves in their blankets and fell asleep under the stars. The rest of us, as was our custom, sat close about the fire that blazed in the circle of tents, discussing the events of the day and the plans for the next. It was a flawlessly clear Himalayan night and K3 tiered up into the blackness like a monstrous sentinel lighted from within. There was no wind, but a great tide of cold air crept down the valley from the ice fields above, penetrating our clothing, pressing gently against the canvas of the tents.

"Another night or two and we'll be needing the sleeping bags," commented Randolph.

Osborn nodded. "We could use them tonight, would be my guess."

Randolph turned to Nace. "What do you say, Martin?"

The Englishman puffed at his pipe a moment. "Rather think it might be better to wait," he said at last.

"Wait? Why?" Osborn jerked his head up.

"Well, it gets pretty nippy high up, you know. I've seen it thirty below at twenty-five thousand on the east ridge. Longer we wait for the bags, better acclimated we'll get."

Osborn snorted. "A lot of good being acclimated will do if we have frozen feet."

"Easy, Paul, easy," cautioned Randolph. "It seems to me Martin's right."

Osborn bit his lip, but said nothing. The

other men entered the conversation, and soon it had veered to other matters: the weather, the porters and pack animals, routes, camps and strategy—the inevitable, inexhaustible topics of the climber's world.

There were all kinds of men among the eight of us, men with a great diversity of background and interest. Sayre Randolph, whom the Alpine Club had named leader of our expedition, had for years been a well-known explorer and lecturer. Now in his middle fifties, he was no longer equal to the grueling physical demands of high climbing, but served as planner and organizer of the enterprise. Wittmer was a Seattle lawyer, who had recently made a name for himself by a series of difficult ascents in the Coast Range of British Columbia. Johns was an Alaskan, a fantastically strong, able sourdough, who had been a ranger in the U.S. Forest Service and had accompanied many famous Alaskan expeditions. Schlapp was a practicing physician from Milwaukee, Bixler a government meteorologist with a talent for photography. I, at the time, was an assistant professor of geology at an eastern university.

Finally, and preeminently, there were Osborn and Nace. I say "preeminently," because even at this time, when we had been together as a party for little more than a month, I believe all of us realized that these were the two key men of our venture. None, to my knowledge, ever expressed it in words, but the conviction was there, nevertheless, that if any of us were eventually to stand on the hitherto unconquered summit of K3, it would be one of them, or both. They were utterly dissimilar men. Osborn was twenty-three and a year out of college, a compact, buoyant mass of energy and high spirits. He seemed to be wholly unaffected by either the physical or mental hazards of

mountaineering and had already, by virtue of many spectacular ascents in the Alps and Rockies, won a reputation as the most skilled and audacious of younger American climbers. Nace was in his forties—lean, taciturn, introspective. An official in the Indian Civil Service, he had explored and climbed in the Himalayas for twenty years. He had been a member of all five of the unsuccessful British expeditions to K3, and in his last attempt had attained to within five hundred feet of the summit, the highest point which any man had reached on the unconquered giant. This had been the famous tragic attempt in which his fellow climber and lifelong friend, Captain Furness, had slipped and fallen ten thousand feet to his death. Nace rarely mentioned his name, but on the steel head of his ice ax were engraved the words: TO MARTIN FROM JOHN. If fate were to grant that the ax of any one of us should be planted upon the summit of K3, I hoped it would be his.

Such were the men who huddled about the fire in the deep, still cold of that Himalayan night. There were many differences among us, in temperament as well as in background. In one or two cases, notably that of Osborn and Nace, there had already been a certain amount of friction, and as the venture continued and the struggles and hardships of the actual ascent began, it would, I knew, increase. But differences were unimportant. What mattered—all that mattered—was that our purpose was one— to conquer the monster of rock and ice that now loomed above us in the night; to stand for a moment where no man, no living thing, had ever stood before. To that end we had come from half a world away, across oceans and continents to the fastnesses of inner Asia. To that end we were prepared to endure cold, exhaustion and danger, even to the very last extremity of human endurance. Why? There is no answer, and at the same time every man among us knew the answer; every man who has ever looked upon a great mountain and felt the fever in his blood to climb and conquer, knows the answer. George Leigh Mallory, greatest of mountaineers, expressed it once and for all when he was asked why he wanted to climb unconquered Everest. "I want to climb it," said Mallory, "because it's there."

Day after day we crept on and upward. The naked desolation of the valley was unrelieved by any motion, color or sound, and, as we progressed, it was like being trapped at the bottom of a deep well or in a sealed court between great skyscrapers. Soon we were thinking of the ascent of the shining mountain not only as an end in itself but as an escape.

In our nightly discussions around the fire, our conversation narrowed more and more to the immediate problems confronting us, and during them I began to realize that the tension between Osborn and Nace went deeper than I had at first surmised. There was rarely any outright argument between them—they were both far too able mountain men to disagree on fundamentals—but I saw that at almost every turn they were rubbing each other the wrong way. It was a matter of personalities chiefly. Osborn was talkative, enthusiastic, optimistic, always chafing to be up and at it, always wanting to take the short, straight line to the given point. Nace, on the other hand, was matter-of-fact, cautious, slow. He was the apostle of trial-and-error and watchful waiting. Because of his far greater experience and intimate knowledge of K3, Randolph almost invariably followed his advice, rather than Osborn's, when a difference of opinion arose. The younger man usually capitulated with good

grace, but I could tell that he was irked.

During the days in the valley I had few occasions to talk privately with either of them, and only once did either mention the other in any but the most casual manner. Even then, the remarks they made seemed unimportant, and I remember them only in view of what happened later.

My conversation with Osborn occurred first. It was while we were on the march, and Osborn, who was directly behind me, came up suddenly to my side.

"You're a geologist, Frank," he began without preamble. "What do you think of Nace's theory about the ridge?"

"What theory?" I asked.

"He believes we should traverse under it from the glacier up. Says the ridge itself is too exposed."

"It looks pretty mean through the telescope."

"But it's been done before. He's done it himself. All right, it's tough—I'll admit that. But a decent climber could make it in half the time the traverse will take."

"Nace knows the traverse is longer," I said, "but he seems certain it will be much easier for us."

"Easier for him is what he means." Osborn paused, looking moodily at the ground. "He was a great climber in his day. It's a shame a man can't be honest enough with himself to know when he's through." He fell silent and a moment later dropped back into his place in line.

It was that same night, I think, that I awoke to find Nace sitting up in his blanket and staring at the mountain.

"How clear it is," I whispered.

The Englishman pointed. "See the ridge?"

I nodded, my eyes fixed on the great, twisting spine of ice that climbed into the sky. I could see now, more clearly than in the blinding sunlight, its huge indentations and jagged, wind-swept pitches.

"It looks impossible," I said.

"No, it can be done. Trouble is, when you've made it, you're too done in for the summit."

"Osborn seems to think its shortness would make up for its difficulty."

Nace was silent a long moment before answering. Then for the first and only time I heard him speak the name of his dead companion. "That's what Furness thought," he said quietly. Then he lay down and wrapped himself in his blanket.

For the next two weeks the uppermost point of the valley was our home and workshop. We established our base camp as close to the mountain as we could, less than half a mile from the tongue of its lowest glacier, and plunged into the arduous tasks of preparation for the ascent. Our food and equipment were unpacked, inspected and sorted, and finally repacked in lighter loads for transportation to more advanced camps. Hours on end were spent poring over maps and charts and studying the monstrous heights above us through telescope and binoculars. Under Nace's supervision, a thorough reconnaissance of the glacier was made and the route across it laid out; then began the backbreaking labor of moving up supplies and establishing the advance stations.

Camps I and II were set up on the glacier itself, in the most sheltered sites we could find. Camp III we built at its upper end, as near as possible to the point where the great rock spine of K3 thrust itself free of ice and began its precipitous ascent. According to our plans, this would be the advance base of operations during the climb; the camps to be established higher up, on the mountain prop-

er, would be too small and too exposed to serve as anything more than one or two nights' shelter. The total distance between the base camp and Camp III was only fifteen miles, but the utmost daily progress of our porters was five miles, and it was essential that we should never be more than twelve hours' march from food and shelter. Hour after hour, day after day, the long file of men wound up and down among the hummocks and crevasses of the glacier, and finally the time arrived when we were ready to advance.

Leaving Doctor Schlapp in command of eight porters at the base camp, we proceeded easily and on schedule, reaching Camp I the first night, Camp II the second and the advance base the third. No men were left at Camps I and II, inasmuch as they were designed simply as caches for food and equipment; and, furthermore, we knew we would need all the man power available for the establishment of the higher camps on the mountain proper.

For more than three weeks now the weather had held perfectly, but on our first night at the advance base, as if by malignant prearrangement of Nature, we had our first taste of the supernatural fury of a high Himalayan storm. It began with great streamers of lightning that flashed about the mountain like a halo; then heavily through the weird glare snow began to fall. The wind howled about the tents with hurricane frenzy, and the wild flapping of the canvas dinned in our ears like machine-gun fire.

There was no sleep for us that night or the next. For thirty-six hours the storm raged without lull, while we huddled in the icy gloom of the tents. At last, on the third morning, it was over, and we came out into a world transformed by a twelve-foot cloak of snow. No single landmark remained as it had been before, and our supplies and equipment were in the wildest confusion. Fortunately, there had not been a single serious injury, but it was another three days before we had regained our strength and put the camp in order.

Then we waited. The storm did not return, and the sky beyond the ridges gleamed flawlessly clear, but night and day we could hear the roaring thunder of avalanches on the mountain above us. To have ventured so much as one step into that savage, vertical wilderness before the new-fallen snow froze tight would have been suicidal. We chafed or waited patiently, according to our individual temperaments, while the days dragged by.

It was late one afternoon that Osborn returned from a short reconnaissance up the ridge. His eyes were shining and his voice jubilant.

"It's tight!" he cried. "Tight as a drum! We can go!" All of us stopped whatever we were doing. His excitement leaped like an electric spark from one to another. "I went about a thousand feet, and it's sound all the way. What do you say, Sayre? Tomorrow?"

Randolph hesitated a moment, then looked at Nace.

"Better give it another day or two," said the Englishman.

Osborn glared at him. "Why?" he challenged.

"It's generally safer to wait until——"

"Wait! Wait!" Osborn exploded. "Don't you ever think of anything but waiting? The snow's firm, I tell you!"

"It's firm down here," Nace replied quietly, "because the sun hits it only two hours a day. Up above it gets the sun twelve hours. It may not have frozen yet."

"The avalanches have stopped."

"That doesn't necessarily mean it will hold a man's weight."

"It seems to me, Martin's point——" Randolph began.

Osborn wheeled on him. "Sure," he snapped. "I know. Martin's right. The cautious bloody English are always right. Let him have his way, and we'll be sitting here twiddling our thumbs until the mountain falls down on us." His eyes flashed to Nace. "Maybe with a little less of that bloody cautiousness, you English wouldn't have made such a mess of Everest. Maybe your pals Mallory and Furness wouldn't be dead."

"Osborn!" commanded Randolph sharply.

The youngster stared at Nace for another moment, breathing heavily. Then, abruptly, he turned away.

The next two days were clear and windless, but we still waited, following Nace's advice. There were no further brushes between him and Osborn, but an unpleasant air of restlessness and tension hung over the camp. I found myself chafing almost as impatiently as Osborn himself for the moment when we would break out of that maddening inactivity and begin the assault.

At last the day came. With the first paling of the sky, a roped file of men, bent almost double beneath heavy loads, began slowly to climb the ice slope just beneath the jagged line of the great east ridge. In accordance with prearranged plan, we proceeded in relays; this first group consisting of Nace, Johns, myself and eight porters. It was our job to ascend approximately two thousand feet in a day's climbing and establish Camp IV at the most level and sheltered site we could find. We would spend the night there and return to the advance base next day, while the second relay, consisting of Osborn, Wittmer and eight more porters, went up with their loads. This process was to continue until all necessary supplies were at

Camp IV, and then the whole thing would be repeated between Camps IV and V, and V and VI. From VI, at an altitude of about 26,000 feet, the ablest and fittest men—presumably Nace and Osborn—would make the direct assault on the summit. Randolph and Bixler were to remain at the advance base throughout the operations, acting as directors and coordinators. We were under the strictest orders that any man, sahib or porter, who suffered illness or injury should be brought down immediately.

How shall I describe those next two weeks beneath the great ice ridge of K3? In a sense, there was no occurrence of importance, and at the same time everything happened that could possibly happen, short of actual disaster. We established Camp IV, came down again, went up again, came down again. Then we crept laboriously higher. The wind increased, and the air grew steadily colder and more difficult to breathe. One

morning two of the porters awoke with their feet frozen black; they had to be sent down. A short while later Johns developed an uncontrollable nosebleed and was forced to descend to a lower camp. Wittmer was suffering from splitting headaches and I from a continually dry throat. But providentially, the one enemy we feared the most in that icy, gale-lashed hell did not again attack us—no snow fell. And day by day, foot by foot, we ascended.

It is during ordeals like this that the surface trappings of a man are shed and his secret mettle laid bare. There were no shirkers or quitters among us—I had known that from the beginning—but now, with each passing day, it became more manifest which were the strongest and ablest among us. Beyond all argument, these were Osborn and Nace.

Osborn was magnificent. All the boyish impatience and moodiness which he had exhibited earlier were gone, and, now that he was at last at work in his natural element, he emerged as the peerless mountaineer he was. His energy was inexhaustible, and his speed, both on rock and ice, almost twice that of any other man in the party. He was always discovering new routes and short cuts; and there was such vigor, buoyancy and youth in everything he did that it gave heart to all the rest of us.

In contrast, Nace was slow, methodical, unspectacular. Since he and I worked in the same relay, I was with him almost constantly, and to this day I carry in my mind the clear image of the man—his tall body bent almost double against endless, shimmering slopes of ice; his lean brown face bent in utter concentration on the problem in hand, then raised searchingly to the next; the bright prong of his ax rising, falling, rising, falling with tireless rhythm, until the steps in the glassy incline were so wide and deep that the most clumsy of the porters could not have slipped from them had he tried. Osborn attacked the mountain, head on. Nace studied it, sparred with it, wore it down. His spirit did not flap from his sleeve like a pennon; it was deep inside him, patient, indomitable.

The day came soon when I learned from him what it is to be a great mountaineer. We were making the ascent from Camp IV to V, and an almost perpendicular ice wall had made it necessary for us to come out for a few yards on the exposed crest of the ridge. There were six of us in the party, roped together, with Nace leading, myself second, and four porters bringing up the rear. The ridge at this particular point was free of snow, but razor-thin, and the rocks were covered with a smooth glaze of ice. On either side the mountain dropped away in sheer precipices of five thousand feet.

Suddenly the last porter slipped. In what seemed to be the same instant I heard the ominous scraping of boot nails and, turning, saw a wildly gesticulating figure plunge sideways into the abyss. There was a scream as the next porter followed him. I remember trying frantically to dig into the ridge with my ax, realizing at the same time it would no more hold against the weight of the falling men than a pin stuck in a wall. Then I heard Nace shout, "Jump!" As he said it, the rope went tight about my waist, and I went hurtling after him into space on the opposite side of the ridge. After me came the nearest porter.

What happened then must have happened in five yards and a fifth of a second. I heard myself cry out, and the glacier, a mile below, rushed up at me, spinning. Then both were blotted out in a violent spasm, as the rope jerked taut. I hung for a moment, an inert mass, feeling that my body had been cut in two; then I swung in slowly to the side of the mountain. Above me the rope lay tight and motionless across the crest of the ridge, our weight exactly counterbalancing that of the men who had fallen on the far slope.

Nace's voice came up from below. "You chaps on the other side!" he shouted. "Start climbing slowly! We're climbing too!"

In five minutes we had all regained the ridge. The porters and I crouched panting on the jagged rocks, our eyes closed, the sweat beading our faces in frozen drops. Nace carefully examined the rope that again hung loosely between us.

"All right, men," he said presently. "Let's get on to camp for a cup of tea."

Above Camp V the whole aspect of the ascent changed. The angle of the ridge eased off, and the ice, which lower down had covered the mountain like a sheath, lay only in scattered patches between the rocks.

Fresh enemies, however, instantly appeared to take the place of the old. We were now laboring at an altitude of more than 25,000 feet—well above the summits of the highest surrounding peaks—and day and night, without protection or respite, we were buffeted by the savage fury of the wind. Worse than this was that the atmosphere had become so rarefied it could scarcely support life. Breathing itself was a major physical effort, and our progress upward consisted of two or three painful steps, followed by a long period of rest in which our hearts pounded wildly and our burning lungs gasped for air. Each of us carried a small cylinder of oxygen in our pack, but we used it only in emergencies, and found that, though its immediate effect was salutary, it left us later even worse off than before.

But the great struggle was now mental rather than physical. The lack of air induced a lethargy of mind and spirit; confidence and the powers of thought and decision waned. The mountain, to all of us, was no longer a mere giant of rock and ice; it had become a living thing, an enemy, watching us, waiting for us, hostile, relentless.

On the fifteenth day after we had first left the advance base, we pitched Camp VI at an altitude of 26,500 feet. It was located near the uppermost extremity of the great east ridge, directly beneath the so-called shoulder of the mountain. On the far side of the shoulder the stupendous north face of K3 fell sheer to the glaciers, two miles below. Above it and to the left rose the symmetrical bulk of the summit pyramid. The topmost rocks of its highest pinnacle were clearly visible from the shoulder, and the intervening fifteen hundred feet seemed to offer no insuperable obstacles.

Camp VI, which was in reality no camp at all but a single tent, was large enough to accommodate only three men. Osborn established it with the aid of Wittmer and one porter; then, the following morning, Wittmer and the porter descended to Camp V, and Nace and I went up. It was our plan that Osborn and Nace should launch the final assault—the next day, if the weather held—with myself in support, following their progress through binoculars and going to their aid or summoning help from below if anything went wrong. As the three of us lay in the tent that night, the summit seemed already within arm's reach, victory securely in our grasp.

And then the blow fell. With fiendishly malignant timing, which no power on earth could have made us believe was a simple accident of nature, the mountain hurled at us its last line of defense. It snowed.

For a day and a night the great flakes drove down upon us, swirling and swooping in the wind, blotting out the summit, the shoulder, everything beyond the tiny white-walled radius of our tent. At last, during the morning of the following day, it cleared. The sun came out in a thin blue sky, and the summit pyramid again appeared above us, now whitely robed in fresh snow. But still we waited. Until the snow either froze or was blown away by the wind, it would have been the rashest courting of destruction for us to have ascended a foot beyond the camp. Another day passed. And another.

By the third nightfall our nerves were at the breaking point. For hours on end we had scarcely moved or spoken, and the only sounds in all the world were the endless moaning of the wind outside and the harsh, sucking noise of our breathing. I knew that, one way or another, the end had come. Our meager food supply was running out; even with careful rationing, there was enough left for only two more days.

Presently Nace stirred in his sleeping bag and sat up. "We'll have to go down tomorrow," he said quietly.

For a moment there was silence in the tent. Then Osborn struggled to a sitting position and faced him.

"No," he said.

"There's still too much loose snow above. We can't make it."

"But it's clear. As long as we can see——"

Nace shook his head. "Too dangerous. We'll go down tomorrow and lay in a fresh supply. Then we'll try again."

"Once we go down we're licked. You know it."

Nace shrugged. "Better to be licked than——" The strain of speech was suddenly too much for him and he fell into a violent paroxysm of coughing. When it had passed, there was a long silence.

Then, suddenly, Osborn spoke again. "Look, Nace," he said, "I'm going up tomorrow."

The Englishman shook his head.

"I'm going—understand?"

For the first time since I had known him, I saw Nace's eyes flash in anger. "I'm the senior member of this group," he said. "I forbid you to go!"

With a tremendous effort, Osborn jerked himself to his feet. "You forbid me? This may be your sixth time on this mountain, and all that, but you don't own it! I know what you're up to. You haven't got it in you to make the top yourself, so you don't want anyone else to get the glory. That's it, isn't it? Isn't it?" He sat down again suddenly, gasping for breath.

Nace looked at him with level eyes. "This mountain has licked me five times," he said softly. "It killed my best friend. It means more to me to lick it than anything else in the world. Maybe I'll make it and maybe I won't. But if I do, it will be as a rational, intelligent human being, not as a fool throwing my life away——"

He collapsed into another fit of coughing and fell back in his sleeping bag. Osborn, too, was still. They lay there inert, panting, too exhausted for speech.

It was hours later that I awoke from dull, uneasy sleep. In the faint light I saw Nace fumbling with the flap of the tent.

"What is it?" I asked.

"Osborn. He's gone."

The words cut like a blade through my lethargy. I struggled to my feet and followed Nace from the tent.

Outside, the dawn was seeping up the eastern sky. It was very cold, but the wind had fallen and the mountain seemed to hang suspended in a vast stillness. Above us the summit pyramid climbed bleakly into space, like the last outpost of a spent lifeless planet. Raising my binoculars, I swept them over the gray waste. At first I saw nothing but rock and ice; then, suddenly, something moved.

"I've got him," I whispered.

As I spoke, the figure of Osborn sprang into clear focus against a patch of ice. He took three or four slow upward steps, stopped, went on again. I handed the glasses to Nace.

The Englishman squinted through them a moment, returned them to me, and re-entered the tent. When I followed, he had already laced his boots and was pulling on his outer gloves.

"He's not far," he said. "Can't have been gone more than half an hour." He seized his ice ax and started out again.

"Wait," I said. "I'm going with you."

Nace shook his head. "Better stay here."

"I'm going with you," I said.

He said nothing further, but waited while I made ready. In a few moments we left the tent, roped up and started off.

Almost immediately we were on the shoulder and confronted with the paralyzing two-mile drop of the north face, but we negotiated the short exposed stretch without mishap and in ten minutes were working up the base of the summit pyramid. Our progress was creepingly slow. There seemed to be literally no air at all to breathe, and after almost every step we were forced to rest.

The minutes crawled into hours, and still we climbed. Presently the sun came up. Its level rays streamed across the clouds far below, and glinted from the summits of distant peaks. But, although the pinnacle of K3 soared a full five thousand feet above anything in the surrounding world, we had scarcely any sense of height. The stupendous wilderness of mountains and glaciers that spread beneath us to the horizon was flattened and remote, an unreal, insubstan-

tial landscape seen in a dream. We had no connection with it, or it with us. All living, all awareness, purpose and will, was concentrated in the last step and the next—to put one foot before the other; to breathe; to ascend. We struggled on in silence.

I do not know how long it was since we had left the camp—it might have been two hours, it might have been six—when we suddenly sighted Osborn. We had not been able to find him again since our first glimpse through the binoculars, but now, unexpectedly and abruptly, as we came up over a jagged outcropping of rock, there he was. He was at a point, only a few yards above us, where the mountain steepened into an almost vertical wall. The smooth surface directly in front of him was obviously unclimbable, but two alternate routes were presented. To the left, a chimney cut obliquely across the wall, forbiddingly steep, but seeming to offer adequate holds. To the right was a gentle slope of snow that curved

Bob & Ira Spring

upward and out of sight behind the rocks. As we watched, Osborn ascended to the edge of the snow, stopped and tested it with his foot; then, apparently satisfied that it would bear his weight, he stepped out on the slope.

I felt Nace's body tense. "Paul!" he cried out.

His voice was too weak and hoarse to carry. Osborn continued his ascent.

Nace cupped his hands and called his name again, and this time Osborn turned. "Wait!" cried the Englishman.

Osborn stood still, watching us, as we struggled up the few yards to the edge of the snow slope. Nace's breath came in shuddering gasps, but he climbed faster than I had ever seen him climb before.

"Come back!" he called. "Come off the snow!"

"It's all right! The crust is firm!" Osborn called back.

"But it's melting! There's"—Nace paused, fighting for air—"there's nothing underneath!"

In a sudden, horrifying flash I saw what he meant. Looked at from directly below, at the point where Osborn had come to it, the slope on which he stood appeared as a harmless covering of snow over the rocks. From where we were now, however, a little to one side, it could be seen that it was in reality no covering at all, but merely a cornice or unsupported platform clinging to the side of the mountain. Below it was not rock, but ten thousand feet of blue air.

"Come back!" I cried. "Come back!"

Osborn hesitated, then took a downward step. But he never took the next. For in that same instant the snow directly in front of him disappeared. It did not seem to fall or to break away. It was just soundlessly and magically no longer there. In the spot where Osborn had been about to set his foot there

was now revealed the abysmal drop of the north face of K3.

I shut my eyes, but only for a second, and when I reopened them Osborn was still, miraculously, there.

Nace was shouting, "Don't move! Don't move an inch!"

"The rope," I heard myself saying.

The Englishman shook his head. "We'd have to throw it, and the impact would be too much. Brace yourself and play it out." As we spoke, his eyes were traveling over the rocks that bordered the snow bridge. Then he moved forward.

I wedged myself into a cleft in the wall and let out the rope which extended between us. A few yards away, Osborn stood in the snow, transfixed, one foot a little in front of the other. But my eyes now were on Nace. Cautiously, but with astonishing rapidity, he edged along the rocks beside the cornice. There was a moment when his only support was an inch-wide ledge beneath his feet, another where there was nothing under his feet at all and he supported himself wholly by his elbows and hands. But he advanced steadily, and at last reached a shelf wide enough for him to turn around on. At this point he was perhaps six feet away from Osborn.

"It's wide enough here to hold both of us," he said in a quiet voice. "I'm going to reach out my ax. Don't move until you're sure you have a grip on it. When I pull, jump."

He searched the wall behind him and found a hold for his left hand. Then he slowly extended his ice ax, head foremost, until it was within two feet of Osborn's shoulder.

"Grip it!" he cried suddenly. Osborn's hands shot out and seized the ax. "Jump!"

There was a flash of steel in the sunlight

and a hunched figure hurtled inward from the snow to the ledge. Simultaneously another figure hurtled out. The haft of the ax jerked suddenly from Nace's hand, and he lurched forward and downward. A violent, sickening spasm convulsed my body as the rope went taut. Then it was gone. Nace did not seem to hit the snow; he simply disappeared through it, soundlessly. In the same instant the snow itself was gone. The frayed, yellow end of broken rope spun lazily in space.

Somehow my eyes went to Osborn. He was crouched on the ledge where Nace had been a moment before, staring dully at the ax he held in his hands. Beyond his head, not two hundred feet above, the white, untrodden pinnacle of K3 stabbed the sky.

Perhaps ten minutes passed, perhaps a half hour. I closed my eyes and leaned forward motionless against the rock, my face against my arm. I neither thought nor felt; my body and mind alike were enveloped in a suffocating numbness. Through it at last came the sound of Osborn moving. Looking up, I saw he was standing beside me.

"I'm going to try to make the top," he said tonelessly.

I merely stared at him.

"Will you come?"

I shook my head slowly. Osborn hesitated a moment, then turned and began slowly climbing the steep chimney above us. Halfway up he paused, struggling for breath. Then he resumed his laborious upward progress and presently disappeared beyond the crest.

I stayed where I was, and the hours passed. The sun reached its zenith above the peak and sloped away behind it. And at last I heard above me the sound of Osborn return-

ing. As I looked up, his figure appeared at the top of the chimney and began the descent. His clothing was in tatters, and I could tell from his movements that only the thin flame of his will stood between him and collapse. In another few minutes he was standing beside me.

"Did you get there?" I asked.

He shook his head slowly. "I couldn't make it," he answered. "I didn't have what it takes."

We roped together silently and began the descent to the camp. There is nothing more to be told of the sixth assault on K3—at least not from the experiences of the men who made it. Osborn and I reached Camp V in safety, and three days later the entire expedition gathered at the advance base. It was decided, in view of the appalling tragedy that had occurred, to make no further attempt on the summit, and we began the evacuation of the mountain.

It remained for another year and other men to reveal the epilogue.

The summer following our attempt a combined English-Swiss expedition stormed the peak successfully. After weeks of hardship and struggle, they attained the topmost pinnacle of the giant, only to find that what should have been their great moment of triumph was, instead, a moment of the bitterest disappointment. For when they came out at last upon the summit, they saw that they were not the first. An ax stood there. Its haft was embedded in rock and ice, and on its steel head were the engraved words: To MARTIN FROM JOHN.

They were sporting men. On their return to civilization they told their story, and the name of the conqueror of K3 was made known to the world. □ □

Discussion

1. There are a number of scenes memorable for their tension and suspense. Which did you find most suspenseful? Why?

2. (a) Explain how the setting is a vital part of this story. (b) To portray a setting vividly, an author frequently appeals to more than one of the reader's five senses: sight, hearing, touch or feeling, taste, and smell. To what senses does Ullman appeal in his description of K3? Cite examples.

3. Conflict creates doubt and contributes importantly to feelings of uncertainty. (a) What external conflicts are present in the story? (b) What internal conflicts are there?

4. Osborn and Nace are both expert mountain climbers, but the personalities of the two men are quite different. Read the following two remarks taken from the story:

(1) "Let's get on to camp for a cup of tea."

(2) "Let him have his way, and we'll be sitting here chewing our nails until the mountain falls down on us."

(a) Who is speaking in the first quotation? (b) What incident occurs just before his remark? (c) What do the remark and the incident show about this man's character? (d) Who is speaking in the second quotation? (e) What is the speaker talking about? (f) What does the sentence reveal about his character?

5. (a) Why do you think the author titled his story "Top Man"? (b) Who do you think is the "top man" in this story? Explain.

Vocabulary
Context, Structure

Many words in English are derived from Latin words. Often if you know the meaning of the Latin word, you can easily figure out the meaning of the related English word.

Each item in the list below includes an English word, the Latin word it is derived from, and the meaning of that Latin word. After reading through the list, choose from it the English word that best completes each numbered sentence below. (You will not use one of the words.)

malignant (from *malignus,* "disposed to do evil")

taciturn (from *tacitum,* "unspoken")

imminent (from *imminentum,* "overhanging, threatening")

precipitous (from *praecipitum,* "steep")

indomitable (from *indomitus,* "untamed")

audacious (from *audax,* "bold")

1. The look on his face was so _____ that I was sure he was going to harm me.

2. How _____ of Joan to tell Mr. Silvestri that she didn't feel like coming to school yesterday!

3. She was a shy, _____ woman, not likely to indulge in idle conversations.

4. The temperature dropped, the skies clouded over, and we knew that a snowstorm was _____.

5. In spite of all her family's criticisms, Sylvia never lost her _____ will to succeed.

James Ramsey Ullman
1907 • 1971

Author of many books and articles about mountaineering, James Ramsey Ullman was not content to write about what he himself had not experienced. Born in New York in 1907, he grew up to become "more familiar with Tibet than Times Square" and traveled widely throughout the world before his death in 1971. He climbed many mountains on all continents, and in 1963 he was a member of the successful American Mount Everest Expedition.

In his early career Ullman was both a newspaper reporter and a Broadway producer, and he devoted the major part of his later life to writing. Among his best-known books are *The White Tower, Banner in the Sky, The Age of Mountaineering, Tiger of the Snows,* and *Americans on Everest.*

Private Hurricane

Elizabeth Bartlett

It blew in on the telephone
and caught me off guard, asleep.

At the first signal
the charcoal sky erupted
5 in a heat wave,
whirling up a cyclone
from the night's deep gorge.

It was a direct hit.

Born off course
10 on an ordinary Sunday,
it arrived without warning
at 7 a.m.,
tearing sheets and blankets
loose from dreams
15 and hurling me dead-center
into its white, electric eye.

As the barometer dropped,
my bloodstream rose;
wind and rain ripped across
20 fields, roads, boulders,
uprooting memories
and flooding the gullies of thought.

Damage was total.

Trees, walls, bridges,
25 everything collapsed,
broke apart, scattered.
People I had known,
houses lived in,
habits collected,
30 all disappeared in the torrent,
cut off
from the passageways of speech.
only the cottonmouth snake
remains,
35 slithering at my feet
as I uncoil it
from my throat, arms, waist.

My shattered nerves
have become a disaster area,
40 waiting for God to provide some relief.
I have declared martial law.

All day I have been searching
through the rubble,
to see what can be salvaged,
45 what may have escaped.

From *Panache*, No. 14, 1975. Reprinted by permission of the author.

Dan Morrill

1. (a) What clues exist in the title and first two lines of the poem to indicate that the poet is not writing about a real storm, but about some news which creates great emotional or psychological distress? (b) What sort of news might cause such a reaction?

2. (a) When does the "storm" hit? (b) What is the speaker doing when it hits? (c) How does the speaker react, physically and mentally, to the "storm" (lines 13–32)?

3. What remains after the "storm" passes?

4. In describing the distressing news in terms of a natural catastrophe, the poet is using hyperbole. What specific effects has the poet achieved through this exaggerated figure of speech?

5. Do you think the speaker will be able to recover from the effects of the "storm"? Why or why not?

2: Uncertainties

CONTENT REVIEW

1. (a) Of all the characters in this unit, which do you think best deals with a problem or predicament? Why? **(b)** Which characters seem to be defeated by their problems?

2. In this unit, even non-human creatures deal with challenges. What might be learned from the examples of "The War Between the Eagle and the Crows" and "The Beetle in the Country Bathtub"?

3. In "The Bracelet" and "Not Poor, Just Broke," two young people are faced with extremely upsetting problems. What other similarities do these two selections have? For example, in what other ways might the two characters be compared?

4. The unexpected (fate, chance, accident) plays an important part in each of the following poems: "Breaking and Entering," "Private Hurricane," and "Fifteen." What *is* the unexpected in each case, and how do those involved respond?

Unit 2, Test I
INTERPRETATION: NEW MATERIAL

Read carefully the short story reprinted below. Then on a separate sheet of paper, write your answers to the questions that follow it.

Old Man at the Bridge

Ernest Hemingway

An old man with steel-rimmed spectacles and very dusty clothes sat by the side of the road. There was a pontoon bridge across the river and carts, trucks, and men, women, and children were crossing it. The mule-drawn carts staggered up the steep bank from the bridge with soldiers helping push against the spokes of the wheels. The trucks ground up and away heading out of it all and the peasants plodded along in the ankle deep dust. But the old man sat there without moving. He was too tired to go any farther.

It was my business to cross the bridge, explore the bridgehead beyond, and find out to what point the enemy had advanced. I did this and returned over the bridge. There were not so many carts now and very few people on foot, but the old man was still there.

"Where do you come from?" I asked him.

"From San Carlos," he said, and smiled.

That was his native town and so it gave him pleasure to mention it and he smiled.

"I was taking care of animals," he explained.

"Oh," I said, not quite understanding.

"Yes," he said, "I stayed, you see, taking care of animals. I was the last one to leave the town of San Carlos."

He did not look like a shepherd nor a herdsman and I looked at his black dusty clothes and his gray dusty face and his steel-rimmed spectacles and said, "What animals were they?"

"Various animals," he said, and shook his head. "I had to leave them."

I was watching the bridge and the African-looking country of the Ebro Delta and wondering how long now it would be before we would see the enemy, and listening all the while for the first noises that would signal that ever-mysterious event called contact, and the old man still sat there.

"What animals were they?" I asked.

"There were three animals altogether," he explained. "There were two goats and a cat and then there were four pairs of pigeons."

"And you had to leave them?" I asked.

"Yes. Because of the artillery. The captain told me to go because of the artillery."

"And you have no family?" I asked, watching the far end of the bridge where a few last carts were hurrying down the slope of the bank.

"No," he said, "only the animals I stated. The cat, of course, will be all right. A cat can look out for itself, but I cannot think what will become of the others."

"What politics have you?" I asked.

"I am without politics," he said. "I am seventy-six years old. I have come twelve kilometers now and I think now I can go no further."

"This is not a good place to stop," I said. "If you can make it, there are trucks up the road where it forks for Tortosa."

"I will wait a while," he said, "and then I will go. Where do the trucks go?"

"Towards Barcelona," I told him.

"I know no one in that direction," he said, "but thank you very much. Thank you again very much."

He looked at me very blankly and tiredly, then said, having to share his worry with someone, "The cat will be all right, I am sure. There is no need to be unquiet about the cat. But the others. Now what do you think about the others?"

"Why, they'll probably come through it all right."

"You think so?"

"Why not?" I said, watching the far bank where now there were no carts.

"But what will they do under the artillery when I was told to leave because of the artillery?"

"Did you leave the dove cage unlocked?" I asked.

"Yes."

"Then they'll fly."

"Yes, certainly they'll fly. But the others. It's better not to think about the others," he said.

"If you are rested I would go," I urged. "Get up and try to walk now."

"Thank you," he said and got to his feet, swayed from side to side and then sat down backwards in the dust.

"I was taking care of animals," he said dully, but no longer to me. "I was only taking care of animals."

There was nothing to do about him. It was Easter Sunday and the Fascists were advancing toward the Ebro. It was a gray overcast day with a low ceiling so their planes were not up. That and the fact that cats know how to look after themselves was all the good luck that old man would ever have. □□

1. The overall feeling in the first paragraph of "Old Man at the Bridge" is one of (a) peace and quiet; (b) bustling activity; (c) anger; (d) disaster.

2. The peasants mentioned in the first paragraph are crossing the bridge to (a) flee from the advancing enemy; (b) establish a camp on the other side of the river; (c) rest their mules; (d) help the old man.

3. The narrator must go back across the bridge to (a) help the people still trying to get across; (b) plant dynamite near the base of the bridge; (c) check the condition of the road beyond the bridge; (d) see how far the enemy has advanced.

4. Judging from his actions, the narrator of the story is probably (a) a peasant fleeing from the enemy; (b) a soldier; (c) a truck driver; (d) an army doctor.

5. The weather conditions at the time of the story are (a) overcast and dry; (b) overcast and rainy; (c) sunny and dry; (d) partly sunny.

6. According to the narrator, why is the old man sitting by the side of the road?

7. The narrator is puzzled when the old man first tells him he was "taking care of animals" (137, 4) because (a) the old man is so tired that he whispers his words; (b) he can't believe that anyone would be interested in animals; (c) the old man doesn't look like a shepherd or a herdsman; (d) animals have no place in a war zone.

8. Why is the old man so concerned about his animals? **(a)** because they have been injured by the artillery; **(b)** because they could not get across the bridge; **(c)** because there will be no one to take care of them; **(d)** because they are very old.

9. Which of the following can be inferred from the old man's statement that he is "without politics" (137, 17)? **(a)** a political situation that has no meaning for him is disrupting his life; **(b)** he doesn't understand what the fighting is about; **(c)** he doesn't care who wins the war; **(d)** all of the above.

10. Why does the narrator urge the old man to move on?

11. The narrator suggests that the old man try to get on a truck going toward **(a)** San Carlos; **(b)** the Ebro Delta; **(c)** Tortosa; **(d)** Barcelona.

12. What is the real dilemma that the old man now faces? **(a)** he wants to go back for his animals, but he is afraid they will be dead; **(b)** he needs help, but he is too proud to ask for it; **(c)** he is tired, but he knows he must keep moving; **(d)** he cannot stay where he is, but he has nowhere to go.

13. Why are the weather conditions "good luck" for the old man?

14. The author's tone in the last line of the story is **(a)** loving; **(b)** bitter; **(c)** impatient; **(d)** frantic.

15. The theme of the story is **(a)** for some people, animals can be just as good friends as human beings; **(b)** a war displaces an old man from his home and his few possessions; **(c)** war is hardest on people who can't take care of themselves; **(d)** it is never wise to become too attached to possessions.

Unit 2, Test II
COMPOSITION

Choose one of the following assignments to write about. Unless you are told otherwise, assume that you are writing for your classmates.

1. Describe what you think are the two most important conflicts in "Top Man" and show how each conflict has an effect on the outcome of the story.

2. Assume that you are the princess in "The Lady, or the Tiger?" It is the night before your lover is to go into the arena, and you have just made your decision about which door you will have him open. Now you are writing in your diary. Explain in your diary entry what your decision is, and what reasons you had for making it.

3. Both Ruri, the narrator of "The Bracelet," and the old man in "Old Man at the Bridge" have been forced to leave their homes because of a war. Discuss each character's reaction to being a "displaced person." In what ways, if any, are their reactions similar? In what ways are they different?

4. Not long after Charlie Gordon in "Flowers for Algernon" has the operation to increase his intelligence, he feels that he is "more alone than ever before." Reread Charlie's journal entries for April 28, May 15, and May 18. Then discuss the possibility that at least some of his loneliness may come from his lack of ability to deal with people realistically.

5. "Breaking and Entering" and "Private Hurricane" both involve a personal tragedy and the narrator's reaction to it. In which poem, in your opinion, is the feeling of loss communicated more effectively? Defend your choice in terms of (1) the way the writer presented a loss in the poem, and (2) the details and images she used to make it vivid.

A poem can be many things, said many ways.

It can touch softly, or it can beat like a fist

against the ear. It can concern everything from

a lamb's wintry birth to a criminal's execution;

from a dog howling at the moon to an act of human

kindness on a crowded bus.

A poem can laugh, cry, sing, rage. **POETRY**

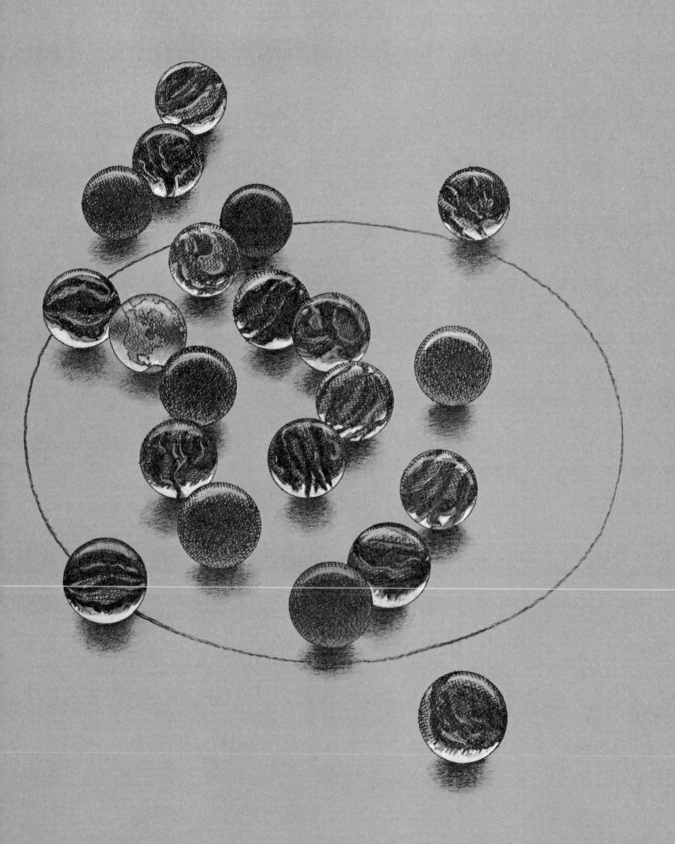

Every Good Boy Does Fine

David Wagoner

1.

*Everyone is striving for
something:
to succeed,
to escape,
or simply to survive.*

I practiced my cornet in a cold garage
Where I could blast it till the oil in drums
Boomed back; tossed free-throws till I couldn't move
    my thumbs;
Sprinted through tires, tackling a headless dummy.

5 In my first contest, playing a wobbly solo,
I blew up in the coda,[1] alone on stage,
And twisting like my hand-tied necktie, saw the judge
Letting my silence dwindle down his scale.

At my first basketball game, gangling away from home
10 A hundred miles by bus to a dressing room,
Under the showering voice of the coach, I stood in a
    towel,
Having forgotten shoes, socks, uniform.

In my first football game, the first play under the lights
I intercepted a pass. For seventy yards, I ran
15 Through music and squeals, surging, lifting my cleats,
Only to be brought down by the safety man.

I took my second chances with less care, but in
    dreams
I saw the bald judge slumped in the front row,
The coach and team at the doorway, the safety man
20 Galloping loud at my heels. They watch me now.

You who have always horned your way through
    passages,
Sat safe on the bench while some came naked to court,
Slipped out of arms to win in the long run,
Consider this poem a failure, sprawling flat on a page.

Reprinted from *The Nesting Ground* by permission of the Indiana University Press.
1.*coda* (kō′də), a final passage of a musical composition, which gives it a satisfactory ending.

David Wagoner 1926 •

Discussion

1. **(a)** What various things does the boy practice in stanza 1? **(b)** What is his first contest? How does he do? **(c)** Why isn't he a success in his first basketball game? **(d)** What happens in the first football game he plays?

2. Explain the meaning of "I took my second chances with less care" (line 17) and "They watch me now" (line 20).

3. **(a)** To whom is the speaker talking in the last stanza? **(b)** In each of lines 21–23, the speaker recalls one of his failures while he describes people who do not fail. Does he totally admire their achievements? Explain. **(c)** Why might the people referred to in these lines consider the poem a failure (line 24)?

4. "Every Good Boy Does Fine" is a sentence many music students learn to help them remember the names of certain musical notes: EGBDF. Why is it ironic as a title for this poem?

In regard to this poem David Wagoner writes: "I think I started to write 'Every Good Boy Does Fine' in an attempt to keep the incidents described therein from bothering me any more. During the work on the poem, I realized I was still having experiences similar to those I'd had in high school, that they were symbolic of many kinds of failure, and that the act of writing the poem itself was just one more example, however necessary, of asking for disappointment. I have judges, coaches, and safety men inside me, doing their jobs strictly and sometimes badly and sometimes not for my benefit.

"Every good boy does not do fine. In my own terms, I consider the poem a success, but I didn't manage to get it down on paper because I was 'good,' but because I had learned how and was still willing to take a chance at outfoxing whatever there is inside me that says 'I can't.' "

See **METAPHOR** Handbook of Literary Terms

Sky Diver

Adrien Stoutenberg

Grotesque, jumping out
like a clothed frog, helmet and glasses,
arms and legs wading the sky,
feet flapping before the cloth flower opens;
5 then suspended, poised,
an exclamation point upside-down,
and going down, swaying over corn and creeks
and highways scribbled
over the bones of fish and eagles.

10 There is the interim between air and earth,
time to study steeples
and the underwings of birds going over,
before the unseen chasm,
the sudden jaw open and hissing.

15 Lying here after the last jump
I see how fanatic roots are,
how moles breathe through darkness,
how deep the earth can be.

Discussion

1. (a) What is a sky diver? Describe the sport of sky diving. **(b)** What metaphors are used to describe the sky diver and equipment in stanza 1?

2. (a) What is actually happening to the sky diver in lines 10–12? **(b)** Describe what feelings you get from stanzas 1 and 2 (lines 1–14). Do your feelings change from line to line?

3. (a) Where is the sky diver in line 15? **(b)** In what ways are the details in lines 16–18 different from those in the rest of the poem? Why might this be so?

Mickey Palmer/DPI

The Sprinters

Lillian Morrison

The gun explodes them.
Pummeling, pistoning they fly
In time's face.
A go at the limit,
5 A terrible try
To smash the ticking glass,
Outpace the beat
That runs, that streaks away
Tireless, and faster than they.

10 Beside ourselves
(It is for us they run!)
We shout and pound the stands
For one to win,
Loving him, whose hard
15 Grace-driven stride
Most mocks the clock
And almost breaks the bands
Which lock us in.

Gerry Cranham/PHOTO RESEARCHERS, INC.

Reprinted by permission of the author
from *Sprints and Distances*, Thomas Y.
Crowell Company, Inc. Copyright © 1965
by Lillian Morrison.

Discussion

1. (a) What is described in this poem? (b) Explain the meaning of the first line.

2. (a) What is the "ticking glass" (line 6)? (b) Who or what else are the sprinters competing against in lines 7–9?

3. (a) In what sense do the sprinters run "for us" (line 11)? (b) What are "the bands" mentioned in lines 17–18? (c) Does it seem possible that these bands will eventually be broken? Support your answer with words or lines from the poem.

(d) What do you think would happen if a runner—or anyone else—succeeded in breaking those bands?

After most of the employees of the New York *Sun* had gone home for the evening, Archy, a cockroach, climbed up on a typewriter and wrote reports to the boss, a columnist. Archy tapped out letters on the typewriter by hurling himself headfirst at the keys. But, being very much a lightweight, he could not operate the shift key; thus his writings contain no capitals or punctuation.

The two poems that follow are samples of the kinds of reports Archy wrote to Don Marquis, the boss.

the hen and the oriole

Don Marquis

well boss did it
ever strike you that a
hen regrets it just as
much when they wring her
5 neck as an oriole but
nobody has any
sympathy for a hen because
she is not beautiful
while everyone gets
10 sentimental over the
oriole and says how
shocking to kill the
lovely thing this thought
comes to my mind
15 because of the earnest
endeavor of a
gentleman to squash me
yesterday afternoon when i
was riding up in the
20 elevator if i had been a
butterfly he would have
said how did that
beautiful thing happen to
find its way into
25 these grimy city streets do
not harm the splendid
creature but let it
fly back to its rural
haunts again beauty always
30 gets the best of
it be beautiful boss
a thing of beauty is a
joy forever[1]
be handsome boss and let
35 who will be clever[2] is
the sad advice
of your ugly little friend
                          archy

Don Marquis (mär′kwis)
1. *a thing of beauty is a/joy forever.* Archy is quoting a line from *Endymion*, a long poem by the English poet, John Keats (1795–1821).
2. *be handsome boss and let/who will be clever,* a paraphrase of a line in Charles Kingsley's "A Farewell." The original line reads: "Be good, sweet maid, and let who can be clever."

Discussion

1. In your own words tell about the incident Archy describes in this poem.

2. (a) What conclusion does Archy's experience lead him to make? (b) What criticism of human values does Archy imply in this poem? (c) Is this criticism valid? Why or why not?

takes talent

Don Marquis

Don Marquis

Discussion

1. Describe and contrast the qualities involved in the "two/kinds of human/beings in the world."

2. (a) What does the title of this poem mean? **(b)** What comment on people is Archy making? **(c)** Does he see any hope for those who lack the "talent"? **(d)** Is Archy justified in separating humans into these two categories? Why or why not?

3. (a) Is the tone of "takes talent" humorous or serious? **(b)** Do you think Archy's comment should be taken seriously? Explain.

Don Marquis   1878 • 1937

Within his lifetime Marquis was poet, playwright, short-story writer, and newspaper columnist. But today he is best remembered for his work in a field where talent is rare—humorous verse. Fame came to Marquis with the creation of Archy and Mehitabel, the cat who claimed to have once been Cleopatra. The quaint philosophies of the cat and the cockroach often filled Marquis's column in the New York *Sun,* and have been collected in a book entitled *the lives and times of archy and mehitabel.*

there are two
kinds of human
beings in the world
so my observation
5 has told me
namely and to wit
as follows
firstly
those who
10 even though they
were to reveal
the secret of the universe
to you would fail
to impress you
15 with any sense
of the importance
of the news
and secondly
those who could
20 communicate to you
that they had
just purchased
ten cents worth
of paper napkins
25 and make you
thrill and vibrate
with the intelligence
                    archy

Highway: Michigan

Theodore Roethke

Here from the field's edge we survey
The progress of the jaded. Mile
On mile of traffic from the town
Rides by, for at the end of day
5 The time of workers is their own.

They jockey for position on
The strip reserved for passing only.
The drivers from production lines
Hold to advantage dearly won.
10 They toy with death and traffic fines.

Acceleration is their need:
A mania keeps them on the move
Until the toughest nerves are frayed.
They are the prisoners of speed
15 Who flee in what their hands have made.

The pavement smokes when two cars meet
And steel rips through conflicting steel.
We shiver at the siren's blast.
One driver, pinned beneath the seat,
20 Escapes from the machine at last.

"Highway: Michigan," copyright 1940 by Theodore Roethke from *The Collected Poems of Theodore Roethke*. Reprinted by permission of Doubleday & Company, Inc. and Faber and Faber Limited.
Theodore Roethke (ret′kē)

Patricia Hollander Gross/STOCK, BOSTON

Discussion

1. (a) Describe the setting. Where is the speaker in relation to what he is describing? (b) What "progress" is the speaker surveying? Explain what is happening. (c) Describe the kind of traffic referred to in stanza 2 (lines 6–10). (d) What kind of attitude do the drivers have toward the possible consequences of their driving?

2. (a) In stanza 3, what does the speaker suggest are the reasons for the behavior of the drivers? (b) Find clues in the poem that suggest the kind of jobs these drivers have.

3. (a) What happens in stanza 4? (b) In what sense does one driver "escape" (lines 19–20)?

4. (a) How does the speaker seem to feel about automobiles, about people who are "prisoners of speed," and about the kind of driving described in this poem? (b) How do you feel about these same things?

Vocabulary
Pronunciation, Dictionary

A. Using your Glossary, figure out which syllable of each italicized word below has a primary stress or accent. Then choose the word that rhymes with that accented syllable and write the letter of your choice on your paper.

1. *grotesque:* (a) low; (b) mess; (c) desk; (d) due.
2. *fanatic:* (a) ran; (b) rain; (c) fat; (d) sick.
3. *intercept:* (a) pin; (b) were; (c) deer; (d) kept.
4. *pummel:* (a) dumb; (b) doom; (c) tell; (d) peel.
5. *acceleration:* (a) tack; (b) tell; (c) pay; (d) fun.
6. *mania:* (a) say; (b) sane; (c) free; (d) the.
7. *chasm:* (a) daze; (b) has; (c) pass; (d) them.

B. Now use each italicized word in a sentence that shows you understand the meaning of the word.

Theodore Roethke
1908 • 1963

Born in Saginaw, Michigan, Theodore Roethke received his education at the University of Michigan and Harvard. During his career as teacher and poet, Roethke received many honors, including a National Book Award and a Pulitzer Prize. He was much admired for his ability to write brilliantly in a wide range of moods, from light to serious.

2.

Memorable portraits—
of good people,
and bad.

How Tuesday Began

Kathleen Fraser

Discussion

1. Where and when does the action in this poem take place?

2. **(a)** What is the speaker's "habit" (line 14)? **(b)** How is the black woman described (lines 15–21)?

3. **(a)** Describe the progress of the old woman on the bus (lines 23–36). **(b)** How does the speaker describe the movements of the other passengers (lines 30–32)? **(c)** What does the black woman do?

4. **(a)** Has the action of the black woman affected the speaker in any particular way? How can you tell? **(b)** Do you think "How Tuesday Began" is an effective title for this poem? Why or why not?

Kathleen Fraser 1937 •

Author of several books of poetry for both children and adults, Kathleen Fraser has also taught poetry and creative writing in New York, at the University of Iowa, and in San Francisco, where she now lives, married to another poet.

Don't let me lose you,
lady. We're jogging up
First Avenue in the sun,
nursing morning with
5 our habits.
I must have boarded before
you, where the bus stops
and the dusty nightgowns
beckon from Orchard St.
10 I must have pulled out
my book, peeled off my gloves,
and settled among the fumes
for a poem or two,
my habit.
15 I didn't see you,
black, filling the aisle
with your green housedress,
lowering each part of you
gently, in front of me,
20 maybe heaving a sigh, your
sorrow and habit.

Still, my eyes pulled
sideways. Someone old
moved without moving,
25 veins, vague eyes resisting
the aisle in front
of her, a journey
to be mastered upright,
seat by seat.

30 We rolled with the bus,
easy as rubber lifeboats
on troubled water.
But she hung to the same
space, sensing the movement
35 around her, sinking
in her own flesh.
Then you reached out, lady,
and pulled her in
beside you.
40 You were fading
and full of troubles, lady,
and you saw her drowning
and you reached out
and said, "I don't see
45 so good myself."

Jamie

Elizabeth Brewster

When Jamie was sixteen,
Suddenly he was deaf. There were no songs,
No voices any more.
He walked about stunned by the terrible silence.
5 Kicking a stick, rapping his knuckles on doors,
He felt a spell of silence all about him,
So loud it made a whirring in his ears.
People moved mouths without a sound escaping:
He shuddered at the straining of their throats.
10 And suddenly he watched them with suspicion,
Wondering if they were talking of his faults,
Were pitying him or seeing him with scorn.
He dived into their eyes and dragged up sneers,
And sauntering the streets, imagined laughter behind him.
15 Working at odd jobs, ploughing, picking potatoes,
Chopping trees in the lumber woods in winter,
He became accustomed to an aimless and lonely labor.
He was solitary and unloquacious as a stone,
And silence grew over him like moss on an old stump.
20 But sometimes, going to town,
He was sore with the hunger for company among the people,
And, getting drunk, would shout at them for friendship,
Laughing aloud in the streets.
He returned to the woods,
25 And dreaming at night of a shining cowboy heaven
Where guns crashed through his deafness, woke morose,
And chopped the necks of pine trees in his anger.

Discussion

1. What do you feel toward Jamie—sympathy, pity, or impatience that he doesn't try harder to adjust to his handicap? Explain your reaction.

2. Do you think Jamie's reactions to going deaf at sixteen are different from the reactions he might have had if he had been born deaf? Explain your answer.

3. (a) In what ways are Jamie's relationships with people affected? (b) What attempts does Jamie make to gain the company of people? (c) Are these attempts likely to win friends? Explain.

4. (a) What does the last line of the poem reveal about Jamie? (b) What do you think will happen to him?

Extension • Speaking

Helen Keller was an extremely gifted woman who lived most of her life deaf and blind. She was once asked which sense she would prefer to regain, sight or hearing. Reportedly, she said she would have chosen her ability to hear. Which would have been your choice? Share with the class your personal reasons for making such a choice.

"Jamie" by Elizabeth Brewster from *East Coast* published by Ryerson Press, 1951.
Reprinted by permission of the author.

The small pine nuts called piñones (pē nyō′nes)
are a treat today as they were in the past.

piñones

Leroy Quintana

Discussion

1. (a) What details does the
speaker mention from his
youth? **(b)** What is different
about what the speaker watches and listens to in this "supersonic age"? **(c)** What single detail remains the same?

2. (a) Does the speaker seem
to prefer his youth or his present life? How can you tell?
(b) How would you describe
the tone of this poem—warm,
sad, bitter, ironic—or what?

Leroy Quintana

Much of Leroy Quintana's
poetry is based on his New
Mexico background, as in his
book *Hijo del Pueblo: New
Mexico Poems*. His work has
appeared in numerous magazines and has been reprinted in
such anthologies as *Chicano
Voices* and *101 Poets of the
60's and 70's*. A teacher of
English, poetry, and creative
writing, Quintana has edited a
number of magazines and an
anthology of Spanish and English poetry.

when i was young
we would sit by
an old firewood stove
watching my grandmother make candy,
5 listening to the stories
my grandparents would tell
about "the old days"
        and eat piñones

now we belong
10 to a supersonic age
and have college degrees.
we sit around color t.v. sets
watching the super bowl
listening to howard cosell,
15 stories of rioting, war, inflation
        and eat piñones

Lord Randal

Old Ballad

"O where ha you been, Lord Randal, my son?
And where ha you been, my handsome young man?"
"I ha been at the greenwood; Mother, mak my bed soon,
For I'm wearied wi huntin, and fain wad lie down."[1]

5 "An wha met ye there, Lord Randal, my son?
An wha met you there, my handsome young man?"
"O I met wi my true-love; Mother, mak my bed soon,
For I'm wearied wi huntin, and fain wad lie down."

"And what did she give you, Lord Randal, my son?
10 And what did she give you, my handsome young man?"
"Eels fried in a pan;[2] Mother, mak my bed soon,
For I'm wearied wi huntin, and fain wad lie down."

"And wha gat your leavins,[3] Lord Randal, my son?
And wha gat your leavins, my handsome young man?"
15 "My hawks and my hounds; Mother, mak my bed soon,
For I'm wearied wi huntin, and fain wad lie down."

"And what becam of them, Lord Randal, my son?
And what becam of them, my handsome young man?"
"They stretched their legs out an died; Mother, mak my bed soon,
20 For I'm wearied wi huntin, and fain wad lie down."

"O I fear you are poisoned, Lord Randal, my son!
I fear you are poisoned, my handsome young man!"
"O yes, I am poisoned; Mother, mak my bed soon,
For I'm sick at the heart, and I fain wad lie down."

English and Scottish Popular Ballads. Helen Child Sargent and George Lymann
Kittredge, eds. Boston: Houghton Mifflin Company, 1904, 1932.
1. *down,* to be pronounced in the Scottish manner (dün) to rhyme with *soon.*
2. *Eels fried in a pan,* a method of poisoning that appears in many old ballads.
3. *wha gat your leavins,* who ate the food you didn't eat?

25 "What d'ye leave to your mother, Lord Randal, my son?
  What d'ye leave to your mother, my handsome young man?"
  "Four and twenty milk kye;[4] Mother, mak my bed soon,
  For I'm sick at the heart, and I fain wad lie down."

  "What d'ye leave to your sister, Lord Randal, my son?
30 What d'ye leave to your sister, my handsome young man?"
  "My gold and my silver; Mother, mak my bed soon,
  For I'm sick at the heart, and I fain wad lie down."

  "What d'ye leave to your brother, Lord Randal, my son?
  What d'ye leave to your brother, my handsome young man?"
35 "My houses and my lands; Mother, mak my bed soon,
  For I'm sick at the heart, and I fain wad lie down."

  "What d'ye leave to your true-love, Lord Randal, my son?
  What d'ye leave to your true-love, my handsome young man?"
  "I leave her hell and fire; Mother, mak my bed soon,
40 For I'm sick at the heart, and I fain wad lie down."

---

4. *kye,* cows.

Discussion

1. (a) Who is asking the question in the first two lines of the poem? (b) Who answers in lines 3–4? (c) How is the story told throughout?

2. (a) What is the situation at the opening of "Lord Randal"? Describe the scene. (b) Why do you think the mother asks Lord Randal what he has eaten (line 9)? (c) What does she suspect has happened? Why?

3. In many ballads, phrases or whole lines are repeated much as they appeared before, with new details added slowly, one by one. (a) At what point does Lord Randal give a new reason for wanting to lie down? What is his real reason? (b) Why do you think he does not tell this to his mother earlier? (c) How do you learn who is responsible for Lord Randal's condition? (d) What do you think are the mother's purposes for asking what Lord Randal will leave her, his sister and brother, and his true-love?

4. Discuss the ways in which the telling of the story creates suspense.

Extension • Writing

Write a brief news article with headlines of the incident told in "Lord Randal" for the newspaper of a small country town.

Or, find a current news article about a sensational story and write a few stanzas of a ballad based on that incident. You may use "Lord Randal" as a model for your stanza form and rhyme scheme.

Old Ballads

During the Middles Ages, wandering minstrels traveled throughout the countryside of England and the rest of Europe singing songs in exchange for food and lodging. These songs the minstrels sang are called *ballads*. No one is certain how old the first ballads are, who their authors were, or how they came to be written. But whatever their origins, ballads were sung for hundreds of years. Different versions arose as people, moving from one place to another, forgot some of the older lines, substituted new ones of their own, or made changes to suit the time and place. Centuries went by before these ballads were written down in any permanent form. Today we have a number of versions of some of the same ballads.

Although ballads sprang from many sources and often underwent drastic revisions in the telling, there are certain distinctive features common to most ballads. First of all, the ballad is a highly dramatic story told in verse, with an emphasis on action. Ballads deal with basic subjects like treachery, cunning, death, love, jealousy. Few of the old ballads are humorous. Most of them are tragic, dealing with sensational events—but they do so objectively, with little or no emotion or moralizing.

Ballads often contain dialogue, and their stories deal with a limited number of characters and incidents. There is little description; only those facts are included which are necessary for narrating the action. To do this, the minstrels often used a kind of shorthand, using stereotyped characters and actions which are sometimes almost symbolic. For example, the crowing of a rooster means "morning" to us now as it did in the Middle Ages, and the giving of a ring still symbolizes engagement or marriage. The making of a bed usually meant preparing a deathbed or coffin, and feeding someone eels meant poisoning, although these actions no longer carry the same significance to us as they did to earlier audiences.

Another feature is the characteristic verse form used in most of the old ballads. The stanzas are composed of four lines, and the second and fourth lines of each stanza rhyme. Phrases or whole lines are very often repeated, and rhythm usually follows a quite definite pattern.

Meditation on His Ninety-First Year

John Haag

This withered clutch of bones, this hand that held
Two oxen and a plow steadily down
An even furrow, now scarcely can hold
The heavy reading-glass. An April sun
5 Could bring me to a sweat when my thin blood
Was warmer; now I'm tissue-dry and shake
In any breeze that giddies this grey head.
"The years have flown," a fellow patriarch
Is fond of saying, but as I reflect
10 Upon nine decades ripening steadily,
Each measured year maturing, act by act,
I wonder at him—could his memory
Remain so barren that life disappears
Into a limbo of forgotten years?

15 It's pleasant for me now to spin the past:
A boyhood full of cows and berry-vines,
Hay-ricks and wild birds, the journey west
When I was seventeen, the evergreens
And rivers and the rocks . . . I took a wife
20 The fall that my first crop was harvested,
And she was fruitful; under our first roof
We reared four sons to carry on the blood.
I've planted every year, yet never known
Two springs so much alike I could not tell
25 One from the other; no two days have been

From *Northwest Review*, Spring, 1959. Reprinted by permission
of the author.
John Haag (häg)

Identical, and I can still recall
Each acre tilled, each crop or foal or calf . . .
The living things—these are my epitaph.

The doctor tells me I should not expect
30 To live forever. After he has gone
I smile to think that he, at thirty-eight,
Cannot conceive how well, at ninety-one,
I have accepted this absurd remark.
Today the teacup chatters at my teeth;
35 I feel the room grow colder, and I break
With reveries and vague regrets that growth
Is over, that the blood wears out, and then
No more of things that breathe and climb, no more.
But, though I feel the minutes growing thin
40 And I've torn the last page from the calendar,
I cannot grudge the passing of my breath—
After so much life, so little death.

Discussion

1. Who is the speaker in this poem?

2. (a) What occupation did the speaker follow as a young man? (b) What are some of the things he remembers about his youth?

3. (a) Does the young doctor understand the speaker's attitude and views? Explain. (b) What things about being old does the speaker regret? (c) What is his attitude toward the life he has lived? toward the death that will come to him shortly?

4. Read the poet's comments on this poem, noting what he has to say about the language. (a) Find images in the poem you consider especially vivid. (b) Considering the subject matter, is the imagery the poet

uses appropriate? Why or why not?

5. The poem begins by pointing out the contrast between the power in the man's hands when he was young and their feebleness in old age. (a) Find other examples of contrast in the poem and explain their functions. (b) Are the contrasts effective? Explain.

John Haag

In regard to this poem John Haag writes: "'Meditation' is a tribute to my paternal Grandfather, and I feel it faithfully represents the pattern and spirit of his life, even though some of the details I employ are not necessarily biographical.

"To express the man I felt I had to use language he might himself have used. His formal education was limited, by today's standards, but his high intelligence and active interest in what went on in the world made him articulate—when he felt it was time to speak up. He might use an image, but no ornate language or poeticisms, so one of my problems was to make poetry out of his direct diction and patterns of speech. In doing so I rediscovered an elemental truth about the relationship between what you say and the way you say it: as I searched out the poetry in the man, I found no better expression for it than his own language, because the language he used to express himself always honestly reflected what he was. So in a way my Grandfather really made this poem—I just put it together."

See **RHYTHM** Handbook of Literary Terms

Danny Deever

Rudyard Kipling

"What are the bugles blowin' for?" said Files-on-Parade.[1]
"To turn you out, to turn you out," the Color-Sergeant[2] said.
"What makes you look so white, so white?" said Files-on-Parade.
"I'm dreadin' what I've got to watch," the Color-Sergeant said.
5   For they're hangin' Danny Deever, you can hear the Dead March play,
    The regiment's in 'ollow square[3]—they're hangin' him today;
    They've taken of his buttons off an' cut his stripes away,[4]
    An' they're hangin' Danny Deever in the mornin'.

"What makes the rear-rank breathe so 'ard?" said Files-on-Parade.
10 "It's bitter cold, it's bitter cold," the Color-Sergeant said.
"What makes that front-rank man fall down?" said Files-on-Parade.
"A touch o' sun, a touch o' sun," the Color-Sergeant said.
    They are hangin' Danny Deever, they are marchin' of 'im round,
    They 'ave 'alted Danny Deever by 'is coffin on the ground;
15   An' 'e'll swing in 'arf a minute for a sneakin', shootin' hound—
    O they're hangin' Danny Deever in the mornin'.

"'Is cot was right-'and cot to mine," said Files-on-Parade.
"'E's sleepin' out an' far tonight," the Color-Sergeant said.
"I've drunk 'is beer a score o' times," said Files-on-Parade.
20 "'E's drinkin' bitter beer alone," the Color-Sergeant said.
    They are hangin' Danny Deever, you must mark 'im to 'is place,
    For 'e shot a comrade sleepin'—you must look 'im in the face;
    Nine 'undred of 'is county an' the regiment's disgrace,
    While they're hangin' Danny Deever in the mornin'.

25 "What's that so black agin' the sun?" said Files-on-Parade.
"It's Danny fightin' 'ard for life," the Color-Sergeant said.

"Danny Deever" by Rudyard Kipling, from *Rudyard Kipling's Verse:* Definitive Edition. Reprinted by permission of The Executors of the Estate of Mrs. George Bambridge, Doubleday & Company, Inc. and the National Trust.
1. *Files-on-Parade,* a term applied to a soldier assigned to close up the files or ranks.
2. *Color-Sergeant,* the noncommissioned officer who carries the regimental colors.
3. *regiment's . . . square.* The soldiers form the four sides of a square, here facing inwards. This is the formation used on ceremonial occasions or when a soldier is to be publicly executed.
4. *taken of his buttons off . . . away,* a custom applied to a disgraced soldier.

"What's that that whimpers over'ead?" said Files-on-Parade.
"It's Danny's soul that's passin' now," the Color-Sergeant said.
    For they're done with Danny Deever, you can 'ear the quick-step[5] play,
30   The regiment's in column, an' they're marchin' us away;
    Ho! the young recruits are shakin', an' they'll want their beer today,
    After hangin' Danny Deever in the mornin'.

---

5. *quick-step,* a lively air played after the funeral march.

Discussion

1. (a) Who is carrying on the conversation recorded in this poem? (b) From their conversation, what do you learn about these men? Does there seem to be any difference between them? (c) Danny Deever is the only person mentioned by name in the poem. What effect is created by referring to the two speakers by their rank rather than by their proper names?

2. (a) Why is Danny Deever being hanged? (b) Does the poem focus more on Danny's plight or on the effect of his execution on others? Explain.

3. Does this poem merely tell a story, or does it make a comment as well? Explain.

4. "Danny Deever" can be considered a modern ballad, in that it shares many characteristics of the old ballads, such as "Lord Randal." In what ways does "Danny Deever" resemble the old ballads? (Reread the Notes and Comments accompanying "Lord Randal" before you answer.)

5. Read enough of the poem aloud to get a sense of the rhythm involved. (a) How many different rhythms do you find? Where are they used? (b) How do these rhythms reflect the mood and action of the poem?

Vocabulary
Context, Dictionary

Particularly when you are reading poetry, it is a great help to know exactly which meaning of a word a writer had in mind. If you see a word used in a way that is not familiar to you, check your dictionary or Glossary. Be sure, however, that you read through all the definitions to find the one that makes the most sense in the context.

A. Each pair of sentences below contains the same word used in two different ways. Using your Glossary, write the correct definition of the italicized word as it is used in each sentence.

1. (a) He was older than his wife by a *score* of years.
(b) Have you heard the *score* of last night's basketball game?

2. (a) Improper *inflation* of a tire can cause a blowout.
(b) More companies should give cost-of-living raises to help their employees stay ahead of *inflation*.

3. (a) At eighty-five, the bearded *patriarch* had lost none of his intelligence or wit.
(b) Henry Ford was the *patriarch* of the automobile industry.

4. (a) When you tune up my car, please adjust the *clutch*.
(b) A whole *clutch* of people crowded into the tiny room. [Hint: Read both entries for *clutch* in your Glossary.]

B. Listed below are the four words you just defined and the poems that the words were used in. Reread the indicated lines in each poem; then write the letter of the definition (a or b) that the writer had in mind.

1. *score:* "Danny Deever," line 19

2. *inflation:* "piñones," line 12–15

3. *patriarch:* "Meditation on His Ninety-First Year," line 8

4. *clutch:* "Meditation on His Ninety-First Year," line 1

Rudyard Kipling
1865 • 1936

Born in India, Kipling was educated in England, where he began writing poetry, some of which was published in the school magazine. When he had finished his education, he rejoined his family at Lahore, India, where he became assistant editor of a newspaper. Some of his poems and stories appeared in the newspaper's columns and later in book form.

Kipling traveled widely in the United States and Europe, and eventually settled in England. He was the youngest person ever to be awarded the Nobel Prize for Literature (1907). Throughout his life, Kipling wrote stories and poems filled with suspense and excitement. Many of these Kipling based on Indian folklore and on his own experiences in India.

notes and comments

Different Ways of Speaking

When you're a little bit hungry, would you go for a bite, a lunch, a piece meal, or a snack? And to satisfy your hunger would you eat bacon, flitch, middlin, middlin meat, salt pork, side pork, side meat, sowbelly, or fatback? You don't have to travel much to be aware that people say things in different ways. Sometimes they use different words, as the terms above for the same kind of meat. Sometimes they use the same word, but pronounce it differently. For example, when you pronounce *toward,* do you say tôrd, tōrd, or tə wôrd'? Or something still different?

Writers are aware of such differences—called *dialects*—and often make use of them to make a point. In the musical comedy *My Fair Lady* a poor flower girl, Eliza, asks a language professor to help her change her speech so that she can get a better job. In one scene the professor tries to teach Eliza to say "the rain in Spain stays mainly on the plain" instead of "the rine in Spine sties minely on the pline."

Written language is a reflection of the way people actually do talk. For example, many people do not always pronounce the *d* in *and.* To suggest this, an author might write *an'.* Some people might shorten the word even more: *'n'.* Sometimes the spellings of certain words reflect this: rock'n'roll, for example.

Rudyard Kipling makes use of the same device. You are probably quite familiar with the pronunciations suggested by spellings like *blowin', dreadin',* and *hangin'.* You may not be familiar with the pronunciations of words like *'ollow, 'ard,* and *'im.* They are simply the words *hollow, hard,* and *him* with the initial *h* dropped to indicate the dialectal pronunciations of the characters. Some others you might not be familiar with are the use of *'arf* for *half, o'* for *of,* and *agin'* for *against.*

It is not just pronunciations that mark the speech of Files-on-Parade and the Color Sergeant. They also make use of certain phrases peculiar to their dialect. Phrases like "taken of his buttons off," and "marchin' of 'im round" may seem difficult at first, but usually when you realize what words are indicated by the spellings, you can tell from context what is meant.

Find the following expressions in "Danny Deever" and explain what the words mean in context.

1. turn you out (line 2)
2. 'arf a minute (line 15)
3. right-'and cot to mine (line 17)
4. out an' far tonight (line 18)

3.

Living in . . .
and with . . .
the natural world.

Sometimes a poem is like a riddle.
Can you solve this one?

Living Tenderly

May Swenson

My body a rounded stone
with a pattern of smooth seams.
My head a short snake,
retractive, projective.
5 My legs come out of their sleeves
or shrink within,
and so does my chin.
My eyelids are quick clamps.

My back is my roof.
10 I am always at home.
I travel where my house walks.
It is a smooth stone.
It floats within the lake,
or rests in the dust.
15 My flesh lives tenderly
inside its bone.

Discussion

1. (a) Who or what is speaking? (b) At what point were you able to guess the identity of the speaker?

2. (a) How does the speaker describe its body in lines 1–2? in line 9? in line 11? (b) How is the head described? the eyelids?

3. (a) Which clue in this "riddle poem" did you find most helpful? (b) Do you think any of the clues are misleading or unfair? Explain.

May Swenson 1919 •

Born and educated in Utah, May Swenson has spent most of her career as a poet, teacher, and editor in New York.

The "riddle poem" is a form that has particularly interested Swenson. One of her collections, *Poems to Solve,* is completely devoted to such poems.

See **RHYME** Handbook of Literary Terms

First Sight

Philip Larkin

Discussion

1. **(a)** At what time of year are these lambs born? Under what kind of weather conditions do they learn to walk? **(b)** Find words in the poem to tell what it is these lambs "meet" and what they "know."

2. **(a)** Find words in the poem to complete this sentence: "_____ lies hidden." **(b)** What is it that will "wake and grow/Utterly unlike the snow"?

3. **(a)** To what does the title "First Sight" refer? **(b)** Tell in your own language what happens in the poem.

4. **(a)** Describe the rhyme scheme in "First Sight." **(b)** Many poems in this book do not rhyme. What effect does the rhyme in this poem have on you?

Philip Larkin 1922 •

Known as one of the finest poets of post-World War II England, Philip Larkin is a librarian at the University of Hull, England. His poems appear in six books of his collected works, but he has also been the feature writer on jazz for the newspaper *Daily Telegraph*.

Lambs that learn to walk in snow
When their bleating clouds the air
Meet a vast unwelcome, know
Nothing but a sunless glare.
5 Newly stumbling to and fro
All they find, outside the fold,
Is a wretched width of cold.

As they wait beside the ewe,
Her fleeces wetly caked, there lies
10 Hidden round them, waiting too,
Earth's immeasurable surprise.
They could not grasp it if they knew,
What so soon will wake and grow
Utterly unlike the snow.

Reprinted by permission of Faber and Faber Ltd. from *The Whitsun Wedding* by Philip Larkin.

Dog at Night

Louis Untermeyer

At first he stirs uneasily in sleep
And, since the moon does not run off, unfolds
Protesting paws. Grumbling that he must keep
Both eyes awake, he whimpers; then he scolds
5 And, rising to his feet, demands to know
The stranger's business. You who break the dark
With insolent light, who are you? Where do you go?
But nothing answers his indignant bark.
The moon ignores him, walking on as though
10 Dogs never were. Stiffened to fury now,
His small hairs stand upright, his howls come fast,
And terrible to hear is the bow-wow
That tears the night. Stirred by this bugle-blast,
The farmer's hound grows active; without pause
15 Summons her mastiff and the cur that lies
Three fields away to rally to the cause.
And the next county wakes. And miles beyond
Throats ring themselves and brassy lungs respond
With threats, entreaties, bellowings and cries,
20 Chasing the white intruder down the skies.

Discussion

1. (a) What disturbs the dog? (b) Why does it disturb him? (c) What makes the dog grow furious? (d) How does he demonstrate his anger?

2. (a) What effect does the dog's howling have on other dogs? (b) Find words that suggest the different noises made by the dogs.

3. What images in the poem appeal to your sense of hearing?

4. (a) Chart the rhyme scheme of "Dog at Night." (b) Does it contain any internal rhymes?

Portrait

King Kuka

Discussion

1. (a) Who is the speaker in this poem, and who is the subject of the portrait? **(b)** How does the speaker seem to feel toward his subject? Give evidence for your answer.

2. (a) What can you tell about the background of the subject from the words the portrait speaks (lines 12–20)? **(b)** Do the colors mentioned by the portrait have the same symbolic meaning to you as they have in the poem? Explain.

I penciled in his features.
Ones that make him unique.
Later I would reveal him.
On 300 lb. paper[1]
5 300 pound I can't afford but
If it were the last paper, for him I
would use it.

Snow was almost to my knees walking
down hospital hill to my studio.
10 There I began to paint.

As I started, the portrait spoke to me.
"Paint my eyes brown for the earth from what we were made.
Make my face red for the spilled blood of brothers.
Put yellow on my cheeks to never turn our backs
15 on the Sun.
Blue on shadows for water from
where we came.
Use white for visions we seek.
But paint the background black
20 for mystery in our lives."

"Portrait" by King D. Kuka from *The First Skin Around Me* published by Territorial Press. Copyright © 1976 by King Kuka. Reprinted by permission.
King Kuka (kü′kä)
1. **300 lb. paper,** very thick, expensive paper used for artwork. The poundage refers to the weight of five hundred sheets of the paper.

The Four Directions

Emerson Blackhorse "Barney" Mitchell

A century and eight more years,
   Since Kit Carson rode from four directions,
Deep into the heart of nomadic Navajos,
   Burning, ravishing the Land of Enchantment.[1]

5 Prairie grasses are once more
   Growing as high as the horse's belly.
Cradles of wrapped babies in colors
   Of the rainbow again span the land.

I know my people will stand and rise again.
10   Now it is time.
Pollen of yellow grain,
   Scatter in the four directions.

"The Four Directions" from *The Whispering Wind*, edited by Terry Allen. Copyright © 1972 by the Institute of American Indian Arts. Reprinted by permission of Doubleday & Company, Inc.

1. *Land of Enchantment.* In 1863 Kit Carson led a military campaign against the Navajos, burning their crops and orchards, destroying their herds. The following winter the starving Navajos finally surrendered and were removed from their homeland to a reservation.

Discussion

1. (a) What actions does the first stanza describe? (b) In what sense might Kit Carson have ridden "from four directions"?

2. (a) What things are happening "once more," one hundred and eight years later? (b) What do these actions and images suggest is happening to the land and to the Navajo people?

3. The ritual sprinkling of pollen or grain in the four directions is part of Navajo religious ceremonies and also plays a part in the seeding of newly plowed fields. What else might lines 11–12 imply about the Navajo people themselves?

Emerson Blackhorse Mitchell
1945 •

Born in a Navajo hogan in New Mexico, "Barney" Mitchell was reared by his grandparents after his father's death in service in World War II. His grandparents instilled in him a love of Navajo life and lore.

His first major piece of writing was the story of his childhood and his experiences on the reservation, entitled *Miracle Hill*. This was completed while he was attending the Institute of American Indian Arts.

"God's Eye Shield" by Robin Whitespear

Living While It May

Denise Levertov

The young elm that must be cut
because its roots push at the house wall

taps and scrapes my window
urgently—but when I look round at it

5 remains still. Or if I turn by chance,
it seems its leaves are eyes, or the whole spray
of leaves and twigs a face flattening
its nose against the glass, breathing a cloud,

longing to see clearly my life whose term
10 is not yet known.

Simon Cherpitel/MAGNUM PHOTOS

1. (a) Why must the elm tree be cut down? **(b)** What seems to be the speaker's attitude toward this coming event? **(c)** Is the speaker suggesting that the tree itself knows what is going to happen?

2. When writers suggest that a nonhuman thing has human characteristics (thoughts, feelings, physical qualities), they are using a figure of speech called *personification.* In what ways has the speaker personified, or "humanized," the elm in this poem?

When you learned in an earlier word study the Latin words that certain English words are derived from, you were learning about the *etymology,* or origins, of the words. Etymologies, usually given in brackets at the end of dictionary entries, include information about the language (or languages) the word came from, its original spelling in that language, and, if different from English, its meaning in that language.

The words in the list below are all derived either from Latin, from French, or from earlier forms of English (Old English or Middle English). Divide your paper into columns labeled "Latin," "French," and "Early English." Then, as you check the etymology of each word in your Glossary, write the word in the appropriate column. Be sure you know the meanings of all the words in the list.

entreaty	fold
wretched	ewe
mastiff	rally
projective	cur

Born in England, Denise Levertov came to the United States after marrying an American. Here she changed her style, learned to write in the American language, and discovered "how one's most ordinary experience could be shown in the poem as it was, invested with wonder." Her poems are compact and intense perceptions of people, things, and feelings. She says of poetry: "Like everything living, it is a mystery. . . . "

See **MOOD** Handbook of Literary Terms

Morning Mood

M. Panegoosho

4.

Time, place, and season.

I wake with morning yawning in my mouth,
With laughter, see a teakettle spout steaming.
I wake with hunger in my belly
And I lie still, so beautiful it is, it leaves me dazed,
5 The timelessness of the light.

Grandma cares for me, and our family needs nothing more.
They share each other for pleasure
As mother knows, who learns of happiness
From her own actions
10 They did not even try to be beautiful, only true,
But beauty is here, it is a custom.

This place of unbroken joy,
Giving out its light today—only today—not tomorrow.

Discussion

1. Describe the setting as you imagine it to be.

2. (a) What can you tell of the family relationships and of how the family members feel toward each other? (b) How can beauty be attained when the family "did not even try" for it (line 10)?

3. (a) How would you describe the mood of this poem? (b) Does the speaker seem to feel it is a good thing that this place gives out its light "today—only today—not tomorrow"? How would you explain this line?

Waiting

Joy Kogawa

Discussion

1. What is happening in the poem? Describe the scene.

2. (a) How do the last three lines reflect the first two lines? (b) What is the mood of the poem?

3. To whom or to what does the title "Waiting" apply? Why do you think so?

A very quiet
            very quiet ticking
In the room where the child
Stays by the window
5 Watching
While outside innumerable snow feathers
Touch melt
            touch melt
                        touch melt

Joy Kogawa (kō gä wä)

The clouds pass

Richard Garcia

The clouds pass in a blue sky
Too white to be true
Before winter sets in
The trees are spending all their money

5 I lie in gold
Above a green valley
Gold falls on my chest
I am a rich man.

Discussion

1. At what time of year is the poem set? How can you tell?

2. (a) What is meant by line 4? (b) Why might the speaker say that he is "rich"?

3. What emotions does the speaker seem to be feeling?

Extension • Writing

Many things besides money can make a person feel "rich"—family, good friends, contentment, small but definite successes, etc.

Write a paragraph describing a time when you felt "rich" in one sense or another. Describe the setting and your actions—other people and their actions, too, if they played a part—as well as your feelings about the whole situation. Can you succeed in making anyone who reads your paragraph share your feeling of richness?

Harald Sund

Winter Sun

Joy Harjo

the winternoon sun
heaves its heavy bear body
between two branches
of a stripped elm tree

5 it nestles but for a moment
then moves west
catching bits of fur on limbs
and leaving mica-thin pieces of skin
between branches

10 i have tried to capture
the winter bear[1]
but can touch only
the soft blue shadows
of bear-life in the snow.

"Winter Sun" by Joy Harjo from *The First Skin Around Me* published by Territorial Press. Copyright © 1976 by Joy Harjo. Reprinted by permission.

1. **winter bear.** On rare occasions, a bear will emerge from its den in the middle of winter. The "winter bear" is regarded with particular fear and respect, because its appearance is so unexpected, and its fur, armored with a thick coating of ice, is capable of deflecting arrows and even bullets.

Discussion

1. (a) To what is the midwinter sun compared? **(b)** In what sense might the sun heave "its . . . body / between two branches," nestle "but for a moment," then move west? **(c)** What are the "bits of fur" and "mica-thin pieces of skin" it leaves on limbs and between branches in lines 7–9?

2. (a) What part of the "winter bear" can the speaker capture? Why? **(b)** How would you describe the mood of this poem?

Joy Harjo

After attending the Institute of American Indian Arts in Santa Fe, New Mexico, Joy Harjo studied fine arts at the University of New Mexico. A member of the Creek people, she has published poetry in such magazines as *Best Friends* and *Thunderbird* and in the anthologies *Settling America* and *Passing Through.*

Nora

Gwendolyn Brooks

Discussion

1. What happens in this poem?
2. (a) Contrast Nora's mood with the mood her brother seems to be in. (b) How do Nora and her brother seem to feel toward each other?
3. What do you think is meant by line 8?

Gwendolyn Brooks 1917 •

At the age of thirteen, Gwendolyn Brooks published her first poem in a national children's magazine. She has been writing and receiving praise ever since. She won several awards with her first collection of poems, *A Street in Bronzeville. Annie Allen,* her second collection of poems, won a Pulitzer Prize in 1950.

Brooks lives in Chicago, where she continues to be involved with writing, teaching, and community work. One of her two children is named Nora.

I was not sleeping when Brother said
'Good-bye!' and laughed and teased my head;
And went, like rockets, out of the door,
As he had done most days before.

5 But it was fun to curl between
The white warm sheets, and not be seen,

And stay, a minute more, alone,
Keeping myself for my very own.

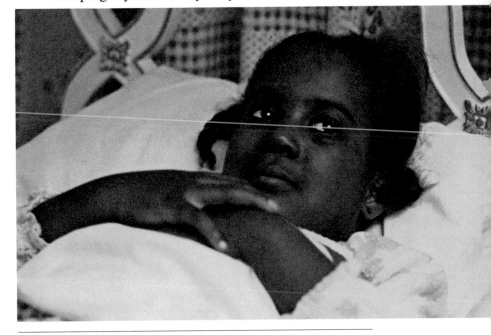

Unit Review Tests 3: Poetry

CONTENT REVIEW

1. Morning is the time setting of several poems in this unit: "How Tuesday Began," "Morning Mood," and "Nora." What feelings about "morning" are expressed or suggested in each poem?

2. "First Sight," "Winter Sun," "The clouds pass," and "Waiting" are set in a particular season of the year. For each of these poems, identify the season and describe how the season influences the mood or feeling of the poem.

3. In your opinion, who among the following does the best job of coping with the circumstances of his or her life: Jamie, the old man in "Meditation on His Ninety-First Year," the black woman in "How Tuesday Began," or the speaker in "Every Good Boy Does Fine"? Explain the reasons for your choice.

4. Which was your favorite of the poems in this unit? Did you base your choice more on the style of language, the emotion or feeling expressed, your feeling of closeness to the speaker, subject, or situation of the poem, or something else? Explain.

Unit 3, Test I
INTERPRETATION: NEW MATERIAL

Read the following poem carefully. Then on a separate sheet of paper, write your answers to the questions that follow on page 180. Do not write in your book.

Sea Lullaby

Elinor Wylie

The old moon is tarnished
With smoke of the flood,
The dead leaves are varnished
With color like blood,

5 A treacherous smiler
With teeth white as milk,
A savage beguiler[1]
In sheathings of silk,

The sea creeps to pillage,[2]
10 She leaps on her prey;
A child of the village
Was murdered today.

She came up to meet him
In a smooth golden cloak,
15 She choked him and beat him
To death, for a joke.

Her bright locks were tangled,
She shouted for joy,
With one hand she strangled
20 A strong little boy.

Now in silence she lingers
Beside him all night
To wash her long fingers
In silvery light.

1. beguiler, a deceitful person.
2. pillage, to rob with violence; loot.

1. The title "Sea Lullaby" suggests that the poem will be about (a) a calm, restful sea; (b) a storm at sea; (c) children playing in the sea; (d) a sea animal.

2. The first line in the poem indicates that the moon is (a) almost full; (b) crescent-shaped; (c) bright; (d) dull.

3. Lines 3 and 4 suggest that the action of the poem takes place in (a) spring; (b) summer; (c) fall; (d) winter.

4. When the writer describes the sea as having "teeth white as milk" (line 6), she is probably referring to the sea's (a) currents; (b) tides; (c) breaking waves; (d) smooth surface.

5. Who is the sea's "prey" (line 10)?

6. The writer's choice of words in the first ten lines of the poem suggests that she wants to create a feeling of (a) anger; (b) alarm; (c) loneliness; (d) bitterness.

7. List at least two words or phrases from the poem that help create the feeling conveyed by the first ten lines.

8. What one word would you yourself use to tell what actually happened to the child in the poem?

9. The sea's "smooth golden cloak" (line 14) probably describes (a) sunlight on the water; (b) sand; (c) seaweed; (d) an oil spill on the water.

10. Lines 19 and 20 mean that (a) killing the boy was an easy job; (b) the boy tried to escape but could not; (c) the killer only had one hand; (d) the boy didn't know what was happening to him.

11. Stanzas 4 and 5 both emphasize the difference between (a) the sea and the sun; (b) the noise of the sea and the silence of the boy; (c) the beauty of the sea and the horror of what it does; (d) the beauty of the sea and the boy's fear of it.

12. After the death of the boy, the sea (a) shouts for joy; (b) becomes quiet; (c) carries his body away; (d) becomes wild and stormy.

13. The poem leaves the reader with the impression that the sea is (a) always angry; (b) usually calm; (c) unchanging; (d) changeable.

14. The writer personifies the sea as a (a) strong little boy; (b) weak little boy; (c) kindly woman; (d) treacherous woman.

15. The imagery in the poem appeals to the senses of (a) touch and hearing; (b) sight and taste; (c) touch, sight, and hearing; (d) sight, taste, and hearing.

16. The rhyme scheme is (a) abcb; (b) aabb; (c) abab; (d) abba.

17. In every line of the poem there are only two stresses. In nearly every line, the syllables stressed are (a) one and four; (b) two and five; (c) two and four; (d) three and five.

18. Considering what happens in the poem, which of the following terms best describes the title? (a) objective; (b) descriptive; (c) rhythmic; (d) ironic.

COMPOSITION

Choose one of the following assignments to write about. Unless you are told otherwise, assume you are writing for your classmates.

1. Both "Portrait" and "Meditation on His Ninety-First Year" are descriptions of people that the poets seem to have great respect for. Write a composition describing some older person that you know and admire. Mention specific qualities of this person that have caused you to respect him or her, and illustrate one or more of these qualities by describing something the person has done.

2. Most of the poems in this unit that create moods do so by describing specific situations that cause the moods. Write a composition re-creating a mood—sorrow, anger, happiness, peacefulness—by describing several specific objects or occurrences that put you into that mood. Make your descriptions as clear and intense as you can; remember that you are trying to communicate your feelings to your audience. (If you wish, you may write this assignment in the form of a poem.)

3. Since the lambs in "First Sight" were born in winter, they had no way of knowing what the weather in any other season would be like. In the same way, people living in certain parts of the world have never experienced weather conditions that you may be familiar with—for example, dust storms, drought, snow, tornadoes, hurricanes. Choose a specific weather event that you yourself have experienced, and try to describe it in such a way that it has meaning for someone who has never encountered it. Use figurative language if you wish, but remember that any details or comparisons that you include must involve things that your reader is familiar with.

4. The descriptions of sports in "Every Good Boy Does Fine," "The Sprinters," and "Sky Diver" are effective because the writers also include information about the setting and about the emotions that the athletes were experiencing. Choose a sport or other activity familiar to you; then describe it in terms of things you hear and see, actions you perform, and emotions you feel while participating in it. Make your description of the activity as vivid as possible by including figurative language wherever it seems appropriate. (If you wish, you may write this assignment in the form of a poem.)

Around a campfire, in a banquet hall,

from a stage; accompanied by music,

or speaking into hushed silence,

storytellers since the beginning of time

have told their tales . . .

And the audience listens . . . and listens . . .

and listens to **THE**

WELL-TOLD TALE

See **FORESHADOWING** Handbook of Literary Terms

*He was alone, and it was seventy-five
degrees below zero. Could he
make it to camp before the cold conquered him?*

To Build a Fire

Jack London

Edward Pieratt/STOCK, BOSTON

Day had broken cold and gray, exceedingly cold and gray, when the man turned aside from the main Yukon trail[1] and climbed the high earth bank, where a dim and little-traveled trail led eastward through the fat spruce timberland. It was a steep bank, and he paused for breath at the top, excusing the act to himself by looking at his watch. It was nine o'clock. There was no sun or hint of sun, though there was not a cloud in the sky. It was a clear day, and yet there seemed an intangible pall over the face of things, a subtle gloom that made the day dark and that was due to the absence of sun. This fact did not worry the man. He was used to the lack of sun. It had been days since he had seen the sun, and he knew that a few more days must pass before that cheerful orb, due south, would just peep above the skyline and dip immediately from view.

The man flung a look back along the way he had come. The Yukon lay a mile wide and hidden under three feet of ice. On top of this ice were as many feet of snow. It was all pure white, rolling in gentle undulations where the ice jams of the freeze-up had formed. North and south, as far as his eye could see, it was unbroken white, save for a dark hairline that curved and twisted from around the spruce-covered island to the south and that curved and twisted away into the north, where it disappeared behind another spruce-covered island. This dark hairline was the trail—the main trail—that led south five hundred miles to the Chilcoot Pass,[2] Dyea,[3] and salt water, and that led

From *Lost Faces* by Jack London. Published by The Macmillan Company (1909). Reprinted by permission of the estate of the author.
1. **Yukon** (ū′kon) **trail,** a trail which runs through the Yukon, a territory in northwestern Canada.
2. **Chilcoot** (chil′kūt) **Pass,** a mountain pass in British Columbia, the territory just south of the Yukon.
3. **Dyea** (di′ā), at the time of the story, a town in western British Columbia, south of Chilcoot Pass.

north seventy miles to Dawson, and still on to the north a thousand miles to Nulato,[4] and finally to St. Michael on the Bering Sea,[5] a thousand miles and half a thousand more.

But all this—the mysterious, far-reaching hairline trail, the absence of sun from the sky, the tremendous cold, and the strangeness and weirdness of it all—made no impression on the man. It was not because he was long used to it. He was a newcomer in the land, a *chechaquo*,[6] and this was his first winter. The trouble with him was that he was without imagination. He was quick and alert in the things of life, but only in the things, not in the significances. Fifty degrees below zero meant eighty-odd degrees of frost. Such a fact impressed him as being cold and uncomfortable, and that was all. It did not lead him to meditate upon his frailty as a creature of temperature, and upon man's frailty in general, able only to live within certain narrow limits of heat and cold; and, from there on, it did not lead him to the conjectural field of immortality and man's place in the universe. Fifty degrees below zero stood for a bite of frost that hurt and that must be guarded against by the use of mittens, ear flaps, warm moccasins, and thick socks. Fifty degrees below zero was to him just precisely fifty degrees below zero. That there should be anything more to it than that was a thought that never entered his head.

As he turned to go on, he spat speculatively. There was a sharp, explosive crackle that startled him. He spat again. And again, in the air, before it could fall to the snow, the spittle crackled. He knew that at fifty below spittle cracked on the snow, but this spittle had crackled in the air. Undoubtedly it was colder than fifty below—how much colder he did not know. But the temperature did not matter. He was bound for the old claim on the left fork of Henderson Creek where the boys were already. They had come over across the divide from the Indian Creek country, while he had come the roundabout way to take a look at the possibilities of getting out logs in the spring from the islands in the Yukon. He would be in to camp by six o'clock; a bit after dark, it was true, but the boys would be there, a fire would be going, and a hot supper would be ready. As for lunch, he pressed his hand against the protruding bundle under his jacket. It was also under his shirt, wrapped up in a handkerchief and lying against the naked skin. It was the only way to keep the biscuits from freezing. He smiled agreeably to himself as he thought of those biscuits, each cut open and sopped in bacon grease, and each enclosing a generous slice of fried bacon.

He plunged in among the big spruce trees. The trail was faint. A foot of snow had fallen since the last sled had passed over, and he was glad he was without a sled, traveling light. In fact, he carried nothing but the lunch wrapped in the handkerchief. He was surprised, however, at the cold. It certainly was cold, he concluded, as he rubbed his numb nose and cheekbones with his mittened hand. He was a warm-whiskered man, but the hair on his face did not protect the high cheekbones and the eager nose that thrust itself aggressively into the frosty air.

At the man's heels trotted a dog, a big native husky, the proper wolf dog, gray-coated and without any visible or temperamental difference from its brother, the wild wolf. The animal was depressed by the tremendous cold. It knew that it was no time

---

4. *Dawson . . . Nulato* (nü lä′tō). Dawson is a city in the western part of the Yukon. Nulato is a city in western Alaska.
5. *St. Michael on the Bering Sea,* a port city on the western coast of Alaska.
6. *chechaquo* (chē chä′kō), a newcomer; greenhorn; tenderfoot.

for traveling. Its instinct told it a truer tale than was told to the man by the man's judgment. In reality, it was not merely colder than fifty below zero; it was colder than sixty below, than seventy below. It was seventy-five below zero. Since the freezing point is thirty-two above zero, it meant that one hundred and seven degrees of frost obtained. The dog did not know anything about thermometers. Possibly in its brain there was no sharp consciousness of a condition of very cold such as was in the man's brain. But the brute had its instinct. It experienced a vague but menacing apprehension that subdued it and made it slink along at the man's heels, and that made it question eagerly every unwonted movement of the man as if expecting him to go into camp or to seek shelter somewhere and build a fire. The dog had learned fire, and it wanted fire, or else to burrow under the snow and cuddle its warmth away from the air.

The frozen moisture of its breathing had settled on its fur in a fine powder of frost, and especially were its jowls, muzzle, and eyelashes whitened by its crystalled breath. The man's red beard and mustache were likewise frosted, but more solidly, the deposit taking the form of ice and increasing with every warm, moist breath he exhaled. Also, the man was chewing tobacco, and the muzzle of ice held his lips so rigidly that he was unable to clear his chin when he expelled the juice. The result was that a crystal beard of the color and solidity of amber was increasing its length on his chin. If he fell down it would shatter itself, like glass, into brittle fragments. But he did not mind the appendage. It was the penalty all tobacco chewers paid in that country, and he had been out before in two cold snaps. They had not been so cold as this, he knew, but by the spirit thermometer at Sixty Mile[7] he knew

they had been registered at fifty below and at fifty-five.

He held on through the level stretch of woods for several miles, crossed a wide flat, and dropped down a bank to the frozen bed of a small stream. This was Henderson Creek, and he knew he was ten miles from the forks. He looked at his watch. It was ten o'clock. He was making four miles an hour, and he calculated that he would arrive at the forks at half-past twelve. He decided to celebrate that event by eating his lunch there.

The dog dropped in again at his heels, with a tail drooping discouragement, as the man swung along the creek bed. The furrow of the old sled trail was plainly visible, but a dozen inches of snow covered the marks of the last runners. In a month no man had come up or down that silent creek. The man held steadily on. He was not much given to thinking, and just then, particularly, he had nothing to think about save that he would eat lunch at the forks and that at six o'clock he would be in camp with the boys. There was nobody to talk to, and, had there been, speech would have been impossible because of the ice muzzle on his mouth. So he continued monotonously to chew tobacco and to increase the length of his amber beard.

Once in a while the thought reiterated itself that it was very cold and that he had never experienced such cold. As he walked along he rubbed his cheekbones and nose with the back of his mittened hand. He did this automatically, now and again changing hands. But, rub as he would, the instant he stopped his cheekbones went numb and the following instant the end of his nose went

---

7. *Sixty Mile,* a village in the western part of the Yukon near the Alaskan border.

numb. He was sure to frost his cheeks; he knew that, and experienced a pang of regret that he had not devised a nose strap of the sort Bud wore in cold snaps. Such a strap passed across the cheeks as well and saved them. But it didn't matter much, after all. What were frosted cheeks? A bit painful, that was all; they were never serious.

Empty as the man's mind was of thoughts, he was keenly observant, and he noticed the changes in the creek, the curves and bends and timber jams, and always he sharply noted where he placed his feet. Once, coming around a bend, he shied abruptly, like a startled horse, curved away from the place where he had been walking, and retreated several paces back along the trail. The creek he knew was frozen clear to the bottom—no creek could contain water in that arctic winter—but he knew also that there were springs that bubbled out from the hillsides and ran along under the snow and on top of the ice of the creek. He knew that the coldest snaps never froze these springs, and he knew likewise their danger. They were traps. They hid pools of water under the snow that might be three inches deep, or three feet. Sometimes a skin of ice half an inch thick covered them, and in turn was covered by the snow. Sometimes there were alternate layers of water and ice skin, so that when one broke through, he kept on breaking through for a while, sometimes wetting himself to the waist.

That was why he had shied in such panic. He had felt the give under his feet and heard the crackle of a snow-hidden ice skin. And to get his feet wet in such a temperature meant trouble and danger. At the very least it meant delay, for he would be forced to stop and build a fire, and, under its protection, to bare his feet while he dried his socks and moccasins. He stood and studied the creek bed and its banks and decided that the flow of water came from the right. He reflected awhile, rubbing his nose and cheeks, then skirted to the left, stepping gingerly and testing the footing for each step. Once clear of the danger, he took a fresh chew of tobacco and swung along at his four-mile gait.

In the course of the next two hours he came upon several similar traps. Usually the snow above the hidden pools had a sunken, candied appearance that advertised the danger. Once again, however, he had a close call, and once, suspecting danger, he compelled the dog to go on in front. The dog did not want to go. It hung back until the man shoved it forward, and then it went quickly across the white, unbroken surface. Suddenly it broke through, floundered to one side, and got away to firmer footing. It had wet its forefeet and legs, and almost immediately the water that clung to it turned to ice. It made quick efforts to lick the ice off its legs, then dropped down in the snow and began to bite out the ice that had formed between the toes. This was a matter of instinct. To permit the ice to remain would mean sore feet. It did not know this. It merely obeyed the mysterious prompting that arose from the deep crypts of its being. But the man knew, having achieved a judgment on the subject, and he removed the mitten from his right hand and helped tear out the ice particles. He did not expose his fingers more than a minute, and was astonished at the swift numbness that smote them. It certainly was cold. He pulled on the mitten hastily, and beat the hand savagely across his chest.

At twelve o'clock the day was at its brightest. Yet the sun was too far south on its winter journey to clear the horizon. The bulge of the earth intervened between it and Henderson Creek, where the man walked

under a clear sky at noon and cast no shadow. At half-past twelve, to the minute, he arrived at the forks of the creek. He was pleased at the speed he had made. If he kept it up, he would certainly be with the boys by six. He unbuttoned his jacket and shirt and drew forth his lunch. The action consumed no more than a quarter of a minute, yet in that brief moment the numbness laid hold of the exposed fingers. He did not put the mitten on, but, instead, struck the fingers a dozen sharp smashes against his leg. Then he sat down on a snow-covered log to eat. The sting that followed upon the striking of his fingers against his leg ceased so quickly that he was startled. He had no chance to take a bite of biscuit. He struck the fingers repeatedly and returned them to the mitten, baring the other hand for the purpose of eating. He tried to take a mouthful but the ice muzzle prevented. He had forgotten to build a fire and thaw out. He chuckled at his foolishness, and as he chuckled he noted the numbness creeping into the exposed fingers. Also, he noted that the stinging which had first come to his toes when he sat down was already passing away. He wondered whether the toes were warm or numb. He moved them inside the moccasins and decided that they were numb.

He pulled the mitten on hurriedly and stood up. He was a bit frightened. He stamped up and down until the stinging returned into the feet. It certainly was cold, was his thought. That man from Sulphur Creek had spoken the truth when telling how cold it sometimes got in the country. And he had laughed at him at the time! That showed one must not be too sure of things. There was no mistake about it, it *was* cold. He strode up and down, stamping his feet and threshing his arms, until reassured by the returning warmth. Then he got out matches and proceeded to make a fire. From the undergrowth, where high water of the previous spring had lodged a supply of seasoned twigs, he got his firewood. Working carefully from a small beginning, he soon had a roaring fire, over which he thawed the ice from his face and in the protection of which he ate his biscuits. For the moment the cold of space was outwitted. The dog took satisfaction in the fire, stretching out close enough for warmth and far enough away to escape being singed.

When the man had finished, he filled his pipe and took his comfortable time over a smoke. Then he pulled on his mittens, settled the ear flaps of his cap firmly about his ears, and took the creek trail up the left fork. The dog was disappointed and yearned back toward the fire. This man did not know cold. Possibly all the generations of his ancestry had been ignorant of cold, of real cold, of cold one hundred and seven degrees below freezing point. But the dog knew; all its ancestry knew, and it had inherited the knowledge. And it knew that it was not good to walk abroad in such fearful cold. It was the time to lie snug in a hole in the snow and wait for a curtain of cloud to be drawn across the face of outer space whence this cold came. On the other hand, there was no keen intimacy between the dog and the man. The one was the toil slave of the other, and the only caresses it had ever received were the caresses of the whip lash and of harsh and menacing throat sounds that threatened the whip lash. So the dog made no effort to communicate its apprehension to the man. It was not concerned in the welfare of the man; it was for its own sake that it yearned back toward the fire. But the man whistled and spoke to it with the sound of whip lashes, and the dog swung in at the man's heels and followed after.

The man took a chew of tobacco and proceeded to start a new amber beard. Also, his moist breath quickly powdered with white his mustache, eyebrows, and lashes. There did not seem to be so many springs on the left fork of the Henderson, and for half an hour the man saw no signs of any. And then it happened. At a place where there were no signs, where the soft, unbroken snow seemed to advertise solidity beneath, the man broke through. It was not deep. He wet himself halfway to the knees before he floundered out to the firm crust.

He was angry and cursed his luck aloud. He had hoped to get into camp with the boys at six o'clock, and this would delay him an hour, for he would have to build a fire and dry out his footgear. This was imperative at that low temperature—he knew that much; and he turned aside to the bank which he climbed. On top, tangled in the underbrush about the trunks of several small spruce trees, was a high-water deposit of dry firewood—sticks and twigs, principally, but also larger portions of seasoned branches and fine, dry, last year's grasses. He threw down several large pieces on top of the snow. This served for a foundation and prevented the young flame from drowning itself in the snow it otherwise would melt. The flame he got by touching a match to a small shred of birch bark that he took from his pocket. This burned even more readily than paper. Placing it on the foundation, he fed the young flame with wisps of dry grass and with the tiniest dry twigs.

He worked slowly and carefully, keenly aware of his danger. Gradually, as the flame grew stronger, he increased the size of the twigs with which he fed it. He squatted in the snow, pulling the twigs out from their entanglement in the brush and feeding directly to the flame. He knew there must be no failure. When it is seventy-five below zero, a man must not fail in his first attempt to build a fire—that is, if his feet are wet. If his feet are dry, and he fails, he can run along the trail for half a mile and restore his circulation. But the circulation of wet and freezing feet cannot be restored by running when it is seventy-five below. No matter how fast he runs, the wet feet will freeze the harder.

All this the man knew. The old-timer on Sulphur Creek had told him about it the previous fall, and now he was appreciating the advice. Already all sensation had gone out of his feet. To build a fire he had been forced to remove his mittens, and the fingers had quickly gone numb. His pace of four miles an hour had kept his heart pumping blood to the surface of his body and to all the extremities. But the instant he stopped, the action of the pump eased down. The cold of space smote the unprotected tip of the planet, and he, being of that unprotected tip, received the full force of the blow. The blood of his body recoiled before it. The blood was alive, like the dog, and like the dog it wanted to hide away and cover itself up from the fearful cold. So long as he walked four miles an hour, he pumped that blood, willy-nilly, to the surface, but now it ebbed away and sank down into the recesses of his body. The extremities were the first to feel its absence. His wet feet froze the faster, and his exposed fingers numbed the faster, though they had not yet begun to freeze. Nose and cheeks were already freezing, while the skin of all his body chilled as it lost its blood.

But he was safe. Toes and nose and cheeks would be only touched by the frost, for the fire was beginning to burn with strength. He was feeding it with twigs the size of his finger. In another minute he would be able to feed it with branches the size of his wrist, and then he could remove his wet footgear, and, while it dried, he could keep his naked feet warm by the fire, rubbing them at first, of course, with snow. The fire was a success. He was safe. He remembered the advice of the old-timer on Sulphur Creek and smiled. The old-timer had been very serious in laying down the law that no man must travel alone in the Klondike[8] after fifty below. Well, here he was; he had had the accident; he was alone; and he had saved himself. Those old-timers were rather womanish, some of them, he thought. All a man had to do was to keep his head, and he was all right. Any man who was a man could travel alone. But it was surprising, the rapidity with which his cheeks and nose were freezing. And he had not thought his fingers could go lifeless in so short a time. Lifeless they were, for he could scarcely make them move together to grip a twig, and they seemed remote from his body and from him. When he touched a twig, he had to look and see whether or not he had hold of it. The wires were pretty well down between him and his finger ends.

All of which counted for little. There was the fire, snapping and crackling and promising life with every dancing flame. He started to untie his moccasins. They were coated with ice; the thick German socks were like sheaths of iron halfway to the knees; and the moccasin strings were like rods of steel all twisted and knotted as by some conflagration. For a moment he tugged with his numb fingers; then, realizing the folly of it, he drew his sheath knife.

But before he could cut the strings, it happened. It was his own fault or, rather, his mistake. He should not have built the fire under the spruce tree. He should have built it in the open. But it had been easier to pull the twigs from the brush and drop them directly on the fire. Now the tree under which he had done this carried a weight of snow on its boughs. No wind had blown for weeks, and each bough was fully freighted. Each time he had pulled a twig he had communicated a slight agitation to the tree—an imperceptible agitation, so far as he was concerned, but an agitation sufficient to bring about the disaster. High up in the tree one bough capsized its load of snow. This fell on the boughs beneath, capsizing them. This process continued, spreading out and involving the whole tree. It grew like an avalanche, and it descended without warning upon the man and the fire, and the fire was blotted out! Where it had burned was a mantle of fresh and disordered snow.

The man was shocked. It was as though he had just heard his own sentence of death. For a moment he sat and stared at the spot where the fire had been. Then he grew very calm. Perhaps the old-timer on Sulphur Creek was right. If he had only had a trail mate he would have been in no danger now. The trail mate could have built the fire. Well, it was up to him to build the fire over again, and this second time there must be no failure. Even if he succeeded, he would most likely lose some toes. His feet must be badly frozen by now, and there would be some time before the second fire was ready.

Such were his thoughts, but he did not sit and think them. He was busy all the time they were passing through his mind. He made a new foundation for a fire, this time in the open, where no treacherous tree could blot it out. Next he gathered dry grasses and tiny twigs from the high-water flotsam. He could not bring his fingers together to pull

---

8. *Klondike* (klon′dīk), a region in the western part of the Yukon territory.

them out, but he was able to gather them by the handful. In this way he got many rotten twigs and bits of green moss that were undesirable, but it was the best he could do. He worked methodically, even collecting an armful of the larger branches to be used later when the fire gathered strength. And all the while the dog sat and watched him, a certain yearning wistfulness in its eyes, for it looked upon him as the fire provider, and the fire was slow in coming.

When all was ready, the man reached in his pocket for a second piece of birch bark. He knew the bark was there, and, though he could not feel it with his fingers, he could hear its crisp rustling as he fumbled for it. Try as he would, he could not clutch hold of it. And all the time, in his consciousness, was the knowledge that each instant his feet were freezing. This thought tended to put him in a panic, but he fought against it and kept calm. He pulled on his mittens with his teeth, and threshed his arms back and forth, beating his hands with all his might against his sides. He did this sitting down, and he stood up to do it; and all the while the dog sat in the snow, its wolf brush of a tail curled around warmly over its forefeet, its sharp wolf ears pricked forward intently as it watched the man. And the man, as he beat and threshed with his arms and hands, felt a great surge of envy as he regarded the creature that was warm and secure in its natural covering.

After a time he was aware of the first faraway signals of sensation in his beaten fingers. The faint tingling grew stronger till it evolved into a stinging ache that was excruciating but which the man hailed with satisfaction. He stripped the mitten from his right hand and fetched forth the birch bark. The exposed fingers were quickly going numb again. Next he brought out his bunch of sulphur matches. But the tremendous cold had already driven the life out of his fingers. In his effort to separate one match from the others, the whole bunch fell in the snow. He tried to pick it out of the snow, but failed. The dead fingers could neither touch nor clutch. He was very careful. He drove the thought of his freezing feet, and nose, and cheeks, out of his mind, devoting his whole soul to the matches. He watched, using the sense of vision in place of that of touch, and when he saw his fingers on each side of the bunch, he closed them—that is, he willed to close them, for the wires were down, and the fingers did not obey. He pulled the mitten on the right hand, and beat it fiercely against his knee. Then, with both mittened hands, he scooped the bunch of matches, along with much snow, into his lap. Yet he was no better off.

After some manipulation he managed to get the bunch between the heels of his mittened hands. In this fashion he carried it to his mouth. The ice crackled and snapped when, by a violent effort, he opened his mouth. He drew the lower jaw in, curled the upper lip out of the way, and scraped the bunch with his upper teeth in order to separate a match. He succeeded in getting one, which he dropped on his lap. He was no better off. He could not pick it up. Then he devised a way. He picked it up in his teeth and scratched it on his leg. Twenty times he scratched before he succeeded in lighting it. As it flamed he held it with his teeth to the birch bark. But the burning brimstone went up his nostrils and into his lungs, causing him to cough spasmodically. The match fell into the snow and went out.

The old-timer on Sulphur Creek was right, he thought in the moment of controlled despair that ensued: after fifty below, a man should travel with a partner. He beat his hands but failed in exciting any sensation. Suddenly he bared both hands, removing the mittens with his teeth. He caught the whole bunch between the heels of his hands. His arm muscles not being frozen enabled him to press the hand heels tightly against the matches. Then he scratched the bunch along his leg. It flared into flame, seventy sulphur matches at once! There was no wind to blow them out. He kept his head to one side to escape the strangling fumes, and held the blazing bunch to the birch bark. As he so held it, he became aware of sensation in his hand. His flesh was burning. He could smell it. Deep down below the surface he could feel it. The sensation developed into pain that grew acute. And still he endured it, holding the flame of the matches clumsily to the bark that would not light readily because his own burning hands were in the way, absorbing most of the flame.

At last, when he could endure no more, he jerked his hands apart. The blazing matches fell sizzling into the snow, but the birch bark was alight. He began laying dry grasses and the tiniest twigs on the flame. He could not pick and choose, for he had to lift the fuel between the heels of his hands. Small pieces of rotten wood and green moss clung to the twigs, and he bit them off as well as he could with his teeth. He cherished the flame carefully and awkwardly. It meant life, and it must not perish. The withdrawal of blood from the surface of his body now made him begin to shiver, and he grew more awkward. A large piece of green moss fell squarely on the little fire. He tried to poke it out with his fingers, but his shivering frame made him poke too far, and he disrupted the nucleus of the little fire, the burning grasses and tiny twigs separating and scattering. He tried to poke them together again, but in spite of the tenseness of the effort, his shivering got away with him, and the twigs were hopelessly scattered. Each twig gushed a puff of smoke and went out. The fire provider had failed. As he looked apathetically about him, his eyes chanced on the dog, sitting across the ruins of the fire from him, in the snow, making restless, hunching movements, slightly lifting one forefoot and then the other, shifting its weight back and forth on them with wistful eagerness.

The sight of the dog put a wild idea into his head. He remembered the tale of the man, caught in a blizzard, who killed a steer and crawled inside the carcass and so was saved. He would kill the dog and bury his hands in the warm body until the numbness went out of them. Then he could build another fire. He spoke to the dog, calling it to him, but in his voice was a strange note of fear that frightened the animal, who had never known the man to speak in such a way before. Something was the matter, and its suspicious nature sensed danger—it knew not what danger, but somewhere, somehow, in its brain arose an apprehension of the man. It flattened its ears down at the sound of the man's voice, and its restless, hunching movements and the liftings and shiftings of its forefeet became more pronounced; but it would not come to the man. He got on his hands and knees and crawled toward the dog. This unusual posture again excited suspicion, and the animal sidled mincingly away.

The man sat up in the snow for a moment and struggled for calmness. Then he pulled on his mittens, by means of his teeth, and got up on his feet. He glanced down at first in order to assure himself that he was really standing up, for the absence of sensation in his feet left him unrelated to the earth. His erect position in itself started to drive the webs of suspicion from the dog's mind, and

John Ebeling

when he spoke peremptorily, with the sound of whip lashes in his voice, the dog rendered its customary allegiance and came to him. As it came within reaching distance, the man lost his control. His arms flashed out to the dog, and he experienced genuine surprise when he discovered that his hands could not clutch, that there was neither bend nor feeling in the fingers. He had forgotten for the moment that they were frozen and that they were freezing more and more. All this happened quickly, and before the animal could get away, he encircled its body with his arms. He sat down in the snow and in this fashion held the dog, while it snarled and whined and struggled.

But it was all he could do, hold its body encircled in his arms and sit there. He realized that he could not kill the dog. There was no way to do it. With his helpless hands he could neither draw nor hold his sheath knife nor throttle the animal. He released it, and it plunged wildly away, with tail between its legs and still snarling. It halted forty feet away and surveyed him curiously, with ears sharply pricked forward.

The man looked down at his hands in order to locate them, and found them hanging on the ends of his arms. It struck him as curious that one should have to use his eyes in order to find out where his hands were. He began threshing his arms back and forth, beating the mittened hands against his sides. He did this for five minutes, violently, and his heart pumped enough blood up to the surface to put a stop to his shivering. But no sensation was aroused in the hands. He had an impression that they hung like weights on the ends of his arms, but when he tried to run the impression down, he could not find it.

A certain fear of death, dull and oppressive, came to him. This fear quickly became poignant as he realized that it was no longer a mere matter of freezing his fingers and toes, or of losing his hands and feet, but that it was a matter of life and death with the chances against him. This threw him into a panic, and he turned and ran up the creek bed along the old, dim trail. The dog joined in behind and kept up with him. He ran blindly, without intention, in fear such as he had never known in his life. Slowly, as he plowed and floundered through the snow, he began to see things again—the banks of the creek, the old timber jams, the leafless aspens, and the sky. The running made him feel better. He did not shiver. Maybe, if he ran on, his feet would thaw out, and, anyway, if he ran far enough, he would reach camp and the boys. Without doubt he would lose some fingers and toes and some of his face, but the boys would take care of him, and save the rest of him when he got there. And at the same time there was another thought in his mind that said he would never get to the camp and the boys, that it was too many miles away, that the freezing had too great a start on him, and that he would soon be stiff and dead. This thought he kept in the background and refused to consider. Sometimes it pushed itself forward and demanded to be heard, but he thrust it back and strove to think of other things.

It struck him as curious that he could run at all on feet so frozen that he could not feel them when they struck the earth and took the weight of his body. He seemed to himself to skim along above the surface and to have no connection with the earth. Somewhere he had once seen a winged Mercury,[9] and he wondered if Mercury felt as he felt when skimming over the earth.

His theory of running until he reached camp and the boys had one flaw in it: he lacked the endurance. Several times he stumbled, and finally he tottered, crumpled up, and fell. When he tried to rise, he failed. He must sit and rest, he decided, and next time he would merely walk and keep on going. As he sat and regained his breath, he noted that he was feeling quite warm and comfortable. He was not shivering, and it even seemed that a warm glow had come to his chest and trunk. And yet, when he touched his nose or cheeks, there was no sensation. Running would not thaw them out. Nor would it thaw out his hands and feet. Then the thought came to him that the frozen portions of his body must be extending. He tried to keep this thought down, to

---

9. Mercury, in Roman mythology, the messenger of the gods. He is usually depicted as having wings on his sandals.

forget it, to think of something else; he was aware of the panicky feeling that it caused, and he was afraid of the panic. But the thought asserted itself and persisted, until it produced a vision of his body totally frozen. This was too much, and he made another wild run along the trail. Once he slowed down to a walk, but the thought of the freezing extending itself made him run again.

And all the time the dog ran with him, at his heels. When he fell down a second time, it curled its tail over its forefeet and sat in front of him, facing him, curiously eager and intent. The warmth and security of the animal angered him, and he cursed it till it flattened down its ears appeasingly. This time the shivering came more quickly upon the man. He was losing in his battle with the frost. It was creeping into his body from all sides. The thought of it drove him on, but he ran no more than a hundred feet when he staggered and pitched headlong. It was his last panic. When he had recovered his breath and control, he sat up and entertained in his mind the conception of meeting death with dignity. However, the conception did not come to him in such terms. His idea of it was that he had been making a fool of himself, running around like a chicken with its head cut off—such was the simile that occurred to him. Well, he was bound to freeze anyway, and he might as well take it decently. With this new-found peace of mind came the first glimmerings of drowsiness. A good idea, he thought, to sleep off to death. It was like taking an anesthetic. Freezing was not so bad as people thought. There were lots worse ways to die.

He pictured the boys finding his body next day. Suddenly he found himself with them, coming along the trail and looking for himself. And, still with them, he came around a turn in the trail and found himself lying in the snow. He did not belong with himself any more, for even then he was out of himself, standing with the boys and looking at himself in the snow. It certainly was cold, was his thought. When he got back to the States he could tell the folks what real cold was. He drifted on from this to a vision of the old-timer on Sulphur Creek. He could see him quite clearly, warm and comfortable, and smoking a pipe.

"You were right, old hoss; you were right," the man mumbled to the old-timer of Sulphur Creek.

Then the man drowsed off into what seemed to him the most comfortable and satisfying sleep he had ever known. The dog sat facing him and waiting. The brief day drew to a close in a long, slow twilight. There were no signs of a fire to be made, and, besides, never in the dog's experience had it known a man to sit like that in the snow and make no fire. As the twilight drew on, its eager yearning for the fire mastered it, and with a great lifting and shifting of forefeet, it whined softly, then flattened its ears down in anticipation of being chidden by the man. But the man remained silent. Later the dog whined loudly. And still later it crept close to the man and caught the scent of death. This made the animal bristle and back away. A little longer it delayed, howling under the stars that leaped and danced and shone brightly in the cold sky. Then it turned and trotted up the trail in the direction of the camp it knew, where were the other food providers and fire providers. □□

Discussion

1. (a) What is the setting in this story? (b) What details in the early part of the story make you aware of the intense cold? (c) Why is the setting important?

2. (a) What advice was given by the old-timer at Sulphur Creek? (b) What was the man's reaction to this advice before he started on his journey?

3. According to medical research, prolonged exposure to cold can have a deadly effect on the mind: one can lose awareness, memory, the ability to think clearly. What evidence is there in the story to support this finding?

4. (a) How do the dog's reactions to the cold differ from those of the man? (b) Why do you think the author includes the dog's reactions?

5. (a) Do you think the ending of this story is appropriate? Explain. (b) At what point in the story were you aware that the author is foreshadowing a tragic ending? (c) Cite passages in the story which foreshadow the ending.

Vocabulary
Context, Pronunciation

Each sentence in the next column contains the pronunciation symbols for a word in the list. For each sentence, (1) write the word the pronunciation symbols stand for (refer to the pronunciation key in your Glossary if you need help fig-

uring out any of the symbols). Then (2) choose the appropriate definition of the word and write its letter after the word. You will not use one of the words on the list.

conjecture	imperceptible
acute	poignant
apathetic	peremptory
imperative	reiterate

1. Let me (re it′ə rāt) what I have already told you: no students are allowed in this lounge. (a) explain; (b) answer; (c) repeat; (d) demand.

2. The movie, a (poi′nyənt) story of two abandoned children, had the audience in tears. (a) somewhat silly; (b) overly long; (c) poorly acted; (d) piercingly sad.

3. Mr. Sheehy is so (ap′ə thet′ ik) about this election that he doesn't even know who the candidates are. (a) deserving of pity; (b) wishing for change; (c) controlling through fear; (d) lacking in interest.

4. Since she hates to drive at night, my (kən jek′chər) is that she won't leave until morning. (a) wild guess; (b) guess based on some evidence; (c) concern; (d) reason.

5. (ə kyüt′) chest pains can sometimes be a sign of a heart attack. (a) intense; (b) narrow; (c) allergic; (d) imaginary.

6. If you don't want your car towed, it is (im per′ə tiv) that you move it immediately. (a) unlucky; (b) fortunate; (c) urgent; (d) avoidable.

7. The (pə remp′tər ē) tone of her statement made it clear that we would get nowhere arguing with her. (a) dictatorial; (b) private; (c) public; (d) shy.

Jack London 1876 • 1916

The financial problems of his family forced Jack London to leave school and go to work at the age of fourteen. After several years of wandering around the country, he returned to San Francisco (where he had been born and raised) and completed high school. Later, London enrolled at the University of California but attended for only a short time.

In 1896, after the gold rush to the Klondike had begun, he went to Alaska. He found no gold, but the experiences of the prospectors and trappers of the region gave him the materials for the stories he was to write. When he returned to San Francisco, he supported himself and his family by working at odd jobs, writing and studying in his spare time. By 1913 he was one of the best-known writers in the country.

Jack London's stories about Alaska during the gold rush are still widely read. Among his best-known books are his novels *Call of the Wild* and *White Fang,* and a collection of shorter pieces, *Sun Dog Trial and Other Stories.*

See **TONE** Handbook of Literary Terms

Bill was to be scalped at daybreak and Sam was to be broiled at the stake. At first, neither took the idea seriously.

The Ransom of Red Chief

O. Henry

It looked like a good thing: but wait till I tell you. We were down South, in Alabama—Bill Driscoll and myself—when this kidnaping idea struck us. It was, as Bill afterward expressed it, "during a moment of temporary mental apparition";[1] but we didn't find that out till later.

There was a town down there, as flat as a flannel-cake, and called Summit, of course. It contained inhabitants of as undeleterious[2] and self-satisfied a class of peasantry as ever clustered around a Maypole.

Bill and me had a joint capital of about six hundred dollars, and we needed just two thousand dollars more to pull off a fraudulent town-lot scheme in western Illinois with. We talked it over on the front steps of the Hotel. Philoprogenitiveness,[3] says we, is strong in semi-rural communities; therefore, and for other reasons, a kidnaping project ought to do better there than in the radius of newspapers that send reporters out in plain clothes to stir up talk about such things. We knew that Summit couldn't get after us with anything stronger than constables and, maybe, some lackadaisical bloodhounds and a diatribe or two in the *Weekly Farmers' Budget*. So, it looked good.

1. *apparition,* Bill means *aberration,* a temporary disorder of the mind.
2. *undeleterious,* harmless.
3. *Philoprogenitiveness,* love of offspring.

We selected for our victim the only child of a prominent citizen named Ebenezer Dorset. The father was respectable and tight, a mortgage fancier and a stern, upright collection-plate passer and forecloser. The kid was a boy of ten, with bas-relief freckles, and hair the color of the cover of the magazine you buy at the newsstand when you want to catch a train. Bill and me figured that Ebenezer would melt down for a ransom of two thousand dollars to a cent. But wait till I tell you.

About two miles from Summit was a little mountain, covered with a dense cedar brake. On the rear elevation of this mountain was a cave. There we stored provisions.

One evening after sundown, we drove in a buggy past old Dorset's house. The kid was in the street, throwing rocks at a kitten on the opposite fence.

"Hey, little boy!" says Bill, "would you like to have a bag of candy and a nice ride?"

The boy catches Bill neatly in the eye with a piece of brick.

"That will cost the old man an extra five hundred dollars," says Bill, climbing over the wheel.

That boy put up a fight like a welterweight cinnamon bear; but, at last, we got him down in the bottom of the buggy and drove away. We took him up to the cave, and I hitched the horse in the cedar brake. After dark I drove the buggy to the little village, three miles away, where we had hired it, and walked back to the mountain.

Bill was pasting court-plaster over the scratches and bruises on his features. There was a fire burning behind the big rock at the entrance of the cave, and the boy was watching a pot of boiling coffee, with two buzzard tail-feathers stuck in his red hair. He points a stick at me when I come up, and says:

"Ha! cursed paleface, do you dare to enter the camp of Red Chief, the terror of the plains?"

"He's all right now," says Bill, rolling up his trousers and examining some bruises on his shins. "We're playing Indian. We're making Buffalo Bill's show look like magic-lantern views of Palestine in the town hall. I'm Old Hank, the Trapper, Red Chief's captive, and I'm to be scalped at daybreak. By Geronimo! that kid can kick hard."

Yes, sir, that boy seemed to be having the time of his life. The fun of camping out in a cave had made him forget that he was a captive himself. He immediately christened me Snake-eye, the Spy, and announced that, when his braves returned from the warpath, I was to be broiled at the stake at the rising of the sun.

Then we had supper; and he filled his mouth full of bacon and bread and gravy, and began to talk. He made a during-dinner speech something like this:

"I like this fine. I never camped out before; but I had a pet 'possum once, and I was nine last birthday. I hate to go to school. Rats ate up sixteen of Jimmy Talbot's aunt's speckled hen's eggs. Are there any real Indians in these woods? I want some more gravy. Does the trees moving make the wind blow? We had five puppies. What makes your nose so red, Hank? My father has lots of money. Are the stars hot? I whipped Ed Walker twice, Saturday. I don't like girls. You dassent catch toads unless with a string. Do oxen make any noise? Why are oranges round? Have you got beds to sleep on in this cave? Amos Murray has got six toes. A parrot can talk, but a monkey or a fish can't. How many does it take to make twelve?"

Every few minutes he would remember that he was a pesky redskin, and pick up his stick rifle and tiptoe to the mouth of the cave to rubber for the scouts of the hated pale-face. Now and then he would let out a war-whoop that made Old Hank the Trapper shiver. That boy had Bill terrorized from the start.

"Red Chief," says I to the kid, "would you like to go home?"

"Aw, what for?" says he. "I don't have any fun at home. I hate to go to school. I like to camp out. You won't take me back home again, Snake-eye, will you?"

"Not right away," says I. "We'll stay here in the cave awhile."

"All right!" says he. "That'll be fine. I never had such fun in all my life."

We went to bed about eleven o'clock. We spread down some wide blankets and quilts and put Red Chief between us. We weren't afraid he'd run away. He kept us awake for three hours, jumping up and reaching for his rifle and screeching: "Hist! pard," in mine and Bill's ears, as the fancied crackle of a twig or the rustle of a leaf revealed to his young imagination the stealthy approach of the outlaw band. At last, I fell into a troubled sleep, and dreamed that I had been kid-naped and chained to a tree by a ferocious pirate with red hair.

Just at daybreak, I was awakened by a series of awful screams from Bill. They weren't yells, or howls, or shouts, or whoops, or yawps, such as you'd expect from a manly set of vocal organs—they were simply indecent, terrifying, humiliating screams, such as women emit when they see ghosts or caterpillars. It's an awful thing to hear a strong, desperate, fat man scream incontinently in a cave at daybreak.

I jumped up to see what the matter was. Red Chief was sitting on Bill's chest, with one hand twined in Bill's hair. In the other he had the sharp case-knife we used for slicing bacon; and he was industriously and realisti-cally trying to take Bill's scalp, according to the sentence that had been pronounced upon him the evening before.

I got the knife away from the kid and made him lie down again. But, from that moment, Bill's spirit was broken. He laid down on his side of the bed, but he never closed an eye again in sleep as long as that boy was with us. I dozed off for a while, but along toward sun-up I remembered that Red Chief had said I was to be burned at the stake at the rising of the sun. I wasn't nervous or afraid; but I sat up and lit my pipe and leaned against a rock.

"What you getting up so soon for, Sam?" asked Bill.

"Me?" says I. "Oh, I got a kind of pain in my shoulder. I thought sitting up would rest it."

"You're a liar!" says Bill. "You're afraid. You was to be burned at sunrise, and you was afraid he'd do it. And he would, too, if he could find a match. Ain't it awful, Sam? Do you think anybody will pay out money to get a little imp like that back home?"

"Sure," said I. "A rowdy kid like that is just the kind that parents dote on. Now, you and the Chief get up and cook breakfast, while I go up on the top of this mountain and reconnoiter."

I went up on the peak of the little moun-tain and ran my eye over the contiguous vicinity. Over towards Summit I expected to see the sturdy yeomanry of the village armed with scythes and pitchforks beating the countryside for the dastardly kidnap-ers. But what I saw was a peaceful land-scape dotted with one man ploughing with a dun mule. Nobody was dragging the creek; no couriers dashed hither and yon, bringing tidings of no news to the distracted parents. There was a sylvan attitude of somnolent sleepiness pervading that section of the external outward surface of Alabama that lay exposed to my view. "Perhaps," says I to myself, "it has not yet been discovered that the wolves have borne away the tender lambkin from the fold. Heaven help the wolves!" says I, and I went down the mountain to breakfast.

When I got to the cave I found Bill backed up against the side of it, breathing hard, and the boy threatening to smash him with a rock half as big as a cocoanut.

"He put a red-hot boiled potato down my back," explained Bill, "and then mashed it with his foot; and I boxed his ears. Have you got a gun about you, Sam?"

I took the rock away from the boy and kind of patched up the argument. "I'll fix you," says the kid to Bill. "No man ever yet struck the Red Chief but he got paid for it. You better beware!"

After breakfast the kid takes a piece of leather with strings wrapped around it out of his pocket and goes outside the cave unwinding it.

"What's he up to now?" says Bill, anxiously. "You don't think he'll run away, do you, Sam?"

"No fear of it," says I. "He don't seem to be much of a home body. But we've got to fix up some plan about the ransom. There don't seem to be much excitement around Summit on account of his disappearance; but maybe they haven't realized yet that he's gone. His folks may think he's spending the night with Aunt Jane or one of the neighbors. Anyhow, he'll be missed today. To-night we must get a message to his father demanding the two thousand dollars for his return."

Just then we heard a kind of war whoop, such as David might have emitted when he knocked out the champion Goliath.[4] It was a sling that Red Chief had pulled out of his pocket, and he was whirling it around his head.

I dodged, and heard a heavy thud and a kind of a sigh from Bill, like a horse gives out when you take his saddle off. A rock the size of an egg had caught Bill just behind his left ear. He loosened himself all over and fell in the fire across the frying pan of hot water for washing the dishes. I dragged him out and poured cold water on his head for half an hour.

By and by, Bill sits up and feels behind his ear and says: "Sam, do you know who my favorite biblical character is?"

"Take it easy," says I. "You'll come to your senses presently."

"King Herod,"[5] says he. "You won't go away and leave me here alone, will you, Sam?"

I went out and caught that boy and shook him until his freckles rattled.

"If you don't behave," says I, "I'll take you straight home. Now, are you going to be good, or not?"

"I was only funning," says he, sullenly. "I didn't mean to hurt Old Hank. But what did he hit me for? I'll behave, Snake-eye, if you won't send me home, and if you'll let me play the Black Scout today."

"I don't know the game," says I. "That's for you and Mr. Bill to decide. He's your playmate for the day. I'm going away for a while, on business. Now, you come in and make friends with him and say you are sorry for hurting him, or home you go, at once."

I made him and Bill shake hands, and then I took Bill aside and told him I was going to Poplar Grove, a little village three miles from the cave, and find out what I

---

4. *Goliath,* in the Bible, a Philistine giant whom David killed with a stone from a sling.
5. *King Herod,* King of Judea, a tyrant who at the time of Jesus Christ's birth ordered all the male infants of Bethlehem killed.

could about how the kidnaping had been regarded in Summit. Also, I thought it best to send a peremptory letter to old man Dorset that day, demanding the ransom and dictating how it should be paid.

"You know, Sam," says Bill, "I've stood by you without batting an eye in earthquakes, fire and flood—in poker games, dynamite outrages, police raids, train robberies, and cyclones. I never lost my nerve yet till we kidnaped that two-legged skyrocket of a kid. He's got me going. You won't leave me long with him, will you, Sam?"

"I'll be back some time this afternoon," says I. "You must keep the boy amused and quiet till I return. And now we'll write the letter to old Dorset."

Bill and I got paper and pencil and worked on the letter while Red Chief, with a blanket wrapped around him, strutted up and down, guarding the mouth of the cave. Bill begged me tearfully to make the ransom fifteen hundred dollars instead of two thousand. "I ain't attempting," says he, "to decry the celebrated moral aspect of parental affection, but we're dealing with humans, and it ain't human for anybody to give up two thousand dollars for that forty-pound chunk of freckled wildcat. I'm willing to take a chance at fifteen hundred dollars. You can charge the difference up to me."

So, to relieve Bill, I acceded, and we collaborated a letter that ran this way:

EBENEZER DORSET, ESQ.:

We have your boy concealed in a place far from Summit. It is useless for you or the most skillful detectives to attempt to find him. Absolutely, the only terms on which you can have him restored to you are these: We demand fifteen hundred dollars in large bills for his return; the money to be left at midnight tonight at the same spot and in the same box as your reply—as hereinafter described. If you agree to these terms, send your answer in writing by a solitary messenger tonight at half-past eight o'clock. After crossing Owl Creek on the road to Poplar Grove, there are three large trees about a hundred yards apart, close to the fence of the wheat field on the right-hand side. At the bottom of the fence post, opposite the third tree, will be found a small pasteboard box.

The messenger will place the answer in this box and return immediately to Summit.

If you attempt any treachery or fail to comply with our demand as stated, you will never see your boy again.

If you pay the money as demanded, he will be returned to you safe and well within three hours. These terms are final, and if you do not accede to them no further communication will be attempted.

TWO DESPERATE MEN

I addressed this letter to Dorset, and put it in my pocket. As I was about to start, the kid comes up to me and says:

"Aw, Snake-eye, you said I could play the Black Scout while you was gone."

"Play it, of course," says I. "Mr. Bill will play with you. What kind of a game is it?"

"I'm the Black Scout," says Red Chief, "and I have to ride to the stockade to warn the settlers that the Indians are coming. I'm tired of playing Indian myself. I want to be the Black Scout."

"All right," says I. "It sounds harmless to me. I guess Mr. Bill will help you foil the pesky savages."

"What am I to do?" asks Bill, looking at the kid suspiciously.

"You are the hoss," says Black Scout. "Get down on your hands and knees. How can I ride to the stockade without a hoss?"

"You'd better keep him interested," said I, "till we get the scheme going. Loosen up."

Bill gets down on his all fours, and a look comes in his eye like a rabbit's when you catch it in a trap.

"How far is it to the stockade, kid?" he asks, in a husky manner of voice.

"Ninety miles," says the Black Scout. "And you have to hump yourself to get there on time. Whoa, now!"

The Black Scout jumps on Bill's back and digs his heels in his side.

"For Heaven's sake," says Bill, "hurry back, Sam, as soon as you can. I wish we hadn't made the ransom more than a thousand. Say, you quit kicking me or I'll get up and warm you good."

I walked over to Poplar Grove and sat around the postoffice and store, talking with the chaw-bacons that came in to trade. One whiskerando says that he hears Summit is all upset on account of Elder Ebenezer Dorset's boy having been lost or stolen. That was all I wanted to know. I bought some smoking tobacco, referred casually to the price of black-eyed peas, posted my letter surreptitiously, and came away. The postmaster said the mail-carrier would come by in an hour to take the mail to Summit.

When I got back to the cave Bill and the boy were not to be found. I explored the vicinity of the cave, and risked a yodel or two, but there was no response.

So I lighted my pipe and sat down on a mossy bank to await developments.

In about half an hour I heard the bushes rustle, and Bill wabbled out into the little glade in front of the cave. Behind him was the kid, stepping softly like a scout, with a broad grin on his face. Bill stopped, took off his hat, and wiped his face with a red handkerchief. The kid stopped about eight feet behind him.

"Sam," says Bill, "I suppose you'll think I'm a renegade, but I couldn't help it. I'm a grown person with masculine proclivities and habits of self-defense, but there is a time

when all systems of egotism and predominance fail. The boy is gone. I sent him home. All is off. There was martyrs in old times," goes on Bill, "that suffered death rather than give up the particular graft they enjoyed. None of 'em ever was subjugated to such supernatural tortures as I have been. I tried to be faithful to our articles of depredation; but there came a limit."

"What's the trouble, Bill?" I asks him.

"I was rode," says Bill, "the ninety miles to the stockade, not barring an inch. Then, when the settlers was rescued, I was given oats. Sand ain't a palatable substitute. And then, for an hour I had to try to explain to him why there was nothin' in holes, how a road can run both ways, and what makes the grass green. I tell you, Sam, a human can only stand so much. I takes him by the neck of his clothes and drags him down the mountain. On the way he kicks my legs black and blue from the knees down; and I've got to have two or three bites on my thumb and hand cauterized.

"But he's gone"—continues Bill—"gone home. I showed him the road to Summit and kicked him about eight feet nearer there at one kick. I'm sorry we lose the ransom; but it was either that or Bill Driscoll to the madhouse."

Bill is puffing and blowing, but there is a look of ineffable peace and growing content on his rose-pink features.

"Bill," says I, "there isn't any heart disease in your family, is there?"

"No," says Bill, "nothing chronic except malaria and accidents. Why?"

"Then you might turn around," says I, "and have a look behind you."

Bill turns and sees the boy, and loses his complexion and sits down plump on the ground and begins to pluck aimlessly at grass and little sticks. For an hour I was afraid of his mind. And then I told him that my scheme was to put the whole job through immediately and that we would get the ransom and be off with it by midnight if old Dorset fell in with our proposition. So Bill braced up enough to give the kid a weak sort of a smile and a promise to play the Russian in a Japanese war with him as soon as he felt a little better.

I had a scheme for collecting that ransom without danger of being caught by counterplots that ought to commend itself to professional kidnapers. The tree under which the answer was to be left—and the money later on—was close to the road fence with big, bare fields on all sides. If a gang of constables should be watching for any one to come for the note, they could see him a long way off crossing the fields or in the road. But no, sirree! At half-past eight I was up in that tree as well hidden as a tree toad, waiting for the messenger to arrive.

Exactly on time, a half-grown boy rides up the road on a bicycle, locates the pasteboard box at the foot of the fencepost, slips a folded piece of paper into it, and pedals away again back toward Summit.

I waited an hour and then concluded the thing was square. I slid down the tree, got the note, slipped along the fence till I struck the woods, and was back at the cave in another half an hour. I opened the note, got near the lantern, and read it to Bill. It was written with a pen in a crabbed hand, and the sum and substance of it was this:

Two Desperate Men.

Gentlemen: I received your letter today by post, in regard to the ransom you ask for the return of my son. I think you are a little high in your demands, and I hereby make you a counter-proposition, which I am inclined to believe you will accept. You bring Johnny home and pay me two hundred and fifty dollars in cash, and I agree to take him off your hands. You had better come at night, for the neighbors believe he is lost, and I couldn't be responsible for what they would do to anybody they saw bringing him back. Very respectfully,

Ebenezer Dorset.

"Great Pirates of Penzance," says I; "of all the impudent——"

But I glanced at Bill, and hesitated. He had the most appealing look in his eyes I ever saw on the face of a dumb or a talking brute.

"Sam," says he, "what's two hundred and fifty dollars, after all? We've got the money. One more night of this kid will send me to a bed in Bedlam.[6] Besides being a thorough gentleman, I think Mr. Dorset is a spendthrift for making us such a liberal offer. You ain't going to let the chance go, are you?"

"Tell you the truth, Bill," says I, "this little he ewe lamb has somewhat got on my

---

6. *Bedlam,* popular name for the hospital of St. Mary of Bethlehem, insane asylum in London, England.

nerves too. We'll take him home, pay the ransom, and make our getaway."

We took him home that night. We got him to go by telling him that his father had bought a silver-mounted rifle and a pair of moccasins for him, and we were to hunt bears the next day.

It was just twelve o'clock when we knocked at Ebenezer's front door. Just at the moment when I should have been abstracting the fifteen hundred dollars from the box under the tree, according to the original proposition, Bill was counting out two hundred and fifty dollars into Dorset's hand.

When the kid found out we were going to leave him at home he started up a howl like a calliope and fastened himself as tight as a leech to Bill's leg. His father peeled him away gradually, like a porous plaster.

"How long can you hold him?" asks Bill.

"I'm not as strong as I used to be," says old Dorset, "but I think I can promise you ten minutes."

"Enough," says Bill. "In ten minutes I shall cross the Central, Southern, and Middle Western States, and be legging it trippingly for the Canadian border."

And, as dark as it was, and as fat as Bill was, and as good a runner as I am, he was a good mile and a half out of Summit before I could catch up with him. □□

Discussion

1. Is "Red Chief" someone you would like to have as a friend or neighbor? Why or why not?

2. (a) What circumstances at first make the kidnaping of the Dorset boy attractive to Bill and the narrator? (b) What kind of boy does he appear to be when they first meet him? (c) Is there any indication in the first few pages of the story that the kidnaping may not succeed? If so, where?

3. (a) How old is the boy? (b) In your opinion, does he act his age? List examples from the story which support your opinion. (c) Of the three, Bill, the narrator, and "Red Chief," who seems the cleverest? Why?

4. (a) Near the middle of the story, who seems to be in control? (b) Is this situation ironic in any way? Why or why not?

5. (a) How would you describe the tone of this story? (b) Is this tone what you would expect in a story about a criminal plot? Why or why not?

6. What is unexpected about the outcome of the story?

Vocabulary
Pronunciation, Dictionary

Use your Glossary to answer the following questions. If more than one pronunciation is given for a word, use the first one to answer the question. Be sure you know the meanings of all of the words.

1. Does the accent in *fraudu-lent* fall on the first, second, or third syllable?

2. Does the accent in *proclivity* fall on the second, third, or fourth syllable?

3. Does the first syllable of *stealthy* rhyme with *reel, tell*, or *mail?*

4. Does the accented syllable in *contiguous* rhyme with *don, dig*, or *flu?*

5. Does the **sc** in *scythe* sound like the **sc** in *scare*, in *scent*, or in *conscience?*

6. Does the first syllable of *bas-relief* rhyme with *ha, lace*, or *glass?*

7. Does the syllable in *reconnoiter* that has a primary accent rhyme with *deck, boy*, or *her?*

8. Does the syllable in *collaborate* that has a primary accent rhyme with *babe, tab, bat*, or *mate?*

Certainly this story didn't happen, couldn't happen, wouldn't happen. But what if . . . ?

The Story Machine

Ron Arias

That summer they discovered him by the river, playing his tape recorder to the weeds and dry rocks along the lower bank. His mouth was like Henry's mother's mouth, turned down at the ends. His thick eyebrows, hair flaring out at the edges, looked like Tina's father's eyebrows. The man's wobbly saucer ears were those of Carmela's uncle's ears. And he had the smooth, muscled arms of Raúl's stepfather.

The children stepped closer to stare at this man with his tape recorder and his green dog.

They hardly noticed the dog, which besides its color was scrawny and had sunken, lazy eyes. Henry Mendoza, oldest of the four children, asked the man what he was doing with the machine.

"Playing stories. . . . Listen."

The children sat down and waited.

"How come it stopped?" Henry asked.

The man glanced at the top of the river bank. "It's better if we go over to the middle of the river."

Tina shook her head. "My mom says I can't go in the river."

"It's dry," the tape recorder announced. "Nothing will happen to you."

"There's still some quicksand," Carmela said, ignoring the machine. "Last year a boy died in the quicksand."

"Nothing will happen," the machine said in a louder voice. "I promise."

"Why is he green?" Raúl asked, pointing.

"Is that you talking in the machine?" Henry followed.

"How do you do it?" Tina asked, wrinkling her nose.

"No more questions until we move," the man said, and he rose like a tired bedspring, lifted the machine by the handle and went off toward the dry river bed. The dog scratched its ribs and waited for the children to follow.

"All right," the man said after they had gathered on a sandbar, "who wants to hear the first story?"

Four hands were up.

"Who was first?"

"Me!" they all yelled.

"Let's start with the littlest first. What's your name, *muchachito*?"[1]

"Raúl."

"Okay, Raúl. This is for you."

The machine spoke. It was Raúl's voice.

Tina's father is mad. She forgot to empty the wastebasket and he punished her. She has to stand in the corner of the kitchen for a long time. Now she sees an ant crawling near the dirty dishes and she asks the ant to take her place so she can play in the sink. The ant says okay, and Tina gets down like an ant and starts to play. It's a lot of fun because she can slide down the knife with the butter,

---

1. *muchachito* (mü chä chē′tō), little boy.

she can jump in the cranberry sauce, she can do somersaults in the spaghetti and she can sail in a tortilla on the dishwater.

Everyone looked at Raúl, who was silent for a moment. Then he smiled, feeling a little proud. "Now it's Carmela's turn!" he said excitedly.

Carmela blushed, and her skin was like an apricot's ripe, red side.

The man never touched the machine; the reels of magnetic tape kept turning round and round. When the machine began to speak with Carmela's voice, which was very deep for a girl, the dog raised its ears and once flicked its tail.

Henry wants to be a frog and hop around the house. But he doesn't know how to be a frog. His mother is always sad and he wants to make her laugh. Finally he meets a big frog, a giant frog with green bumpy skin. Can I borrow your skin? Henry asks, and the frog says, here, but don't take too long, it's all I've got. When Henry goes up to his mother, at first she thinks he's a frog. Then she sees his socks are inside out, and she starts to laugh.

The children laughed too, and even more when the man's green dog began to hop over the sandbar making sounds like a frog.

Then it was Tina's turn, and the machine spoke with her small, squeaky voice. *"Raúl asked his stepfather if he would like to have a real son, not just a stepson. But his father wouldn't answer; right away they went to see the monkeys at the zoo. For a long time Raúl watched the father monkeys share each other's baby monkeys. I get it, Raúl said, you think I'm a monkey. And his father tickled him on his throat and made funny noises the way monkeys sometimes do.*

After an easy yawn, the dog put its head in Carmela's lap and completely relaxed under the soft strokes along its back.

It was Henry's turn.

Carmela's Tío[2] Fausto is always bringing home bums and winos. One time he brought a lady who looked like she was lost. She also looked very poor because she had holes in her sweater. Fausto gave her food, then drove her to where she lived under the bridge. Everyone knew she was bad, and Fausto even let her steal the clock that was on the television. Later on he said he was glad she didn't take the TV too.

"I have to go now," the man said, switching off the machine. "I'll see you tomorrow."

Carmela petted the dog's green hair once more, then it trotted after the man who climbed up the concrete slope and disappeared over the top.

"That was neat," Henry said, breaking the silence.

The others nodded, slowly like grown-ups, then ran across the sand, over the gravel and back to their homes.

The stories were not kept secret. The four children told everyone about the man and his machine. Their parents smiled or asked silly questions or said something about not speaking to strangers. No one really worried. They were just kid stories.

But the stories came true. The next day Tina's father punished her and she played on the dirty dishes.

And Henry forgot to take off his socks, and his mother laughed.

And because it was Saturday, Raúl went to the zoo with his father, heading straight for the monkey cages.

Even Carmela's story about her uncle and the lady came true. Only she didn't take the clock; instead, it was a bar of Dial soap and an old bottle of her aunt's perfume.

Every afternoon the children went to the river. The man seemed to like it there, but he would always leave in a hurry as soon as the machine finished its stories. The only thing he told them was never to follow him and his dog. And they never did, mostly because they didn't want him to get mad and maybe go away for good.

Even though the stories came true, the older people still weren't too curious about the stranger. After all, they were harmless stories, something that made their children happy.

But one day Carmela's voice spoke from the machine and said that Henry's older sister had died in a car accident. Henry felt like crying when he heard the words.

When the children went home, as usual they repeated their stories. Henry choked when he came to the end of his, and soon the

2. **Tío** (tē′ō), uncle.

prediction spread throughout the neighborhood and his older sister was locked in her room.

The parents were furious. Tina's father got his neighbors to follow him like a posse behind the sheriff. They were going to find the stranger, and who knew what they would do to him? The four children tagged behind, hoping their friend would not be found.

After a long search, the posse discovered the stranger and fell on him like a flock of crows. He had been sitting with his machine and green dog, quietly chewing a carrot among the tumbleweeds under the freeway bridge. Before they could reach him, he turned to the crowd and hesitated, as if waiting for the children to catch up and go with him. Then he jerked to his feet and sprinted away with his dog. He seemed to fly, barely touching the ground, over the far bank, quickly losing himself among the freightyard trains.

Henry's mother found the machine. She raised it high in the air and flung it hard on the concrete slope. Then she tore the plastic tape into little crinkled pieces.

That night hardly anyone slept, thinking that Henry's sister would die, somehow killed in her car. But the next day came and went, and nothing happened to her. She even slipped out the window of her room so she could see her boyfriend in the park.

Since the story never came true, all the parents were relieved. And the children were almost glad they would never see the man with the green dog again. ☐☐

Discussion

1. (a) What would you want to know about the immediate future if you had a similar tape recorder? (b) What would you not want to know?

2. Describe the following in terms of their fantastic, or magical, qualities: (a) the man; (b) the man's dog; (c) the tape recorder.

3. In what ways does the man resemble the children's relatives?

4. Reread the four stories told by the story machine. (a) What does the first one reveal about Tina's family life? (b) How is Henry's mother characterized? (c) What does the third story tell you about Raúl's feelings about his stepfather? (d) How is Carmela's uncle characterized in the last story?

5. (a) Why do the parents get angry at the man and his machine? (b) What actions do they take?

6. Do you think either the parents or the children will regret that the man and his story machine are gone forever? Explain.

Extension • Writing

1. In twenty-five words or less, write an advertisement for the tape recorder described in the story. What features would you stress? At whom would you direct the ad?

2. You are the police chief in the community where this story occurs. Write a one-paragraph report for neighboring police officials, warning them to be on the look-out for the man and his dog. What facts would you include in your report? Where would you recommend that the police concentrate their search?

Ron Arias 1941 •

A graduate of the University of California at Los Angeles with a degree in Spanish and journalism, Ronald Arias served with the Peace Corps in Peru. He has also worked on newspapers in Argentina and Venezuela. His work as a free-lance writer is published widely.

The Story-Teller

Mark Van Doren

Discussion

1. What seems to be the speaker's reaction to the story-teller?

2. How does the story-teller affect the listener's world?

3. In the last stanza what might "the worm in the world's brain" refer to?

He talked, and as he talked
Wallpaper came alive;
Suddenly ghosts walked,
And four doors were five;

5 Calendars ran backward,
And maps had mouths;
Ships went tackward
In a great drowse;

Trains climbed trees,
10 And soon dripped down
Like honey of bees
On the cold brick town.

He had wakened a worm
In the world's brain,
15 And nothing stood firm
Until day again.

Reprinted with the permission of Farrar, Straus & Giroux, Inc. and Mrs. Mark Van Doren from *Collected Poems* by Mark Van Doren, Copyright © 1963 by Mark Van Doren.

*What is it about the old man's eye
that makes the narrator's blood run cold?*

The Tell-Tale Heart

Edgar Allan Poe

True!—nervous—very, very dreadfully nervous I had been and am; but why *will* you say that I am mad? The disease had sharpened my senses—not destroyed—not dulled them. Above all was the sense of hearing acute. I heard all things in the heavens and in the earth. I heard many things in hell. How, then, am I mad? Hearken! and observe how healthily—how calmly I can tell you the whole story.

It is impossible to say how first the idea entered my brain; but once conceived, it haunted me day and night. Object there was none. Passion there was none. I loved the old man. He had never wronged me. He had never given me insult. For his gold I had no desire. I think it was his eye! Yes, it was this! One of his eyes resembled that of a vulture—a pale blue eye, with a film over it. Whenever it fell upon me, my blood ran cold; and so by degrees—very gradually—I made up my mind to take the life of the old man, and thus rid myself of the eye forever.

Now this is the point. You fancy me mad. Madmen know nothing. But you should have seen *me.* You should have seen how wisely I proceeded—with what caution—with what foresight—with what dissimulation I went to work! I was never kinder to the old man than during the whole week before I killed him. And every night, about midnight, I turned the latch of his door and opened it—oh, so gently! And then, when I had made an opening sufficient for my head, I put in a dark lantern,[1] all closed, closed, so that no light shone out, and then I thrust in my head. Oh, you would have laughed to see how cunningly I thrust it in! I moved it slowly—

The Complete Works of Edgar Allan Poe, edited by James A. Harrison (17 vols.). New York: AMS Press, 1902.

1. dark lantern, a lantern whose light can be hidden by a cover over the opening.

very, very slowly, so that I might not disturb the old man's sleep. It took me an hour to place my whole head within the opening so far that I could see him as he lay upon his bed. Ha!—would a madman have been so wise as this? And then, when my head was well in the room, I undid the lantern cautiously—oh, so cautiously—cautiously (for the hinges creaked)—I undid it just so much that a single thin ray fell upon the vulture eye. And this I did for seven long nights—every night just at midnight—but I found the eye always closed; and so it was impossible to do the work; for it was not the old man who vexed me, but his Evil Eye. And every morning, when the day broke, I went boldly into the chamber, and spoke courageously to him, calling him by name in a hearty tone, and inquiring how he had passed the night. So you see he would have been a very profound old man, indeed, to suspect that every night, just at twelve, I looked in upon him while he slept.

Upon the eighth night I was more than usually cautious in opening the door. A watch's minute hand moves more quickly than did mine. Never before that night had I *felt* the extent of my own powers—of my sagacity. I could scarcely contain my feelings of triumph. To think that there I was, opening the door, little by little, and he not even to dream of my secret deeds or thoughts. I fairly chuckled at the idea; and perhaps he heard me; for he moved on the bed suddenly, as if startled. Now you may think that I drew back—but no. His room was as black as pitch with the thick darkness (for the shutters were close fastened, through fear of robbers), and so I knew that he could not see the opening of the door, and I kept pushing it on steadily, steadily.

I had my head in, and was about to open the lantern, when my thumb slipped upon the tin fastening, and the old man sprang up in the bed, crying out—"Who's there?"

I kept quite still and said nothing. For a whole hour I did not move a muscle, and in the meantime I did not hear him lie down. He was still sitting up in the bed listening—just as I have done, night after night, hearkening to the death watches[2] in the wall.

Presently I heard a slight groan, and I knew it was the groan of mortal terror. It was not a groan of pain or of grief—oh, no!—it was the low stifled sound that arises from the bottom of the soul when overcharged with awe. I knew the sound well. Many a night, just at midnight, when all the world slept, it has welled up from my own bosom, deepening, with its dreadful echo, the terrors that distracted me. I say I knew it well. I knew what the old man felt, and pitied him, although I chuckled at heart. I knew that he had been lying awake ever since the first slight noise, when he had turned in the bed. His fears had been ever since growing upon him. He had been trying to fancy them causeless, but could not. He had been saying to himself: "It is nothing but the wind in the chimney—it is only a mouse crossing the floor," or "It is merely a cricket which has made a single chirp." Yes, he had been trying to comfort himself with these suppositions; but he had found all in vain. *All in vain;* because Death, in approaching him, had stalked with his black shadow before him, and enveloped the victim. And it was the mournful influence of the unperceived shadow that caused him to feel—although he neither saw nor heard—to *feel* the presence of my head within the room.

2. *death watches,* small beetles that live in wood and make a ticking sound.

When I had waited a long time, very patiently, without hearing him lie down, I resolved to open a little—a very, very little crevice in the lantern. So I opened it—you cannot imagine how stealthily, stealthily—until, at length, a single dim ray, like the thread of the spider, shot from out the crevice and full upon the vulture eye.

It was open—wide, wide open—and I grew furious as I gazed upon it. I saw it with perfect distinctness—all a dull blue, with a hideous veil over it that chilled the very marrow in my bones; but I could see nothing else of the old man's face or person, for I had directed the ray as if by instinct, precisely upon the spot.

And now have I not told you that what you mistake for madness is but over-acuteness of the senses?—now, I say, there came to my ears a low, dull, quick sound, such as a watch makes when enveloped in cotton. I knew *that* sound well too. It was the beating of the old man's heart. It increased my fury, as the beating of a drum stimulates the soldier into courage.

But even yet I refrained and kept still. I scarcely breathed. I held the lantern motionless. I tried how steadily I could maintain the ray upon the eye. Meantime the hellish tattoo of the heart increased. It grew quicker and quicker, and louder and louder every instant. The old man's terror *must* have been extreme! It grew louder, I say, louder every moment!—do you mark me well? I have told you that I am nervous: so I am. And now at the dead hour of the night, amid the dreadful silence of that old house, so strange a noise as this excited me to uncontrollable terror. Yet, for some minutes longer I refrained and stood still. But the beating grew louder, louder! I thought the heart must burst. And now a new anxiety seized me—the sound

would be heard by a neighbor! The old man's hour had come! With a loud yell, I threw open the lantern and leaped into the room. He shrieked once—once only. In an instant I dragged him to the floor, and pulled the heavy bed over him. I then smiled gaily, to find the deed so far done. But, for many minutes, the heart beat on with a muffled sound. This, however, did not vex me; it would not be heard through the wall. At length it ceased. The old man was dead. I removed the bed and examined the corpse. Yes, he was stone, stone dead. I placed my hand upon the heart and held it there many minutes. There was no pulsation. He was stone dead. His eye would trouble me no more.

If still you think me mad, you will think so no longer when I describe the wise precautions I took for the concealment of the body. The night waned, and I worked hastily, but in silence. First of all I dismembered the corpse. I cut off the head and the arms and the legs.

I then took up three planks from the flooring of the chamber, and deposited all between the scantlings. I then replaced the boards so cleverly, so cunningly, that no human eye—not even *his*—could have detected anything wrong. There was nothing to wash out—no stain of any kind—no bloodspot whatever. I had been too wary for that. A tub had caught all—ha! ha!

When I had made an end of these labors, it was four o'clock—still dark as midnight. As the bell sounded the hour, there came a knocking at the street door. I went down to open it with a light heart—for what had I *now* to fear? There entered three men, who introduced themselves, with perfect suavity, as officers of the police. A shriek had been heard by a neighbor during the night; suspicion of foul play had been aroused; informa-tion had been lodged at the police office, and they (the officers) had been deputed to search the premises.

I smiled—for *what* had I to fear? I bade the gentlemen welcome. The shriek, I said, was my own in a dream. The old man, I mentioned, was absent in the country. I took my visitors all over the house. I bade them search—search *well*. I led them, at length, to *his* chamber. I showed them his treasures, secure, undisturbed. In the enthusiasm of my confidence, I brought chairs into the room, and desired them *here* to rest from their fatigues, while I myself, in the wild audacity of my perfect triumph, placed my own seat upon the very spot beneath which reposed the corpse of the victim.

The officers were satisfied. My *manner* had convinced them. I was singularly at ease. They sat, and while I answered cheerily, they chatted of familiar things. But, ere long, I felt myself getting pale and wished them gone. My head ached, and I fancied a ringing in my ears: but still they sat and still chatted. The ringing became more distinct; it continued and became more distinct; I talked more freely to get rid of the feeling; but it continued and gained definiteness—until, at length, I found that the noise was *not* within my ears.

No doubt I now grew *very* pale—but I talked more fluently, and with a heightened voice. Yet the sound increased—and what could I do? It was *a low, dull, quick sound—much such a sound as a watch makes when enveloped in cotton.* I gasped for breath—and yet the officers heard it not. I talked more quickly—more vehemently; but the noise steadily increased. I arose and argued about trifles, in a high key and with violent gesticulations, but the noise steadily increased. Why *would* they not be gone? I paced the floor to and fro with heavy strides, as if excited to fury by the observation of the men—but the noise steadily increased. Oh, what *could* I do? I foamed—I raved—I swore! I swung the chair upon which I had been sitting, and grated it upon the boards, but the noise arose over all and continually increased. It grew louder—louder—*louder!* And still the men chatted pleasantly, and smiled. Was it possible they heard not? No, no! They heard!—they suspected!—they *knew!*—they were making a mockery of my horror!—this I thought, and this I think. But anything was better than this agony! Anything was more tolerable than this derision! I could bear those hypocritical smiles no longer! I felt that I must scream or die!—and now—again!—hark! louder! louder! louder! *louder!*——

"Villains!" I shrieked, "dissemble no more! I admit the deed!—tear up the planks!—here, here!—it is the beating of his hideous heart!" □□

Discussion

1. (a) Why does the narrator want to kill the old man? (b) How does he go about carrying out his plans? (c) Why do his plans go wrong?

2. (a) What is the setting for the events of this story? (b) Why is this setting important?

3. Throughout the story, the narrator insists that he is not mad. Do you feel he is correct? Cite passages from the selection to justify your answer.

4. Read the biography of Poe on this page. (a) What single emotional effect does Poe create in this story? (b) Pick out phrases and sentences that help create this effect.

5. This story was written over one hundred years ago. Why do you think it is still widely read?

Edgar Allan Poe
1809 • 1849

The life of Edgar Allan Poe was, for the most part, a tragic one. Orphaned at an early age, Poe was taken in by the wealthy Allan family of Virginia. Following his attendance at English schools and instruction by private tutors, Poe attended the University of Virginia for a year. He also attended the military academy at West Point for a short time but was expelled. Increasing friction between Poe and his foster father led to a final break between the two men when Poe was twenty-three.

Forced to make his own living, Poe turned to writing and editing. He achieved success as a poet and literary critic but especially as a short-story writer. Poe believed that a short story should be written so as to produce a single emotional effect within the reader: all events, characters, ideas, and words should be chosen and manipulated solely for the purpose of achieving this effect. Few writers have used this formula more effectively than did Poe himself. Among his most famous short stories are "The Pit and the Pendulum," "The Cask of Amontillado," "The Fall of the House of Usher," and his detective stories "The Gold Bug" and "The Purloined Letter."

See SIMILE Handbook of Literary Terms

The Highwayman

Alfred Noyes

Part One:
The wind was a torrent of darkness among the gusty trees;
The moon was a ghostly galleon tossed upon cloudy seas;
The road was a ribbon of moonlight over the purple moor;
And the highwayman came riding—
5   Riding—riding—
The highwayman came riding, up to the old inn door.

He'd a French cocked hat on his forehead, a bunch of lace at his chin,
A coat of the claret velvet, and breeches of brown doeskin;
They fitted with never a wrinkle; his boots were up to the thigh!
10 And he rode with a jeweled twinkle,
       His pistol butts a-twinkle,
His rapier hilt a-twinkle, under the jeweled sky.

Over the cobbles he clattered and clashed in the dark inn yard;
And he tapped with his whip on the shutters, but all was locked and barred;
15 He whistled a tune to the window, and who should be waiting there
But the landlord's black-eyed daughter,
       Bess, the landlord's daughter,
Plaiting a dark red love knot into her long black hair.

And dark in the dark old inn yard a stable-wicket creaked
20 Where Tim the ostler listened; his face was white and peaked;
His eyes were hollows of madness, his hair like moldy hay,
But he loved the landlord's daughter,
       The landlord's red-lipped daughter;
Dumb as a dog he listened, and he heard the robber say—

25 "One kiss, my bonny sweetheart; I'm after a prize tonight;
But I shall be back with the yellow gold before the morning light;
Yet, if they press me sharply, and harry me through the day,
Then look for me by moonlight,
       Watch for me by moonlight,
30 I'll come to thee by moonlight, though hell should bar the way."

He rose upright in the stirrups; he scarce could reach her hand,
But she loosened her hair i' the casement! His face burned like a brand
As the black cascade of perfume came tumbling over his breast;
And he kissed its waves in the moonlight
35   (Oh, sweet black waves in the moonlight!);
Then he tugged at his rein in the moonlight, and galloped away to the West.

Part Two:
He did not come in the dawning; he did not come at noon;
And out o' the tawny sunset, before the rise o' the moon,
When the road was a gypsy's ribbon, looping the purple moor,
40 A redcoat troop came marching—
            Marching—marching—
King George's men came marching, up to the old inn door.

They said no word to the landlord; they drank his ale instead;
But they gagged his daughter and bound her to the foot of her narrow bed;
45 Two of them knelt at her casement, with muskets at their side!
There was death at every window,
            And hell at one dark window,
For Bess could see, through her casement, the road that *he* would ride.

They had tied her up to attention, with many a sniggering jest;
50 They had bound a musket beside her, with the barrel beneath her breast!
"Now keep good watch!" and they kissed her.
She heard the dead man say:
Look for me by moonlight,
            Watch for me by moonlight,
55 *I'll come to thee by moonlight, though hell should bar the way!*

She twisted her hands behind her, but all the knots held good!
She writhed her hands till her fingers were wet with sweat or blood!
They stretched and strained in the darkness, and the hours crawled by like years,
Till, now, on the stroke of midnight,
60   Cold on the stroke of midnight,
The tip of one finger touched it! The trigger at least was hers!

The tip of one finger touched it; she strove no more for the rest!
Up she stood, to attention, with the barrel beneath her breast.
She would not risk their hearing; she would not strive again;
65 For the road lay bare in the moonlight,
            Blank and bare in the moonlight,
And the blood of her veins in the moonlight throbbed to her love's refrain.

Tlot-tlot; tlot-tlot! Had they heard it? The horse-hoofs ringing clear;
Tlot-tlot, tlot-tlot, in the distance! Were they deaf that they did not hear?
70 Down the ribbon of moonlight, over the brow of the hill,
The highwayman came riding—
      Riding—riding—
The redcoats looked to their priming! She stood up, straight and still!

Tlot-tlot, in the frosty silence! *Tlot-tlot,* in the echoing night!
75 Nearer he came and nearer! Her face was like a light!
Her eyes grew wide for a moment; she drew one last deep breath;
Then her finger moved in the moonlight,
      Her musket shattered the moonlight,
Shattered her breast in the moonlight and warned him—with her death.

80 He turned; he spurred to the westward; he did not know who stood
Bowed, with her head o'er the musket, drenched with her own red blood!
Not till the dawn he heard it; and slowly blanched to hear
How Bess, the landlord's daughter,
      The landlord's black-eyed daughter,
85 Had watched for her love in the moonlight, and died in the darkness there.

Back he spurred like a madman, shrieking a curse to the sky,
With the white road smoking behind him, and his rapier brandished high!
Blood-red were his spurs i' the golden noon; wine-red was his velvet coat,
When they shot him down on the highway,
90   Down like a dog on the highway,
And he lay in his blood on the highway, with the bunch of lace at his throat.

And still of a winter's night, they say, when the wind is in the trees,
When the moon is a ghostly galleon tossed upon cloudy seas,
When the road is a ribbon of moonlight over the purple moor,
95 *A highwayman comes riding—*
      Riding—riding—
A highwayman comes riding, up to the old inn door.

Over the cobbles he clatters and clangs in the dark inn yard;
And he taps with his whip on the shutters, but all is locked and barred;
100 *He whistles a tune to the window, and who should be waiting there*
But the landlord's black-eyed daughter,
      Bess, the landlord's daughter,
Plaiting a dark red love knot into her long black hair.

Discussion

1. Poems, too, sometimes have plots and tell stories. What are the major incidents in the plot of "The Highwayman"?

2. (a) How would you describe the mood, or atmosphere, of this poem? (b) What details are particularly important in creating this mood?

3. "The Highwayman" is famous for its driving rhythm, which suggests the sound of hoofbeats. The poem is also a showcase of other literary techniques. (a) For example, what is the effect of alliteration in line 13? What other examples of alliteration can you find? (b) List at least three metaphors to be found in the poem. (c) In the fourth stanza, what similes are used to describe Tim the ostler? Why do you think he is portrayed in this way?

4. Tim, Bess, and the highwayman all take an action because they love someone. (a) What is the result in each case? (b) Would you say that one character's love is greater or better than the others'? Why or why not?

5. Alfred Noyes once commented, "The point of the poem is not that the highwayman was a highwayman, but that the heroine was a heroine." What do you think the author means?

notes and comments

Highwaymen, Footpads, and Rufflers

If you were a wealthy person in eighteenth-century England, a journey of any kind could be an extremely dangerous venture. The streets and roads about London were infested with highwaymen, footpads (highwaymen without horses), and rufflers (today we would call them "muggers"). Highway robbery was an almost daily occurrence. The outlaws grew so bold, according to one source, that they once posted notices on the doors of the rich, warning everyone who ventured out of town to carry at least ten gold coins and a watch—or risk a penalty of death.

During this "golden age of crime" a Prime Minister, the Prince of Wales, and the Lord Mayor of London all had expensive encounters with robbers. Queen Anne once narrowly missed an ambush when her coach was delayed: a waiting band of highwaymen attacked another coach by mistake. A later monarch, George II, was not so fortunate. While walking in Kensington Gardens, he was confronted by a lone highwayman and was forced to give up his money, his watch, and the buckles of his shoes.

In a time when organized police forces were unheard of, the principal means of fighting crime was to offer large rewards for the capture of criminals. An unfortunate side effect of this system was that it made possible the extraordinary double career of Jonathan Wild. On one hand, Wild was a master criminal, plotting thefts, receiving stolen goods. On the other hand, Wild was the most successful "thief-taker" of all, and made an additional profit by returning stolen goods to their owners—for a fee. If a thief objected to Wild's leadership, he was quickly betrayed to the authorities, and Wild pocketed another reward. Like many of the highwaymen he dealt with, Wild eventually finished his career at the end of a rope, betrayed in his own turn.

There are many obvious parallels between the highwaymen of eighteenth-century England and the outlaws of the American West. A further parallel exists in the mysterious process by which brutal and greedy men of both eras have become figures of folklore and legend.

He needed the reward desperately, but was he ready to die for it?

The Inspiration
of
Mr. Budd

Dorothy Sayers

Wanted   Wanted

£500 Reward

The *Evening Messenger,* ever anxious to further the ends of justice, has decided to offer the above reward to any person who shall give information leading to the arrest of the man, William Strickland, alias Bolton, who is wanted by the police in connection with the murder of the late Emma Strickland at 59 Acacia Crescent, Manchester.

DESCRIPTION OF THE WANTED MAN

The following is the official description of William Strickland: Age 43; height 6 ft. 1 or 2; complexion rather dark; hair silver-gray and abundant, may dye same; full gray mustache and beard, may now be clean-shaven; eyes light gray, rather close-set; hawk nose; teeth strong and white, displays them somewhat prominently when laughing, left upper eye-tooth stopped with gold; left thumb-nail disfigured by a recent blow.

- Speaks in rather loud voice; quick, decisive manner. Good address.

- May be dressed in a gray or dark blue lounge suit, with stand-up collar (size 15) and soft felt hat.

- Absconded 5th inst., and may have left, or will endeavor to leave, the country.

Wanted   Wanted

Mr. Budd read the description through carefully once again and sighed. It was in the highest degree unlikely that William Strickland should choose his small and unsuccessful saloon, out of all the barbers' shops in London, for a haircut or a shave, still less for "dyeing same"; even if he was in London, which Mr. Budd saw no reason to suppose.

Three weeks had gone by since the murder, and the odds were a hundred to one that William Strickland had already left a country too eager with its offer of free hospitality. Nevertheless, Mr. Budd committed the description, as well as he could, to memory. It was a chance—just as the Great Crossword Tournament had been a chance, just as the Ninth Rainbow Ballot had been a chance, and the Bunko Poster Ballot, and the Monster Treasure Hunt organized by the *Evening Clarion*. Any headline with money in it could attract Mr. Budd's fascinated eye in these lean days, whether it offered a choice between fifty thousand pounds down and ten pounds a week for life, or merely a modest hundred or so.

It may seem strange, in an age of shingling and bingling,[1] Mr. Budd should look enviously at Complete Lists of Prizewinners. Had not the hairdresser across the way, who only last year had eked out his mean ninepences with the yet meaner profits on cheap cigarettes and comic papers, lately bought out the greengrocer next door, and engaged a staff of exquisitely coiffed assistants to adorn his new "Ladies' Hairdressing Department" with its purple and orange curtains, its two rows of gleaming marble basins, and an apparatus like a Victorian chandelier for permanent waving?

Had he not installed a large electric sign surrounded by a scarlet border that ran round and round perpetually, like a kitten chasing its own tail? Was it not his sandwich-man[2] even now patrolling the pavement with a luminous announcement of Treatment and Prices? And was there not at this moment an endless stream of young ladies hastening into those heavily-perfumed parlors in the desperate hope of somehow getting a shampoo and a wave "squeezed in" before closing-time?

If the reception clerk shook a regretful head, they did not think of crossing the road to Mr. Budd's dimly lighted window. They made an appointment for days ahead and waited patiently, anxiously fingering the bristly growth at the back of the neck and the straggly bits behind the ears that so soon got out of hand.

Day after day Mr. Budd watched them flit in and out of the rival establishment, willing, praying even, in a vague, ill-directed manner, that some of them would come over to him; but they never did.

And yet Mr. Budd knew himself to be the finer artist. He had seen shingles turned out from over the way that he would never have countenanced, let alone charged three shillings and sixpence for. Shingles with an ugly hard line at the nape, shingles which were a slander on the shape of a good head or brutally emphasized the weak points of an ugly one; hurried, conscienceless shingles, botched work, handed over on a crowded afternoon to a girl who had only served a three years' apprenticeship and to whom the final mysteries of "tapering" were a sealed book.

And then there was the "tinting"—his own pet subject, which he had studied *con*

---

1. **shingling and bingling,** methods of cutting women's hair. A shingle is a tapered haircut; a bingle is a somewhat shorter cut.
2. **sandwich man,** a man carrying two advertising boards hung from his shoulders, one in front and one behind.

amore[3]—if only those too-sprightly matrons would come to him! He would gently dissuade them from that dreadful mahogany dye that made them look like metallic robots—he would warn them against that widely advertised preparation which was so incalculable in its effects; he would use the cunning skill which long experience had matured in him—tint them with the infinitely delicate art which conceals itself.

Yet nobody came to Mr. Budd but the navvies[4] and the young loungers and the men who plied their trade beneath the naphtha-flares[5] in Wilton Street.

And why could not Mr. Budd also have burst out into marble and electricity and swum to fortune on the rising tide?

The reason is very distressing, and, as it fortunately has no bearing on the story, shall be told with merciful brevity.

Mr. Budd had a younger brother, Richard, whom he had promised his mother to look after. In happier days Mr. Budd had owned a flourishing business in their native town of Northampton, and Richard had been a bank clerk. Richard had got into bad ways (poor Mr. Budd blamed himself dreadfully for this). There had been a sad affair with a girl, and a horrid series of affairs with bookmakers, and then Richard had tried to mend bad with worse by taking money from the bank. You need to be very much more skillful than Richard to juggle successfully with bank ledgers.

The bank manager was a hard man of the old school: he prosecuted. Mr. Budd paid the bank and the bookmakers, and saw the girl through her trouble while Richard was in prison, and paid for their fares to Australia when he came out, and gave them something to start life on.

But it took all the profits of the hairdress-ing business, and he couldn't face all the people in Northampton any more, who had known him all his life. So he had run to vast London, the refuge of all who shrink from the eyes of their neighbors, and bought this little shop in Pimlico, which had done fairly well, until the new fashion which did so much for other hairdressing businesses killed it for lack of capital.

That is why Mr. Budd's eye was so painfully fascinated by headlines with money in them.

He put the newspaper down, and as he did so, caught sight of his own reflection in the glass and smiled, for he was not without a sense of humor. He did not look quite the man to catch a brutal murderer single-handed. He was well on in the middle forties—a trifle paunchy, with fluffy pale hair, getting a trifle thin on top (partly hereditary, partly worry, that was), five feet six at most, and soft-handed, as a hairdresser must be.

Even razor in hand, he would hardly be a match for William Strickland, height six feet one or two, who had so ferociously battered his old aunt to death, so butcherly hacked her limb from limb, so horribly disposed of her remains in the copper.[6] Shaking his head dubiously, Mr. Budd advanced to the door, to cast a forlorn eye at the busy establishment over the way, and nearly ran into a bulky customer who dived in rather precipitately.

"I beg your pardon, sir," murmured Mr.

---

3. *con amore* (kōn ä mōr′ä), an Italian expression meaning "with love, with tenderness."
4. *navvies* (nav′ēz), unskilled laborers, especially those who work on canals, railways, etc.
5. *naphtha flares,* street lamps fueled by naphtha (naf′thə), a flammable liquid.
6. *copper,* a large kettle used for cooking or for boiling laundry.

Budd, fearful of alienating ninepence; "just stepping out for a breath of fresh air, sir. Shave, sir?"

The large man tore off his overcoat without waiting for Mr. Budd's obsequious hands.

"Are you prepared to die?" he demanded abruptly.

The question chimed in so alarmingly with Mr. Budd's thoughts about murder that for a moment it quite threw him off his professional balance.

"I beg your pardon, sir," he stammered, and in the the same moment decided that the man must be a preacher of some kind. He looked rather like it, with his odd, light eyes, his bush of fiery hair and short, jutting chinbeard. Perhaps he even wanted a subscription. That would be hard, when Mr. Budd had already set him down as ninepence, or, with tip, possibly even a shilling.

"Do you do dyeing?" said the man impatiently.

"Oh!" said Mr. Budd, relieved, "yes, sir, certainly, sir."

A stroke of luck, this. Dyeing meant quite a big sum—his mind soared to seven-and-sixpence.

"Good," said the man, sitting down and allowing Mr. Budd to put an apron about his neck. (He was safely gathered in now—he could hardly dart away down the street with a couple of yards of white cotton flapping from his shoulders.)

"Fact is," said the man, "my young lady doesn't like red hair. She says it's conspicuous. The other young ladies in her firm make jokes about it. So, as she's a good bit younger than I am, you see, I like to oblige her, and I was thinking perhaps it could be changed into something quieter, what? Dark brown, now—that's the color she has a fancy for. What do you say?"

It occurred to Mr. Budd that the young ladies might consider this abrupt change of coat even funnier than the original color, but in the interests of business he agreed that dark brown would be very becoming and a great deal less noticeable than red. Besides, very likely there was no young lady. A woman, he knew, will say frankly that she wants different colored hair for a change, or just to try, or because she fancies it would suit her, but if a man is going to do a silly thing he prefers, if possible, to shuffle the responsibility on to someone else.

"Very well, then," said the customer, "go ahead. And I'm afraid the beard will have to go. My young lady doesn't like beards."

"A great many young ladies don't, sir," said Mr. Budd. "They're not so fashionable nowadays as they used to be. It's very fortunate that you can stand a clean shave very well, sir. You have just the chin for it."

"Do you think so?" said the man, examining himself a little anxiously. "I'm glad to hear it."

"Will you have the mustache off as well, sir?"

"Well, no—no, I think I'll stick to that as long as I'm allowed to, what?" He laughed loudly, and Mr. Budd approvingly noted well-kept teeth and a gold stopping. The customer was obviously ready to spend money on his personal appearance.

In fancy, Mr. Budd saw this well-off and gentlemanly customer advising all his friends to visit "his man"—"wonderful fellow—wonderful—round at the back of Victoria Station—you'd never find it by yourself—only a little place, but he knows what he's about—I'll write it down for you." It was imperative that there should be no fiasco. Hair-dyes were awkward things—there had been a case in the paper lately.

"I see you have been using a tint before, sir," said Mr. Budd with respect. "Could you tell me——?"

"Eh?" said the man. "Oh, yes—well, fact is, as I said, my fiancée's a good bit younger than I am. As I expect you can see I began to go gray early—my father was just the same—all our family—so I had it touched up—streaky bits restored, you see. But she doesn't take to the color, so I thought, if I have to dye it at all, why not a color she does fancy while we're about it, what?"

It is a common jest among the unthinking that hairdressers are garrulous. This is their wisdom. The hairdresser hears many secrets and very many lies. In his discretion he occupies his unruly tongue with the weather and the political situation, lest, restless with inaction, it plunge unbridled into a mad career of inconvenient candor.

Lightly holding forth upon the caprices of the feminine mind, Mr. Budd subjected his customer's locks to the scrutiny of trained eye and fingers. Never—never in the process of Nature could hair of that texture and quality have been red. It was naturally black hair, prematurely turned, as some black hair will turn, to a silvery gray. However that was none of his business. He elicited the information he really needed— the name of the dye formerly used, and noted that he would have to be careful. Some dyes do not mix kindly with other dyes.

Chatting pleasantly, Mr. Budd lathered his customer, removed the offending beard, and executed a vigorous shampoo, preliminary to the dyeing process. As he wielded the roaring drier, he reviewed Wimbledon, the Silk-tax and the Summer Time Bill—at that moment threatened with sudden strangulation—and passed naturally on to the Manchester murder.

"The police seem to have given it up as a bad job," said the man.

"Perhaps the reward will liven things up a bit," said Mr. Budd, the thought being naturally uppermost in his mind.

"Oh, there's a reward, is there? I hadn't seen that."

"It's in tonight's paper, sir. Maybe you'd like to have a look at it."

"Thanks, I should."

Mr. Budd left the drier to blow the fiery bush of hair at its own wild will for a moment, while he fetched the *Evening Messenger*. The stranger read the paragraph carefully and Mr. Budd, watching him in the glass, after the disquieting manner of his craft, saw him suddenly draw back his left hand, which was resting carelessly on the arm of the chair, and thrust it under the apron.

But not before Mr. Budd had seen it. Not before he had taken conscious note of the horny, misshapen thumbnail. Many people had such an ugly mark, Mr. Budd told himself hurriedly—there was his friend, Bert Webber, who had sliced the top of his thumb right off in a motorcycle chain—his nail looked very much like that. Mr. Budd thought and thought.

The man glanced up, and the eyes of his reflection became fixed on Mr. Budd's face with a penetrating scrutiny—a horrid warning that the real eyes were steadfastly interrogating the reflection of Mr. Budd.

"Not but what," said Mr. Budd, "the man is safe out of the country, I reckon. They've put it off too late."

The man laughed in a pleasant, conversational way.

"I reckon they have," he said. Mr. Budd wondered whether many men with smashed left thumbs showed a gold left upper eye-tooth. Probably there were hundreds of people like that going about the country. Likewise with silver-gray hair ("may dye same") and aged about forty-three. Undoubtedly.

Mr. Budd folded up the drier and turned off the gas. Mechanically he took up a comb and drew it through the hair that never, never in the process of Nature had been that fiery red.

There came back to him, with an accuracy which quite unnerved him, the exact number and extent of the brutal wounds inflicted upon the Manchester victim—an elderly lady, rather stout, she had been. Glaring through the door, Mr. Budd noticed that his rival over the way had closed. The streets were full of people. How easy it would be——

"Be as quick as you can, won't you?" said the man, a little impatiently, but pleasantly enough. "It's getting late. I'm afraid it will keep you overtime."

"Not at all, sir," said Mr. Budd. "It's of no consequence—not the least."

No—if he tried to bolt out of the door, his terrible customer would leap upon him, drag him back, throttle his cries, and then with one frightful blow like the one he had smashed in his aunt's skull with——

Yet surely Mr. Budd was in a position of advantage. A decided man would do it. He would be out in the street before the customer could disentangle himself from the chair. Mr. Budd began to edge round towards the door.

"What's the matter?" said the customer.

"Just stepping out to look at the time, sir," said Mr. Budd, meekly pausing. (Yet he might have done it then, if he only had the courage to make the first swift step that would give the game away.)

"It's five-and-twenty past eight," said the man, "by tonight's broadcast. I'll pay extra for the overtime."

"Not on any account," said Mr. Budd. Too late now, he couldn't make another effort. He vividly saw himself tripping on the threshold—falling—the terrible fist lifted to smash him into a pulp. Or, perhaps, under the familiar white apron, the disfigured hand was actually clutching a pistol.

Mr. Budd retreated to the back of the shop, collecting his materials. If only he had been quicker—more like a detective in a book—he would have observed that thumbnail, that tooth, put two and two together, and run out to give the alarm while the man's beard was wet and soapy and his face buried in the towel. Or he could have dabbed lather in his eyes—nobody could possibly commit a murder or even run away down the street with his eyes full of soap.

Even now—Mr. Budd took down a bottle, shook his head and put it back on the shelf—even now, was it really too late? Why could he not take a bold course? He had only to open a razor, go quietly up behind the unsuspecting man and say in a firm, loud, convincing voice: "William Strickland, put up your hands. Your life is at my mercy. Stand up till I take your gun away. Now walk straight out to the nearest policeman." Surely, in his position, that was what Sherlock Holmes would do.

But as Mr. Budd returned with a little trayful of requirements, it was borne in upon him that he was not of the stuff of which great man-hunters are made. For he could not seriously see that attempt "coming off." Because if he held the razor to the man's throat and said: "Put up your hands," the man would probably merely catch him by the wrists and take the razor away. And greatly as Mr. Budd feared his customer unarmed, he felt it would be a perfect crescendo of madness to put a razor in his hands.

Or, supposing he said, "Put up your hands," and the man just said, "I won't." What was he to do next? To cut his throat then and there would be murder, even if Mr. Budd could possibly have brought himself to do such a thing. They could not remain there, fixed in one position, till the boy came to do out the shop in the morning.

Perhaps the policeman would notice the light on and the door unfastened and come in? Then he would say, "I congratulate you, Mr. Budd, on having captured a very dangerous criminal." But supposing the policeman didn't happen to notice—and Mr. Budd would have to stand all the time, and he would get exhausted and his attention would relax, and then——

After all, Mr. Budd wasn't called upon to arrest the man himself. "Information leading to arrest"—those were the words. He would be able to tell them the wanted man had been there, that he would now have dark brown hair and mustache and no beard. He might even shadow him when he left —he might—

It was at this moment that the great Inspiration came to Mr. Budd.

As he fetched a bottle from the glass-fronted case he remembered with odd vividness, an old-fashioned wooden paper-knife that had belonged to his mother. Between sprigs of blue forget-me-not, hand-painted, it bore the inscription "Knowledge Is Power."

A strange freedom and confidence were vouchsafed to Mr. Budd; his mind was alert; he removed the razors with an easy, natural movement, and made nonchalant conversation as he skillfully applied the dark-brown tint.

The streets were less crowded when Mr. Budd let his customer out. He watched the tall figure cross Grosvenor Place and climb on to a 24 bus.

"But that was only his artfulness," said Mr. Budd, as he put on his hat and coat and extinguished the lights carefully, "he'll take another at Victoria, like as not, and be making tracks from Charing Cross or Waterloo."[7]

He closed the shop door, shook it, as was his wont, to make sure that the lock had caught properly, and in his turn made his way, by means of a 24, to the top of Whitehall.

The policeman was a little condescending at first when Mr. Budd demanded to see "somebody very high up," but finding the little barber insist so earnestly that he had news of the Manchester murderer, and that there wasn't any time to lose, he consented to pass him through.

Mr. Budd was interviewed first by an important-looking inspector in uniform, who listened very politely to his story and made him repeat very carefully about the gold tooth and the thumbnail and the hair which had been black before it was gray or red and now dark-brown.

The inspector then touched a bell, and said, "Perkins, I think Sir Andrew would like to see this gentleman at once," and he was taken to another room where sat a very shrewd, genial gentleman in mufti,[8] who heard him with even greater attention, and called in another inspector to listen too, and to take down a very exact description of— yes, surely the undoubted William Strickland as he now appeared.

"But there's one thing more," said Mr. Budd—" and I'm sure to goodness," he added, "I hope, sir, it is the right man, because if it isn't it'll be the ruin of me——"

He crushed his soft hat into an agitated

---

7. *Charing Cross or Waterloo,* major railroad stations in London.
8. *mufti* (muf'tē), ordinary "civilian" clothes. Sir Andrew was not in uniform.

ball as he leaned across the table, breathlessly uttering the story of his great betrayal.

"Tzee—z-z-z—tzee—tzee—z-z—tzee—z-z——"

"Dzoo—dz-dz-dz—dzoo—dz—dzoo—dzoo—dz."

"Tzee—z—z."

The fingers of the wireless operator on the packet[9] *Miranda* bound for Ostend moved swiftly as they jotted down the messages of the buzzing wireless mosquito-swarms.

One of them made him laugh.

"The Old Man'd better have this, I suppose," he said.

The Old Man scratched his head when he read and rang a little bell for the steward. The steward ran down to the little round office where the purser was counting his money and checking it before he locked it away for the night. On receiving the Old Man's message, the purser put the money quickly into the safe, picked up the passenger list and departed aft. There was a short

consultation, and the bell was rung again—this time to summon the head steward.

"Tzee—z-z—tzeez-z-z—tzee—tzee—z—tzee."

All down the Channel, all over the North Sea, up to the Mersey Docks, out into the Atlantic soared the busy mosquito-swarms. In ship after ship the wireless operator sent his message to the captain, the captain sent for the purser, the purser sent for the head steward and the head steward called his staff about him. Huge liners, little packets, destroyers, sumptuous private yachts—every floating thing that carried aerials—every port in England, France, Holland, Germany, Denmark, Norway, every police center that could interpret the mosquito message, heard, between laughter and excitement, the tale of Mr. Budd's betrayal. Two Boy Scouts at Croydon, practicing their Morse with a home-made valve set, decoded it laboriously into an exercise book.

"Cripes," said Jim to George, "what a joke! D'you think they'll get the beggar?"

The *Miranda* docked at Ostend at 7 A.M. A man burst hurriedly into the cabin where the wireless operator was just taking off his headphones.

"Here!" he cried; "this is to go. There's something up and the Old Man's sent over for the police. The Consul's coming on board."

The wireless operator groaned, and switched on his valves.[10]

"Tzee—z—tzee——" a message to the English police.

"Man on board answering to description. Ticket booked name of Watson. Has locked himself in cabin and refuses to come out.

9. *packet,* a boat that carries mail, passengers, and goods regularly on a fixed route.
10. *switched on his valves,* that is, he turned on the transmitter to warm up the vacuum tubes.

Insists on having hairdresser sent out to him. Have communicated Ostend police. Await instructions."

The Old Man with sharp words and authoritative gestures cleared a way through the excited little knot of people gathered about First Class Cabin No. 36. Several passengers had got wind of "something up." Magnificently he herded them away to the gangway with their bags and suitcases. Sternly he bade the stewards and the boy, who stood gaping with his hands full of breakfast dishes, to stand away from the door. Terribly he commanded them to hold their tongues. Four or five sailors stood watchfully at his side. In the restored silence, the passenger in No. 36 could be heard pacing up and down the narrow cabin, moving things, clattering, splashing water.

Presently came steps overhead. Somebody arrived, with a message. The Old Man nodded. Six pairs of Belgian police boots came tip-toeing down the companion. The Old Man glanced at the official paper held out to him and nodded again.

"Ready?"

"Yes."

The Old Man knocked at the door of No. 36.

"Who is it?" cried a harsh, sharp voice.

"The barber is here, sir, that you sent for."

"Ah!" There was relief in the tone. "Send him in alone if you please. I—I have had an accident."

"Yes, sir."

At the sound of the bolt being cautiously withdrawn, the Old Man stepped forward. The door opened a chink, and was slammed to again, but the Old Man's boot was firmly wedged against the jamb. The policemen surged forward. There was a yelp and a shot which smashed harmlessly through the window of the first-class saloon, and the passenger was brought out.

"Strike me pink!" shrieked the boy, "strike me pink if he ain't gone green in the night!"

Green!

Not for nothing had Mr. Budd studied the intricate mutual reactions of chemical dyes. In the pride of his knowledge he had set a mark on his man, to mark him out from the billions of this overpopulated world. Was there a port in all Christendom where a murderer might slip away, with every hair on him green as a parrot—green mustache, green eyebrows, and that thick, springing shock of hair, vivid, flaring midsummer green?

Mr. Budd got his five hundred pounds. The *Evening Messenger* published the full story of his great betrayal. He trembled, fearing this sinister fame. Surely no one would ever come to him again.

On the next morning an enormous blue limousine rolled up to his door, to the immense admiration of Wilton Street. A lady, magnificent in musquash[11] and diamonds, swept into the saloon.

"You are Mr. Budd, aren't you?" she cried. "The great Mr. Budd? Isn't it too wonderful? And now, dear Mr. Budd, you must do me a favor. You must dye my hair green, at once. Now. I want to be able to say I'm the very first to be done by you. I'm the Duchess of Winchester, and that awful Melcaster woman is chasing me down the street—the cat!"

If you want it done, I can give you the number of Mr. Budd's parlors in Bond Street. But I understand it is a terribly expensive process. □□

---

11. *musquash* (mus′kwosh), a coat made of muskrat fur.

Discussion

1. Reread the headnote for this story. If it had said, "He needed the reward desperately, but was he ready to dye for it?" how might it have helped you guess the ending?

2. (a) At what point in the story did you know what Mr. Budd's inspiration would be? **(b)** What details prepared you for the outcome?

3. (a) What is Mr. Budd's financial condition at the beginning of the story? **(b)** Why is he so interested in the newspaper's offer of a reward? **(c)** What is the reward for?

4. Reread the official description of the wanted man. **(a)** Which details are included in Mr. Budd's observations of his new customer? **(b)** Which aspect of the man's appearance obviously does not fit the description? **(c)** Is this difference enough to account for Mr. Budd's lack of suspicion? Why or why not?

5. At one point the narrator states a "hairdresser hears . . . lies." **(a)** Which of the customer's comments does Mr. Budd think *may* be lies? **(b)** Which statement is certainly a lie, according to Mr. Budd? **(c)** What peculiarity finally arouses Mr. Budd's suspicion that the customer might be the wanted man?

6. (a) What is Mr. Budd's opinion of his own courage in this situation? **(b)** Do you think it is an accurate judgment? Why or why not?

7. (a) In what sense is Mr. Budd guilty of "betrayal"? **(b)** How does Mr. Budd feel after he gets the reward? **(c)** What is ironic about the events that follow his "betrayal"?

8. Mr. Budd recalls an old paper-knife that bears the inscription, "Knowledge Is Power." Why might that be an appropriate title for this story?

Vocabulary
Context, Structure

Often when you know the meanings of the various parts of a word (that is, its root word and its affixes), you can figure out the meaning of the entire word. But sometimes you will discover that knowing the meanings of the parts is not enough—that the definition you have come up with for the word doesn't make sense in context. Before reaching for a dictionary, try the following: Think about the root word a little further. What underlying meanings, or connotations, does it suggest to you? Do you know any other words with the same root? What do they mean? After testing the various meanings you have thought about to see if they fit the context, often you will be able to come up with a reasonable definition for the word in question.

Using the process just described, determine the meaning of the italicized words as they are used in the sentences below. Then write the letters of the appropriate definitions on your paper.

1. His nonstop talking about nothing was beginning to *unnerve* me. **(a)** remove the nervous system of; **(b)** make relaxed; **(c)** cause to lose self-control; **(d)** strengthen.

2. Most company managers know that business will suffer if they *alienate* their employees. **(a)** send to other countries; **(b)** speak foreign languages to; **(c)** discuss UFO's with; **(d)** cause to become unfriendly.

3. Considering her usual lack of interest in sports, her *unbridled* enthusiasm at the rodeo was quite surprising. **(a)** not excited; **(b)** not married; **(c)** not held back; **(d)** not having a bridle on her horse.

4. Our opponents' high batting averages caused us some *disquiet* as we practiced for the game. **(a)** anxiety; **(b)** noise; **(c)** calm; **(d)** eagerness.

5. She was not happy that the car thief got away, but she had to admire the *artfulness* of his escape. **(a)** ability to draw; **(b)** cleverness; **(c)** ability to steal works of art; **(d)** quality of being artificial.

4: The Well-Told Tale

CONTENT REVIEW

1. (a) Which of the stories in this unit are basically realistic? (b) What elements or techniques do the authors use in these stories to make them seem true to life?

2. In which of the stories does the author use fantasy?

3. Some of the main characters in this unit face unusual stress. Identify the stress that each of the following characters faces and explain how each reacts to it. (a) the man in "To Build a Fire"; (b) the murderer in "The Tell-Tale Heart"; (c) the man in "The Story Machine"; (d) Mr. Budd.

4. Which of the characters listed above seem most believable to you? Why?

Unit 4, Test I
INTERPRETATION: NEW MATERIAL

Read the following story carefully. Then on a separate sheet of paper, write your answers to the questions that follow it.

Lazy Peter and
His Three-Cornered Hat

adapted by Ricardo E. Alegría

This is the story of Lazy Peter, a shameless rascal of a fellow who went from village to village making mischief.

One day Lazy Peter learned that a fair was being held in a certain village. He knew that a large crowd of country people would be there selling horses, cows, and other farm animals and that a large amount of money would change hands. Peter, as usual, needed money, but it was not his custom to work for it. So he set out for the village, wearing a red three-cornered hat.

The first thing he did was to stop at a stand and leave a big bag of money with the owner, asking him to keep it safely until he returned for it. Peter told the man that when he returned for the bag of money, one corner of his hat would be turned down, and that was how the owner of the stand would know him. The man promised to do this, and Peter thanked him. Then he went to

From *The Three Wishes: A Collection of Puerto Rican Folktales*, copyright © 1969 by Ricardo E. Alegría. Reprinted by permission of Harcourt Brace Jovanovich, Inc.
Ricardo Alegría (ä lā grē′ä)

the drugstore in the village and gave the druggist another bag of money, asking him to keep it until he returned with one corner of his hat turned up. The druggist agreed, and Peter left. He went to the church and asked the priest to keep another bag of money and to return it to him only when he came back with one corner of his hat twisted to the side. The priest said fine, that he would do this.

Having disposed of three bags of money, Peter went to the edge of the village where the farmers were buying and selling horses and cattle. He stood and watched for a while until he decided that one of the farmers must be very rich indeed, for he had sold all of his horses and cows. Moreover, the man seemed to be a miser who was never satisfied but wanted always more and more money. This was Peter's man! He stopped beside him. It was raining; and instead of keeping his hat on to protect his head, he took it off and wrapped it carefully in his cape, as though it were very valuable. It puzzled the farmer to see Peter stand there with the rain falling on his head and his hat wrapped in his cape.

After a while he asked, "Why do you take better care of your hat than of your head?"

Peter saw that the farmer had swallowed the bait, and smiling to himself, he said that the hat was the most valuable thing in all the world and that was why he took care to protect it from the rain. The farmer's curiosity increased at this reply, and he asked Peter what was so valuable about a red three-cornered hat. Peter told him that the hat worked for him; thanks to it, he never had to work for a living because, whenever he put the hat on with one of the corners turned over, people just handed him any money he asked for.

The farmer was amazed and very interested in what Peter said. As money-getting was his greatest ambition, he told Peter that he couldn't believe a word of it until he saw the hat work with his own eyes. Peter assured him that he could do this, for he, Peter, was hungry, and the hat was about to start working since he had no money with which to buy food.

With this, Peter took out his three-cornered hat, turned one corner down, put it on his head, and told the farmer to come along and watch the hat work. Peter took the farmer to the stand. The minute the owner looked up, he handed over the bag of money Peter had left with him. The farmer stood with his mouth open in astonishment. He didn't know what to make of it. But of one thing he was sure—he had to have that hat!

Peter smiled and asked if he was satisfied, and the farmer said yes, he was. Then he asked Peter if he would sell the hat. This was just what Lazy Peter wanted, but he said no, that he was not interested in selling the hat because, with it, he never had to work and he always had money. The farmer said he thought that was unsound reasoning because thieves could easily steal a hat, and wouldn't it be safer to invest in a farm with cattle? So they talked, and Peter pretended to be impressed with the farmer's arguments. Finally he said yes, that he saw the point, and if the farmer would make him a good offer, he would sell the hat. The farmer, who had made up his mind to have the hat at any price, offered a thousand pesos. Peter laughed aloud and said he could make as much as that by just putting his hat on two or three times.

As they continued haggling over the price, the farmer grew more and more determined to have that hat until, finally, he offered all he had realized from the sale of his horses and cows—ten thousand pesos in gold. Peter still pretended not to be interested, but he chuckled to himself, thinking of the trick he was about to play on the farmer. All right, he said, it was a deal. Then the farmer grew cautious and told Peter that, before he handed over the ten thousand pesos, he would like to see the hat work again. Peter said that was fair enough. He put on the hat with one of the corners turned up and went with the farmer to the drugstore. The moment the druggist saw the turned-up corner, he handed over the money Peter had left with him. At this the farmer was convinced and very eager to set the hat to work for himself. He took out a bag containing ten thousand pesos in gold and was about to hand it to Peter when he had a change of heart and thought better of it. He asked Peter please to excuse him, but he had to see the hat work just once more before he could part with his gold. Peter said that that was fair enough, but now he would have to ask the farmer to give him the fine horse he was riding as well as the ten thousand pesos in gold. The farmer's interest in the hat revived, and he said it was a bargain!

Lazy Peter put on his hat again, doubled over one of the corners, and told the farmer that, since he still seemed to have doubts, this time he could watch the hat work in the church. The farmer was delighted with this, his doubts were stilled, and he fairly beamed thinking of all the money he was going to make once that hat was his.

They entered the church. The priest was hearing confession, but when he saw Peter with his hat, he said, "Wait here, my son," and he went to the sacristy and returned with the bag of money Peter had left with him. Peter thanked the priest, then knelt and asked for a blessing before he left. The farmer had seen every-thing and was fully convinced of the hat's magic powers. As soon as they left the church, he gave Peter the ten thousand pesos in gold and told him to take the horse, also. Peter tied the bag of pesos to the saddle, gave the hat to the farmer, begging him to take good care of it, spurred his horse, and galloped out of town.

As soon as he was alone, the farmer burst out laughing at the thought of the trick he had played on Lazy Peter. A hat such as this was priceless! He couldn't wait to try it. He put it on with one corner turned up and entered the butcher shop. The butcher looked at the hat, which was very handsome indeed, but said nothing. The farmer turned around, then walked up and down until the butcher asked him what he wanted. The farmer said he was waiting for the bag of money. The butcher laughed aloud and asked if he was crazy. The farmer thought that there must be something wrong with the way he had folded the hat. He took it off and doubled another corner down. But this had no effect on the butcher. So he decided to try it out some other place. He went to the Mayor of the town.

The Mayor, to be sure, looked at the hat but did nothing. The farmer grew desperate and decided to go to the druggist who had given Peter a bag of money. He entered and stood with the hat on. The druggist looked at him but did nothing.

The farmer became very nervous. He began to suspect that there was something very wrong. He shouted at the druggist, "Stop looking at me and hand over the bag of money!"

The druggist said he owed him nothing, and what bag of money was he talking about, anyway? As the farmer continued to shout about a bag of money and a magic hat, the druggist called the police. When they arrived, he told them that the farmer had gone out of his mind and kept demanding a bag of money. The police questioned the farmer, and he told them about the magic hat he had bought from Lazy Peter. When he heard the story, the druggist explained that Peter had left a bag of money, asking that it be returned when he appeared with a corner of his hat turned up. The owner of the stand and the priest told the same story. And I am telling you the farmer was so angry that he tore the hat to shreds and walked home. □□

1. Peter went to the fair in order to **(a)** see the exhibits of farm products; **(b)** buy a horse; **(c)** complete a business deal with a certain farmer; **(d)** find someone to swindle money from.

2. How many people did Peter give bags of money to?

3. The people that Peter gave money to were supposed to recognize him by **(a)** the fact that he would be carrying his three-cornered hat; **(b)** what he did to a corner of the hat; **(c)** the color of the hat; **(d)** all of the above.

4. Peter was interested in the farmer because the farmer **(a)** had agreed to sell him some horses; **(b)** had tricked him out of money in the past; **(c)** seemed to be a rich and important man; **(d)** seemed to be a rich man who wanted to be richer.

5. Peter attracted the farmer's attention by **(a)** approaching the farmer and introducing himself; **(b)** examining the farmer's horses and cattle; **(c)** taking off his hat when it started to rain; **(d)** bragging about his hat.

6. According to Peter, what did people give him when he put on his hat?

7. When the farmer heard Peter's claims about the hat, he **(a)** was interested but wanted proof; **(b)** pretended he was not interested; **(c)** offered to buy the hat immediately; **(d)** told Peter he was a liar and a cheat.

8. The farmer tried to convince Peter to sell the hat by telling him that **(a)** the hat might not always work; **(b)** they could both use the hat and share the profits; **(c)** someone might steal the hat; **(d)** no one else would offer him so much money for it.

9. Peter finally agreed to accept in trade for the hat **(a)** the farmer's horses and cattle; **(b)** the farmer's horse and ten thousand pesos; **(c)** a large bag of gold; **(d)** half of the farmer's land.

10. After the farmer had the hat, his first reaction was **(a)** curiosity as to why Peter was so stupid; **(b)** concern over whether the hat actually worked; **(c)** pleasure because he had tricked Peter; **(d)** anger because Peter had tricked him.

11. From whom did the farmer learn the real value of the hat? **(a)** Peter; **(b)** the police; **(c)** the Mayor; **(d)** the people to whom Peter had given bags of money.

12. Which of the following statements best describes the story? **(a)** the plot is realistic and the characters are believable individuals; **(b)** the plot is not very realistic and the characters are types; **(c)** the plot is not very realistic but the characters are believable individuals; **(d)** the plot is realistic but the characters are types.

13. Many folktales have a moral, either directly stated or implied. The moral of this story is **(a)** misers should learn to spend money more freely; **(b)** greed can make fools of people who should know better; **(c)** neither a borrower nor a lender be; **(d)** people who live in glass houses shouldn't throw stones.

Unit 4, Test II
COMPOSITION

Choose one of the following assignments to write about. Unless you are told otherwise, assume you are writing for your classmates.

1. Assume that you are "Red Chief." Soon after you return to school, you are asked to write an account of your kidnaping for the school newspaper. In writing your account, you might want to include any or all of the following points: how you were captured by Sam and Bill, what you did while you were with them, what you thought of the two men, how you felt when they took you back home.

2. People with clever ideas or plans often make the mistake of thinking that no one can outsmart them. Choose one of the characters listed below, and explain what the character's idea or plan was and what people and circumstances caused him to be outsmarted.

a. the farmer ("Lazy Peter and His Three-Cornered Hat")

b. the murderer ("The Inspiration of Mr. Budd")

c. Sam ("The Ransom of Red Chief")

3. Imagine that the narrator of "The Tell-Tale Heart" is about to go on trial for murder and that he has pleaded "not guilty by reason of insanity." You, as one of the officers who arrested him, have been asked by the court to provide evidence about the narrator's mental state. Write a short report for the court describing what you noticed about the narrator's actions from the time you entered his house until he confessed the murder.

4. Mr. Budd in "The Inspiration of Mr. Budd" and the man in "To Build a Fire" both tried to work out problems that were confronting them. Compare the two men. Why did one succeed and the other fail? Was it the methods they used, something in their own opinions of themselves, or a combination of both of these? Use evidence from the stories to back up the statements you make.

A kaleidoscope: bits of colored glass tumble

at the end of a tube, reflecting in mirrors

to form brilliant patterns, endlessly changing.

The American Kaleidoscope is as colorful—

as varied—as changing—as the places, events,

and people of our land. **AMERICAN**

KALEIDOSCOPE

It was a special day for Cephas (sē′fəs),
a day for which he had waited
for over ten years.

Upon the Waters

Joanne Greenberg

It was a bright green day. The big trees on the side streets were raining seeds and the wind stirred in its second sleep. A long flatbed truck came rattling down Grant Street and stopped by the new steel, chrome, and glass building. The building's lines were so austere it made Cephas wonder if anyone really worked in it. Then he saw some women going in. Good. He checked his appearance by hitching up to the rearview mirror. He was wearing a clean white shirt and a bow tie, and his thin grey hair had been slicked down with water. When he was sure he was presentable, he got down out of the cab of the truck, dusted himself off and began to walk slowly toward the building. It had been many years—perhaps they had moved. No, there was the sign: BOONE COUNTY DEPARTMENT OF WELFARE. The last time he had been here the building was a temporary shed and the people were lined up outside waiting for the relief trucks to come. That was in 1934, in the winter. His father had been proud of holding out till '34. He stopped and looked at the building again. Some secretaries came out, laughing and talking. They didn't look at him, being used to seeing people who came hesitantly to their offices to acknowledge failure in life. Cephas checked himself again in the big glass door and then went in. There was a large booth with a woman behind it and eight or nine rows of benches facing it. People were sitting quietly, staring at nothing, waiting. To the right there were a series of chutes with numbers over them. Cephas went up to the booth.

"Take a number," the woman said, without looking at him.

"Ma'am?"

"You take a number and wait your turn. We'll call you."

He took one of the plastic number cards.

It said 15. He went back, sat down and waited. "Five," the woman called. A heavy woman got up slowly and went to the booth and then to one of the chutes. Cephas waited. Minutes were born, ripened, aged, and died without issue. "Number six." Around him the springtime asthmatics whistled and gasped. He looked at the cracks in his fingers. "Number seven." An hour went by, another. A number, another. He was afraid to go out and check his truck lest the line speed up and he lose his place. "Number thirteen," the woman called.

So they came to his number at last and he went up to the desk, gave back the plastic card and was directed to his chute. Another woman was there at another desk. She took his name, Cephas Ribble, and his age, sixty-eight. Had he been given aid before? Yes. Had he been on General Assistance, Aid to the Needy Disabled? Tuberculosis?

"It was what they called Relief."

"Yes, but under what category was it?"

"It was for the people that was off their farms or else didn't have nothin' to eat. They called it Goin' On The County. It was back in 19 and 34. We held out till '34."

"I see. Now you are applying for the old age pension?" He said he wasn't.

"Are you married, Mr. Ribble?" She sighed. "Never had the pleasure," he said.

"Are you in emergency status?" He said he wasn't.

"All right, then, take this card and go to room 11, on your left." She pressed a little light or something and he felt the people shifting their weight on the benches behind him. Number sixteen, he expected. He made his way to room 11.

The lady there was nice; he could see it

right off. She told him about the different kinds of what they called Aid, and then she had him sign some forms: permission to inquire into his bank account, acceptance of surplus or donated food, release of medical information, and several others. Then she said sympathetically, "In what way are you disabled?"

He thought about all the ways a man might be disabled and checked each one off. It was a proud moment, a man sixty-eight without one thing in the world to complain of in his health.

"I ain't disabled no way, but I'm pleased you asked me, though. A man don't take time to be grateful for things like his health. If the shoe don't pinch, you don't take notice, do you." He sat back, contented. Then he realized that the sun was getting hotter and what with everything in the truck, he'd better get on. The woman had put down her ball point pen. "Mr. Ribble, if you aren't disabled or without funds, what kind of aid do you want?" A shadow of irritation crossed her face.

"No aid at all," he said. "This is about somethin' different." He tried to hold down his excitement. It was his special day, a day for which he had waited for over a decade, but it was no use bragging and playing the boy, so he said no more. The woman was very annoyed. "Then why didn't you tell the worker at the desk?"

"She didn't give me no chance, ma'am, an' neither did that other lady. I bet you don't have many repair men comin' in here to fix things—not above once, anyway."

"Well, Mr. Ribble, what is it you want?" She heard the noise of co-workers leaving and returning from their coffee breaks. She sighed and began to drum her fingers, but he wasn't aware of her impatience. He was beginning back in 1934. She would have to listen to all of it!

"Thirty-four cleaned us out—cleaned us to bone. You wonder how *farmers* could go hungry. I don't know, but we did. After the drought hit there was nothin' to do but come in town an' sign up on the County. Twice a month my pa would come in an' bring back food. Sometimes I came with him. I seen them lines of hungry men just standin' out there like they was poleaxed an' hadn't fallen yet. I tell you, them days was pitiful, *pitiful."* He glanced up at her and then smiled. "I'm glad to see *you* done good since—got a new buildin' an' all. Yes, you come right up." He looked around with approval at the progress they had made.

"Mr. Ribble . . . ?" He returned. "See, we taken the Relief, but we never got to tell nobody the good it done for us. After that year, things got a little better, and soon we was on toward bein' a payin' farm again. In '46 we built us a new house—every convenience, an' in '56 we got some of them automated units for cattle care. Two years ago we was doin' good, an' last year, I knew it was time to think about My Plan for real. It was time to Thank The Welfare."

"Mr. Ribble, thanks are not necessary. . . ."

"Don't you mind, ma'am, you just get your men an' come with me."

"I beg your pardon. . . ."

"I do more than talk, ma'am. You come on out an' bring your men."

Mr. Morrissey had come back from his coffee break and was standing in the hall. She signaled him with her eyes as she followed Cephas Ribble, now walking proud and sure out to his truck. He sighed and followed, wondering why he was always around when somebody needed to make a madness plain. Why did it never happen to McFarland?

Cephas was reaching into his pocket and they thought: *gun.* He took out a piece of paper and turned to them as they stood transfixed and pale and thinking of violence. "I got it all here, all of what's in the truck. Get your men, ma'am; no use wastin' time. It's all in the truck and if it don't get unloaded soon, it's gonna spoil."

"What is this about, Mr. Ribble?"

"My donation, ma'am, I told you. I'm givin' the Relief six hundred chickens, thirty bushels of tomatoes, thirty bushels of apricots—I figured for variety, an' don't you think the apricots was a good idea, though?—ten bushels of beans, six firkins of butter—ma'am, you better get them chickens out, it don't do to keep 'em in this sun. I thought about milk, so I give two cans— that's one hundred gallons of milk, you know, for the babies."

They were dumbfounded. Cephas could see that. He wanted to tell them that he wasn't trying to be big. Everybody gives what he can. He'd even signed a form right there in the office about promising to accept donated food and clothing. Their amazement at his gift embarrassed him. Then he realized that it was probably the only way they could thank him—by making a fuss. People on the state payroll must have to walk a pretty narrow line. They'd have to be on the lookout for people taking advantage. That was it. It was deep work, that welfare, mighty deep work.

"What are we supposed to do with all that food?" Mr. Morrissey said. Cephas saw that the man was making sure it wasn't a bribe. "Why, give it to the poor. Call 'em in an' let 'em get it. You can have your men unload it right now, an' I'd do it quick if I was you—like I said, it won't be long till it starts to turn in all this heat."

Mr. Morrissey tried to explain that modern welfare methods were different from those of 1934. Even then, the food had been U.S. surplus and not privately donated. It had come from government warehouses. Cephas spoke of the stupidity and waste of Government and rained invective on the Soil Bank and the Department of Agriculture. Mr. Morrissey tried again. "We don't give out any *food.* There hasn't been any *donated* since 1916!"

No doubt of it, these welfare people had to be awful careful. Cephas nodded. "The others do what they can—don't blame 'em if it don't seem like much," he said sympathetically. "I signed that slip in there about the donated food, so there must *be* some donated."

"It's done because of an obsolete law," Mrs. Traphagen argued, "one of the old Poor Laws that never got taken off the books."

"—an' here you folks are followin' it, right today," Cephas mused, "it must make you mighty proud."

"Mr. Ribble, *we have no place to store all this!*"

Cephas found his throat tightening with happiness. He had come in humility, waited all the morning just so he could show his small gratitude and be gone, and here were these people thunderstruck at the plenty. "Mister," he said, "I pay my taxes without complainin', but I never knowed how hard you people was workin' for your money. You got to guard against every kind of bribes and invitations to break the law; you got to find ways to get this food to the poor people so fast, you can't even store it! Mister, you make me proud to be an American!"

A policeman had stopped by the truck and was tranquilly writing a ticket. Cephas excused himself modestly and strode off to defend his situation. The two workers stood staring after him as he engaged the officer. It was, after all, state law that food could be donated. Had the department no parking place for donors? The policeman looked over at the stunned bearers of the state's trust. He had stopped writing.

"Could that truck fit in the workers' parking lot?" Morrissey murmured.

"What are we going to *do* with it all?" whimpered Mrs. Traphagen.

"All those chickens—six hundred chickens!"

"The poor will never stand for it," Mrs. Traphagen sighed.

"First things first," Mr. Morrissey decided, and went to confront the policeman.

Cephas's truck in the workers' parking lot blocked all their cars. As a consequence, the aid applications of eight families were held pending investigation. Six discharged inmates of the state hospital remained incarcerated for a week longer pending home checkups. Thirty-seven women washed floors and children's faces in the expectation of home visits which were not made. A meeting on disease at the Midtown Hotel was one speaker short, and high school students scheduled to hear Social Work, Career of Tomorrow, remained unedified. Applicants who came to apply for aid that afternoon were turned away. There was no trade in little plastic cards and the hive of offices was empty. But the people of the Boone County Department of Public Welfare were not idle. It was only that the action had moved from the desks and files and chutes to the workers' parking lot and into the hands of its glad tyrant, Cephas Ribble.

All afternoon Cephas lifted huge baskets of apricots and tomatoes into the arms of the welfare workers. All afternoon they went from his truck to their cars carrying the baskets, chickens festooned limply over their arms. When they complained to Mr. Morrissey, he waved them off. Were they to go to every home and deliver the food, they asked? Were big families to get the same amount as small families?

Cephas was a titan. He lifted smiling, and loaded with a strong arm. He never stopped for rest or to take a drink. The truck steamed in the hot spring light, but he was living at height, unbothered by the heat or the closeness or the increasing rankness of his chickens. Of course he saw that the welfare people weren't dressed for unloading food. They were dressed for church, looked like. It was deep work, very deep, working for the state. You had to set a good example. You had to dress up and talk very educated so as to give the poor a moral uplift.

You had to be honest. A poor man could lie—he'd been poor himself so he knew, but it must be a torment to deal with people free to lie and not be able to do it yourself.

By 3:30 the truck had been unloaded into the cars and Cephas was free to go home and take up his daily life again. He shook hands with the director and the casework supervisor, the head bookkeeper and the statistician. To them he presented his itemized list, carefully weighed and given the market value as of yesterday, in case they needed it for their records. Then he carefully turned the truck out of the parking lot, waved goodbye to the sweating group, nosed into the sluggish mass of afternoon traffic and began to head home. The lot burst into a cacophony of high-pitched voices:

"I've got three mothers of dropouts to visit!"

"What am I going to *do* with all this stuff?"

"Who do we give this to? My people won't take the Lady Bountiful bit!"

"Does it count on their food allowance? Do we go down Vandalia and hand out apricots to every kid we see?"

"I don't have the time!"

"Which families get it?"

"Do we take the value off next month's check?"

"It's hopeless to try to distribute this fairly," the supervisor said.

"It will cost us close to a thousand dollars to distribute it at all," the statistician said.

"It would cost us close to two thousand to alter next month's checks," the bookkeeper said, "and the law specifies that we have to take extra income-in-kind off the monthly allowance."

"If I were you," Morrissey said, "I would take all this home and eat it and not let anyone know about it."

"Mr. Morrissey!" Mrs. Traphagen's face paled away the red of her exertion. "That is fraud! You know as well as I do what would happen if it got out that we had diverted welfare commodities to our own use! Can you imagine what the mayor would say, what the governor would say, the state legislature, the Department of Health, Education, and Welfare, the National Association of Social Workers!" She had begun to tremble and the two chickens that were hanging over her arm nodded to one another, with a kind of slow decorum, their eyes closed righteously against the thought. Motors started, horns sounded and cars began to clot the exit of the parking lot. The air was redolent.

As the afternoon wore on, apricots began to appear in the hands of children from Sixteenth and Vandalia Street all the way to the Boulevard. Tomatoes flamed briefly on the windowsills of the ghetto between Fourteenth and Kirk, and on one block, there was a chicken in every pot.

The complaints began early the next day. Sixteen people called the Mayor's Committee on Discrimination claiming that chickens, fruit, and vegetables had been given to others while they had received tomatoes, half of them rotten. A rumor began that the food had been impregnated with medicine to test on the poor and that three people had died from it. The Health Department finally issued a denial, which brought a score of reporters to its door. During the questioning by reporters, a chemist at the department called the whole affair "the blatherings of a bunch of pinheads on the lunatic fringe." On the following day, the department received complaints from the ACLU, the Black Muslims, and the Diocesan Council, all of whom demanded apologies. There were eighteen calls at the Department of Welfare protesting a tomato "bombing" which had taken place on Fourteenth and Vandalia, in which passersby had been hit with tomatoes dropped from the roofs of slum houses. The callers demanded that the families of those involved be stricken from the welfare rolls as relief cheaters, encouraging waste and damaging the moral fiber of the young. Twenty-two mothers on the Aid to Dependent Children program picketed the governor's mansion carrying placards saying *Hope, Not Handouts* and *Jobs, Not Charity*. Sixty-eight welfare clients called to say that they had received no food at all and demanded equal service. When they heard that the Vandalia Street mothers were picketing, a group of them went down to protest. Words were exchanged between the two groups and a riot ensued in which sixteen people were hospitalized for injuries, including six members of the city's riot squad. Seven of the leaders and four who were bystanders were jailed pending investigation. The FBI was called into the case in the evening to ascertain if the riot was Communist-inspired. At ten o'clock, the mayor went on TV with a plea for reason and patience. He stated that the riot was a reflection of the general decline in American morals and a lack of respect for the law. He ordered a six-man commission to be set up to hear testimony and make recommendations. A political opponent demanded a thorough investigation of the county welfare system and the local university's hippies. On the following day, Mrs. Traphagen was unable to go to work at the welfare office, having been badly scalded on the hand while canning a bushel of apricots.

Cephas Ribble remembered everyone at the Welfare Office in his prayers. After work he would think about the day he had spent in the city and of his various triumphs. The surprise and wonder on the faces of the workers, and the modest awe of the woman who had said, "Mr. Ribble, you don't need to thank us," humbled and moved him. It had been a wonderful day. He had given his plenty unto the poor, plenty that was the doing of his own hands. He rose refreshed into his work, marveling at the meaning and grandeur in which his simplest chores were suddenly invested. He said, as he checked his chickens, "A man has his good to do. I'm gonna do it every year. I'm gonna have a day for the poor. Yessir, every year!" And he smiled genially on the chickens, the outbuildings, and the ripening fields of a generous land. ☐☐

Discussion

1. Do you think that Cephas is sincere in his wish to give food to the welfare department for distribution to the poor? Why or why not?

2. Give a short description of Cephas's history. What has he experienced that makes him want to donate food?

3. (a) How is Cephas treated when he goes to the welfare office? (b) What is his attitude toward the office building and those who work in it?

4. (a) What reasons do the welfare workers have for not wanting to accept Cephas's donation? (b) Do you think the workers are correct? Explain.

5. (a) When the welfare workers finally accept the donation and distribute the food, what are the consequences? (b) Is this situation a believable one? Why or why not?

6. (a) What makes Cephas decide to donate again next year? (b) How do you think the welfare workers might react when they see Cephas again?

7. The title of this story comes from the biblical quotation: "Cast your bread upon the waters and it will return a hundredfold." (a) How does this quotation relate to the story? (b) In what way is the title ironic?

Joanne Greenberg   1932 •

For one who does most of her writing as a "hobby," Joanne Greenberg has achieved huge success. She is best known for *I Never Promised You a Rose Garden,* an account of a young girl's recovery from mental illness. This best-selling novel was recently made into a motion picture. Greenberg has published several other novels and two story collections. She lives in Colorado with her family.

Dan Morrill

Dreams

Langston Hughes

Hold fast to dreams
For if dreams die
Life is a broken-winged bird
That cannot fly.

5   Hold fast to dreams
For when dreams go
Life is a barren field
Frozen with snow.

Discussion

1. (a) What kind of dreams do you think the poet is talking about? **(b)** With what two things does he compare a life without dreams? **(c)** In what ways are the comparisons appropriate?

2. (a) How important do you think dreams are? **(b)** Suggest some comparisons of your own that could be applied to a life without dreams.

Langston Hughes
1902 • 1967

A man who lived to see many of his dreams come true, Langston Hughes expressed himself in many types of writing—novels, stories, plays, songs, movie screenplays, travel articles, and children's books. He is best known, however, as a poet.

Born in Joplin, Missouri, he attended high school in Cleveland, Ohio, where he began writing poetry. Before graduating from college he spent a year in Mexico, worked as a seaman on trans-Atlantic voyages, and held a job as a cook in Paris. While working as a busboy in a hotel, he one day left some poems beside the plate of the American poet Vachel Lindsay. Lindsay picked them up and later recited them before an audience. Lindsay's reading gave Hughes his first public hearing and launched him on a highly successful career.

*In this remembrance of life on a farm, Ben Logan describes
the effects of a drouth on the land, on animals . . . and on people.*

Drouth

Ben Logan

There was a gentleness in most summers, the land staying green and moist even in the boiling sun of August. The summer the drouth was at its peak was different. That summer had violence in it. The thirsty land dried, cracked open as though to better receive the rain—and the rain didn't come. The stunted corn curled up its leaves, trying to save moisture. The oats, which needed cool weather when the grains were forming, cooked in the hot dry sun, producing grains light as chaff. The alfalfa was short-stemmed and had the pale green look of cured hay even before it was mowed.

Down in the valleys the creeks ran warm and sluggish, half clogged with moss and slime. The leaves on the elm trees in our yard rattled like the dried oak leaves of fall and began to turn yellow by the middle of July. By then the pastures were brown as old straw, the cattle thin, ribs showing halfway across a forty-acre field, and we could milk any two of them into one twelve-quart pail.

As the land dried out the days grew hotter. The sun came up a violent red through the dust and smoke, heat pulling at the moisture in us before we had finished the morning milking. For the first time anyone

could remember, there was no morning fog filling the big valley that led down to the Kickapoo.

The bawling of cattle woke us at night. Any other summer it would have meant a cow had been left in the barnyard by accident when the others were put out to night pasture. This summer it meant they wanted to get back into the barnyard for water.

"Even the grass doesn't have any moisture in it," Father said.

The drouth was not ours alone. Day after day the northwest wind carried the soil of the Great Plains to us in a never-ending cloud of yellow-brown. The fine dust that rode the wind was everywhere. It gritted between our teeth when we ate. Freshly washed clothes turned brown on the clothesline. I could draw faces on the dark wood of a tabletop that had been wiped clean an hour before.

Newspapers carried pictures of houses half-covered with dust, roads being cleared of dust drifts with snowplows, and caravans of farmers leaving the land, possessions piled high in old pickup trucks. There was talk that half the soil of the Great Plains was going to end up east of the Mississippi.

The endless summer went on. Father suffered with the suffering land. Each morning his eyes swept the horizon, looking for some sign that rain might come. He walked out into the fields, feeling the wilted plants, poking at the concrete hardness of the dry soil. He would come back to the house, face drawn, shaking his head. "If there was just something a man could do. I don't know anything to do but wait for it to rain."

Lyle tried to cheer Father up. "You always said it would be nice to have one of those rich Iowa farms. Few more weeks of this dust and you'll have one, delivered right to you."

The old men at the filling station, who whittled and argued their days away, compared the summer to the ancient-sounding past. Any time we stopped there they were at it. "Figure it's the worst one we ever had," old Charlie said. "Lot worse than back in ninety-five. I tell you, there's never been a summer like this one before."

He said it with great authority, and no one argued. I had never seen that happen before.

Men reacted to the drouth in different ways. Some gave up and moved away. Some prayed to God for help. Some went through the days cursing steadily at the Devil, the weatherman, the Republicans, and whoever invented farming in the first place.

Some, like Lyle, kept trying to make jokes. "Joking about it's a lot better than shooting yourself," he said.

A neighbor offered Lyle a chew of tobacco one day.

"Nope," Lyle said. "Had to give it up."

"How come?"

"Too dry. Last time I tried some, I chewed all day. It was seven o'clock that night before I worked up enough juice to spit. Going to try it again some day if it ever rains."

It didn't rain.

The grasshoppers came in a horde, as though they were blown in from the West with the dust. There was a story about them, too, passed on by one of the men at the filling station.

"I heard a fellow over by Mount Zion was out cultivating corn. He noticed the grasshoppers was pretty thick but didn't pay them no mind. Finally he got thirsty. He was in a field close to the house so he left the horses there and started to go get some water. It was when he was climbing over the fence he noticed them grasshoppers had gone through all the grass along the fence row and was starting on the fence posts."

"Wood fence posts or steel fence posts?" someone interrupted.

"Fellow didn't say. Anyway, he went on to the house and got his drink of water. When he got back to the field, the cultivator and team of horses was gone. He figured they'd run away until he saw what the grasshoppers was doing. You know they'd ate up the horses and cultivator and was pitching horseshoes to see who got him."

As the summer went on, a new and pungent blue joined with the brown of the dust. Forest fires were raging out of control in the pine woods to the north.

Along the ridge wells began drying up. Neighbors came in wagons and pickup trucks to fill ten-gallon milk cans or sometimes drove a whole herd of cattle to water at our stock tank. Father kept checking the flow from our pump, but it held out, the windmill going steadily.

Storms rolled up the northwest. We watched them coming, hopeful even when they looked violent and dangerous. White windclouds boiled ahead of black clouds, the day going so dark the nighthawks came out and filled the sky with their whirling and diving. But the storm had a way of going around us or just seeming to dissolve into the dry air. Or they came on, driving us to cover, and turned out to be nothing but a giant wind.

Someone said, "The wind's doing its best to bring us rain. It's like there just ain't any rain out there to bring."

We put up forty-eight loads of hay that summer. No one could remember a year when we had put up less than a hundred. One field of oats was so light we cut it for hay and made a stack behind the barn. That night one of the rainless windstorms came. Lightning struck the hay poles and set the stack on fire. The flickering glow coming through the window woke Father. We rushed out, but all we saved were the hay poles and rope.

Father reported the loss to the fire-insurance company and a check came in the mail. He opened the letter at the dinner table, looked at it, and started shaking his head.

"They didn't pay very much?" Laurance asked.

"They paid too much. They must think that was good hay—like alfalfa."

And in that violent summer, when the crops were a failure, the cows drying up, money short, and it seemed it might never rain again, Father sent the check back to the insurance company and said he'd take half that much.

Mother suffered through that summer, worrying about Father, worrying about her garden and about a fall and winter coming with a family to keep fed. Her garden withered, only the brave-colored zinnias seeming to flourish in the drouth. Birds were scarce. "Gone on farther north maybe," she said, "to where it's cooler." And having said that, she began to worry about the birds getting caught in the forest fires.

Looking ahead to a lean harvest, we canned all the summer apples we could, even searching in the old orchards of deserted farms. Lee and I picked more than a hundred quarts of blackberries, still a decent crop, deep in the shaded woods along the moist ditches. When the ears of the field corn were in the milk stage, we picked bushels of them and cut off the kernels for canning.

"Good idea," Lyle said. "We won't be able to put it in the corncrib anyway."

"What are you talking about?" Father asked.

Lyle had on his deadpan look. "Why the ears are so small they're just going to come rolling out through the slats in the crib fast as we can shovel them in."

Father didn't even smile.

Rain finally came in the fall, breaking the drouth, and the land began to heal itself. But the costs of drouth were not yet paid. Ditches appeared where none had ever been as the rain pounded at soil that was cracked and protected only by the stunted plants and close-cropped grass. Hundreds of oak trees stood bare of leaves the following spring. Some of the wells and springs that had dried up never had water again.

We didn't farm quite the same after that summer. The reaction of the land to the drouth told us we had made mistakes, had taken the harvest too much for granted, and left the land too little safety margin to allow for the dry years.

We learned to cultivate corn just deep enough to cut off the weeds, leaving the moisture protected instead of rolling it up to dry out in the sun.

Most important of all, we began laying out fields in long narrow strips, planted alternately in oats, hay, and corn so that a plowed field and a cultivated crop never laid open a wide piece of hillside to the rain. When water had a free run across a big cornfield, it picked up enough speed to carry the soil with it. In the new strip-cropping, water was slowed by running into the hay or oats before it could pick up the soil.

Laurance came home from high school with word that strip-cropping had been used more than fifty years before by farmers from

Switzerland who lived in Mormon Coulee, near La Crosse, sixty miles to the north.

At first we laid out our strips in straight lines, but the hillsides were not straight. Later, we ran them along the contours of the hills and our fields began to look like pictures in my geography book of mountainside terraces in China.

From the drying up of the wells we learned that the need to protect the land was not just local. A state geologist explained what he thought had happened. Much of the well water in southwestern Wisconsin came from a layer of limestone buried three hundred feet or more below the surface of the ridges. That layer of limestone slanted upward, to the north, so that a hundred miles away, in north central Wisconsin, the limestone lay at the surface. There, it picked up water. That water seeped slowly southward through the limestone to our wells, taking perhaps seventy-five years to make the trip. And about seventy-five years before, the geologist pointed out, men had drained the surface water from the north central Wisconsin marshes to make more farmland.

The story of the seventy-five-year-old well water and the draining of the marshes made a deep impression on Father. "There's just too much we don't know," he said. "How could somebody way up there know he was draining away our water supply? For that matter, what are we doing right here that's changing things someplace else? We know what cutting off the timber has done—making floods in the valleys."

"I guess we can't be expected to know everything in advance," Mother said gently.

"That's right. But we can go slow when we start changing things. We can admit that we're playing around with something that's a lot bigger than we are."

I suddenly remembered old Charlie Harding, teetered back in his chair at the filling station, fussing about the timber being cut out of the Mississippi bottoms. "I don't know just what it's all about," he said. "Might even be a good idea. But it's another thing being changed that ain't ever going to be changed back again."

An age of innocence had ended. Father had thought of man in general as being an enemy of the land. The summer of the drouth made him examine everything we were doing to see in what ways we, personally, were enemies of the land. □□

Discussion

1. Did the drouth described by Logan happen in recent years or several decades ago? Support your answer with details from the selection.

2. (a) What were some of the ways land and livestock were affected by the dry weather? (b) Describe some of the specific ways people responded to the drouth.

3. (a) How did the farmers change their farming methods as a result of the drouth? (b) Though the drouth eventually came to an end, some of the dried-up wells never had water again. What explanation is given for these dry wells?

4. In addition to describing the drouth, Logan also presents an effective portrait of his father. Describe the character of the father in two or three sentences.

Extension • Reading

"Drouth" is an excerpt from Ben Logan's *The Land Remembers* (Viking, 1975), a recollection of family life and farming in the Middle West.

*When John Steinbeck set out to rediscover the United States,
he traveled in a well-stocked camper truck.
His only companion was a large French poodle
named Charley, a dog Steinbeck thought he knew well—
until they visited Yellowstone National Park.*

from Travels with Charley

John Steinbeck

I must confess to a laxness in the matter of National Parks. I haven't visited many of them. Perhaps this is because they enclose the unique, the spectacular, the astounding—the greatest waterfall, the deepest canyon, the highest cliff, the most stupendous works of man or nature. And I would rather see a good Brady photograph[1] than Mount Rushmore.[2] For it is my opinion that we enclose and celebrate the freaks of our nation and of our civilization. Yellowstone National Park is no more representative of America than is Disneyland.

This being my natural attitude, I don't know what made me turn sharply south and cross a state line to take a look at Yellowstone. Perhaps it was a fear of my neighbors. I could hear them say, "You mean you were that near to Yellowstone and didn't go? You must be crazy." Again it might have been the American tendency in travel. One goes, not so much to see but to tell afterward. Whatever my purpose in going to Yellowstone, I'm glad I went because I discovered something about Charley I might never have known.

A pleasant-looking National Park man checked me in and then he said, "How about that dog? They aren't permitted in except on leash."

"Why?" I asked.

"Because of the bears."

"Sir," I said, "this is an unique dog. He does not live by tooth or fang. He respects the right of cats to be cats although he doesn't admire them. He turns his steps rather than disturb an earnest caterpillar. His greatest fear is that someone will point out a rabbit and suggest that he chase it. This is a dog of peace and tranquillity. I suggest that the greatest danger to your bears will be pique at being ignored by Charley."

The young man laughed. "I wasn't so much worried about the bears," he said. "But our bears have developed an intolerance for dogs. One of them might demon-

From *Travels with Charley* by John Steinbeck. Copyright © 1961, 1962 by The Curtis Publishing Co., Inc. Copyright © 1962 by John Steinbeck. Reprinted by permission of The Viking Press and William Heinemann Ltd.
1. Brady photograph. Photographic portraits of famous people were the specialty of Mathew B. Brady, an American photographer of the Civil War period.
2. Mount Rushmore, a national memorial in the Black Hills of South Dakota. On one face of the mountain are sculptured the heads of Washington, Jefferson, Lincoln, and Theodore Roosevelt.

strate his prejudice with a clip on the chin, and then—no dog."

"I'll lock him in the back, sir. I promise you Charley will cause no ripple in the bear world, and as an old bear-looker, neither will I."

"I just have to warn you," he said. "I have no doubt your dog has the best of intentions. On the other hand, our bears have the worst. Don't leave food about. Not only do they steal but they are critical of anyone who tries to reform them. In a word, don't believe their sweet faces or you might get clobbered. And don't let the dog wander. Bears don't argue."

We went on our way into the wonderland of nature gone nuts, and you will have to believe what happened. The only way I can prove it would be to get a bear.

Less than a mile from the entrance I saw a bear beside the road, and it ambled out as though to flag me down. Instantly a change came over Charley. He shrieked with rage. His lips flared, showing wicked teeth that have some trouble with a dog biscuit. He screeched insults at the bear, which hearing, the bear reared up and seemed to me to overtop Rocinante.[3] Frantically I rolled the windows shut and, swinging quickly to the left, grazed the animal, then scuttled on while Charley raved and ranted beside me, describing in detail what he would do to that bear if he could get at him. I was never so astonished in my life. To the best of my knowledge Charley had never seen a bear, and in his whole history had showed great tolerance for every living thing. Besides all this, Charley is a coward, so deep-seated a coward that he has developed a technique for concealing it. And yet he showed every evidence of wanting to get out and murder a bear that outweighed him a thousand to one. I don't understand it.

A little farther along two bears showed up, and the effect was doubled. Charley became a maniac. He leaped all over me, he cursed and growled, snarled and screamed. I didn't know he had the ability to snarl. Where did he learn it? Bears were in good supply, and the road became a nightmare. For the first time in his life Charley resisted reason, even resisted a cuff on the ear. He became a primitive killer lusting for the blood of his enemy, and up to this moment he had had no enemies. In a bearless stretch, I opened the cab, took Charley by the collar, and locked him in the house. But that did no good. When we passed other bears he leaped on the table and scratched at the windows trying to get out at them. I could hear canned goods crashing as he struggled in his mania. Bears simply brought out the Hyde in my Jekyll-headed dog.[4] What could have caused it? Was it a pre-breed memory of a time when the wolf was in him? I know him well. Once in a while he tries a bluff, but it is a palpable lie. I swear that this was no lie. I am certain that if he were released he would have charged every bear we passed and found victory or death.

It was too nerve-wracking, a shocking spectacle, like seeing an old, calm friend go insane. No amount of natural wonders, of rigid cliffs and belching waters, of smoking springs could even engage my attention while that pandemonium went on. After about the fifth encounter I gave up, turned Rocinante about, and retraced my way. If I had stopped the night and bears had gathered to my cooking, I dare not think what would have happened.

---

3. **Rocinante** (rō sə nän′tā), the camper truck. Steinbeck named it after the horse of Don Quixote (don ki hō′tē), the hero of a novel about chivalry by Miguel de Cervantes.
4. **Bears . . . Jekyll-headed dog,** a reference to *The Strange Case of Dr. Jekyll and Mr. Hyde,* a novel by Robert Louis Stevenson. It is the story of Dr. Jekyll, who compounds a drug which turns him into a murdering beast called Mr. Hyde.

At the gate the park guard checked me out. "You didn't stay long. Where's the dog?"

"Locked up back there. And I owe you an apology. That dog has the heart and soul of a bear-killer and I didn't know it. Hereto-fore he has been a little tender-hearted to-ward an underdone steak."

"Yeah!" he said. "That happens some-times. That's why I warned you. A bear dog would know his chances, but I've seen a Pomeranian go up like a puff of smoke. You know, a well-favored bear can bat a dog like a tennis ball."

I moved fast, back the way I had come, and I was reluctant to camp for fear there might be some unofficial non-government bears about. That night I spent in a pretty auto court near Livingston. I had my dinner in a restaurant, and when I had settled in with a drink and a comfortable chair and my bathed bare feet on a carpet with red roses, I inspected Charley. He was dazed. His eyes held a faraway look and he was totally exhausted, emotionally no doubt. Mostly he reminded me of a man coming out of a long, hard drunk—worn out, depleted, collapsed. He couldn't eat his dinner, he refused the evening walk, and once we were in he collapsed on the floor and went to sleep. In the night I heard him whining and yapping, and when I turned on the light his feet were making running gestures and his body jerked and his eyes were wide open, but it was only a night bear. I awakened him and gave him some water. This time he went to sleep and didn't stir all night. In the morning he was still tired. I wonder why we think the thoughts and emotions of animals are simple. □□

Discussion

1. (a) What are Steinbeck's feelings about national parks? **(b)** Do you agree or disagree with him? Explain. **(c)** Why does Steinbeck decide to visit Yellowstone Park?

2. (a) Why must dogs be strictly controlled while in the park? **(b)** What kind of "personality" had Charley displayed before the visit to Yellowstone? **(c)** What does Steinbeck think is the reason for Charley's reaction to the bears?

3. At the end of his account, Steinbeck suggests that animals have more complicated thoughts and emotions than we usually give them credit for. From your own experiences with a pet, or from your reading, can you support this idea? If so, explain.

Vocabulary • Context

Use the context clues provided to figure out the meaning of the italicized word in each sentence below. Write the letter of the correct answer.

1. When it was announced that the star performer was not going to appear, *pandemonium* broke out in the angry audience. **(a)** wild cheers; **(b)** wild disorder; **(c)** flags and banners; **(d)** bored yawns.

2. Their provisions were so *depleted* that they would have run out of water in two days. **(a)** used up; **(b)** extensive; **(c)** controlled; **(d)** appetizing.

3. I wanted to shout at him to stop, but fear of what he might do next made me *inarticulate.* **(a)** frightened; **(b)** angry; **(c)** unable to think; **(d)** unable to speak.

4. Why should Carlos react with such *pique* just because he can't have his own way? **(a)** annoyance; **(b)** charm; **(c)** charity; **(d)** flowery speech.

5. Gina said she was happy, but that was such a *palpable* lie that no one was fooled. **(a)** clever; **(b)** unhappy; **(c)** obvious; **(d)** nervous.

John Steinbeck
1902 • 1968

Born in the fertile valley of Salinas, California, John Steinbeck worked as a fruit picker, bricklayer, ranch hand, and reporter before achieving success as a full-time writer. His most famous novel was *The Grapes of Wrath*, which won a Pulitzer Prize in 1940. In 1962 Steinbeck was awarded the Nobel Prize for Literature.

In Search of America

He took to the road after Labor Day: a man, his dog, and a thoroughly equipped camper truck. He traveled alone, as a "nobody." He avoided the big cities, major highways, hotels and motels. He wanted to see people "at home in their own places." He intended to experience the flavor and the sound of his own country. John Steinbeck, in search of America.

From Long Island, New York, he traveled north to Maine, then zigzagged across the Midwest, through Montana and Idaho to Seattle, then south to California, then across the Southwest and South toward home. In all he covered over 10,000 miles and visited thirty-four states.

Not once on his journeys was he recognized as a famous writer (though a roving actor encountered at a roadside rest area did mistake Steinbeck for a fellow actor). Steinbeck's camper and the fishing rods and hunting gear inside it gave a ready excuse for his presence. Charley the poodle provided the opening for many conversations ("What degree of a dog is that?"). Steinbeck talked with scores of people on his journey: with truckers, waitresses, mechanics, farmers, cooks, rangers, toll collectors, veterinarians (Charley was ill twice on the trip). Steinbeck even "conversed" with four Maine moose by means of a cattle-calling horn on his truck—a conversation which ended quickly when the moose began trotting toward the truck with what seemed to be romantic intentions.

The journey provided Steinbeck with episodes of comedy, surprise, loneliness, friendship, hostility, frustration, awe, and wonder. A visit to his hometown of Salinas, California, was a bittersweet experience for Steinbeck. Later in his journey Steinbeck was a sorrowing witness to an example of the country's racial problems.

The long hours of driving gave Steinbeck time to ponder what he had seen of America: the sheer hugeness of it, the vitality and busyness of its people, the rapidity of change and development. His account of his travels—what he discovered and what he thought—was published in 1962 as *Travels with Charley,* one of the last books of Steinbeck's long and productive writing career.

See **INVERSION** Handbook of Literary Terms

Jukebox Showdown

Victor Hernández Cruz

Two men got into a fight with a jukebox
The air was night and warm
Splattered all over the avenue
Was screws and bolts
5 Broken 45's all over the place
The police came and arrested all three
The police asked the jukebox questions
Then dropped quarters in

Discussion

1. (a) Why do you think the two men got into a fight with the jukebox? **(b)** Have you ever felt like "fighting" with a vending machine? If so, explain the circumstances.

2. What details in the poem are unreal or fantastic?

3. (a) In lines 3–4, the normal word order is inverted. What word is emphasized by this inversion? **(b)** What else is unusual about these lines?

Extension • Writing

What sort of questions do you ask an arrested jukebox? How does a jukebox answer? Write out an imaginary dialogue between a police officer and the jukebox. The questions of the officer should be serious and straightforward; the answers from the jukebox should consist of appropriate titles or lyrics from songs in the Top Forty.

Victor Hernández Cruz
1949 •

Born in Puerto Rico, Victor Hernández Cruz came to New York City when he was four years old. His poems have appeared in many publications, and he has published several collections of his work.

"This is your journal," read the English assignment. "Express yourself." As you read this story, note how Jessie reveals her own character, and also how she manages to reveal the characters of others.

Up on Fong Mountain

Norma Fox Mazer

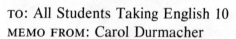

TO: All Students Taking English 10
MEMO FROM: Carol Durmacher
DATE: February 3

"That favorite subject, Myself."—JAMES BOSWELL

Your term project will be to keep a weekly Journal. Purchase a 7³/₄ × 5-inch ruled, wire-bound notebook. (Woolworth's at the Mall stocks them, so does Ready's Stationers on East Avenue.) Date each entry. Note the day, also. Make a minimum of two entries each week. The Journal must be kept to the end of the school year. It is to be handed in June 24.

I will not read these Journals—only note that they have been kept faithfully. There will be two marks for this project—Pass and Fail. Only those students not handing in a Journal or blatantly disregarding the few rules I have set down will receive a Fail.

In writing in your Journal, try to be as free as possible. This is *your* Journal: express *yourself.* Use the language that comes naturally to you. Express your true feelings without reservation. Remember, I will not read what you have written (unless you ask me to). Once I record your mark I will hand the Journal back to you. (You may be present while I check to see that the Journal has been kept in the required manner.)

These Journals are for YOU. To introduce you to the joys of record-keeping. To help you think about your lives, the small events, the little graces, the funny, sad, or joyful moments. Record these as simply and directly as possible.

A moment recorded is a moment forever saved.

Carol Durmacher

February 6, Thursday

I don't know what to write really. I have never kept a journal before. Well, I better write something. I have to do this two times in the next three days. Miss Durmacher, you said, Write your true feelings. My true feelings are that I actually have nothing to write. Well, I'll describe myself. My name is Jessie Granatstein. I'm fifteen years old. My coloring is sandy (I think you would call it that). I ought to lose ten pounds. My eyes are brown. I have thick eyebrows that my sister Anita says I ought to pluck. My father says I'm stubborn as a bulldog. He said that last week when we fought over the Sunday papers. I was up first and started to read it, then he got up and took it away from me. He says he ought to get it first, the whole paper, every single section, because he's the father, the head of the household, and that I should learn to wait patiently. We argued for an hour. He didn't change my mind and I didn't change his. He got the paper first.

February 8, Saturday

Anita and I made a *huge* bowl of popcorn tonight, then ate it watching TV. Then we were still hungry, so we made a pot of spaghetti, slathered it with butter, and ate it straight from the pot. We had a good time till Mark came over, then Anita acted like I didn't exist.

February 12, Wednesday

Lincoln's birthday, also my parents' anniversary. Mom made a rib roast, baked Idaho potatoes with sour cream and chives, frozen corn on the cob, and strawberry shortcake with real whipped cream for topping. I stuffed myself like a pig. It half rained, half snowed all day. Why would anyone want to get married on Feb. 12, in the middle of winter? Mom just laughs when I ask her, and looks at Dad.

February 14, Friday

I don't have anything to write. I'm sorry, Miss Durmacher, but all I seem to be writing about is food. I had tuna fish with celery and mayo for lunch, plus two ice cream sandwiches which I should have resisted. Mom says not to worry about my weight, that I'm "appealing." She's nice.

February 18, Tuesday

Yesterday I was talking to Anita and we got called to supper right in the middle of a sentence. "Girls!" That's my father, he won't eat till we're all at the table, and he's hungry when he sits down, so he doesn't want to wait very long for us. Like, not one extra second.

But, anyway, that wasn't what I was going to write about today. I was going to write about Brian Marchant—Brian Douglas Marchant III. Kids call him BD. I'm pretty sure he was watching me in geometry class today. Fairly sure, although not positive. What I am positive of is that *I* was watching *him*. In fact—well, I'm not going to write any more about it. I thought I wanted to, but I take it back. And that's all I have to say today.

Feb. 21, Fri.

Well, Miss D., it's a Friday, it's winter, I feel sort of depressed. I wish I had someone I could really talk to. It snowed again today. I've always loved snow, loved to see it caked in big thick white clumps on all the trees when it first falls, loved to jump around in it. Today, for the first time ever I didn't like it. I *hated* it. And that depressed me even more.

And to tell the truth, Miss D., while we're on depressing subjects, I just can't believe this journal. Almost three more *months* of my real thoughts and feelings—that's depressing!

Monday, February 24

Brian Marchant borrowed paper from me, and winked at me. I have always hated winking boys.

Feb 28, last day of the month, Friday

BD winked at me again.

I said, "Why are you winking at me?"

"What do you mean? I'm winking at you because I feel like winking at you."

"Don't," I said.

"Don't?" He looked at me in astonishment and amazement. I mean it, Miss Durmacher, like nobody ever said don't to him before.

"I think winking is dumb," I said.

He stared at me some more. Then he gave me a double wink.

March 3, Monday

I saw BD in the cafeteria today. I said, Hi. He said, Hi. I said, Have you given up winking? He said, What? Then he laughed. He has a nice big laugh.

Tues. Mar. 4

BD and I ate lunch together today. No winking.

Thursday, March 6

Lunch again with BD. I forgot to bring mine and didn't have any money with me, either. BD brings *enormous* lunches. Two peanut butter jelly sandwiches, one tuna fish with pickle relish, one salami with cheese, three Hostess Twinkies, one bag of chips, an apple, an orange, a banana, plus he bought three cartons of milk and two ice cream sandwiches. And parted reluctantly with one of the pbj's for me. Also, he bigheartedly gave me half his apple.

And that makes *three* entries for this week, Miss Durmacher. Not bad, huh?

Tuesday, March 11

BD walked home with me and came in for cocoa. Then we went outside and he looked up at the pignut tree in the backyard which is almost the tallest tree around. "I think I could climb that, Jess," he said.

"Don't, BD," I said.

"Why not? I like to climb trees."

"I don't like heights, and it might be slippery."

"You don't have to climb it," he said. And up he went. I could hardly bear to look. All I could think was, He's going to fall. He's going to fall and crack his head.

When he got nearly to the top he yelled, "Jess-eee! Jess-eee!" I yelled back, "I hear you, Beee-Deee!" Then he came down, laughing all the way.

Wednesday, March 12

Anita said she thought BD was funny-looking. I said I didn't think he was any funnier-looking than most human beings.

She said, "You have to admit he's, one, shorter than you, and two, has got big pop eyes. Green pop eyes, like a frog. Also, a big mouth which looks like he could swallow your whole face when he kisses you."

"How do you know he kisses me, Anita?"

"Well, sister, I hope he kisses you! At your age, you're not going to tell me you're sweet fifteen and never been kissed! I had boys running after me and kissing me since I was nine years old!" She laughed merrily.

Are you reading this, Miss Durmacher? Don't, please. The truth is, I have only been kissed a few times—well, not even a few, three to be exact—at parties. But I'm not going to tell Anita that.

March 21, Friday

Anita doesn't stop making cracks about BD's looks. I just don't understand it. Her

boyfriend, Mark Maloff, is supposed to be super-good-looking, but I really can't stand him. He wears pink ties and has a little green ring on his left hand. It's true BD looks as if he never thinks about what he's wearing. Nothing ever matches. But something about him really pleases me. Maybe it's the way he walks around with his hands stuck in his back pockets, sort of jaunty and jolly and swaggering. (The other day he was wearing one green sock and one dark blue. When I pointed it out to him, he said, "Really?" and looked down at his feet, very interested. Then he said that his eyes were never really open in the morning, not till about ten o'clock, and by then, for better or worse, he was dressed.)

Saturday night, March 22

Miss Durmacher, don't read this—you said you wouldn't. I love kissing BD. I love it!

Wednesday, March 26

Mom thinks she and I are alike. She's always saying it. (She thinks Dad and Anita are alike, she says they are both very good-looking. True. While she and I are both chunky and sandy-haired.) *But* Mom doesn't say boo to Dad, she's always very sweet to him. (Actually she's sort of sweet to everybody.) I'm not like her in that way *at all. I'm not sweet.* In that regard, I'm more like my father than Anita is. I became aware of this because of BD. I have been noticing that he likes things his own way. Most of the time he gets it. I have noticed, too, that I don't feel sweet about this at all!

March 29, Sat. afternoon

BD came over last night and said we were going bowling. I said why didn't we do something else, as we went bowling last week. He said he liked bowling and what else was there to do, anyway? I said we could go roller skating. BD laughed a lot. I said what's the problem with roller skating. I like roller skating. (Which I do.) BD said, "Jessie, why are you being so picky? Why are you being hard to get along with?" I thought, Right! Why am I?

And we went bowling. And then, later, I realized, just like that, he had talked me out of what I wanted to do and into what he wanted to do.

Monday, March 31, last day of the month

I don't even mind writing in here anymore, Miss Durmacher. I have plenty to write all the time. Now, lately, I've been thinking about what you wrote at the top of our assignment sheet. That favorite subject, Myself. Everyone got a laugh out of that when we first read it. Who wants to admit they are their own best, most favorite topic of conversation?

But I think it's the truth. Last night, at supper, Dad was talking, and I noticed how I was pretty much waiting to get my own two cents in. It seems Anita was, too, because

she actually beat me to the punch. The only one who didn't rush to talk about herself was Mom, and sometimes I think that's just from long years of practice listening to Dad.

Also, today, I noticed when BD and I were hanging around school that he is another one whose most favorite subject is—myself. That is—*him*self. The thing is, I really like to listen to him go on because, mainly, I like him. But if he never wants to listen to me, after a while, I get this horrible lonely feeling. I think that's it. A lonely feeling. Sad.

April 2, Tuesday, no I mean, Wednesday

A dumb fight with BD today. He came home from school with me and not for the first time got going on his ancestors who came over here about two hundred years ago. *Pioneers,* he said with a big happy delighted smile. As if because they got on a boat about one hundred fifty years earlier than my family this made them really special. So I said, "Well, BD, I think there's another word for your ancestors. Thieves."

"Thieves!" His cheeks puffed up.

"They stole Indian land, didn't they?" (I have just become aware of this lately from Mr. Happy's American History class.)

BD whipped out his map of the Northeast from his pocket and stabbed his finger about a dozen places all over Maine and Vermont. "Here's Marchantville, Jessie. Marchant River. Marchant's Corners. East Marchant! West Marchant, and Marchant's Falls!" He looked at me very triumphantly.

"BD," I said, "I've seen all that before." Which, indeed, I have. In fact, the first time I realized BD actually carried that map around with him, I burst out laughing. And at the time he didn't take too kindly to that. But this time, I made him truly furious.

"You think thieves were the founders

of all these places, Jessie? You think that's why all these rivers and towns were named after the Marchants? They were pioneers, Jess——" And he got that fanatical happy look on his face again at the mere sound of the word. "Pioneers, people who had the intelligence and foresight to go to the new country, the unexplored territory, the virgin lands——"

"Now listen, BD," I said, and I had to talk loud to slow him down. "Suppose a boatload of people came over here tomorrow from China and landed smack in the middle of our town, and pushed us all out——"

"The boat's in the middle of our town?" BD said.

"You know what I mean! The people, BD. The people from across the ocean. And they say to us, From now on, we're going to call this Fong City after our leader, Mao Tze Fong, and this river here, this is going to be Fong River, and over here we've got Fong Mountain——"

"Jessie, that's dumb," BD yelled. "That's inaccurate, the comparison just won't work——"

Well! I can yell, too. *"Like I was saying,* BD, although we don't know it, the Chinese have developed this ray gun. Instant death. Superior to anything we have. Okay? Now——"

"No, it's not okay. We've got atomic weapons, we've got sophisticated weapons, an army, police——"

"So here comes Mao Tze Fong," I went on, "and all the others with him and they've got these ray guns which we can't do *any-thing* against. They kill off a bunch of us, take over our houses and land, and the rest of us run to hide in the mountains——"

"Fong Mountain, I presume?" BD said.

"Right! We're up on Fong Mountain. From there we survivors would try to get our homes back, but after quite a few years of battling, the invaders would beat us enough so we'd have to agree to anything they said. Because, remember, we have just a few old hunting rifles against their ray guns. They, after a while, would let us have some land they didn't care about, some swamps and stuff, and they'd stick us all on it and call it a reservation. And meanwhile, *meanwhile*—BD, are you listening?—they'd have been wiping out all the old maps and

making new ones. With Fong Mountain, East Fong, West Fong, Fong's Corners, BD."

April 3, Thursday

In geometry class today: "How's your revered ancestors, BD?"

"How're things up on Fong Mountain, Jessie?"

April 6, Sunday

I talked to BD on the phone. We were peaceful. That's good. Because we have been fighting a good bit lately.

April 12, Saturday

Mom came into my room with a sweater she'd washed for me. "Oh, by the way, honey," she said (which is always the signal that she's going to be serious), "aren't you and Brian seeing an awful lot of each other?"

"Me and BD?" I said, sort of stalling for time.

"Yes. You saw him every single night this week. Do you think that's wise?"

"Wise?"

"I don't want you to be in a terrible hurry like I was."

"Terrible hurry?"

"To grow up," she said.

"Grow up?"

"Jessie! Do you have to repeat everything I say?" She flashed me a funny little smile. "When two people see a lot of each other, it's not always so wise. They might get too—they might get carried away."

"Oh," I said. "You don't have to worry, Mom. No one is going to carry me away."

Sunday, April 20

A fight with BD last night. I wanted to get out of the car and walk but he wouldn't let me. He started the car and drove me home. I was furious. He won't even let me get mad in my own way.

Monday, April 21

Miss Durmacher, you didn't say how long or short the entries had to be. I'll describe the weather today. Sletty gray air and the smell of garbage everywhere.

Tuesday, April 22

Today, in school, I saw BD in the halls, and I saw him in geometry class, and I saw him in the cafeteria. We looked at each other. He didn't say anything, and I didn't say anything.

After school I started home. After a few blocks I felt someone was following me. I turned around. There was BD behind me. I started walking again. Then I turned around. He was right behind me. He grabbed me in a big hug, knocking my books every which way and said, "Kiss! Kiss!" I was sort of shocked, but I couldn't help kissing him back. And then he laughed and laughed.

Wednesday, April 30

Today I tried to talk to BD. He says it's my fault we fight so much. He says I pick the fights, that I'm aggressive, he's peaceful. This might be true. He is peaceful when he gets his way. He said I didn't know how to give in gracefully. He might be right about this, too. I hate to lose a game or an argument. He says I'm a prickly character. He's started calling me Porky, short for porcupine.

Saturday, May 10

I have kind of a problem here. What I want to write about is BD and me, but I keep thinking you'll read this, Miss Durmacher. Your eyes might just slip and catch this or that. And if they do, you're going to just keep reading. That's human nature. So this is going to be my second entry for the week.

Friday, May 16

Oh, BD, you mix me up . . . I love you . . . but . . . .

Friday, May 23

BD came over last night. I thought we could just walk around, buy ice cream, and maybe talk. Be restful with each other. It was a nice night, warm, and I didn't feel like doing anything special. Also, BD couldn't get the car, which was a relief to me because we wouldn't have to park and then fight over me.

But the minute we set foot on the sidewalk, BD said, "We're going to the movies," and he starts walking fast, getting ahead of me, like he wanted me to have to run to catch up with him.

So I just kept walking along at my usual pace, and I said to his back, "How do you know that's what I want to do?"

"There's a new movie at the Cinema," he said. "You'll like it."

"How do you know that?"

He turned around, gave me one of his smiles. He really has the nicest smile in the world! But he uses it unfairly. "Oh, listen, Jessie, if I like it, you'll like it. Right?"

"Wrong!" I yelled.

"Say it again, Porky. They couldn't hear you in Rochester."

"Very funny, BD. And I told you not to call me Porky!"

"Why don't you smile more? When you frown like that it makes you look like a teacher."

"What's wrong with teachers?" I said.

"Who said anything was wrong with teachers. Don't change the subject, Jessie."

"BD, you said if I frowned that made me look like a teacher. You meant ugly!"

"I didn't mean anything of the sort," he said. "I was just talking, just using a metaphor."

I knew he thought he had me there, but Miss Durmacher you had just reviewed all this stuff. "You mean a simile," I said. "The moon *is* a balloon is a metaphor. The moon *looks like* a balloon is a simile."

"Don't act smart! Come on, walk faster, or we'll miss the opening of the movie."

"What movie?"

"The movie we're going to see." BD wasn't smiling now. Neither was I.

"I don't believe I'm going to any movie," I said. "I haven't made up my mind what I want to do tonight. Nobody asked me what I wanted to do, only told me what they wanted to do."

"They," BD said. "There's only one of me."

"Oh, BD," I said, "no, you're a whole government. You're a president, vice-president, and secretary of defense all rolled into one."

"What are you talking about?"

"You know what I'm talking about, BD. How you always have to be Top Banana. The Big Cheese. Always telling me. You're a regular Mao Tze Fong! We're going to do this, we're going to do that, we're going here, we're eating this—don't you think I have a mind of my own? You want your own way all the time. You never ask me anything. You just barrel on ahead. You want to lead me around by the nose!"

"You're being difficult tonight," he said. He was smiling. Only not his usual, regular beautiful smile, more of a toothy mean smile, as if he would like to really bite off my arm instead of talking to me. "You've been difficult just about every time we see each other lately. Now, do you want to see that movie, or don't you?"

"I don't care about the movie," I said. "What I care about is that I have a mind of my own, I am a free person also, and I don't want to be in any dictatorship relationship!"

"Dictatorship relationship," he said. And he laughed. Hee-hee-hee. "You mean a dictatorial relationship. Dictatorial, not dictatorship."

I stared at him. Then I turned around and walked in the other direction. And he didn't come after me, and I didn't go back after him.

Wednesday, May 28

I guess everything really is over with BD and me. We really have broken up. I never would have thought it—breaking up over grammar.

June 2, Monday

I know I missed making a couple of entries, Miss Durmacher, but I was sort of upset. I'll make some extra ones to make up for it. Anita has a job after school at the telephone company. Mom has been going over every day to help Aunt Peggy, who just had her fifth baby. I don't have anything to do except hang around the house, feeling crummy.

June 4, Wednesday

Sometimes, thinking about BD, which I can't help doing a lot, I think I was the biggest fool in the world, because it's true I never loved a boy the way I loved BD. Then I go over everything in my mind, and I don't see what else I could have done.

June 5, Thursday

Why should I miss someone who all I could do was fight with, anyway.

Friday, June 6

I'm sick of hanging around the house, I'm sick of thinking about BD. Two whole weeks is enough. I'm going to get a job.

Saturday, June 7

Everyone at every place I go says, "Leave your name, we'll call you." Or else, "Fill out this application." Then they ask you a hundred questions about your whole life for a job which they don't mean to give you, anyway.

Sunday, June 8

I got a job!

It happened just by accident, this way. Yesterday, I was really discouraged after spending the whole day looking for work. I stopped into Dippin DoNuts on the Blvd. I ordered coffee and a plain doughnut, and just out of habit told the lady behind the counter I was looking for work.

She looked me over. I sat up straighter. She said, "Are you prepared to start next week, and then work all summer?"

I said, "Sure!"

She looked me over again. She asked me how old I was. She asked me where I lived. She said she was Mrs. Richmondi and she owned the place. Then she said that her regular girl had gotten smashed up in a car accident the day before. She needed someone right away. I start tomorrow afternoon.

Sunday, June 15

I've worked a whole week, every day after school from four to seven. (Then Mrs. Richmondi comes in for the last three hours and to close up.) And I worked all day Saturday. I'm a little bit tired today, but I like working. Yesterday morning I got up at five o'clock. Everyone was asleep. I crept around the house and let myself out as quiet as I could. The birds were racketing while I walked to work, but everything else was quiet. The streets were empty. Not even one car. And the houses all quiet. It was nice. I was never out early in the morning like that.

Monday, June 16

I have to wear a horrible uniform, orange with white trim (Mrs. Richmondi is big on orange—all the cups are orange, also the napkins), but other than that, I really like my job. Mrs. Richmondi is nice, too, but she *hates* bare feet. She's got a sign on the door: NO BARE FEET.

Wednesday, June 18

I see BD every day in school and we never say a word, just look at each other and then keep walking.

Mom came in to Dippin DoNuts today and ordered coffee and a jelly doughnut. Then a bunch of kids came pouring in yelling orders, and before I'd really taken in who was there, I thought—BD's here! And my hands got sweaty.

Thursday, June 19

BD came into the doughnut shop today. It was 6:30. At first I almost didn't recog-

nize him. He was wearing a funny-looking hat that was too big for him, a gray, crumpled fedora with a wide brim like something out of a thirties gangster movie. And a red wool shirt and enormous, huge red-and-white sneakers.

He sat down at the counter. I wiped my hands down the sides of my uniform. "Yes?" I said, just like I did to anyone who came in. "Can I help you?"

"Cupacawfee," he said.

I poured coffee into the orange mug and

set it in front of him. "Would you like a doughnut with your coffee?" I said, which is the next thing I always say to regular customers.

"Yup," he said.

I was nervous. Some of the coffee spilled. I wiped it up. "Cinnamon, plain, sugar, jelly, chocolate, banana, peach, orange, cream, or cinnamon-chocolate?"

"What kind would you recommend?"

"Whatever you like."

"What do *you* think is the best?"

"That depends on your taste," I said.

"Well, what is your taste? What is your favorite?"

"The cinnamon-chocolate."

"Then that's what I'll have," BD said. "Cinnamon-chocolate."

"I thought you didn't like chocolate, BD," I said, putting the doughnut down in front of him.

"Everyone needs an open mind in this world," he said. "I haven't eaten chocolate in quite a few years, so I might just as well try it again, don't you agree, Jessie?"

I stared at him. I wanted to say, BD, is that you?

I went into the kitchen and took a tray of fresh jelly doughnuts back into the shop. With a piece of waxed paper I began arranging them on the shelf.

"You like working here?" BD said to my back.

"Yes."

"I heard from some of the kids you were working here."

"Oh."

"What do you like best about it?"

"The people," I said. I finished arranging the doughnuts.

"You eat a lot of doughnuts?" he said.

I nodded. "Too many."

"I wouldn't mind working in a doughnut shop. They'd lose money on me."

I nodded. I had missed BD an awful lot. I had thought about him nearly every single day. Sometimes I had loved him so much in my thoughts, in my mind, that I could hardly stand it. Sometimes I had hated him just as hard. Now here he was, not more than two feet from me, and all we were talking about was doughnuts.

The door opened and a woman and two little boys came in and sat down. I wiped the counter in front of them. "One coffee, and two hot chocolates," the woman said. "And—let's see, oh, let's splurge, three jelly doughnuts." She smiled at me. The little boys were twirling on the stools.

I took care of them. BD was brushing up the last crumbs of his doughnut and eating them. "Anything else?" I said. "More coffee?" BD nodded. I could feel him watching me as I got the Silex and poured his coffee. I took a creamer out of the refrigerator under the counter and put it next to his cup.

The woman and two boys finished and she paid. She left me a dime tip on the counter. I put it into my apron pocket and wiped up everything.

"How do you like my hat?"

"Your hat?"

He took off the hat, twirling it on his fingers. "My hat. This venerable, antique, genuine gangster hat. You don't like it, do you?"

"Well——"

"No, I can tell, you don't have to say anything, you think it's an ancient, grungy piece of junk. Okay, Jessie, if that's what you think, then I don't want to wear this hat," BD said. And he opened the door and flipped the hat through. I could see it sailing out into the parking lot.

"You dope, BD," I said. "I liked that hat all right, it's your sneakers I'm not so wild about."

"My sneakers? These genuine red-and-white Converse All-Americans? Jessie! That's all you have to say." He kicked off his sneakers one after the other, and sent them sailing through the door into the parking lot where they joined his hat.

"You're crazy, BD," I said. "You're really impossible."

And just then my boss, Mrs. Richmondi, parked her car outside in the lot. I looked down at BD's bare feet and then at the sign Mrs. Richmondi had tacked on the door. NO BARE FEET.

"BD, here comes my boss," I said, sort of fast. "You better leave." I put his bill on the counter. "Eighty-one cents." My voice was froggy. I felt kind of sick. Because BD and I hadn't said anything real.

BD reached in one pocket, then in another pocket, then into both back pockets. His forehead got red. He reached into his shirt pockets. "I don't have any money," he said.

Mrs. Richmondi was opening the trunk of her car and taking out packages.

"I don't have any money!" he said again. "I must have come out without my wallet." He turned out his pockets, piling a bunch of stuff on the counter. Movie ticket stubs, keys, his map, a pair of sunglasses.

I pushed his stuff toward him. "Put it away," I said. "My boss hates bare feet. BD, you better just *go*. I'll pay for you."

"You will?"

"Yes!" I took eighty-one cents out of my apron pocket and put it in the cash register.

"I'll bring you back the money," he said. "I'll go right home and get it and bring it back."

Mrs. Richmondi was coming to the door now.

"BD, you don't have to do that."

"But, Jessie——"

"BD, she's coming!"

Mrs. Richmondi pushed open the door with her shoulder. And the first thing she saw was BD's feet. "Young man! You have bare feet. You shouldn't have let him in, Jessie. I've told you, no bare feet!" She dropped her packages on the counter with a thud.

"I didn't come in with bare feet," BD said.

Mrs. Richmondi glared at him. "Out!" She pointed to the door.

"I'm going," BD said, "but don't blame——"

"Out!"

BD left. I watched him through the window, cutting across the parking lot. Mrs. Richmondi was talking to me.

"I'm sorry, Mrs. Richmondi," I said.

"Excuse me, please." I bolted through the door, snatched up BD's sneakers and hat, and ran after him. "BD! BD!" I thrust the sneakers into his hand and clapped the hat on his head. "Perfectly good sneakers, BD," I said, which wasn't what I wanted to say, at all.

"If you don't like 'em, Jessie, I don't want 'em."

Oh, BD, I thought. Oh, BD! I knew I had to go back in the shop. Mrs. Richmondi was watching us through the window. But we still hadn't said *anything.* Neither of us. And we were just standing there, looking at each other.

"BD," I said. "BD, do you want to be friends?"

"That's what I mean," he said. And then he gave me a smile, that terrific smile which I'd missed all this time. "That's what I really mean, Jessie."

Friday, June 20

Today I hand in my journal.

When I started writing it way back in February, I didn't even know BD. It's funny. Odd, I mean. So much has happened. And now, this is the last time I'm writing here. I'm not going to do it anymore. I don't care about the past that much. Not when there's tomorrow to think about and look forward to! So, Miss Durmacher, this is it. Please remember your promise not to read this journal. I trust you, Miss Durmacher. □□

Discussion

1. What do you think was Miss Durmacher's purpose in asking students to write journals that she herself would never read?

2. Reread Miss Durmacher's instructions to her students and then refer to Jessie's journal to do the following: (a) Show that Jessie used language that came naturally to her. (b) Show that Jessie did express her true feelings without reservation. (c) Show that Jessie did record "the small events, the little graces, the funny, sad, or joyful moments of her life" (three or four examples will do).

3. Miss Durmacher didn't read Jessie's journal; you have. Based on Miss Durmacher's instructions, what letter grade (A to F, with A the highest) would you give Jessie's journal? Why?

4. In the time period covered by her journal, (a) what changes occurred in her relationship with BD? (b) What indications are there that she has grown up somewhat? (c) What indications are there that BD has grown up somewhat?

5. (a) Where does "Fong Mountain" appear in the journal? (b) What personal meaning does "Fong Mountain" come to have for Jessie? (c) What meaning does "Fong Mountain" have for BD?

6. (a) Based on what you have learned from reading the journal, describe Jessie in three or four sentences. (b) In a similar way, describe BD. (c) Do you think Jessie and BD will continue their friendship during the next school year? Why or why not?

Extension • Writing

1. Write journal entries for a few of the days Jessie omitted.

2. Assume that BD is in Jessie's English class and write a few journal entries for him. Focus these entries on specific episodes of the story.

3. Keep a journal of your own for the next few weeks, writing two or three entries each week, at least five in all. Arrange in advance whether or not your journal will be read by your teacher.

Erich Hartmann/MAGNUM PHOTOS

See **SATIRE** Handbook of Literary Terms

Nightmare Number Three

Stephen Vincent Benét

We had expected everything but revolt
And I kind of wonder myself when they started thinking—
But there's no dice in that now.
               I've heard fellows say
They must have planned it for years and maybe they did.
5 Looking back, you can find little incidents here and there,
Like the concrete-mixer in Jersey eating the guy
Or the roto press that printed "Fiddle-dee-dee!"
In a three-color process all over Senator Sloop,
Just as he was making a speech. The thing about that
10 Was, how could it walk upstairs? But it was upstairs,
Clicking and mumbling in the Senate Chamber.
They had to knock out the wall to take it away

And the wrecking-crew said it grinned.
                                        It was only the best
Machines, of course, the superhuman machines,
15 The ones we'd built to be better than flesh and bone,
But the cars were in it, of course . . .
                                        and they hunted us
Like rabbits through the cramped streets on that Bloody Monday,
The Madison Avenue buses leading the charge.
The buses were pretty bad—but I'll not forget
20 The smash of glass when the Duesenberg[1] left the show-room
And pinned three brokers to the Racquet Club steps
Or the long howl of the horns when they saw men run,
When they saw them looking for holes in the solid ground . . .

I guess they were tired of being ridden in
25 And stopped and started by pygmies for silly ends,
Of wrapping cheap cigarettes and bad chocolate bars
Collecting nickels and waving platinum hair
And letting six million people live in a town.
I guess it was that. I guess they got tired of us
And the whole smell of human hands.
30   But it was a shock
To climb sixteen flights of stairs to Art Zuckow's office
(Nobody took the elevators twice)
And find him strangled to death in a nest of telephones,
The octopus-tendrils waving over his head,
35 And a sort of quiet humming filling the air. . . .
Do they eat? . . . There was red . . . But I did not stop to look.
I don't know yet how I got to the roof in time
And it's lonely, here on the roof.
                                  For a while, I thought
That window-cleaner would make it, and keep me company.
40 But they got him with his own hoist at the sixteenth floor
And dragged him in, with a squeal.
You see, they cooperate. Well, we taught them that
And it's fair enough, I suppose. You see, we built them.
We taught them to think for themselves.
45 It was bound to come. You can see it was bound to come
And it won't be so bad, in the country. I hate to think
Of the reapers, running wild in the Kansas fields,
And the transport planes like hawks on a chickenyard,

---

1. **Duesenberg**, an American-made, luxury automobile.

But the horses might help. We might make a deal with the horses.
50 At least, you've more chance, out there.
                                                    And they need us, too.
They're bound to realize that when they once calm down.
They'll need oil and spare parts and adjustments and tuning up.
Slaves? Well, in a way, you know, we were slaves before.
There won't be so much real difference—honest, there won't.
55 (I wish I hadn't looked into that beauty-parlor
And seen what was happening there.
But those are female machines and a bit high-strung.)
Oh, we'll settle down. We'll arrange it. We'll compromise.
It wouldn't make sense to wipe out the whole human race.
60 Why, I bet if I went to my old Plymouth now
(Of course you'd have to do it the tactful way)
And said, "Look here! Who got you the swell French horn?"
He wouldn't turn me over to those police cars;
At least I don't think he would.
                                                    Oh, it's going to be jake.
65 There won't be so much real difference—honest, there won't—
And I'd go down in a minute and take my chance—
I'm a good American and I always liked them—
Except for one small detail that bothers me
And that's the food proposition. Because, you see,
70 The concrete-mixer may have made a mistake,
And it looks like just high spirits.
But, if it's got so they like the flavor . . . well . . .

Discussion

1. (a) Where is the speaker as he describes the events in the poem? (b) Why is the speaker afraid to leave his position?

2. (a) What happened on "Bloody Monday"? (b) What were the first signs that the machines were revolting? (c) According to the speaker, why did the machines revolt?

3. (a) Why does the speaker think the machines will not kill everyone? (b) However, he is still afraid of something. What worries him?

4. (a) What do you think the author is satirizing in this poem? (b) Do you or do you not share his concern? Explain.

5. The speaker suggests that people have already been slaves ("in a way") to machines. Would you agree? For example, is there a sense in which people are slaves to the automobile? to atomic energy?

Stephen Vincent Benét
1898 • 1943

Among Benét's writings are radio scripts and plays, short stories, American folk tales, and poems ranging from long narratives to science fantasies. His many works dealing with America's traditions and ideals reveal Benét's love for his country and his pride in its achievements.

Charla discovers on a visit home that her schooling and modern ideas make her a stranger to her family and its traditions. Is it because she knows too much—or too little?

When the Fire Dies

Ramona Maher

CHARACTERS

CHARLA

ANITA

MRS. ESCALANTE (es′kä län′tā)

MR. ESCALANTE

HALUSITALA (ha lü′sə tä′lä)

On one of the Southwest's Indian reservations, vulnerable to the wind and the blowing dusty heat, is the home of VERO ESCALANTE *and his family.*

The scene is the combined kitchen and living-room of his home. The walls are a tan-wash color, the color adobe becomes when it has been fretted clean by whirling sand. The door in the Right wall leads outside. Another doorway, black-lintelled, in the down Left corner, leads into the bedroom, which is being shared by ANITA *and* CHARLA. *A door Left in rear wall leads into a hall and the parents' bedroom. The kitchen arrangements are up Center. An indentation in a wooden cabinet serves the function of a sink, as there is no running water. To the Right of* *the cabinet is a slender, upright wooden cupboard with a perennially open door. On top of the cupboard are two kerosene lanterns and a box of matches. A scarred table is on the Left of the cabinet. A small, clean stove is Left of sink. A bucket sits on one of*

the burners of the stove. The living-room furniture is concentrated Right, facing the outside entrance. There are two armchairs, both covered with brightly-woven blankets for protection. Back of table another chair. Between the armchairs is a flat, low table which has obviously been used often as a foot-rest. Below table is a stool. A bench is at Right. There are windows down Right and up Right; shelf on upper Left wall; armchair down Left.

As the Curtain opens, MRS. ESCALANTE, with the aid of a tin, oval-shaped cutter, is pressing round cakes from a sheet of mealy dough. From time to time she reaches in a canister on the table for a handful of flour. She is wearing a maroon dress with a full

skirt, and there is a long string of silver beads around her neck. Her hairdress is Chiricahua Indian, and she wears dark, flat moccasins. The door Right opens, and ANITA rushes in carrying an armful of schoolbooks. ANITA is small and dark, and she gives the effect of flashes of static in her speech and her movements.

ANITA. Did Charla come home, Mama? Is she here yet? (She places her books on the table between the armchairs.)

MRS. ESCALANTE (with an inclination of her head, not ceasing her work). She is in there—in your room.

ANITA. I watched the train come from the school window, but it was too far away for me to tell if anybody got off. So I ran all the way here.

MRS. ESCALANTE. You're getting too big to run like that, I think. You a big, awkward girl now.

ANITA. Don' waste your words on me. I already skinned my knee an' that was lesson enough. (She pulls up her skirt to demonstrate.)

MRS. ESCALANTE. You know where the red iodine is. Get it an' use it.

ANITA (dropping her skirt and crossing over to see what her mother is doing). It's not skinned that bad. Besides, I wan' to hurry up an' see Charla.

MRS. ESCALANTE. Then don' you come to me when your leg gets all infected up.

ANITA. Who do you want me to go to?

MRS. ESCALANTE. Oh, go on in an' see your sister. (with a gesture of dismissal) An' hurry her up to get dressed if you can. We have to leave for the home of the Gormans, right away soon as your father comes home.

ANITA (starting Left). On Charla's first night home?

MRS. ESCALANTE. Don' be foolish, Anita. Their ceremony is tonight. So should we go—tomorrow?

ANITA. Still, it's foolish for us to go, I think. What diff'rence will it make to that old man? *(opens door Left)* Charla? *(excited scream)* You've got your hair cut off? Did you get sick an' have to have it clipped off? *(exits, closing door)*

(MRS. ESCALANTE shakes her head, crosses over and places the canister in the cupboard. She takes a towel from the cupboard, and spreading it out on the table, she begins wrapping the flat meal cakes in it. The bedroom door opens again, and ANITA catapults through it.)

ANITA. Mama, why didn' you tell me she had cut her hair off like that?

CHARLA *(Following ANITA slowly, closing the door behind her. She is a pretty, rather petulant-looking Indian girl, dressed much in the style of the college girl on U.S. campuses).* I don't think Mama cares much for it, Anita.

MRS. ESCALANTE *(small shrug).* I will get used to it.

CHARLA *(defiantly, ruffling her hair the wrong way).* It's an Italian hair-cut. Every girl at the school has one.

MRS. ESCALANTE *(deftly re-folding the towel).* That should be a good coupling. *(She pauses.)* Sioux, Apache, and Navajo Indians with Italian hair-cuts.

ANITA. *I* like it. Do you think you could cut mine that way, Charla?

CHARLA. Sure, it's easy. I watched the girl who cut mine.

MRS. ESCALANTE *(to ANITA).* You better wait an' see what your father has to say about that.

ANITA. Charla didn't wait to see what he would say about it. She went ahead an' did it!

MRS. ESCALANTE. An' if you go away to the boarding school, I think you too will do things without asking your father or me. But for now, you will mind us.

ANITA. An' did you see Charla's new dress, Mama? It's like something out of a fairy-tale! Real sparkly!

MRS. ESCALANTE *(strangely).* Yes—I saw Charla's dress. *(turning to* CHARLA*)* An' I don' think it would be too smart for you to let your father see it on you while you're here.

ANITA. Why not?

CHARLA *(languidly, from the Left arm-chair).* Oh, he'd think it was wicked. I hate to say it, but he's what we call a "yesterday Indian."

ANITA *(sitting Right of table).* What's a "yesterday Indian"?

CHARLA. You know. *(She raises her hand in a movie-Indian gesture.)* "Heap-big Indian. Live in wickiup. Grind maize. Hunt deer. Live the good life, close to Nature. Squaw wear blankets, ugh! Good enough for squaw." Heap-big "yesterday Indian."

MRS. ESCALANTE *(swiftly).* I think if that is what you learn at that school—your father an' I, we are proud to be what you call "yesterday Indians." If that is what you learn at the white man's school from the Bellacana, is to make fun of your family, then it is bad, an' it would not be a thing to be proud of, this to be a "today Indian."

CHARLA. Oh, don't worry, I won't let him see the dress. And I guess I'm sorry if I hurt your feelings.

ANITA. Am I a "yesterday Indian," Charla? *(CHARLA is silent, looking at her mother, whose face is turned away.)* Well, tell me.

CHARLA *(turning and scrutinizing her sister carefully).* You could be. If you aren't careful. In a couple of years, you can come to the boarding school with me, and then you'll see the difference and decide what you want to be.

MRS. ESCALANTE. I think it was a mistake to let you go to that school. I don't see any good in sight from it.

CHARLA (without turning). You didn't have any choice. You had to send me. It's the law.

MRS. ESCALANTE. An' don't forget, then, that it is also the law, the law that you will have to come back to the reservation after you finish going through the school. An' what help will your Italian hair-cut an' your bare-back dress an' your painted fingernails do you back here? That is also your law.

CHARLA. Of course it's the law—unless you decide you want to leave the reservation and live with the white men.

MRS. ESCALANTE. I don't see any other help for you.

ANITA. Mama!

MRS. ESCALANTE (moving toward door up Left). I go get dressed now. Don't you two waste time, because we leave as soon as your father gets here. (She exits, closing the door behind her.)

CHARLA. You know—for a minute there, she sounded as if she didn't want me to come back.

ANITA. Oh, of course she does.

CHARLA. I don't know why she should care—I'm not trying to change her ways or her life.

(Silence.)

ANITA. Come on, we got to get ready to leave.

CHARLA. Leave for where? (disinterestedly) Where are we supposed to be going?

ANITA. We're all going. To the Gormans'. The old grandfather is dying, an' he asked his children to have the old ceremony for him—the one where friends of the family bring one of their most precious possessions each an' throw into the fire. You know—you been to one.

CHARLA. Not in a long time. And I'm not going this time.

ANITA. You got to.

CHARLA (mimicking her sister). No, I don't "got to." I'm not going to listen to a bunch of that mumbo-jumbo, medicine man junk. It makes me sick. And it doesn't do anybody any good. What good will it do that old man, who probably has tuberculosis in the first place, for somebody to throw a lizard in the fire and hoo-rah over it? You don't believe in it, do you?

ANITA. I don't know whether I do or not. But Charla, it's just the idea that the old man wanted it.

CHARLA. There'll be enough people there without me. Most precious possession, what good would that do?

ANITA. I guess it's mostly to show your respect.

CHARLA. Respect for what? That he's dying? Why can't we just send a card of sincere sympathy?

ANITA. That just doesn't happen. That's not the way to do it.

CHARLA. When on the reservation live as the Indians do. But I guess it's like Mama said: I guess I'm not Indian anymore, I guess the only help for me is to live with the white men, because I've been living like them for so long. Well, anyway, I'm still not going tonight. It's not my affair, and that ends it.

ANITA. I suppose I'll have to go.

CHARLA. That's up to you. It'll be easy for you to go, because you don't know the difference.

ANITA. An' it's easy for you to just say you

won't go. But I got to live here, an' you can go back to school.

CHARLA. I belong there anyway, more than I belong here.

ANITA. Tell me about the school, Charla. Do all the girls really cut their hair that way?

CHARLA. Almost all of them. The only ones who don't are the blanket Indians.

ANITA. Why don' you say what you mean, instead of "yesterday Indian" an' "blanket Indian"?

CHARLA. They're the same thing. Anyway, we got some of those "blanket Indian" girls at the school. They're so dumb. One of them drank a bottle of strawberry soda one day and then the rest of us told her it was blood. And in her tribe it is said that a woman who drinks blood will become heavy with child. She cried all night, until the matron came and found out what was wrong with her.

ANITA. The spirit of the *Chindi* must have been with you, Charla!

CHARLA *(her attention fully captured for the first time).* The spirit of the what?

ANITA *(timidly).* Of—of the *Chindi!*

CHARLA *(scornfully).* Of the *Chindi,* huh? You're just as ignorant as that little blanket Indian girl. *Chindi* is just a boogeyman to frighten superstitious Indians. You know there aren't any *Chindi,* Anita.

ANITA. People like you say there aren't. But I know old people who say the *Chindi* have visited them.

CHARLA. And I suppose the *Chindi* came booming down from Heaven, spitting flame.

ANITA. Oh, I really don't believe in them, Charla.

CHARLA. Don't lie to me. I guess I used to believe in them too when I still lived here. But even at the reservation school they

should have enough sense to teach you that there aren't any such things.

ANITA. Tell me some more about your school, Charla. Do they let you wear lipsticks like that to class?

CHARLA. Sure. An' you meet a lot of students from different parts of the United States. There's a lot of different classes—there's even a class in dancing.

ANITA. Do you study history or arithmetic or anything like that?

CHARLA. Sure. All those things. They give you an allowance, too, that you can spend for anything you want. That's how I bought my dress—and this locket. *(She pulls a small gold locket on a chain from the top of her dress and shows it to ANITA.)*

ANITA. It's pret-ty! Did you show it to Mama?

CHARLA. No. She wouldn't like it anyhow. Look—it opens.

ANITA. Whose picture?

CHARLA. That's just a boy at school. If you like the locket, I'll try to save up enough money to get you one. *(She tucks the locket out of sight.)*

ANITA. That would be wonderful, Charla! Nobody else aroun' here has a gold necklace like that one.

CHARLA. All these people around here have are silver beads and sandy turquoise.

ANITA. You don' like the people on the reservation, do you?

CHARLA. I don' know. But I just don't belong with them—I don't think I even want to belong.

ANITA. Were you honest about what you said to Mama? About not coming back to the reservation?

CHARLA. I haven't decided yet. I could take some office courses and prepare myself good enough so I could get a job, and I wouldn't have to come back here. Besides,

what can I hope to do if I stay here? End up selling pottery or rugs at a roadside stand? I'm tired of hearing stories about Coyote and the White Shell Woman and Dawn-Boy and all those little Indian lies. I want to get away and believe in calendars and clocks and Saturday night.

ANITA. Is that what a "today Indian" believes?

CHARLA. Sure. You know what the Indian is in history books? He killed Custer. He scalped white men. He sold New York for twenty-four dollars. Spit on him. Today's Indian is dirty, he bathes in bear-grease, and he eats horse-meat.

ANITA. Why do the books say that?

CHARLA. I don't ask why. I'm just going to prove that I don't.

ANITA. Are things like that really so much important at the school?

CHARLA. Well, what would you expect to be important? Maybe you think we study the science of war-paint and methods of scalping. We try to get away from all that.

MRS. ESCALANTE *(has silently opened the door up Left. She has changed her dress to a dark blue, and her hair is freshly combed into a bun at the back of her neck).* Your trouble is you care too much about what people say. (CHARLA *mumbles)* What?

CHARLA *(clearly).* I just said, "What school did you study philosophy in?"

MRS. ESCALANTE. I don't want to quarrel with you. I did not go to a school like you, but I am glad I am an Inyan. And I'm not sorry of my great-gran'father fought the white men for his land an' that he was killed doing it. These things, no, I am not sorry of.

CHARLA. That is—regrettable.

MRS. ESCALANTE. Are you sick, Charla? Or why are you acting like this?

CHARLA. Don't worry. After the holidays are over, you won't have to put up with me. I'll go back to the school. Isn't that what you want me to do?

MRS. ESCALANTE. I don' want to have any more words about it. Anita, go wash your face, an' comb through your hair. Charla, you change your dress.

(ANITA *rises and starts for door down Left. She halts when* CHARLA *speaks.)*

CHARLA. I'm not going, Mama.

MRS. ESCALANTE *(calmly).* It's a custom, Charla. I think it would be best if you go.

CHARLA. And I do not think it would be best.

MRS. ESCALANTE *(after a pause).* Very well.

ANITA. She doesn't have to go?

MRS. ESCALANTE. No. She does not have to go. But you do. Because I hope you still have enough clear thoughts to see that you ought to go.

(ANITA *exits.)*

CHARLA. It's stupid for you to make her go. You can tell she doesn't want to.

MRS. ESCALANTE. There are something we "yesterday Inyans" do, Charla, because they are kind. (MRS. ESCALANTE *exits through the door up Left.)*

(CHARLA *is alone in the room. She crosses and lifts the towel, views the cakes, then drops the towel again, disdainfully. The door Right opens, and* MR. ESCALANTE *enters. He wears khakis and a wide-brimmed hat. Rubber boots, which have obviously been wet and then filmed over with dust, reach to his knees. He takes off his hat as he comes through the door and tosses it on bench.)*

CHARLA *(after a pause, she rises).* The word is hello.

MR. ESCALANTE *(coming close to her and looking down at her keenly).* So we have you home for two weeks, um, Charla?

CHARLA *(nodding).* Two whole weeks.

MR. ESCALANTE. You learning anything?

CHARLA. Sure. Last week I memorized a poem. After the holidays I'll probably memorize something else. But you don't want to talk about what I do at school. Why don't you tell me about the irrigation ditches.

MR. ESCALANTE. You make fun of the irrigation project, Charla. But that is something that should matter to you. It is your land.

CHARLA. My land?

MR. ESCALANTE. The land you have to live on. This week we put in irrigation over on the Flat. It as dry as pollen out there. I guess you maybe noticed how low all the dams were if you saw from the train window.

CHARLA. I didn't see much out of the train window. I slept most of the way.

MR. ESCALANTE. What's wrong, don' they have beds at that school?

CHARLA *(nodding)*. Complete with mattresses. They're really spoiling us.

MR. ESCALANTE *(resting his hand briefly on her hair)*. Don't joke so much with things, Charla. I know your home does not seem as grand to you as your school must be. But you will grow used to it again. Now I got to clean up some. We have to go by the home of the gran'father of the Gormans. Did Mama or Anita tell you?

CHARLA *(casually)*. I think they did say something about it.

MR. ESCALANTE *(peering in the bucket on the stove)*. Never any water kep' where it should be. I dig irrigation canals all day, an' at night I get home an' have to pump water to wash in. *(He swings the bucket down.)*

CHARLA. You ought to get the radio fixed. I tried to play it a while ago, and it won't work. It probably needs a new tube.

MR. ESCALANTE. I know. Your mother, she order a tube, an' it supposed to be here by next week.

CHARLA. What's it coming by, mule train?

MR. ESCALANTE. What?

CHARLA. Nothing.

MR. ESCALANTE. You hurry your mother an' sister up. *(He takes the bucket and exits through the Right door.)*

(CHARLA gazes after him, sits down, crosses her legs, swinging one petulantly. The door down Left opens and ANITA enters. Her manner is sober and intent.)

ANITA *(crossing)*. You really mean it, that you aren't going?

CHARLA. Of course I mean it. I don't see any use in it. I'd feel out of place.

ANITA. You tell Dad yet?

CHARLA. Not yet.

ANITA. Why don't you change your mind? Mama is already mad at you.

CHARLA. I can't help that. Now just keep quiet, I'm tired of hearing about it.

(There is a silence during which CHARLA apparently becomes absorbed in chipping away the fingernail polish from her nails.)

ANITA. What are you doing?

CHARLA. Just scraping off some of this old polish. Would you like me to paint your nails for you?

ANITA. Does it take very long?

CHARLA. No, just a few minutes. Run and look in my suitcase and find it. *(ANITA returns to the down Left bedroom. After a few moments she enters again, carrying a small bottle of violently red polish.)* Now sit down and hold out one of your hands. *(ANITA sits on stool. Carelessly CHARLA begins to paint ANITA's fingernails. In her excitement, ANITA wiggles.)* Hold still or I'll smear it. *(in exasperation)* Now, look! You made me get it on wrong.

ANITA. I didn't even move!

CHARLA. Here—you try. Go real slow.

ANITA (*takes the brush and makes several painstaking strokes across her fingernails*). Like this?

CHARLA. That's fine.

(MR. ESCALANTE *enters with the bucket filled with water. He pauses on the threshold of the door, observing them.*)

ANITA (*catching sight of her father*). I'm painting my fingernails with Charla's polish. (*She holds up the bottle.*) It's called "Scarlet Stoplight." Isn't it pretty? (*She extends her hand for him to admire.*)

MR. ESCALANTE. I guess it all right, if that is what you want to look like. (*He sets the bucket on the cabinet and pours water from it into a flat pan and washes his hands. He wipes them on his shirt and takes a comb from his pocket, and, carefully wetting his hair, he combs it.*) Maybe I should let my hair grow a little bit longer, eh? (*He holds one lock out from his head.*) Then maybe it might look like Charla's.

CHARLA. I didn't know you had noticed it.

MR. ESCALANTE (*rolling down his sleeves*). I notice it all right. Anita, you go tell your mother to hurry up. (ANITA *exits through the up Left door. Sitting.*) How old are you now, Charla?

CHARLA (*flippantly*). Eighteen grasses, eighteen snows.

MR. ESCALANTE. An' how old is Anita?

CHARLA. Fourteen or fifteen, I suppose.

MR. ESCALANTE. She is not old enough for the things you try to show her, Charla. Like that fingernail paint—people around here will just laugh at her if she wear it.

CHARLA. Well, for heaven's sake, I'm not forcing her to wear it.

MR. ESCALANTE. I know. But you understand what I mean. She wants to copy you.

CHARLA. And you don't want her to? Is that what you mean?

MR. ESCALANTE. A year ago, I would have said it would be fine for Anita to try to be like you. But now—I don' think so.

CHARLA. Thanks very much. (*She turns away. There is a pause.*)

ANITA (*returning*). She's ready.

MRS. ESCALANTE (*entering*). I guess I am. I'm stitched together with pins almost.

MR. ESCALANTE. Hope they hold. (*reaches out his hand to* CHARLA.) Charla, come on an' get inna car.

CHARLA. I'm not going.

MRS. ESCALANTE. Charla doesn' feel good. I tell her she can stay home.

CHARLA (*innocently*). I feel fine. I just don't want to go.

MR. ESCALANTE. It will not harm you to go. The Gormans, they will wonder why if you are not with us.

CHARLA. Why? Will it hurt their feelings? Just tell them I don't believe in their little hoo-doo ceremonies. If their grandfather is going to die, he can die just the same without me there to throw something in the fire. Elder Brother and the Great Spirit won't know the difference.

MR. ESCALANTE. Just a minute. Anita, go outside and wait. (*He opens the door Right and* ANITA *exits slowly. Then* MR. ESCALANTE *closes it and turns his attention toward* CHARLA *once more.*) I think you should go.

CHARLA. How are you going to force me to go?

MR. ESCALANTE. Force you?

CHARLA. Don't you get it? Do I have to send smoke signals to you? I'm not going.

MR. ESCALANTE. You're my daughter, an' if I tell you—

CHARLA. I don't think I am your daughter anymore.

MR. ESCALANTE. You go if I tell you to, an' I guess I can force you to go.

CHARLA (rises). Oh, no, you can't. I won't go into any old smoky house where some old Indian is dying.

MR. ESCALANTE. Who are you to talk that way?

CHARLA. Who do I have to be?

MR. ESCALANTE. Sit down, Charla. (CHARLA complies, unwillingly.) I'm going to tell you something an' you are going to listen. There was a time in the world, before men had grown up and had grown apart. Then Elder Brother put the Apaches in the mountains and they grew up there away from everyone else. An' when a man died, he walked away over the mountains, an' he turned around once to see the fire his friends has built for him. But that was before the white men, the weak-knees, came and shuffled the Indians like cards and made fences and buildings and laws. So some of the children of the Apaches had to go away to school. An' they came back—talking about the "dirty old Indians."

CHARLA. But you forgot. The children who came back were no longer Indians. The Indian had been educated out of them. They couldn't go back even if they wanted to.

MR. ESCALANTE. No. They did not forget. But it has not yet been shown what the children shall be.

CHARLA (steadily). I'm not going.

MRS. ESCALANTE (intervening). Let her stay. She got her mind set not to go. Come, Vero— (She marshals her husband to the door Right.) We come back in a couple hours, Charla. If you get hungry, maybe you can find something. I cook when we get back.

CHARLA (without turning). Have a good time.

(The door closes. CHARLA crosses to the bedroom down Left and returns with a book. She sits once more and removes a piece of paper from the book which has been serving as a bookmark. After a few moments, from beyond the door Right, drifts in the sound of an old woman crooning tunelessly.

HALUSITALA (off stage).
Vatâ masi, vatâ masi, siâmu, tâny kokopaimu
Vatâ masi, vatâ masi, siâmu, tâny kokopaimu
Vatâ masi, vatâ masi, siâmu, tâny kokopaimu—
(The crooning stops and there is a knock on the door. Impatiently CHARLA lays her book aside and goes to answer it.)

HALUSITALA (just outside the door). You girl. I Halusitala. I come to ride with you.

CHARLA. I'm sorry. The last, great white stallion just left.

HALUSITALA. I come to ride-a-a-to the Gormans' with you.

CHARLA. They've already gone.

HALUSITALA. Uh?

CHARLA. My mother and father have gone already. I am not going to the Gormans'. Do you understand? They have already left.

HALUSITALA. Let me come in. (She enters, pushing past CHARLA. She is carrying a woven basket with the lid fastened down. She is old and very slight. Her hair is gray and wispy, and her cheeks are leathery and hollow.) You their daughter that gone to the white man's school.

CHARLA. I don't seem able to get away from that. But my mother and father have gone already. They are not here.

HALUSITALA. You mean they forgot that I was to ride with them?

CHARLA. I guess so. They didn't say anything about it.

HALUSITALA (nodding). It easy to forget. I

walk on, if I rest here after a while or so. *(She sits down in the armchair Right of table.)* I walk far already. *(motioning)* You know, from where I live. (CHARLA *sits and resumes her reading. The old woman watches her intently.)* I would thank you for a drink of water, girl.

CHARLA *(rises and removes a glass from the cupboard. She scoops the glass down into the bucket and brings it up, brimming with water).* Here you are.

HALUSITALA *(drinking).* Taste is good. Clean.

CHARLA. Glad you like it.

HALUSITALA *(holding the glass).* What book you reading?

CHARLA. Just a novel. It's called *This Side of Paradise.*

HALUSITALA. Could I hold it—see it? (CHARLA *bends down the corner of the page she is reading and hands the book to the old woman, who takes it eagerly.)* What it about?

CHARLA. Nothing very much. It's just the story of a boy's life.

HALUSITALA *(ruffling the pages wistfully).* I never learn to read. When I a girl they did not yet have the schools like the ones you go to. I never even see a book when I as old as you are. *(She turns the pages of the book reverently.)*

CHARLA. I'll take the glass if you're through with it. *(She takes the glass and places it on the table.)*

HALUSITALA *(nodding wisely).* An' now— you go many miles to school an' you come back, and someday you will teach many of us the ways you learn to read an' write—

CHARLA. I'm afraid it won't work out that way.

HALUSITALA. I remember, long time 'go, when little Apache boy was stolen in Apache war, an' a white man an' woman

take him an' raise him for their own boy. An' he went far 'way to school an' learn about sickness, an' one day he came back to help the Inyan with what he had learned. An' he did help his people. But he work too hard for them, an' one day he fin' out that he had one of the sicknesses himself, so bad it would never get well again. So—he die too. Nobody has come back since then. So now, we go back to what we know before. Like this—this thing where we give to the fire. *(She gestures toward her little wicker basket.)* That is what you should do—learn, an' then someday come back an' help us what to do.

CHARLA. Not me. I don't have any wish to be a saint among the Indians.

HALUSITALA *(as if she had not heard).* Maybe you will come back an' help us— like the boy. You know, I am friends with Hoshala Gorman, so I will go now, while he is dying but still alive, so he may know I yet his friend. An' I take this *(her hand touches the basket)* to throw in fire before his eyes, so he will know even more that I am his friend. But he an' I—we both know that it does no good. Inyan say those who die during the hours of darkness are killed by Night—an' the fire makes only a very little blaze, an' it cannot frighten the night away.

CHARLA. What is in the basket?

HALUSITALA. I show you. *(She opens the basket slowly.)* My gran'father got them from his enemy who he had kill. They're strong—an' worth much money.

CHARLA *(lifting them from the basket).* Silver spurs! But these are valuable, Halusitala! You aren't going to throw them in the fire, are you? *(She holds the spurs to the light from the window.)*

HALUSITALA. They are as good there as

where I have to keep them. To my gran'father they were his victory. To my father, they were his father's. An' to me they are the only thing I have to show Hoshala Gorman that I do not want to see him die.

CHARLA. But you don't understand. You can sell these—for money. You can use money, can't you?

HALUSITALA. The government give me enough.

CHARLA. At least why don't you pry out the turquoise sets. They're big settings—then you won't be wasting everything.

HALUSITALA. I don' need the turquoise. *(The sunlight begins to fade.)*

CHARLA. I still don't see any use in *cremating* them! Even though I don't like turquoise, some people might like these stones.

HALUSITALA. Why that you no like turquoise?

CHARLA. Oh, it's all right. I'm just tired of it. When I was about eight, my best dress was the color of turquoise. It was my best dress for two years.

HALUSITALA. You ever hear the story about it?

CHARLA. I'd need a filing system in my head to keep track of all of the Indian fairy-tales.

HALUSITALA. At the time when Elder Brother changed Vantre into an eagle strange things happened to the people of Casa Grande. One day the women were playing takal, an' among them was the daughter of Sial Sivan. Sudden, a strange little green lizard drop in front of her while she was standing 'mong the other women. The earth about the spot became like the green part of the rainbow. They dug an' found the green stone, the turquoise.

CHARLA. No, I didn't remember that one.

HALUSITALA. Even the stories are lost anymore. But there is no lack of green stone. Besides, I have nothing else to give to the fire. It is only right. These spurs bruised many. horses, an' now they will be bruised by fire.

CHARLA. They belong to you. But if they were mine, I wouldn't dream of throwing them away like that. In fact, I wouldn't throw anything into a fire to be burned up.

HALUSITALA. Then you sent nothing to the fire?

CHARLA. No. *(She lifts her head defiantly.)* I don't believe in it.

HALUSITALA. In what? The fire ceremony?

CHARLA. In anything. I don't believe the story of thunder. I don't believe that the Milky Way was formed from the ashes on the end of Earth Doctor's walking-stick. Or any of those stories.

HALUSITALA. You said you did not remember the stories. How can you not believe when you do not take the trouble to remember?

CHARLA. About the only one I do remember is the one about the mescal and the thunder. It was my favorite for a long time.

HALUSITALA. That is the story of when Coyote was after the Boy Twins.

CHARLA. During a thunderstorm or something like that.

HALUSITALA. Go on an' tell me the rest of it.

CHARLA. And to save them from Coyote, their father changed them into mescal—the two strongest, hardiest bushes of mescal on the mountain. *(as if reciting from memory)* And—and that is the reason why mescal yet grows on the mountains and why the thunder and lightning go from place to place—because the children did. That's supposed to be the reason why it rains when we go to gather mescal. Not that anybody does anymore.

HALUSITALA. Don' the Americanos—the Bellacana, too, have stories—*leyendas?*

CHARLA. Sure, I suppose so.

HALUSITALA. Maybe they don' believe in their stories anymore—but they tell them besides. An' you know what I think about you? I think you 'most believe the *leyenda* of the boy twins, or you would not have remembered it.

CHARLA. To me it's just a fairy-tale. Just like the fire is a fairy-tale. And everything else.

HALUSITALA. And an Inyan—like Hoshala Gorman? Is he too a fairy-tale to you?

CHARLA. I don't know.

HALUSITALA. The fire will show him his friends. It will warm his cold eyes for a while before he dies. It will burn for a long time for him, even though it has gone out. He will be shut in at day dawn.

CHARLA.
"All night he will be free to run,
But he will be shut in at day dawn."

HALUSITALA. You remember the songs too. Maybe someday I tell you all the songs I know an' you can put them down an' save them for other Inyans long time off to read.

CHARLA. At least it might be better than selling baskets.

HALUSITALA (*picking up her basket*). An' that day maybe the basket we take will have medicine in it or something else that will help. (*She fastens the lid and rises.*) I must go now, or I will not get there before they have finish'. An' I will ride back with your mother an' father. (*She crosses with tiny steps to the door Right and turns.*) Goodbye, girl. (*noticing the falling light*) It getting dark. I have to hurry.

CHARLA (*rises with a restraining motion of her hand*). Wait a minute. Halusitala—

HALUSITALA. You will go with me?

CHARLA (*dropping her hand*). No—no. But what you say to his family—say it for me, too. An' tell Hoshala Gorman that I, Charla Escalante—that I am sorry I am not there.

HALUSITALA. One day you will be there. Listen a moment to me. Many times has it been said to the young and many times has it all been forgotten. We do not want to die with the coughing and the dirt. We did not make our stories to have them die with us. But the children learn an' yet they will not share it. An' they turn their backs on what their fathers have to give—the stories an' the songs. So no one is helped.

CHARLA. But what can I do? I am but me—I am but one.

HALUSITALA. It is better to light one lamp than to curse the darkness. Well— (*She opens her hands and then refolds them.*) I go now. An' you think of what I say to you.

(HALUSITALA *exits, and* CHARLA *closes the door after her and leans against it. The song of the old woman drifts faintly through the closed door.* CHARLA *looks around the room, and with a slight shiver takes a kerosene lantern from the top of the cupboard with one hand and the box of matches with the other. She strikes one of the matches and it flares vividly.* CHARLA *watches it in fascination as the Curtain falls.*)

Discussion

1. (a) How does Mrs. Escalante feel about Charla as the play opens? (b) How does Anita feel?

2. (a) How does Charla feel about being home again? (b) At the beginning of the play, what are her opinions of her parents, their friends, and life on the reservation? (c) Do her opinions seem justified to you? Explain.

3. (a) Describe the major points of difference between Mr. and Mrs. Escalante and Charla. (b) At what point in the play do these differences become most obvious?

4. (a) Briefly describe the fire ceremony being held at the Gormans'. What is the purpose of this ceremony? (b) What is Charla's opinion of this custom? (c) What is your opinion?

5. A set of silver spurs starts a discussion between Charla and Halusitala about values. (a) How does Charla measure the worth of the spurs? (b) What is the value of the spurs to Halusitala? (c) Do you think either one of these methods of evaluating the spurs is better than the other? Explain.

6. Has Charla changed her opinions by the end of the play? Support your answer with evidence from the play.

7. (a) What "fire" does the title of the play refer to? (b) Does the title have more than one level of meaning? Explain.

Vocabulary • Structure

Most of the words whose structures you have analyzed so far have been words with English roots and affixes. Words containing word parts from other languages can sometimes be more difficult to figure out.

Look carefully at the meanings of the foreign-word parts as you answer the following word-structure questions.

1. The English word *vulnerable* means "capable of being hurt or damaged." Do you think the Latin word *vulnus*, from which *vulnerable* is derived, means "battle," "injury," or "ability"?

2. The Latin word that *intervene* is derived from is made up of these parts: *inter* "between" + *venire* "to come." In which of the following situations should you probably *intervene?* Your parents are having a private discussion; an older boy is threatening your little brother; a police officer has a motorist pulled over to the side of the road.

3. The English word *perennial* comes from a Latin word made up of these parts: *per* "through" + *annus* "year." (a) If your mother accused you of being a *perennial* complainer, would she mean that you complained once in a while, just around holidays, or constantly? (b) Which of these words do you think is also derived from the Latin word *annus: animal, anniversary, annoy?*

Ramona Maher   1934 •

A native of Arizona, Ramona Maher writes poetry, stories, and drama on a variety of subjects. One of her major interests is the people and history of the southwestern United States, and their traditions and folklore. For her writing she has received many awards, including one for *When the Fire Dies.*

Printed Words Liz Sohappy Bahe

I stared at the printed words
hazed, blurred, they became grey.
I trailed down the page
to a picture shouting what I read.

5 I thought about my people
up North—
far from here.
My land, the hot dry basin,
the pine on the mountain ranges
10 and the snowcapped peaks.

I thought of the killing word:
Civilization.
The steel buildings stabbing the earth,
stabbing old religions
15 now buried on the hilltop,
to have their tears drip black
from Industry's ash clouds.

I thought of the unseen tears
in eyes watching our valley
20 gashed by plows,
proud trees uprooted, dragged aside,
giving way to smothering tar roads.

And river veins pumped away
never knowing the path to the Columbia River.

25 I glanced at the blurring printed words
and felt an ancient anger swell,
bubble like a volcano in birth,
anger blackening the printed words
about your land being only a swamp
30 useless to Civilization.

I saw in a flash
the unknowing eyes of the Everglades—
alligators, egrets, water turkeys, ibises.
Animals I've never seen, never known
35 except from sadness that their fate lies
in printed words.

The words about the Everglades—
moist, mysterious, very much a land—
useless.
40 Words forgetting the animal people,
the Seminole, the Miccosukie,
who are standing in the way of the thing called
Civilization.

From *Carriers of the Dream Wheel* published by Harper & Row, Publishers, 1975.
Reprinted by permission of the author.
Liz Sohappy Bahe (bä′hē)

Discussion

1. (a) What "printed words" is the speaker reading? (b) What are the words saying? (c) What does the speaker mean when she says a picture "shouts" what she has just read?

2. The speaker describes Civilization as "killing." What specific details in the poem support this idea?

3. According to the speaker, the printed words "forget" or ignore several things. What are they?

4. (a) What would you say is the tone of this poem? (b) Cite several of the words or phrases that suggest the author's feelings about the subject of the poem.

Liz Sohappy Bahe 1947 •

A Yakima Indian, Liz Sohappy Bahe was born and raised in the state of Washington. She was educated at the Institute of American Indian Arts and resides in Arizona with her husband and two sons.

*In this autobiographical selection
Gordon Parks, a renowned photographer
and film maker, tells how he became interested
in music as a youth and how he tried to
get the world of music interested in him.*

Music
Inside My Head

Gordon Parks

It was natural that we hoped for an early spring. But winter was deep in the earth and unwilling to be hurried. So spring would sneak in a bit at a time, breathe upon the cold, and then retreat. It gnawed at the snow, dwindling it with rain and sun, but the cold wind never slept. It roamed the nights, repairing the damage that had been done during the day. It was good when finally the icicles fell and melted into the earth and the smoke left our breath and the frozen Mississippi moved again.

By now the land was stricken with poverty.[1] Every newspaper and magazine I read showed photographs of men queued up at breadlines[2] and employment halls seeking food and work. And this poverty attacked my family wherever it caught us. Yet hunger, I learned, was less frightening in the summer. I could walk slower and give more freely of what energy I had. And it was

easier when the moon shone and the stars twinkled over the warm evenings, and love was close at hand.

July brought such evenings and also my first quarrel with Sally.[3] It happened over some minor thing, but it kept us apart for months. And during those hours I worried and worked at a composition that spoke my feelings. The song was called "No Love," and I wrote it at an upright piano my sister inherited with the house. And now that I had started writing songs again, I worked at it late into the nights and on weekends; music was the one thing that kept me hopeful. A peculiar experience had kindled my love for

---

Abridged from pp. 80–90 in *A Choice of Weapons* by Gordon Parks. Copyright © 1965, 1969 by Gordon Parks. Reprinted by permission of Harper & Row, Publishers, Inc. and the Lantz Office, Incorporated.
1. *By now . . . poverty.* The author is referring to the great depression of the 1930's.
2. *breadlines,* lines of people waiting to receive food given as charity or relief.
3. *Sally,* the girl who later became Parks's wife.

it long before Casamala[4] decided that I should become a composer.

I was seven at the time. The Kansas day was hot and I was hunting June bugs in our cornfield when I heard a murmuring in the cornstalks. The murmuring grew into music, and I stood there, my mouth full of mulberries, puzzled, looking up at the slow-drifting clouds to see if they were the music's source. The violins, horns, and drums were as true to me as the sunlight, and I had a feeling that the music was trapped inside my head, that it would be there even if I had no ears. I covered them with my hands, and the sounds were still there and they continued until all the clouds moved away and there was nothing but pale sky. Then it was gone as mysteriously as it had come, and I ran toward the house a little frightened, a little joyful, eager to tell my experience. But no one was around and I scooted up on the piano stool and started banging our old Kimball upright—trying to reproduce the sounds I had heard. The noise reached my father in another part of the field and he dropped his hoe and rushed to the house. He opened the door and watched me with astonishment; I was screaming as loud as I could.

"Have you gone batty, boy?"

I jumped down and started telling my story, but he only looked at me, at the mulberry stains around my mouth, and shook his head. "I declare, if you don't quit fondin' yourself on those mulberries, you're goin' to be swearin' you saw the devil. Now stop that bangin' and git to your chores."

Perhaps I never forgave my father's reactions to those delirious moments, for never again did we talk about things bordering on fantasy—not even a bedtime story. On that day, however (and to the woe of my good father), I began to play the piano. Several years later, Earl McCray, a music professor at the white school, offered me free music lessons. I was assigned a trombone and placed in our junior-high-school orchestra. But by now I was accustomed to playing by ear, and the slow process of learning to read music seemed unnecessary. I indulged in trickery. Each Saturday morning, before my appointment with Mr. McCray, my sister fingered my lesson on the piano and I memorized it; then I went off to astonish the professor with my "sight reading." He recommended me as soloist at the graduation concert. And everyone said I played "The Rosary" with great feeling that night. Only my sister knew I couldn't read a note.

This was long past. But now at nineteen, five years later, I regretted the tricks I had played upon the professor. I had never learned to read or write music, though I was determined to compose; it seemed the one way to avoid a less-than-ordinary existence. I worked out a notation system of my own by referring to the piano keys as numbers instead of notes—a process that proved more complicated than the conventional way.

The next consideration was a publisher; it was disheartening to discover that all the important ones were in Chicago or farther east. And there were warnings against dishonest publishers who stole songs; but this didn't bother me. It would have been flattering, I thought, to have composed something worthy of a professional's theft. The difficulty would be to get someone to transpose my numbers to notes and then have the final work accepted. But I knew I couldn't depend on music alone. That first winter[5] had

<hr />

4. **Casamala,** a girl of Parks's acquaintance, who encouraged him in his musical studies.
5. **That first winter,** 1928–1929. When his mother died the previous year, Parks had come to live with his sister and her family in St. Paul, Minnesota.

taught me that I would have to fight with everything that came to hand. Learning, I knew, would be the most effective weapon against the coming years. So once again I seized upon books. After school I searched the local library shelves for authors who might help me in different ways. I pushed my mind into the foreign worlds of Thomas Mann, Dostoevski, James Joyce[6] and others whom I had never read before. I tried stone sculpture, short-story writing, poetry and, when I could hustle the material, painting. I did everything I could to protect myself against another such winter. Somewhere in between I played basketball for the Diplomats[7] and my high school as well.

A collapse was inevitable, and it came during a basketball game in October, 1931. I had dribbled past two guards and arched the ball perfectly, knowing it would swish through the hoop. But a blackness suddenly covered the court and the ball disappeared into it like a balloon into a cloud, and I felt myself falling. The coach had my teammates carry me to the locker room, where I was examined by the school nurse. Her only comment was that I looked awful hungry and thin to be playing such a strenuous game. But at home later that evening a doctor whom my sister called said I was on the verge of a physical breakdown. I had wasted from 165 pounds to 124 in less than three months. If I was to regain my health, he said, I would have to leave school for the remainder of the year and rest.

So at twenty I found myself an invalid. There was no chance of graduating with my class. I was already too far behind. In fact, I knew that I would never go back to school. For the next five months I sat in the dark of my room rejecting time, light, and reason. I never heard from Sally during that time, but my sister helped me through the long convalescence and tried to get me to read, to write, to do anything that would divert my eyes from the blank wall opposite my bed. I finally opened a book one rainy afternoon. And gradually I began to read, think, and hope again. One thing was clear. I couldn't escape my fate by trying to outrun it. I would have to take my time from now on, and grow in the light of my own particular experience—and accept the slowness of things that were meant to be slow. Spring was back again, but I was afraid to look upon its coming with any pleasure. It had deceived me once too often.

By April I had regained my weight and strength. And before long I was hanging out at Jim's pool hall again, for it was a good place to get back into the stream of things. Arguments were always going; they flared, blossomed, and faded by the dozens. Some of them were senseless, some were heated, some were comical.

During one argument, one man claimed that Glen Gray, the band leader, had a mustache. The other denied it. My interest was casual until one of the men, a waiter at the Hotel St. Paul, boasted that he should know since he "rubbed shoulders with Gray every night." He was lying of course about the shoulder rubbing, but he did see the orchestra leader regularly; anyone working there had the same opportunity. I wondered why I hadn't thought of this before. Many of the best orchestras played at the large Twin City hotels;[8] if only I could get one of them to broadcast my songs. The thought grew and I hurried home, sorted out several of my compositions, and set my alarm clock for six o'clock. And by seven-thirty the next morn-

6. *Thomas Mann, Dostoevski* (dos′tə yef′skē), *James Joyce,* important novelists of the 19th and 20th centuries.
7. *the Diplomats,* a boys' club.
8. *Twin City hotels.* Minneapolis and St. Paul, Minnesota, are known as the Twin Cities.

ing I was at the Hotel St. Paul servants' entrance, the songs tucked in my pocket, applying for a waiter's job.

The timekeeper, an old gray-haired man, looked me over and asked me to wait around until he saw the day's work schedule. And for the next four hours I paced the corridor, looking expectantly at him now and then. At eleven-thirty, he motioned for me.

"Are you an experienced waiter?"

"Yessir. Yessir." (I had never waited on table in my life.)

"You ever work here before?"

"Not yet, no, sir."

"Where have you worked?"

"The Minnesota Club, the Lowry, the——"

"Okay, okay. There's a Rotary[9] luncheon today, nothing steady. You want to work it?"

"Is that where the orchestra plays?"

"Orchestra? What's the orchestra got to do with it?" he asked.

"Oh nothing, nothing. Just thought I'd ask." My heart thumped like a drum.

"Well, do you want it or not?" he snapped.

"Yessir, I'll take it." I stepped up to his table and signed in.

The banquet captain changed my status from waiter to bus boy the instant he saw me pick up a tray. And as I trudged back and forth between the kitchen and the banquet hall, under the weight of the trays of drinks, I could hear the music coming from the main dining room. It was frustrating to have Glen Gray so close and not to be able to talk with him. But the driving captain kept his eye on me, pointing to tray after tray. And only once, when the dining-room door swung open, did I glimpse the tall, debonair orchestra leader directing his orchestra. And I noticed then that he did have a mustache.

Much later, the Rotarians were enjoying coffee, puffing cigars and asking silly questions of a mind reader they had hired for entertainment. I hung around, clearing dirty dishes from the tables—and listening to the questions and answers.

"Who's going to be the most famous in this room?" someone asked.

"Good question," the mind reader said. He then covered his eyes and turned his back to the audience. There was snickering as he supposedly searched the future. Whomever he chose was in for a good razzing. The laughter was already building.

"Gentlemen." There was a momentary quiet. "There is a boy in the back of this room in a white uniform" (every eye in the room turned on me). "He will be more widely acclaimed than any——"

That was enough. Bedlam broke loose. "Boy! Boy! Come up here!" It was the mind reader's voice screaming over the others. "Bring him up, somebody!"

Two men started toward me, but I grabbed a tray of dishes, and, fleeing the banquet hall, I tripped and threw the dishes in all directions. But I got to my feet and kept going until I reached the dressing room.

In spite of that fiasco, I was hired three days later as a regular bus boy, and assigned to the main dining room.

Glen Gray left soon after, without my having had a chance to speak to him. But Kay Kyser, Bert Lown, Jack Teagarden and others, who came later, didn't get off so easy. Each of them suffered through my inexhaustible efforts—and they encouraged me. But none of them acted as though Tin Pan Alley[10] was overlooking a great talent.

---

9. *Rotary.* The Rotary Club is a men's service organization.
10. *Tin Pan Alley,* the body of composers and publishers of popular music.

Late that summer, I was offered the head bus boy job at the Hotel Lowry, by the *maître d'hôtel*,[11] a former wrestler whose name was Gleason. I took it. And for nearly three hours each day, after the luncheon crowd left, I had the main dining room and the huge grand piano all to myself. Once the tables were set for the evening, I played away before an imagined audience—using the light-control switches for color combinations that added to the mood. On one such afternoon I was playing and singing "No Love" when I felt someone was behind me. Embarrassed, I stopped, turned and looked into the shadows. It was Larry Duncan, the orchestra leader who was currently engaged by the hotel.

"Is that your music?" he asked.

"Yes."

"Go ahead. Play it again."

I played it again and he listened attentively. When I finished he asked me if I would like to have it orchestrated.

"I sure would," I said, and it was probably the understatement of my lifetime. The orchestra's arranger spent the rest of that afternoon with me, taking the piece down as I played it. And, as I watched him work, I hoped that my afternoons of fantasy were coming to an end.

This happened on a Wednesday.

During dinner on the following Friday night, Larry motioned me toward the bandstand. "We're broadcasting 'No Love' on the network show tomorrow night—with your permission, of course," he said.

I got Sally on the telephone and, without knowing whether she cared or not, I excitedly spilled out the good news. "I composed it for you—don't forget to listen." Her voice didn't reveal the slightest interest. She said, very casually, that she would listen—but, I found out later, she spent the next two hours telephoning all her friends. And I spent the rest of that evening and the next day drifting about in a trance.

On the night of the broadcast, Abby, the drummer, congratulated me and showed a group of waiters and myself the program. Fate had arranged things. There was my name among those of Irving Berlin, Duke Ellington, Cole Porter and Jerome Kern.[12] Now, in spite of my imagining the worst—a broken microphone, a broken promise, a canceled broadcast—it was going to happen. I knew that Gleason kept a death watch on unfilled water glasses, so I went about filling them to the brim. I wanted to hear every word, every note, without being disturbed.

When at last the moment came, people continued to eat, drink, and talk, as if they were unaware of the miracle taking place. I wanted to shout, to command everyone to listen, to ascend with me—far above ordinary things. But they kept on eating, drinking, laughing, and talking. And, just before the vocalist approached the microphone, I took refuge near the bandstand where I could hear him sing my lyrics. But now, at such a moment, a drunk started rapping his glass with a spoon. He wanted more water. I ignored him. He rapped louder and I hated him for it.

"What is it, sir?" A shiver went up my back. It was Gleason's voice.

"Water! Water! Tell that boy our party wants water!"

Such was my lot, I thought, and I turned toward the table only to have Gleason wave me away. He was filling the glasses and proudly explaining that the music the orchestra was playing was mine. The drunk

---

11. *maître d'hôtel* (meˈtrə dō telˈ), headwaiter. [*French*]
12. *Irving Berlin . . . Jerome Kern,* well-known songwriters.

whispered the news to his party, and his party whispered the news to the next table, and soon everyone in the entire dining room was looking toward me. When the orchestra finished, a burst of applause filled the air. I smiled nervously, picked up a tray of dirty dishes and left the room amidst the ovation. Then, slipping into an empty room, I telephoned Sally. "Yes, I listened," she said, "and it was beautiful. Would you like to come over sometime, maybe tonight?"

"As soon as I can get out of here," I answered. The sky was overcast and it was chilly when I boarded the street car; but I couldn't accept such a night. There were stars and a moon instead, and a ridiculous hint of spring in the fall air. My heart, in its joy, would have it no other way. □□

Discussion

1. (a) Under what financial conditions is Parks living when he writes "No Love"? Explain. (b) Why does he write the song? (c) What causes his physical breakdown?

2. (a) What inspires Parks to look for work at the Hotel St. Paul? (b) Are his expectations there fulfilled? Explain. (c) How does Parks meet Larry Duncan, the bandleader?

3. What important personal qualities does Gordon Parks reveal in this selection? Illustrate these qualities by referring to passages throughout the selection.

4. What do you think Parks means by his statement: ". . . learning, I knew, would be the most effective weapon against the coming years"?

5. Reread the last paragraph of the selection. (a) What does Parks mean when he says, "There were stars and a moon instead, and a ridiculous hint of spring in the fall air"? (b) How does this last paragraph contrast with the opening one?

Vocabulary • Dictionary

Now that you have learned about the type of information given in etymologies (see page 171 if you don't remember), you should get in the habit of reading them when you look up words. Since many words have interesting or unusual origins, becoming familiar with their histories can often help you recall their present meanings.

Use the etymologies in your Glossary to answer the questions about the words in the following list. Be sure you know the meaning of each word.

queue	acclaim
delirious	razz
fiasco	orchestrate
bedlam	debonair

1. Which word is derived from a Latin word meaning "cry out"?

2. Which word means "flask" in Italian?

3. (a) Which word is derived from "raspberry"? (b) What slang meaning of "raspberry" is similar to the meaning of this word?

4. Which word is derived from three French words meaning "of good disposition"?

5. (a) Which word comes from the name of an English insane asylum? (b) How is the source of this word related to its present meaning?

6. (a) Which word originally meant "tail"? (b) How is "tail" related to the present meaning of the word?

7. Which word originally had a meaning related to dancing?

8. Which word originally had a meaning related to plowing?

Gordon Parks 1912 •

Though his musical composition gave Gordon Parks his first taste of success, he has since won fame as a fashion photographer, photojournalist, writer, and filmmaker.

Midwest Town

Ruth De Long Peterson

Farther east it wouldn't be on the map—
Too small—but here it rates a dot and name.
In Europe it would wear a castle cap
Or have a cathedral rising like a flame.

5 But here it stands where the section roadways meet,
Its houses dignified with trees and lawn;
The stores hold tête-à-tête across Main Street;
The red brick school, a church—the town is gone.

America is not all traffic lights
10 And beehive homes and shops and factories;
No, there are wide green days and starry nights,
And a great pulse beating strong in towns like these.

Discussion

1. (a) How large is the town described in this poem? Support your answer with details from the poem. (b) What specific things would you see as you drove down Main Street?

2. *Tête-à-tête* (tāt′ə tāt′) is a French expression for a private conversation (literally it means "head to head"). Why might the stores be said to be holding tête-à-tête?

3. (a) What qualities of larger towns does this Midwest town *not* have? (b) What kind of life would one probably lead in such a Midwest town? What phrases in the poem suggest this?

4. (a) What seems to be the speaker's attitude toward this town? (b) What type of town—large or small, country or city—would you prefer to live in? Why?

See **STEREOTYPE** Handbook of Literary Terms

*"It's seventy-five miles of mountains and swamps and lakes. . . .
Every year some of you get lost. And when you get lost,
you panic. And the panic kills you. . . ."*

The Warden

Georges Carousso

The searching party was gathered on the open hotel porch, smoking silently, casting uneasy glances up at the shrouded mountains. It was snowing hard up there. It would be a nasty search. Harlan Bellamy, the game warden, walked heavily up and down the porch, chewing viciously on the stem of his pipe. There was a man lost somewhere on the Big Panther range. Some fool tenderfoot deer hunter with not enough sense to carry a compass, or know how to use it if he did.

Having a man lost in your district meant trouble. It meant you had to make out reports to the Department; you had to gather up state troopers and the fire ranger and what guides did not happen to be working and as many natives as you could get; you had to go out and find the dumb tenderfoot, and then you had to start making reports all over again. And all that while, every violator who had a piece of illegal doe meat could sneak right out of the country without a man to check him. If Game Warden Bellamy had his way, lost hunters could stay lost.

A little apart from the natives, the lost man's hunting companions formed a small, restless group. They were city slickers. They talked too much. They argued too much, in nervous little sentences that blamed Bill, the lost man, and the weather, and Joe, who should have stuck by Bill, and the country in general, and Big Panther Mountain in particular. The natives sat passively by. They listened and said nothing.

"What the devil are we waiting around here for?" a big man asked. He seemed to be the leader of the hunting party.

Bellamy looked the man over coolly. "We're waiting for Bert Ellis," he said, trying to keep the anger out of his voice. "Best guide up Big Panther country. Knows it better than any of us."

Then suddenly, because he was scared, anger came into his voice. "We don't go off half-cocked," he said irritably. "And if you folks didn't go off half-cocked, there wouldn't be men getting lost around here!" He knew he was scared. Big Panther country was plenty big. And Bear Trap Swamp, in back of it, was bigger still. The chances of finding the lost hunter were small. Bellamy faced the hunters, hemming them in with his bulk and anger.

"Just because there's a hard-surface road through here, you city folks think that this is tame country. It ain't! It's seventy-five miles of mountains and swamps and lakes straight west to the next road. You fellers think you can hunt this country without guides or compasses, or without even studying a topographical map.[1] Every year some of you get lost. And when you get lost, you panic. And the panic kills you, if the cold don't."

The hunters did not answer but they looked up at the snow clouds on the mountains. A battered jitney[2] pulled up and Bert Ellis, a small, wiry middle-aged man with a week's growth of beard, got out. He passed a critical eye over the men on the porch.

"This all the men you got?" he asked.

The warden nodded. "That's all, Bert."

The little man shrugged. "That Panther country's mighty big," he said thoughtfully. He got back in his car. Bellamy got in beside him. The rest of the men walked to their cars and started piling in.

"How're you goin' to run this search?" the warden asked.

"Dunno," said Ellis. "Most lost men sort

"The Warden" by Georges Carousso. From *Collier's*, Vol. 118, No. 22, November 30, 1946.
1. *topographical map* (top′ə graf′ ə kəl), a detailed map which indicates surface features (such as mountains, hills, and valleys) as well as roads and towns.
2. *jitney,* a small passenger bus or taxi that follows a regular route.

of swing around the shoulder of the mountain and get theirselves tangled up in Bear Trap Swamp. Need a thousand men to spook 'em out of there."

"This feller's pals claim he ain't lost," the warden said. "Claim he must be hurt because they didn't hear no signal shots."

"Most likely throwed his gun away minute he found he was lost. Most of 'em do. They get excited."

They drove the cars to the foot of Panther Mountain and pulled them in along the old tote road that cut off the main highway. They went single file along the tote road, Ellis leading, then the natives, then the city hunters. Bellamy brought up the rear.

Ellis walked with his shoulders hunched against the snow, his hands in his pockets, and the gun hanging loosely from the crook of his arm. Most of the natives walked that way, loose-hipped, slouched, their guns an integral part of them. They walked fast— faster now that they had a bunch of city slickers with them, showing off a bit with a subconscious mixture of pride and malice.

The hunters were walking stiffly, their bodies tensed against the dangers of the unfamiliar footing. The guns they carried were alien to them, and they shifted them from one hand to the other, from one shoulder to the other, unable to make them part of the balance of their motions. The gap between them was widening. One of them kept at the heels of the close-packed group of natives for a while, then he too dropped back.

Ellis sure is setting a pace, Bellamy thought. *He sure is giving them the works.*

Bellamy himself was puffing. Well, he was not as young as he had been, and he had put on a bit of weight, too. There had been a time, ten-fifteen years ago, when he could have walked the whole bunch of them off

their feet—Ellis included. In those days he could shoulder a pack basket full of traps and grub, head out over the range and drop down to Little Wolf Pond without even stopping to roll a smoke or get a breather. Fifteen—? It must have been a good twenty years ago. He had been in the Service that long. In the Service there wasn't much call for a warden to go traipsing around the woods. A warden had to cover a lot of territory, but he covered most of it in a car. Now a wiry little squirt like Bert Ellis could walk the legs off him.

Ellis stopped up ahead, and the thin single line of men blunted around him. He had rolled and smoked half a cigarette before the last of the hunters and Bellamy reached the group. Yes, sir, he had certainly set a pace! You could see the steam coming off the hunters. It must be cold to see steam like that, but Bellamy didn't feel cold. Sweat drenched his backbone. He took out a red bandanna and blew his nose, fumbling with it before his face so they would not notice his gasping breaths.

"I guess we'd better start droppin' off men from here," Ellis said. "You take this here end of the line, Warden. I'll take the rest up yonder along the tote road, and drop them off say every couple or three hundred yard. I'll drop one of you folks next, then somebody who knows the woods. We're gonna keep hollering, 'Hey, Jack!'—or whatever the feller's name is."

"Bill," one of the hunters volunteered.

"Okay, then, 'Hey, Bill!' And keep listenin' for the man on your right and left. By gosh, I ain't aimin' to get any more of you lost. I got chores aplenty to do." He dropped his cigarette in the snow and stepped on it from force of habit. "And no shootin' unless we find this feller Bill. Shoot two quick ones if you find him. We'll answer with one.

Shoot a couple every fifteen minutes to guide us to you."

He turned to Bellamy. "We'll spread out and work up the range, far as the rock cliffs. If he's hurt down here somewhere, we might find him. I dunno what else to say."

The warden nodded. He wanted to offer some suggestions, but breath was still choking in his throat. Ellis's plan was good enough.

"How about the swamp?" one of the hunters asked.

"A man ain't got no call to go into that swamp. It'd take the Army, with some Marines to boot, to find a man in there unless he signals. Your friend don't seem to be the signaling kind." He turned away and led the searching party on.

There was a half-rotted log at the side of the trail, and the warden sat down. He could breathe more evenly now but his knees trembled from the exertion.

I guess I'm not as young as I was, he thought. *Ellis sure set a pace.* Dry pellets of snow almost as heavy as hail hissed through the evergreens. Bellamy shivered. The cold was already working inside of him, spreading along his spine. After a while he got up and started beating his arms together, and twice he looked at his watch to see how long it was since Ellis had left him.

He began to think maybe the starting signal had gone down the line and he had not heard it in the hissing of the wind and snow. When he strained his ears, he could hear "Hey, Bill! Hey, Bill!" far away, blending into the sounds of the wind, and he was ready to shout himself when he heard other voices calling, and far away the strains of ghostly music, and the bugle tones of a hound baying, and the voice of his wife saying, "The wood . . . the wood . . . the wood . . . ."

When the real voices came, they were unmistakable, and the ghost sounds of the woods disappeared instantly. He heard a faint voice shouting "Hey, Bill!" Then another voice, nearer, repeating the cry, and then the man directly to his left, so near that it startled him. He started to shout and his voice croaked in his tight throat and he swallowed a couple of times and cleared it and then shouted.

I could always hear things in the sound of running water, he thought. *When I was a kid, I used to sit by the brook and hear whole conversations and hear a girl laughing.*

He cut at right angles from the trail and headed into the thicket of young beech seedlings not much higher than his head, but so thick that he had to shoulder his way through them. The beech seedlings kept tangling him up and whipping across his face. To his left, the man shouted, "Hey, Bill!" and he stopped and shouted back.

The ground sloped upward, and he came out of the belt of young beeches to a small clearing where the trees had been cut down. The logs had been dragged out but the tops lay in a tangled heap. He was breathing hard again when he came out into the hardwood timber. He wanted to rest, but the cry of the man on his left sounded, fainter this time and farther up the slope, and he kept on going.

"City slicker," he murmured. "Race horse." Showing off up there somewhere, going fast just because the going under *his* feet was good and solid. No thought that somebody else might have it tough. Well, it would take more than a burst of speed by a city hunter to leave him behind, even if he wasn't as young as he used to be.

The snow stopped for a few moments, and he could see the mist-shrouded hulk of the mountain through the bare tree branches. It looked immense in the dim light. A tough mountain, uncompromising and sinister, and for a moment Bellamy felt sympathy for the man who was lost somewhere in its grasp.

Poor feller, he thought. *What chance has he got?* And then the resentment welled up in him again. *Well, they got no business tanglin' with mountains like this one. They ain't got no right to be so cocksure and sassy.*

It began to snow again, big soft flakes. The giant mountain drew back into the haze and disappeared. He could no longer see the crest of the ridges in front of him. Once he had scrambled to their tops, he could not see the bottoms of the ravines he had left. *It's like walking inside of a cocoon,* he thought. He stopped and called the lost man's name, feeling the futility of it for the first time. If the man had slipped and fallen and knocked himself out, his body would long ago have been covered by the snow.

It occurred to him that he had not heard the man on his left for some time. He cupped his hands and called out. He shouted again and again, trying to pierce the muffling snow, but it was like shouting with his face buried in a pillow. He needed a rest and the comfort of tobacco, but here was another guy straying off his post. He took off his mittens and tried whistling through his fingers. Only a couple of off-key sounds came out. He walked on for a few hundred yards, calling all the while, then suddenly stopped.

There was something wrong. He was supposed to be skirting the base of the mountain. The swamp had been to his right, and now it should be in back of him. The man to his left should be uphill from him. Yet, in spite of the rise and fall of the ground, he was definitely going downhill. He tried to peer through the thick curtain of snow. He took a few steps in one direction, stopped and looked around him again. Then he trotted back to where the snow was churned up by his turning feet. He looked all around. But there was nothing to see, and he felt fear growing inside him.

It was ridiculous. The swamp had been to his right. The other man had been to his left and farther up the slope. But the ground was dipping away from him. He cupped his hands to his mouth and shouted. In the mute fluttering of the snow, he heard an answer to his cry. He stood still and held his breath. He heard the cry again. It was from the direction he had expected and he thought with relief, *I was right all the time.*

Then he heard the cry again and it came from in back of him, and then it came from his right and from his left, until it was all around him, until it became a part of the soft music he had not noticed before and the sound of a girl's laughter, and his wife's voice saying, "The wood . . . the wood . . . "

I can back track, he thought. *I can follow my own tracks until I get to a spot I recognize, then set myself right again.* He looked around him, picked up his dim track in the snow, and started to follow it. But after a few steps, the track curved back, and came to the churned place in the snow where he had been standing. The tight fist of fear in his chest grew bigger.

"That's the track I made looking around trying to get located," he muttered. "Sure! The other one must head off that way."

He started to circle, looking for the track, and he almost stepped over it before he saw the dim rounded outline in the snow. The snow was filling the track fast; he followed it, bent almost double. Once he thought he had lost it but he was able to pick it up again where his boot had brushed the snow off a stump. He began to trot, racing against time, racing against the endless curtain of snow, against the inevitability of defeat softly stamped in each dimming print.

The prints disappeared. He stopped. His eyes darted in all directions. There was no avenue of escape, no opening in the white cocoon of snow.

"I'm lost," he said. The mute voices of the woods echoed his words and flung them back at him, the voices blending with the music and the girl's laughter and his wife's words. Lost——

He began to run, as if running would rend the invisible veil that hemmed him in, and still the mute voices. He scrambled up the side of a ravine that he did not remember crossing, his mouth gaping, his breath coming in wheezing gasps. He almost reached its crest when the choking feathers in his chest filled it completely. Hot wires of pain tightened across his chest. They crossed and recrossed in a spot over his heart. They touched and exploded in a blinding shower of pain-filled sparks. He clutched at his chest, staggered a few steps, and sank against the base of a tree.

Take it easy, he thought. *Got to take it easy.*

He was not conscious of the pain diminishing, but he began to hear the sharp rasping of his breath and feel the rapid thumping of his heart. He sat where he had fallen, his cheek pressed against the rough bark of the tree, and stared at his mittened hand lying palm upward in the snow, and watched the snowflakes settling softly on it. The pain over his heart gradually diminished.

I'm lost, he thought. *Lost!*

The desire to run swept over him in uncontrollable waves. He would have started running if he had been standing up instead of lying in the snow. He would have started running again, blindly, unthinkingly.

But in the time and effort of raising his body, of clawing his way upward along the tree trunk, he stifled the impulse. He stood up with his arms still clutched around the tree trunk, holding himself from running.

You're acting like a tenderfoot, he thought. *You're acting like a city slicker. You've got to stop and think.*

He dug out his pipe and tobacco, and took off his mittens. But his hands were trembling so that the tobacco spilled. He dropped the pipe and, in an unreasoning fit of anger, threw the tobacco pouch down. He forgot them immediately and started to put on his mittens. He got the right one on but when the left one fell in the snow at his feet, he forgot that, too, in the welter of thoughts racing through his mind.

He was lost. A mile from the trail. Maybe more. Maybe a lot more. The snow was a heavy, muffling curtain that closed in all around him. The trail was somewhere to the south of him. Only there was no way of telling which way was south. The wind usually blew in from the north and the snow was usually stuck on the north sides of the trees. But it did not work out that way all the time. Some of the worst storms came in from the south. The mountains made their own wind currents. You couldn't tell, except with a compass, and he never carried one. No native ever carried one.

"Shucks, I wouldn't give pocket room to one of them things. All's I got to do is follow my nose back to one of Ma's pies." All natives said that to city slickers. Or else they said, "Comes a time I get turned around, I just set my gun down on its feet and follow it plumb into camp."

There was a bunch of men in the woods. There might be one of them just beyond the curtain of snow, for all he knew, and if there was he could set himself right; he wouldn't have to admit that he was lost. He cupped his hands around his mouth and shouted, "Hey, Bill!" He was not thinking of the lost man; he shouted that name because he'd shouted it before. He walked and he shouted, lifting his face to the falling snow, but there was no answer.

He thought of his pistol then—the .45 strapped around his waist. They would hear that. They were bound to, in spite of the muffling snow. He opened the holster, rested his hand on the butt. But he didn't draw the gun out. "No shooting unless we find the lost man," Ellis had said. He hadn't found the lost man. If he shot, they would answer him, and they would converge on him, the natives and the city hunters. He couldn't tell them that he had shot because *he* was lost. He couldn't stand before them and say, "I'm the warden, but I got lost. I got lost and panicky, and I got a pain across my heart, and I needed help." He couldn't say that to the city slickers. Not even to the natives. He couldn't be the warden and say that.

He kept on walking, shuffling with heavy feet through the snow. He was lost and he must get out of there, and walking was the only way that he could get out. He must not run. If he started to run, he must wind his arms around a tree and hold on until the impulse to run left him. *I'm lost,* he thought. *Lost—lost—lost—* The words became the rhythm of his motions, the total of his reasoning. When the pain returned to his chest, now dull and heavy and constant, he did not think of it as pain containing a meaning and a warning of its own but only as part of being lost.

He walked with head lolling on his neck and downcast eyes that seldom raised above the obstacles before his feet. The wind had begun to blow again. The snowflakes were heavy and hard-driven. It was getting much colder, but he did not notice that. He stumbled blindly forward, sometimes falling. Once he twisted his wrist in a fall, but the pain of it mingled with the rhythm throbbing in his head.

Time became a blank infinity that held no meaning for him. Once he ran headlong into a tree, and the shock startled him. He touched his skinned forehead with his hand and looked vaguely at the blood on his fingers. A deer bounded out of its bed beside a small fir; he watched it dully as it disappeared into the haze with noiseless leaps. He came to a spruce thicket and crashed through the dead, interlocked branches with the full weight of his body.

It was much lighter now. But he failed to notice he was out of the big timber, walking in tall, matted beaver-meadow grass. His feet broke through the surface of small ice-crusted puddles. He did not notice them until he stepped into one deeper than the others, and the water welled over his boot tops.

He was in a swamp clustered with thickets of alder. On the drier ground, here and there, were even thicker clusters of spruce and cedar. He climbed over rotted tree trunks, half hidden in the tall grass. He skirted many ice-covered pools and once, very carefully, crossed a large one along the branch network of an old beaver dam. He felt proud of having crossed the beaver dam; floundering forward, he thought about it, but there was no meaning to his thoughts.

He was shouldering his way through a thicket of low snow-covered spruce when suddenly he stopped. It was the first time he had stopped voluntarily. He raised his head and looked dully around him. He became aware of the pelting of the wind-driven

snow, of the heavy pain in his chest, and the dull pain of his forehead, and the sharper pain of his wrist. He became conscious of the icy water inside his boots and the throbbing of his leg muscles.

I'm lost, he thought in surprise. The thought held a meaning once more.

He looked around carefully. He was standing on a low, flat ridge that rose out of the swamp like a whale's back out of a heaving sea. He was somewhere out on a swamp. On Bear Trap Swamp—the terror of the whole district! Yet, somehow, the thought did not startle him. The *thing* that had stopped him suddenly still lingered in his subconscious, driving out panic. He turned slowly, looked all around him. His senses were alert. Suddenly, he knew. He had smelled wood smoke!

He sniffed the air hungrily. There it was! Unmistakable! It had been there all along—a thin link between the wilderness that surrounded him and civilization. His eyes spied a twisting, transparent wraith, thicker than the haze of snow. A cry escaped his lips. He started to run. But he stopped suddenly and his eyes narrowed. It must be the lost hunter. He had forgotten completely about him. There would be no one else out here in this dismal swamp but that fool hunter hunching over a little fire. It would never do to go up to him, panting and gasping like a worn-out old engine.

He moved cautiously through the screen of spruce until he saw the cone of rising smoke, and then the small fire and the figure of the man hunched down beside it. Bellamy crouched down out of sight and breathed carefully until the fierce panting of his chest subsided. Then he stood up and walked toward the man.

He said evenly, "Hi, Bill. Kind of cold out, ain't it?"

The man by the fire leaped up with a strangled cry. He gazed with wide, terrified eyes for a moment; then the cry came from his open lips again, and he stumbled toward the warden, hopping on one leg and dragging the other one grotesquely behind him. He threw his arms around the warden and sagged against him, and buried his face against his coat, and sobbed.

"Easy, feller," the warden said. "Take it easy. You're all right now." The sobbing slowed and stopped. The man rubbed his face back and forth against the warden's coat, then straightened himself up slowly. "You'll be all right," the warden said. "Here, lean on me, and let's get over to that fire."

"I'm all right now," the man said.

He leaned on the warden's shoulder and hobbled back to the fire.

"Pulled my ankle sometime yesterday. Guess it was yesterday——"

"It was," said the warden. "Here—you lie down here and let me pile up some wood on this fire. I guess I'd better signal. There's a reg'lar army out lookin' for you."

He took out his pistol and fired two quick shots. There was no answer for a moment, and fear inside him began to mount again. Then he heard an answer dimly from somewhere in back of him. He turned and faced that way, and the gust of wind in his face brought the sound of other shots more clearly.

"Have a gang here in less than an hour," he said cheerily.

The hunter smiled up at him.

"Here, let me take a look at that foot," Bellamy said.

"It's all right," the hunter said.

Bellamy found a dead spruce near by, and broke off an armful of branches and piled them on the fire. "That's what I call a fire," he said. "Only city folks believe that bunk about Indians building little fires. Any man wants to keep from freezing builds a heaping big fire."

Suddenly he remembered something. He dug into his pocket and brought out a small vacuum of coffee and poured out a steaming cup. The hunter reached out for it. His eyes opened in sudden amazement.

"Say, I've got a sandwich in my pocket!" he said. "I thought a while ago that I was going to starve to death out here—and I never remembered that sandwich in my pocket."

"Lost men do mighty queer things," the warden said. "Why the devil didn't you shoot when you found out you was lost?"

The man sipped the hot coffee thoughtfully as if trying to remember. "I couldn't," he said at last. "I slipped and fell and banged my head. Knocked myself cold. When I came to, it was just getting dark and my ankle was on fire. I started to look for the gun, but I couldn't find it. Then I started out for home. I—I guess I got lost then—I found myself out here when it got light."

"You mean you traveled all night?"

"Yes, I think I did."

"You ought to be darned glad you didn't drown yourself in one of them ponds down there. The ice would never hold you up. Of all the stupid——"

"I know," the man said.

The warden got up and fired two quick shots with his pistol. The answers were much more distinct.

"I'm sorry," the man said. "I guess I led you through some tough going. That's a nasty cut on your forehead."

Bellamy reached up his unmittened hand and touched the spot tenderly. "Ducked one branch and ran smack into another I hadn't seen."

His hat was gone, too. He didn't remem-ber losing it. He remembered going through a real tough thicket once. That must have been the place he lost it. It would be just like Ellis to find it in that thicket and start asking questions. Ellis had a nose for such things. The two men sat by the fire, staring into the leaping flames and thinking their own thoughts. The hunter finally said:

"Warden, when I first saw you—I mean—I guess I acted sort of like a fool."

"Shucks," the warden said. "Rest easy. There's some things one man never tells about another."

"Thanks," the man said.

And later, when a new armful of branch-es blazed high against the darkening sky, the hunter looked up once more.

"I've been wondering how you found me," he said.

Warden Bellamy thought for a long time before answering. "Years ago, when we used to run deer with dogs," he said slowly, "every deer we started on a certain moun-tain would go pretty near along the same ridges, and through the same notches, and finally cross the brooks at certain places. A wounded deer will pretty near always travel over a certain way. Maybe the going is easier that way—maybe, for generations, they've gone that way, to some thicket or swamp, to die. I guess maybe all lost men travel in the same paths without even knowin' it——"

The hunter thought that over, nodding slowly. "You ever been lost, Warden?"

This time there was no need to stop and think.

"Shucks, no! Been turned around for two-three days, a couple of times. But lost——"

He chuckled at the idea, and his arm came up and he rubbed his sleeve absently over his badge, the way he always chuckled, the way he always rubbed his badge when he was telling it to a tenderfoot, to a fool city slicker. The hunter believed him. They all did. Sometime, he might even grow to believe it himself again. He had to. He was a native. He belonged to these mountains. He was the warden. □□

Discussion

1. There are two groups of people in this story, the "natives" and the hunters from the city. **(a)** What kinds of traits and behavior are typical of each group? **(b)** Would you say that these two groups are presented as stereotypes? Why or why not?

2. (a) What is Bellamy's opinion of the hunters from the city? **(b)** Which character does he seem to admire and respect at the beginning of the story? **(c)** In what ways is Bellamy like or different from this person?

3. The first few pages of the story give many clues about Bellamy. **(a)** About how old is he? **(b)** What is his physical condition? **(c)** What is the extent of his experience in the woods?

4. (a) When does Bellamy first realize he is lost? **(b)** At what point does he panic?

5. When Bellamy realizes he is lost, he reaches for his pistol. **(a)** Why doesn't he fire the signal shots? **(b)** What does this indicate about Bellamy?

6. (a) Why is it ironic that Bellamy finds the lost hunter? **(b)** Several of Bellamy's subsequent statements to the hunter are also ironic, in view of the warden's experiences. Explain the irony of at least two of Bellamy's statements.

7. How do you think the warden's reputation will be affected by his "finding" of the lost hunter?

8. Has Bellamy changed in any way by the end of the story? Explain.

Extension • Writing

1. This story may remind you of a time when you yourself were lost. Perhaps you can recall a childhood incident of being lost in a crowded store, museum, or ballpark. In two or three paragraphs, describe your reactions to being "lost and found."

2. Which of the two statements below more nearly reflects your own view of "The Warden"? Write a paragraph explaining your agreement or your disagreement with one of the statements.

(a) Bellamy is a phony at the beginning and the end of the story. Even after his frightening ordeal in the woods, he is still pretending to be what he most definitely is not: a wise and able woodsman.

(b) Bellamy is humbled and changed by the discovery he makes about himself while lost. Though he does not "confess" his weaknesses to the lost hunter, we can be sure he no longer believes in his stereotyped opinions of "natives" and "city slickers."

5: American Kaleidoscope

CONTENT REVIEW

1. In several selections in this unit, characters make important discoveries about themselves—about what they want or need, for example, or what they can or cannot do. What "self-discoveries" are made by **(a)** Jessie in "Up on Fong Mountain"; **(b)** Gordon Parks in "Music Inside My Head"; **(c)** Bellamy in "The Warden"?

2. The issue of "progress" —of modern ideas, of technology and machines, of new ways of using the land—is touched on in many selections in this unit. What attitude toward "progress" is expressed by **(a)** the speaker in "Printed Words"; **(b)** the father in "Drouth"; **(c)** the speaker in "Nightmare Number Three"; **(d)** Charla in "When the Fire Dies"?

3. In the poem "Dreams," the speaker emphasizes the importance of holding onto one's hopes and ideals. What other selections in this unit might be used to illustrate this idea?

Unit 5, Test I
INTERPRETATION: NEW MATERIAL

Read carefully the short story reprinted below. Then on a separate sheet of paper, write your answers to the questions that follow it.

Thank You, Ma'am
Langston Hughes

She was a large woman with a large purse that had everything in it but a hammer and nails. It had a long strap, and she carried it slung across her shoulder. It was about eleven o'clock at night, and she was walking alone, when a boy ran up behind her and tried to snatch her purse. The strap broke with the tug the boy gave it from behind. But the boy's weight and the weight of the purse caused him to lose his balance. Instead of taking off full blast, the boy fell on his back on the sidewalk, and his legs flew up. The large woman simply turned around and kicked him right square in his blue-jeaned sitter. Then she reached down and picked the boy up by his shirt. She shook him until his teeth rattled.

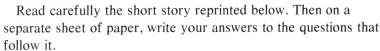

After that the woman said, "Pick up my pocketbook, boy, and give it here."

She still held him tightly. But she bent down enough to let him pick up her purse. Then she said, "Now ain't you ashamed of yourself?"

Firmly gripped by his shirt front, the boy said, "Yes'm."

The woman said, "What did you want to do it for?"

The boy said, "I didn't aim to."

She said, "You lie!"

By that time two or three people passed, turned to look, and some stood watching.

"If I turn you loose, will you run?" asked the woman.

"Yes'm," said the boy.

"Then I won't turn you loose," said the woman. She did not release him.

"Lady, I'm sorry," whispered the boy.

"Um-hum! Your face is dirty. I got a great mind to wash your face for you. Ain't you got nobody home to tell you to wash your face?"

"No'm," said the boy.

"Then it will get washed this evening," said the large woman, starting up the street, dragging the frightened boy behind her.

He looked as if he were fourteen or fifteen, thin and wild, in tennis shoes and blue jeans.

The woman said, "You ought to be my son. I would teach you right from wrong. Least I can do right now is to wash your face. Are you hungry?"

"No'm," said the boy. "I just want you to turn me loose."

"Was I bothering you when I turned that corner?" asked the woman.

"No'm."

"But you put yourself in contact with *me*," said the woman. "If you think that contact is not going to last a while, you got another thought coming. When I get through with you, sir, you are going to remember Mrs. Luella Bates Washington Jones."

Sweat popped out on the boy's face, and he began to struggle. Mrs. Jones stopped, jerked him around in front of her, put a half nelson about his neck, and continued to drag him up the street. When she got to her door, she dragged the boy inside, down a hall, and into a large room at the rear of the house. She switched on the light and left the door open. The boy could hear other roomers laughing and talking. Some of their doors were open, too; so he knew he and the woman were not alone. The woman still had him by the neck in the middle of her room.

She said, "What is your name?"

"Roger," answered the boy.

"Then, Roger, you go to that sink and wash your face," said the woman. She turned him loose—at last. Roger looked at the door—and went to the sink.

"Let the water run until it gets warm," she said. "Here's a clean towel."

"You gonna take me to jail?" asked the boy, bending over the sink.

"Not with that face. I would not take you nowhere," said the woman. "Here I am trying to get home to cook me a bite to eat, and you snatch my pocketbook! Maybe you ain't been to your supper, either, late as it be. Have you?"

"There's nobody home at my house," said the boy.

"Then we'll eat," said the woman. "I believe you're hungry—or been hungry—to try to snatch my pocketbook!"

"I want a pair of suede shoes," said the boy.

"Well, you didn't have to snatch *my* pocketbook to get some suede shoes," said Mrs. Luella Bates Washington Jones. "You could of asked me."

"Ma'am?"

The water dripping from his face, the boy looked at her. There was a long pause. A very long pause. After drying his face and not knowing what else to do, the boy dried it again. Then he turned around. The door was open. He would make a dash for it down the hall. He would run, run, run, *run!*

The woman was sitting on the day bed. After a while she said, "I were young once and I wanted things I could not get."

There was another long pause. The boy's mouth opened. Then he frowned, not knowing he frowned.

The woman said, "Um-hum! You thought I was going to say, *but I didn't snatch people's pocketbooks.* Well, I wasn't going to say that." Pause. Silence. "I have done things, too, which I would not tell you, son—neither tell God, if He didn't already know. Everybody's got something in common. Sit you down while I fix us something to eat. You might run that comb through your hair so you will look presentable."

In another corner of the room behind a screen was a gas plate and an icebox. Mrs. Jones got up and went behind the screen. The woman did not watch the boy to see if he was going to run now. She didn't watch her purse, which she left behind her on the day bed. But the boy took care to sit on the far side of the room, away from the purse. He thought she could easily see him out of the corner of her eye if she wanted to. He did not trust the woman *not* to trust him. And he did not want to be mistrusted now.

"Do you need somebody to go to the store," asked the boy, "to get some milk or something?"

"Don't believe I do," said the woman, "unless you want sweet milk yourself. I was going to make cocoa out of this canned milk I got here."

"That will be fine," said the boy.

She heated some lima beans and ham, made the cocoa, and set the table. The woman did not ask the boy anything about where he lived, or his folks, or anything else that would embarrass him. Instead, as they ate, she told him about her job in a hotel beauty shop, what the work was like, and how all kinds of women came in and out. Then she cut him half of her ten-cent cake.

"Eat some more, son," she said.

When they finished eating, she got up and said, "Now here, take this ten dollars and buy yourself some suede shoes. And, next time, do not make the mistake of latching onto my pocketbook nor nobody *else's*—because shoes got by devilish ways will burn your feet. I got to get my rest now. But from here on in, son, I hope you will behave yourself."

She led him down the hall to the front door and opened it. "Good night! Behave yourself, boy!" she said as he went down the steps.

The boy wanted to say something more than "Thank you, ma'am," to Mrs. Luella Bates Washington Jones. Although his lips moved, he couldn't even say that as he turned at the foot of the stairs and looked up at the large woman in the door. Then she shut the door. □□

1. Roger tries to rob Mrs. Jones (a) early in the morning; (b) in the middle of the day; (c) during evening rush hour; (d) late at night.

2. What happens to Roger as he grabs Mrs. Jones's purse?

3. When Mrs. Jones catches Roger, she tells him that she wants to (a) wash his face; (b) turn him in to the police; (c) take him home to his mother; (d) buy him dinner.

4. Roger goes to Mrs. Jones's house because (a) the police take him there to have Mrs. Jones identify him; (b) he wants to get revenge on Mrs. Jones; (c) his mother has sent him there to apologize; (d) Mrs. Jones drags him there.

5. Which of the following words best describes Roger's reaction while all this is happening? (a) amusement; (b) fear; (c) anger; (d) unconcern.

6. What does Roger tell Mrs. Jones he wanted money for?

7. Based on the evidence in the story, Mrs. Jones (a) has no money; (b) has a limited amount of money; (c) is fairly well to do; (d) is rich.

8. The longer Roger is with Mrs. Jones, the more he **(a)** finds the whole situation ridiculous; **(b)** wants to get away; **(c)** is frightened of what Mrs. Jones will do to him; **(d)** wants Mrs. Jones to believe he is trustworthy.

9. Which of the following best describes Roger? **(a)** He steals because he is hungry; **(b)** He knows that he will get away with criminal acts because he is not sixteen yet; **(c)** He needs guidance to keep him from being a criminal; **(d)** He is too far along the road to crime for anyone to help him.

10. In her dealings with Roger, Mrs. Jones **(a)** tries to provide him with guidance; **(b)** convinces him that he will never amount to anything; **(c)** threatens to call the police if he ever comes near her again; **(d)** indicates that because he is poor, he is not responsible for what he does.

11. What does Mrs. Jones give Roger just before she lets him go?

12. The conflict in this story is between **(a)** Roger and his environment; **(b)** Mrs. Jones and her environment; **(c)** Mrs. Jones and her fears; **(d)** Roger and Mrs. Jones.

13. The personalities of Roger and Mrs. Jones are mainly revealed through **(a)** descriptions of their physical traits; **(b)** their speech and behavior; **(c)** their thoughts; **(d)** the setting of the story.

14. The theme of this story is **(a)** kindness sometimes has a better effect on wrongdoers than punishment does; **(b)** a boy tries to steal a woman's purse and ends up having dinner with her; **(c)** poverty and crime always go hand in hand; **(d)** there is no such thing as a perfect crime.

15. When Roger tries to say "Thank you, ma'am" at the end of the story, he wants to thank Mrs. Jones for **(a)** food; **(b)** money; **(c)** taking time to talk with him; **(d)** all of the above.

Unit 5 Test II
COMPOSITION

Choose one of the following assignments to write about. Unless you are told otherwise, assume you are writing for your classmates.

1. Assume that you are Roger in "Thank You, Ma'am." Several months have passed since the episode with Mrs. Jones, and now you want to thank her for the way you think she helped you change your life. Write her a letter expressing your gratitude. Begin by reminding her who you are, and tell her how she helped you by explaining specifically how your feelings changed from the moment you tried to rob her until she finally let you go.

2. One of the problems of both Harlan Bellamy in "The Warden" and Charla Escalante in "When the Fire Dies" is that they are not tolerant of people whose ideas about how to live are different from their own. Choose one of these characters, and write a composition discussing **(a)** the specific ways the character shows lack of acceptance of others' life-styles; and **(b)** what you think the character's attitudes reveal about his or her own personality.

3. Do inventions and other advances of society sometimes create more problems than they solve? The authors of at least some of the selections listed below seem to think so. Choose a selection in which you think the author is making a statement against some element of society's "progress." Explain what it is that the author is finding fault with, and how he or she makes a case against it.

    a. "Drouth"

    b. "Nightmare Number Three"

    c. from *Travels with Charley*

    d. "Upon the Waters"

4. A kaleidoscope is a tube containing colored glass pieces that form different patterns when the tube is turned. In what way is this unit an "American Kaleidoscope"? Choose two selections from the unit that you think convey different or contrasting pictures of life in this country (for example, city life—country life, happiness—unhappiness, poverty—comfort). In an essay entitled "Two Views of America," discuss the contrasting pictures of American life presented in the two selections.

The old were young once . . .

and the young do not grow younger.

GENERATIONS

An elegy (el′ə jē) is a mournful poem that expresses grief at someone's death. But how—and why—would an elegy be written in a junkyard?

Elegy: Written at the County Junkyard

James D. Houston

At the county dump I am throwing away my father. His old paint rags, and stumps of brushes. Color catalogues. The caked leather suitcase he used for so many years carrying small tools and tiny jars of his trade, suitcase so cracked and bent and buckle-ripped it's no good for anything now, not even what he used it for. I start to toss it on top of the brushes and the rags, but hesitate, toss instead the five-gallon drums that once held primer. He stacked them against one wall of his shop, for nothing, kept dozens more than he'd ever use. Around these fall the ointments from his medicine chest. And cracked galoshes, filled with dust, as if in his closet it's been raining dust for years. And magazines. His fishing hat. Notes to himself:

Fix window
Grease car
Call Ed
Call Harlow about job

Bent nails in a jar, rolls of old wire, pipe sections, fiddle he always intended to mend, embossed cards some salesman left, old paid bills, check stubs, pencils his teeth chewed.

Ragtaggle bits of this and that he touched, stacked, stored, useless to anyone but him, and he's gone now, so toss it all out there among the refrigerators and lettuce leaves and seven hundred truck tires, busted sofas, flower pots, and grass from the overgrown gardens of every household. Into it I throw my father, saving for last that suitcase of his, first seen twenty years back, and old

then, the first day he took me out on a job, pair of his spattered overalls to wear, rolled thick at the cuff, and Sherwin-Williams white billcap,[1] and us two squatting while he unbuckles the case and touches dark labels of pigment tubes, deciding something.

Crusted with splats of seventy colors now, lid corners split as if somebody sat on it. The ragged straps dangle. One shred of leather holds the chromium buckle, yet the buckle itself hasn't worn much at all, still catches the sun, where paint doesn't cover

---

Reprinted with the permission of Capra Press from *Three Songs for My Father* by James D. Houston. Copyright © 1974 by James D. Houston.
1. Sherwin-Williams white billcap, a hat provided by a well-known paint company.

it, relic from those days before things tarnished in a week.

One last glance. By five tonight it'll be gone for good, when the bulldozer comes around to shove it over the side with the rest of today's arms and toes and parts of hearts.

"What're ya gonna do, dad?"

He doesn't answer. He never answers, as if it offends him to be interrupted. And I always wait, as if all those previous silences were exceptions, and this time he will turn and speak. It's a big reason for coming along this morning, the chance that out here on the job something might pass between us. I would never have been able to describe it ahead of time, but . . . something.

I wait and watch two minutes of puckering lips and long slow blinks while he studies the labels, then selects one tube, smudged and wrinkled, unscrews its top and squeezes out a little on his fingertips.

Five feet away a canvas dropcloth covers a few square yards of hardwood floor. I follow him to a five-gallon drum he's mixing paint in. A narrow stick of plywood holds the color he's shooting for—pale pale green. He's proud of his eye, his knack for figuring just how pale this green will be when it's dry. Squeeze a green strip from the tube and stir it in, wide easy stirs while the green spreads out like taffy strips. Stir and stir. Then test: dip another stick in. Pair it. Stir.

"Okay, Jim. Take half this green paint and git that wall there covered."

He hands me a clean brush, black bristles glistening with yesterday's thinner. He pours a gallon bucket full, deft tilt, and cuts the fall off clean.

"I'll be back in a minute," he says.

It's the first time I've painted anything away from home. I do not yet know that this wall is the beginning of the end, that before the summer is out I will dread the look of yet another long, unpainted wall and wince at the smell of thinner. I want this one to be a good job. I want to live up to the paint he's just mixed. I start by the living room door, taking my time, keeping the molding clear for a white trim later.

Ten minutes pass, and this first wall becomes my world, each piece I cover is a quadrant on my map of it. I am moving across the wide-open middle country—working my brush like dad told me to the time we painted the back side of our house, using the wrist, lapping strokes over—when I feel compelled to turn around.

In the far doorway the lady of the house stands glaring at me, her eyes a blend of terror and hate. I realize how dangerous I must look to her: next to the wall of her priceless living room she finds Tom Sawyer with his cuffs rolled thick, whitewashing away an afternoon.

Under green freckles my face turns scarlet.

She disappears.

From the hallway comes her loud whisper. "Mr. *Hous*ton! That boy painting my living room wall couldn't be over fifteen!"

"He's thirteen, ma'am."

"He's what?"

"It's my boy, Jim. He's giving me a hand this summer."

"I just wonder if he knows what he's *doing* in there."

"I painted my first house when I was ten."

"Well . . . I . . . if . . . I'd certainly be keeping an eye on him if I were you."

"Don't worry, ma'am, he knows what to do."

Behind me I hear her walking slowly across the room. I keep painting, don't look at her this time. Plenty of paint on the brush. But don't let it run. Feather it at the overlap. Cover. Cover.

Dad comes in and fills up another gallon bucket and helps me finish the wall. He catches my eye once and winks at the fast one we have pulled on Mrs. So-and-so. Then we are covering the middle country together, in a curiously enclosed stillness, broken only by the whish of bristles and cluck of brush handle against the can. Somewhere in the back of the house a radio is playing, but its faraway music doesn't penetrate our territory.

We finish the room by quitting time. Dad looks over the sections I've painted, finds a couple of holidays[2] along the baseboard and has me fill these in before we clean the brushes, saying only, "Keep an eye out for them holidays," and then a little later, when the sash tools are thinned, and the pigment tubes lined up the way he wants them, next to the knives he uses for cutting linoleum and spreading putty and spackling cracks, he drops the lid shut on his kit of a suitcase, snaps the buckle to, straps it, says, "Might as well take that on out to the truck."

I have never paid much attention to his kit. Now I know just enough about what's inside for its contents to be mysteries. A year from now I will know too much about what's inside, and I will be able to read his half smile, already on the verge of apologizing for having only this to reward me with. But today it is an honor. No one has ever carried that kit but him. It has mysterious weight, with gypsy daubs of ivory, burnt umber, and vermilion all across the ancient leather. A fine weight for carrying from the house downstairs to the curb.

At the county dump I am throwing away my father, hefting this suitcase to toss the last of him onto the smoking heap, when that shred of leather gives and the buckle breaks. The kit flies open. As if compressed inside, waiting to escape, the pungent smell of oil and rare pigments cuts through smoke and rot and fills the air around me. The few tubes still in there begin to topple. My throwing arm stays. My other hand reaches. I'm holding the suitcase, inhaling the smell that always surrounded him, even after he had scrubbed. It rose from the creases in his hands, from permanent white liners rimming his fingernails, from the paint-motes he sometimes missed with thinner, at the corners of his eyes.

I breathe deep. Close the suitcase slowly. Prepare to heave it once and for all. This time with both hands. Out among all those things you only find by losing them. Out and up. And onto the truck bed. Where it lands with a thunk. And sits solid. Those aromatic tubes give it density. I wait for him to tie his ladder on the overhead rack, and we climb onto the cab. He winks once more, as we prepare to leave Mrs. So-and-so behind. Reeking of paint and turpentine, billcaps shoved back, we are Sherwin and Williams calling it a day, with no way to talk much over the stuttering engine of this metal-floored chevvy, and no need to talk. The sticky clutch leaps. Wind rushes in, mixing paint and gasoline fumes, and all you need to do is stay loose for the jolts and the whole long rumble ride home. ☐☐

---

2. *holidays*, painters' slang word for places accidentally left unpainted.

Discussion

1. Do you think you would have liked Jim's father? Why or why not?

2. Jim presents his father as he sees him from two different points in Jim's life. What are the two different time periods and how does the reader know what these are?

3. The narrator tells us in the first sentence that he is throwing away his father. (a) What does he *really* throw away? (b) How are these things connected to "throwing away a father"?

4. (a) Of the objects he throws away, what most represents Jim's father to him? (b) What specific effect does this object have on Jim's thoughts?

5. Jim says he went on that first painting job on the chance that something important would pass between his father and himself. (a) What does Jim learn about his father that he probably hadn't known before? (b) How does this first commercial work with his father probably change the relationship between Jim and his father?

6. (a) Reread the last paragraph. At what point in time are we viewing events depicted there—when Jim is thirteen, when he is thirty-three, or both? Explain. (b) What does this paragraph suggest about how Jim will remember his father?

Vocabulary
Context, Pronunciation

The sentences in this exercise include the pronunciations of five of the words listed below. For each sentence, (1) figure out which word the pronunciation symbols stand for and write it (use the pronunciation key in your Glossary if necessary). Then (2) choose the appropriate definition of the word and write its letter after the word.

quadrant	pigment
pungent	compress
primer	compel

1. You will have better luck painting unfinished furniture if you start by applying (prī′mər). (a) color; (b) white wallpaper; (c) paneling; (d) base coat of paint.

2. Those white spots on her hand are areas where the skin has lost its (pig′mənt). (a) substance causing warts; (b) substance causing burns; (c) substance causing pain; (d) substance causing color.

3. Now they are asking him to (kəm pres′) his thirty-minute speech into only ten minutes. (a) squeeze together; (b) expand; (c) eliminate; (d) strengthen.

4. The (pun′jənt) smell of Dad's cheap cigar had us all begging him to open a window. (a) sweet; (b) sharp; (c) delicate; (d) inviting.

5. It is easy to urge that people stop smoking but difficult to (kəm pel′) them to do so. (a) promise; (b) advise; (c) force; (d) reward.

Extension • Writing

Can you recall an experience of doing something for the first time with a parent or other adult? Write two paragraphs in which you tell about the event and how you felt about it. You may write about either a pleasant experience or an unpleasant one. The first paragraph should tell what the event was. The second paragraph should explain how you felt and why.

for sapphires[1]

Carolyn M. Rodgers

(for mama and daddy)

Discussion

1. Is a child's view of "reali-ty" usually different from an adult's? Why or why not?

2. There are two pictures of "mama" presented here. **(a)** How does the child see her mother? **(b)** What is the second picture that is presented? **(c)** Which do you think is the "true" picture? Why?

Carolyn M. Rodgers

Formerly a counselor and language arts instructor, Carolyn Rodgers began a full-time writing career after being encouraged by Gwendolyn Brooks, the Pulitzer-Prize-winning poet.

Rodgers's first work appeared in *Black World;* since then she has published several volumes of poetry and has served as writer-in-residence at Malcolm X College in Chicago.

my daddy don't know
the same lady
i do. i know mama
he knows "suga."
5   and when daddy looks at mama
i wonder does he see
the wrinkles around
the tight mouth, stiff
factory used fingers
10   uh yellow skin,
begun to fade. . . .

and when mama talks
how does he hear? i hear
anger, pride, strength and love
15 crouched low in the throat,
any, ready to spring.
but daddy calls mama "suga"
and uh beacon is behind his eyes,
he buys Chanel and coats
with fur collars. . . .

i wonder what lady does daddy know?

In this excerpt from Child of the Owl, *Casey Young is twelve years old.*
Her mother is dead, her father is in the hospital after an accident.
She has spent an uncomfortable time with the family of her Uncle Phil,
and now is being taken to live with her maternal grandmother,
in San Francisco's Chinatown.

Paw-Paw

Laurence Yep

It was like we'd gone through an invisible wall into another world. There was a different kind of air in Chinatown, lighter and brighter. I mean, on the north side there were the American bars and joints; on the west, the mansions and hotels of Nob Hill; and on the other two sides were the tall skyscrapers where insurance men or lawyers spent the day. And they were pushing all the sunshine and all the buildings of Chinatown together—like someone had taken several square miles of buildings and squeezed it until people and homes were compressed into a tiny little half of a square mile. I didn't know what to make of the buildings either. They were mostly three- or four-story stone buildings but some had fancy balconies, and others had decorations on them like curved tile roofs—one building had bright yellow balconies decorated with shiny, glazed purple dolphins—and there was a jumble of neon signs, dark now in the daytime, jammed all together. Most of the buildings, though, had some color to them—bright reds and rich golds with some green thrown in.

But it was the people there that got me. I don't think I'd ever seen so many Chinese in my life before this. Some were a rich, dark tan while others were as pale as Caucasians. Some were short with round faces and wide, full-lipped mouths and noses squashed flat, and others were tall with thin faces and high cheekbones that made their eyes look like the slits in a mask. Some were dressed in regular American style while others wore padded silk jackets. All of them crowding into one tiny little patch of San Francisco.

Funny, but I felt embarrassed. Up until then I had never thought about skin colors because in the different places where we had lived, there were just poor people in all different colors. But now all of a sudden I saw all these funny brown people running around, a lot of them gabbling away at one another. I started to roll up the car window to try to shut out the sound and I noticed that my hand on the window handle was colored a honey kind of tan like some of the

people outside. I took my hand off the handle and stared at it.

"What's the matter now?" Uncle Phil asked. We'd gotten caught in a momentary traffic snarl. I turned to see that Phil's face was brown as my hand. Phil adjusted his tie uneasily and growled, "What're you looking at?"

I looked ahead, keeping my eyes on the glove compartment. My father and I had never talked much about stuff like this. I knew more about race horses than I knew about myself—I mean myself as a Chinese. I looked at my hands again, thinking they couldn't be my hands, and then I closed my eyes and felt their outline, noticing the tiny fold of flesh at the corners. Maybe it was because I thought of myself as an American and all Americans were supposed to be white like on TV or in books or in movies, but now I felt like some mad scientist had switched bodies on me like in all those monster movies, so that I had woken up in the wrong one.

Suddenly I felt like I was lost. Like I was going on this trip to this place I had always heard about and I was on the only road to that place but the signs kept telling me I was going to some other place. When I looked in the glove compartment to check my maps, I found I'd brought the wrong set of maps. And the road was too narrow to turn around in and there was too much traffic anyway so I just had to keep on going . . . and getting more and more lost. It gave me the creeps so I kept real quiet.

Phil headed up Sacramento Street—a steep, slanting street that just zoomed on and on up to the top of Nob Hill, where the rich people lived and where they had the swanky hotels. Phil turned suddenly into a little dead-end alley wide enough for only one car. On one side was a one-story Chinese school of brick so old or so dirty that the bricks were practically a purple color. On the other side as we drove by was a small parking lot with only six spaces for cars. Phil stopped the car in the middle of the alley and I could see the rest of it was filled with apartment houses. Somewhere someone had a window open and the radio was blaring out. I couldn't find the place where it was coming from but I did see someone's diapers and shirts hung in the windows and on the fire escape of one apartment.

"Why do they hang their laundry in the windows?" I asked Phil.

"That's what people from Hong Kong use for curtains," Phil grumbled.

The sidewalk in front of the house was cracked like someone had taken a sledge-hammer to it, and there were iron grates over the lower windows. The steps up to the doorway were old, worn concrete painted red. To the left were the mailboxes, which had Chinese words for the names or had no labels at all. To the right were the doorbells to all the nine apartments. Phil picked out the last and rang. He jabbed his thumb down rhythmically. Three short. Three long. Three short.

"Why are you doing that?" I asked.

"Signaling your grandmother," he grumbled. "She never answers just one buzz like any normal person, or even just three bursts. It's got to be nine buzzes in that way or she doesn't open the door. She says her friends know what she means."

So did I. It was Morse code for SOS.[1] The buzzer on the door sounded like an

---

1. *SOS.* These three letters, in telegraphic code, are the international signal for help.

angry bee. Phil opened the door, putting his back against it and fighting against the heavy spring that tried to swing it shut. "Go on. Up three flights. Number nine. Remember now. You call her Paw-Paw."

"What's Paw-Paw?"

"Maternal grandmother. Chinese have a different word for every relation. Like I'm your *kauh-fu*—your maternal uncle. Actually your grandmother's name is *Ah Paw* but when you're close to someone, you repeat the word, so it's Paw-Paw."

"I don't know any Chinese," I said.

Phil grunted. "You don't have to worry about talking to her. She learned pretty good English when she was a maid to some rich Americans."

"When did she do that?"

"Just after your grandfather died. I was only a baby then. But she quit once Jeanie finished high school. She got tired of leaving Chinatown."

I walked into an old, dim hallway and climbed up the wooden steps. As I turned an angle on the stairs, I saw light burning fierce and bright from a window. When I came to it, I looked out at the roof of the Chinese school next door. Someone had thrown some old 45's and a pair of sneakers down there. If I were some kind of kid that felt sorry for herself, I would almost have said that was the way I felt: like some piece of old, ugly junk that was being kicked around on the discard pile.

I didn't stay by the window long, though, because Phil was coming up the stairs and I didn't want to act like his kids' stories about Paw-Paw had scared me. Anybody could be better than Uncle Phil and his family . . . I hoped. I stopped by the number-nine room, afraid to knock. It could not be the right place because I could hear rock music com-

ing through the doorway. I scratched my head and checked the numbers on the other doors on the landing. Phil was still a flight down, huffing and puffing up the steps with my duffel bag—it wasn't that heavy; Phil was just that much out of shape. "Go on. Go on. Knock, you little idiot," he called up the stairwell.

I shrugged. It wasn't any of my business. I knocked at the door. I heard about six bolts and locks being turned. Finally the door swung open and I saw a tiny, pleasant, round-faced woman smiling at me. Her cheeks were a bright red. Her gray hair was all curly and frizzy around her head and a pair of rimless, thick eyeglasses perched on her nose. She was round and plump, wearing a sweater even on a hot day like this, a pair of cotton black slacks, and a pair of open-heeled, flat slippers.

"Paw-Paw?" I asked.

"Hello. Hello." She opened up her arms and gave me a big hug, almost crushing me. It was funny, but I suddenly found myself holding on to her. Underneath all the soft layers of clothing I could feel how hard and tough she was. She patted me on the back three times and then left me for a moment to turn down her radio. It really was her old, white, beat-up radio playing rock music.

"Hey, how about a hand?" Phil puffed as he finally got to the landing.

Paw-Paw shuffled out to the landing in her slippered feet and made shooing motions. "You can go home now. We can do all right by ourselves."

Phil heaved his shoulders up and down in a great sigh and set the bag down. "Now, Momma——"

"Go on home," she said firmly. "We need time by ourselves."

I saw that Phil must have had some fine

speech all prepared, probably warning Paw-Paw about me and warning me about ingratitude. He was not about to give up such an opportunity to make a speech.

"Now, Momma——"

"Go on. You're still not too old for a swat across the backside."

Phil ran his hand back and forth along the railing. "Really, Momma. You oughtn't——"

"Go on," Paw-Paw raised her hand.

Phil gulped. The thought of having a former district president of the lawyers spanked by his own mother must have been too much for him. He turned around and started down the steps. He still had to get in the last word though.

"You mind your Paw-Paw, young lady. You hear me?" he shouted over his shoulder.

I waited till I heard the door slam. "Do you know what those buzzes stand for?"

"Do you?" Her eyes crinkled up.

"It stands for SOS. But where did you learn it?"

"When I worked for the American lady, her boy had a toy . . . what do you call it?" She made a tapping motion with her finger.

"Telegraph?"

"Yes. It's a good joke on such a learned man, no?" Her round red face split into a wide grin and then she began to giggle and when she put her hand over her mouth, the giggle turned into a laugh.

I don't think that I had laughed in all that time since my father's accident a month ago. It was like all the laughter I hadn't been able to use came bubbling up out of some hidden well—burst out of the locks and just came up. Both of us found ourselves slumping on the landing, leaning our heads against the banister, and laughing.

Finally Paw-Paw tilted up her glasses and wiped her eyes. "Philip always did have too much dignity for one person. Ah." She leaned back against the railing on the landing before the stairwell, twisting her head to look at me. "You'll go far," she nodded. "Yes, you will. Your eyebrows are beautifully curved, like silkworms. That means you'll be clever. And your ears are small and close to your head and shaped a certain way. That means you're adventurous and win much honor."

"Really?"

She nodded solemnly. "Didn't you know? The face is the map of the soul." Then she leaned forward and raised her glasses and pointed to the corners of her eyes where there were two small hollows, just shadows, really. "You see those marks under my eyes?"

"Yes." I added after a moment, "Paw-Paw."

"Those marks, they mean I have a temper."

"Oh." I wondered what was to happen next.

She set her glasses back on her nose. "But I will make a deal with you. I can keep my temper under control if you can do the same with your love of adventure and intelligence. You see, people, including me, don't always understand a love of adventure and intelligence. Sometimes we mistake them for troublemaking."

"I'll try." I grinned.

I went and got my bag then and brought it inside Paw-Paw's place and looked around, trying to figure out where I'd put it. Her place wasn't more than ten by fifteen feet and it was crowded with her stuff. Her bed was pushed lengthwise against the wall next to the doorway leading out to the landing. To the right of the door was another doorway, leading to the small little cubicle of a kitchen, and next to that door was her bureau.

The wall opposite the bed had her one window leading out to the fire escape and giving a view of the alley, which was so narrow that it looked like we could have shaken hands with the people in the apartment house across from us. Beneath the window was a stack of newspapers for wrapping up the garbage. Next to the window was a table with a bright red-and-orange-flower tablecloth. Paw-Paw pulled aside her chair and her three-legged stool and told me to put my bag under the table. A metal cabinet and stacks of boxes covered the rest of the wall and the next one had hooks from which coats and other stuff in plastic bags hung.

In the right corner of the old bureau were some statues and an old teacup with some dirt in it and a half-burnt incense stick stuck into it. The rest of the top, though, was covered with old photos in little cardboard covers. They filled the bureau top and the mirror too, being stuck into corners of the mirror or actually taped onto the surface.

Next to the photos were the statues. One was about eight inches high in white porcelain of a pretty lady holding a flower and with the most patient, peaceful expression on her face. To her left was a statue of a man with a giant-sized, bald head. And then there were eight little statues, each only about two inches high. "Who are they?" I asked.

"Statues of some holy people," Paw-Paw said reluctantly.

There was something familiar about the last statue on Paw-Paw's bureau. It was of a fat, balding god with large ears, who had little children crawling over his lap and climbing up his shoulders. "Hey," I said. "Is that the happy god?"

Paw-Paw looked puzzled. "He's not the god of happiness."

"But they call him the happy god. See?" I pulled my father's little plastic charm out of my pocket and pointed to the letters on the back. *Happy God—Souvenir of Chinatown.*

Paw-Paw didn't even try to read the lettering. Maybe my father had already shown it to her long ago. "He's not the god of happiness. He just looks happy. He's the Buddha—the Buddha who will come in the future. He's smiling because everyone will be saved by that time and he can take a vacation. The children are holy people who become like children again."

"What about the others, Paw-Paw?"

"I don't have the words to explain," Paw-Paw said curtly, like the whole thing was embarrassing her.

I sat down by the table on the stool, which was painted white with red flowers. "Sure you do. I think your English is better than mine."

"You don't want to know any of that stuff." With her index finger Paw-Paw rubbed hard against some spot on the table-cloth. "That stuff's only for old people. If I tell you any more, you'll laugh at it like all other young people do." There was bitter hurt and anger in her voice.

I should have left her alone, I guess; but we had been getting close to one another and suddenly I'd found this door between us—a door that wouldn't open. I wasn't so much curious now as I was desperate: I didn't want Paw-Paw shutting me out like that. "I won't laugh, Paw-Paw. Honest."

"That stuff's only for old people who are too stupid to learn American ways," she insisted stubbornly.

"Well, maybe I'm stupid too."

"No." Paw-Paw pressed her lips together tightly; and I saw that no matter how much I pestered her, I wasn't going to get her to tell me any more about the statues on her bureau. We'd been getting along so great before that I was sorry I'd ever started asking questions.

We both sat, each in our own thoughts, until almost apologetically Paw-Paw picked up a deck of cards from the table. "Do you play cards?"

"Some," I said. "Draw poker. Five-card stud. Things like that."

Paw-Paw shuffled the cards expertly. "Poker is for old men who like to sit and think too much. Now I know a game that's for the young and quick."

"What's that?"

"Slapjack." She explained that each of us took half of a deck and stacked it in front without looking at it. Then we would take turns taking the top card off and putting it down in the middle. Whenever a jack appeared, the first one to put her hand over the pile of cards got it. She then mixed the new cards with all the cards she still had in front of her. The first one to get all the cards won the game. It would sound like the advantage was with the person who was putting out the card at that time, but she was supposed to turn up the card away from her so she couldn't see it before the other player.

Paw-Paw had played a lot of card games, since she lived by herself, so she seemed to know when the jacks were going to come up. For a while all you could hear was the *slap-slap-slap*ping of cards and sometimes our hands smacking one another trying to get the pile. And sometimes I'd have more cards and sometimes Paw-Paw would. Eventually, though, she beat me. She shuffled the deck again. "You're a pretty good player," she grudged.

"Not as good as you, though."

Paw-Paw shuffled the cards, tapping them against the table so the cards in the pack were all even. "We used to play all the time. Your mother, Phil, everyone. We'd hold big contests and make plenty of noise. Only when Phil got older, he only wanted to play the games fancy Americans played like—what's that word for a road that goes over water?"

"A bridge? Phil wanted to play bridge."

"Yes." Paw-Paw put the deck on the table. I wandered over to the bed.

The radio was in a little cabinet built into the headboard of the bed. I lay down on the bed and looked at the radio dial. "Do you like rock music, Paw-Paw?"

"It's fun to listen to," Paw-Paw said, "and besides, *Chinese Hour* is on that station every night."

"Chinese Hour?"

"An hour of news and songs all in Chinese." Paw-Paw slipped the cards back carefully into their box. "They used to have some better shows on that station like mystery shows."

"I bet I could find some." I started to reach for the dial.

"Don't lose that station." Paw-Paw seemed afraid suddenly.

"Don't worry, Paw-Paw, I'll be able to get your station back for you." It was playing "Monster Mash" right then. I twisted the dial to the right and the voices and snatches of song slid past and then I turned the dial back to her station, where "Monster Mash" was still playing. "See?"

"As long as you could get it back," Paw-Paw said reluctantly.

I fiddled with the dial some more until I got hold of *Gunsmoke.* It'd gone off the air years ago but some station was playing reruns. Paw-Paw liked that, especially the deep voice of the marshal. It was good to sit there in the darkening little room, listening to Marshal Dillon inside your head and picturing him as big and tall and striding down the dusty streets of Dodge City. And I got us some other programs too, shows that Paw-Paw had never been able to listen to before.

Don't get the idea that Paw-Paw was stupid. She just didn't understand American machines that well. She lived with them in a kind of truce where she never asked much of them if they wouldn't ask much of her.

"It's getting near eight," Paw-Paw said anxiously. It was only when I got the station back for her that she began to relax. "I was always so worried that I would not be able to get back the station, I never tried to listen to others. Look what I missed."

"But you have me now, Paw-Paw," I said.

"Yes," Paw-Paw smiled briefly, straightening in her chair. "I guess I do." ☐☐

Discussion

1. Although the girl in the story is of Chinese ancestry, she reports that she knew more about horses than about herself as Chinese. (a) What makes the girl conscious of her Chinese origin? (b) How does she feel when she becomes aware of the physical characteristics which identify her as Chinese? (c) What evidence is there that she knows little about Chinese people, their customs, culture, or beliefs?

2. (a) Why is the girl staying with Paw-Paw? (b) What do you infer about the girl's past actions and reputation? How might these be connected to her stay?

3. How is Paw-Paw able to make the girl feel comfortable and accepted?

4. Paw-Paw twice refers to herself as old. What evidence is there in the story that she is "youthful" in spirit, if not in actual age?

Chinatown

There are Chinatowns in many cities, but San Francisco's Chinatown has the largest Chinese population of any city outside Asia. Today it is one of the major tourist attractions in the San Francisco area. Shops, restaurants, even school buildings have been constructed especially to imitate a picturesque Oriental-style architecture— upward-curving tiled roofs which are supposed to throw back to the skies any bad luck or misfortune that may rain down from heaven. Oriental clothing, art, furniture, porcelain, and toys fill the shops, and food of all descriptions is available for tourists as well as residents.

Although there are historical records to show that people from China settled in the Americas more than 2500 years ago, the first large group of Chinese immigrants came to California as a result of the discovery of gold in the 1840's. These adventurous pioneers came to mine gold, along with the other "forty-niners" who flocked to the state from all over the world hoping to make their fortunes.

Later, when the first transcontinental railroad was being constructed, the railroad companies recruited and imported men from China as laborers. Soon the Chinese made up a large percentage of the work crews; they often did the most hazardous work and were an important reason why the railroad was completed in record time. But they were always isolated because of their differences in language and culture, and there was no effective communication between the Chinese and white workers. After the railroad was completed in 1869, thousands of Chinese men were left without a way to earn a living. Since there was a financial depression in California at the time, many unemployed Americans were quick to blame the Chinese workers for allegedly accepting a lower pay scale and for taking jobs away from them. Such anti-Chinese feeling produced many discriminatory state laws and local ordinances. These laws not only prevented other Chinese from entering the United States but also prevented the men who were here from bringing over their families, from owning land, from attending public schools, and from applying for U.S. citizenship. Mob violence occasionally occurred during this time; some Chinese were abused physically and even killed, and others were ruined financially when crowds invaded Chinatowns and destroyed their shops and burned their homes.

In 1943, 1952, and 1965 the discriminatory laws against the Chinese were repealed. Equality of rights and opportunities finally became the law in the United States.

Gold miners in California

Brown Brothers

Grandfather

James K. Cazalas

Discussion

1. Do you know anyone like Grandfather, someone who sometimes seems much younger than his actual age? What specific abilities does the person have that create this impression?

2. In stanza one, the speaker in this poem suggests that Grandfather is a puzzle. **(a)** Under what conditions or circumstances did the speaker discover the puzzle? **(b)** What is the nature of the puzzle?

3. What possible explanation is there for the fact that Grandfather "sees" better and moves along the trail with greater ease than someone much younger?

4. What change takes place in Grandfather when he returns home?

It puzzles me
That I cannot see
What grandfather can:
He is eighty with the eyes
5 Of a young Indian
Proving his manhood.

I stumbled in the deep yellow sand
And he walked over it easily.
I breathed hard and perspired
10 And he paced himself
Like an animal
With a long way to go.

A dollar-sized turtle
Struggling on its back
15 Was dying ten feet off the sand:
It was he who saw it
And turned it over.

When we returned home,
He took off his sneakers,
20 Took out his teeth,
And was an old, dying man.
But on the trail
He was Seneca[1]
And more a part of the earth
25 Than the sand we trod.

"Grandfather" by James K. Cazalas from *Southwest Review,* Winter 1977, Vol. 62, No. 1. Reprinted by permission.
1. *Seneca,* member of the Seneca people, one of the five American Indian tribes which formed the powerful Iroquois nation.

See **CONNOTATION/DENOTATION** Handbook of Literary Terms

Buffalo Dusk

Carl Sandburg

The buffaloes are gone.
And those who saw the buffaloes are gone.
Those who saw the buffaloes by thousands and
    how they pawed the prairie sod into dust
5   with their hoofs, their great heads down
    pawing on in a great pageant of dusk,
Those who saw the buffaloes are gone.
And the buffaloes are gone.

From *Smoke and Steel* by Carl Sandburg, copyright, 1920 by Harcourt Brace Jovanovich, Inc.; renewed 1948 by Carl Sandburg. Reprinted by permission of the publishers.

Montana Historical Society

Carl Sandburg 1878 • 1967

As a young man, Carl Sandburg traveled widely across America, riding the freight trains from city to city, viewing the land, and meeting people. He loved the common people and took great pains to collect and record their folklore. He was instrumental in popularizing the folk music of his day, singing and accompanying himself on the guitar.

Sandburg was awarded two Pulitzer Prizes during his lifetime: one for his *Complete Poems* (1951) and the other for *Abraham Lincoln: The War Years* (1939). The poem that appears here is a simple, sad lament for a part of America that is gone forever. In language and thought it is characteristic of Sandburg's most famous poems.

See **POINT OF VIEW** Handbook of Literary Terms

*"Please . . . I don't want a high grade,
all I want is to pass. . . . I don't want
to pass this exam for myself only. I mean,
it means a lot to my family. My father
will be very disappointed if I flunk the
exam. . . ."*

So Much Unfairness of Things

C. D. B. Bryan

The Virginia Preparatory School lies just off the Shirley Highway between Washington, D.C., and Richmond. It is a small Southern school with dull-red brick dormitories and classroom buildings, quiet old school buildings with quiet old Southern names—Page House, Stuart Hall, Randolph Hall, Breckinridge, Pinckney, and Coulter. The high brick wall that surrounds the school is known as the Breastworks, and the shallow pond behind the football field is the Crater. V.P.S. is an old school, with an old school's traditions. A Virginia Department of Conservation sign commemorates the use of the school by Union troops as a military hospital in 1861, and every October the school celebrates "Liberation Day," in honor of the day in 1866 when the school reopened.

Graduates of the Virginia Preparatory School who have not returned for some years are shocked by the glass-and-steel apartment houses and cinderblock ramblers that have sprung up around the school grounds, but once they have driven along the Breastworks and passed through the ornate wrought-iron East Gate, they see, with satisfaction, that the school has not changed. Neither have its customs. For example, new boys, or "toads," still must obey the Toad Code. They must be courteous to old boys and faculty. They must know the school song and cheers by the end of the second week. They must know the names of all members of the faculty and the varsity football team. They must hold doors open for old boys and see that old boys are served first in the dining room. And they must "run relay"—meaning that they have to wake up the old boys in the morning when they wish to be wakened and see that they are not disturbed when they wish to sleep.

Philip Sadler Wilkinson was fourteen; he was an old boy. The new boy shook him lightly. "Mr. Wilkinson? Mr. Wilkinson? It's five-thirty, sir. You asked me to wake you up!"

Next year the new boy would be permitted to call Philip Sadler Wilkinson "P.S.," like the others. He watched P.S. stretch, turn over, and go back to sleep. "Sir? Hey! Wake up!"

P.S. rolled out of his metal cot, rubbed his eyes, felt around the top of his desk for his glasses, put them on, and looked at the new boy.

"Toad?"

"Yes, sir?"

"What is the date?"

"Thursday, the seventh of June."

"How much longer do we have until the end of the school year?"

"Seven days, twenty-three hours, and"—the new boy looked at his wristwatch—"and thirteen minutes, sir."

P.S. smiled. "Are you sure?"

"No, sir."

"Ah-hah! Ah-HAH! Toad, assume the position."

The new boy locked his knees and bent over and grabbed his ankles.

"What is a 'toad,' toad?" P.S. asked.

"Sir, a toad is a loathsome warty creature who eats insects and worms, sir. A toad is the lowest form of amphibian. A toad is despicable."

"Well, well, now, straighten those knees, toad." P.S. looked at the new boy and saw that his face was turning red with strain. "Toad, are you in pain?"

"No, sir," the new boy lied.

"Then you may straighten up."

The new boy massaged his calves. "Honest to Pete, P.S., you're a sadist."

"No, no, wait till next year. You'll be pulling the same thing on some toad yourself. I had it done to me, you had it done to you. And did I detect you calling me by my rightful name?"

The new boy smiled.

"Ah, you toads will never learn. Assume the position."

The new boy started to bend over again.

"Oh, go away," P.S. said. The new boy started out of the door and P.S. called him back. "Hey, toad? You gonna kill the Latin exam?"

"I hope so."

"How do you conjugate the verb 'to spit'?"

"Exspuo, exspuere, exspui——"

"Heck, no!" P.S. laughed. "It's *spitto, spittere, ach tui, splattus!*"

The new boy groaned and left the room.

P.S. looked at his watch. It was twenty minutes to six. He could hear the new boy waking up the boy in the next room. P.S. picked up his water glass and toothbrush and tiptoed down the corridor. He stopped at Charlie Merritt's room and knocked softly.

"Who is it?"

"It's me, Charlie."

"Oh, hey, P.S. Come on in."

P.S. pushed aside the curtain of the cubicle. Charlie was sitting at his desk, studying.

"Morning," P.S. whispered.

"Morning."

"Studying the Latin?"

"Yep."

"You know how to conjugate the verb 'to spit'?"

"Yep," Charlie said. *"Spitto, spittere, ach——"*

"O.K., O.K.!" P.S. laughed. "You gonna kill the exam?"

"I hope so. You think you'll pass it?"

"Doubt it. I haven't passed one yet." P.S. looked over at Charlie's bureau. "Say, Charlie? Can I borrow your toothpaste? I'm out."

"Sure, but roll it from the bottom of the tube, will you?"

P.S. picked up the toothpaste and went down the hall to the bathroom. Mabrey, the head monitor, was shaving. P.S. watched him in the mirror.

"You must have had a porcupine for a father," P.S. said. "You've got the heaviest beard in school."

Mabrey began to shave the length of his neck.

"Wilkinson, you're about as funny as a rubber crutch."

"Cut your throat! Cut your throat!" P.S. began to dance around behind Mabrey, sprinkling voodoo potions on the top of the older student's head. "Monkey dust! Monkey dust! Oh, black Pizzoola! Great Kubla of the Ancient Curse! Make this bad man cut his throat!"

Mabrey cursed and a small red stain began to seep through the lather on his throat. "P.S., will you *get out of here!*"

P.S. stared, eyes wide open, at the broadening stain. "My gosh! Hey! It worked!"

Mabrey undid the towel from around his waist and snapped P.S.'s skinny behind. P.S. yelped and jumped away. "Hey, Mr. Mabrey, sir? Hey, Mabrey? I'm sorry, I really am. I didn't know it would work."

"What would work?"

"My voodoo curse. I didn't know it would make you cut yourself."

"For heaven's sake, P.S., what're you talking about? I cut a pimple. Will you leave me alone before I throw you out of a closed window?"

P.S. was quiet for a moment. Then he moved over to the washbasin next to Mabrey and looked at himself in the mirror. He ran his fingers through his light-brown hair and pushed his glasses higher on his nose. "Hey, Mabrey? Do you think I'm fresh? I mean, I have great respect for you—you being the head monitor and all. I mean it. Sometimes I worry. I mean, do you think I'm too fresh?"

Mabrey finished rinsing his face. "P.S., kid," he said as he dried himself, "you're all right. You're a nice guy. And I'm willing to bet that if you could only learn to throw a baseball from center field to second base overhand, you might turn out to be a pretty fair little baseball player."

"Overhand! Whaddya mean 'overhand'? They call me 'Deadeye Wilkinson.'" P.S. wound up with an imaginary baseball and threw it as hard as he could. Then he pantomimed being the second baseman. He crouched and caught the incoming baseball at his knees and thrust his hand down to tag out the runner. "Safe!" he shouted. "I mean, out! Out! Out!"

"Too late," Mabrey said, and laughed. "An umpire never changes his decision."

"I meant out," P.S. said.

Mabrey disappeared down the hall.

P.S. brushed his teeth, being careful to squeeze the toothpaste from the bottom of the tube. He looked at himself in the mirror and chanted, *"Fuero, fueris, fuerit, fuerimus, fueritis, fuerint!"*[1] He examined his upper lip and was disappointed. He wished that he didn't have such a young face. He wished he had a heavy beard, like Mabrey. He washed his face, wet his hair down, and walked back into Charlie's room. Charlie was P.S.'s best friend. He was very short. The other boys kidded him about being an engineer for Lionel trains. P.S. was very tall and thin, and he had not yet grown into his height. At fourteen he was already six feet tall, and he had a tendency to stoop to compensate. He and Charlie were known as Mutt and Jeff. When P.S. entered the room, Charlie was curled up on his bed studying his Latin notes. He didn't look up until P.S. dropped the toothpaste tube on his pillow.

"Rolled from the bottom," P.S. said.

"Hey, how do you expect to pass your Latin exam if you don't study? I heard you and Mabrey clowning around in the can."

"If I don't study!" P.S. said. "Do you know how long I've studied for this exam? Two years! If I flunk it again this year, I get to keep the trophy."

"What trophy?"

"For Pete's sake, I don't know what trophy. But I'll get something, for sure. I've spent the last two weeks practically doing nothing but studying Latin. I recopied all my notes. I underlined practically the whole book. And I memorized all the irregular verbs. Come on, come on, ask me anything. Gosh, if I don't pass it this year, I've had it. Come on, ask me anything."

"O.K., what's the word for 'ridge'?"

"The word for 'ridge'?" P.S. stalled.

"Yep."

P.S. thought for a moment. "Look, I don't know. Make it two out of three."

"The word for 'ridge' is *iugum.*" Charlie looked at his notes. "O.K., two out of three. What's the word for 'crowd'? And 'troop,' as in 'a troop of cavalry'?"

"The word for 'crowd' is *turba, turbae.* . . . What was the other one?"

" 'Troop of cavalry,' "

"'Cavalry' is *equitatus.* . . . I don't know. What is 'troop'?"

"'Troop' is *turma.*" Charlie laughed. "Well, you got one out of three."

"Did I get partial credit for the 'cavalry'?"

"Nope."

"I hope Dr. Fairfax is more lenient than you are."

"He won't be," Charlie said.

"If I flunk the Latin exam again this year. . . ."

"How come you flunked it last year?"

"How come anybody flunks an exam? I didn't know the answers. Boy, Charlie, I don't know what I'm going to do with you. If you weren't such a nice guy and lend me your toothpaste and things like that all the time, I'd probably feed you to the—to the

---

1. *"Fuero, . . . fuerint!"* P.S. is conjugating one tense of the Latin verb "to be."

what's-their-name fish. Those fish who eat people in South America all the time."

"Well, since you don't know what to do with me, as a start why don't you let me study?"

"Sure. Sure, O.K. . . . O.K., be a grind. See if I care."

P.S. walked back to his cubicle and pulled his Ullman and Henry *Latin II* from his unpainted bookcase. First he studied the irregular verbs in the back of the book. Then he went over his vocabulary list. He concentrated for as long as he could; then he leaned out of his window to look at the shadows of the trees directly below, dropped a penny

out of the window to see if a squirrel would pick it up, checked his window sill to see if the cookie crumbs he had left for the mockingbird were still there. He turned back to his Latin book and leafed through the Forestier illustrations of Roman soldiers. He picked up the picture his father had given him last Christmas. Within the frame were

four small round photographs of Wilkinsons in uniform. There was his father as an infantry major during the Second World War, his grandfather as a captain in the field artillery during the First World War, his great-great-grandfather as a corporal in a soft gray Confederate uniform, and a great-great-great-great something or other in a dark uniform with a lot of bright buttons. P.S. didn't know who the last picture was of. He imagined it to be somebody from the Revolutionary War. P.S. had seen the oil portrait the photograph had been taken from hanging in the hallway of his grandfather's house. P.S. had the long, thin nose of the other Wilkinsons in the pictures, but he still had the round cheeks of youth and the perfect eyebrows. He was the fifteenth of his family to attend the Virginia Preparatory School. Among the buildings at V.P.S. there was a Wilkinson Memorial Library and a Sadler Gymnasium. When P.S. was packing to begin his first year at the school, his father had said, "Son, when your great-grandfather went off to V.P.S., his father gave him a dozen silk handkerchiefs and a pair of warm gloves. When your grandfather went off to V.P.S., his father gave him a dozen silk handkerchiefs and a pair of warm gloves. When I went off to V.P.S., your grandfather gave me a dozen silk handkerchiefs and a pair of warm gloves. And now here are a dozen silk handkerchiefs and a pair of warm gloves for you."

P.S. looked at the brightly patterned Liberty-silk handkerchiefs[2] and the fuzzy red mittens. No thirteen-year-old ever wore red mittens, except girls, and particularly not fuzzy red mittens. And P.S. knew he would never dare to wear the silk handkerchiefs.

---

2. *Liberty-silk handkerchiefs,* handkerchiefs from Liberty and Company, a well-known firm in London, England.

"Well, thank you very much, Dad," he had said.

"That's all right, son."

P.S. left the red mittens behind when he went away to V.P.S. He used two of the silk handkerchiefs to cover the top of his bureau and bookcase, gave one other away to a girl, and hid the rest beneath his underwear on the second shelf of his bureau. His father had done very well at the school; he had been a senior monitor, editor-in-chief of the yearbook, and a distance runner in winter and spring track. P.S. hoped he would do as well, but he knew he had disappointed his father so far. When he flunked the Latin examination last year and tried to explain to his father that he just could not do Latin, he could see the disbelief in his father's eyes. "Son, you just didn't study. 'Can't do Latin,' what nonsense!" But P.S. knew that studying had nothing to do with it. His father said that no Wilkinson had ever flunked at V.P.S.; P.S. was the first. His father was not the kind to lose his temper. P.S. wished he were. When P.S. had done something wrong, his father would just look at him and smile sadly and shake his head. The boy had never felt particularly close to his father. He had never been able to talk to or with his father. He had found the best means of getting along with his father was to keep out of his way. He had given up their ever sharing anything. He had no illusions about leading a calendar-picture life with his father—canoeing or hunting together. He could remember trying to get his father to play catch with him and how his father would always say, "Not now, son, not now." But there were certain occasions that his father felt should be shared with P.S. These were the proper father-son occasions that made P.S. feel like some sort of ornament. There would be Father's Day, or the big football

game of the season. P.S. would be told to order two tickets, and the afternoon of the game he and his father would watch the first half together. His father remembered all of the cheers and was shocked when P.S. didn't remember some of the words to the school song. At the half, his father would disappear to talk to his friends and P.S. would be left alone to watch the overcoats or umbrellas. After the game, P.S. would wander back to the field house, where the alumni tables were set up. He would locate his father and stand next to him until his father introduced him to the persons he was talking to. Then his father would say, "Run along, son. I'll meet

you back in your room." So P.S. would go back to his room and wait for his father to come by. The boy would straighten up the bed, dust the bureau, and sweep the floor. And then after a long wait his father would come in and sit down. "Well, how are you, son?" the conversation would always start. And P.S. would answer, "Fine, thank you, sir." His father would look around the room and remark about its not being large enough to swing a cat in, then there would be two or three anecdotes about the times when he was a boy at V.P.S., and then he would look at his watch and say, "Well, I guess I'd better be pushing off." His father would ask him if there was anything he needed, and P.S. would say that he didn't think there was anything. His father would give him a five-dollar bill and drive away. And P.S., with enormous relief, would go look for Charlie. "Did you and your dad have a good time?" Charlie would ask. "Sure," P.S. would say. And that would end the conversation.

P.S. knew that his father loved him, but he also knew better than to expect any sign of affection. Affection always seemed to embarrass his father. P.S. remembered his first year at school, when his father had first come up to see him. He had been very happy to see his father, and when they were saying goodbye P.S. stepped forward as usual to kiss him and his father drew away. P.S. always made it a point now to shake hands with his father. And at fourteen respect and obedience had taken the place of love.

P.S. picked up his Latin notes and went over the translations he had completed. He wished he knew what questions would be asked. In last year's exam there were questions from all over the book, and it made the exam very difficult to study for, if they were going to do that. He pictured himself handing in the finished examination to Dr. Fairfax and saying, "Sir? Wilkinsons do not flunk. Please grade my exam accordingly."

P.S. looked at his wristwatch. The dining hall would begin serving breakfast in fifteen minutes. He made his bed and put on a clean pair of khakis and a button-down shirt. He slipped into his old white bucks and broke a lace tying them, and pulled out the shorter piece and threaded what was left through the next eyelet up, as the older boys did. He tidied up his room for inspection, picked up his notes, and went back to Charlie's room. Charlie was sweeping the dust into the hall. The new boy on duty that day would be responsible for sweeping the halls and emptying all trash baskets. P.S. entered and sat down on the bed.

"For Pete's sake, P.S.! I just made the bed!"

"O.K., O.K., I'll straighten it up when I leave." P.S. ran his fingers across the desk top. "Merritt, two demerits—dust. . . . Hey, the exam's at ten-thirty, isn't it?"

"Yep. If you flunk Latin again, will they make you go to summer school?"

"Probably. I really think it's archaic the way they make you pass Latin to get out of this place."

"Boy, I sure hope I pass it," Charlie said.

"You will. You will. You're the brain in the class."

"Come on, let's go to chow."

"That's what I've been waiting for, my good buddy, my good friend, old pal of mine." P.S. jumped off the bed, scooped up his notebook, and started out of the room.

"Hey!" Charlie said. "What about the bed?"

At eight o'clock chapel, P.S. knelt in the pew and prayed: "Dear God, I pray that I pass my Latin exam this morning. . . . If I can pass this exam, then I'll do anything you want me to do. . . . God, please. If I don't pass this exam, I've really had it. . . . *They must have made these pews for midgets; I never fit in them right. . . . How am I ever going to get out to Colorado this summer unless I pass that exam? . . .* Please God, I don't want a high grade, all I want is to pass . . . and you don't have to help me on the others. . . . I don't want to pass this exam for myself only. I mean, it means a lot to my family. My father will be very disappointed if I flunk the exam. . . . *I wonder if Charlie will be able to go out to Colorado with me. . . .* God bless Mom, God bless Dad, God bless Grandpa Sadler and Grandma Sadler, God bless Grandpa Wilkinson and Granny Wilkinson, God bless all my relatives I haven't mentioned. . . . Amen. And . . . and, God, please, please help me to pass this exam."

At ten-fifteen, P.S. and Charlie fell in step and walked over to Randolph Hall, where the examination was to be held.

"Well, if we don't know it now, we never will," Charlie said.

"Even if I did know it now, I wouldn't know it tomorrow." P.S. reached into his pants pocket and pulled out his lucky exam tie. It was a stained and unraveled blue knit. As they walked up the path, he was careful to tie the tie backwards, the wide end next to his shirt, the seam facing out. Then he checked his watch pocket to see that his lucky silver dollar was there.

"What's the Latin for 'then'?" Charlie asked.

"'*Tum,*'" P.S. answered. "Tums for your tummy."

"What's the word for 'thence,' or 'from there'?"

"*Inde.*" P.S. began to sing: "*Inde* evening *byde* moonlight you could *hearde*——"

"For Pete's sake, P.S.!" Charlie laughed.

"You don't like my singing?"

"Not much."

"You know? I'm thinking of joining the choir and glee club next year. You know why? They've got a couple of dances next fall. One with St. Catherine's and another with St. Tim's. You wanta try out with me?"

"I don't know. I can't sing."

"Who's gonna sing?" P.S. grabbed Charlie's arm and growled, "Baby, I'm no singer, I'm a lover!"

"Lover? Who says you're a lover?"

"Ask me no questions and I'll tell you no lies."

P.S. and Charlie walked up the worn wooden steps of Randolph Hall to the third-floor study hall, where the Latin examination was to be given. They both were in the upper study hall, since they were underclassmen still. P.S.'s desk was in the back corner of the study hall, against the wall. He sat down and brushed the dust off the top of his desk with his palm. Someone had traced a hand into the wood. Others had traced and retraced the hand and deepened the grooves. They had added fingernails and rings. P.S. had added a Marlboro tattoo.[3] He lifted the desk top and, searching for his pencil sharpener, saw that he had some more Latin translations in his desk. He read them through quickly and decided it was too late to learn anything from them. He pulled out his pencil sharpener and closed his desk. The study hall was filling with boys, who took their places at their desks and called back and forth to each other in their slow Southern voices. It was a long, narrow room with high windows on either side, and the walls were painted a dirty yellow. Between the windows were framed engravings of Roman ruins and Southern generals. The large fluorescent lights above the desks buzzed and blinked into life. A dark, curly-haired boy sat down in the desk next to P.S. and began to empty his pockets of pencils and pens.

"Hey, Jumbo," P.S. said. "You gonna kill the exam?"

"I hope so. If I can get a good grade on it,

---

3. **Marlboro tattoo.** A tattoo on the back of a man's hand was the advertising symbol of Marlboro cigarettes.

then I don't have to worry so much about my math exam tomorrow."

"Well, if we don't know it now we never will."

"You're right."

Jumbo had played second-string tackle on the varsity this year. He was expected to be first-string next year, and by his final year, the coaches thought, he might become All-Virginia High School tackle. Jumbo was a sincere, not very bright student who came from a farm in Virginia and wanted to be a farmer when he finished college. P.S. had sat next to Jumbo all year, but they had never become particularly close friends. Jumbo lived in a different dormitory and had a tendency to stick with the other members of the football team. But P.S. liked him, and Jumbo was really the only member of the football team that he knew at all.

P.S. looked up at the engraving of General Robert E. Lee and his horse, Traveller. He glanced over at Jumbo. Jumbo was cleaning his fingernails with the tip of his automatic pencil.

"Well, good luck," P.S. said.

"Good luck to you."

"I'll need it."

P.S. stood up and looked for Charlie. "Hey! Hey, Charlie?"

Charlie turned around. "Yeah?"

"*Piggo, piggere, squeely, gruntum!*"

"For Pete's sake, P.S.!"

"Hey, P.S.?" someone shouted. "You gonna flunk it again this year?"

"No, no, I don't think so," P.S. answered in mock seriousness. "In point of fact, as the good Dr. Fairfax would say—in point of fact, I might just come out with the highest grade in class. After all, I'm such a brain."

The noise in the study hall suddenly stopped; Dr. Fairfax had entered. The Latin instructor walked to the back of the study hall, where P.S. was sitting.

"And what was all that about, Wilkinson?"

"Sir, I was telling the others how I'm the brain in your class."

"Indeed?" Dr. Fairfax asked.

"Yes, sir. But I was only kidding."

"Indeed," the Latin instructor said, and the other students laughed.

Dr. Fairfax was a large man with a lean, aesthetic face, which he tried to hide with a military mustache. He had taught at the Virginia Preparatory School since 1919. P.S.'s father had had Dr. Fairfax for a Latin instructor. When P.S. read *Goodbye, Mr. Chips,*[4] he had kept thinking of Dr. Fairfax. The Latin instructor wore the same suit and vest all winter. They were always immaculate. The first day of spring was marked by Dr. Fairfax's appearance in a white linen suit, which he always wore with a small blue bachelor's-button. Before a study hall last spring, someone had placed an alarm clock set to go off during the middle of study hall in one of the tall wastepaper baskets at the rear of the room. The student had then emptied all of the pencil sharpeners and several ink bottles into the basket and covered all this with crumpled-up pad paper. When the alarm clock went off, Dr. Fairfax strode down the aisle and reached into the wastepaper basket for the clock. When he lifted it out, the sleeve of his white linen jacket was covered with ink and pencil shavings. There was a stunned silence in the study hall as Dr. Fairfax looked at his sleeve. And then Dr. Fairfax began to laugh. The old man sat down on one of the desk

---

4. *Goodbye, Mr. Chips,* a novel by James Hilton. Mr. Chips is an old and beloved teacher in a private school for boys.

tops and laughed and laughed, until finally the students had enough nerve to join him. The next day, he appeared in the same linen suit, but it was absolutely clean. Nobody was given demerits or punished in any manner. Dr. Fairfax was P.S.'s favorite instructor. P.S. watched him separate the examination papers and blue books[5] into neat piles at the proctor's desk. Dr. Fairfax looked up at the electric clock over the study-hall door and then at his thin gold pocket watch. He cleared his throat. "Good morning, gentlemen."

"GOOD MORNING, SIR!" the students shouted.

"Gentlemen, there will be no talking during the examination. In the two hours given you, you will have ample time to complete all of the necessary work. When the bell sounds signifying the end of the examination, you will cease work immediately. In point of fact, anyone found working after the bell will be looked upon most unfavorably. When you receive your examinations, make certain that the print is legible. Make sure that you place your names on each of your blue books. If you have any difficulty reading the examination, hold your hand above your head and you will be given a fresh copy. The tops of your desks should be cleared of all notes, papers, and books. Are there any questions? . . . If not, will Baylor and you, Grandy, and . . . and Merritt . . . will the three of you please pass out the examinations."

P.S. watched Charlie get up and walk over to the desk.

Dr. Fairfax reached into his breast pocket and pulled out a pair of steel-rimmed spectacles. He looked out across the room. "We are nearing the end of the school year," he said. "Examinations always seem to cause students an undue amount of concern.

I assure you, I can well remember when I was a student at V.P.S. In point of fact, I was not so very different from some of you——"

The instructor was interrupted by a rasping Bronx cheer.[6] He looked quickly over in the direction of the sound. "Travers, was that you?"

"No, sir."

"Brandon, was that you?"

The student hesitated, then answered, "Yes, sir."

"Brandon, I consider that marked disrespect, and it will cost you ten demerits."

"Aww, sir——"

"Fifteen." Dr. Fairfax cleared his throat again. "Now, if I may continue? . . . Good. There are a few important things to remember when taking an examination. First, do not get upset when you cannot at once answer all of the questions. The examination is designed——"

P.S. stopped listening. Charlie was walking down the aisle toward him.

"Hey, Charlie," he whispered, "give me an easy one."

"There will be no favoritism on my part."

"How does it look?"

"Tough."

"Merritt and Wilkinson?" Dr. Fairfax said. "That last little bit of conversation will cost you each five demerits."

The Latin instructor looked up at the electric clock again. "When you receive your examinations, you may begin. Are there any questions? . . . If not, gentlemen, it might be well for us to remember this ancient Latin proverb: *'Abusus non tollit usum.'*" Dr. Fairfax waited for the laugh.

---

5. *blue books,* blue-covered booklets of blank paper in which tests are to be written.
6. *Bronx cheer,* slang for a sound of contempt made by trilling the tongue between the protruded lips.

There was none. He cleared his throat again. "Perhaps . . . perhaps we had better ask the class brain what the proverb means. Wilkinson?"

P.S. stood up. " '*Abusus non tollit usum*,' sir?"

"That's right."

"Something like 'Abuse does not tolerate the use,' sir?"

"What does the verb *tollo, tollere, sustuli, sublatus* mean?"

"To take away, sir."

"That's right. The proverb, then, is 'Abuse does not take away the use,' or, in the context I was referring to, just because you gentlemen cannot do Latin properly does not mean that it should not be done at all."

"Yes, sir," P.S. said, and he sat down.

Dr. Fairfax unfolded his newspaper, and P.S. began to read the examination. He picked up his pencil and printed in large letters on the cover of his blue book:

PHILIP SADLER WILKINSON
LATIN EXAMINATION
LATIN II—DR. FAIRFAX
VIRGINIA PREPARATORY
SCHOOL
7 JUNE 1962—BOOK ONE (1)

Then he put down his pencil, stretched, and began to work.

P.S. read the examination carefully. He saw that he would be able to do very little of it from memory, and felt the first surge of panic moisten his palms. He tried to translate the first Latin-to-English passage. He remembered that it fell on the right-hand side of the page in his Ullman and Henry, opposite the picture of the Roman galley. The picture was a still taken from the silent-movie version of *Ben-Hur*.[7] He recognized some of the verbs, more of the nouns, and finally he began to be able to translate. It was about the Veneti ships, which were more efficient than the Roman galleys because they had high prows and flat keels. He translated the entire passage, put down his pencil, and stretched again.

An hour later P.S. knew he was in trouble. The first translation and the vocabulary section were the only parts of the exam he had been able to do without too much difficulty. He was able to give the rule and examples for the datives of agent and possession. The English-to-Latin sentences were the most difficult. He had been able to do only one of those. For the question, "How do you determine the tense of the infinitive in indirect statement?" he wrote, "You can determine the tense by the construction of the sentence and by the word endings," and hoped he might get some credit. The two Latin-to-English passages counted twenty points apiece. If he could only do that second translation, he stood a chance of passing the examination. He recognized the adverb *inde*, but saw that it didn't help him very much. The examination was halfway over. He tried to count how many points he had made so far on the examination. He thought he might have somewhere between fifty and fifty-five. Passing was seventy. If he could just translate that second passage, he would have the points he needed to pass. Dr. Fairfax never scaled the grades.[8] P.S. had heard that one year the Latin instructor had flunked everybody but two.

He glanced over at Jumbo. Then he looked back down at his own examination

---

7. *Ben Hur*, a novel by Lew Wallace about the life of Jesus.
8. *scaled the grades*, distributed the grades according to a planned percentage of A's, B's, etc.

and swore under his breath. Jumbo looked over at him and smiled. P.S. pantomimed that he could not answer the questions, and Jumbo smiled again. P.S. slid his glasses off and rubbed his eyes. He fought down the panic, wiped his hands on his pants legs, and looked at the passage again. He couldn't make any sense out of the blur of the words. He squinted, looked at them, put on his glasses again, and knew that he was in trouble.

He leaned over his desk and closed his eyes. *Dear God, please help me on this examination . . . please, God, please . . . I must pass this examination.* He opened his eyes and looked carefully around to see if anyone had seen him praying. The others were all working hard on the examination. P.S. looked up again at the engraving on the wall above his desk. Beneath the portrait was the caption "Soon after the close of the War Between the States, General Robert E. Lee became the head of a school for young men. General Lee made this statement when he met with his students for the first time: 'We have but one rule in this school, and that is that every student must be a gentleman.'" *They left out that other rule,* P.S. thought. *They left out the one that says you have to have Latin to graduate! Or is that part of being a gentleman, too?*

He read the Latin-to-English passage through twice, then he read it through backwards. He knew he had seen the passage before. He even remembered seeing it recently. But where? He knew that the passage dealt with the difficulties the Romans were having in fortifying their positions, but there were so many technical words in it that he could not get more than five of the twenty points from the translation, and he needed at least fifteen to pass. . . . He was going to flunk. *But I can't flunk! I can't flunk! I've got to pass!*

P.S. knew if he flunked he wouldn't be able to face his father. No matter what excuse P.S. gave, his father would not believe he hadn't loafed all term.

He looked at the passage and tried to remember where he had seen it. And then his mouth went dry. He felt the flush burn into the back of his neck and spread to his cheeks. He swallowed hard. *The translation's in my desk! . . . It's in my desk! . . . It's the translation on the top of the stack in my desk . . . in my desk!*

All he would have to do would be to slip the translation out of his desk, copy it, put it away, and he would pass the examination. All of his worries would be over. His father would be happy that he passed the examination. He wouldn't have to go to summer school. He and Charlie could go out to Colorado together to work on that dude ranch. He would be through with Latin forever. His Latin grade would never pull his average down again. Everything would be all right. Everything would be fine. All he would have to do would be to copy that one paragraph. Everyone cheated. Maybe not at V.P.S. But in other schools they bragged about it. . . . Everyone cheated in one way or another. Why should that one passage ruin everything? Who cared what problems the Romans had!

P.S. glanced over at Jumbo. Jumbo was chewing on his pencil eraser as he worked on the examination. Dr. Fairfax was still reading his newspaper. P.S. felt his heart beat faster. It began beating so hard that he was certain Jumbo could hear it. P.S. gently raised his desk top and pretended to feel around for a pencil. He let his blue book slide halfway off his desk so it leaned in his lap. Then he slid the translation under his blue book and slid the blue book and notes back onto his desk. He was certain that everyone had seen him—that everyone knew he was about to cheat. He slowly raised his eyes to look at Dr. Fairfax, who

went on reading. P.S. covered part of the notes with his examination and began to copy the rest into his blue book. He could feel the heat in his cheeks, the dryness in his mouth. *Dear God . . . God, please don't let them catch me! . . . Please!*

He changed the smooth translation into a rough one as he copied, so that it would match his other translations.

From these things the army was taught the nature of the place and how the slope of the hill and the necessity of the time demanded more than one plan and order for the art of war.

Different legions, some in one part, others in another, fought the enemy. And the view was obstructed by very thick hedges. Sure support could not be placed, nor could it be seen what work would be necessary in which part, nor could all the commands be administered by one man. Therefore, against so much unfairness of things, various consequences ensued.

He put down his pencil and looked around the study hall. No one was watching. P.S. carefully slid the translation back into his desk. He looked to see if the translation had given him any words that might help him on the rest of the examination. His heart was still beating wildly in his chest, and his hands shook. He licked his lips and concentrated on behaving normally. *It's over. . . . It's over. . . . I've cheated, but it's all over and no one said anything!*

He began to relax.

Fifteen minutes later Dr. Fairfax stood up at his desk, looked at the electric clock, then down at his pocket watch. He cleared his throat and said, "Stop!"

Several students groaned. The rest gathered up their pencils and pens.

"Make certain you have written out the pledge in full and signed it," Dr. Fairfax said.

P.S. felt the physical pain of fear again. He opened his blue book and wrote, "I pledge on my honor as a gentleman that I have neither given nor received unauthorized assistance on this examination." He hesitated; then he signed his name.

"Place your examination inside your blue book," Dr. Fairfax continued. "Make certain that you put your name on your blue book. . . . Baylor? If you and, uh, Ferguson and Showalter will be good enough to pick up the examinations, the rest of you may go. And, um, gentlemen, your grades will be posted on the front door of my office no sooner than forty-eight hours from now. In point of fact, any attempt to solicit your grade any sooner than that will result in bad temper on my part and greater severity in the marking of papers. Are there any questions? . . . If not, gentlemen, dismissed."

The students stood up and stretched. An immediate, excited hum of voices filled the study hall. P.S. looked down at his exam paper. He slid it into his blue book and left it on his desk.

Charlie was waiting at the door of the study hall.

"Well, P.S., how'd the brain do?"

"You know it's bad luck to talk about an exam before the grades are posted."

"I know. I'm just asking how you think you did."

"I don't know," P.S. said.

"Well, well, I mean, do you think you passed?"

"I don't know!"

"Whooey!" Charlie whistled. "And you called *me* a grump!"

They walked down the stairs together. At the bottom, Charlie asked P.S. if he was going to go to lunch.

"No, I don't think so," P.S. said. "I'm not feeling so well. I think I'll lie down for a while. I'll see ya."

"Sure," Charlie said. "See ya."

In his cubicle in Memorial Hall, P.S. took off his lucky exam tie. He put his silver dollar back onto his bookcase. He reached inside the hollow copy of *Gulliver's Travels* for the pack of cigarettes he kept there. Then he walked down the corridor to the bathroom, stepped into one of the stalls, and locked the door. He lit the cigarette and leaned his forehead against the cool green marble divider. He was sick with fear and dread. *It's over! It's all over!* he said, trying to calm himself. He did not like the new knowledge he had of himself. He was a cheater. He rolled his forehead back and forth against the stone, pressing his forehead into it, hurting himself. P.S. had broken the Honor Code of the school, and he was scared.

I shouldn't have cheated! What if someone had seen me! I shouldn't have cheated! . . . Maybe somebody did see me. . . . Maybe Dr. Fairfax will know I cheated when he sees my exam. . . . Maybe somebody will check my desk after the exam and find the copy of the translation. . . . I cheated! . . . Stupid fool. . . . What if somebody finds out! . . . Maybe I should turn myself in. . . . I wonder if they'd kick me out if I turned myself in. . . . It would prove that I really am honest, I just made a mistake, that's all. . . . I'll tell them I couldn't help it. . . . Maybe they'll just give me a reprimand.

But P.S. knew that if he turned himself in, they would still tell his parents he had cheated, so what good would that do? His father would be just as angry. Even more so, since Wilkinsons don't cheat, either. P.S. knew how ashamed his father would make him feel. His father would have to tell others that P.S. had cheated. It was a part of the Southern tradition. "My son has disgraced me. It is better that you hear it from me than somebody else." His father would do something like that. And having other people know he had cheated would be too much shame to bear. And even if he did turn himself in, the school would make him take another exam. . . . And he'd flunk that one, too. . . . He knew it. . . . *What am I going to do?*

If he didn't turn himself in and no one

had seen him, then who would know? He would never cheat again. If he could just get away with it this one time. Then everything would be O.K. Nobody need ever know—except himself. And P.S. knew he would never be able to forget that he had cheated. Maybe if he turned himself in, it would be better in the long run. *What long run? What kind of long run will I have if I turn myself in? Everybody in the school will know I cheated, no matter whether I turn myself in or not. . . . They won't remember me for turning myself in. . . . They'll remember that I cheated in the first place. . . .*

P.S. wanted to cry, but he couldn't. He dropped the cigarette into the toilet and flushed it down. Then he went over to the sink and rinsed his mouth out. He had some chewing gum in his room; that would cover the smell of his smoking. He looked at himself in the mirror. He couldn't see any change since this morning, and yet he felt so different. He looked at his eyes to see if there were lines under them now. *What shall I do?* he asked his reflection. *What shall I do?* He turned on the cold water and rinsed his face. He dried himself on a towel someone had left behind, and walked back down the corridor to his room. He brushed aside the curtain, entered the cubicle, and stopped, frozen with fear. Mabrey, the head monitor, was sitting on P.S.'s bed.

"Wilkinson," Mabrey said, "would you mind coming with me?"

He called me Wilkinson, not P.S. . . . not P.S.! "Where do you want to go?"

"Just outside for a few minutes."

"What about?"

Mabrey got up from the bed. "Come on, P.S."

"What . . . what do you want me for?"

"We want to talk to you."

We! WE! P.S. picked up his jacket and started to put it on.

"You won't need your jacket," Mabrey said.

"It doesn't matter, I'll wear it anyway."

P.S. followed Mabrey out of the dormitory. *I didn't have a chance to turn myself in,* he thought. *I didn't have a chance to choose. . . .*

"You think you'll make the varsity baseball team next year?" Mabrey asked.

"I don't know," P.S. said. *What is he talking about baseball for?*

The new boy who had wakened P.S. passed them on the walk. He said hello to both Mabrey and P.S. He received no answer, and shrugged.

Mabrey and P.S. took the path to the headmaster's office. P.S. could feel the enormous weight of the fear building up inside him again. Mabrey opened the door for P.S. and ushered him into the headmaster's waiting room. Nelson, a pale, fat-faced senior, was sitting there alone. He was the secretary of the Honor Committee. P.S. had always hated him. The other members of the Honor Committee were Mabrey, the vice-president; Linus Hendricks, the president; Mr. Seaton, the headmaster; and Dr. Fairfax, who served as faculty adviser. Mabrey motioned that P.S. was to sit down in the chair facing the others—the only straight-backed wooden chair in the room. Every now and then Nelson would look up at P.S. and shake his head. The door to the headmaster's office opened and Mr. Seaton came out, followed by Linus Hendricks, Dr. Fairfax, and—*What is Jumbo doing here! Don't tell me he cheated, too! He was sitting right next to me!* Jumbo walked out of the room without looking at P.S.

Linus Hendricks waited for the others to

seat themselves, then he sat down himself and faced P.S. "Well, P.S., I imagine you know why you're here."

P.S. looked at Hendricks. Hendricks was the captain of the football team. He and Mabrey were the two most important undergraduates in the school.

"Well, P.S.?" Hendricks repeated.

"Yes, sir," P.S. said.

He could feel them all staring at him. He looked down at his hands folded in his lap. He could see clearly every line in his thumb knuckle. He could see the dirt caught under the corner of his fingernail, and the small blue vein running across the knuckle.

He looked up at Dr. Fairfax. He wanted to tell him not to worry. He wanted to tell him that he was sorry, so very sorry.

The headmaster, Mr. Seaton, was a young man. He had just become the headmaster of V.P.S. this year. He liked the students, and the students liked him. He was prematurely bald, and smiled a lot. He had a very young and pretty wife, and some of the students were in love with her and fought to sit at her table in the dining room. Mr. Seaton liked to play tennis. He would play the students and bet his dessert that he would win. And most of the time he would lose, and the students were enormously pleased to see the headmaster of the school have to get up from the table and pay his bets. Mr. Seaton would walk very quickly across the dining hall, his bald head bent to hide his smile. He would swoop up to a table, drop the dessert, and depart, like a bombing airplane. P.S. could tell that the headmaster was distressed he had cheated.

Linus Hendricks crossed his legs and sank back into the deep leather armchair. Mabrey and Nelson leaned forward as though they were going to charge P.S.

"P.S.," Hendricks said, "you're here this afternoon because the Honor Committee has reason to suspect that you may have cheated on the Latin exam this morning. We must ask you whether or not this is true."

P.S. raised his head and looked at Hendricks. Hendricks was wearing a bright striped tie. P.S. concentrated on the stripes. Thick black, thin white, medium green, thin white, and thick black.

"P.S., did you, or did you not, cheat on the Latin examination?"

P.S. nodded.

"Yes or no, P.S.?" Hendricks asked.

P.S. no longer felt anything. He was numb with misery. "Yes," he said, in a small, tired voice. "Yes, I cheated on the examination. But I was going to turn myself in. I was going to turn myself in. I swear I was."

"If you were going to turn yourself in, why didn't you?" Nelson asked.

"I couldn't. . . . I couldn't yet. . . ." P.S. looked at Dr. Fairfax. "I'm sorry, sir. I'm terribly sorry. . . ." P.S. began to cry. "I'm so ashamed. . . ." P.S. tried to stop crying. He couldn't. The tears stung his eyes. One tear slipped into the inside of his glasses and puddled across the bottom of the lens. He reached into his back pocket for a handkerchief, but he had forgotten to bring one. He started to pull out his shirttail, and decided he'd better not. He wiped his face with the side of his hand.

Mr. Seaton walked over to P.S. and gave him his handkerchief. The headmaster rested his hand on P.S.'s shoulder. "Why, P.S.? Why did you cheat?"

P.S. couldn't answer.

"P.S., you were the last boy I expected this of. Why did you feel you had to cheat on this exam?"

"I don't know, sir."

"But, P.S., you must have had some reason."

Nelson said, "Answer the headmaster when he's asking you a question, Wilkinson."

P.S. looked up at him with such loathing that Nelson looked away.

Mr. Seaton crouched down next to P.S. "You must have been aware of the penalty for cheating."

P.S. nodded.

"Then why, in heaven's name, did you risk expulsion just to pass the examination?"

"Sir—sir, I flunked Latin last year, sir. I knew I'd flunk it this year, too. I—I knew I couldn't pass a Latin exam ever."

"But why did you *cheat?*"

"Because . . . because, sir, I had to pass the exam."

The headmaster ran his hand across his forehead. "P.S., I'm not trying to trick you, I'm only trying to understand why you did this thing. Why did you bring the notes into the exam with you?"

"Sir, Mr. Seaton, I didn't bring the notes in, they were in my desk. If they hadn't been, I wouldn't be here. I didn't want to cheat. I didn't mean to cheat. I—It was just the only way I could pass the exam."

Nelson rested his pudgy arms on the sides of his leather armchair and looked at the headmaster and then back to P.S. Then he said, "Wilkinson, you have been in V.P.S. for two years. You must be familiar, I imagine, with the Honor Code. In fact, in your study hall there is a small wooden plaque above the proctor's desk. On it are carved the four points of the Honor Code: 'I will not lie. I will not steal. I will not cheat. I will report anyone I see doing so.' You are familiar with them, aren't you?"

"Of course I'm familiar with them," P.S. said impatiently.

"Why did you think you were so much better than everyone else that you could ignore it?"

"I don't think I'm better than everyone else, Nelson," P.S. said.

"Well, you sure aren't! The others don't cheat." Nelson sat back again, very satisfied with himself.

Dr. Fairfax came from behind the chairs and stood next to P.S. "Unless you hold your tongue, Nelson—unless you hold your tongue, I shall personally escort you out of here."

"But, sir," Nelson whined. "I'm only trying to—"

"SHUT UP!" Dr. Fairfax roared. He returned to the back of the room.

Mr. Seaton spoke again. "P.S., if you had flunked this exam, you would have been able to take another. Perhaps you would have passed the reexamination. Most boys do."

"I wouldn't have, sir," P.S. said. "I just cannot do Latin. You could have given me fifty examinations, sir. And I don't mean any disrespect, but I would have flunked all fifty of them."

Mabrey asked the headmaster if he could speak, then he turned to P.S. "P.S., we—all of us have been tempted at some time or another to cheat. All of us have either resisted that temptation or, perhaps, we were lucky enough to get away with it. I think that what we want to know is what *made* you cheat. Just having to pass the exam isn't enough. I know you, P.S. I may know you better than anyone else in the room, because I've shared the same floor in the dorm with you for this year. And we were on the same floor when you were a toad. You're not the kind who cheats unless . . . . What I mean is this, P.S. I know you don't care how high your grade is, just so long as you keep out of trouble. . . . You're one of the most popular boys in your class. Everybody likes you.

Why would you throw all of this over, just to pass a Latin exam?"

"I don't know. I don't know. . . . I had to pass the exam. If I flunked it again, my father would kill me."

"What do you mean he would kill you?" Mr. Seaton asked.

"Oh, nothing, sir. I mean—I don't mean he would hurt me. He would just—Oh, I don't know how to explain it to you. If I flunked the exam again, he'd just make me feel so, I don't know . . . *ashamed* . . . so terrible. I just couldn't take it again."

There was a moment of silence in the room. P.S. began to cry again. He could tell the headmaster still didn't understand why he had cheated. He looked down at his hands again. With his index finger he traced the veins that crossed the back of his hand. He looked over at the wooden arm of his straight-backed chair. He could see the little drops of moisture where his hand had squeezed the arm of the chair. He could make out every grain of wood, every worn spot. He took off his glasses and rubbed his eyes. He tried taking deep breaths, but each time his breath would be choked off.

Hendricks cleared his throat and re-crossed his legs. "P.S.," he said, "we have your examination here. You signed your name to the pledge at the end of the exam. You swore on your honor that you had not cheated." Hendricks paused. P.S. knew what he was driving at.

"If I hadn't signed my name to the pledge, you would have known I had cheated right away," P.S. explained. "I didn't want to break my honor again. I was going to turn myself in, honest I was."

"You didn't, though," Nelson said.

"I would have!" P.S. said. But he still wasn't sure whether he would have or not. He knew he never would be certain.

"So, we've got you on lying and cheating," Nelson said. "How do we know you haven't stolen, too?"

Dr. Fairfax grabbed the lapels of Nelson's jacket, pulled him out of the chair, and pushed him out of the room. The old man closed the door and leaned against it. He wiped his brow and said, "Mr. Seaton, sir, I trust you won't find fault with my actions. That young Nelson has a tendency to bother me. In point of fact, he irritates me intensely."

P.S. looked gratefully at Dr. Fairfax. The old man smiled sadly. Mabrey was talking quietly to Hendricks. Mr. Seaton sat down in Nelson's chair and turned to P.S. "I know this is a difficult question. Would you—would you have turned Jumbo in had you seen him cheating?"

P.S. felt the blood drain from his face. *So Jumbo turned me in! . . . Jumbo saw me! . . . Sitting next to me all year! . . . Jumbo turned me in! Why?*

He looked up at the others. They were all waiting for his answer. He had the most curious feeling of aloofness, of coldness. If he said yes, that he would have turned Jumbo in, it would be a lie, and he knew it. If he answered yes, it would please the headmaster, though. Because it would mean that P.S. still had faith in the school system. If he said no, he wouldn't have turned Jumbo in, it would be as good as admitting that he would not obey the fourth part of the Honor Code—"I will report anyone I see doing so." He waited a moment and then answered, "I don't know. I don't know whether I would have turned Jumbo in or not."

"Thank you very much, P.S.," the headmaster said.

P.S. could tell that Mr. Seaton was disappointed in his answer.

"Gentlemen, do you have any further

questions you would like to ask Wilkinson?"

"Nothing, sir," Hendricks answered.

The headmaster looked over at Dr. Fairfax, who shook his head. "Well, then, P.S., if you don't mind, we'd like you to sit in my office until we call for you."

P.S. got up and started for the door.

"Have you had any lunch?" Dr. Fairfax asked.

"No, sir. But I'm not very hungry."

"I'll have Mrs. Burdick bring in some milk and cookies."

"Thank you, sir."

The door opened and P.S. stood up as Mr. Seaton walked over to his desk and eased himself into the swivel chair. P.S. had been sitting alone in the headmaster's office for several hours.

"Sit down, please," the headmaster said. He picked up a wooden pencil and began to roll it back and forth between his palms. P.S. could hear the click of the pencil as it rolled across the headmaster's ring. Mr. Seaton laid the pencil aside and rubbed his cheek. His hand moved up the side of his face and began to massage his temple. Then he looked up at P.S. and said, "The Honor Committee has decided that you must leave the school. The penalty for cheating at V.P.S. is immediate expulsion. There cannot be any exceptions."

P.S. took a deep breath and pushed himself back into the soft leather seat. Then he dropped his hands into his lap and slumped. He was beyond crying; there was nothing left to cry about.

"We were able to reach your father before he left Washington, and he is waiting for you in the other room," Mr. Seaton said. "I've asked him to wait outside for a few minutes, because I want to speak to you alone. I want you to understand why the school had to make the decision to expel you. The school—this school—is only as good as its honor system. And the honor system is only as good as the students who live by it."

P.S. cleared his throat and looked down at his fingernails. He wished the headmaster wouldn't talk about it. He knew why the school had to expel him. It was done. It was over with. What good would it do to talk about it?

"The honor system, since it is based on mutual trust and confidence, no doubt makes it easier for some students to cheat," the headmaster said. "I am not so naïve as to believe that there aren't any boys who cheat here. Unfortunately, our honor system makes it easy for them to do so. These boys have not been caught. Perhaps they will never be caught. But I feel that it was far better for you to have been caught right away, P.S., because you are not a cheater. Notice that I said you *are* not a cheater instead of you *were* not a cheater. . . . Yes, you cheated this one time. I do not need to ask whether you cheated before. I know you haven't. I know also that you will not cheat again. I was frankly stunned when I heard that you had cheated on Dr. Fairfax's examination. You were the last boy I would have expected to cheat. I am still not entirely satisfied by the reasons you gave for cheating. I suppose a person never is. Maybe it is impossible to give reasons for such an act." Mr. Seaton began massaging his temple again. "P.S., the most difficult thing that you must try to understand is that Jumbo did the right thing. Jumbo was correct in turning you in."

P.S. stiffened in the chair. "Yes, sir," he said.

"If no one reported infractions, we would have no Honor Code. The Code would be obeyed only when it was convenient to obey it. It would be given lip service. The whole system would break down. The school would become just another private school, instead of the respected and loved institution it now is. Put yourself in Jumbo's shoes for a moment. You and Jumbo are friends—*believe me,* you are friends. If you had heard what Jumbo said about you in here, and how it hurt him to turn you in, you would know what a good friend Jumbo is. You have been expelled for cheating. You will not be here next fall. But Jumbo will be. Jumbo will stay on at V.P.S., and the other students will know that he was the one who turned you in. When I asked you whether you would have turned Jumbo in, you said that you didn't know. You and I both know from your answer that you wouldn't have turned Jumbo in. Perhaps the schoolboy code is still stronger in you than the Honor Code. Many students feel stronger about the schoolboy code than the Honor Code. No one likes to turn in a friend. A lot of boys who don't know any better, a lot of your friends, will never forgive Jumbo. It will be plenty tough for him. Just as it is rough on anybody who does his duty. I think—I honestly think that Jumbo has done you a favor. I'm not going to suggest that you be grateful to him. Not yet. That would be as ridiculous as my saying something as trite as 'Someday you will be able to look back on this and laugh.' . . . P.S., you will never be able to look back on this and laugh. But you may be able to understand." The headmaster looked at his wristwatch and then said, "I'm going to leave you alone with your father for a few minutes; then I suggest you go back to your room and pack. The other students won't be back in the dormitories yet, so you can be alone." He got up from behind the desk. P.S. rose also. He looked down at the milk and cookies Mrs. Burdick had left him. There was half a glass of milk and three cookies left.

The headmaster looked at P.S. for a moment and then he said, "I'm sorry you have been expelled, P.S. You were a good student here. One of the most popular boys in your class. You will leave behind a great many good friends."

"Thank you, sir," P.S. said.

"I'll see you before you and your father leave?"

"Yes, sir."

The headmaster walked into the waiting room. P.S. could hear Dr. Fairfax talking, and then his father. The door closed, and P.S. sat down to wait for his father. He could feel the fear building up inside him again. He did not know what to say to his father. What could he say? He sipped the last of the milk as the door opened. P.S. put down the glass and stood up.

Stewart Wilkinson closed the door behind him and looked at his son. He wanted to hold the boy and comfort him, but Phil looked so solid, so strong standing there. Why isn't he crying, he wondered, and then he told himself that he wouldn't have cried either; that the boy had had plenty of time to cry; that he would never cry in front of his father again. He tried to think of something to say. He knew that he often was clumsy in his relations with Phil, and said the wrong thing, and he wondered whether he had been that sensitive at his son's age. He looked down at the plate of cookies and the empty milk glass.

"Where did you get the milk and cookies, son?"

"Mrs. Burdick brought them to me, sir."

He never calls me "Dad" now, Stewart Wilkinson said to himself. Always "sir." . . . My own son calls me "sir." . . .

"Did you thank her?"

"Yes, sir."

Stewart Wilkinson walked over to the couch next to his son and sat down. The boy remained standing.

"Phil, son, sit down, please."

"Yes, sir."

Looking at his son, Stewart Wilkinson could not understand why they had grown apart during the last few years. He had always remained close to his father. Why wasn't it the same between him and the boy who sat so stiff beside him, so still in spite of the horror he must have gone through during the past few hours?

"I'm sorry, sir."

"Yes . . . yes, son, I know you are. . . . I'm terribly sorry myself. Sorry for you. . . . Mr. Seaton told me another boy turned you in, is that right?"

P.S. nodded.

"He also told me that he believes you would have turned yourself in had you been given enough time."

"I don't know whether I would have or not. I never had the chance to find out."

"I think you would have. I think you would have."

He waited for his son to say something; then, realizing there was nothing the boy could say, he spoke again. "I was talking to Dr. Fairfax outside—you knew he was my Latin teacher, too?"

"Yes, sir."

"We always used to be able to tell when the first day of spring came, because Dr. Fairfax put on his white linen suit."

"Yes, sir."

"At any rate, that man thinks very highly of you, Phil. He is very upset that you had to be expelled. I hope you will speak to him before we go. He's a good man to have on your side."

"I want to speak to him."

"Phil . . . Phil . . . " Stewart Wilkinson thought for a minute. He wanted so desperately what he said to be the right thing to say. "Phil, I know that I am partly responsible for what has happened. I must have in some way pressured you into it. I wanted your marks to be high. I wanted you to get the best education that you could. V.P.S. isn't the best school in the country, but it's a very fine one. It's a school that has meant a lot to our family. But that doesn't matter so much. I mean, that part of it is all over with. I'm sorry that you cheated, because I know you're not the cheating kind. I'm also sorry because you are going to have to face the family and get it over with. This is going to be tough. But they'll all understand. I doubt that there is any of us who has never cheated in one way or another. But it will make them very proud of you if you can go see them and look them in the eye."

He picked up one of the cookies and began to bite little pieces out of the edge. Then he shook his head sadly, in the gesture P.S. knew so well. "Ah, son, it's so terrible that you have to learn these lessons when you are young. I know that you don't want me to feel sorry for you, but I can't help it. I'm not angry with you. I'm a little disappointed, perhaps, but I can understand it, I think. I suppose I must appear as an ogre to you at times. But Phil, I—If I'm tough with you, it's just because I'm trying to help you. Maybe I'm too tough." Stewart Wilkinson looked over at his son. He saw that the boy was watching him. He felt a little embarrassed to have revealed so much of himself before his son. But he knew they were alike. He knew that Phil was really his son. They already spoke alike, already laughed at the same sort of things, appreciated the same things. Their tastes were pretty much the

same. He knew that, if anything, he was too much like the boy to be able to help him. And also that the problem was the boy's own, and that he would resent his father's interfering.

"Phil, I'll go speak with Mr. Seaton for a little while, and then I'll come on over and help you pack. If you'd like, I'll pack for you and you can sit in the car."

"No, that's all right, sir. I'll pack. I mean, most of the stuff is packed up already. I'll meet you over there."

Stewart Wilkinson rose with his son. Again he wanted to hold the boy, to show him how much he loved him.

"I'll be through packing in a few minutes. I'll meet you in my room," P.S. said.

"Fine, son."

Together they carried the footlocker down the staircase of Memorial Hall. P.S. stopped at the door, balanced the footlocker with one hand, then pulled the heavy door open. The door swung back before they could get through. Stewart Wilkinson stumbled and P.S. said, "I'm sorry."

They carried the footlocker across the small patch of lawn between the front of Memorial Hall and the main drive and slid the footlocker into the back of the station wagon.

"How much more is there, son?"

"A couple of small boxes, some books, and a couple of pictures."

Stewart Wilkinson pulled a silk handkerchief out of his back pocket and wiped his brow. "You think we can get all of them in one more trip?"

"I think so, sir. At least, we can try."

They turned back toward the dormitory. Stewart Wilkinson rested his hand on his son's shoulder as they walked back across the lawn. "Phil, Mr. Seaton told me that he thinks he might be able to get you into Hotchkiss. How does that sound to you?"

"It's a funny name for a school."

"Hotchkiss, funny? Why?"

"I don't know, it just sounds funny."

"Well, do you think you'd like to go there?"

"Sure. I mean I don't know. I haven't given it much thought."

Stewart Wilkinson laughed. "I guess you haven't."

The boy looked worriedly at his father for a moment. He wondered whether his father was making fun of him. And then he saw the humor in his remark and laughed too.

They brought the last of the boxes down from the room and slid them into the car and closed the tailgate.

"Did you get a chance to talk to Dr. Fairfax?"

"Yes, sir. He came by the room while I was packing."

"What did he say?"

"I don't know. I mean he was sorry I was going and all that, but he said I'd get along fine anywhere and that it wasn't the end of the world."

"Did he say 'in point of fact'?"

"Yeah." P.S. laughed. "He said, 'Well, boy, you'll do all right. In point of fact, you have nothing to worry about.' I really like old Doc Fairfax."

They went around the side of the car and climbed in.

"Anything you've forgotten? Books out of the library, equipment in the gym? Anybody special you want to see before we go home?"

"No, Dad, thanks, that's all—Hey, wait a minute, could you, Dad?" P.S. got out of the car. "It's Charlie—Charlie Merritt. I'd like to say goodbye to him."

"Sure, son, take your time."

The two boys spoke together for a moment, standing in the road; then they shook hands. Stewart Wilkinson turned off the engine and watched as the boys walked back up the road toward him. As they drew near, he got out of the station wagon.

"Dad, this is Charlie Merritt . . . . Charlie, you remember my father."

"Yes, sir. How are you, sir?"

"Fine, thank you, Charlie."

"Sir, Mr. Wilkinson, I'm sorry about P.S. getting kicked out and all."

Stewart Wilkinson nodded.

"He's just sorry because I won't be around to borrow his toothpaste any more. He likes to lend it to me because I always roll it from the top and lose the cap."

P.S. and Charlie laughed.

"Hey, P.S.?" Charlie said. "Does this mean you're not going to have to work off the five demerits Doc Fairfax gave us this morning?"

"What did you two get five demerits for?" Stewart Wilkinson asked.

"We were talking before the exam," P.S. said.

Father and son looked at each other, and then P.S. turned away. It was clear that he was thinking about the exam and his cheating again. And then the boy took a deep breath and smiled. "You know? It's funny," he said. "I mean, it seems that that exam took place so long ago. . . . Well, Charlie?" P.S. stuck out his hand and Charlie took it. "Well, I guess we'd better get going. I'll see you around, O.K.?"

"Sure, P.S.," Charlie said.

The two boys shook hands again solemnly. Then Charlie shook hands with P.S.'s father. P.S. and Stewart Wilkinson got back into the station wagon.

Charlie walked around to P.S.'s window. "Hey, P.S.! Make sure you let me hear from you this summer, O.K.?"

"Sure, Charlie. Take care of yourself."

They drove around the school drive, past the Wilkinson Memorial Library and the Sadler Gymnasium, and then they turned down the slight hill toward the Breastworks, and as they passed through the ornate, wrought-iron gate P.S. began to cry. □□

Discussion

1. (a) What is your opinion of the Honor Code of the Virginia Preparatory School? (b) Do you think such an "honor system" would work in your own school? (c) Would you report another student, if you saw that student cheat on an exam? Explain.

2. (a) How has P.S. Wilkinson changed from the beginning to the end of the story? (b) What narrative point of view has the author used in telling the story? (c) How does the point of view help you to know P.S.?

3. P.S.'s family background is important in showing the kind of boy P.S. is. Point out specific details which show: (a) The things which are important to his family. (b) His relationship with his father before they meet in the headmaster's office.

4. (a) What place does the Honor Code have in the life of V.P.S.? (b) Why does P.S. break the Honor Code? (c) How well has P.S. prepared for the Latin exam? (d) How does he react to the decision of the Honor Committee?

5. (a) What releases the tension between P.S. and his father as they are packing the car? (b) How does P.S. then address his father to show that

he is beginning to realize that his father is on his side? (c) What does P.S.'s crying at the end of the story tell you about the change in his relationship with his father?

6. The headmaster says that perhaps the "schoolboy" code is stronger in P.S. than the Honor Code. (a) What does he mean by the schoolboy code? (b) Would P.S. have turned Jumbo in for cheating? Give reasons for your answer. (c) Do you think that P.S. would have turned himself in? Explain.

7. (a) Point out the place in the second half of the story where the author changes the focus of his point of view. (b) On which character is the last portion of the story focused? (c) What do we learn about Mr. Wilkinson by the change of focus?

8. Find the place in the story from which the title is taken. (a) What does "so much unfairness of things" mean in the Latin passage? (b) What does the phrase mean as the title of the story?

Vocabulary
Structure, Pronunciation, Dictionary

A. Use your Glossary, if necessary, to answer the following questions about the structure or pronunciation of the listed words. Be sure you know the meaning of each word.

artillery	infraction
commemorate	liberation
disbelief	reprimand
footlocker	underclassman

1. Which words from the list are compound words?

2. Which word has a prefix that means "lack of"?

3. Which word goes back to the Latin word meaning "act of setting free"?

4. Which word is pronounced (in frak′shən)?

5. Which word is derived from an Old French word meaning "large guns; cannon"?

6. Which word is derived from a Latin word meaning "bring to mind"?

7. Which word is pronounced (rep′rə mand)?

B. Choose five of the words from a list in part A and use each in a sentence that shows that you understand its meaning.

Extension • Writing

Early in this story we learn that P.S. is expected to preserve a strong family tradition and thereby keep one generation of Wilkinsons very much like the another. P.S. broke a family tradition by being expelled from V.P.S. Write a paragraph in which you explain how you think the breaking of this tradition might be (or might *not* be) a good thing to have happened to P.S.

Before you begin writing, consider the kind of person P.S. might have become if he had graduated—what characteristics and attitudes he might have held. Consider as well how his *not* graduating may affect his future, especially his relationship with a son of his own.

The Secret Heart

Robert P. Tristram Coffin

Across the years he could recall
His father one way best of all.

In the stillest hour of night
The boy awakened to a light.

5 Half in dreams, he saw his sire
With his great hands full of fire.

The man had struck a match to see
If his son slept peacefully.

He held his palms each side the spark
10 His love had kindled in the dark.

His two hands were curved apart
In the semblance of a heart.

He wore, it seemed to his small son,
A bare heart on his hidden one,

15 A heart that gave out such a glow
No son awake could bear to know.

It showed a look upon a face
Too tender for the day to trace.

One instant, it lit all about,
20 And then the secret heart went out.

But it shone long enough for one
To know that hands held up the sun.

Women

Alice Walker

They were women then
My mama's generation
Husky of voice—Stout of
Step
5 With fists as well as
Hands
How they battered down
Doors
And ironed
10 Starched white
Shirts
How they led
Armies
Headragged Generals
15 Across mined
Fields
Booby-trapped
Ditches
To discover books
20 Desks
A place for us
How they knew what we
Must know
Without knowing a page
25 Of it
Themselves.

I shall write of the old men I knew
And the young men
I loved
30 And of the gold toothed women
Mighty of arm
Who dragged us all
To church.

Discussion

1. What does the speaker mean when she says the women of her mother's generation had fists as well as hands?

2. The speaker presents us with a kind of riddle at the end of the first stanza. What is it that the women knew "Without knowing a page/Of it/ Themselves"?

3. What seems to be the speaker's attitude toward the women of "mama's generation"? Is she admiring or critical, grateful or resentful? Explain.

Alice Walker 1944 •

Born in Georgia as the eighth child of sharecropping parents, Alice Walker graduated from Sarah Lawrence College. In addition to lecturing on writing and literature, Walker has published a biography of Langston Hughes, a novel, and collections of her stories and poetry.

*"Man, I don't get you. You got
a whole apartment next door all to yourself—
six rooms! And you gotta come here to
eat in this crowded kitchen. Why?"*

Mr. Mendelsohn

Nicholasa Mohr

Psst . . . psst, Mr. Mendelsohn, wake up.
Come on now!" Mrs. Suárez said in a low
quiet voice. Mr. Mendelsohn had fallen
asleep again, on the large armchair in the
living room. He grasped the brown shiny
wooden cane and leaned forward, his chin
on his chest. The small black skullcap that
was usually placed neatly on the back of his
head had tilted to one side, covering his right
ear. "Come on now. It's late, and time to go
home." She tapped him on the shoulder and
waited for him to wake up. Slowly, he lifted
his head, opened his eyes, and blinked.

"What time is it?" he asked.

"It's almost midnight. Caramba! I didn't
even know you was still here. When I came
to shut off the lights, I saw you was sleeping."

"Oh . . . I'm sorry. O.K., I'm leaving."
With short, slow steps he followed Mrs.
Suárez over to the front door.

"Go on now," she said, opening the door.
"We'll see you tomorrow."

He walked out into the hallway, stepped
about three feet to the left, and stood before
the door of his apartment. Mrs. Suárez waited, holding her door ajar, while he carefully
searched for the right key to each lock. He
had to open seven locks in all.

A small fluffy dog standing next to Mrs.
Suárez began to whine and bark.

"Mr. Mendelsohn" from *El Bronx Remembered* by Nicholasa
Mohr. Copyright © 1975 by Nicholasa Mohr. Reprinted by permission of Harper & Row, Publishers, Inc.

"Shh—sh, Sporty! Stop it!" she said. "You had your walk. Shh."

"O.K.," said Mr. Mendelsohn, finally opening his door. "Good night." Mrs. Suárez smiled and nodded.

"Good night," she whispered, as they both shut their doors simultaneously.

Mr. Mendelsohn knocked on the door and waited; then tried the doorknob. Turning and pushing, he realized the door was locked, and knocked again, this time more forcefully. He heard Sporty barking and footsteps coming toward the door.

"Who's there?" a child's voice asked.

"It's me—Mr. Mendelsohn! Open up, Yvonne." The door opened, and a young girl, age nine, smiled at him.

"Mami! It's el Señor Mr. Mendelsohn again."

"Tell him to come on in, muchacha!" Mrs. Suárez answered.

"My mother says come on in."

He followed Yvonne and the dog, who leaped up, barking and wagging his tail. Mr. Mendelsohn stood at the kitchen entrance and greeted everyone.

"Good morning to you all!" He had just shaved and trimmed his large black mustache. As he smiled broadly, one could see that most of his teeth were missing. His large bald head was partially covered by his small black skullcap. Thick dark grey hair grew in abundance at the lower back of his head, coming around the front above his ears into short sideburns. He wore a clean white shirt, frayed at the cuffs. His worn-out pinstripe trousers were held up by a pair of dark suspenders. Mr. Mendelsohn leaned on his brown shiny cane and carried a small brown paper bag.

"Mr. Mendelsohn, come into the kitchen," said Mrs. Suárez, "and have some coffee with us." She stood by the stove. A boy of eleven, a young man of about seventeen, and a young pregnant woman were seated at the table.

"Sit here," said the boy, vacating a chair. "I'm finished eating." He stood by the entrance with his sister Yvonne, and they both looked at Mr. Mendelsohn and his paper bag with interest.

"Thank you, Georgie," Mr. Mendelsohn said. He sat down and placed the bag on his lap.

The smell of freshly perked coffee and boiled milk permeated the kitchen.

Winking at everyone, the young man asked, "Hey, what you got in that bag you holding onto, huh, Mr. Mendelsohn?" They all looked at each other and at the old man, amused. "Something special, I bet!"

"Well," the old man replied. "I thought your mama would be so kind as to permit me to make myself a little breakfast here today . . . so." He opened the bag, and began to take out its contents. "I got two slices of rye bread, two tea bags. I brought one extra, just in case anybody would care to join me for tea. And a jar of herring in sour cream."

"Sounds delicious!" said the young man, sticking out his tongue and making a face. Yvonne and Georgie burst out laughing.

"Shh . . . sh." Mrs. Suárez shook her head and looked at her children disapprovingly. "Never mind, Julio!" she said to the young man. Turning to Mr. Mendelsohn, she said, "You got the same like you brought last Saturday, eh? You can eat with us anytime. How about some fresh coffee? I just made it. Yes?" Mr. Mendelsohn looked at her, shrugging his shoulders. "Come on, have some," she coaxed.

"O.K.," he replied. "If it's not too much bother."

"No bother," she said, setting out a place

for the old man. "You gonna have some nice fresh bread with a little butter—it will go good with your herring." Mrs. Suárez cut a generous slice of freshly baked bread with a golden crust and buttered it. "Go on, eat. There's a plate and everything for your food. Go on, eat. . . ."

"Would anyone care for some?" Mr. Mendelsohn asked. "Perhaps a tea bag for a cup of tea?"

"No . . . no thank you, Mr. Mendelsohn," Mrs. Suárez answered. "Everybody here already ate. You go ahead and eat. You look too skinny; you better eat. Go on, eat your bread."

The old man began to eat vigorously.

"Can I ask you a question?" Julio asked the old man. "Man, I don't get you. You got a whole apartment next door all to yourself—six rooms! And you gotta come here to eat in this crowded kitchen. Why?"

"First of all, today is Saturday, and I thought I could bring in my food and your mama could turn on the stove for me. You know, in my religion you can't light a fire on Saturday."[1]

"You come here anytime; I turn on the stove for you, don't worry," Mrs. Suárez said.

"Man, what about other days? We been living here for about six months, right?" Julio persisted. "And you do more cooking here than in your own place."

"It doesn't pay to turn on the gas for such a little bit of cooking. So I told the gas company to turn it off . . . for good! I got no more gas now, only an electric hot plate," the old man said.

Julio shook his head and sighed. "I don't know——"

"Julio, chico!" snapped Mrs. Suárez, interrupting him, "Basta—it doesn't bother nobody." She looked severely at her son and shook her head. "You gotta go with your sister to the clinic today, so you better get ready now. You too, Marta."

"O.K., Mama," she answered, "but I wanted to see if I got mail from Ralphy today."

"You don't got time. I'll save you the mail; you read it when you get back. You and Julio better get ready; go on." Reluctantly, Marta stood up and yawned, stretching and arching her back.

"Marta," Mr. Mendelsohn said, "you taking care? . . . You know, this is a very delicate time for you."

"I am, Mr. Mendelsohn. Thank you."

"I raised six sisters," the old man said. "I ought to know. Six . . . and married them off to fine husbands. Believe me, I've done my share in life." Yvonne and Georgie giggled and poked each other.

"He's gonna make one of his speeches," they whispered.

". . . I never had children. No time to get married. My father died when I was eleven. I went to work supporting my mother and six younger sisters. I took care of them, and today they are all married, with families. They always call and want me to visit them. I'm too busy and I have no time. . . ."

"Too busy eating in our kitchen," whispered Julio. Marta, Georgie, and Yvonne tried not to laugh out loud. Mrs. Suárez reached over and with a wooden ladle managed a light but firm blow on Julio's head.

". . . Only on the holidays, I make some time to see them. But otherwise, I cannot be bothered with all that visiting." Mr. Mendelsohn stopped speaking and began to eat again.

---

1. **can't light . . . on Saturday.** Saturday is the Jewish Sabbath, a day of rest and worship. For many Jews, the restrictions against work on the Sabbath apply to such tasks as the lighting of stoves.

"Go on, Marta and Julio, you will be late for the clinic," Mrs. Suárez said. "And you two? What are you doing there smiling like two monkeys? Go find something to do!"

Quickly, Georgie and Yvonne ran down the hallway, and Julio and Marta left the kitchen.

Mrs. Suárez sat down beside the old man.

"Another piece of bread?" she asked.

"No, thank you very much. . . . I'm full. But it was delicious."

"You too skinny—you don't eat right, I bet." Mrs. Suárez shook her head. "Come tomorrow and have Sunday supper with us."

"I really couldn't."

"Sure, you could. I always make a big supper and there is plenty. All right? Mr. Suárez and I will be happy to have you."

"Are you sure it will be no bother?"

"What are you talking for the bother all the time? One more person is no bother. You come tomorrow. Yes?"

The old man smiled broadly and nodded. This was the first time he had been invited to Sunday supper with the family.

Mrs. Suárez stood and began clearing away the dishes. "O.K., you go inside; listen to the radio or talk to the kids or something. I got work to do."

Mr. Mendelsohn closed his jar of herring and put it back into the bag. "Can I leave this here till I go?"

"Leave it; I put it in the refrigerator for you."

Leaning on his cane, Mr. Mendelsohn stood up and walked out of the kitchen and down the long hallway into the living room. It was empty. He went over to a large armchair by the window. The sun shone through the window, covering the entire armchair and Mr. Mendelsohn. A canary cage was also by the window, and two tiny yellow birds chirped and hopped back and forth energetically. Mr. Mendelsohn felt drowsy; he shut his eyes. So many aches and pains, he thought. It was hard to sleep at night, but here, well . . . the birds began to chirp in unison and the old man opened one eye, glancing at them, and smiled. Then he shut his eyes once more and fell fast asleep.

When Mr. Mendelsohn opened his eyes, Georgie and Yvonne were in the living room. Yvonne held a deck of playing cards and Georgie read a comic book. She looked at the old man and, holding up the deck of cards, asked "Do you wanna play a game of War? Huh, Mr. Mendelsohn?"

"I don't know how to play that," he answered.

"It's real easy. I'll show you. Come on . . . please!"

"Well," he shrugged, "sure, why not? Maybe I'll learn something."

Yvonne took a small maple end table and a wooden chair, and set them next to Mr. Mendelsohn. "Now . . ." she began, "I'll shuffle the cards and you cut, and then I throw down a card and you throw down a card and the one with the highest card wins. O.K.? And then, the one with the most cards of all wins the game. O.K.?"

"That's all?" he asked.

"That's all. Ready?" she asked, and sat down. They began to play cards.

"You know, my sister Jennie used to be a great card player," said Mr. Mendelsohn.

"Does she still play?" asked Yvonne.

"Oh . . ." Mr. Mendelsohn laughed. "I don't know any more. She's already married and has kids. She was the youngest in my family—like you."

"Did she go to P.S. 39? On Longwood Avenue?"

"I'm sure she did. All my sisters went to school around here."

"Wow! You must be living here a long time, Mr. Mendelsohn."

"Forty-five years!" said the old man.

"Wowee!" Yvonne whistled. "Georgie, did you hear? Mr. Mendelsohn been living here for forty-five whole years!"

Georgie put down his comic book and looked up.

"Really?" he asked, impressed.

"Yes, forty-five years this summer we moved here. But in those days things were different, not like today. No sir! The Bronx has changed. Then, it was the country. That's right! Why, look out the window. You see the elevated trains on Westchester Avenue? Well, there were no trains then. That was once a dirt road. They used to bring cows through there."

"Oh, man!" Georgie and Yvonne both gasped.

"Sure. These buildings were among the first apartment houses to go up. Four stories high, and that used to be a big accomplishment in them days. All that was here was mostly little houses, like you still see here and there. Small farms, woodlands . . . like that."

"Did you see any Indians?" asked Georgie.

"What do you mean, Indians?" laughed the old man. "I'm not that old, and this here was not the Wild West." Mr. Mendelsohn saw that the children were disappointed. He added quickly, "But we did have carriages with horses. No cars and lots of horses."

"That's what Mami says they have in Puerto Rico—not like here in El Bronx," said Yvonne.

"Yeah," Georgie agreed. "Papi says he rode a horse when he was a little kid in Puerto Rico. They had goats and pigs and all them things. Man, was he lucky."

"Lucky?" Mr. Mendelsohn shook his head. "You—you are the lucky one today! You got school and a good home and clothes. You don't have to go out to work and support a family like your papa and I had to do, and miss an education. You can learn and be somebody someday."

"Someday," said Yvonne, "we are gonna get a house with a yard and all. Mami says that when Ralphy gets discharged from the Army, he'll get a loan from the government and we can pay to buy a house. You know, instead of rent."

Mrs. Suárez walked into the living room with her coat on, carrying a shopping bag.

"Yvonne, take the dog out for a walk, and Georgie come on! We have to go shopping. Get your jacket."

Mr. Mendelsohn started to rise. "No," she said, "stay . . . sit down. It's O.K. You can stay and rest if you want."

"All right, Mrs. Suárez," Mr. Mendelsohn said.

"Now don't forget tomorrow for Sunday supper, and take a nap if you like."

Mr. Mendelsohn heard the front door slam shut, and the apartment was silent. The warmth of the bright sun made him drowsy once more. It was so nice here, he thought, a house full of people and kids—like it used to be. He recalled his sisters and his parents . . . the holidays . . . the arguments . . . the laughing. It was so empty next door. He would have to look for a smaller apartment, near Jennie, someday. But not now. Now, it was just nice to sleep and rest right here. He heard the tiny birds chirping and quietly drifted into a deep sleep.

Mr. Mendelsohn rang the bell, then opened the door. He could smell the familiar cooking odors of Sunday supper. For two years he had spent every Sunday at his neighbors'. Sporty greeted him, jumping affectionately and barking.

"Shh—sh . . . down. Good boy," he said, and walked along the hallway toward the kitchen. The room was crowded with people and the stove was loaded with large pots of food, steaming and puffing. Mrs. Suárez was busy basting a large roast. Looking up, she saw Mr. Mendelsohn.

"Come in," she said, "and sit down." Motioning to Julio, who was seated, she continued, "Julio, you are finished, get up and give Mr. Mendelsohn a seat." Julio stood up.

"Here's the sponge cake," Mr. Mendelsohn said, and handed the cake box he carried to Julio, who put it in the refrigerator.

"That's nice. . . . Thank you," said Mrs. Suárez, and placed a cup of freshly made coffee before the old man.

"Would anyone like some coffee?" Mr. Mendelsohn asked. Yvonne and Georgie giggled, looked at one another, and shook their heads.

"You always say that!" said Yvonne.

"One of these days," said Ralphy, "I'm gonna say, 'Yes, give me your coffee,' and you won't have none to drink." The children laughed loudly.

"Don't tease him," Mrs. Suárez said, half smiling. "Let him have his coffee."

"He is just being polite, children," Mr. Suárez said, and shifting his chair closer to Mr. Mendelsohn, he asked, "So . . . Mr. Mendelsohn, how you been? What's new? You O.K.?"

"So-so, Mr. Suárez. You know, aches and pains when you get old. But there's nothing you can do, so you gotta make the best of it."

Mr. Suárez nodded sympathetically, and they continued to talk. Mr. Mendelsohn saw the family every day, except for Mr. Suárez and Ralphy, who both worked a night shift.

Marta appeared in the entrance, holding a small child by the hand.

"There he is, Tato," she said to the child, and pointed to Mr. Mendelsohn.

"Oh, my big boy! He knows, he knows he's my best friend," Mr. Mendelsohn said, and held the brown shiny cane out toward Tato. The small boy grabbed the cane and, shrieking with delight, walked toward Mr. Mendelsohn.

"Look at that, will you?" said Ralphy. "He knows Mr. Mendelsohn better than me, his own father."

"That's because they are always together," smiled Marta. "Tato is learning to walk with his cane!"

Everyone laughed as they watched Tato climbing the old man's knee. Bending over, Mr. Mendelsohn pulled Tato onto his lap.

"Oh . . . he's getting heavy," said Mrs. Suárez. "Be careful."

"Never mind," Mr. Mendelsohn responded, hugging Tato. "That's my best boy. And look how swell he walks, and he's not even nineteen months."

"What a team," Julio said. "Tato already walks like Mr. Mendelsohn and pretty soon he's gonna complain like him, too. . . ." Julio continued to tease the old man, who responded good-naturedly, as everyone laughed.

After coffee, Mr. Mendelsohn sat on the large armchair in the living room, waiting for supper to be ready. He watched with delight as Tato walked back and forth with the cane. Mr. Mendelsohn held Tato's blanket, stuffed bear, and picture book.

"Tato," he called out, "come here. Let me read you a book—come on. I'm going to read you a nice story."

Tato climbed onto the chair and into Mr.

Mendelsohn's lap. He sucked his thumb and waited. Mr. Mendelsohn opened the picture book.

"O.K. Now . . . ." He pointed to the picture. "A is for Alligators. See that? Look at that big mouth and all them teeth. . . ." Tato yawned, nestled back, and closed his eyes. The old man read a few more pages and shut the book.

The soft breathing and sucking sound that Tato made assured Mr. Mendelsohn that the child was asleep. Such a smart kid. What a great boy, he said to himself. Mr. Mendelsohn was vaguely aware of a radio program, voices, and the small dog barking now and then, just before he too fell into a deep sleep.

This Sunday was very much like all the others; coffee first, then he and Tato would play a bit before napping in the large armchair. It had become a way of life for the old man. Only the High Holy Days and an occasional invitation to a family event, such as a marriage or funeral and so on, would prevent the old man from spending Sunday next door.

It had all been so effortless. No one ever asked him to leave, except late at night when he napped too long. On Saturdays, he tried to observe the Sabbath and brought in his meal. They lit the stove for him.

Mrs. Suárez was always feeding him, just like Mama. She also worried about me not eating, the old man had said to himself, pleased. At first, he had been cautious and had wondered about the food and the people that he was becoming so involved with. That first Sunday, the old man had looked suspiciously at the food they served him.

"What is it?" he had asked. Yvonne and Georgie had started giggling, and had looked at one another. Mrs. Suárez had responded quickly and with anger, cautioning her children; speaking to them in Spanish.

"Eat your food, Mr. Mendelsohn. You too skinny," she had told him.

"What kind of meat is it?" Mr. Mendelsohn insisted.

"It's good for you, that's what it is," Mrs. Suárez answered.

"But I——" Mr. Mendelsohn started.

"Never mind—it's good for you. I prepare everything fresh. Go ahead and eat it," Mrs. Suárez had interrupted. There was a silence as Mr. Mendelsohn sat still, not eating.

"You know, I'm not allowed to eat certain things. In my religion we have dietary laws. This is not—pork or something like it, is it?"

"It's just . . . chicken. Chicken! That's what it is. It's delicious . . . and good for you," she had said with conviction.

"It doesn't look like chicken to me."

"That's because you never ate no chicken like this before. This here is—is called Puerto Rican chicken. I prepare it special. So you gonna eat it. You too skinny."

Mr. Mendelsohn had tried to protest, but Mrs. Suárez insisted. "Never mind. Now I prepare everything clean and nice. You eat the chicken; you gonna like it. Go on!"

And that was all.

Mr. Mendelsohn ate his Sunday supper from then on without doubt or hesitation, accepting the affection and concern that Mrs. Suárez provided with each plateful.

That night in his own apartment, Mr. Mendelsohn felt uneasy. He remembered that during supper, Ralphy had mentioned that his G.I. loan had come through. They would be looking for a house soon, everyone agreed. Not in the Bronx; farther out, near

Yonkers: It was more like the country there.

The old man tossed and turned in his bed. That's still a long way off. First, they have to find the house and everything. You don't move just like that! he said to himself. It's gonna take a while, he reasoned, putting such thoughts out of his mind.

Mr. Mendelsohn looked at his quarters.

"I told you, didn't I? See how nice this is?" his sister Jennie said. She put down the large sack of groceries on the small table.

It was a fair-sized room with a single bed, a bureau, a wooden wardrobe closet, a table, and two chairs. A hot plate was set on a small white refrigerator, and a white metal kitchen cabinet was placed alongside.

"We'll bring you whatever else you need, Louis," Jennie went on. "You'll love it here, I'm sure. There are people your own age, interested in the same things. Here—let's get started. We'll put your things away and you can get nicely settled."

Mr. Mendelsohn walked over to the window and looked out. He saw a wide avenue with cars, taxis, and buses speeding by. "It's gonna take me two buses, at least, to get back to the old neighborhood," he said.

"Why do you have to go back there?" Jennie asked quickly. "There is nobody there any more, Louis. Everybody moved!"

"There's shul. . . ."[2]

"There's shul right here. Next door you have a large temple. Twice you were robbed over there. It's a miracle you weren't hurt! Louis, there is no reason for you to go back. There is nothing over there, nothing," Jennie said.

"The trouble all started with that rooming house next door. Those people took in all kinds. . . . " He shook his head. "When the Suárez family lived there we had no prob-

lems. But nobody would talk to the landlord about those new people—only me. Nobody cared."

"That's all finished," Jennie said, looking at her watch. "Now look how nice it is here. Come on, let's get started." She began to put the groceries away in the refrigerator and cabinet.

"Leave it, Jennie," he interrupted. "Go on. . . . I'll take care of it. You go on home. You are in a hurry."

"I'm only trying to help," Jennie responded.

"I know, I know. But I lived in one place for almost fifty years. So don't hurry me." He looked around the room. "And I ain't going nowhere now. . . ."

Shaking her head, Jennie said, "Look— this weekend we have a wedding, but next weekend Sara and I will come to see you. I'll call the hotel on the phone first, and they'll let you know. All right?"

"Sure." He nodded.

"That'll be good, Louis. This way you will get a chance to get settled and get acquainted with some of the other residents." Jennie kissed Mr. Mendelsohn affectionately. The old man nodded and turned away. In a moment, he heard the door open and shut.

Slowly, he walked to the sack of groceries and finished putting them away. Then, with much effort, he lifted a large suitcase onto the bed. He took out several photographs. Then he set the photographs upright, arranging them carefully on the bureau. He had pictures of his parents' wedding and of his sisters and their families. There was a photograph of his mother taken just before she died, and another one of Tato.

---

2. **shul** (shül), synagogue; a Jewish place of worship and religious study.

That picture was taken when he was about two years old, the old man said to himself. Yes, that's right, on his birthday. . . . There was a party. And Tato was already talking. Such a smart kid, he thought, smiling. Last? Last when? he wondered. Time was going fast for him. He shrugged. He could hardly remember what year it was lately. Just before they moved! He remembered. That's right, they gave him the photograph of Tato. They had a nice house around Gunhill Road someplace, and they had taken him there once. He recalled how exhausted he had been after the long trip. No one had a car, and they had had to take a train and buses. Anyway, he was glad he remembered. Now he could let them know he had moved, and tell them all about what happened to the old neighborhood. That's right, they had a telephone now. Yes, he said to himself, let me finish here, then I'll go call them. He continued to put the rest of his belongings away.

Mr. Mendelsohn sat in the lobby holding on to his cane and a cake box. He had told the nurse at the desk that his friends were coming to pick him up this Sunday. He looked eagerly toward the revolving doors. After a short while, he saw Ralphy, Julio, and Georgie walk through into the lobby.

"Deliveries are made in the rear of the building," he heard the nurse at the desk say as they walked toward him.

"These are my friends, Mrs. Read," Mr. Mendelsohn said, standing. "They are here to take me out."

"Oh, well," said the nurse. "All right; I didn't realize. Here he is then. He's been talking about nothing else but this visit." Mrs. Read smiled.

Ralphy nodded, then spoke to Georgie. "Get Mr. Mendelsohn's overcoat."

Quickly, Mr. Mendelsohn put on his coat, and all four left the lobby.

"Take good care of him now . . ." they heard Mrs. Read calling. "You be a good boy now, Mr. Mendelsohn."

Outside, Mr. Mendelsohn looked at the young men and smiled.

"How's everyone?" he asked.

"Good," Julio said. "Look, that's my pickup truck from work. They let me use it sometimes when I'm off."

"That's a beautiful truck. How's everyone? Tato? How is my best friend? And Yvonne? Does she like school? And your Mama and Papa? . . . Marta? . . ."

"Fine, fine. Everybody is doing great. Wait till you see them. We'll be there in a little while," said Julio. "With this truck, we'll get there in no time."

Mr. Mendelsohn sat in the kitchen and watched as Mrs. Suárez packed food into a shopping bag. Today had been a good day for the old man; he had napped in the old armchair and spent time with the children. Yvonne was so grown up, he almost had not recognized her. When Tato remembered him, Mr. Mendelsohn had been especially pleased. Shyly, he had shaken hands with the old man. Then he had taken him into his room to show Mr. Mendelsohn all his toys.

"Now I packed a whole lotta stuff in this shopping bag for you. You gotta eat it. Eat some of my Puerto Rican chicken—it's good for you. You too skinny. You got enough for tomorrow and for another day. You put it in the refrigerator. Also I put some rice and other things."

He smiled as she spoke, enjoying the attention he received.

"Julio is gonna drive you back before it gets too late," she said. "And we gonna pick you up again and bring you back to eat with

us. I bet you don't eat right." She shook her head. "O.K.?"

"You shouldn't go through so much bother," he protested mildly.

"Again with the bother? You stop that! We gonna see you soon. You take care of yourself and eat. Eat! You must nourish yourself, especially in such cold weather."

Mr. Mendelsohn and Mrs. Suárez walked out into the living room. The family exchanged good-byes with the old man. Tato, feeling less shy, kissed Mr. Mendelsohn on the cheek.

Just before leaving, Mr. Mendelsohn embraced Mrs. Suárez for a long time, as everybody watched silently.

"Thank you," he whispered.

"Thank you? For what?" Mrs. Suárez said. "You come back soon and have Sunday supper with us. Yes?" Mr. Mendelsohn nodded and smiled.

It was dark and cold out. He walked with effort. Julio carried the shopping bag. Slowly, he got into the pickup truck. The ride back was bumpy and uncomfortable for Mr. Mendelsohn. The cold wind cut right through into the truck, and the old man was aware of the long winter ahead.

His eyelids were so heavy he could hardly open them. Nurses scurried about busily. Mr. Mendelsohn heard voices.

"Let's give him another injection. It will help his breathing. Nurse! Nurse! The patient needs . . . ."

The voices faded. He remembered he had gone to sleep after supper last—last when? How many days have I been here . . . here in the hospital? Yes, he thought, now I know where I am. A heart attack, the doctor had said, and then he had felt even worse. Didn't matter; I'm too tired. He heard voices once more, and again he barely opened his eyes. A tall thin man dressed in white spoke to him.

"Mr. Mendelsohn, can you hear me? How do you feel now? More comfortable? We called your family. I spoke to your sister, Mrs. Wiletsky. They should be here very soon. You feeling sleepy? Good. . . . Take a little nap—go on. We'll wake you when they get here, don't worry. Go on now. . . ."

He closed his eyes, thinking of Jennie. She'll be here soon with Esther and Rosalie and Sara. All of them. He smiled. He was so tired. His bed was by the window and a bright warm sash of sunshine covered him almost completely. Nice and warm, he thought, and felt comfortable. The pain had lessened, practically disappeared. Mr. Mendelsohn heard the birds chirping and Sporty barking. That's all right, Mrs. Suárez would let him sleep. She wouldn't wake him up, he knew that. It looked like a good warm day; he planned to take Tato out for a walk later. That's some smart kid, he thought. Right now he was going to rest.

"This will be the last of it, Sara."

"Just a few more things, Jennie, and we'll be out of here."

The two women spoke as they packed away all the items in the room. They opened drawers and cabinets, putting things away in boxes and suitcases.

"What about these pictures on the bureau?" asked Sara.

Jennie walked over and they both looked at the photographs.

"There's Mama and Papa's wedding picture. Look, there's you, Sara, when Jonathan was born. And Esther and . . . look, he's got all the pictures of the entire family." Jennie burst into tears.

"Come on, Jennie; it's all over, honey. He was sick and very old." The older woman comforted the younger one.

Wiping her eyes, Jennie said, "Well, we did the best we could for him, anyway."

"Who is this?" asked Sara, holding up Tato's photo.

"Let me see," said Jennie. "Hummm . . . that must be one of the people in that family that lived next door in the old apartment on Prospect Avenue. You know—remember that Spanish family? He used to visit with them. Their name was . . . Díaz or something like that, I think. I can't remember."

"Oh yes," said Sara. "Louis mentioned them once in a while, yes. They were nice to him. What shall we do with it? Return it?"

"Oh," said Jennie, "that might be rude. What do you think?"

"Well, I don't want it, do you?"

"No," Jennie hesitated. " . . . But let's just put it away. Maybe we ought to tell them what happened. About Louis." Sara shrugged her shoulders. "Maybe I'll write to them," Jennie went on, "if I can find out where they live. They moved. What do you say?"

"I don't care, really," Sara sighed. "I have a lot to do yet. I have to meet Esther at the lawyer's to settle things. And I still have to make supper. So let's get going."

Both women continued to pack, working efficiently and with swiftness. After a while, everything was cleared and put away in boxes and suitcases.

"All done!" said Sara.

"What about this?" asked Jennie, holding up Tato's photograph.

"Do what you want," said Sara. "I'm tired. Let's go."

Looking at the photograph, Jennie slipped it into one of the boxes. "I might just write and let them know."

The two women left the room, closing the door behind them. □□

Discussion

1. Would you describe Mr. Mendelsohn's life as "happy" and "fortunate"? Why or why not?

2. What kind of man is Mr. Mendelsohn? What qualities or characteristics does he have?

3. (a) How does Mrs. Suárez feel about Mr. Mendelsohn? How does she show this? (b) What is the attitude of the Suárez children toward Mr. Mendelsohn? Does their relationship with him change during the course of the story? (c) How is Tato's relationship with Mr. Mendelsohn different from Julio's or Georgie's? Why do you think this is so?

4. Early in the story Julio asks Mr. Mendelsohn why he comes to eat in their crowded kitchen when he has six rooms all to himself in his apartment. (a) What answers does Mr. Mendelsohn give him? (b) In your opinion, are these the only or even the most important reasons Mr. Mendelsohn chooses their crowded kitchen over his six rooms?

5. (a) How long has Mr. Mendelsohn lived in the Bronx before he first gets to know the Suárez family? (b) How long does the Suárez family live in their apartment next to Mr. Mendelsohn before they move to a new house? (c) How long does Mr. Mendelsohn remain in his own apartment in the Bronx after the Suárez family has moved to their new home?

6. Near the end of the story, after her brother has died, Jennie says to Sara, "Well, we did the best we could for him, anyway." (a) Describe the relationship between Mr. Mendelsohn and his sisters. (b) In your opinion, did the sisters do the best they could for him?

Vocabulary • Dictionary

Replace the italicized phrase in each of the following sentences with the word from the list that has the same meaning. (You will not use one of the listed words.) Refer to your Glossary if you need help.

ajar	permeated
conviction	unison
injection	vacated

1. At the end of the concert the whole chorus sang in *harmonious combination*.

2. It is his *firm belief* that all it takes to be successful is strong will power.

3. The police stated that the hotel room had been *abandoned and left empty* just thirty minutes before they arrived.

4. By leaving the back door *slightly open*, they hoped to encourage their wandering cat to return home.

5. The poisonous gas fumes soon *spread throughout* the windowless workroom.

Nicholasa Mohr 1935 •

Trained as a graphic artist, Nicholasa Mohr gained a high reputation; her work was featured in exhibitions in New York and Puerto Rico. Since then, Mohr has begun a new career as a writer. "I am learning a new craft," she says of her books, but she has found that much of her knowledge as an artist applies to her work as a writer. She has published a novel and two collections of stories, *El Bronx Remembered* and *In Neuva York*.

6: Generations

CONTENT REVIEW

1. To what extent do the stories and poems in this unit point out the influence of people on each other, especially the influence of one *generation* upon another? Give examples from stories and poems.

2. (a) Do the selections in this unit show youths and adults in conflict or in relative harmony? **(b)** Which selection do you think best displays the relationship that ought to exist between youths and adults?

3. Select one story and one poem from the unit and explain how you think the events and ideas might change if a different point of view were used. For example, how would the picture of "Grandfather" change if Grandfather explained his own feelings about being out on the trail and then returning home? How, for example, would events in "Mr. Mendelsohn" change if we were restricted to seeing them only from the point of view of Julio? How might the story be affected if we saw things exclusively from the point of view of P.S. in "So Much Unfairness of Things"?

4. Who is the most admirable character you have encountered in your readings in this unit? What makes the character most admirable in your judgment? Does the admiration you feel have anything especially to do with the age or the generation of the character? Explain.

Unit 6, Test I
INTERPRETATION: NEW MATERIAL

This selection is taken from the autobiography of Margaret Mead. Mead is well known for her work in anthropology—that is, the study of the human race's origin, development, and cultures. Read the selection carefully; then answer the questions that follow it.

On Being a Granddaughter

Margaret Mead

My paternal grandmother, who lived with us from the time my parents married until she died in 1927, while I was studying anthropological collections in German museums, was the most decisive influence in my life. She sat at the center of our household. Her room—and my mother always saw to it that she had the best room, spacious and sunny, with a fireplace if possible—was the place to which we immediately went when we came in from

---

playing or home from school. There my father went when he arrived in the house. There we did our lessons on the cherry-wood table with which she had begun housekeeping and which, later, was my dining room table for twenty-five years. There, sitting by the fire, erect and intense, she listened to us and to all of Mother's friends and to our friends. In my early childhood she was also very active—cooking, preserving, growing flowers in the garden, and attentive to all the activities of the country and the farm. . . .

My mother was trustworthy in all matters that concerned our care. Grandma was trustworthy in a quite different way. She meant exactly what she said, always. If you borrowed her scissors, you returned them. In like case, Mother would wail ineffectually, "Why does everyone borrow my scissors and never return them?" and Father would often utter idle threats. But Grandma never threatened. She never raised her voice. She simply commanded respect and obedience by her complete expectation that she would be obeyed. And she never gave silly orders. . . . Grandma never said, "Do this because Grandma says so," or "because Grandma wants you to do it." She simply said, "Do it," and I knew from her tone of voice that it was necessary.

My grandmother grew up in the little town of Winchester, in Adams County, Ohio, which two of my great-great-grandfathers had founded. She was one of nine children who reached adulthood. . . .

My grandmother began school teaching quite young, at a time when it was still somewhat unusual for a girl to teach school. When my grandfather, who was also a teacher, came home from the Civil War, he married my grandmother and they went to college together. They also graduated together. She gave a graduation address in the morning and my grandfather, who gave one in the afternoon, was introduced as the husband of Mrs. Mead who spoke this morning.

My grandfather was a school superintendent. . . . He died when my father was six. Two days later the principal took his place and my grandmother took the principal's place. From then on she taught, sometimes in high school, sometimes small children, until she came to live with us when my parents married. It was the small children in whom she was most interested, and I have the notes she took on the schools she observed during a visit to Philadelphia before my parents' marriage.

She understood many things that are barely recognized in the wider educational world even today. . . . She thought that memorizing mere facts was not very important and that drill was stultifying. The result was that I was not well drilled in geography or spelling. But I learned to observe the world around me and to

note what I saw—to observe flowers and children and baby chicks. She taught me to read for the sense of what I read and to enjoy learning.

With the exception of the two years I went to kindergarten . . . and the year I was eight, . . . she taught me until I went to high school and even then helped me with my lessons when my teachers were woefully inadequate, as they often were. I never expected any teacher to know as much as my parents or my grandmother did. . . .

Grandma was a wonderful storyteller, and she had a set of priceless, individually tailored anecdotes with which American grandparents of her day brought up children. There was the story of the little boys who had been taught absolute, quick obedience. One day when they were out on the prairie, their father shouted, "Fall down on your faces!" They did, and the terrible prairie fire swept over them *and they weren't hurt*. There was also the story of three boys at school, each of whom received a cake sent from home. One hoarded his, and the mice ate it; one ate all of his, and he got sick; and who do you think had the best time?—why, of course, the one who shared his cake with his friends. Then there was the little boy who ran away from home and stayed away all day. When he came home after supper, he found the family sitting around the fire and nobody said a word. Not a word. Finally, he couldn't stand it anymore and said, "Well, I see you have the same old cat!" And there was one about a man who was so lazy he would rather starve than work. Finally, his neighbors decided to bury him alive. On the way to the cemetery they met a man with a wagonload of unshelled corn. He asked where they were going. When they told him that they were going to bury that no-good man alive, the owner of the corn took pity on him and said, "I tell you what. I will give you this load of corn. All you will have to do is shell it." But the lazy man said, "Drive on, boys!"

Because Grandma did so many things with her hands, a little girl could always tag after her, talking and asking questions and listening. Side by side with Grandma, I learned to peel apples, to take the skin off tomatoes by plunging them into scalding water, to do simple embroidery stitches, and to knit. Later, during World War I, when I had to cook for the whole household, she taught me a lot about cooking, for example, just when to add a lump of butter, something that always had to be concealed from Mother, who thought that cooking with butter was extravagant.

While I followed her about as she carried out the endless little household tasks that she took on, supplementing the work of the maids or doing more in between maids—and we were often in between—she told me endless tales about Winchester. She told me about her school days and about the poor children who used to beg the cores of apples from the rich children who had whole apples for lunch. She told me about Em Eiler, who pushed Aunt Lou off a rail fence into a flooded pasture lot; about Great-aunt Louisian, who could read people's minds and tell them everything they had said about her and who had been a triplet and was so small when she was born that she would fit into a quart cup; about Grace, who died from riding a trotting horse too hard, which wasn't good for girls; and about the time Lida cut off Anna Louise's curls and said, "Now they won't say 'pretty little girl' anymore." My great-grandfather used to say such a long grace, she told me, that one of her most vivid memories was of standing, holding a log she had started to put on the fire, for what seemed to be hours for fear of interrupting him. All this was as real to me as if I had lived it myself. . . .

Mother never ceased to resent the fact that Grandma lived with us, but she gave her her due. Grandma never "interfered"—never tried to teach the children anything religious that had not previously been introduced by my mother, and in disagreements between my mother and father she always took my mother's side. When my father threatened to leave my mother, Grandma told him firmly that she would stay with her and the children.

When Grandma was angry, she sat and held her tongue. I used to believe that this involved some very mysterious . . . trick. She was so still, so angry, and so determined not to speak, not to lose her temper. And she never did. But not losing her temper came out of her eyes like fire. Years later, when I was given a picture of her as a young woman, I felt that I had looked very like her at the same age. But when I actually compared pictures of me with the one of her, I looked milky mild. Not until the birth of her great-great-granddaughter, my daughter's daughter Sevanne Margaret, did that flashing glance reappear in the family. . . .

I think it was my grandmother who gave me my ease in being a woman. She was unquestionably feminine—small and dainty and pretty. . . . She had gone to college when this was a very unusual thing for a girl to do, she had a firm grasp of anything she paid attention to, she had married and had a child, and she had a career of her own. All this was true of my mother, as well. But my mother was filled with passionate resentment about the condition of women, as perhaps my grandmother might have been had my grandfather lived and had she borne five children and had little opportunity to use her special gifts and training. As it was, the two women I knew best were mothers and had professional training. So I had no reason to doubt that brains were suitable for a woman. And as I had my father's kind of mind—which was also his mother's—I learned that the mind is not sex-typed.

The content of my conscience came from my mother's concern for other people and the state of the world, and from my father's insistence that the only thing worth doing is to add to the store of exactly known facts. But the strength of my conscience came from Grandma, who meant what she said. . . . ☐☐

1. Was the grandmother who lived with Margaret Mead her mother's mother or her father's mother?

2. In the Mead household, Grandma **(a)** usually stayed in her room by herself; **(b)** took little responsibility for raising the children; **(c)** was at the center of the family's life; **(d)** had everyone else wait on her.

3. What job had Grandma been trained for?

4. Margaret Mead thinks her grandmother was trustworthy because Grandma **(a)** never told on the children; **(b)** took Margaret's part in many family arguments; **(c)** secretly lent Margaret money; **(d)** always meant what she said.

5. Grandma's view of education was that children **(a)** need strict discipline; **(b)** need complete freedom; **(c)** can learn a lot by observing; **(d)** should learn by memorizing.

6. The message behind Grandma's story about the little boys and the prairie fire (386, 2) was **(a)** children should not go into the wilderness without their parents; **(b)** children should always obey their elders; **(c)** there are steps people can take to protect themselves in a fire; **(d)** people should not build fires in dry areas.

7. What part of Grandma's face always gave away the fact that she was angry?

8. Margaret Mead thinks the reason that her mother felt "passionate resentment about the condition of women" (387, 3) was that her mother **(a)** had little chance to use her own education; **(b)** was a widow with five children to support; **(c)** knew that Margaret could not get a good job because she was a woman; **(d)** grew up at a time when women's rights were becoming an important issue.

9. When Margaret Mead says her grandmother gave her "ease in being a woman" (387, 3) she means her grandmother showed her that **(a)** a woman's life is easy; **(b)** a woman's life is not easy; **(c)** a woman can be comfortable being intelligent and successful; **(d)** a woman's first responsibility is to try to act feminine.

10. Which of the following statements best describes the Mead family as they are seen in this selection? **(a)** They had many beautiful family traditions; **(b)** they spent much of their time arguing; **(c)** they were poorly educated; **(d)** they were a family that stressed mutual respect and learning.

Choose one of the following assignments to write about. Unless you are told otherwise, assume you are writing for your classmates.

1. It is sometimes said that the older that people get, the more set in their ways they become. To what extent is this true of the older characters you have read about in this unit? Choose one of the characters listed below, and discuss (1) beliefs, habits, or attitudes from earlier years that the character continues to cling to as he or she grows older; and (2) things the character says or does that indicate a willingness to adapt to new ideas.

    a. Paw-Paw
    b. Mr. Mendelsohn

2. Although the author of "Elegy Written at the County Junkyard" talks as much about himself as he does about his father, he nevertheless communicates a fairly clear picture of what his father was like. Using information taken from the selection, write a brief character sketch of the author's father.

3. Mr. Wilkinson in "So Much Unfairness of Things" and Grandma in "On Being a Granddaughter" seem to have different ideas about what a "good education" is. Using specific examples from the two selections, write a composition explaining the difference in the two characters' educational values—that is, in the types of teaching and schooling each character thinks a young person should have in order to be properly educated.

4. Several selections in this unit deal with somewhat special relationships between a young person and a grandparent (or someone of a grandparent's age). Do you think that a strong bond of admiration, affection, or respect is more likely to occur between a young person and someone of a grandparent's generation or between a young person and the immediate parent generation? Discuss this question in terms of evidence presented in various selections in this unit as well as in terms of your own personal experience.

The ancient Greeks believed their gods to be

immortal. In a way that they might not have

expected, they were right, for the gods

live on in our language, in our literature,

and most of all in those timeless stories,

the myths themselves. **GREEK**

MYTHS

GREEK MYTHS

Introduction

A series of feathery clouds moves in formation across the sky. After a heavy downpour, a rainbow appears near the horizon. Thunder rumbles in the sky, and a tree—or a man—is laid low on earth. The seasons change regularly in a never ending cycle. Night follows day, the tide is high for six hours, then low for six. Today we see these phenomena and explain them through science. Ancient peoples saw them too, and wondered. Their wonder led to the composition of myths, stories that often involve gods and goddesses, and that usually attempt to explain the marvels of nature.

By the time the civilization of Greece had become established, these myths, thousands of years older, had become more detailed. The sky, the earth, the sea, the underworld—each had its own deities, who had responsibilities that were more or less clearly defined.

As the myths matured, they were passed by word of mouth from person to person and re-

gion to region, often carried by professional storytellers. With the passage of time, as different storytellers retold the myths, the details sometimes blurred or came into conflict, so that there are often several different versions of the same basic story.

In addition, some of the myths became more sophisticated as the storytellers included elements of symbolism and philosophy. For example, one myth tells us that Zeus, who ruled the gods, developed a dreadful headache. To give him relief, another god split open his head and out sprang Athene, adult and fully clad in armor. We can marvel, or we can laugh. But Athene was the Greek goddess of wisdom—and where should wisdom have its source, if not in the mind of the ruler of the gods?

It may surprise us that some Greek myths show the gods in a comic, irreverent, even unfavorable light. The ancient Greeks saw their gods as complete beings, possessing both good and bad traits, and they

did not limit their myths to the good traits.

The major gods, called the Olympians, were twelve in number, headed by Zeus. Most of them dwelt with Zeus in a huge palace, enveloped by clouds, on the top of Mount Olympus, the highest mountain in Greece. Lesser deities lived on earth, in the sea, and in the underworld. Sometimes the gods fell in love with humans. Their children could then be either human or immortal. The word *demigod* is usually used to describe one of those half-human, half-divine beings who had attained immortal status. On the other hand, the familiar word *hero* was originally used to identify those half-human, half-divine beings who retained their mortal status but were unusually strong and brave.

Greek mythology also provided creatures that were part human, part animal. Almost always these were dangerous or man-eating monsters like the Minotaur, part man and part bull, who appears in the "Daedalus and Icarus" and

"Theseus" myths in the following pages. On rare occasions these monsters could be relatively harmless, or even helpful, like Chiron, one of the centaurs—creatures who were part human, part horse.

We may dispute the origin or meaning of individual myths, but we must agree on one thing: they show us that the ancient Greeks had inquiring minds and excellent imaginations.

We no longer believe that the sun is a golden chariot, that lightning is a spear, that the constellations were once living beings. And yet the heritage of myth that has come down to us across the centuries remains fascinating.

The ancient Greeks believed their gods to be immortal. In a way that they might not have expected, they were right, for the gods live on in our language, in our literature, and most of all in those timeless stories, the myths themselves.

"There was a great rushing and tumult in the skies. The people on earth heard mighty thunder and saw mountains shatter"—the young gods were battling the old for supremacy.

Zeus

as told by Bernard Evslin

Cronos, father of the gods, who gave his name to time, married his sister Rhea, goddess of earth. Now, Cronos had become king of the gods by killing his father, Oranos, the First One. The dying Oranos had prophesied, saying, "You murder me now and steal my throne—but one of your own sons will dethrone you, for crime begets crime."

So Cronos was very careful. One by one, he swallowed his children as they were born. First three daughters—Hestia, Demeter, and Hera; then two sons—Hades and Poseidon. One by one, he swallowed them all.

Rhea was furious. She was determined that he should not eat her next child who she felt sure would be a son. When her time came, she crept down the slope of Olympus to a dark place to have her baby. It was a son, and she named him Zeus. She hung a golden cradle from the branches of an olive tree and put him to sleep there. Then she went back to the top of the mountain. She took a rock and wrapped it in swaddling clothes and held it to her breast, humming a lullaby. Cronos came snorting and bellowing out of his great bed, snatched the bundle

from her and swallowed it, clothes and all.

Rhea stole down the mountainside to the swinging golden cradle and took her son down into the fields. She gave him to a shepherd family to raise, promising that their sheep would never be eaten by wolves.

Here Zeus grew to be a beautiful young boy, and Cronos, his father, knew nothing about him. Finally, however, Rhea became lonely for him and brought him back to the court of the gods, introducing him to Cronos as the new cupbearer. Cronos was pleased because the boy was beautiful.

One night Rhea and Zeus prepared a special drink. They mixed mustard and salt with the nectar. Next morning, after a mighty swallow, Cronos vomited up first a stone, and then Hestia, Demeter, Hera, Hades, and Poseidon—who, being gods, were still undigested, still alive. They thanked Zeus and immediately chose him to be their leader.

Then a mighty battle raged. Cronos was joined by the Titans, his half-brothers, huge, twisted, dark creatures taller than trees, whom he kept pent up in the mountains until there was fighting to be done. They attacked the young gods furiously. But Zeus had allies too. He had gone to darker caverns— caves under caves under caves, deep in the mountainside—formed by the first bubbles of the cooling earth. Here Cronos thousands of centuries before (a short time in the life of a god) had pent up other monsters, the one-eyed Cyclopes and the Hundred-handed Ones. Zeus unshackled these ugly cousins and led them against the Titans.

There was a great rushing and tumult in the skies. The people on earth heard mighty thunder and saw mountains shatter. The earth quaked and tidal waves rolled as the gods fought. The Titans were tall as trees, and old Cronos was a crafty leader. He attacked fiercely, driving the young gods before him. But Zeus had laid a trap. Halfway up the slope of Olympus, he whistled for his cousins, the Hundred-handed Ones, who had been lying in ambush. They took up huge boulders, a hundred each, and hurled them downhill at the Titans. The Titans thought the mountain itself was falling on them. They broke ranks and fled.

The young goat-god Pan was shouting with joy. Later he said that it was his shout that made the Titans flee. That is where we get the word "panic."

Now the young gods climbed to Olympus, took over the castle, and Zeus became their king. No one knows what happened to Cronos and his Titans. But sometimes mountains still explode in fire and the earth still quakes, and no one knows exactly why.

□□

Gods and Mortals

Cronos (krō′ nəs)

Cyclopes (sī klō′ pēz), sons of Oranos. Each had only one eye, located in the middle of his forehead.

Demeter (di mē′ tər), daughter of Cronos and Rhea who became goddess of agriculture and the harvest. Emblem: sheaf of wheat.

Hades (hā′ dēz), son of Cronos and Rhea who became ruler of the underworld, which is often called by his name.

Hera (hir′ ə), daughter of Cronos and Rhea who became wife of Zeus and queen of the gods. She is goddess of women and marriage. Emblem: peacock.

Hestia (hes′ tē ə), daughter of Cronos and Rhea who became goddess of hearth and home.

Oranos (ôr ān′ əs)

Pan, the god of flocks, forests, and shepherds. His body was half human, but with horns, ears, and legs of a goat. Emblem: syrinx, or shepherd's pipe.

Poseidon (pə sīd′ n), son of Cronos and Rhea who became ruler of the sea. Emblems: trident, dolphins, horses.

Rhea (rē′ ə)

Titans (tīt′ nz), gigantic offspring of Oranos. Called "the first race," their number is uncertain, but usually given as twelve, six male and six female.

Zeus (züs), son of Cronos and Rhea who became the chief god, ruling gods and humanity from his throne on Mount Olympus. Emblems: thunderbolt, eagle.

Discussion

1. We might reasonably expect gods to be more dignified and better behaved than human beings—but are they? Explain.

2. (a) Why does Cronos swallow his children? (b) How is the infant Zeus spared this fate? (c) How is the prophecy of Oranos fulfilled?

3. How did the battle of the gods affect the earth?

4. Does strength or cleverness win the battle between the young gods and the old? Explain.

Poseidon's character is unpredictable—
like the wild and changeful sea that he chose for his kingdom.

Poseidon

as told by Bernard Evslin

After Cronos was deposed, the three sons threw dice for his empire. Zeus, the youngest, won and chose the sky. Poseidon smiled to himself because the sky was empty, and he knew that the impulsive Zeus had chosen it because it looked so high. And now, he, Poseidon, could choose as he would have done if he had won. He chose the sea. He had always wanted it; it is the best place for adventures and secrets and makes claim on land and sky. Hades, who was always unlucky, had to take the underworld. The earth was held as a commonwealth and left to the goddesses to manage.

Poseidon left Olympus and came to his kingdom. He immediately set about building a huge underwater palace with a great pearl and coral throne. He needed a queen and chose Thetis, a beautiful Nereid, or water nymph. But it was prophesied that any son born to Thetis would be greater than his father, so Poseidon decided to try elsewhere. The prophecy came true. The son of Thetis was Achilles.

Poseidon chose another Nereid named Amphitrite. But like his brother Zeus, he was a great traveler and had hundreds of children in different places. He was a very difficult god, changeful and quarrelsome. He did bear grudges; but he could be pleased, and then his smile was radiant. He liked jokes and thought up very curious forms for his creatures. He liked to startle nymphs with monsters, and concocted the octopus, the squid, the sea-polyp or jellyfish, the swordfish, blowfish, sea cow, and many others. Once, trying to appease Amphitrite's jealous rage, he thought up the dolphin and gave it to her as a gift.

He was greedy and aggressive, always trying to add to his kingdom. Once he claimed Attica as his own and stabbed his trident into the hillside where the Acropolis[1] still stands, and a spring of salt water spouted. Now, the people of Athens did not want to belong to the kingdom of the sea. They were afraid of Poseidon, who had a habit of seizing all the youth of a town when he was in the mood. So they prayed to be put under the protection of another god. Athene heard their prayers. She came down and planted an olive tree by the side of the spring. Poseidon was enraged. His face darkened, and he roared with fury, raising a storm. A fishing fleet was blown off the sea and never came

Reprinted by permission of Scholastic Magazines, Inc. from *Heroes, Gods, and Monsters of the Greek Myths* by Bernard Evslin. Copyright © 1966, 1967 by Scholastic Magazines, Inc.

1. Attica . . . Acropolis. Attica (at′ə kə) is a southern region of Greece and includes the city of Athens. The Acropolis (ə krop′ə lis) is a high, fortified section of Athens. Some of its ruins are still standing.

to port. He challenged Athene to single combat and threatened to stir up a tidal wave to break over the city if she refused. She accepted. But Zeus heard the sound of this quarreling and came down and decreed a truce. Then all the gods sat in council to hear the rival claims. After hearing both Athene and Poseidon, they voted to award the city to Athene because her olive tree was the better gift. After that, Athenians had to be very careful when they went to sea, and were often unfortunate in their naval battles.

Poseidon was very fond of Demeter and pursued her persistently.

Finally Demeter said, "Give me a gift. You have made creatures for the sea; now make me a land animal. But a beautiful one, the most beautiful ever seen."

She thought she was safe, because she believed he could make only monsters. She was amazed when he made her a horse, and gasped with delight when she saw it. And Poseidon was so struck by his handiwork that he swiftly made a herd of horses that began to gallop about the meadow, tossing their heads, flirting their tails, kicking up their back legs, and neighing joyously. And he was so fascinated by the horses that he forgot all about Demeter and leaped on one and rode off. Later he made another herd of green ones for his undersea stables. But Demeter kept the first herd; from that all the horses in the world have descended.

Another story says it took Poseidon a full week to make the horse. During that time he made and cast aside many other creatures that didn't come out right. But he simply threw them away without killing them, and they made their way into the world. From them have come the camel, the hippopotamus, the giraffe, the donkey, and the zebra.

□□

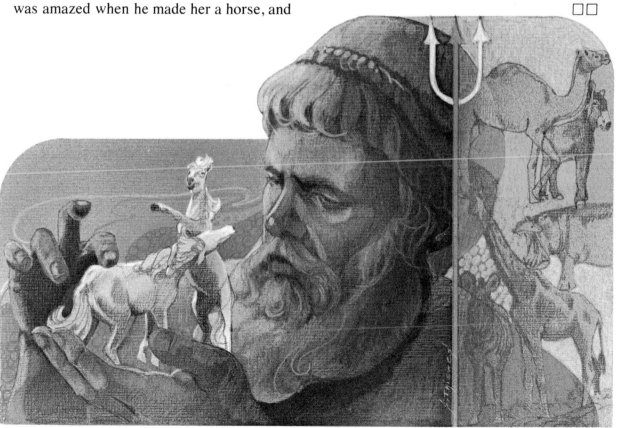

Gods and Mortals

Achilles (ə kil′ēz), the son of Thetis who became a great Greek hero and the most famous warrior of the Trojan War. He was ultimately killed by an arrow which pierced his heel, his only vulnerable spot.

Amphitrite (am′fə trī′tē), wife of Poseidon.

Athene (ə thē′nē), daughter of Zeus who sprang from his aching head full-grown. She is goddess of wisdom, of weaving and other household arts, and of warfare. Emblems: owl, olive, helmet, shield.

Nereid (nir′ē id), any one of fifty daughters of Nereus (nir′ē əs), a sea god.

Thetis (thē′tis)

Discussion

1. Do you agree with Poseidon that the sea "is the best place for adventures and secrets"? Explain.

2. **(a)** Describe the division of Cronos's empire after he was deposed. **(b)** What are Poseidon's feelings about the division?

3. **(a)** Why does Poseidon not marry Thetis? **(b)** Who does become his queen? **(c)** What special creature does he later think up and give his queen?

4. **(a)** How does Athene come to be the protector of Athens? **(b)** How does Poseidon seem to react to this?

5. This myth explains the origin of some natural phenomena. Which are explained and what are some of the explanations?

Vocabulary
Context, Structure, Pronunciation, Dictionary

Write the answers to the following questions. Use your Glossary for questions 2, 3a, and 4.

1. "The noblemen's plan was to *depose* Mary Queen of Scots so that they could make her son James the new ruler of the country." *Depose* means **(a)** put out of office; **(b)** take for granted; **(c)** study; **(d)** worship.

2. **(a)** Is the first *u* in *tumult* pronounced like the *u* in *futile* or the *u* in *drum?* **(b)** Write the definition of *tumult.*

3. **(a)** Write the meanings of the two Latin word parts that are found in the word *trident.* **(b)** What English word containing the prefix *tri-* is the name of something a child rides? **(c)** Complete this sentence with an English word that contains the root *dent:* "The _____ asked me what kind of toothpaste I use."

4. **(a)** Does the last syllable of *prophecy* rhyme with *be* or with *lie?* **(b)** Does the last syllable of *prophesy* rhyme with *be* or with *lie?* **(c)** Which word, *prophecy* or *prophesy,* is correct to use in this sentence: "Who can _____ what the world will be like in ten years?"

Extension • Writing

Myths that contain an explanation of some element of nature are called nature myths, or science myths. Write a brief "nature myth" of your own to explain one of the following: rainbows, the color of the sky, eclipses of the sun, the difference between raindrops and snowflakes, why crickets chirp, why elephants have trunks. Be sure to include a Greek god or goddess in your account.

*"If Athene resents my words, let her answer them herself."
From the moment Arachne made that arrogant statement,
her fate hung by a slender thread.*

Arachne

as told by Olivia Coolidge

Arachne was a maiden who became famous throughout Greece, though she was neither wellborn nor beautiful and came from no great city. She lived in an obscure little village, and her father was a humble dyer of wool. In this he was very skillful, producing many varied shades, while above all he was famous for the clear, bright scarlet which is made from shellfish, and which was the most glorious of all the colors used in ancient Greece. Even more skillful than her father was Arachne. It was her task to spin the fleecy wool into a fine, soft thread and to weave it into cloth on the high-standing loom within the cottage. Arachne was small and pale from much working. Her eyes were light and her hair was a dusty brown, yet she was quick and graceful, and her fingers, roughened as they were, went so fast that it was hard to follow their flickering movements. So soft and even was her thread, so fine her cloth, so gorgeous her embroidery, that soon her products were known all over Greece. No one had ever seen the like of them before.

At last Arachne's fame became so great that people used to come from far and wide to watch her working. Even the graceful nymphs would steal in from stream or forest and peep shyly through the dark doorway, watching in wonder the white arms of Arachne as she stood at the loom and threw the shuttle from hand to hand between the hanging threads, or drew out the long wool, fine as a hair, from the distaff[1] as she sat spinning. "Surely Athene herself must have taught her," people would murmur to one another. "Who else could know the secret of such marvelous skill?"

Arachne was used to being wondered at, and she was immensely proud of the skill that had brought so many to look on her. Praise was all she lived for, and it displeased her greatly that people should think anyone, even a goddess, could teach her anything. Therefore when she heard them murmur, she would stop her work and turn round indignantly to say, "With my own ten fingers I gained this skill, and by hard practice from early morning till night. I never had time to stand looking as you people do while another maiden worked. Nor if I had, would I give Athene credit because the girl was more skillful than I. As for Athene's weaving, how could there be finer cloth or more beautiful embroidery than mine? If Athene herself were to come down and compete with me, she could do no better than I."

From *Greek Myths* by Olivia Coolidge. Copyright 1949 by Olivia E. Coolidge. Reprinted by permission of Houghton Mifflin Company.
1. *distaff,* a stick, slit at one end, to hold wool or flax for spinning into thread by hand.

One day when Arachne turned round with such words, an old woman answered her, a grey old woman, bent and very poor, who stood leaning on a staff and peering at Arachne amid the crowd of onlookers. "Reckless girl," she said, "how dare you claim to be equal to the immortal gods themselves? I am an old woman and have seen much. Take my advice and ask pardon of Athene for your words. Rest content with your fame of being the best spinner and weaver that mortal eyes have ever beheld."

"Stupid old woman," said Arachne indignantly, "who gave you a right to speak in this way to me? It is easy to see that you were never good for anything in your day, or you would not come here in poverty and rags to gaze at my skill. If Athene resents my words, let her answer them herself. I have challenged her to a contest, but she, of course, will not come. It is easy for the gods to avoid matching their skill with that of men."

At these words the old woman threw down her staff and stood erect. The wondering onlookers saw her grow tall and fair and stand clad in long robes of dazzling white. They were terribly afraid as they realized that they stood in the presence of Athene. Arachne herself flushed red for a moment, for she had never really believed that the goddess would hear her. Before the group that was gathered there she would not give in; so pressing her pale lips together in obstinacy and pride, she led the goddess to one of the great looms and set herself before the other. Without a word both began to thread the long woolen strands that hang from the rollers, and between which the shuttle moves back and forth. Many skeins lay heaped beside them to use, bleached white, and gold, and scarlet, and other shades, varied as the rainbow. Arachne had never thought of giving credit for her success to her father's skill in dyeing, though in actual truth the colors were as remarkable as the cloth itself.

Soon there was no sound in the room but the breathing of the onlookers, the whirring of the shuttles, and the creaking of the wooden frames as each pressed the thread up into place or tightened the pegs by which the whole was held straight. The excited crowd in the doorway began to see that the skill of both in truth was very nearly equal, but that, however the cloth might turn out, the goddess was the quicker of the two. A pattern of many pictures was growing on her loom. There was a border of twined branches of the olive, Athene's favorite tree, while in the middle, figures began to appear. As they looked at the glowing colors, the spectators realized that Athene was weaving into her pattern a last warning to Arachne. The central figure was the goddess herself competing with Poseidon for possession of the city of Athens; but in the four corners were mortals who had tried to strive with gods and pictures of the awful fate that had overtaken them. The goddess ended a little before Arachne and stood back from her marvelous work to see what the maiden was doing.

Never before had Arachne been matched against anyone whose skill was equal, or even nearly equal to her own. As she stole glances from time to time at Athene and saw the goddess working swiftly, calmly, and always a little faster than herself, she became angry instead of frightened, and an evil thought came into her head. Thus as Athene stepped back a pace to watch Arachne finishing her work, she saw that the maiden had taken for her design a pattern of scenes which showed evil or unworthy actions of the gods, how they had deceived fair maid-

ens, resorted to trickery, and appeared on earth from time to time in the form of poor and humble people. When the goddess saw this insult glowing in bright colors on Arachne's loom, she did not wait while the cloth was judged, but stepped forward, her grey eyes blazing with anger, and tore Arachne's work across. Then she struck Arachne across the face. Arachne stood there a moment, struggling with anger, fear, and pride. "I will not live under this insult," she cried, and seizing a rope from the wall, she made a noose and would have hanged herself.

The goddess touched the rope and touched the maiden. "Live on, wicked girl," she said. "Live on and spin, both you and your descendants. When men look at you they may remember that it is not wise to strive with Athene." At that the body of Arachne shrivelled up; and her legs grew tiny, spindly, and distorted. There before the eyes of the spectators hung a little dusty brown spider on a slender thread.

All spiders descend from Arachne, and as the Greeks watched them spinning their thread wonderfully fine, they remembered the contest with Athene and thought that it was not right for even the best of men to claim equality with the gods. ☐☐

Gods and Mortals

Arachne (ə rak′ nē). This name, in the Greek language, means "spider" and "spider's web."

Discussion

1. Do you think Arachne deserves her fate? Why or why not?

2. (a) Describe Arachne's physical appearance. (b) Why has she become famous throughout Greece? (c) What part does her father have in her fame? (d) Does she acknowledge her father's role?

3. To the ancient Greeks one of the greatest sins was *hubris* (hyü′ bris), excessive pride that leads to rudeness and disrespect, especially to the gods. (a) Is Arachne guilty of this sin? Explain. (b) What advice does the old woman give to her? (c) How does she react to the warning? (d) How does she react when the old woman turns out to be Athene?

4. (a) Describe the pattern that Athene weaves. (b) Why might she have selected this pattern? (c) Describe the pattern that Arachne weaves. (d) Why might she have selected this pattern? (e) How does the weaving contest end?

5. You probably have read other stories which have a moral like "pride goes before a fall." Choose one and compare it with the story of Arachne.

The god of the underworld falls in love . . .
the goddess of the harvest mourns her lost daughter . . .
and the earth withers under a cruel punishment.

Persephone

retold by Anne Terry White

Deep under Mt. Aetna,[1] the gods had buried alive a number of fearful, fire-breathing giants. The monsters heaved and struggled to get free. And so mightily did they shake the earth that Hades, the king of the underworld, was alarmed.

"They may tear the rocks asunder and leave the realm of the dead open to the light of day," he thought. And mounting his golden chariot, he went up to see what damage had been done.

Now the goddess of love and beauty, fair Aphrodite, was sitting on a mountainside playing with her son, Eros. She saw Hades as he drove around with his coal-black horses and she said:

"My son, there is one who defies your power and mine. Quick! Take up your darts! Send an arrow into the breast of that dark monarch. Let him, too, feel the pangs of love. Why should he alone escape them?"

At his mother's words, Eros leaped lightly to his feet. He chose from his quiver his sharpest and truest arrow, fitted it to his bow, drew the string, and shot straight into Hades' heart.

The grim King had seen fair maids enough in the gloomy underworld over which he ruled. But never had his heart been

"The Bride of Pluto" adapted from *Golden Treasury of Myths and Legends* by Anne Terry White. Copyright © 1959 by Western Publishing Company, Inc. Used by permission.
1. Mt. Aetna (et′nə), a volcano located in northeast Sicily. It is still active.

touched. Now an unaccustomed warmth stole through his veins. His stern eyes softened. Before him was a blossoming valley, and along its edge a charming girl was gathering flowers. She was Persephone, daughter of Demeter, goddess of the harvest. She had strayed from her companions, and now that her basket overflowed with blossoms, she was filling her apron with lilies and violets. The god looked at Persephone and loved her at once. With one sweep of his arm he caught her up and drove swiftly away.

"Mother!" she screamed, while the flowers fell from her apron and strewed the ground. "Mother!"

And she called on her companions by name. But already they were out of sight, so fast did Hades urge the horses on. In a few moments they were at the River Cyane. Persephone struggled, her loosened girdle fell to the ground, but the god held her tight. He struck the bank with his trident. The earth opened, and darkness swallowed them all—horses, chariot, Hades, and weeping Persephone.

From end to end of the earth Demeter sought her daughter. But none could tell her where Persephone was. At last, worn out and despairing, the goddess returned to Sicily. She stood by the River Cyane, where Hades had cleft the earth and gone down into his own dominions.

Now a river nymph had seen him carry off his prize. She wanted to tell Demeter where her daughter was, but fear of Hades kept her dumb. Yet she had picked up the girdle Persephone had dropped, and this the nymph wafted on the waves to the feet of Demeter.

The goddess knew then that her daughter was gone indeed, but she did not suspect Hades of carrying her off. She laid the blame on the innocent land.

"Ungrateful soil!" she said. "I made you fertile. I clothed you in grass and nourishing grain, and this is how you reward me. No more shall you enjoy my favors!"

That year was the most cruel mankind had ever known. Nothing prospered, nothing grew. The cattle died, the seed would not come up, men and oxen toiled in vain. There was too much sun. There was too much rain. Thistles and weeds were the only things that grew. It seemed that all mankind would die of hunger.

"This cannot go on," said mighty Zeus. "I see that I must intervene." And one by one he sent the gods and goddesses to plead with Demeter.

But she had the same answer for all: "Not till I see my daughter shall the earth bear fruit again."

Zeus, of course, knew well where Persephone was. He did not like to take from his brother the one joyful thing in his life, but he saw that he must if the race of man was to be preserved. So he called Hermes to him and said:

"Descend to the underworld, my son. Bid Hades release his bride. Provided she has not tasted food in the realm of the dead, she may return to her mother forever."

Down sped Hermes on his winged feet, and there in the dim palace of the king, he found Persephone by Hades' side. She was pale and joyless. Not all the glittering treasures of the underworld could bring a smile to her lips.

"You have no flowers here," she would say to her husband when he pressed gems upon her. "Jewels have no fragrance. I do not want them."

When she saw Hermes and heard his message, her heart leaped within her. Her cheeks grew rosy and her eyes sparkled, for she knew that Hades would not dare to

disobey his brother's command. She sprang up, ready to go at once. Only one thing troubled her—that she could not leave the underworld forever. For she had accepted a pomegranate from Hades and sucked the sweet pulp from four of the seeds.[2]

With a heavy heart Hades made ready his golden car. He helped Persephone in while Hermes took up the reins.

"Dear wife," said the King, and his voice trembled as he spoke, "think kindly of me, I pray you. For indeed I love you truly. It will be lonely here these eight months you are away. And if you think mine is a gloomy palace to return to, at least remember that your husband is great among the immortals. So fare you well—and get your fill of flowers!"

Straight to the temple of Demeter at Eleusis, Hermes drove the black horses. The goddess heard the chariot wheels and, as a deer bounds over the hills, she ran out swiftly to meet her daughter. Persephone flew to her mother's arms. And the sad tale of each turned into joy in the telling.

So it is to this day. One third of the year Persephone spends in the gloomy abode of Hades—one month for each seed that she tasted. Then Nature dies, the leaves fall, the earth stops bringing forth. In spring Persephone returns, and with her come the flowers, followed by summer's fruitfulness and the rich harvest of fall. ☐☐

Gods and Mortals

Aphrodite (af′rə dī′tē)

Eros (ir′os, er′os)

Hermes (hər′mēz), messenger of the gods and guide who brings the souls of the dead to the underworld. He is also the god of travel, business, invention, and cunning. Emblems: winged cap and sandals; caduceus (kə dü′sē əs), a staff with two snakes wound about it.

Persephone (pər sef′ə nē)

---

2. *four of the seeds.* Technically, Persephone would have to remain in the underworld permanently because she had eaten those seeds. But Zeus arranged a compromise allowing her to leave, on condition she spend a portion of each year with Hades.

Discussion

1. With whom do you sympathize most—Hades, Demeter, or Persephone? Explain.

2. (a) How does it happen that Hades abducts Persephone? (b) Whom does Demeter wrongfully blame for Persephone's disappearance and how does she avenge the loss? (c) What causes Zeus to intervene with Demeter? (d) What is Demeter's answer? (e) What decision does Zeus finally make?

3. (a) Describe the physical changes that have taken place in Persephone while in the underworld. (b) How do you account for these? (c) Under what conditions may Persephone be released from the underworld? (d) Since Persephone has eaten the pulp of four seeds, what is to be her fate?

4. This myth is somewhat different from most in that the gods are shown displaying "human" emotions, such as love, despair, sympathy. Cite several instances of their display of these emotions.

5. (a) How does this myth explain the changing of the seasons? (b) In this version of the myth, Persephone eats four seeds. Other retellings give different numbers—five, six, or seven seeds. How would you account for this variation? (c) One reader has commented, "At the end of the myth, Persephone herself is like a seed." What do you think is meant by that statement?

"The Fates will spin out lasting happiness for no man . . . .
Within twelve months it is your fate to die."

The Fortunate King

as told by Olivia Coolidge

Admetus, king of Pherae in Thessaly,[1] was thought by many to be among the luckiest of men. He was young, strong, and handsome, the only son of a father who had given up the kingdom to him as soon as he came of age. Admetus was an affectionate son, and the old people felt proud and pleased that, though they had given him all their power, he still paid them every attention which could make their old age a happy one. Nor was this all. The wealth of the king lay largely in his immense flocks and herds, for which he had the good fortune to obtain a marvelous herdsman.

Apollo himself had been condemned to spend a year on earth in the form of a servant as a punishment for an offense he had committed in anger against Zeus. He came in this way to Admetus, and since the young king was a just master, the year was a good one for them both. Admetus saw much of his chief herdsman and came to respect him, while Apollo mightily increased the flocks of the king in return for his upright dealing. When the year came to an end, Admetus learned that not only was he a much richer man than before, but he had also acquired a powerful friend and protector.

One of the first uses he made of Apollo's friendship was to gain himself a wife whom any prince in Greece would have been proud to marry.

Pelias, ruler of another Thessalian kingdom which he had seized by force from his cousin, had several daughters, but Alcestis was by far the loveliest. Not only was she beautiful, but she was skilled in all the arts of women. She was a notable spinner and maker of cloth, a good housewife, and performed everything with a charm which really came from a gentle, affectionate, and honorable nature. Even her dark and sinister father was fond of her and by no means anxious to let her marry and go to live in some other land. Nevertheless from the first moment she was old enough Pelias had been bothered by suitors for Alcestis. Every young man who saw her and a great many who only heard of her asked her father for her hand. At last Pelias became weary of the

From *Greek Myths* by Olivia Coolidge. Copyright 1949 by Olivia E. Coolidge. Reprinted by permission of Houghton Mifflin Company.
1. *Pherae in Thessaly.* Thessaly (thes′ə lē) is an eastern region of Greece. Pherae (fēr′ē) was an ancient city-state in that region.

business and let it be known that he would marry his daughter only to the prince who could come to ask for her in a chariot drawn by a wild boar and a lion. Of course, no man could do this without help from the gods, so Pelias thought it most likely that he would be able to keep his daughter. But when Admetus accomplished the feat with Apollo's aid, Pelias at least could be satisfied that she was marrying a prosperous king who had the help of a powerful protector. He made the best of it, therefore, and the wedding was held with much rejoicing.

For several years after this Admetus was even happier than before. His parents thoroughly approved of his bride, who treated them with loving respect. Alcestis was a gentle, dignified queen, a beloved mistress of the household, and an affectionate mother. Towards her husband, even though she had not chosen him herself, she showed all the love he could desire. Nothing seemed to be lacking. Admetus's face was radiant as he moved among his people; everything he did, he enjoyed. Men would mention him in conversation as an example of one who did not know what misfortune meant.

Meanwhile Apollo had not forgotten his friend, and loved to appear in human form from time to time and talk with him. But at last one day he came with a very grave face. "Admetus, my friend," he said seriously, "the Fates[2] will spin out lasting happiness for no man. Each must have fortune and misfortune too, and so it is with you. It is decreed that in this very year your luck shall change. Within twelve months it is your fate to die."

The "fortunate" king went pale as ashes. His legs failed beneath him so that he sat down heavily, his hands limp at his sides. Then in a moment he leapt up and began to beg and implore Apollo. "You are powerful," he said desperately. "Save me from this. I am young. I am strong, no man enjoys life as I do. Why should I die? Life is full and rich for me; I enjoy every moment. Why, they say I even smile in sleep, and my dreams are glad ones. People point at me in the streets, 'There goes a happy man,' they say. And it is true. Why should I die when so many live who are weary of life, who are old, poor, sick, or lonely? Why should I die?"

"It is not possible to alter Fate," said Apollo gravely, "that is, not entirely. What I could do I have done. Someone, at least, must die, but I have won for you the promise that if another will die instead of you when the time comes, you may live." And with that hope the king was forced to be content.

From that time on nobody pointed to Admetus in the streets and called him the fortunate king. Indeed he made no secret of his misfortune, hoping always that someone who was tired of life would offer to change with him. But time went forward, and no one came. Other people who had envied his luck did not see why a less happy man should take on his load now that it was his turn to suffer. The year went on, and in all his kingdom no one offered the service that Admetus was too proud to ask. He found himself wandering past mean hovels, casting imploring glances at poor or crippled people. He fancied they understood what he wanted of them and that they looked at him mockingly. At last he could bear the city no longer and went out to manage his estate as he had been used. But the bleating of the countless lambs and the lowing of the cows in his great

---

2. *Fates* (fātz), three goddesses who controlled human destiny by spinning, then snipping, the "thread" of a person's life.

milking sheds only drove him to desperation. Finally his courage failed him, and as the long year came to an end, he went to see his father.

His father was outraged at the proposition Admetus put before him. "How dare you suggest such a thing?" he shouted. "I have ten more good years of life and it is my own. I earned it and I shall enjoy it. Nobody ever called me the fortunate king. I toiled hard all my life for what I had. And now you, who have had everything given you and made no effort, want my last years of peace and happiness as well. What do you think a father is for, my son? Do you expect him always to give what you need? Oh no, I have given already and far too much. A father should receive—receive respect and affection and obedience from his children as the gods have ordained it. And this is all you offer: respect when it takes no trouble, affection when it is the easiest way. Get out of my sight."

"Selfish old man," answered Admetus, beside himself with fury at the direct refusal. "Now I know how much your only son is worth to you, not even a few miserable, toothless years of life."

"Get out of my sight," yelled the old man.

"I will," shouted Admetus, "and gladly, for you are no true parent of mine. At least I have a mother."

Admetus's mother was no more willing than her husband. "Look after yourself," she said indignantly. "You are not a baby any more. As long as you were one, I watched over you, fed you, dressed you, and sat up with you. You owe your life to me in any case. I never asked you as a baby to look after me. Now it is your turn."

"Now may you be cursed," retorted Ad-metus in a passion. "May the gods remember you as an unworthy mother, a hard, unfeeling woman. What use was it to give me life and nurse me up for this? A fine gift you gave! May you die unwept and unhonored."

"May Hera, the great queen mother, and Leto hear me," screamed the old woman. "They know what it is to have children. May they . . . ." But Admetus turned away without hearing, for he felt that his time was come.

Admetus lay down on his couch and groaned aloud in bitter despair as he hid his face and waited for the coming of death. Meanwhile in her inner chamber the queen Alcestis quietly arose, kissed her two children, and gave them to her attendants. Then she bathed herself and put on fresh, white garments and went to the sacrifice. There she prayed the gods to take her life. Then as faintness came over her, she lay down on a couch and died quietly, while the groaning Admetus felt health surging back again and sat suddenly bolt upright. It was the miracle! His luck had saved him; he was not to die!

Even as he felt sure of this, he heard wails of women from the inner chamber and, rushing in, beheld the body of his wife. Admetus fell on his knees beside the corpse and kissed it, tears running down his cheeks. It had never occurred to him to ask Alcestis. He loved her, and she was so young. Everybody was so fond of her. She had as much to look forward to as he; there was no possible reason why she should die. Then as the greatness of the queen's sacrifice became clear to him, he saw for the first time how selfish he had been. Of course, he should shoulder his own misfortunes just like everybody else. What right had he running to his parents? He had had more luck than

other people in any case. Why should it not be his turn? Admetus groaned again and would gladly have died if by so doing he could have brought his Alcestis to life, but it was too late.

An attendant touched him timidly on the shoulder. There was a stranger shouting for him in the great hall. It was Heracles, the mightly hero, returned from one of his deeds of strength and bursting to celebrate his achievement. He could not have come at a worse time, but he had to be met, so Admetus roused himself to go out and explain to him that this was a house of mourning. On the way, however, he thought better of it. Why should the happiness of Heracles be spoiled? Admetus had brought this sorrow

on himself, and it was fitting he should bear it alone. He was utterly tired of his own selfishness. He stopped and gave orders to his servants to prepare a feast. He spoke firmly to them and they went obediently at last, muttering among themselves. Admetus went out to see his guest and made himself smile as he welcomed him.

The great, good-humored Heracles was not a sensitive man, and just now he was in an excited mood. He noticed nothing curious about Admetus or the servants; he was bent only on having a good time. And Admetus gave him a good time with wine, and song, and feasting. There was much laughter and a lot of noise. The disapproving servants, who had loved their mistress far more than they did Admetus, looked as gloomy as they dared. They grouped together in corners muttering, but for a long time Heracles noticed nothing at all. When finally the revelry was dying down and the excitement was nearly over, Heracles perceived their disapproval and, not liking it, called loudly for more wine. It was brought to him, but with an air of reluctance which made him strike his fist on the table and demand indignantly why they could not serve him better. Admetus was out of the room, and there was no one to restrain the anger of the servants at what was going on. They told him exactly what was the matter in the plainest terms.

Heracles was appalled at the trouble he had caused, but he was also touched by Admetus. Never, he felt, had he been entertained in so princely a fashion before. It was like a great prince to put aside his grief and celebrate with a guest, even while his beloved wife lay dead within his halls. Heracles questioned the servants as to how long ago the queen had died, for he knew the way to Hades well and he had a plan. He had been down to Hades, and so great was his strength that not all the monsters of that place had availed to keep him there. He had bound the mighty Cerberus[3] and brought him up to earth alive. In fact, there was no feat that Heracles was not equal to, for he was half divine and, though he was a man

now, he would be a god in time. It might be possible to pursue Death and wrestle with him for the spirit of Alcestis as they went hand in hand down the steep path to the underworld. He said nothing to Admetus as yet and told the servants to keep silence, but he took up his great club from the corner where he laid it, threw his lionskin over his shoulders, and strode off in the direction of the dreadful path he had trodden once before.

It was early morning when Heracles came back, and with him walked a muffled figure. Admetus, summoned haggard and sleepless from his chamber, came, much tried but still courteous, to answer his guest's unreasonable demands. Heracles put back the cloak, and Alcestis looked at her husband as though she were just waking from sleep. As he ran forward and clasped her, he felt her come to life in his arms.

Alcestis and Admetus lived long after that time, happy yet generous to the poor and ailing. Admetus had learned both seriousness and sympathy. Though he was as prosperous as before, he had found that there were qualities more admirable than good luck, and he never cared again to be known by the title of "the fortunate king." □□

---

3. **Cerberus** (sėr′bər əs), the three-headed dog that guarded the entrance to Hades.

Gods and Mortals

Admetus (ad mē′ təs)

Alcestis (al ses′tis)

Apollo (ə pol′ō), god of the sun who lighted the world by driving his blazing chariot across the skies. He is also god of prophecy, music, and the arts. Emblems: golden chariot, lyre.

Heracles (her′ə clēz′), son of Zeus and a mortal woman, he is the most famous of Greek demigods. Fantastically strong, Heracles is best known for his Twelve Labors.

Leto (lē′tō), the mother of Apollo by Zeus.

Pelias (pē′lē əs)

1. Do you think Admetus was right to ask others to die for him? Why or why not?

2. (a) Explain how Admetus gains the protection of Apollo. (b) Why does Admetus come to be called "the fortunate king"?

3. (a) What bad news does Apollo bring Admetus? (b) Describe Admetus's reaction to it.

(c) How might the decree of the Fates be partially altered?

4. (a) What response does Admetus receive when he asks others to die for him? (b) Who does die in his place?

5. (a) Why does Admetus decide to entertain Heracles? (b) How does Heracles find out what Admetus has done? (c) What does he do to repay Admetus?

6. Why does Admetus want never again to be known as "the fortunate king"?

7. The topic of luck has inspired many proverbs or sayings. According to some of them, it is better to be lucky than to be rich . . . or wise . . . or beautiful . . . or good. (a) Would Admetus agree? (b) Would you agree? Explain.

"How thrilling it was to rise to a height, close his wings, and speed down, like a thunderbolt . . . .
'Not even the eagle soars as high as this!' the boy thought."

Daedalus

retold by Anne Terry White

In the days when King Minos ruled Crete[1] and his mighty navy ranged the seas, there lived in Athens a man by the name of Daedalus. And his name was known as far and wide as that of Minos. For Daedalus was the greatest architect and sculptor of his time. There was nothing his ingenious mind could not design or his skillful hands execute. And his statues were so real that people said they lived. It seemed that at any moment they might move a hand or take a step or open their lips and speak.

His young nephew, Talus, also had clever hands and a creative mind. So his mother placed him with her brother that the boy might learn his marvelous skills. But Talus had a genius of his own and even more imagination. Walking on the shore one day, he picked up the backbone of a fish. Idly he drew the strong, sharp spines forward and

"Daedalus" from *Golden Treasury of Myths and Legends* by Anne Terry White. Copyright © 1959 by Western Publishing Company, Inc. Used by permission.
1. *Crete* (krēt), a Greek island in the Mediterranean, southeast of Greece.

back across a piece of driftwood. They cut deep into the wood. He went home and notched a metal blade all along one edge—and he had a saw. Another time he fixed two iron rods together at the tip. He held one firmly upright against the earth and moved the other slowly around. It made a perfect circle—he had invented the compass.

Talus was a pupil to make any teacher excited and proud. But not Daedalus. Instead of being pleased, he was frightened and sorely jealous.

"Talus will soon surpass me!" he thought.

He could not bear the idea of a rival, and came to hate the boy. And one day, when they stood together on a height, Daedalus pushed Talus off to his death.

He had not planned the deed. It had been a sudden, crazy impulse. The next instant, horrified at what he had done, he rushed down to the boy. But it was too late. Talus was dead, and not all the wonderful skills of Daedalus could call him back. Clearly, if Daedalus wished to save his own life, he must flee. So he left Athens and wandered miserably from place to place, until at last he left Greece altogether and crossed the sea to Crete.

King Minos was delighted to have the Athenian in his realm. The King had something in mind that called for the genius of Daedalus. Minos possessed a fearful monster, with the head and shoulders of a bull and the legs and trunk of a man. The creature was called the Minotaur—that is, the Bull of Minos. The King wanted a suitable place to keep the Minotaur. The building must be such that neither the monster himself nor any victim sent in to be devoured by him could possibly escape from it.

So, at the King's command, Daedalus designed the labyrinth. The building was a bewildering maze of passages. They turned back upon themselves, crisscrossed, and went round and round without leading anywhere. Once inside the labyrinth, it was all but impossible to find the way out again. Even Daedalus himself was once nearly lost.

King Minos was delighted with Daedalus's work and held him in highest favor. Yet Daedalus was less than pleased, for he felt himself to be no better than a prisoner in Crete. The King was so afraid Daedalus would reveal the secret of the labyrinth that he would not let him leave the island. And for that very reason Daedalus yearned to go. With what envy he watched the birds winging their way through the sky!

One day, as his eyes followed the graceful sea birds cleaving the ocean of air, an idea came to him.

"King Minos may shut my way out by land and by sea," he thought, "but he does not control the air."

And he began to study the flight of birds and to observe how their wings are fashioned. He watched the little song birds fold and unfold their wings, watched how they rose from the ground, flew down from the trees, and went to and fro. He also watched the herons slowly flapping their great wings. He watched the eagles soar and swoop. He saw, too, how their feathers overlapped one another—where they were large and where they were small.

When he thought he understood the secrets of flight, Daedalus went to a nesting place he knew of and gathered feathers of various sizes. And in a chamber close to the roof he began to build wings. First he laid down a row of the tiniest feathers, then a row of larger ones overlapping them, and yet larger ones beyond these. He fastened the feathers together in the middle with thread and at the bottom with wax. And when he had built on enough rows, he bent them around into a gentle curve to look like real birds' wings.

His young son Icarus stood by and watched his father work. Laughing, the boy caught the feathers when they blew away in the wind. He pressed his thumb into the yellow wax to soften it for his father, hindering more than he helped.

When Daedalus had finished the pair of wings, he put them on. He raised himself in the air and hovered there. He moved the wings just as he had seen birds do, and lo! he could fly. Icarus clapped his hands together in delight.

"Make me a pair of wings, too, father!" he cried.

Then Daedalus made a second pair of wings and prepared his son to fly.

"Now I warn you, Icarus," Daedalus said, "not to be reckless. Be wise, not bold. Take a course midway between heaven and earth. For if you fly too high, the sun will scorch your feathers. And if you fly too low, the sea will wet them. Take me for your guide. Follow me and you will be safe."

All the time he was speaking, Daedalus was fastening the wings to his son's shoulders. His hands trembled as he thought of the great adventure before them. At the same time, he was worried about the boy. He did not know whether he could quite trust Icarus to obey. As he adjusted his own wings and kissed the excited child, tears ran down Daedalus's face.

"Remember," he repeated for the last time. "Heed my words and stay close to me!"

Then he rose on his wings and flew from the housetop. Icarus followed.

Daedalus kept a watchful eye on the boy, even as a mother bird does when she has brought a fledgling out of its nest in the

treetops and launched it in the air. It was early morning. Few people were about. But here and there a plowman in the field or a fisherman tending his nets caught sight of them.

"They must be gods!" the simple toilers cried, and they bent their bodies in reverent worship.

Father and son flew far out over the sea. Daedalus was no longer worried about Icarus, who managed his wings as easily as a bird. Already the islands of Delos and Paros were behind them. Calymne, rich in honey, was on their right hand. But now Icarus began to yield to the full delight of his new-found powers. He wanted to soar and swoop. How thrilling it was to rise to a height, close his wings, and speed down, down, like a thunderbolt, then turn and rise again!

Time after time Icarus tried it, each time daring greater heights. Then, forgetting his father's warning, he soared higher still, far up into the cloudless sky.

"Not even the eagle soars as high as this!" the boy thought. "I am like the gods that keep the wide heaven."

As the words crossed his mind, he felt a warm stream flow over his shoulders. He had come too close to the blazing sun, and the sweet-smelling wax that bound the feathers was melting. With a shock of terror he felt himself hurtling downward. His wings, broken in a thousand parts, were hurtling downward, too. In vain Icarus moved his arms up and down—he could get no hold on the air.

"Father!" he shrieked. "Father! Help! I am falling."

Even as he cried, the deep blue water of the sea—that ever since has been called Icarian—closed over him.

"Icarus! Icarus! Where are you?" Daedalus cried, turning in every direction and searching the air behind, above, and all around. Then his eyes fell on the sea. Tufts of feathers were floating on the crest of the waves.

Too well he understood their meaning. Folding his great wings, he came to earth on the nearest island and fixed his streaming eyes upon the sea. He beat his breast. Wildly he clutched his hair.

"O Icarus, my son!" he wailed. "Even so fell Talus whom my envy slew! The gods have avenged him." He ripped off his glorious wings and stamped upon them. "Cursed be the skill that wrought my son's destruction!" he cried.

Days afterwards, the body of Icarus washed to the shore. There, on the lonely island which bears the boy's name, Daedalus buried his only son. □□

Gods and Mortals

Daedalus (ded′l əs)
Icarus (ik′ər əs)
Minos (mī′nəs, mī′nos)
Minotaur (min′ə tôr)
Talus (tā′ləs)

Discussion

1. Did Icarus deserve his fate, or was he a victim of his father's sins? Explain.

2. (a) Why must Daedalus flee from Athens? (b) Why does King Minos welcome him? (c) How does Daedalus plan to escape from Crete with his son Icarus?

3. Like many fathers before him, Daedalus tells his son, "Take me for your guide. Follow me and you will be safe." (a) What happens when Icarus disobeys? (b) How might Daedalus's warning to Icarus be updated to apply to advice given by a modern father to his son?

4. This myth touches on two concepts important to the Greeks. The first of these is *hubris* (hyü′bris), excessive pride that leads to insolence, especially disrespect to the gods. (a) Is Daedalus guilty of hubris? (b) Is Icarus guilty of it? Explain.

5. A second concept important to the Greeks is *nemesis* (nem′ə sis), or retribution, by which a past evil deed is appropriately punished. (Nemesis was the goddess of vengeance or divine punishment.) In what sense might the story of Daedalus serve as an illustration of nemesis?

6. The phrase "the price of progress" suggests that an invention or development can have bad as well as good results. (a) What "price" does Talus pay for his ingenuity? (b) What "price" does Daedalus pay for building the labyrinth? for achieving flight? (c) Do you think this myth expresses a definite attitude about science and human progress? Explain.

Greek and Roman Gods

The fourteen major gods and goddesses of classical Greece are listed in the chart below, along with their Roman counterparts. Twelve of these gods made up the family that lived on Mount Olympus. Hades, god of the underworld, was not included among the Olympians. Dionysus, god of wine, in some versions replaces Hestia, goddess of hearth and home.

Greek	Roman
Zeus	Jupiter, Jove
Poseidon	Neptune
Apollo	Phoebus Apollo
Ares	Mars
Hermes	Mercury
Hephaestus	Vulcan
Dionysus	Bacchus
Hades	Pluto
Hera	Juno
Athene	Minerva
Demeter	Ceres
Artemis	Diana
Aphrodite	Venus
Hestia	Vesta

The Romans were famous for "borrowing" from the cultures of people they conquered, and it is generally true that they borrowed most of their mythology from the Greeks. This process began long before the Greeks were completely conquered by the Romans, and involved more than a simple substitution of Roman names for Greek.

In a few cases—Apollo is one—a Greek god was adopted as a deity completely new to the Romans. Usually, however, Greek gods and goddesses were linked with existing Roman deities. These native Roman gods did not have the vivid, complex personalities of the Greek gods and, apparently, no myths were told about them. Roman gods tended to be abstract symbols of a single virtue or power; so abstract, in many cases, that the Romans were unsure whether the god was male or female.

These Roman gods were transformed when they were given the attributes of their Greek counterparts. Neptune, a minor god of freshwater, became lord of the sea when he was identified as Poseidon. Similarly, Ceres and Venus were lifted from lowly positions when they were equated with Demeter and Aphrodite.

The Greeks had fourteen major gods; the Romans had a more restricted focus. Major deities were Jupiter, Juno, and Minerva. Possibly the most important god to the Romans—outstripping even Jupiter—was Mars, the god of war and agriculture and father of the legendary founder of the city of Rome. The Roman worship of their god of war is in sharp contrast to the Greek attitude. The Greeks seemed to have despised Ares: there are few myths which feature him, and he is almost always portrayed unfavorably.

One result of the Roman "adoption" of Greek gods and goddesses is that the Roman names tend to be more familiar to us. Mercury, Mars, and Cupid are more commonly used than Hermes, Ares, and Eros. This Roman influence should not disguise the fact that the myths themselves are almost entirely Greek in origin.

*"I will not live this way!" Thesus cried to the wind.
"I will not be small and weak and poor. I will be a king,
a warrior . . . or I will not be at all."*

Theseus

as told by Bernard Evslin

Young Theseus had a secret. He lived with his mother in a little hut on a wild sea-battered part of the coast called Troezen.[1] For all his poor house and worn-out clothes, he was very proud, for he had a secret: he knew that he was the son of a king. His mother had told him the story one night when their day's catch of fish had been very bad and they were hungry.

"A king, truly," she said. "And one day you will know his name."

"But mother, then why are you not a queen and I a prince? Why don't we live in a palace instead of a hovel?"

"Politics, my son," she said sadly. "All politics . . . . You're too young to understand, but your father has a cousin, a very powerful lord with fifty sons. They are waiting for your father to die so they can divide the kingdom. If they knew he had a son of his own to inherit it, they would kill the son immediately."

"When can I go to him? When can I go there and help my father?"

"When you're grown. When you know how to fight your enemies."

This was Theseus's secret . . . and he needed a secret to keep him warm in those long, cold, hard years. One of his worst troubles was his size. His being small for his age bothered him terribly, for how could he become a great fighter and help his father against terrible enemies if he couldn't even hold his own against the village boys? He exercised constantly by running up and down the cliffs, swimming in the roughest seas, lifting logs and rocks, bending young trees; and indeed he grew much stronger, but he was still very dissatisfied with himself.

A Voice from the Sea

One day, when he had been beaten in a fight with a larger boy, he felt so gloomy that he went down to the beach and lay on the sand watching the waves, hoping that a big one would come along and cover him.

"I will not live this way!" he cried to the wind. "I will not be small and weak and poor. I will be a king, a warrior . . . or I will not be at all."

And then it seemed that the sound of the

Reprinted by permission of Scholastic Magazines, Inc. from *Heroes, Gods, and Monsters of the Greek Myths* by Bernard Evslin. Copyright © 1966, 1967 by Scholastic Magazines, Inc.
1. *Troezen* (trē′zən), an ancient seacoast town in Greece.

waves turned to a deep-voiced lullaby, and Theseus fell asleep—not quite asleep, perhaps, because he was watching a great white gull smashing clams open by dropping them on the rocks below. Then the bird swooped down and stood near Theseus's head looking at him, and spoke, "I can crack clams open because they are heavy. Can I do this with shrimps or scallops? No . . . they are too light. Do you know the answer to my riddle?"

"Is it a riddle?"

"A very important one. The answer is this: do not fear your enemy's size, but use it against him. Then his strength will become yours. When you have used this secret, come back, and I will tell you a better one."

Theseus sat up, rubbing his eyes. Was it a dream? Had the gull been there, speaking to him? Could it be? What did it all mean? Theseus thought and thought; then he leaped to his feet and raced down the beach, up the cliff to the village where he found the boy who had just beaten him and slapped him across the face. When the boy, who was almost as big as a man, lunged toward him swinging his big fist, Theseus caught the fist and pulled in the same direction. The boy, swung off balance by his own power, went spinning off his feet and landed headfirst.

"Get up," said Theseus. "I want to try that again."

The big fellow lumbered to his feet and rushed at Theseus, who stooped suddenly. The boy went hurtling over him and landed in the road again. This time he lay still.

"Well," said Theseus, "that was a smart gull."

One by one, Theseus challenged the largest boys of the village; and, by being swift and sure and using their own strength against them, he defeated them all.

Then, he returned to the beach and lay on the sand, watching the waves, and listening as the crashing became a lullaby. Once again, his eyes closed, then opened. The great white seagull was pacing the sand near him.

"Thank you," said Theseus.

"Don't thank me," said the gull. "Thank your father. I am but his messenger."

"My father, the king?"

"King, indeed. But not the king your mother thinks."

"What do you mean?"

"Listen now . . . . Your father rules no paltry stretch of earth. His domain is as vast as all the seas, and all that is beneath them, and all that the seas claim. He is the Earth-shaker, Poseidon."

"Poseidon . . . my father?"

"You are his son."

"Then why does my mother not know? How can this be?"

"You must understand, boy, that the gods sometimes fall in love with beautiful maidens of the earth, but they cannot appear to the maidens in their own forms. The gods are too large, too bright, too terrifying, so they must disguise themselves. Now, when Poseidon fell in love with your mother, she had just been secretly married to Aegeus, king of Athens. Poseidon disguised himself as her new husband, and you, you are his son. One of many, very many; but he seems to have taken a special fancy to you and plans great and terrible things for you . . . if you have the courage."

"I have the courage," said Theseus. "Let me know his will."

"Tomorrow," said the seagull, "you will receive an unexpected gift. Then you must bid farewell to your mother and go to Athens to visit Aegeus. Do not go by sea. Take the dangerous overland route, and your adventures will begin."

The waves made great crashing music. The wind crooned. A blackness crossed the boy's mind. When he opened his eyes the gull was gone, and the sun was dipping into the sea.

"Undoubtedly a dream," he said to himself. "But the last dream worked. Perhaps this one will too."

The next morning there was a great excitement in the village. A huge stone had appeared in the middle of the road. In this stone was stuck a sword halfway up to its hilt; and a messenger had come from the oracle at Delphi[2] saying that whoever pulled the sword from the stone was a king's son and must go to his father.

When Theseus heard this, he embraced his mother and said, "Farewell."

"Where are you going, my son?"

"To Athens. This is the time we have been waiting for. I shall take the sword from the stone and be on my way."

"But, son, it is sunk so deeply. Do you think you can? Look . . . look . . . the

2. *oracle at Delphi.* An oracle (ôr′ə kəl) is a shrine or place where it was thought that a god provided answers in response to questions. The shrine of Apollo in the town of Delphi (del′fī) was one of the most famous oracles.

strongest men cannot budge it. There is the smith trying . . . and there the Captain of the Guard . . . and look . . . look at that giant herdsman trying. See how he pulls and grunts. Oh, son, I fear the time is not yet."

"Pardon me," said Theseus, moving through the crowd. "Let me through, please. I should like a turn."

When the villagers heard this, heard the short fragile-looking youth say these words, they exploded in laughter.

"Delighted to amuse you," said Theseus. "Now, watch this."

Theseus grasped the sword by the hilt and drew it from the stone as easily as though he were drawing it from a scabbard; he bowed to the crowd and stuck the sword in his belt. The villagers were too stunned to say anything. They moved apart as he approached, making room for him to pass. He smiled, embraced his mother again, and set out on the long road to Athens.

Gods and Mortals

Aegeus (ē′jüs, ē jē′əs)
Theseus (thē′süs, thē′sē əs)

The Road

The overland road from Troezen to Athens was the most dangerous in the world. It was infested not only by bandits but also giants, ogres, and sorcerers who lay in wait for travelers and killed them for their money, or their weapons, or just for sport. Those who had to make the trip usually went by boat, preferring the risk of shipwreck and pirates to the terrible mountain brigands. If the trip overland had to be made, travelers banded together, went heavily armed, and kept watch as though on a military march.

Theseus knew all this, but he did not give it a second thought. He was too happy to be on his way . . . leaving his poky little village and his ordinary life. He was off to the great world and adventure. He welcomed the dangers that lay in wait. "The more, the better," he thought. "Where there's danger, there's glory. Why, I shall be disappointed if I am *not* attacked."

He was not to be disappointed. He had not gone far when he met a huge man in a bearskin carrying an enormous brass club. This was Corynetes, the cudgeler, terror of travelers. He reached out a hairy hand, seized Theseus by the throat and lifted his club, which glittered in the hot sunlight.

"Pardon me," said Theseus. "What are you planning to do?"

"Bash in your head."

"Why?"

"That's what I do."

"A beautiful club you have there, sir," said Theseus. "So bright and shiny. You know, it's a positive honor to have my head bashed in with a weapon like this."

"Pure brass," growled the bandit.

"Mmm . . . but is it really brass? It might be gilded wood, you know. A brass club would be too heavy to lift."

"Not too heavy for me," said the bandit, "and it's pure brass. Look . . . ."

He held out his club, which Theseus accepted, smiling. Swinging it in a mighty arc he cracked the bandit's head as if it were an egg.

"Nice balance to this," said Theseus. "I think I'll keep it." He shouldered the club and walked off.

The road ran along the edge of the cliff above the burning blue sea. He turned a bend in the road and saw a man sitting on a rock. The man held a great battle-ax in his hand; he was so large that the ax seemed more like a hatchet.

"Stop!" said the man.

"Good day," said Theseus.

"Now listen, stranger, everyone who passes this way washes my feet. That's the toll. Any questions?"

"One. Suppose I don't?"

"Then I'll simply cut off your head," said the man, "unless you think that little twig you're carrying will stop this ax."

"I was just asking," said Theseus. "I'll be glad to wash your feet, sir. Personal hygiene is very important, especially on the road."

"What?"

"I said I'll do it."

Theseus knelt at the man's feet and undid his sandals, thinking hard. He knew who this man was; he had heard tales of him. This was Sciron who was notorious for keeping a pet turtle that was as large for a turtle as Sciron was for a man and was trained to eat human flesh. This giant turtle swam about at the foot of the cliff waiting for Sciron to kick his victims over. Theseus glanced swiftly down the cliffside. Sure enough, he saw the great blunt head of the turtle lifted out of the water, waiting.

Theseus took Sciron's huge foot in his hand, holding it by the ankle. As he did so, the giant launched a mighty kick. Theseus was ready. When the giant kicked, Theseus pulled, dodging swiftly out of the way as the enormous body hurtled over him, over and down, splashing the water cliff-high as it hit. Theseus saw the turtle swim toward the splash. He arose, dusted off his knees, and proceeded on his journey.

The road dipped now, running past a grove of pines.

"Stop!"

He stopped. There was another huge brute of a man facing him. First Theseus thought that Sciron had climbed back up the cliff somehow; but then he realized that this must be Sciron's brother, of whom he had also heard. This fellow was called Pityocamptes, which means "pine-bender." He was big enough and strong enough to press pine trees to the ground. It was his habit to bend a tree just as a passerby approached and ask the newcomer to hold it for a moment. The traveler, afraid not to oblige, would grasp the top of the tree. Then Pityocamptes with a great jeering laugh would release his hold. The pine tree would spring mightily to its full height, flinging the victim high in the air, so high that the life was dashed out of him when he hit the ground. Then the bandit would search his pockets, chuckling all the while, as he was a great joker. Now he said to Theseus, "Wait, friend. I want you to do me a favor."

He reached for a pine tree and bent it slowly to earth like an enormous bow. "Just hold this for a moment like a good fellow, will you?"

"Certainly," said Theseus.

Theseus grasped the tree, set his feet, clenched his teeth, let his mind go dark and all his strength flow downward, through his legs, into the earth, anchoring him to the earth like a rock. Pityocamptes let go, expecting to see Theseus fly into the air. Nothing happened. The pine stayed bent. The lad was holding it, legs rigid, arms trembling. The giant could not believe his eyes. He thought he must have broken the pine while bending it. He leaned his head closer to see. Then Theseus let go. The tree snapped up, catching the giant under the chin, knocking him unconscious. Theseus bent the tree again, swiftly bound the giant's wrists to it. He pulled down another pine and tied Pityocamptes' legs to that . . . and then let both pines go. They sprang apart. Half of Pityocamptes hung from one tree, half from the other. Vultures screamed with joy and fed on both parts impartially. Theseus wiped the

pine tar from his hands and continued on his
way.

By now it was nightfall, and he was very
weary. He came to an inn where light was
coming from the window, smoke from the
chimney. But it was not a cozy sight as the
front yard was littered with skulls and other
bones.

"They don't do much to attract guests,"
thought Theseus. "Well . . . I'm tired. It has
been a gruesome day. I'd just as soon go to
bed now without any more fighting. On the
other hand, if an adventure comes my way, I
must not avoid it. Let's see what this bone-
collector looks like."

He strode to the door and pounded on it,
crying, "Landlord! Landlord, ho!"

The door flew open. In it was framed a
greasy-looking giant, resembling Sciron and
the pine-bender, but older, filthier, with long,
tangled gray hair and a blood-stained gray
beard. He had great meaty hands like grap-
pling hooks.

"Do you have a bed for the night?" said
Theseus.

"A bed? That I have. Come with me."

He led Theseus to a room where a bed
stood—an enormous ugly piece of furniture,
hung with leather straps, and chains, and
shackles.

"What are all those bolts and bindings
for?" said Theseus.

"To keep you in bed until you've had
your proper rest."

"Why should I wish to leave the bed?"

"Everyone else seems to. You see, this is
a special bed, exactly six feet long from head
to foot. And I am a very neat, orderly
person. I like things to fit. Now, if the guest
is too short for the bed, we attach those
chains to his ankles and stretch him. Simple."

"And if he's too long?" said Theseus.

"Oh, well then we just lop off his legs to
the proper length."

"I see."

"But don't worry about that part of it.
You look like a stretch job to me. Go ahead,
lie down."

"And if I do, then you will attach chains
to my ankles and stretch me—if I understand you correctly."

"You understand me fine. Lie down."

"But all this stretching sounds uncomfortable."

"You came here. Nobody invited you.
Now you've got to take the bad with the
good."

"Yes, of course," said Theseus. "I suppose if I decided not to take advantage of

your hospitality . . . I suppose you'd *make* me lie down, wouldn't you?"

"Oh, sure. No problem."

"How? Show me."

The inn-keeper, whose name was Procrustes, reached out a great hand, put it on Theseus's chest, and pushed him toward the bed. Theseus took his wrist, and, as the big man pushed, he pulled . . . in the swift shoulder-turning downward snap he had taught himself. Procrustes flew over his shoulder and landed on the bed. Theseus bolted him fast, took up an ax, and chopped off his legs as they dangled over the footboards. Then, because he did not wish the fellow to suffer, chopped off his head too.

"As you have done by travelers, so are you done by," said Theseus. "You have made your bed, old man. Now lie on it."

He put down the ax, picked up his club, and resumed his journey, deciding to sleep in the open because he found the inn unpleasant.

Gods and Mortals

Corynetes (kôr′ə nē′tēz)
Pityocamptes (pit′ē ō kamp′tēz)
Procrustes (prō krus′tēz). The adjective *Procrustean* is now used to describe anything that tends to produce conformity by violent or unfair means.
Sciron (sī′ron)

Athens

Athens was not yet a great city in those days, but it was far more spendid than any Theseus had seen. He found it quite beautiful with arbors and terraces and marble temples. After the adventures of the road, however, he found it strangely dull. He suffered too from humiliation for, although he was the king's son, his father was in a very weak position so he could not be a real prince. It was his father's powerful cousin, the tall black-browed Pallas with his fifty fierce sons, who actually ran things. Their estate was much larger and finer than the castle, their private army stronger than the Royal Guard, and Theseus could not bear it.

"Why was I given the sign?" he stormed. "Why did I pull the sword from the stone and come here to Athens? To skulk in the castle like a runaway slave? What difference does it make, Father, how *many* there are? After we fight them, there will be many less. Let's fight! Right now!"

"No," said Aegeus, "we cannot. Not yet. It would not be a battle, it would be suicide. They must not know you are here. I am sorry now I had you come all the way to Athens. It is too dangerous. I should have kept you in some little village somewhere, outside of town, where we could have seen each other every day, but where you would not be in such danger."

"Well, if I am no use here, let me go to Crete!" cried Theseus. "If I can't fight our enemies at home, let me try my hand abroad."

"Crete! . . . Oh, my dear boy, no, no . . ." and the old man fell to lamenting for it was in these days that Athens, defeated in a war with Crete, was forced by King Minos to pay a terrible tribute. He demanded that each year the Athenians send him seven of their most beautiful maidens, seven of their strongest young men. These were taken to the labyrinth and offered to the monster who lived there—the dread Minotaur, half man and half bull. Year after year they were taken from their parents, these seven maidens and seven youths, and were never heard of again. Now the day of tribute was approaching again.

Theseus offered to go himself as one of the seven young men and take his chances with the monster. He kept hammering at his father, kept producing so many arguments, was so electric with impatience and rage, that finally his father consented, and the name Theseus was entered among those who were to be selected for tribute. The night before he left, he embraced Aegeus and said, "Be of good heart, dear sire. I traveled a road that was supposed to be fatal before and came out alive. I met quite a few unpleasant characters on my journey and had a few anxious moments, but I learned from them that the best weapon you can give an enemy is your own fear. So . . . who can tell? I may emerge victorious from the labyrinth and lead my companions home safely. Then I will be known to the people of Athens and will be able to rouse them against your tyrant cousins and make you a real king."

"May the gods protect you, son," said Aegeus. "I shall sacrifice to Zeus and to Ares, and to our own Athene, every day, and pray for your safety."

"Don't forget Poseidon," said Theseus.

"Oh, yes, Poseidon too," said Aegeus. "Now do this for me, son. Each day I shall climb the Hill of the Temple, and from there watch over the sea . . . watching for your ship to return. It will depart wearing black sails, as all the sad ships of tribute do; but if you should overcome the Minotaur, please, I pray you, raise a white sail. This will tell me that you are alive and save a day's vigil."

"That I will do," said Theseus. "Watch for the white sail . . . ."

Gods and Mortals

Ares (er′ēz, ar′ēz), the god of war. Emblems: armor, dogs, vultures.
Pallas (pal′əs)

Crete

All Athens was at the pier to see the black-sailed ship depart. The parents of the victims were weeping and tearing their clothing. The maidens and the young men, chosen for their beauty and courage, stood on the deck trying to look proud; but the sound of lamentation reached them, and they wept to see their parents weep. Then Theseus felt the cords of his throat tighten with rage. He stamped his foot on the deck and shouted, "Up anchor, and away!" as though he were the captain of the vessel. The startled crew obeyed, and the ship moved out of the harbor.

Theseus immediately called the others to him. "Listen to me," he said. "You are not to look upon yourselves as victims, or victims you will surely be. The time of tribute has ended. You are to regard this voyage not as a submission but as a military expedition. Everything will change, but first you must change your own way of looking at things.

Place your faith in my hands, place yourselves under my command. Will you?"

"We will!" they shouted.

"Good. Now I want every man to instruct every girl in the use of the sword and the battle-ax. We may have to cut our way to freedom. I shall also train you to respond to my signals—whistles, hand-movements—for if we work as a team, we may be able to defeat the Minotaur and confound our enemies."

They agreed eagerly. They were too young to live without hope, and Theseus's words filled them with courage. Every day he drilled them, man and maiden alike, as though they were a company of soldiers. He taught them to wrestle in the way he had invented. And this wild young activity, this sparring and fencing, so excited the crew, that they were eager to place themselves under the young man's command.

"Yes," he said, "I will take your pledges. You are Athenians. Right now that means you are poor, defeated, living in fear. But one day 'Athenian' will be the proudest name in the world, a word to make warriors quake in their armor, kings shiver upon their thrones!"

Now Minos of Crete was the most powerful king in all the world. His capital, Knossos, was the gayest, richest, proudest city in the world; and the day, each year, when the victims of the Minotaur arrived from Athens, was always a huge feast-day. People mobbed the streets—warriors with shaven heads and gorgeous feathered cloaks, women in jewels, children, farmers, great swaggering bullherders, lithe bullfighters, dwarfs, peacocks, elephants, and slaves, slaves, slaves from every country known to man. The streets were so jammed no one could walk freely, but the King's Guard kept a lane open from quayside to palace. And here, each year, the fourteen victims were marched so that the whole city could see them—marched past the crowds to the palace to be presented to the king to have their beauty approved before giving them to the Minotaur.

On this day of arrival, the excited harbormaster came puffing to the castle, fell on his knees before the throne, and gasped, "Pity, great king, pity . . . ."

And then in a voice strangled with fright the harbormaster told the king that one of the intended victims, a young man named Theseus, demanded a private audience with Minos before he would allow the Athenians to disembark.

"My warships!" thundered Minos. "The harbor is full of triremes.[3] Let the ship be seized, and this Theseus and his friends dragged here through the streets."

"It cannot be, your majesty. Their vessel stands over the narrow neck of the harbor. And he swears to scuttle it right there, blocking the harbor, if any of our ships approach."

"Awkward . . . very awkward," murmured Minos. "Quite resourceful for an Athenian, this young man. Worth taking a look at. Let him be brought to me."

Thereupon Theseus was informed that the king agreed to see him privately. He was led to the palace, looking about eagerly as he was ushered down the lane past the enormous crowd. He had never seen a city like this. It made Athens look like a little fishing village. He was excited and he walked proudly, head high, eyes flashing. When he came to the palace, he was introduced to the king's daughters, two lovely young princesses, Ariadne and Phaedra.

"I regret that my queen is not here to greet you," said Minos. "But she has be-come attached to her summer house in the labyrinth and spends most of her time there."

The princesses were silent, but they never took their eyes off Theseus. He could not decide which one he preferred. Ariadne, he supposed—the other was really still a little girl. But she had a curious cat-faced look about her that intrigued him. However, he could not give much thought to this; his business was with the king.

Finally, Minos signaled the girls to leave the room, and motioned Theseus toward his throne. "You wanted to see me alone," he said. "Here I am. Speak."

"I have a request, your majesty. As the son of my father, Aegeus, King of Athens, and his representative in this court, I ask you formally to stop demanding your yearly tribute."

"Oh, heavens," said Minos. "I thought you would have something original to say. And you come with this threadbare old petition. I have heard it a thousand times and refused·it a thousand times."

"I know nothing of what has been done before," said Theseus. "But only of what I must do. You laid this tribute upon Athens to punish the city, to show the world that you were the master. But it serves only to degrade you and show the world that you are a fool."

"Feeding you to the Minotaur is much too pleasant a finale for such an insolent rascal," said Minos. "I shall think of a much more interesting way for you to die—perhaps several ways."

"Let me explain what I mean," said Theseus. "Strange as it seems, I do not hate you. I admire you. You're the most powerful

---

3. *trireme* (trī′rēm′), a Greek warship having three rows of oars on each side.

king in the world and I admire power. In fact, I intend to imitate your career. So what I say, I say in all friendliness, and it is this: when you take our young men and women and shut them in the labyrinth to be devoured by the Minotaur, you are making the whole world forget Minos, the great general Minos, the wise king. What you are forcing upon their attention is Minos, the betrayed husband, the man whose wife disliked him so much she ran away. And this image of you is what people remember. Drop the tribute, I say, and you will once again live in man's mind as warrior, law-giver, and king."

"You are an agile debater," said Minos, "as well as a very reckless young man, saying these things to me. But there is a flaw in your argument. If I were to drop the tribute, my subjects would construe this as an act of weakness. They would be encouraged to launch conspiracies against me. Other countries under my sway would be encouraged to rebel. It cannot be done."

"I can show you a graceful way to let the tribute lapse. One that will not be seen as a sign of weakness. Just tell me how to kill the monster."

"Kill the monster, eh? And return to Athens a hero? And wipe out your enemies there? And then subdue the other cities of Greece until you become leader of a great alliance? And then come visit me again with a huge fleet and an enormous army, and topple old Minos from his throne . . . ? Do I describe your ambitions correctly?"

"The future does not concern me," said Theseus. "I take one thing at a time. And the thing that interests me now is killing the Minotaur."

"Oh, forget the Minotaur," said Minos. "How do you know there is one? How do you know it's not some maniac there who ties sticks to his head? Whatever it is, let him rot there in the labyrinth with his mad mother. I have a better plan for you. My sons are dead. My daughter Ariadne, I notice, looks upon you with favor. Marry her, and become my heir. One day you will rule Crete and Athens both . . . and all the cities of the sea."

"Thank you, sir. I appreciate your offer. But I came here to fight a monster."

"You are mad."

"Perhaps. But this is the only way I know how to be. When I am your age, when the years have thinned my blood, when rage has cooled into judgment, then I will go in for treaties, compromises. Now, I must fight."

"Why is the young fool so confident?" thought Minos to himself. "He acts like a man who knows he is protected by the gods. Can it be true what they say? Is he really the son of Poseidon? Do I have that kind of enemy on my hands? If so, I will make doubly sure to get rid of him."

Then he said aloud, "You are wrong to refuse my offer. I suppose you are made so wildly rash by some old gossip in your little village that you are the son of this god or that. Those mountain villages of yours, they're ridiculous. Every time a child does something out of the way, all the crones and hags get together and whisper, 'He's the son of a god, really the son of a god.' Is that the way of it? Tell the truth now."

"My truth," said Theseus, "is that I am the son of Poseidon."

"Poseidon, eh? No less. Well, how would you like to prove it?"

"Why should I care to prove it? *I* know. That's enough for me. The whole world has heard that you are the son of Zeus, who courted your mother, Europa, in the guise of a white bull. Everyone has heard this tale; few disbelieve it. But can you prove it?"

"Come with me," said Minos.

He led him out of the palace, beyond the wall, to a cliff overlooking the sea. He stood tall, raised his arms, and said, "Father Zeus, make me a sign."

Lightning flashed so furiously that the night became brighter than day, and the sky spoke in thunder. Then Minos dropped his arms; the light stopped pulsing in the sky, and the thunder was still.

"Well," said Minos. "Have I proved my parentage?"

"It's an impressive display. I suppose it proves something."

"Then show me you are the son of Poseidon."

Minos took the crown from his head and threw it over the cliff into the sea. They heard the tiny splash far below.

"If you are his son, the sea holds no terror for you. Get me my crown," said Minos.

Without a moment's hesitation, Theseus stepped to the edge of the cliff and leaped off. As he fell, he murmured, "Father, help me now."

Down he plunged, struck the black water and went under, shearing his way through until he felt his lungs bursting. But he did not kick toward the surface. He let out the air in his chest in a long tortured gasp, and then, breathed in. No strangling rush of water, but a great lungfull of sweet cool air . . . and he felt himself breathing as naturally as a fish. He swam down, down, and as he swam his eyes became accustomed to the color of the night sea; he moved in a deep green light. And the first thing he saw was the crown gleaming on the bottom. He swam down and picked it up.

Theseus stood on the ocean bottom holding the crown in his hand and said, "All thanks, Father Poseidon."

He waited there for the god to answer him, but all he saw were dark gliding shapes, creatures of the sea passing like shadows. He swam slowly to the surface, climbed the cliff, and walked to where Minos was waiting.

"Your crown, sir."

"Thank you."

"Are you convinced now that Poseidon is my father?"

"I am convinced that the water is more shallow here than I thought. Convinced that you are lucky."

"Luck? Is that not another word for divine favor?"

"Perhaps. At any rate, I am also convinced that you are a dangerous young man. So dangerous that I am forced to strip you of certain advantages allowed those who face the Minotaur. You will carry neither sword nor ax, but only your bare hands . . . and your luck, of course. I think we will not meet again. So farewell." He whistled sharply. His Royal Guard appeared, surrounded Theseus, and marched him off to a stone tower at the edge of the labyrinth. There they locked him up for the night.

An hour before dawn Ariadne appeared in his cell and said, "I love you, Theseus. I will save you from death if you promise to take me back to Athens with you."

"And how do you propose to save me, lovely princess?"

"Do you know what the labyrinth is? It is a hedge of a thousand lanes, all leading in, and only one leading out. And this one is so concealed, has so many twists and turns and secret windings that no one can possibly find his way out. Only I can travel the labyrinth freely. I will lead you in and hide you. I will also lead you around the central chamber where the Minotaur is and lead you out again. You will not even see the monster. Since no one has ever found his way out of the maze, Minos will assume that you have killed the Minotaur, and you will have a chance to get to your ship and escape before the trick is discovered. But you must take me with you."

"It cannot be," said Theseus.

"Don't you believe me? It's all true. Look . . . ."

She took from her tunic a ball of yellow silk thread and dropped it on the floor. The ball swiftly rolled across the room, unwinding itself as it went. It rolled around the bench, wrapped itself around one of Theseus's ankles, rolled up the wall, across the ceiling and down again. Then Ariadne tugged sharply on her end of the thread, and the ball reversed itself, rolling back the way it had come, reeling in its thread as it rolled. Back to Ariadne it rolled and leaped into her hand.

"This was made for me by old Daedalus," said Ariadne. "It was he who built the labyrinth, you know. And my father shut him up in it too. I used to go visit him there. He made me this magic ball of thread so that I would always be able to find my way to him, and find my way back. He was very fond of me."

"I'm getting very fond of you too," said Theseus.

"Do you agree?" cried Ariadne. "Will you let me guide you in the labyrinth and teach you how to avoid the monster, and fool my father? Say you will. Please . . . ."

"I'll let you guide me through the maze," said Theseus. "Right to where the monster dwells. You can stay there and watch the fight. And when it's over, you can lead me back."

"No, no, I won't be able to. You'll be dead! It's impossible for you to fight the Minotaur."

"It is impossible for me not to."

"You won't even be armed."

"I have always traveled light, sweet princess, and taken my weapons from the enemy. I see no reason to change my habits now. Are you the kind of girl who seeks to change a man's habits? If you are, I don't think I will take you back to Athens."

"Oh, please, do not deny me your love," she said. "I will do as you say."

The next morning when the Royal Guard led Theseus out of the tower and forced him into the outer lane of the labyrinth, Ariadne was around the first bend, waiting. She tied one end of the thread to a branch of the hedge, then dropped the ball to the ground. It rolled slowly, unwinding; they followed, hand in hand. It was pleasant, walking in the labyrinth. The hedge grew tall above their heads and was heavy with little white sweet-smelling flowers. The lane turned and twisted and turned again, but the ball of thread ran ahead, and they followed it. Theseus heard a howling.

"Sounds like the wind," he said.

"No, it is not the wind. It is my mad mother, howling."

They walked farther. They heard a rumbling, crashing sound.

"What's that?"

"That is my brother. He's hungry."

They continued to follow the ball of thread. Now the hedges grew so tall the branches met above their heads, and it was dark. Ariadne looked up at him, sadly. He bent his head and brushed her lips in a kiss.

"Please don't go to him," she said. "Let me lead you out now. He will kill you. He has the strength of a bull and the cunning of a man."

"Who knows?" said Theseus. "Perhaps he has the weakness of a man and the stupidity of a bull." He put his hand over her mouth. "Anyway, let me think so because I must fight him, you see, and I'd rather not frighten myself beforehand."

The horrid roaring grew louder and louder. The ball of thread ran ahead, ran out of the lane, into an open space. And here, in a kind of meadow surrounded by the tall hedges of the labyrinth, stood the Minotaur.

Theseus could not believe his eyes. The thing was more fearsome than in his worst dreams. What he had expected was a bull's head on a man's body. What he saw was something about ten feet tall shaped like a man, like an incredibly huge and brutally muscular man, but covered with a short dense brown fur. It had a man's face, but a squashed, bestialized one, with poisonous red eyes, great blunt teeth, and thin leathery lips. Sprouting out of its head were two long, heavy, polished horns. Its feet were hooves, razor sharp; its hands were shaped like a man's hands, but much larger and hard as horn. When it clenched them they were great fists of bone.

It stood pawing the grass with a hoof, peering at Theseus with its little red eyes. There was a bloody slaver on its lips.

Now, for the first time in all his battles, Theseus became unsure of himself. He was confused by the appearance of the monster. It filled him with a kind of horror that was beyond fear, as if he were wrestling a giant spider. So when the monster lowered its

head and charged, thrusting those great bone lances at him, Theseus could not move out of the way.

There was only one thing to do. Drawing himself up on tiptoe, making himself as narrow as possible, he leaped into the air and seized the monster's horns. Swinging himself between the horns, he somersaulted onto the Minotaur's head, where he crouched, gripping the horns with desperate strength. The monster bellowed with rage and shook its head violently. But Theseus held on. He thought his teeth would shake out of his head; he felt his eyeballs rattling in their sockets. But he held on.

Now, if it can be done without one's being gored, somersaulting between the horns is an excellent tactic when fighting a real bull; but the Minotaur was not a real bull; it had hands. So when Theseus refused to be shaken off but stood on the head between the horns trying to dig his heels into the beast's eyes, the Minotaur stopped shaking his head, closed his great horny fist, big as a cabbage and hard as a rock, and struck a vicious backward blow, smashing his fist down on his head, trying to squash Theseus as you squash a beetle.

This is what Theseus was waiting for. As soon as the fist swung toward him, he jumped off the Minotaur's head, and the fist smashed between the horns, full on the skull. The Minotaur's knees bent, he staggered and fell over; he had stunned himself. Theseus knew he had only a few seconds before the beast would recover his strength. He rushed to the monster, took a horn in both hands, put his foot against the ugly face, and putting all his strength in a sudden tug, broke the horn off at the base. He leaped away. Now he, too, was armed, and with a weapon taken from the enemy.

The pain of the breaking horn goaded the Minotaur out of his momentary swoon. He scrambled to his feet, uttered a great choked bellow, and charged toward Theseus, trying to hook him with his single horn. Bone cracked against bone as Theseus parried with his horn. It was like a duel now, the beast thrusting with his horn, Theseus parrying, thrusting in return. Since the Minotaur was much stronger, it forced Theseus back—back until it had Theseus pinned against the hedge. As soon as he felt the first touch of the hedge, Theseus disengaged, ducked past the Minotaur, and raced to the center of the meadow, where he stood, poised, arm drawn back. For the long pointed horn made as good a javelin as it did a sword, and so could be used at a safer distance.

The Minotaur whirled and charged again. Theseus waited until he was ten paces away, and then whipped his arm forward, hurling the javelin with all his strength. It entered the bull's neck and came out the other side. But so powerful was the Minotaur's rush, so stubborn his bestial strength, that he trampled on with the sharp horn through his neck and ran right over Theseus, knocking him violently to the ground. Then it whirled to try to stab Theseus with its horn; but the blood was spouting fast now, and the monster staggered and fell on the ground beside Theseus.

Ariadne ran to the fallen youth. She turned him over, raised him in her arms; he was breathing. She kissed him. He opened his eyes, looked around, and saw the dead Minotaur; then he looked back at her and smiled. He climbed to his feet, leaning heavily on Ariadne.

"Tell your thread to wind itself up again, Princess. We're off for Athens."

When Theseus came out of the labyrinth there was an enormous crowd of Cretans gathered. They had heard the sound of fighting, and, as the custom was, had gathered to learn of the death of the hostages. When they saw the young man covered with dirt and blood, carrying a broken horn, with Ariadne clinging to his arm, they raised a great shout.

Minos was there, standing with his arms folded. Phaedra was at his side. Theseus bowed to him and said, "Your majesty, I have the honor to report that I have rid your kingdom of a foul monster."

"Prince Theseus," said Minos. "According to the terms of the agreement, I must release you and your fellow hostages."

"Your daughter helped me, king. I have promised to take her with me. Have you any objection?"

"I fancy it is too late for objections. The women of our family haven't had much luck in these matters. Try not to be too beastly to her."

"Father," said Phaedra, "she will be lonesome there in far-off Athens. May I not go with her and keep her company?"

"You too?" said Minos. He turned to Theseus. "Truly, young man, whether or not Poseidon has been working for you, Aphrodite surely has."

"I will take good care of your daughters, king," said Theseus. "Farewell."

And so, attended by the Royal Guard, Theseus, his thirteen happy companions, and the two Cretan princesses, walked through the mobbed streets from the palace to the harbor. There they boarded their ship.

It was a joyous ship that sailed northward from Crete to Athens. There was feasting and dancing night and day. And every young man aboard felt himself a hero too, and every maiden a princess. And Theseus was lord of them all, drunk with strength and joy. He was so happy he forgot his promise to his father—forgot to tell the crew to take down the black sail and raise a white one.

King Aegeus, keeping a lonely watch on the Hill of the Temple, saw first a tiny speck on the horizon. He watched it for a long time and saw it grow big and then bigger. He could not tell whether the sail was white or black; but as it came nearer, his heart grew heavy. The sail seemed to be dark. The ship came nearer, and he saw that it wore a black sail. He knew that his son was dead.

"I have killed him," he cried. "In my weakness, I sent him off to be killed. I am unfit to be king, unfit to live. I must go to Tartarus[4] immediately and beg his pardon there."

And the old king leaped from the hill, dived through the steep air into the sea far below, and was drowned. He gave that lovely blue, fatal stretch of water its name for all time—the Aegean Sea.

Theseus, upon his return to Athens, was hailed as king. The people worshipped him. He swiftly raised an army, wiped out his powerful cousins, and then led the Athenians forth into many battles, binding all the cities of Greece together in an alliance. Then, one day he returned to Crete to reclaim the crown of Minos which once he had recovered from the sea. □□

Gods and Mortals

Ariadne (ar′ē ad′nē)
Europa (yù rō′ pə)
Phaedra (fē′drə)

---

4. *Tartarus* (tär′tər əs), a region of punishment located below Hades. Sometimes the term simply refers to the whole underworld.

Discussion

1. (a) In what ways would you say Theseus is a typical hero? **(b)** In what ways is he unusual?

2. Theseus's early years are difficult. **(a)** What secret helps him to get through this period? **(b)** What is the point of the riddle that the gull tells Theseus, and how does Theseus test it? **(c)** What does the gull later tell Theseus about his father? **(d)** What feat does Theseus perform in the presence of the villagers before he leaves, and what does it signify?

3. We often speak of poetic justice—of people being defeated or punished by the same weapons they customarily use on others. Cite at least three examples of poetic justice from Theseus's experiences on the road to Athens.

4. Theseus's stay in Athens is short. **(a)** Why is he anxious to journey to Crete? **(b)** Why is Aegeus so reluctant to allow Theseus to make the journey? **(c)** What signal is Theseus supposed to make to Aegeus if he is successful?

5. (a) In which episodes in Crete is Theseus mainly dependent on cleverness? **(b)** In which episodes is he dependent on his strength? **(c)** In which does he rely on assistance from others, human and divine?

6. (a) How would you describe Theseus's attitude toward his enemies? What is his tone of voice in speaking to them? **(b)** Do you think this tone is appropriate for the story? Why or why not?

7. Repeated throughout this myth is a pattern of the larger and stronger being defeated by the smaller and weaker. **(a)** List as many examples of this pattern as you can. **(b)** What is the effect of this repetition, and what does it suggest to you?

Vocabulary
Context, Structure

The italicized words in the statements below explain or define the *root* of the listed words. Read each statement; then write the word from the list that best completes it. (You will not use one of the listed words.)

alliance	disembark
bestialized	parentage
disengage	submission

1. Alice does not know who her *mother and father* are; in other words, she is not sure of her _____.

2. He thinks that Fred's crimes have turned him into an *animal,* that they have _____ him.

3. If you *give in* to what she wants with no argument now, she will only expect more acts of _____ from you in the future.

4. If you don't want to *take part* in conversations that waste your time, try to _____ yourself gracefully and walk away.

5. In 1961, many Western Hemisphere *nations joined together* and formed an organization called the _____ for Progress.

Strange Combinations

The half-man, half-bull Minotaur is only one of a bizarre collection of monsters and strange creatures that appear in Greek myths. Other well-known oddities include:

The Gorgons

The Gorgons were three monstrous sisters who had brass claws, gold wings, and a scalpful of wriggling snakes instead of hair. Anyone unfortunate enough to look at the Gorgons was instantly turned to stone. Medusa (mə dü′sə), the youngest Gorgon, was mortal, and she was eventually beheaded by the great hero Perseus (pėr′sē əs), who approached the sleeping monster by looking at her reflection in a highly polished shield. (From Medusa's body sprang another fantastic creature, the snow-white flying horse, Pegasus.) Medusa's head retained its statue-making power, which for a time gave Perseus a convenient way of disposing of his enemies ("See what I have . . .").

The Chimera

A dreaded, fire-breathing monster, the Chimera (kə mir′ə) was a zoo on four legs. She was a lion in front, a goat in the middle, and a snake (or dragon) behind—complete with the heads of each creature. (You may have some difficulty visualizing this combination. The word *chimera* today is used to refer to an absurd, impossible idea or fancy.) The Chimera was eventually killed by the hero Bellerophon (bə-ler′ə fon), mounted on the flying horse Pegasus. According to one version, Bellerophon defeated the monster by poking a lump of lead into her fiery mouth: the lead melted and the Chimera was choked to death.

The Hydra

The Hydra (hī′drə) was a monstrous serpent with nine poisonous heads. As part of his Twelve Labors, the great hero Heracles was ordered to kill the Hydra. At first Heracles had a terrible time: when he cut off one head, two more sprouted in its place. Heracles solved the problem by using fire to sear the necks. The Hydra's last head was immortal, so Heracles buried it under a large rock. Before leaving, he tipped some of his arrows with the deadly poison of the Hydra's blood.

The Centaurs

Centaurs (sen′tôrz) had four legs like horses, but their heads, arms, and chests were human. Most centaurs were brutal, ill-tempered creatures who lived on raw flesh, but one, Chiron (kī′ron), was wise and gentle. He trained many of the Greek heroes in music, hunting, and medicine. Heracles, a former pupil, accidentally wounded Chiron with one of his poisoned arrows. The wound could never be healed and Chiron, though immortal, could not endure the pain. He gave away his immortality and was allowed to die.

The Sirens

The Sirens were sisters with the faces of maidens and the feathered bodies of birds. The Sirens could sing beautifully—but it was fatal to hear them do so. Sailors were lured to shipwreck, drowning, or starvation by Siren songs (in some accounts, the Sirens devoured their spellbound listeners); human bones cluttered the island on which the Sirens lived. One man who heard the Sirens and survived to tell about it was wise Odysseus (ō dis′ē-əs), who plugged the ears of his crew and had himself tied securely to the ship's mast. The Sirens were so enraged by this clever escape that they flung themselves in the sea and drowned.

"Let everything I touch turn to gold!"

Midas

as told by Bernard Evslin

There was a king named Midas, and what he loved best in the world was gold. He had plenty of his own, but he could not bear the thought of anyone else having any. Each morning he awoke very early to watch the sunrise and said, "Of all the gods, if gods there be, I like you least, Apollo. How dare you ride so unthriftily in your sun-chariot scattering golden sheaves of light on rich and poor alike—on king and peasant, on merchant, shepherd, warrior? This is an evil thing, oh wastrel god, for only kings should have gold; only the rich know what to do with it."

After a while these words of complaint, uttered each dawn, came to Apollo, and he was angry. He appeared to Midas in a dream and said, "Other gods would punish you, Midas, but I am famous for my even temper. Instead of doing you violence, I will show you how gracious I can be by granting you a wish. What is it to be?"

Midas cried, "Let everything I touch turn to gold!"

He shouted this out of his sleep in a strangling greedy voice, and the guards in

Reprinted by permission of Scholastic Magazines, Inc. from *Heroes, Gods, and Monsters of the Greek Myths* by Bernard Evslin. Copyright © 1966, 1967 by Scholastic Magazines, Inc.

the doorway nodded to each other and said, "The king calls out. He must be dreaming of gold again."

Wearied by the dream, Midas slept past sunrise; when he awoke it was full morning. He went out into his garden. The sun was high, the sky was blue. A soft breeze played among the trees. It was a glorious morning. He was still half asleep. Tatters of the dream were in his head.

"Can it be true?" he said to himself. "They say the gods appear in dreams. That's how men know them. On the other hand I know that dreams are false, teasing things. You can't believe them. Let us put it to the test."

He reached out his hand and touched a rose. It turned to gold—petals and stalk, it turned to gold and stood there rigid, heavy, gleaming. A bee buzzed out of its stiff folds, furious; it lit on Midas's hand to sting him. The king looked at the heavy golden bee on the back of his hand and moved it to his finger.

"I shall wear it as a ring," he said.

Midas went about touching all his roses, seeing them stiffen and gleam. They lost their odor. The disappointed bees rose in swarms and buzzed angrily away. Butterflies departed. The hard flowers tinkled like little bells when the breeze moved among them, and the king was well pleased.

His little daughter, the princess, who had been playing in the garden, ran to him and said, "Father, Father, what has happened to the roses?"

"Are they not pretty, my dear?"

"No! They're ugly! They're horrid and sharp and I can't smell them any more. What happened?"

"A magical thing."

"Who did the magic?"

"I did."

"Unmagic it, then! I hate these roses."

She began to cry.

"Don't cry," he said, stroking her head. "Stop crying, and I will give you a golden doll with a gold-leaf dress and tiny golden shoes."

She stopped crying. He felt the hair grow spiky under his fingers. Her eyes stiffened and froze into place. The little blue vein in her neck stopped pulsing. She was a statue, a figure of pale gold standing in the garden path with lifted face. Her tears were tiny golden beads on her golden cheeks. He looked at her and said, "This is unfortunate. I'm sorry it happened. I have no time to be sad this morning. I shall be busy turning things into gold. But, when I have a moment, I shall think about this problem; I promise." He hurried out of the garden which had become unpleasant to him.

On Midas's way back to the castle he amused himself by kicking up gravel in the path and watching it tinkle down as tiny nuggets. The door he opened became golden; the chair he sat upon became solid gold like his throne. The plates turned into gold, and the cups became gold cups before the amazed eyes of the servants, whom he was careful not to touch. He wanted them to continue being able to serve him; he was very hungry.

With great relish Midas picked up a piece of bread and honey. His teeth bit metal; his mouth was full of metal. He felt himself choking. He reached into his mouth and pulled out a golden slab of bread, all bloody now, and flung it through the window. Very lightly now he touched the other food to see what would happen. Meat . . . apples . . . walnuts . . . they all turned to gold even when he touched them with only the tip of his finger . . . and when he did not touch them with his fingers, when he lifted them on his fork, they became gold as soon as they touched his lips, and he had to put them back onto the plate. He was savagely hungry. Worse than hunger, when he thought about drinking, he realized that wine, or water, or milk would turn to gold in his mouth and choke him if he drank. As he thought that he could not drink, thirst began to burn in his belly. He felt himself full of hot dry sand, felt that the lining of his head was on fire.

"What good is all my gold?" he cried, "if I cannot eat and cannot drink?"

He shrieked with rage, pounded on the table, and flung the plates about. All the servants ran from the room in fright. Then Midas raced out of the castle, across the bridge that spanned the moat, along the golden gravel path into the garden where the stiff flowers chimed hatefully, and the statue of his daughter looked at him with scooped and empty eyes. There in the garden, in the blaze of the sun, he raised his arms heavenward, and cried, "You, Apollo, false god, traitor! You pretended to forgive me, but you punished me with a gift!"

Then it seemed to him that the sun grew brighter, that the light thickened, that the sun-god stood before him in the path, tall, stern, clad in burning gold. A voice said, "On your knees, wretch!"

He fell to his knees.

"Do you repent?"

"I repent. I will never desire gold again. I will never accuse the gods. Pray, revoke the fatal wish."

Apollo reached his hand and touched the roses. The tinkling stopped, they softened, swayed, blushed. Fragrance grew on the air. The bees returned, and the butterflies. He touched the statue's cheek. She lost her stiffness, her metallic gleam. She ran to the roses, knelt among them, and cried, "Oh, thank you, Father. You've changed them back again." Then she ran off, shouting and laughing.

Apollo said, "I take back my gift. I remove the golden taint from your touch, but you are not to escape without punishment. Because you have been the most foolish of men, you shall wear always a pair of donkey's ears."

Midas touched his ears. They were long and furry. He said, "I thank you for your forgiveness, Apollo . . . even though it comes with a punishment."

"Go now," said Apollo. "Eat and drink. Enjoy the roses. Watch your child grow. Life is the only wealth, man. In your great thrift, you have been wasteful of life, and that is the sign you wear on your head. Farewell."

Midas put a tall pointed hat on his head so that no one would see his ears. Then he went in to eat and drink his fill.

For years he wore the cap so that no one would know of his disgrace. But the servant who cut his hair had to know so Midas swore him to secrecy, warning that it would cost him his head if he spoke of the king's ears. But the servant who was a coward was also a gossip. He could not bear to keep a secret, especially a secret so mischievous. Although he was afraid to tell it, he felt that he would burst if he didn't.

One night he went out to the banks of the river, dug a little hole, put his mouth to it, and whispered, "Midas has donkey's ears, Midas has donkey's ears . . ." and quickly filled up the hole again, and ran back to the castle, feeling better.

But the river-reeds heard him, and they always whisper to each other when the wind seethes among them. They were heard whispering, "Midas has donkey's ears . . . donkey's ears . . ." and soon the whole country was whispering, "Have you heard about Midas? Have you heard about his ears?"

When the king heard, he knew who had told the secret and ordered the man's head cut off; but then he thought, "The god forgave me, perhaps I had better forgive this blabbermouth." Therefore he let the treacherous man keep his head.

Then Apollo appeared again and said, "Midas, you have learned the final lesson, mercy. As you have done, so shall you be done by."

And Midas felt his long hairy ears dwindling back to normal.

He was an old man now. His daughter, the princess, was grown. He had grandchildren. Sometimes he tells his smallest granddaughter the story of how her mother was turned into a golden statue, and he says, "See, I'm changing you too. Look, your hair is all gold."

And she pretends to be frightened. □□

Discussion

1. If you had Midas's chance, and had the gift of one wish, what would you wish for?

2. Midas's weakness is his greed, or lust for gold. (a) Explain how he first shows this greed with regard to Apollo. (b) Apollo is angry, yet he grants Midas a wish. Why do you think he does so? (c) When does Midas first become aware of the awfulness of the gift? What does this imply about the type of man he is? (d) Do you think Midas deserves the mercy Apollo shows him in taking back the gift of the golden touch? Explain.

3. (a) How is Midas punished for being "the most foolish of men"? (b) In your opinion, is this punishment appropriate? (c) How does Apollo show mercy to Midas a second time, and why does he do so?

4. This myth is really two stories in one. (a) What are the two stories? (b) Does their joining appear logical? Explain.

5. The English author Oscar Wilde once wrote: "In this world there are only two tragedies: One is not getting what one wants and the other is getting it." (a) Which of the two "tragedies" might Midas feel was the greater? Why? (b) Which "tragedy" do you feel is the greater?

Vocabulary • Structure

The names of characters from Greek myths are found in a good number of words and expressions that we use today. Answer the following questions about Greek names that you have encountered in this unit. You may refer to selections in the unit if necessary.

1. The term "Midas touch" comes from Midas's ability to make anything he touched turn into gold. Which of the following people do you think could be described as having a "Midas touch": a jeweler who makes elaborate gold rings and necklaces, a dentist who generally puts gold fillings in his patients' teeth, or a businesswoman who never fails to make money on a deal?

2. The Titans are described as "huge . . . creatures taller than trees." Of the following three items, which would most likely be described as *titanic:* the Rocky Mountains, a twenty-story building, or the White House?

3. In the story "Zeus" you read that Cronos gave his name to time. (a) What do you think a *chronometer* does? [Hint: What does a *speedometer* do?] (b) Put these dates in *chronological* order: May 8, 1946; August 9, 1974; April 2, 1969; July 1, 1917.

4. Arachne gave her name to a class of living creatures called *arachnids*. Which of the following animals do you think belongs to that class—dogs, spiders, or squirrels?

5. If you wanted to name your new solar-energy company after one of the Greek gods, would it be most appropriate to name it after Hermes, Apollo, or Zeus? Why?

6. Why is *The Poseidon Adventure* a good name for a movie dealing with a ship?

"A bachelor is bad enough, a happy bachelor is intolerable"
—so Pygmalion is forced to choose a wife.

Pygmalion

as told by Bernard Evslin

The women of Cyprus[1] were displeased with Pygmalion. He was one of the few unmarried young men on the island, and it seemed that he meant to stay that way. He was a sculptor who lived alone in a house he had knocked together out of an old stable, one enormous room on a hill overlooking the sea, far away from any neighbor. Here he spent the days very happily. Great unhewn blocks of marble stood about, and tubs of clay, and a crowd of figures, men and women, nymphs, satyrs, wolves, lions, bulls, and dolphins. Some of them were half-carved, some of them clay daubs, almost shapeless; and others were finished statues, marvelous gleaming shapes of white marble.

Sometimes people came and bought Pygmalion's figures. He sold only those he was tired of looking at, but would never set a price. He took anything offered. Often, he would give his work away, if he thought that someone enjoyed looking at it and had no money to pay. He ate when he was hungry, slept when he was tired, worked when he felt like it, swam in the sea when hot, and spent days without seeing anyone.

"Oh, I have plenty of company," he'd say. "Plenty of statues around, you know. Not very good conversationalists, but they listen beautifully."

Now, all this irritated the mothers and daughters of Cyprus exceedingly. A bachelor is bad enough, a happy bachelor is intolerable. And so they were resolved that he should marry.

"He's earning enough to keep a wife . . . or he would be if he charged properly. That's another reason he needs one. My Althea is a very shrewd girl. She'd see he got the right prices for his work . . . ."

Reprinted by permission of Scholastic Magazines, Inc. from *Heroes, Gods, and Monsters of the Greek Myths* by Bernard Evslin. Copyright © 1966, 1967 by Scholastic Magazines, Inc.
1. **Cyprus** (si′prəs), an island in the Mediterranean, south of Turkey.

"My Laurel is an excellent housekeeper. She'd clean out that pig-sty of his, and make it fit to live in . . . ."

"My daughter has very strict ideas. She'd make him toe the mark. Where does he get the models for those nymph statues? Tell me that? Who knows what goes on in that stable of his? . . ."

"*My* daughter . . . ."

And so it went. They talked like this all the time, and Pygmalion was very much aware of their plans for him. More than ever he resolved to keep himself to himself.

Now Cyprus was an island sacred to Aphrodite, for it was the first land she touched when she arose from the sea. The mothers of the island decided to use her favor for their own purposes. They crowded into the temple of Aphrodite and recited this prayer:

"Oh, great goddess of Love, you who rose naked and dripping from the sea and walked upon this shore, making it blossom with trees and flowers, you, Aphrodite, hear our plea: touch the heart of young Pygmalion, who has become as hard as his own marble. Weave your amorous spell, plaiting it into the tresses of one of our maidens, making it a snare for his wild loneliness. Bid your son, the Archer of Love,[2] plant one of his arrows in that indifferent young man so that he becomes infected with a sweet sickness for which there is only one cure. Please, goddess, forbid him all solitary joy. Bind him to one of our maidens. Make him love her and take her as his wife."

That night Pygmalion, dreaming, was visited by the goddess who said, "Pygmalion, I have been asked to marry you off. Do you have any preferences?"

---

2. *Archer of Love,* Eros. His more familiar, Roman name is Cupid.

Pygmalion, being an artist, was acquainted with the terrible reality of dreams and knew that the matter was serious, that he was being threatened. He said, "There is one lady I fancy. But she is already married."

"Who?"

"You."

"Me?"

"You, Aphrodite, queen of beauty, lady of delight. How can you think that I who in my daily work will accept nothing less than the forms of ideal beauty, how can you think that I could pin my highest aspiration on any but the most perfect face and form? Yours, Aphrodite. Yours, yours. I love you, and you alone. And until I can find a mortal maid of the same perfection, I will not love."

Now, Aphrodite, although a goddess, was also a woman. In fact, her divinity was

precisely this, womanliness raised to its highest power. She was much pleased by this ardent praise. She knelt beside Pygmalion and, stroking his face, said, "Truly, you are a fair-spoken young man. I find your arguments very persuasive. But what am I to do? I have promised the mothers of Cyprus that you shall wed, and I must not break my promise."

"Did you tell them *when?*"

"No, I set no time."

"Then grant me this: permit me to remain unwed until I do one more statue. It will be my masterwork, the thing I have been training myself for. Let me do it now, and allow me to remain unmarried until I complete it for the vision is upon me, goddess. The time has come. I must do this last figure."

"Of whom?"

"Of you, of course! Of you, of you! I told you that I have loved you all my life without ever having seen you. And now that you have appeared to me, now that I do see you, why then I must carve you in marble. It is simple. This is what my life is for; it is my way of loving you, a way that you cannot deny me."

"I see . . . . And how long will this work take?"

"Until it is finished. What else can I say? If you will be good enough to visit me like this whenever you can spare the time, I will fill my eyes with you and work on your image alone, putting all else aside. Once and for all I shall be able to cast in hard cold marble the flimsy, burning dream of man, his dream of beauty, his dream of you . . . ."

"Very well," said Aphrodite, "you may postpone your marriage until my statue is completed." She smiled at him. "And every now and again I shall come to pose."

Pygmalion worked first in clay. He took it between his hands and thought of Aphrodite—of her round arms, of the strong column of her neck, of her long, full thighs, of the smooth swimming of her back muscles when she turned from the waist—and his hands followed his thinking, pressing the clay to the shape of her body. She came to him at night, sliding in and out of his dreams, telling him stories about herself. He used a whole tub-full of clay making a hundred little Aphrodites, each in a different pose. He caught her at that moment when she emerged from the sea, shaking back her wet hair, lifting her face to the sky which she saw for the first time. He molded her in the Hall of the Gods receiving marriage offers, listening to Poseidon, and Hermes, and Apollo press their claims, head tilted, shoulders straight, smiling to herself, pleasing everyone, but refusing to answer. He molded her in full magnificent fury, punishing Narcissus, kneeling on the grass, teasing the shy Adonis, and then mourning him, slain.

He caught her in a hundred poses, then stood the little clay figures about, studying them, trying to mold them in his mind to a total image that he could carve in marble. He had planned to work slowly. After all, the whole thing was a trick of his to postpone marriage; but as he made the lovely little dolls and posed them among her adventures, his hands took on a schedule of their own. The dream invaded daylight, and he found himself working with wild fury.

When the clay figures were done, he was ready for marble. He set the heavy mass of polished stone in the center of the room and arranged his clay studies about it. Then he took mallet and chisel, and began to work— it was as if the cold tools became living parts of himself. The chisel was like his own finger, with a sharp fingernail edge; the mallet was his other hand, curled into a fist. With these living tools he reached into the marble and worked the stone as if it were clay, chopping, stroking, carving, polishing. And from the stone a body began to rise as Aphrodite had risen from the white foam of the sea.

He never knew when he had finished. He had not eaten for three days. His brain was on fire, his hands flying. He had finished carving; he was polishing the marble girl now with delicate files. Then, suddenly, he knew that it was finished. His head felt full of ashes; his hands hung like lumps of meat. He fell onto his pallet and was drowned in sleep.

He awoke in the middle of the night. The goddess was standing near his bed, he saw. Had she come to pose for him again? It was too late. Then he saw that it was not Aphrodite, but the marble figure standing in the center of the room, the white marble gathering all the moonlight to her. She shone in the darkness, looking as though she were trying to leap from the pediment.

He went to the statue and tried to find something unfinished, a spot he could work on. But there was nothing. She was complete. Perfect. A masterwork. Every line of her drawn taut by his own strength stretched to the breaking point, the curvings of her richly rounded with all the love he had never given to a human being. There she was, an image of Aphrodite. But no Aphrodite. She was herself, a marble girl, modeled after the goddess, but different; younger; human.

"You are Galatea," he said. "That is your name."

He went to a carved wooden box and took out jewels that had belonged to his mother. He decked Galatea in sapphires and diamonds. Then he sat at the foot of the statue, looking at it, until the sun came up. The birds sang, a donkey brayed; he heard the shouting of children, the barking of dogs. He sat there, looking at her. All that day he sat, and all that night. Still he had not eaten. And now it seemed that all the other marble figures in the room were swaying closer, were shadows crowding about, threatening him.

She did not move. She stood there, tall, radiant. His mother's jewels sparkled on her throat and on her arms. Her marble foot spurned the pediment.

Then Aphrodite herself stepped into the room. She said, "I have come to make you keep your promise, Pygmalion. You have finished the statue. You must marry."

"Whom?"

"Whomever you choose. Do you not wish to select your own bride?"

"Yes."

"Then choose. Choose any girl you like.

Whoever she is, whatever she is, she shall love you. For I am pleased with the image you have made of me. Choose."

"I choose—her," said Pygmalion, pointing to the statue.

"You may not."

"Why not?"

"She does not live. She is a statue."

"My statues will outlive all who are living now," said Pygmalion.

"That is just a way of speaking. She is not flesh and blood; she is a marble image. You must choose a living girl."

"I must choose where I love. I love her who is made in your image, goddess."

"It cannot be."

"You said, 'whoever she is, whatever she is . . . .' "

"Yes, but I did not mean a statue."

"I did. You call her lifeless, but I say my blood went into her making. My bones shaped hers. My fingers loved her surfaces. I polished her with all my knowledge, all my wit. She has seen all my strength, all my weakness, she has watched me sleep, played with my dreams. We *are* wed, Aphrodite, in a fatal incomplete way. Please, dear goddess, give her to me."

"Impossible."

"You are a goddess. Nothing is impossible."

"I am the Goddess of Love. There is no love without life."

"There is no life without love. I know how you can do it. Look . . . I stand here. I place my arm about her; my face against hers. Now, use your power, turn me to marble too. We shall be frozen together in this moment of time, embracing each other through eternity. This will suffice. For I tell you that without her my brain is ash, my hands are meat; I do not wish to breathe, to see, to be."

Aphrodite, despite herself, was warmed by his pleas. After all, he had made the statue in her image. It was pleasing to know that her beauty, even cast in lifeless marble, could still drive a young man mad.

"You are mad," she said. "Quite mad. But in people like you, I suppose, it is called inspiration. Very well, young sir, put your arms about her again."

Pygmalion embraced the cold marble. He kissed the beautiful stiff lips. And then he felt the stone flush with warmth. He felt the hard polished marble turn to warm silky flesh. He felt the mouth grow warm and move against his. He felt arms come up and hug him tight. He was holding a live girl in his arms.

He stepped off the pediment, holding her hand. She stepped after him. They fell on their knees before Aphrodite and thanked her for her gift.

"Rise, beautiful ones," she said. "It is the morning of love. Go to my temple, adorn it with garlands. You, Pygmalion, set about the altar those clever little dolls of me you have made. Thank me loudly for my blessings for I fear the mothers of Cyprus will not be singing my praises so ardently for some time."

She left. Galatea looked about the great dusty studio, littered with tools, scraps of marble, and spillings of clay. She looked at Pygmalion—tousled, unshaven, with bloodshot eyes and stained tunic—and said, "Now, dear husband, it's my turn to work on you." □□

Gods and Mortals

Adonis (ə don′is, ə dōn′is), an extremely handsome young man, with whom Aphrodite once fell in love. Killed by a wild boar while hunting, Adonis was deeply mourned by the goddess.

Galatea (gal′ə tē′ə)

Narcissus (när sis′əs), a young man so proud of his handsome appearance that he offended Aphrodite. His punishment was to fall helplessly in love with his own reflection in a pool. He remained rooted to that place, gazing at himself, until he was finally transformed into the flower that bears his name.

Pygmalion (pig mā′lē ən)

Discussion

1. What causes Aphrodite to visit Pygmalion in a dream?

2. (a) What reason does Pygmalion give at first for not marrying? (b) Realizing that he must marry, Pygmalion makes one request of Aphrodite. What is it? (c) In his responses to Aphrodite, do you think Pygmalion is being sincere, or is he only trying to flatter the goddess, make excuses, and delay his wedding date? Explain.

3. How does Pygmalion change during the course of the story?

4. In this myth, as in the story of Midas, mortals have their wishes fulfilled. (a) Is Pygmalion's wish fulfilled in the way he expects? (b) Are the wishes of the Cyprus women fulfilled? Explain.

5. In his masterwork, Pygmalion accomplishes all he can ever hope to achieve as an artist. Do you think he will continue to carve statues? Why or why not?

7: Greek Myths

CONTENT REVIEW

1. Many of the myths explain natural phenomena. Where and how are each of the following explained: **(a)** earthquakes; **(b)** volcanic eruptions; **(c)** seasonal changes; **(d)** creation of various animals?

2. Reread the myths dealing with Zeus, Poseidon, and Hades (the "Persephone" myth), and think of other myths in which these gods are mentioned or appear briefly. Characterize each as best you can, keeping in mind—and making reference to—the part of the world which each rules.

3. Many mortals in this unit have a particular skill or are unusually clever. **(a)** In which stories does skill or cleverness lead to success? **(b)** In which stories does skill or cleverness lead to disaster? **(c)** How would you account for these different outcomes?

4. The introduction to this unit explains that the word *hero* was originally applied to a mortal who had a god as one parent and a human as the other, and who was unusually brave and strong. Discuss the extent to which Theseus meets these qualifications.

5. Both Pygmalion and Admetus ("The Fortunate King") are befriended by deities. How do they earn this friendship, and what is the result for each?

6. The ancient Greeks believed in "the golden mean,"— in being moderate and sensible in all things, in avoiding extremes and excess. Which of the myths in this unit seem to demonstrate this principle, by showing that moderation is good, or that excess is bad?

Unit 7, Test I
INTERPRETATION: NEW MATERIAL

Read the myth reprinted below. Then on a separate sheet of paper, write your answers to the questions that follow it.

Baucis and Philemon[1]

retold by Olivia Coolidge

One time Zeus and Hermes came down to earth in human form and traveled through a certain district, asking for food and shelter as they went. For a long time they found nothing but refusals from both rich and poor until at last they came to a little, one-room cottage rudely thatched with reeds from the nearby marsh, where dwelled a poor old couple, Baucis and Philemon.

The two had little to offer, since they lived entirely from the

---

"Baucis and Philemon" from *Greek Myths* by Olivia Coolidge. Copyright 1949 by Olivia E. Coolidge. Reprinted by permission of Houghton Mifflin Company.
1. *Baucis and Philemon* (bô′sis, fi lē′mon)

produce of their plot of land and a few goats, fowl, and pigs.
Nevertheless they were prompt to ask the strangers in and to set
their best before them. The couch that they pulled forward for
their guests was roughly put together from willow boughs, and
the cushions on it were stuffed with straw. One table leg had to
be propped up with a piece of broken pot, but Baucis scrubbed
the top with fragrant mint and set some water on the fire. Meanwhile Philemon ran out into the garden to fetch a cabbage and
then lifted down a piece of home-cured bacon from the blackened
beam where it hung. While these were cooking, Baucis set out her
best delicacies on the table. There were ripe olives, sour cherries
pickled in wine, fresh onions and radishes, cream cheese, and
eggs baked in the ashes of the fire. There was a big earthenware
bowl in the midst of the table to mix their crude, homemade wine
with water.

The second course had to be fruit, but there were nuts, figs,
dried dates, plums, grapes, and apples, for this was their best
season of the year. Philemon had even had it in mind to kill their
only goose for dinner, and there was a great squawking and
cackling that went on for a long time. Poor old Philemon wore
himself out trying to catch that goose, but somehow the animal
always got away from him until the guests bade him let it be, for
they were well served as it was. It was a good meal, and the old
couple kept pressing their guests to eat and drink, caring nothing
that they were now consuming in one day what would ordinarily
last them a week.

At last the wine sank low in the mixing bowl, and Philemon
rose to fetch some more. But to his astonishment as he lifted the
wineskin to pour, he found the bowl was full again as though it
had not been touched at all. Then he knew the two strangers must
be gods, and he and Baucis were awed and afraid. But the gods
smiled kindly at them, and the younger, who seemed to do most
of the talking, said, "Philemon, you have welcomed us beneath
your roof this day when richer men refused us shelter. Be sure
those shall be punished who would not help the wandering stranger, but you shall have whatever reward you choose. Tell us what
you will have."

The old man thought for a little with his eyes bent on the
ground, and then he said: "We have lived together here for many
years, happy even though the times have been hard. But never yet
did we see fit to turn a stranger from our gate or to seek a reward
for entertaining him. To have spoken with the immortals face to
face is a thing few men can boast of. In this small cottage,
humble though it is, the gods have sat at meat. It is as unworthy
of the honor as we are. If, therefore, you will do something for
us, turn this cottage into a temple where the gods may always be

served and where we may live out the remainder of our days in worship of them."

"You have spoken well," said Hermes, "and you shall have your wish. Yet is there not anything that you would desire for yourselves?"

Philemon thought again at this, stroking his straggly beard, and he glanced over at old Baucis with her thin, grey hair and her rough hands as she served at the table, her feet bare on the floor of trodden earth. "We have lived together for many years," he said again, "and in all that time there has never been a word of anger between us. Now, at last, we are growing old and our long companionship is coming to an end. It is the only thing that has helped us in the bad times and the source of our joy in the good. Grant us this one request, that when we come to die, we may perish in the same hour and neither of us be left without the other."

He looked at Baucis and she nodded in approval, so the old couple turned their eyes on the gods.

"It shall be as you desire," said Hermes. "Few men would have made such a good and moderate request."

Thereafter the house became a temple, and the neighbors, amazed at the change, came often to worship and left offerings for the support of the aged priest and priestess there. For many years Baucis and Philemon lived in peace, passing from old to extreme old age. At last, they were so old and bowed that it seemed they could only walk at all if they clutched one another. But still every evening they would shuffle a little way down the path that they might turn and look together at the beautiful little temple and praise the gods for the honor bestowed on them. One evening it took them longer than ever to reach the usual spot, and there they turned arm in arm to look back, thinking perhaps that it was the last time their limbs would support them so far. There as they stood, each one felt the other stiffen and change and only had time to turn and say once, "Farewell," before they disappeared. In their place stood two tall trees growing closely side by side with branches interlaced. They seemed to nod and whisper to each other in the passing breeze. □□

1. The two gods involved in this selection are (a) Ares and Hermes; (b) Hermes and Apollo; (c) Zeus and Hermes; (d) Apollo and Zeus.

2. In what form did the two gods come down to earth?

3. As they traveled, the gods were looking for (a) someone to bow down and worship them; (b) the most beautiful woman on the earth; (c) temples that had been built in their honor; (d) food and shelter.

4. Baucis and Philemon lived on (a) the sale of their livestock; (b) their animals and their land; (c) gifts from their children; (d) Philemon's work as a carpenter.

5. Baucis and Philemon offered their guests (a) lodging for the night; (b) a donkey to carry their belongings for them; (c) a fine woodcarving that Philemon had made; (d) a large meal.

6. At first the old couple thought that their guests were (a) gods; (b) officials from the village; (c) long-forgotten friends of theirs; (d) passing strangers.

7. What did Baucis and Philemon realize when the wine bowl was suddenly full again?

8. Why did the guests want to give some reward to Baucis and Philemon? (a) Because they had given shelter to wandering strangers; (b) because they had been properly respectful to the gods; (c) because they were getting too old to take care of themselves; (d) because they were very poor.

9. When the guests told Baucis and Philemon that they could have whatever gift they wanted, the first thing they asked for was (a) that their cottage be turned into a temple; (b) that the gods would visit them again; (c) that they might never have to go hungry; (d) that they could die together.

10. When were Baucis and

Philemon transformed into trees? (a) Immediately after the gods left; (b) as soon as they had built a temple to the gods; (c) after a year; (d) after many years.

11. As trees, the two stood "closely side by side with branches interlaced." This symbolizes that (a) neither tree could support its weight without help from the other; (b) Baucis and Philemon were not afraid to die; (c) Baucis and Philemon would always be together; (d) Baucis and Philemon continued to worship the gods even after they were turned into trees.

12. List at least three virtues or good qualities that Baucis and Philemon possessed.

Unit 7, Test II
Composition

Choose one of the following assignments to write about. Assume you are writing for your classmates.

1. The gods and goddesses you have read about in this unit possess many of the same qualities or characteristics, both good and bad, that humans have. Using examples from the selections "Zeus," "Poseidon," and "Persephone," describe some of these human characteristics displayed by the gods.

2. Theseus's punishments of the giants along the road are

examples of poetic justice because they are punishments that are particularly appropriate to the situations. Which of the situations below involve poetic justice? Choose two that you think do, and explain why you think so. [Hint: Remember that poetic justice can involve appropriate rewards as well as appropriate punishments.]

   a. Midas receiving the golden touch

   b. Icarus falling to his death

   c. Baucis and Philemon being changed into interlaced trees

   d. Alcestis in "The Fortunate King" dying in place of Admetus

3. One of the virtues most admired by the ancient Greeks was hospitality—that is, generous treatment of guests or strangers who come to one's door. Describe two situations you have read about in this unit in which characters have acted hospitably, and explain how these characters are rewarded for their generosity.

4. Write a brief character sketch of Theseus, describing several outstanding traits that you think he possesses. Back up your opinions by presenting examples from the story that reveal those traits.

"I see the eight of us . . . as if we were a little piece

of blue heaven, surrounded by heavy black rain clouds.

The round, clearly defined spot where we stand

is still safe, but the clouds gather more closely about us

and the circle which separates us from the

approaching danger closes more and more tightly."

THE DIARY
OF
ANNE FRANK

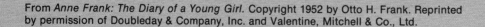

Introduction

When Anne Frank was thirteen years old, her family had to leave their home in Amsterdam to take refuge in a hidden apartment. The Franks were Jews, and no Jew was safe in lands controlled by the Nazis.

Earlier Otto Frank, his wife Edith, and their two daughters Margot and Anne had fled Frankfort, Germany. In Amsterdam Mr. Frank became an importer for Travis, Inc. In May, 1940, the Nazi army captured the Netherlands, and in July, 1942, the Franks were driven into hiding to escape persecution.

On her thirteenth birthday Anne's father presented her with a diary. Into the diary Anne recorded the hopes, fears, joys, and frustrations of living for twenty-five months in cramped quarters under constant tension. That diary, on which this drama is based, remains a living tribute to the dignity, courage, and perseverance of the human spirit.

The Diary of Anne Frank

Dramatized by

Frances Goodrich and Albert Hackett
(based upon the book, *Anne Frank: The Diary of a Young Girl*)

CHARACTERS

MR. OTTO FRANK (frängk)

MIEP (mēp) GIES (Hēs)

MRS. PETRONELLA (pet′rə nel′ə) VAN DAAN (fän dän′)

MR. VAN DAAN

PETER VAN DAAN

MRS. EDITH FRANK

MARGOT (mär′gət) FRANK

ANNE FRANK

MR. KRALER (krä′lər)

MR. DUSSEL (düs′əl)

The Time: During the years of World War II and immediately thereafter. The Place: Amsterdam. There are two acts.

ACT ONE

SCENE ONE

The scene remains the same throughout the play. It is the top floor of a warehouse and office building in Amsterdam, Holland. The sharply peaked roof of the building is outlined against a sea of other rooftops, stretching away into the distance. Nearby is the belfry of a church tower, the Westertoren, whose carillon rings out the hours. Occasionally faint sounds float up from below: the voices of children playing in the street, the tramp of marching feet, a boat whistle from the canal.

The three rooms of the top floor and a small attic space above are exposed to our view. The largest of the rooms is in the center, with two small rooms, slightly raised, on either side. On the right[1] is a bathroom, out of sight. A narrow steep flight of stairs at the back leads up to the attic. The rooms are sparsely furnished with a few chairs, cots, a table or two. The windows are painted over, or covered with makeshift blackout curtains. In the main room there is a sink, a gas ring for cooking, and a woodburning stove for warmth.

The room on the left is hardly more than a closet. There is a skylight in the sloping ceiling. Directly under this room is a small steep stairwell, with steps leading down to a door. This is the only entrance from the building below. When the door is opened we see that it has been concealed on the outer side by a bookcase attached to it.

The curtain rises on an empty stage. It is late afternoon, November, 1945.

The rooms are dusty, the curtains in rags. Chairs and tables are overturned.

The door at the foot of the small stairwell swings open. MR. FRANK *comes up the steps into view. He is a gentle, cultured European in his middle years. There is still a trace of a German accent in his speech.*

He stands looking slowly around, making a supreme effort at self-control. He is weak, ill. His clothes are threadbare.

After a second he drops his rucksack on the couch and moves slowly about. He opens the door to one of the smaller rooms, and then abruptly closes it again, turning away. He goes to the window at the back, looking off at the Westertoren as its carillon strikes the hour of six; then he moves restlessly on.

From the street below we hear the sound of a barrel organ and children's voices at play. There is a many-colored scarf hanging from a nail. MR. FRANK *takes it, putting it around his neck. As he starts back for his rucksack, his eye is caught by something lying on the floor. It is a woman's white glove. He holds it in his hand and suddenly all of his self-control is gone. He breaks down, crying.*

We hear footsteps on the stairs. MIEP GIES *comes up, looking for* MR. FRANK. MIEP *is a Dutch girl of about twenty-two. She wears a coat and hat, ready to go home. She is pregnant. Her attitude toward* MR. FRANK *is protective, compassionate.*

MIEP. Are you all right, Mr. Frank?

MR. FRANK *(quickly controlling himself).* Yes, Miep, yes.

MIEP. Everyone in the office has gone home . . . It's after six. *(Then pleading)* Don't stay up here, Mr. Frank. What's the use of torturing yourself like this?

MR. FRANK. I've come to say good-by . . . I'm leaving here, Miep.

MIEP. What do you mean? Where are you going? Where?

---

1. *On the right.* Stage directions are given from the actor's viewpoint. It is the *actor's* right, not that of the audience, that is meant here.

MR. FRANK. I don't know yet. I haven't decided.

MIEP. Mr. Frank, you can't leave here! This is your home! Amsterdam is your home. Your business is here, waiting for you . . . You're needed here . . . Now that the war is over, there are things that . . .

MR. FRANK. I can't stay in Amsterdam, Miep. It has too many memories for me. Everywhere there's something . . . the house we lived in . . . the school . . . that street organ playing out there . . . I'm not the person you used to know, Miep. I'm a bitter old man. *(Breaking off)* Forgive me. I shouldn't speak to you like this . . . after all that you did for us . . . the suffering . . .

MIEP. No. No. It wasn't suffering. You can't say we suffered. *(As she speaks, she straightens a chair which is overturned.)*

MR. FRANK. I know what you went through, you and Mr. Kraler. I'll remember it as long as I live. *(He gives one last look around.)* Come, Miep. *(He starts for the steps, then remembers his rucksack, going back to get it.)*

MIEP *(hurrying up to a cupboard)*. Mr. Frank, did you see? There are some of your papers here. *(She brings a bundle of papers to him.)* We found them in a heap of rubbish on the floor . . . after you left.

MR. FRANK. Burn them. *(He opens his rucksack to put the glove in it.)*

MIEP. But, Mr. Frank, there are letters, notes . . .

MR. FRANK. Burn them. All of them.

MIEP. Burn *this?* *(She hands him a paper-bound notebook.)*

MR. FRANK *(quietly)*. Anne's diary. *(He opens the diary and begins to read.)* "Monday, the sixth of July, nineteen forty-two." *(To MIEP)* Nineteen forty-two. Is it possible, Miep? . . . Only three years ago. *(As he continues his reading, he sits down on the couch.)* "Dear Diary, since you and I are going to be great friends, I will start by telling you about myself. My name is Anne Frank. I am thirteen years old. I was born in Germany the twelfth of June, nineteen twenty-nine. As my family is Jewish, we emigrated to Holland when Hitler came to power."

(As MR. FRANK reads on, another voice joins his, as if coming from the air. It is ANNE'S VOICE.)

MR. FRANK *and* ANNE. "My father started a business, importing spice and herbs. Things went well for us until nineteen forty. Then the war came, and the Dutch capitulation, followed by the arrival of the Germans. Then things got very bad for the Jews."

(MR. FRANK'S VOICE dies out. ANNE'S VOICE continues alone. The lights dim slowly to darkness. The curtain falls on the scene.)

ANNE'S VOICE. You could not do this and you could not do that. They forced Father out of his business. We had to wear yellow stars. I had to turn in my bike. I couldn't go to a Dutch school any more. I couldn't go to the movies, or ride in an automobile, or even on a streetcar, and a million other things. But somehow we children still managed to have fun. Yesterday Father told me we were going into hiding. Where, he wouldn't say. At five o'clock this morning Mother woke me and told me to hurry and get dressed. I was to put on as many clothes as I could. It would look too suspicious if we walked along carrying suitcases. It wasn't until we were on our way that I learned where we were going. Our hiding place was to be upstairs in the building where Father used to have his business. Three other people were coming in with us . . . the Van Daans and their son Peter . . . Father knew the Van Daans but we had never met them . . .

(During the last lines the curtain rises on the scene. The lights dim on. ANNE'S VOICE *fades out.)*

Discussion

1. (a) What information do you get about Anne from the first entry in the diary? (b) What do you learn about her father? (c) What information does the diary give you about the war and its effect on the Jews?

2. What reason does Mr. Frank give Miep for his decision to leave Amsterdam?

3. (a) What is the time setting for this scene? (b) What is the general appearance of the rooms?

SCENE TWO

It is early morning, July, 1942. The rooms are bare, as before, but they are now clean and orderly.

MR. VAN DAAN, *a tall, portly man in his late forties, is in the main room, pacing up and down, nervously smoking a cigarette. His clothes and overcoat are expensive and well cut.*

MRS. VAN DAAN *sits on the couch, clutching her possessions, a hatbox, bags, etc. She is a pretty woman in her early forties. She wears a fur coat over her other clothes.*

PETER VAN DAAN *is standing at the window of the room on the right, looking down at the street below. He is a shy, awkward boy of sixteen. He wears a cap, a raincoat, and long Dutch trousers, like "plus fours." At his feet is a black case, a carrier for his cat.*

The yellow Star of David[1] is conspicuous on all of their clothes.

MRS. VAN DAAN *(rising, nervous, excited).* Something's happened to them! I know it!

MR. VAN DAAN. Now, Kerli![2]

MRS. VAN DAAN. Mr. Frank said they'd be here at seven o'clock. He said . . .

MR. VAN DAAN. They have two miles to walk. You can't expect . . .

MRS. VAN DAAN. They've been picked up. That's what's happened. They've been taken . . .

*(*MR. VAN DAAN *indicates that he hears someone coming.)*

MR. VAN DAAN. You see?

*(*PETER *takes up his carrier and his schoolbag, etc. and goes into the main room as* MR. FRANK *comes up the stairwell from below.* MR. FRANK *looks much younger now. His movements are brisk, his manner confident. He wears an overcoat and carries his hat and a small cardboard box. He crosses to the* VAN DAANS, *shaking hands with each of them.)*

MR. FRANK. Mrs. Van Daan, Mr. Van Daan, Peter. *(Then, in explanation of their lateness)* There were too many of the Green Police[3] on the streets . . . We had to take the long way around.

(Up the steps come MARGOT FRANK, MRS. FRANK, MIEP—*not pregnant now—and* MR. KRALER. *All of them carry bags, packages, and so forth. The Star of David is conspicu-*

---

1. *Star of David*, a six-pointed star, a religious symbol of the Jewish people. In Nazi-occupied countries all Jews were required to wear a Star of David prominently displayed on their clothing.
2. *Kerli* (ker′lē)
3. *Green police*, a branch of the Nazi police who wore green uniforms.

ous on all of the FRANKS' *clothing.* MARGOT *is eighteen, beautiful, quiet, shy.* MRS. FRANK *is a young mother, gently bred, reserved. She, like* MR. FRANK, *has a slight German accent.* MR. KRALER *is a Dutchman, dependable, kindly.*

As MR. KRALER *and* MIEP *go upstage[4] to put down their parcels,* MRS. FRANK *turns back to call* ANNE.*)*

MRS. FRANK. Anne?

*(*ANNE *comes running up the stairs. She is thirteen, quick in her movements, interested in everything, mercurial in her emotions. She wears a cape, long wool socks and carries a schoolbag.)*

MR. FRANK *(introducing them).* My wife, Edith. Mr. and Mrs. Van Daan *(*MRS. FRANK *hurries over, shaking hands with them.)* . . . their son, Peter . . . my daughters, Margot and Anne.

*(*ANNE *gives a polite little curtsy as she shakes* MR. VAN DAAN'S *hand. Then she immediately starts off on a tour of investigation of her new home, going upstairs to the attic room.*

MIEP *and* MR. KRALER *are putting the various things they have brought on the shelves.)*

MR. KRALER. I'm sorry there is still so much confusion.

MR. FRANK. Please. Don't think of it. After all, we'll have plenty of leisure to arrange everything ourselves.

MIEP *(to* MRS. FRANK*).* We put the stores of food you sent in here. Your drugs are here . . . soap, linen here.

MR. FRANK. Thank you, Miep.

MIEP. I made up the beds . . . the way Mr. Frank and Mr. Kraler said. *(She starts out.)* I have to hurry. I've got to go to the other side of town to get some ration books[5] for you.

MRS. VAN DAAN. Ration books? If they see our names on ration books, they'll know we're here.

MR. KRALER. There isn't anything . . .

MIEP. Don't worry. Your names won't be on them. *(As she hurries out)* I'll be up later. } *(Together)*

MR. FRANK. Thank you, Miep.

MRS. FRANK *(to* MR. KRALER*).* It's illegal, then, the ration books? We've never done anything illegal.

MR. FRANK. We won't be living here exactly according to regulations.

(As MR. KRALER *reassures* MRS. FRANK, *he takes various small things, such as matches, soap, etc., from his pockets, handing them to her.)*

MR. KRALER. This isn't the black market, Mrs. Frank. This is what we call the white market[6] . . . helping all of the hundreds and hundreds who are hiding out in Amsterdam.

(The carillon is heard playing the quarter-hour before eight. MR. KRALER *looks at his watch.* ANNE *stops at the window as she comes down the stairs.)*

ANNE. It's the Westertoren!

MR. KRALER. I must go. I must be out of here and downstairs in the office before the workmen get here. *(He starts for the stairs leading out.)* Miep or I, or both of us, will be up each day to bring you food and news and find out what your needs are. Tomorrow I'll get you a better bolt for the door at the foot of the stairs. It needs a bolt that you can throw yourself and open

---

4. *upstage,* toward the back of the stage. *Down,* or *downstage,* means toward the front of the stage.
5. *ration books,* books of coupons which allowed the bearer to buy a fixed amount of provisions or food.
6. *black market . . . white market.* Black market goods are sold illegally, usually at a very high price. The goods the Franks were receiving (white market) were donated by people wishing to help the Jews.

only at our signal. *(To* MR. FRANK*)* Oh . . . You'll tell them about the noise?

MR. FRANK. I'll tell them.

MR. KRALER. Good-by then for the moment. I'll come up again, after the workmen leave.

MR. FRANK. Good-by, Mr. Kraler.

MRS. FRANK *(shaking his hand).* How can we thank you?

(The others murmur their good-bys.)

MR. KRALER. I never thought I'd live to see the day when a man like Mr. Frank would have to go into hiding. When you think—

(He breaks off, going out. MR. FRANK *follows him down the steps, bolting the door after him. In the interval before he returns,* PETER *goes over to* MARGOT, *shaking hands with her. As* MR. FRANK *comes back up the steps,* MRS. FRANK *questions him anxiously.)*

MRS. FRANK. What did he mean, about the noise?

MR. FRANK. First let us take off some of these clothes.

(They all start to take off garment after garment. On each of their coats, sweaters, blouses, suits, dresses, is another yellow Star of David. MR. *and* MRS. FRANK *are underdressed quite simply. The others wear several things—sweaters, extra dresses, bathrobes, aprons, nightgowns, etc.)*

MR. VAN DAAN. It's a wonder we weren't arrested, walking along the streets . . . Petronella with a fur coat in July . . . and that cat of Peter's crying all the way.

ANNE *(as she is removing a pair of panties).* A cat?

MRS. FRANK *(shocked).* Anne, please!

ANNE. It's all right. I've got on three more.

(She pulls off two more. Finally, as they have all removed their surplus clothes, they look to MR. FRANK, *waiting for him to speak.)*

MR. FRANK. Now. About the noise. While the men are in the building below, we must have complete quiet. Every sound can be heard down there, not only in the workrooms, but in the offices too. The men come at about eight-thirty, and leave at about five-thirty. So, to be perfectly safe, from eight in the morning until six in the evening we must move only when it is necessary, and then in stockinged feet. We must not speak above a whisper. We must not run any water. We cannot use the sink, or even, forgive me, the w.c.[7] The pipes go down through the workrooms. It would be heard. No trash . . . (MR. FRANK *stops abruptly as he hears the sound of marching feet from the street below. Everyone is motionless, paralyzed with fear.* MR. FRANK *goes quietly into the room on the right to look down out of the window.* ANNE *runs after him, peering out with him. The tramping feet pass without stopping. The tension is relieved.* MR. FRANK, *followed by* ANNE, *returns to the main room and resumes his instructions to the group.*) . . . No trash must ever be thrown out which might reveal that someone is living up here . . . not even a potato paring. We must burn everything in the stove at night. This is the way we must live until it is over, if we are to survive.

(There is silence for a second.)

MRS. FRANK. Until it is over.

MR. FRANK (*reassuringly*). After six we can move about . . . we can talk and laugh and have our supper and read and play games . . . just as we would at home. (*He looks at his watch.*) And now I think it would be wise if we all went to our rooms, and were settled before eight o'clock. Mrs. Van Daan, you and your husband will be upstairs. I regret that there's no place up there for Peter. But he will be here, near us. This will be our common room, where we'll meet to talk and eat and read, like one family.

MR. VAN DAAN. And where do you and Mrs. Frank sleep?

MR. FRANK. This room is also our bedroom.

MRS. VAN DAAN. That isn't right. We'll sleep here and you take the room upstairs. } *(Together)*

MR. VAN DAAN. It's your place.

MR. FRANK. Please. I've thought this out for weeks. It's the best arrangement. The only arrangement.

MRS. VAN DAAN (*to* MR. FRANK). Never, never can we thank you. (*Then to* MRS. FRANK) I don't know what would have happened to us, if it hadn't been for Mr. Frank.

MR. FRANK. You don't know how your husband helped me when I came to this country . . . knowing no one . . . not able to speak the language. I can never repay him for that. (*Going to* VAN DAAN) May I help you with your things?

MR. VAN DAAN. No. No. (*To* MRS. VAN DAAN) Come along, *liefje.*[8]

MRS. VAN DAAN. You'll be all right, Peter? You're not afraid?

PETER (*embarrassed*). Please, Mother.

(They start up the stairs to the attic room above. MR. FRANK *turns to* MRS. FRANK.)

MR. FRANK. You too must have some rest, Edith. You didn't close your eyes last night. Nor you, Margot.

ANNE. I slept, Father. Wasn't that funny? I knew it was the last night in my own bed, and yet I slept soundly.

MR. FRANK. I'm glad, Anne. Now you'll be

---

7. *w. c.*, water closet, the bathroom.
8. *liefje* (lēf′Hyə), darling.

able to help me straighten things in here. *(To* MRS. FRANK *and* MARGOT*)* Come with me . . . You and Margot rest in this room for the time being. *(He picks up their clothes, starting for the room on the right.)*

MRS. FRANK. You're sure . . . ? I could help . . . And Anne hasn't had her milk . . .

MR. FRANK. I'll give it to her. *(To* ANNE *and* PETER*)* Anne, Peter . . . it's best that you take off your shoes now, before you forget. *(He leads the way to the room, followed by* MARGOT*.)*

MRS. FRANK. You're sure you're not tired, Anne?

ANNE. I feel fine. I'm going to help Father.

MRS. FRANK. Peter, I'm glad you are to be with us.

PETER. Yes, Mrs. Frank.

*(*MRS. FRANK *goes to join* MR. FRANK *and* MARGOT*.)*

(During the following scene MR. FRANK *helps* MARGOT *and* MRS. FRANK *to hang up their clothes. Then he persuades them both to lie down and rest. The* VAN DAANS *in their room above settle themselves. In the main room* ANNE *and* PETER *remove their shoes.* PETER *takes his cat out of the carrier.)*

ANNE. What's your cat's name?

PETER. Mouschi.[9]

ANNE. Mouschi! Mouschi! Mouschi! *(She picks up the cat, walking away with it. To* PETER*)* I love cats. I have one . . . a darling little cat. But they made me leave her behind. I left some food and a note for the neighbors to take care of her . . . I'm going to miss her terribly. What is yours? A him or a her?

PETER. He's a tom. He doesn't like strangers. *(He takes the cat from her, putting it back in its carrier.)*

ANNE *(unabashed).* Then I'll have to stop being a stranger, won't I? Is he fixed?

PETER *(startled).* Huh?

ANNE. Did you have him fixed?

PETER. No.

ANNE. Oh, you ought to have him fixed—to keep him from—you know, fighting. Where did you go to school?

PETER. Jewish Secondary.

ANNE. But that's where Margot and I go! I never saw you around.

PETER. I used to see you . . . sometimes . . .

ANNE. You did?

PETER. . . . in the school yard. You were always in the middle of a bunch of kids. *(He takes a penknife from his pocket.)*

ANNE. Why didn't you ever come over?

PETER. I'm sort of a lone wolf. *(He starts to rip off his Star of David.)*

ANNE. What are you doing?

PETER. Taking it off.

ANNE. But you can't do that. They'll arrest you if you go out without your star.

(He tosses his knife on the table.)

PETER. Who's going out?

ANNE. Why, of course! You're right! Of course we don't need them any more. *(She picks up his knife and starts to take her star off.)* I wonder what our friends will think when we don't show up today?

PETER. I didn't have any dates with anyone.

ANNE. Oh, I did. I had a date with Jopie to go and play ping-pong at her house. Do you know Jopie de Waal?[10]

PETER. No.

ANNE. Jopie's my best friend. I wonder what she'll think when she telephones and

---

9. *Mouschi* (müs′kē)
10. *Jopie de Waal* (yo′pē də väl′)

there's no answer? . . . Probably she'll go over to the house . . . I wonder what she'll think . . . we left everything as if we'd suddenly been called away . . . breakfast dishes in the sink . . . beds not made . . . *(As she pulls off her star the cloth underneath shows clearly the color and form of the star.)* Look! It's still there! (PETER *goes over to the stove with his star.)* What're you going to do with yours?

PETER. Burn it.

ANNE. *(She starts to throw hers in, and cannot.)* It's funny, I can't throw mine away. I don't know why.

PETER. You can't throw . . . ? Something they branded you with . . . ? That they made you wear so they could spit on you?

ANNE. I know. I know. But after all, it *is* the Star of David, isn't it?

(In the bedroom, right, MARGOT *and* MRS. FRANK *are lying down.* MR. FRANK *starts quietly out.)*

PETER. Maybe it's different for a girl.

(MR. FRANK *comes into the main room.)*

MR. FRANK. Forgive me, Peter. Now let me see. We must find a bed for your cat. *(He goes to a cupboard.)* I'm glad you brought your cat. Anne was feeling so badly about hers. *(Getting a used small washtub.)* Here we are. Will it be comfortable in that?

PETER *(gathering up his things).* Thanks.

MR. FRANK *(opening the door of the room on the left).* And here is your room. But I warn you, Peter, you can't grow any more. Not an inch, or you'll have to sleep with your feet out of the skylight. Are you hungry?

PETER. No.

MR. FRANK. We have some bread and butter.

PETER. No, thank you.

MR. FRANK. You can have it for luncheon then. And tonight we will have a real supper . . . our first supper together.

PETER. Thanks. Thanks.

(He goes into his room. During the following scene he arranges his possessions in his new room.)

MR. FRANK. That's a nice boy, Peter.

ANNE. He's awfully shy, isn't he?

MR. FRANK. You'll like him, I know.

ANNE. I certainly hope so, since he's the only boy I'm likely to see for months and months.

(MR. FRANK *sits down, taking off his shoes.)*

MR. FRANK. Annele,[11] there's a box there. Will you open it?

(He indicates a carton on the couch. ANNE *brings it to the center table. In the street below there is the sound of children playing.)*

ANNE *(as she opens the carton).* You know the way I'm going to think of it here? I'm going to think of it as a boarding house. A very peculiar summer boarding house, like the one that we—*(She breaks off as she pulls out some photographs.)* Father! My movie stars! I was wondering where they were! I was looking for them this morning . . . and Queen Wilhelmina![12] How wonderful!

MR. FRANK. There's something more. Go on. Look further.

(He goes over to the sink, pouring a glass of milk from a thermos bottle.)

ANNE *(pulling out a pasteboard-bound book).* A diary! *(She throws her arms around her father.)* I've never had a diary. And I've always longed for one. *(She looks around the room.)* Pencil, pencil, pencil, pencil. *(She starts down the stairs.)* I'm going down to the office to get a pencil.

---

11. ***Annele*** (än′ə lə), little Anne. *Anneke* (än′ə kə), used later, is a similar term of endearment.
12. ***Queen Wilhelmina*** (wil′hel mē′nə), queen of the Netherlands from 1890 to 1948.

MR. FRANK. Anne! No!

(He goes after her, catching her by the arm and pulling her back.)

ANNE *(startled).* But there's no one in the building now.

MR. FRANK. It doesn't matter. I don't want you ever to go beyond that door.

ANNE *(sobered).* Never . . . ? Not even at night time, when everyone is gone? Or on Sundays? Can't I go down to listen to the radio?

MR. FRANK. Never. I am sorry, Anneke. It isn't safe. No, you must never go beyond that door.

(For the first time ANNE *realizes what "going into hiding" means.)*

ANNE. I see.

MR. FRANK. It'll be hard, I know. But always remember this, Anneke. There are no walls, there are no bolts, no locks that anyone can put on your mind. Miep will bring us books. We will read history, poetry, mythology. *(He gives her the glass of milk.)* Here's your milk. *(With his arm about her, they go over to the couch, sitting down side by side.)* As a matter of fact, between us, Anne, being here has certain advantages for you. For instance, you remember the battle you had with your mother the other day on the subject of overshoes? You said that you'd rather die than wear overshoes? But in the end you had to wear them? Well now, you see, for as long as we are here you will never have to wear overshoes! Isn't that good? And the coat that you inherited from Margot, you won't have to wear that any more. And the piano! You won't have to practice on the piano. I tell you, this is going to be a fine life for you!

*(*ANNE'S *panic is gone.* PETER *appears in the doorway of his room, with a saucer in his hand. He is carrying his cat.)*

PETER. I . . . I . . . I thought I'd better get some water for Mouschi before . . .

MR. FRANK. Of course.

(As he starts toward the sink the carillon begins to chime the hour of eight. He tiptoes to the window at the back and looks down at the street below. He turns to PETER, *indicating in pantomime that it is too late.* PETER *starts back for his room. He steps on a creaking board. The three of them are frozen for a minute in fear. As* PETER *starts away again,* ANNE *tiptoes over to him and pours some of the milk from her glass into the saucer for the cat.* PETER *squats on the floor, putting the milk before the cat.* MR. FRANK *gives* ANNE *his fountain pen, and then goes into the room at the right. For a second* ANNE *watches the cat, then she goes over to the center table, and opens her diary.*

In the room at the right, MRS. FRANK *has sat up quickly at the sound of the carillon.* MR. FRANK *comes in and sits down beside her on the settee, his arm comfortingly around her.*

Upstairs, in the attic room, MR. *and* MRS. VAN DAAN *have hung their clothes in the closet and are now seated on the iron bed.* MRS. VAN DAAN *leans back exhausted.* MR. VAN DAAN *fans her with a newspaper.*

ANNE *starts to write in her diary. The lights dim out, the curtain falls.*

In the darkness ANNE'S VOICE *comes to us again, faintly at first, and then with growing strength.)*

ANNE'S VOICE. I expect I should be describing what it feels like to go into hiding. But I really don't know yet myself. I only know it's funny never to be able to go outdoors . . . never to breathe fresh air . . . never to run and shout and jump. It's the silence in the nights that frightens me most. Every time I hear a creak in the house, or a step on the street outside, I'm sure they're coming for us. The days aren't so bad. At least we know that Miep and Mr. Kraler are down there below us in the office. Our protectors, we call them. I asked Father what would happen to them if the Nazis found out they were hiding us. Pim[13] said that they would suffer the same fate that we would . . . Imagine! They know this, and yet when they come up here, they're always cheerful and gay as if there were nothing in the world to bother them . . . Friday, the twenty-first of August, nineteen forty-two. Today I'm going to tell you our general news. Mother is unbearable. She insists on treating me like a baby, which I loathe. Otherwise things are going better. The weather is . . .

(*As* ANNE'S VOICE *is fading out the curtain rises on the scene.*)

---

13. *Pim,* a nickname Anne gave to her father.

Discussion

1. (a) What is the time setting for this scene? (b) What difference is there in the appearance of the rooms?

2. The refugees speak of their apartment as the Secret Annex. (a) What advantages does the annex have as a hiding place? (b) What are the disadvantages? (c) Why does Mr. Kraler want a better bolt at the foot of the stairs?

3. (a) What are your impressions of the Van Daans? (b) Why has Mr. Frank invited the Van Daans to join his family in hiding?

4. (a) What are your impressions of Mr. Frank? (b) How does he show that he hopes to keep life in the annex as normal as possible? (c) How does he try to reconcile Anne to "going into hiding"?

5. (a) Why does Peter burn the Star of David? (b) Why can't Anne do the same?

6. Reread the diary entry that concludes the scene. This is the second time so far that we have heard Anne's voice reading from her diary. (a) What might be the playwrights' purpose in including this entry? (b) What is signified by the dimming light and the curtain falling?

Vocabulary
Pronunciation, Dictionary

Use your Glossary to answer the following questions.

1. (a) What is another word for *rucksack?* (b) What language does *rucksack* come from?

2. Look up the word *portly* and read the synonym study that immediately follows it. In which of these sentences would *portly* be the correct word to use? (a) That little girl is much too _____; or (b) The _____ lawyer wore only expensive, hand-tailored suits.

3. Write the definition of *reserved* as it is used in this sentence: Her *reserved* manner in dealing with the unfair criticism won the admiration of all of her friends.

4. Use the word *unabashed* in a sentence that shows that you understand its meaning.

5. Read the complete Glossary entry for *emigrate.* In which of these sentences is *emigrate* used correctly? (a) Nate's family plans to *emigrate* to Canada next year; or (b) The potato famine in the 1840s caused many of the Irish to *emigrate* from their country.

6. Is the *th* in *loathe* pronounced like the *th* in *there* or the *th* in *theory?*

7. Does the accented syllable in *mercurial* rhyme with *her, sure,* or *tea?*

8. Use the word *capitulation* in a sentence that shows that you understand its meaning.

SCENE THREE

It is a little after six o'clock in the evening, two months later.

MARGOT is in the bedroom at the right, studying. MR. VAN DAAN is lying down in the attic room above.

The rest of the "family" is in the main room. ANNE and PETER sit opposite each other at the center table, where they have been doing their lessons. MRS. FRANK is on the couch. MRS. VAN DAAN is seated with her fur coat, on which she has been sewing, in her lap. None of them are wearing their shoes.

Their eyes are on MR. FRANK, waiting for him to give them the signal which will release them from their day-long quiet. MR. FRANK, his shoes in his hand, stands looking down out of the window at the back, watching to be sure that all of the workmen have left the building below.

After a few seconds of motionless silence, MR. FRANK turns from the window.

MR. FRANK *(quietly to the group)*. It's safe now. The last workman has left.
(There is an immediate stir of relief.)
ANNE *(Her pent-up energy explodes)*. WHEE!
MRS. FRANK *(startled, amused)*. Anne!
MRS. VAN DAAN. I'm first for the w.c.
(She hurries off to the bathroom. MRS. FRANK puts on her shoes and starts up to the sink to prepare supper. ANNE sneaks PETER'S shoes from under the table and hides them behind her back. MR. FRANK goes into MARGOT'S room.)
MR. FRANK *(to MARGOT)*. Six o'clock. School's over.
(MARGOT gets up, stretching. MR. FRANK sits down to put on his shoes. In the main room PETER tries to find his.)

PETER *(to ANNE)*. Have you seen my shoes?
ANNE *(innocently)*. Your shoes?
PETER. You've taken them, haven't you?
ANNE. I don't know what you're talking about.
PETER. You're going to be sorry!
ANNE. Am I?
(PETER goes after her. ANNE, with his shoes in her hand, runs from him, dodging behind her mother.)
MRS. FRANK *(protesting)*. Anne, dear!
PETER. Wait till I get you!
ANNE. I'm waiting! *(PETER makes a lunge for her. They both fall to the floor. PETER pins her down, wrestling with her to get the shoes.)* Don't! Don't! Peter, stop it. Ouch!
MRS. FRANK. Anne! . . . Peter!
(Suddenly PETER becomes self-conscious. He grabs his shoes roughly and starts for his room.)
ANNE *(following him)*. Peter, where are you going? Come dance with me.
PETER. I tell you I don't know how.
ANNE. I'll teach you.
PETER. I'm going to give Mouschi his dinner.
ANNE. Can I watch?
PETER. He doesn't like people around while he eats.
ANNE. Peter, please.
PETER. No!
(He goes into his room. ANNE slams his door after him.)
MRS. FRANK. Anne, dear, I think you shouldn't play like that with Peter. It's not dignified.
ANNE. Who cares if it's dignified? I don't want to be dignified.
(MR. FRANK and MARGOT come from the room on the right. MARGOT goes to help her mother. MR. FRANK starts for the center table to correct MARGOT'S school papers.)

MRS. FRANK (to ANNE). You complain that I don't treat you like a grownup. But when I do, you resent it.

ANNE. I only want some fun . . . someone to laugh and clown with . . . After you've sat still all day and hardly moved, you've got to have some fun. I don't know what's the matter with that boy.

MR. FRANK. He isn't used to girls. Give him a little time.

ANNE. Time? Isn't two months time? I could cry. (Catching hold of MARGOT.) Come on, Margot . . . dance with me. Come on, please.

MARGOT. I have to help with supper.

ANNE. You know we're going to forget how to dance . . . When we get out we won't remember a thing.

(She starts to sing and dance by herself. MR. FRANK takes her in his arms, waltzing with her. MRS. VAN DAAN comes in from the bathroom.)

MRS. VAN DAAN. Next? (She looks around as she starts putting on her shoes.) Where's Peter?

ANNE (as they are dancing). Where would he be!

MRS. VAN DAAN. He hasn't finished his lessons, has he? His father'll kill him if he catches him in there with that cat and his work not done. (MR. FRANK and ANNE finish their dance. They bow to each other with extravagant formality.) Anne, get him out of there, will you?

ANNE (at PETER'S door). Peter? Peter?

PETER (opening the door a crack). What is it?

ANNE. Your mother says to come out.

PETER. I'm giving Mouschi his dinner.

MRS. VAN DAAN. You know what your father says.

(She sits on the couch, sewing on the lining of her fur coat.)

PETER. For heaven's sake, I haven't even looked at him since lunch.

MRS. VAN DAAN. I'm just telling you, that's all.

ANNE. I'll feed him.

PETER. I don't want you in there.

MRS. VAN DAAN. Peter!

PETER (to ANNE). Then give him his dinner and come right out, you hear?

(He comes back to the table. ANNE shuts the door of PETER'S room after her and disappears behind the curtain covering his closet.)

MRS. VAN DAAN (to PETER). Now is that any way to talk to your little girl friend?

PETER. Mother . . . for heaven's sake . . . will you please stop saying that?

MRS. VAN DAAN. Look at him blush! Look at him!

PETER. Please! I'm not . . . anyway . . . let me alone, will you?

MRS. VAN DAAN. He acts like it was something to be ashamed of. It's nothing to be ashamed of, to have a little girl friend.

PETER. You're crazy. She's only thirteen.

MRS. VAN DAAN. So what? And you're sixteen. Just perfect. Your father's ten years older than I am. (To MR. FRANK) I warn you, Mr. Frank, if this war lasts much longer, we're going to be related and then . . .

MR. FRANK. Mazeltov![1]

MRS. FRANK (deliberately changing the conversation). I wonder where Miep is. She's usually so prompt.

(Suddenly everything else is forgotten as they hear the sound of an automobile coming to a screeching stop in the street below. They are tense, motionless in their terror. The car starts away. A wave of relief sweeps over

---

1. **Mazeltov** (mä′zəl tof), an expression used among Jews to express congratulations or wish good luck.

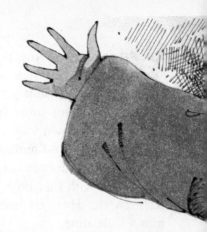

them. They pick up their occupations again. ANNE *flings open the door of* PETER'S *room, making a dramatic entrance. She is dressed in* PETER'S *clothes.* PETER *looks at her in fury. The others are amused.)*

ANNE. Good evening, everyone. Forgive me if I don't stay. *(She jumps up on a chair.)* I have a friend waiting for me in there. My friend Tom. Tom Cat. Some people say that we look alike. But Tom has the most beautiful whiskers, and I have only a little fuzz. I am hoping . . . in time . . .

PETER. All right, Mrs. Quack Quack!

ANNE *(outraged—jumping down).* Peter!

PETER. I heard about you . . . How you talked so much in class they called you Mrs. Quack Quack. How Mr. Smitter made you write a composition . . . "'Quack, quack,' said Mrs. Quack Quack."

ANNE. Well, go on. Tell them the rest. How it was so good he read it out loud to the class and then read it to all his other classes!

PETER. Quack! Quack! Quack . . . Quack . . . Quack . . .

(ANNE pulls off the coat and trousers.)

ANNE. You are the most intolerable, insufferable boy I've ever met!

(She throws the clothes down the stairwell. PETER goes down after them.)

PETER. Quack, quack, quack!

MRS. VAN DAAN *(to* ANNE*).* That's right, Anneke! Give it to him!

ANNE. With all the boys in the world . . . Why I had to get locked up with one like you! . . .

PETER. Quack, quack, quack, and from now on stay out of my room!

(As PETER *passes her,* ANNE *puts out her foot, tripping him. He picks himself up, and goes on into his room.)*

MRS. FRANK *(quietly).* Anne, dear . . .

your hair. *(She feels* ANNE'S *forehead.)* You're warm. Are you feeling all right?

ANNE. Please, Mother.

(She goes over to the center table, slipping into her shoes.)

MRS. FRANK *(following her).* You haven't a fever, have you?

ANNE *(pulling away).* No. No.

MRS. FRANK. You know we can't call a doctor here, ever. There's only one thing to do . . . watch carefully. Prevent an illness before it comes. Let me see your tongue.

ANNE. Mother, this is perfectly absurd.

MRS. FRANK. Anne, dear, don't be such a baby. Let me see your tongue. *(As* ANNE *refuses,* MRS. FRANK *appeals to* MR. FRANK.*)* Otto . . . ?

MR. FRANK. You hear your mother, Anne.

*(ANNE *flicks out her tongue for a second, then turns away.)*

MRS. FRANK. Come on—open up! *(As* ANNE *opens her mouth very wide)* You seem all right . . . but perhaps an aspirin . . .

MRS. VAN DAAN. For heaven's sake, don't give that child any pills. I waited for fifteen minutes this morning for her to come out of the w.c.

ANNE. I was washing my hair!

MRS. FRANK. I think there's nothing the matter with our Anne that a ride on her

bike, or a visit with her friend Jopie de-Waal wouldn't cure. Isn't that so, Anne?

(MR. VAN DAAN *comes down into the room. From outside we hear faint sounds of bombers going over and a burst of ack-ack.²*)

MR. VAN DAAN. Miep not come yet?

MRS. VAN DAAN. The workmen just left, a little while ago.

MR. VAN DAAN. What's for dinner tonight?

MRS. VAN DAAN. Beans.

MR. VAN DAAN. Not again!

MRS. VAN DAAN. Poor Putti!³ I know. But what can we do? That's all that Miep brought us.

(MR. VAN DAAN *starts to pace, his hands behind his back.* ANNE *follows behind him, imitating him.*)

ANNE. We are now in what is known as the "bean cycle." Beans boiled, beans *en casserole*,⁴ beans with strings, beans without strings . . .

(PETER *has come out of his room. He slides into his place at the table, becoming immediately absorbed in his studies.*)

MR. VAN DAAN *(to* PETER*).* I saw you . . . in there, playing with your cat.

MRS. VAN DAAN. He just went in for a second, putting his coat away. He's been out here all the time, doing his lessons.

MR. FRANK *(looking up from the paper).* Anne, you got an excellent in your history paper today . . . and very good in Latin.

ANNE *(sitting beside him).* How about algebra?

MR. FRANK. I'll have to make a confession. Up until now I've managed to stay ahead of you in algebra. Today you caught up with me. We'll leave it to Margot to correct.

ANNE. Isn't algebra *vile*, Pim!

---

2. *ack-ack,* antiaircraft fire.
3. *Putti* (pùt′ē)
4. *en casserole* (aN käs rôl′), prepared and served in a covered baking dish.

MR. FRANK. Vile!

MARGOT *(to* MR. FRANK*).* How did I do?

ANNE *(getting up).* Excellent, excellent, excellent, excellent!

MR. FRANK *(to* MARGOT*).* You should have used the subjunctive here . . .

MARGOT. Should I? . . . I thought . . . look here . . . I didn't use it here . . .

(The two become absorbed in the papers.)

ANNE. Mrs. Van Daan, may I try on your coat?

MRS. FRANK. No, Anne.

MRS. VAN DAAN *(giving it to* ANNE*).* It's all right . . . but careful with it. (ANNE *puts it on and struts with it.)* My father gave me that the year before he died. He always bought the best that money could buy.

ANNE. Mrs. Van Daan, did you have a lot of boy friends before you were married?

MRS. FRANK. Anne, that's a personal question. It's not courteous to ask personal questions.

MRS. VAN DAAN. Oh I don't mind. *(To* ANNE*)* Our house was always swarming with boys. When I was a girl we had . . .

MR. VAN DAAN. Oh, God. Not again!

MRS. VAN DAAN *(good-humored).* Shut up! *(Without a pause, to* ANNE. MR. VAN DAAN *mimics* MRS. VAN DAAN, *speaking the first few words in unison with her.)* One summer we had a big house in Hilversum.[5] The boys came buzzing round like bees around a jam pot. And when I was sixteen! . . . We were wearing our skirts very short those days and I had good-looking legs. *(She pulls up her skirt, going to* MR. FRANK.*)* I still have 'em. I may not be as pretty as I used to be, but I still have my legs. How about it, Mr. Frank?

MR. VAN DAAN. All right. All right. We see them.

MRS. VAN DAAN. I'm not asking you. I'm asking Mr. Frank.

PETER. Mother, for heaven's sake.

MRS. VAN DAAN. Oh, I embarrass you, do I? Well, I just hope the girl you marry has as good. *(Then to* ANNE*)* My father used to worry about me, with so many boys hanging round. He told me, if any of them gets fresh, you say to him . . . "Remember, Mr. So-and-So, remember I'm a lady."

ANNE. "Remember, Mr. So-and-So, remember I'm a lady."

(She gives MRS. VAN DAAN *her coat.)*

MR. VAN DAAN. Look at you, talking that way in front of her! Don't you know she puts it all down in that diary?

MRS. VAN DAAN. So, if she does? I'm only telling the truth!

*(*ANNE *stretches out, putting her ear to the floor, listening to what is going on below. The sound of the bombers fades away.)*

MRS. FRANK *(setting the table).* Would you mind, Peter, if I moved you over to the couch?

ANNE *(listening).* Miep must have the radio on.

*(*PETER *picks up his papers, going over to the couch beside* MRS. VAN DAAN.*)*

MR. VAN DAAN *(accusingly, to* PETER*).* Haven't you finished yet?

PETER. No.

MR. VAN DAAN. You ought to be ashamed of yourself.

PETER. All right. All right. I'm a dunce. I'm a hopeless case. Why do I go on?

MRS. VAN DAAN. You're not hopeless. Don't talk that way. It's just that you haven't anyone to help you, like the girls have. *(To* MR. FRANK*)* Maybe you could help him, Mr. Frank?

MR. FRANK. I'm sure that his father . . . ?

MR. VAN DAAN. Not me. I can't do any-

---

5. *Hilversum* (hil ́vər səm), a health resort and residential area some miles from Amsterdam.

thing with him. He won't listen to me. You go ahead . . . if you want.

MR. FRANK (going to PETER). What about it, Peter? Shall we make our school coeducational?

MRS. VAN DAAN (kissing MR. FRANK). You're an angel, Mr. Frank. An angel. I don't know why I didn't meet you before I met that one there. Here, sit down, Mr. Frank . . . (She forces him down on the couch beside PETER.) Now, Peter, you listen to Mr. Frank.

MR. FRANK. It might be better for us to go into Peter's room.

(PETER jumps up eagerly, leading the way.)

MRS. VAN DAAN. That's right. You go in there, Peter. You listen to Mr. Frank. Mr. Frank is a highly educated man.

(As MR. FRANK is about to follow PETER into his room, MRS. FRANK stops him and wipes the lipstick from his lips. Then she closes the door after them.)

ANNE (on the floor, listening). Shh! I can hear a man's voice talking.

MR. VAN DAAN (to ANNE). Isn't it bad enough here without your sprawling all over the place?

(ANNE sits up.)

MRS. VAN DAAN (to MR. VAN DAAN). If you didn't smoke so much, you wouldn't be so bad-tempered.

MR. VAN DAAN. Am I smoking? Do you see me smoking?

MRS. VAN DAAN. Don't tell me you've used up all those cigarettes.

MR. VAN DAAN. One package. Miep only brought me one package.

MRS. VAN DAAN. It's a filthy habit anyway. It's a good time to break yourself.

MR. VAN DAAN. Oh, stop it, please.

MRS. VAN DAAN. You're smoking up all our money. You know that, don't you?

MR. VAN DAAN. Will you shut up? (During this, MRS. FRANK and MARGOT have studiously kept their eyes down. But ANNE, seated on the floor, has been following the discussion interestedly. MR. VAN DAAN turns to see her staring up at him.) And what are you staring at?

ANNE. I never heard grownups quarrel before. I thought only children quarreled.

MR. VAN DAAN. This isn't a quarrel! It's a discussion. And I never heard children so rude before.

ANNE (rising, indignantly). I, rude!

MR. VAN DAAN. Yes!

MRS. FRANK (quickly). Anne, will you get me my knitting? (ANNE goes to get it.) I must remember, when Miep comes, to ask her to bring me some more wool.

MARGOT (going to her room). I need some hairpins and some soap. I made a list.

(She goes into her bedroom to get the list.)

MRS. FRANK (to ANNE). Have you some library books for Miep when she comes?

ANNE. It's a wonder that Miep has a life of her own, the way we make her run errands for us. Please, Miep, get me some starch. Please take my hair out and have it cut. Tell me all the latest news, Miep. (She goes over, kneeling on the couch beside MRS. VAN DAAN.) Did you know she was engaged? His name is Dirk, and Miep's afraid the Nazis will ship him off to Germany to work in one of their war plants. That's what they're doing with some of the young Dutchmen . . . they pick them up off the streets—

MR. VAN DAAN (interrupting). Don't you ever get tired of talking? Suppose you try keeping still for five minutes. Just five minutes.

(He starts to pace again. Again ANNE follows him, mimicking him. MRS. FRANK jumps up and takes her by the arm up to the sink, and gives her a glass of milk.)

MRS. FRANK. Come here, Anne. It's time for your glass of milk.

MR. VAN DAAN. Talk, talk, talk. I never heard such a child. Where is my . . . ? Every evening it's the same, talk, talk, talk. *(He looks around.)* Where is my . . . ?

MRS. VAN DAAN. What're you looking for?

MR. VAN DAAN. My pipe. Have you seen my pipe?

MRS. VAN DAAN. What good's a pipe? You haven't got any tobacco.

MR. VAN DAAN. At least I'll have something to hold in my mouth! *(Opening* MARGOT'S *bedroom door)* Margot, have you seen my pipe?

MARGOT. It was on the table last night.

*(*ANNE *puts her glass of milk on the table and picks up his pipe, hiding it behind her back.)*

MR. VAN DAAN. I know. I know. Anne, did you see my pipe? . . . Anne!

MRS. FRANK. Anne, Mr. Van Daan is speaking to you.

ANNE. Am I allowed to talk now?

MR. VAN DAAN. You're the most aggravating . . . The trouble with you is, you've been spoiled. What you need is a good old-fashioned spanking.

ANNE *(mimicking* MRS. VAN DAAN*).* "Remember, Mr. So-and-So, remember I'm a lady."

(She thrusts the pipe into his mouth, then picks up her glass of milk.)

MR. VAN DAAN *(restraining himself with difficulty).* Why aren't you nice and quiet like your sister Margot? Why do you have to show off all the time? Let me give you a little advice, young lady. Men don't like that kind of thing in a girl. You know that? A man likes a girl who'll listen to him once in a while . . . a domestic girl, who'll keep her house shining for her husband . . . who loves to cook and sew and . . .

ANNE. I'd cut my throat first! I'd open my veins! I'm going to be remarkable! I'm going to Paris . . .

MR. VAN DAAN *(scoffingly).* Paris!

ANNE. . . . to study music and art.

MR. VAN DAAN. Yeah! Yeah!

ANNE. I'm going to be a famous dancer or singer . . . or something wonderful.

(She makes a wide gesture, spilling the glass of milk on the fur coat in MRS. VAN DAAN'S *lap.* MARGOT *rushes quickly over with a towel.* ANNE *tries to brush the milk off with her skirt.)*

MRS. VAN DAAN. Now look what you've done . . . you clumsy little fool! My beautiful fur coat my father gave me . . .

ANNE. I'm so sorry.

MRS. VAN DAAN. What do you care? It isn't yours . . . So go on, ruin it! Do you know what that coat cost? Do you? And now look at it! Look at it!

ANNE. I'm very, very sorry.

MRS. VAN DAAN. I could kill you for this. I could just kill you!

*(*MRS. VAN DAAN *goes up the stairs, clutching the coat.* MR. VAN DAAN *starts after her.)*

MR. VAN DAAN. Petronella . . . *liefje! Liefje!* . . . Come back . . . the supper . . . come back!

MRS. FRANK. Anne, you must not behave in that way.

ANNE. It was an accident. Anyone can have an accident.

MRS. FRANK. I don't mean that. I mean the answering back. You must not answer back. They are our guests. We must always show the greatest courtesy to them. We're all living under terrible tension. *(She stops as* MARGOT *indicates that* VAN DAAN *can hear. When he is gone, she continues.)* That's why we must control ourselves . . . You don't hear Margot getting into arguments with them, do you? Watch Margot. She's always courteous with them. Never familiar. She keeps her distance. And they respect her for it. Try to be like Margot.

ANNE. And have them walk all over me, the way they do her? No, thanks!

MRS. FRANK. I'm not afraid that anyone is going to walk all over you, Anne. I'm afraid for other people, that you'll walk on them. I don't know what happens to you, Anne. You are wild, self-willed. If I had ever talked to my mother as you talk to me . . .

ANNE. Things have changed. People aren't like that any more. "Yes, Mother." "No, Mother." "Anything you say, Mother." I've got to fight things out for myself! Make something of myself!

MRS. FRANK. It isn't necessary to fight to do it. Margot doesn't fight, and isn't she . . .?

ANNE *(violently rebellious).* Margot! Margot! Margot! That's all I hear from everyone . . . how wonderful Margot is . . . "Why aren't you like Margot?"

MARGOT *(protesting).* Oh, come on, Anne, don't be so . . .

ANNE *(paying no attention).* Everything she does is right, and everything I do is wrong! I'm the goat around here! . . . You're all against me! . . . And you worst of all!

(She rushes off into her room and throws herself down on the settee, stifling her sobs. MRS. FRANK *sighs and starts toward the stove.)*

MRS. FRANK *(to* MARGOT*).* Let's put the soup on the stove . . . if there's anyone who cares to eat. Margot, will you take the bread out? *(*MARGOT *gets the bread from the cupboard.)* I don't know how we can go on living this way . . . I can't say a word to Anne . . . she flies at me . . .

MARGOT. You know Anne. In half an hour she'll be out here, laughing and joking.

MRS. FRANK. And . . . *(She makes a motion upwards, indicating the* VAN DAANS.*)* . . . I told your father it wouldn't work . . . but no . . . no . . . he had to ask them, he said . . . he owed it to him, he said. Well, he knows now that I was right! These quarrels! . . . This bickering!

MARGOT *(with a warning look).* Shush. Shush.

(The buzzer for the door sounds. MRS. FRANK *gasps, startled.)*

MRS. FRANK. Every time I hear that sound, my heart stops!

MARGOT *(starting for* PETER'S *door).* It's Miep. *(She knocks at the door.)* Father?

*(*MR. FRANK *comes quickly from* PETER'S *room.)*

MR. FRANK. Thank you, Margot. *(As he goes down the steps to open the outer door)* Has everyone his list?

MARGOT. I'll get my books. *(Giving her mother a list)* Here's your list. *(*MARGOT *goes into her and* ANNE'S *bedroom on the right.* ANNE *sits up, hiding her tears, as* MARGOT *comes in.)* Miep's here.

*(*MARGOT *picks up her books and goes back.* ANNE *hurries over to the mirror, smoothing her hair.)*

MR. VAN DAAN *(coming down the stairs).* Is it Miep?

MARGOT. Yes. Father's gone down to let her in.

MR. VAN DAAN. At last I'll have some cigarettes!

MRS. FRANK *(to* MR. VAN DAAN*).* I can't tell you how unhappy I am about Mrs. Van Daan's coat. Anne should never have touched it.

MR. VAN DAAN. She'll be all right.

MRS. FRANK. Is there anything I can do?

MR. VAN DAAN. Don't worry.

(He turns to meet MIEP. *But it is not* MIEP *who comes up the steps. It is* MR. KRALER, *followed by* MR. FRANK. *Their faces are grave.* ANNE *comes from the bedroom.* PETER *comes from his room.)*

MRS. FRANK. Mr. Kraler!

MR. VAN DAAN. How are you, Mr. Kraler?

MARGOT. This is a surprise.

MRS. FRANK. When Mr. Kraler comes, the sun begins to shine.

MR. VAN DAAN. Miep is coming?

MR. KRALER. Not tonight.

(KRALER goes to MARGOT and MRS. FRANK and ANNE, shaking hands with them.)

MRS. FRANK. Wouldn't you like a cup of coffee? . . . Or, better still, will you have supper with us?

MR. FRANK. Mr. Kraler has something to talk over with us. Something has happened, he says, which demands an immediate decision.

MRS. FRANK *(fearful).* What is it?

(MR. KRALER sits down on the couch. As he talks he takes bread, cabbages, milk, etc., from his briefcase, giving them to MARGOT and ANNE to put away.)

MR. KRALER. Usually, when I come up here, I try to bring you some bit of good news. What's the use of telling you the bad news when there's nothing that you can do about it? But today something has happened . . . Dirk . . . Miep's Dirk, you know, came to me just now. He tells me that he has a Jewish friend living near him. A dentist. He says he's in trouble. He begged me, could I do anything for this man? Could I find him a hiding place? . . . So I've come to you . . . I know it's a terrible thing to ask of you, living as you are, but would you take him in with you?

MR. FRANK. Of course we will.

MR. KRALER *(rising).* It'll be just for a night or two . . . until I find some other place. This happened so suddenly that I didn't know where to turn.

MR. FRANK. Where is he?

MR. KRALER. Downstairs in the office.

MR. FRANK. Good. Bring him up.

MR. KRALER. His name is Dussel . . . Jan Dussel.

MR. FRANK. Dussel . . . I think I know him.

MR. KRALER. I'll get him.

(He goes quickly down the steps and out. MR. FRANK *suddenly becomes conscious of the others.)*

MR. FRANK. Forgive me. I spoke without consulting you. But I knew you'd feel as I do.

MR. VAN DAAN. There's no reason for you to consult anyone. This is your place. You have a right to do exactly as you please. The only thing I feel . . . there's so little food as it is . . . and to take in another person . . .

(PETER turns away, ashamed of his father.)

MR. FRANK. We can stretch the food a little. It's only for a few days.

MR. VAN DAAN. You want to make a bet?

MRS. FRANK. I think it's fine to have him. But, Otto, where are you going to put him? Where?

PETER. He can have my bed. I can sleep on the floor. I wouldn't mind.

MR. FRANK. That's good of you, Peter. But your room's too small . . . even for *you.*

ANNE. I have a much better idea. I'll come in here with you and Mother, and Margot can take Peter's room and Peter can go in our room with Mr. Dussel.

MARGOT. That's right. We could do that.

MR. FRANK. No, Margot. You mustn't sleep in that room . . . neither you nor Anne. Mouschi has caught some rats in there. Peter's brave. He doesn't mind.

ANNE. Then how about *this?* I'll come in

here with you and Mother, and Mr. Dussel can have my bed.

MRS. FRANK. No. No. *No!* Margot will come in here with us and he can have her bed. It's the only way. Margot, bring your things in here. Help her, Anne.

(MARGOT *hurries into her room to get her things.*)

ANNE *(to her mother).* Why Margot? Why can't I come in here?

MRS. FRANK. Because it wouldn't be proper for Margot to sleep with a . . . Please, Anne. Don't argue. Please.

(ANNE *starts slowly away.*)

MR. FRANK *(to* ANNE). You don't mind sharing your room with Mr. Dussel, do you, Anne?

ANNE. No. No, of course not.

MR. FRANK. Good. (ANNE *goes off into her bedroom, helping* MARGOT. MR. FRANK *starts to search in the cupboards.*) Where's the cognac?

MRS. FRANK. It's there. But, Otto, I was saving it in case of illness.

MR. FRANK. I think we couldn't find a better time to use it. Peter, will you get five glasses for me?

(PETER *goes for the glasses.* MARGOT *comes out of her bedroom, carrying her possessions, which she hangs behind a curtain in the main room.* MR. FRANK *finds the cognac and pours it into the five glasses that* PETER *brings him.* MR. VAN DAAN *stands looking on sourly.* MRS. VAN DAAN *comes downstairs and looks around at all of the bustle.*)

MRS. VAN DAAN. What's happening? What's going on?

MR. VAN DAAN. Someone's moving in with us.

MRS. VAN DAAN. In here? You're joking.

MARGOT. It's only for a night or two . . . until Mr. Kraler finds him another place.

MR. VAN DAAN. Yeah! Yeah!

(MR. FRANK *hurries over as* MR. KRALER *and* DUSSEL *come up.* DUSSEL *is a man in his late fifties, meticulous, finicky . . . bewildered now. He wears a raincoat. He carries a briefcase, stuffed full, and a small medicine case.*)

MR. FRANK. Come in, Mr. Dussel.

MR. KRALER. This is Mr. Frank.

DUSSEL. Mr. Otto Frank?

MR. FRANK. Yes. Let me take your things. *(He takes the hat and briefcase, but* DUSSEL *clings to his medicine case.)* This is my wife Edith . . . Mr. and Mrs. Van Daan . . . their son, Peter . . . and my daughters, Margot and Anne.

(DUSSEL *shakes hands with everyone.*)

MR. KRALER. Thank you, Mr. Frank. Thank you all. Mr. Dussel, I leave you in good hands. Oh . . . Dirk's coat.

(DUSSEL *hurriedly takes off the raincoat, giving it to* MR. KRALER. *Underneath is his white dentist's jacket, with a yellow Star of David on it.*)

DUSSEL *(to* MR. KRALER*).* What can I say to thank you . . . ?

MRS. FRANK *(to* DUSSEL*).* Mr. Kraler and Miep . . . They're our life line. Without them we couldn't live.

MR. KRALER. Please, please. You make us seem very heroic. It isn't that at all. We simply don't like the Nazis. *(To* MR. FRANK, *who offers him a drink)* No, thanks. *(Then going on)* We don't like their methods. We don't like . . .

MR. FRANK *(smiling).* I know. I know. "No one's going to tell us Dutchmen what to do with our damn Jews!"

MR. KRALER *(to* DUSSEL*).* Pay no attention to Mr. Frank. I'll be up tomorrow to see that they're treating you right. *(To* MR. FRANK*)* Don't trouble to come down again. Peter will bolt the door after me, won't you, Peter?

PETER. Yes, sir.

MR. FRANK. Thank you, Peter. I'll do it.

MR. KRALER. Good night. Good night.

GROUP. Good night, Mr. Kraler. We'll see you tomorrow, etc., etc.

(MR. KRALER *goes out with* MR. FRANK. MRS. FRANK *gives each one of the "grownups" a glass of cognac.*)

MRS. FRANK. Please, Mr. Dussel, sit down.

(MR. DUSSEL *sinks into a chair.* MRS. FRANK *gives him a glass of cognac.*)

DUSSEL. I'm dreaming. I know it. I don't believe my eyes. Mr. Otto Frank here! *(To* MRS. FRANK*)* You're not in Switzerland then? A woman told me . . . She said she'd gone to your house . . . the door was open, everything was in disorder, dishes in the sink. She said she found a piece of paper in the wastebasket with an address scribbled on it . . . an address in Zurich. She said you must have escaped to Zurich.

ANNE. Father put that there purposely . . . just so people would think that very thing!

DUSSEL. And you've been *here* all the time?

MRS. FRANK. All the time . . . ever since July.

(ANNE *speaks to her father as he comes back.*)

ANNE. It worked, Pim . . . the address you left! Mr. Dussel says that people believe we escaped to Switzerland.

MR. FRANK. I'm glad . . . And now let's have a little drink to welcome Mr. Dussel. *(Before they can drink,* MR. DUSSEL *bolts his drink.* MR. FRANK *smiles and raises his glass.)* To Mr. Dussel. Welcome. We're very honored to have you with us.

MRS. FRANK. To Mr. Dussel, welcome.

(The VAN DAANS *murmur a welcome. The "grownups" drink.*)

MRS. VAN DAAN. Um. That was good.

MR. VAN DAAN. Did Mr. Kraler warn you that you won't get much to eat here? You can imagine . . . three ration books among the seven of us . . . and now you make eight.

(PETER *walks away, humiliated. Outside a street organ is heard dimly.*)

DUSSEL *(rising).* Mr. Van Daan, you don't realize what is happening outside that you should warn me of a thing like that. You don't realize what's going on . . . *(As* MR. VAN DAAN *starts his characteristic pacing,* DUSSEL *turns to speak to the others.)* Right here in Amsterdam every day hundreds of Jews disappear . . . They surround a block and search house by house. Children come home from school to find their parents gone. Hundreds are being deported . . . people that you and I know . . . the Hallensteins . . . the Wessels . . .

MRS. FRANK *(in tears).* Oh, no. No!

DUSSEL. They get their call-up notice . . . come to the Jewish theatre on such and such a day and hour . . . bring only what you can carry in a rucksack. And if you refuse the call-up notice, then they come and drag you from your home and ship you off to Mauthausen.[6] The death camp!

MRS. FRANK. We didn't know that things had got so much worse.

DUSSEL. Forgive me for speaking so.

ANNE *(coming to DUSSEL).* Do you know the deWaals? . . . What's become of them? Their daughter Jopie and I are in the same class. Jopie's my best friend.

DUSSEL. They are gone.

ANNE. Gone?

DUSSEL. With all the others.

ANNE. Oh, no. Not Jopie!

(She turns away, in tears. MRS. FRANK *motions to* MARGOT *to comfort her.* MARGOT *goes to* ANNE, *putting her arms comfortingly around her.)*

MRS. VAN DAAN. There were some people called Wagner. They lived near us . . . ?

MR. FRANK *(interrupting with a glance at* ANNE*).* I think we should put this off until later. We all have many questions we want to ask . . . But I'm sure that Mr. Dussel would like to get settled before supper.

DUSSEL. Thank you. I would. I brought very little with me.

MR. FRANK *(giving him his hat and brief-case).* I'm sorry we can't give you a room alone. But I hope you won't be too uncomfortable. We've had to make strict rules here . . . a schedule of hours . . . We'll tell you after supper. Anne, would you like to take Mr. Dussel to his room?

ANNE *(controlling her tears).* If you'll come with me, Mr. Dussel?

(She starts for her room.)

DUSSEL *(shaking hands with each in turn).* Forgive me if I haven't really expressed my gratitude to all of you. This has been such a shock to me. I'd always thought of myself as Dutch. I was born in Holland. My father was born in Holland, and my grandfather. And now . . . after all these years . . . *(He breaks off.)* If you'll excuse me.

(DUSSEL gives a little bow and hurries off after ANNE. MR. FRANK *and the others are subdued.)*

ANNE *(turning on the light).* Well, here we are.

(DUSSEL looks around the room. In the main room MARGOT *speaks to her mother.)*

MARGOT. The news sounds pretty bad, doesn't it? It's so different from what Mr. Kraler tells us. Mr. Kraler says things are improving.

MR. VAN DAAN. I like it better the way Kraler tells it.

(They resume their occupations, quietly. PETER *goes off into his room. In* ANNE'S *room,* ANNE *turns to* DUSSEL.)*

ANNE. You're going to share the room with me.

DUSSEL. I'm a man who's always lived alone. I haven't had to adjust myself to others. I hope you'll bear with me until I learn.

ANNE. Let me help you. *(She takes his briefcase.)* Do you always live all alone? Have you no family at all?

DUSSEL. No one.

(He opens his medicine case and spreads his bottles on the dressing table.)

ANNE. How dreadful. You must be terribly lonely.

---

6. Mauthausen (mout′houz ən), a Nazi concentration camp located in Austria.

DUSSEL. I'm used to it.

ANNE. I don't think I could ever get used to it. Didn't you even have a pet? A cat, or a dog?

DUSSEL. I have an allergy for fur-bearing animals. They give me asthma.

ANNE. Oh, dear. Peter has a cat.

DUSSEL. Here? He has it here?

ANNE. Yes. But we hardly ever see it. He keeps it in his room all the time. I'm sure it will be all right.

DUSSEL. Let us hope so. (He takes some pills to fortify himself.)

ANNE. That's Margot's bed, where you're going to sleep. I sleep on the sofa there. (Indicating the clothes hooks on the wall.) We cleared these off for your things. (She goes over to the window.) The best part about this room . . . you can look down and see a bit of the street and the canal. There's a houseboat . . . you can see the end of it . . . a bargeman lives there with his family . . . They have a baby and he's just beginning to walk and I'm so afraid he's going to fall into the canal some day. I watch him . . .

DUSSEL (interrupting). Your father spoke of a schedule.

ANNE (coming away from the window). Oh, yes. It's mostly about the times we have to be quiet. And times for the w.c. You can use it now if you like.

DUSSEL (stiffly). No, thank you.

ANNE. I suppose you think it's awful, my talking about a thing like that. But you don't know how important it can get to be, especially when you're frightened . . . About this room, the way Margot and I did . . . she had it to herself in the afternoons for studying, reading . . . lessons, you know . . . and I took the mornings. Would that be all right with you?

DUSSEL. I'm not at my best in the morning.

ANNE. You stay here in the mornings then. I'll take the room in the afternoons.

DUSSEL. Tell me, when you're in here, what happens to me? Where am I spending my time? In there, with all the people?

ANNE. Yes.

DUSSEL. I see. I see.

ANNE. We have supper at half past six.

DUSSEL (going over to the sofa). Then, if you don't mind . . . I like to lie down quietly for ten minutes before eating. I find it helps the digestion.

ANNE. Of course. I hope I'm not going to be too much of a bother to you. I seem to be able to get everyone's back up.

(DUSSEL lies down on the sofa, curled up, his back to her.)

DUSSEL. I always get along very well with children. My patients all bring their children to me, because they know I get on well with them. So don't worry about that.

(ANNE leans over him, taking his hand and shaking it gratefully.)

ANNE. Thank you. Thank you, Mr. Dussel. (The lights dim to darkness. The curtain falls on the scene. ANNE'S VOICE comes to us faintly at first, and then with increasing power.)

ANNE'S VOICE. . . . And yesterday I finished Cissy Van Marxvelt's latest book. I think she is a first-class writer. I shall definitely let my children read her. Monday the twenty-first of September, nineteen forty-two. Mr. Dussel and I had another battle yesterday. Yes, Mr. Dussel! According to him, nothing, I repeat . . . nothing, is right about me . . . my appearance, my character, my manners. While he was going on at me I thought . . . sometime I'll give you such a smack that you'll fly right up to the ceiling! Why is it that every grownup thinks he knows the way to bring up children? Particularly the grownups that never had any. I keep wishing that Peter was a girl instead of a boy. Then I would have someone to talk to. Margot's a darling, but she takes everything too seriously. To pause for a moment on the subject of Mrs. Van Daan. I must tell you that her attempts to flirt with Father are getting her nowhere. Pim, thank goodness, won't play.

(As she is saying the last lines, the curtain rises on the darkened scene. ANNE'S VOICE *fades out.)*

Discussion

1. Much of this scene is composed of incidents which provide a clearer idea of thirteen-year-old Anne. **(a)** What are some of her characteristics? Cite incidents to illustrate these character traits. **(b)** Does Anne seem to you a normal thirteen-year-old girl? Why or why not?

2. What does the behavior of Mr. Van Daan, Mrs. Van Daan, and Peter tell you about each?

3. (a) How are members of the audience suddenly reminded early in the scene, amidst the horseplay and teasing on stage, that they are not observing a normal household? **(b)** What effect does this reminder create?

4. (a) What effect does Mr. Dussel's arrival have upon arrangements in the household? **(b)** How do various members of the household react to his coming? **(c)** What information of the outside world does Mr. Dussel provide?

Vocabulary
Context, Dictionary

Look up the words listed below in your Glossary. Then write the word that best completes each sentence. You will not use one of the words.

deported   meticulous
domestic   subdued
insufferable   scoffingly

1. Listening to him constantly brag about that dog of his is becoming _____.

2. He planned even the less important parts of the program with _____ care.

3. John Martin was _____ from Canada because he had entered the country illegally.

4. Men and women with full-time jobs often have difficulty finding time for _____ tasks.

5. Once Marta realized that she was upsetting Frank, she _____ her criticism of his art.

SCENE FOUR

It is the middle of the night, several months later. The stage is dark except for a little light which comes through the skylight in PETER'S *room.*

Everyone is in bed. MR. *and* MRS. FRANK *lie on the couch in the main room, which has been pulled out to serve as a makeshift double bed.*

MARGOT *is sleeping on a mattress on the floor in the main room, behind a curtain stretched across for privacy. The others are all in their accustomed rooms.*

From outside we hear two drunken soldiers singing "Lili Marlene." A girl's high giggle is heard. The sound of running feet is heard coming closer and then fading in the distance. Throughout the scene there is the distant sound of airplanes passing overhead.

A match suddenly flares up in the attic. We dimly see MR. VAN DAAN. *He is getting his bearings. He comes quickly down the stairs, and goes to the cupboard where the food is stored. Again the match flares up, and is as quickly blown out. The dim figure is seen to steal back up the stairs.*

There is quiet for a second or two, broken only by the sound of airplanes, and running feet on the street below.

Suddenly, out of the silence and the dark, we hear ANNE *scream.*

ANNE *(screaming).* No! No! Don't . . . don't take me!

(She moans, tossing and crying in her sleep. The other people wake, terrified. DUSSEL *sits up in bed, furious.)*

DUSSEL. Shush! Anne! Anne, for God's sake, shush!

ANNE *(still in her nightmare).* Save me! Save me!

(She screams and screams. DUSSEL *gets out of bed, going over to her, trying to wake her.)*

DUSSEL. For God's sake! Quiet! Quiet! You want someone to hear?

(In the main room MRS. FRANK *grabs a shawl and pulls it around her. She rushes in to* ANNE, *taking her in her arms.* MR. FRANK *hurriedly gets up, putting on his overcoat.* MARGOT *sits up, terrified.* PETER'S *light goes on in his room.)*

MRS. FRANK *(to* ANNE, *in her room).* Hush, darling, hush. It's all right. It's all right. *(Over her shoulder to* DUSSEL*)* Will you be kind enough to turn on the light, Mr. Dussel? *(Back to* ANNE*)* It's nothing, my darling. It was just a dream.

*(*DUSSEL *turns on the light in the bedroom.*

MRS. FRANK *holds* ANNE *in her arms. Gradually* ANNE *comes out of her nightmare, still trembling with horror.* MR. FRANK *comes into the room, and goes quickly to the window, looking out to be sure that no one outside has heard* ANNE'S *screams.* MRS. FRANK *holds* ANNE, *talking softly to her. In the main room* MARGOT *stands on a chair, turning on the center hanging lamp. A light goes on in the* VAN DAANS' *room overhead.* PETER *puts his robe on, coming out of his room.)*

DUSSEL *(to* MRS. FRANK, *blowing his nose).* Something must be done about that child, Mrs. Frank. Yelling like that! Who knows but there's somebody on the streets? She's endangering all our lives.

MRS. FRANK. Anne, darling.

DUSSEL. Every night she twists and turns. I don't sleep. I spend half my night shushing her. And now it's nightmares!

*(*MARGOT *comes to the door of* ANNE'S *room, followed by* PETER. MR. FRANK *goes to them, indicating that everything is all right.* PETER *takes* MARGOT *back.)*

MRS. FRANK *(to* ANNE*).* You're here, safe, you see? Nothing has happened. *(To* DUSSEL*)* Please, Mr. Dussel, go back to bed. She'll be herself in a minute or two. Won't you, Anne?

DUSSEL *(picking up a book and a pillow).* Thank you, but I'm going to the w.c. The one place where there's peace!

(He stalks out. MR. VAN DAAN, *in underwear and trousers, comes down the stairs.)*

MR. VAN DAAN *(to* DUSSEL*).* What is it? What happened?

DUSSEL. A nightmare. She was having a nightmare!

MR. VAN DAAN. I thought someone was murdering her.

DUSSEL. Unfortunately, no.

(He goes into the bathroom. MR. VAN DAAN *goes back up the stairs.* MR. FRANK, *in the*

main room, sends PETER *back to his own bedroom.)*

MR. FRANK. Thank you, Peter. Go back to bed.

(PETER goes back to his room. MR. FRANK follows him turning out the light and looking out the window. Then he goes back to the main room, and gets up on a chair, turning out the center hanging lamp.)

MRS. FRANK *(to* ANNE*).* Would you like some water? (ANNE *shakes her head.)* Was it a very bad dream? Perhaps if you told me . . . ?

ANNE. I'd rather not talk about it.

MRS. FRANK. Poor darling. Try to sleep then. I'll sit right here beside you until you fall asleep. *(She brings a stool over, sitting there.)*

ANNE. You don't have to.

MRS. FRANK. But I'd like to stay with you . . . very much. Really.

ANNE. I'd rather you didn't.

MRS. FRANK. Good night, then. *(She leans down to kiss* ANNE. ANNE *throws her arm up over her face, turning away.* MRS. FRANK, *hiding her hurt, kisses* ANNE'S *arm.)* You'll be all right? There's nothing that you want?

ANNE. Will you please ask Father to come.

MRS. FRANK *(after a second).* Of course, Anne dear. *(She hurries out into the other room.* MR. FRANK *comes to her as she comes in.) Sie verlangt nach Dir!*[1]

MR. FRANK *(sensing her hurt). Edith, Liebe, schau . . .*[2]

MRS. FRANK. *Es macht nichts! Ich danke dem lieben Herrgott, dass sie sich wenigstens an Dich wendet, wenn sie Trost braucht! Geh hinein, Otto, sie ist ganz hysterisch vor Angst.*[3] *(As* MR. FRANK *hesitates) Geh zu ihr.*[4] *(He looks at her for a second and then goes to get a cup of water for* ANNE. MRS. FRANK *sinks down on the bed, her face in her hands, trying to keep from sobbing aloud.* MARGOT *comes over to her, putting her arms around her.)* She wants nothing of me. She pulled away when I leaned down to kiss her.

MARGOT. It's a phase . . . You heard Father . . . Most girls go through it . . . they turn to their fathers at this age . . . they give all their love to their fathers.

MRS. FRANK. You weren't like this. You didn't shut me out.

MARGOT. She'll get over it . . .

(She smooths the bed for MRS. FRANK *and sits beside her a moment as* MRS. FRANK *lies down. In* ANNE'S *room* MR. FRANK *comes in, sitting down by* ANNE. ANNE *flings her arms around him, clinging to him. In the distance we hear the sound of ack-ack.)*

ANNE. Oh, Pim. I dreamed that they came to get us! The Green Police! They broke down the door and grabbed me and started to drag me out the way they did Jopie.

MR. FRANK. I want you to take this pill.

ANNE. What is it?

MR. FRANK. Something to quiet you.

(She takes it and drinks the water. In the main room MARGOT *turns out the light and goes back to her room.)*

MR. FRANK *(to* ANNE*).* Do you want me to read to you for a while?

ANNE. No. Just sit with me for a minute. Was I awful? Did I yell terribly loud? Do you think anyone outside could have heard?

MR. FRANK. No. No. Lie quietly now. Try to sleep.

ANNE. I'm a terrible coward. I'm so disappointed in myself. I think I've conquered

---

1. *Sie verlangt nach Dir!* She wants to see you.
2. *Edith, Liebe, schau . . .* Edith, my dear, look . . .
3. *Es macht nichts! . . . vor Angst.* It doesn't matter. Thank God that she at least turns to you when she is in need of consolation. Go, Otto, she is hysterical with fear.
4. *Geh zu ihr.* Go to her.

my fear . . . I think I'm really grown-up . . . and then something happens . . . and I run to you like a baby . . . I love you, Father. I don't love anyone but you.

MR. FRANK (reproachfully). Annele!

ANNE. It's true. I've been thinking about it for a long time. You're the only one I love.

MR. FRANK. It's fine to hear you tell me that you love me. But I'd be happier if you said you loved your mother as well . . . She needs your help so much . . . your love . . .

ANNE. We have nothing in common. She doesn't understand me. Whenever I try to explain my views on life to her she asks me if I'm constipated.

MR. FRANK. You hurt her very much now. She's crying. She's in there crying.

ANNE. I can't help it. I only told the truth. I didn't want her here . . . (Then, with sudden change) Oh, Pim, I was horrible, wasn't I? And the worst of it is, I can stand off and look at myself doing it and know it's cruel and yet I can't stop doing it. What's the matter with me? Tell me. Don't say it's just a phase! Help me.

MR. FRANK. There is so little that we parents can do to help our children. We can only try to set a good example . . . point the way. The rest you must do yourself. You must build your own character.

ANNE. I'm trying. Really I am. Every night I think back over all of the things I did that day that were wrong . . . like putting the wet mop in Mr. Dussel's bed . . . and this thing now with Mother. I say to myself, that was wrong. I make up my mind, I'm never going to do that again. Never! Of course I may do something worse . . . but at least I'll never do *that* again . . . I have a nicer side, Father . . . a sweeter, nicer side. But I'm scared to show it. I'm afraid that people are going to laugh at me if I'm serious. So the mean Anne comes to the outside and the good Anne stays on the inside, and I keep on trying to switch them around and have the good Anne outside and the bad Anne inside and be what I'd like to be . . . and might be . . . if only . . . only . . .

(She is asleep. MR. FRANK *watches her for a moment and then turns off the light, and starts out. The lights dim out. The curtain falls on the scene.* ANNE'S VOICE *is heard dimly at first, and then with growing strength.)*

ANNE'S VOICE. . . . The air raids are getting worse. They come over day and night. The noise is terrifying. Pim says it should be music to our ears. The more planes, the sooner will come the end of the war. Mrs. Van Daan pretends to be a fatalist. What will be, will be. But when the planes come over, who is the most frightened? No one else but Petronella! . . . Monday, the ninth of November, nineteen forty-two. Wonderful news! The Allies[5] have landed in Africa. Pim says that we can look for an early finish to the war. Just for fun he asked each of us what was the first thing we wanted to do when we got out of here. Mrs. Van Daan longs to be home with her own things, her needlepoint chairs, the Beckstein piano her father gave her . . . the best that money could buy. Peter would like to go to a movie. Mr. Dussel wants to get back to his dentist's drill. He's afraid he is losing his touch. For myself, there are so many things . . . to ride a bike again . . . to laugh till my belly aches . . . to have new clothes from the skin out . . . to have a hot tub filled to

---

5. The Allies (al ´īz), the countries (including Britain and the United States) which fought against Germany, Italy, and Japan in World War II.

overflowing and wallow in it for hours
. . . to be back in school with my
friends . . .

*(As the last lines are being said, the curtain
rises on the scene. The lights dim on as
ANNE'S VOICE fades away.)*

Discussion

1. Anne's nightmare serves more than one dramatic purpose. (a) What does it tell you about Anne? (b) What do you think it may foreshadow?

2. What does the scene reveal about the feelings of: (a) Mr. Dussel toward Anne? (b) Anne toward her mother? (c) Her mother toward Anne? (d) Anne toward her father? (e) Mr. Frank toward his wife? (f) Margot toward her mother? Find statements to support your answers.

3. Toward the end of the scene, what does Anne say that indicates she is struggling for greater maturity?

4. Just before Anne's nightmare, Mr. Van Daan has come downstairs. (a) What is his purpose? (b) Have there been any clues to this kind of action on his part? Explain.

SCENE FIVE

It is the first night of the Hanukkah[1] celebration. MR. FRANK *is standing at the head of the table on which is the Menorah.[2] He lights the Shamos, or servant candle, and holds it as he says the blessing. Seated listening is all of the "family," dressed in their best. The men wear hats,* PETER *wears his cap.*

MR. FRANK *(reading from a prayer book).* "Praised be Thou, oh Lord our God, Ruler of the universe, who has sanctified us with Thy commandments and bidden us kindle the Hanukkah lights. Praised be Thou, oh Lord our God, Ruler of the universe, who has wrought wondrous deliverances for our fathers in days of old. Praised be Thou, oh Lord our God, Ruler of the universe, that Thou has given us life and sustenance and brought us to this happy season." (MR. FRANK *lights the one candle of the Menorah as he continues.)* "We kindle this Hanukkah light to celebrate the great and wonderful deeds wrought through the zeal with which God filled the hearts of the heroic Maccabees, two thousand years ago. They fought against indifference, against tyranny and oppression, and they restored our Temple to us. May these lights remind us that we should ever look to God, whence cometh our help." Amen. *(Pronounced O-mayn.)*

ALL. Amen.

(MR. FRANK *hands* MRS. FRANK *the prayer book.)*

MRS. FRANK *(reading).* "I lift up mine eyes unto the mountains, from whence cometh my help. My help cometh from the Lord who made heaven and earth. He will not

---

1. *Hanukkah* (hä′nə kə), a Jewish festival usually held in December. The festival commemorates the rededication of the temple in Jerusalem after the Maccabees (mak′ə bēz′), a family of Jewish patriots, led the Jews to victory over the Syrians in 165 B.C.
2. *Menorah* (mə nôr′ə), a candlestick with various numbers of branches used primarily in Jewish religious services. The *Shamos* (shäm′əs), or servant candle, is lit first, then used to light the Menorah.

suffer thy foot to be moved. He that keepeth thee will not slumber. He that keepeth Israel doth neither slumber nor sleep. The Lord is thy keeper. The Lord is thy shade upon thy right hand. The sun shall not smite thee by day, nor the moon by night. The Lord shall keep thee from all evil. He shall keep thy soul. The Lord shall guard thy going out and thy coming in, from this time forth and forevermore.'' Amen.

ALL. Amen.

(MRS. FRANK *puts down the prayer book and goes to get the food and wine.* MARGOT *helps her.* MR. FRANK *takes the men's hats and puts them aside.*)

DUSSEL (*rising*). That was very moving.

ANNE (*pulling him back*). It isn't over yet!

MRS. VAN DAAN. Sit down! Sit down!

ANNE. There's a lot more, songs and presents.

DUSSEL. Presents?

MRS. FRANK. Not this year, unfortunately.

MRS. VAN DAAN. But always on Hanukkah everyone gives presents . . . everyone!

DUSSEL. Like our St. Nicholas' Day.[3]

(*There is a chorus of "no's" from the group.*)

MRS. VAN DAAN. No! Not like St. Nicholas! What kind of a Jew are you that you don't know Hanukkah?

MRS. FRANK (*as she brings the food*). I remember particularly the candles . . . First one, as we have tonight. Then the second night you light two candles, the next night three . . . and so on until you have eight candles burning. When there are eight candles it is truly beautiful.

MRS. VAN DAAN. And the potato pancakes.

MR. VAN DAAN. Don't talk about them!

MRS. VAN DAAN. I make the best *latkes*[4] you ever tasted!

MRS. FRANK. Invite us all next year . . . in your own home.

MR. FRANK. God willing!

MRS. VAN DAAN. God willing.

MARGOT. What I remember best is the presents we used to get when we were little . . . eight days of presents . . . and each day they got better and better.

MRS. FRANK (*sitting down*). We are all here, alive. That is present enough.

ANNE. No, it isn't. I've got something . . . (*She rushes into her room, hurriedly puts on a little hat improvised from the lamp shade, grabs a satchel bulging with parcels and comes running back.*)

MRS. FRANK. What is it?

ANNE. Presents!

MRS. VAN DAAN. Presents!

DUSSEL. Look!

MRS. VAN DAAN. What's she got on her head?

PETER. A lamp shade!

ANNE (*She picks out one at random*). This is for Margot. (*She hands it to* MARGOT, *pulling her to her feet.*) Read it out loud.

MARGOT (*reading*).
"You have never lost your temper.
You never will, I fear,
You are so good.
But if you should,
Put all your cross words here."
(*She tears open the package.*) A new crossword puzzle book! Where did you get it?

ANNE. It isn't new. It's one that you've done. But I rubbed it all out, and if you wait a little and forget, you can do it all over again.

MARGOT (*sitting*). It's wonderful, Anne.

---

3. *St. Nicholas' Day.* On December 6, the feast of St. Nicholas, Dutch children are given gifts. St. Nicholas, actually a fourth-century saint, is today a figure like Santa Claus. The feast has no real religious significance.

4. *latkes* (lät′kəs), potato pancakes.

Thank you. You'd never know it wasn't new.

(From outside we hear the sound of a street-car passing.)

ANNE *(with another gift)*. Mrs. Van Daan.

MRS. VAN DAAN *(taking it)*. This is awful . . . I haven't anything for anyone . . . I never thought . . .

MR. FRANK. This is all Anne's idea.

MRS. VAN DAAN *(holding up a bottle)*. What is it?

ANNE. It's hair shampoo. I took all the odds and ends of soap and mixed them with the last of my toilet water.

MRS. VAN DAAN. Oh, Anneke!

ANNE. I wanted to write a poem for all of them, but I didn't have time. *(offering a large box to* MR. VAN DAAN*)* Yours, Mr. Van Daan, is *really* something . . . something you want more than anything. *(as she waits for him to open it)* Look! Cigarettes!

MR. VAN DAAN. Cigarettes!

ANNE. Two of them! Pim found some old pipe tobacco in the pocket lining of his coat . . . and we made them . . . or rather, Pim did.

MRS. VAN DAAN. Let me see . . . Well, look at that! Light it, Putti! Light it.

(MR. VAN DAAN hesitates.)

ANNE. It's tobacco, really it is! There's a little fluff in it, but not much.

(Everyone watches as MR. VAN DAAN *cautiously lights it. The cigarette flares up. Everyone laughs.)*

PETER. It works!

MRS. VAN DAAN. Look at him.

MR. VAN DAAN *(spluttering)*. Thank you, Anne. Thank you.

(ANNE rushes back to her satchel for another present.)

ANNE *(handing her mother a piece of paper)*. For Mother, Hanukkah greeting.

(She pulls her mother to her feet.)

MRS. FRANK *(She reads)*.
   "Here's an I.O.U. that I promise to pay. Ten hours of doing whatever you say. Signed, Anne Frank."

(MRS. FRANK, touched, takes ANNE in her arms, holding her close.)

DUSSEL *(to ANNE)*. Ten hours of doing what you're told? *Anything* you're told?

ANNE. That's right.

DUSSEL. You wouldn't want to sell that, Mrs. Frank?

MRS. FRANK. Never! This is the most precious gift I've ever had!

(She sits, showing her present to the others. ANNE *hurries back to the satchel and pulls out a scarf, the scarf that* MR. FRANK *found in the first scene.)*

ANNE *(offering it to her father)*. For Pim.

MR. FRANK. Anneke . . . I wasn't supposed to have a present!

(He takes it, unfolding it and showing it to the others.)

ANNE. It's a muffler . . . to put round your neck . . . like an ascot, you know. I made it myself out of odds and ends . . . I knitted it in the dark each night, after I'd gone to bed. I'm afraid it looks better in the dark!

MR. FRANK *(putting it on)*. It's fine. It fits me perfectly. Thank you, Annele.

(ANNE hands PETER a ball of paper, with a string attached to it.)

ANNE. That's for Mouschi.

PETER *(rising to bow)*. On behalf of Mouschi, I thank you.

ANNE *(hesitant, handing him a gift)*. And . . . this is yours . . . from Mrs. Quack Quack. *(As he holds it gingerly in his hands)* Well . . . open it . . . Aren't you going to open it?

PETER. I'm scared to. I know something's going to jump out and hit me.

ANNE. No. It's nothing like that, really.

MRS. VAN DAAN (as he is opening it). What is it, Peter? Go on. Show it.

ANNE (excitedly). It's a safety razor!

DUSSEL. A what?

ANNE. A razor!

MRS. VAN DAAN (looking at it). You didn't make that out of odds and ends.

ANNE (to PETER). Miep got it for me. It's not new. It's second-hand. But you really do need a razor now.

DUSSEL. For what?

ANNE. Look on his upper lip . . . you can see the beginning of a mustache.

DUSSEL. He wants to get rid of that? Put a little milk on it and let the cat lick it off.

PETER (starting for his room). Think you're funny, don't you.

DUSSEL. Look! He can't wait! He's going in to try it!

PETER. I'm going to give Mouschi his present!

(He goes into his room, slamming the door behind him.)

MR. VAN DAAN (disgustedly). Mouschi, Mouschi, Mouschi.

(In the distance we hear a dog persistently barking. ANNE brings a gift to DUSSEL.)

ANNE. And last but never least, my roommate, Mr. Dussel.

DUSSEL. For me? You have something for me? (He opens the small box she gives him.)

ANNE. I made them myself.

DUSSEL (puzzled). Capsules! Two capsules!

ANNE. They're ear-plugs!

DUSSEL. Ear-plugs?

ANNE. To put in your ears so you won't hear me when I thrash around at night. I saw them advertised in a magazine. They're not real ones . . . I made them out of cotton and candle wax. Try them . . .

See if they don't work . . . see if you can hear me talk . . .

DUSSEL (putting them in his ears). Wait now until I get them in . . . so.

ANNE. Are you ready?

DUSSEL. Huh?

ANNE. Are you ready?

DUSSEL. Good God! They've gone inside! I can't get them out! (They laugh as MR. DUSSEL jumps about, trying to shake the plugs out of his ears. Finally he gets them out. Putting them away.) Thank you, Anne! Thank you!

MR. VAN DAAN. A real Hanukkah! } (Together)

MRS. VAN DAAN. Wasn't it cute of her?

MRS. FRANK. I don't know when she did it.

MARGOT. I love my present.

ANNE (sitting at the table). And now let's have the song, Father . . . please . . . (To DUSSEL) Have you heard the Hanukkah song, Mr. Dussel? The song is the whole thing! (She sings) "Oh Hanukkah! Oh, Hanukkah! The sweet celebration . . ."

MR. FRANK (quieting her). I'm afraid, Anne, we shouldn't sing that song tonight. (To DUSSEL) It's a song of jubilation, of rejoicing. One is apt to become too enthusiastic.

ANNE. Oh, please, please. Let's sing the song. I promise not to shout!

MR. FRANK. Very well. But quietly now . . . I'll keep an eye on you and when . . .

(As ANNE starts to sing, she is interrupted by DUSSEL, who is snorting and wheezing.)

DUSSEL (pointing to PETER). You . . . You! (PETER is coming from his bedroom, ostentatiously holding a bulge in his coat as if he were holding his cat, and dangling ANNE'S present before it.). How many times . . . I told you . . . Out! Out!

MR. VAN DAAN (going to PETER). What's

the matter with you? Haven't you any sense? Get that cat out of here.

PETER (innocently). Cat?

MR. VAN DAAN. You heard me. Get it out of here!

PETER. I have no cat. (Delighted with his joke, he opens his coat and pulls out a bath towel. The group at the table laugh, enjoying the joke.)

DUSSEL (still wheezing). It doesn't need to be the cat . . . his clothes are enough . . . when he comes out of that room . . .

MR. VAN DAAN. Don't worry. You won't be bothered any more. We're getting rid of it.

DUSSEL. At last you listen to me.

(He goes off into his bedroom.)

MR. VAN DAAN (calling after him). I'm not doing it for you. That's all in your mind . . . all of it! (He starts back to his place at the table.) I'm doing it because I'm sick of seeing that cat eat all our food.

PETER. That's not true! I only give him bones . . . scraps . . .

MR. VAN DAAN. Don't tell me! He gets fatter every day! Damn cat looks better than any of us. Out he goes tonight!

PETER. No! No!

ANNE. Mr. Van Daan, you can't do that! That's Peter's cat. Peter loves that cat.

MRS. FRANK (quietly). Anne.

PETER (to MR. VAN DAAN). If he goes, I go.

MR. VAN DAAN. Go! Go!

MRS. VAN DAAN. You're not going and the cat's not going! Now please . . . this is Hanukkah . . . Hanukkah . . . this is the time to celebrate . . . What's the matter with all of you? Come on, Anne. Let's have the song.

ANNE (singing).
"Oh, Hanukkah! Oh, Hanukkah!
The sweet celebration."

MR. FRANK (rising). I think we should first blow out the candle . . . then we'll have something for tomorrow night.

MARGOT. But, Father, you're supposed to let it burn itself out.

MR. FRANK. I'm sure that God understands shortages. (Before blowing it out) "Praised be Thou, oh Lord our God, who hast sustained us and permitted us to celebrate this joyous festival."

(He is about to blow out the candle when suddenly there is a crash of something falling below. They all freeze in horror, motionless. For a few seconds there is complete silence. MR. FRANK slips off his shoes. The others noiselessly follow his example. MR. FRANK turns out a light near him. He motions to PETER to turn off the center lamp. PETER tries to reach it, realizes he cannot and gets up on a chair. Just as he is touching the lamp he loses his balance. The chair goes out from under him. He falls. The iron lamp shade crashes to the floor. There is a sound of feet below, running down the stairs.)

MR. VAN DAAN (under his breath). God almighty! (The only light left comes from the Hanukkah candle. DUSSEL comes from his room. MR. FRANK creeps over to the stairwell and stands listening. The dog is heard barking excitedly.) Do you hear anything?

MR. FRANK (in a whisper). No. I think they've gone.

MRS. VAN DAAN. It's the Green Police. They've found us.

MR. FRANK. If they had, they wouldn't have left. They'd be up here by now.

MRS. VAN DAAN. I know it's the Green Police. They've gone to get help. That's all, they'll be back.

MR. VAN DAAN. Or it may have been the Gestapo[5] looking for papers . . .

---

5. **Gestapo** (gə stä′pō), the Secret Police of Nazi Germany.

MR. FRANK *(interrupting).* Or a thief, looking for money.

MRS. VAN DAAN. We've got to do something . . . Quick! Quick! Before they come back.

MR. VAN DAAN. There isn't anything to do. Just wait.

(MR. FRANK holds up his hand for them to be quiet. He is listening intently. There is complete silence as they all strain to hear any sound from below. Suddenly ANNE begins to sway. With a low cry she falls to the floor in a faint. MRS. FRANK goes to her quickly, sitting beside her on the floor and taking her in her arms.)

MRS. FRANK. Get some water, please! Get some water!

(MARGOT starts for the sink.)

MR. VAN DAAN *(grabbing MARGOT).* No! No! No one's going to run water!

MR. FRANK. If they've found us, they've found us. Get the water. (MARGOT *starts again for the sink.* MR. FRANK, *getting a flashlight)* I'm going down.

(MARGOT rushes to him, clinging to him. ANNE struggles to consciousness.)

MARGOT. No, Father, no! There may be someone there, waiting . . . It may be a trap!

MR. FRANK. This is Saturday. There is no way for us to know what has happened until Miep or Mr. Kraler comes on Monday morning. We cannot live with this uncertainty.

MARGOT. Don't go, Father!

MRS. FRANK. Hush, darling, hush. (MR. FRANK *slips quietly out, down the steps and out through the door below.)* Margot! Stay close to me.

(MARGOT goes to her mother.)

MR. VAN DAAN. Shush! Shush!

(MRS. FRANK *whispers to* MARGOT *to get the water.* MARGOT *goes for it.*)

MRS. VAN DAAN. Putti, where's our money? Get our money. I hear you can buy the Green Police off, so much a head. Go upstairs quick! Get the money!

MR. VAN DAAN. Keep still!

MRS. VAN DAAN (*kneeling before him, pleading*). Do you want to be dragged off to a concentration camp? Are you going to stand there and wait for them to come up and get you? Do something, I tell you!

MR. VAN DAAN (*pushing her aside*). Will you keep still!

(*He goes over to the stairwell to listen.* PETER *goes to his mother, helping her up onto the sofa. There is a second of silence. Then* ANNE *can stand it no longer.*)

ANNE. Someone go after Father! Make Father come back!

PETER (*starting for the door*). I'll go.

MR. VAN DAAN. Haven't you done enough?

(*He pushes* PETER *roughly away. In his anger against his father* PETER *grabs a chair as if to hit him with it, then puts it down, burying his face in his hands.* MRS. FRANK *begins to pray softly.*)

ANNE. Please, please, Mr. Van Daan. Get Father.

MR. VAN DAAN. Quiet! Quiet!

(ANNE *is shocked into silence.* MRS. FRANK *pulls her closer, holding her protectively in her arms.*)

MRS. FRANK (*softly, praying*). "I lift up mine eyes unto the mountains, from whence cometh my help. My help cometh from the Lord who made heaven and earth. He will not suffer thy foot to be moved . . . He that keepeth thee will not slumber . . ."

(*She stops as she hears someone coming. They all watch the door tensely.* MR. FRANK *comes quietly in.* ANNE *rushes to him, holding him tight.*)

MR. FRANK. It was a thief. That noise must have scared him away.

MRS. VAN DAAN. Thank God.

MR. FRANK. He took the cash box. And the radio. He ran away in such a hurry that he didn't stop to shut the street door. It was swinging wide open. (*A breath of relief sweeps over them.*) I think it would be good to have some light.

MARGOT. Are you sure it's all right?

MR. FRANK. The danger has passed. (MARGOT *goes to light the small lamp.*) Don't be so terrified, Anne. We're safe.

DUSSEL. Who says the danger has passed? Don't you realize we are in greater danger than ever?

MR. FRANK. Mr. Dussel, will you be still!

(MR. FRANK *takes* ANNE *back to the table, making her sit down with him, trying to calm her.*)

DUSSEL (*pointing to* PETER). Thanks to this clumsy fool, there's someone now who knows we're up here! Someone now knows we're up here, hiding!

MRS. VAN DAAN (*going to* DUSSEL). Someone knows we're here, yes. But who is the someone? A thief! A thief! You think a thief is going to go to the Green Police and say . . . I was robbing a place the other night and I heard a noise up over my head? You think a thief is going to do that?

DUSSEL. Yes. I think he will.

MRS. VAN DAAN (*hysterically*). You're crazy!

(*She stumbles back to her seat at the table.* PETER *follows protectively, pushing* DUSSEL *aside.*)

DUSSEL. I think some day he'll be caught and then he'll make a bargain with the

Green Police . . . if they'll let him off, he'll tell them where some Jews are hiding!

(He goes off into the bedroom. There is a second of appalled silence.)

MR. VAN DAAN. He's right.

ANNE. Father, let's get out of here! We can't stay here now . . . Let's go . . .

MR. VAN DAAN. Go! Where?

MRS. FRANK *(sinking into her chair at the table).* Yes. Where?

MR. FRANK *(rising, to them all).* Have we lost all faith? All courage? A moment ago we thought that they'd come for us. We were sure it was the end. But it wasn't the end. We're alive, safe. (MR. VAN DAAN *goes to the table and sits.* MR. FRANK *prays.)* "We thank Thee, oh Lord our God, that in Thy infinite mercy Thou hast again seen fit to spare us." *(He blows out the candle, then turns to* ANNE.) Come on, Anne. The song! Let's have the song! *(He starts to sing.* ANNE *finally starts falteringly to sing, as* MR. FRANK *urges her on. Her voice is hardly audible at first.)*

ANNE *(singing).*

"Oh, Hanukkah! Oh, Hanukkah!
The sweet . . . celebration . . ."

(As she goes on singing, the others gradually join in, their voices still shaking with fear. MRS. VAN DAAN *sobs as she sings.)*

GROUP.

"Around the feast . . . we . . . gather
In complete . . . jubilation . . .
Happiest of sea . . . sons
Now is here.
Many are the reasons for good cheer."

*(*DUSSEL *comes from the bedroom. He comes over to the table, standing beside* MARGOT, *listening to them as they sing.)*

"Together
We'll weather
Whatever tomorrow may bring."

(As they sing on with growing courage, the lights start to dim.)

"So hear us rejoicing
And merrily voicing
The Hanukkah song that we sing.
Hoy!"

(The lights are out. The curtain starts slowly to fall.)

"Hear us rejoicing
And merrily voicing
The Hanukkah song that we sing."

(They are still singing, as the curtain falls.)

CURTAIN

Discussion

1. (a) What significance can you find in the fact that the "family" celebrates Hanukkah? **(b)** Why does Mr. Frank lead the family in the observance? **(c)** Is the gift Anne gives to each occupant of the annex appropriate? Explain your answers. **(d)** Why does Mr. Frank not want Anne to sing the Hanukkah song?

2. (a) What incident reveals that Peter has a sense of humor? **(b)** What effect does his behavior have on Mr. Dussel? on Mr. Van Daan?

3. (a) What event ends the celebration abruptly? **(b)** Do you think there is any significance in this event? **(c)** What do you learn about each of the following from the way in which each reacts to the incident: Anne, Mr. Dussel, Mrs. Van Daan, Mr. Van Daan?

4. What decisions does Mr. Frank make throughout the scene that show him still to be the person in charge?

5. (a) Why at the end of the scene does Mr. Frank urge Anne to sing the Hanukkah song when earlier he had discouraged her? **(b)** Why do you think the playwrights conclude Act One with the singing of this song?

Dramatic License

Since a drama is a series of events that can be acted out rather than a description, Frances Goodrich and Albert Hackett had to adapt Anne's diary entries to make them suitable for presentation on a stage. These changes, made for the sake of the overall effect desired by the dramatists, are referred to as the use of dramatic license.

From Anne's descriptions of events in the annex, the dramatists had to create dialogue for the persons involved. Too, they had to compress journal entries to provide necessary exposition, or background, for the play. For example, the first diary entry, which Mr. Frank begins to read aloud on stage, was drawn from parts of a number of entries. Finally, so as not to crowd the stage unduly with actors, in Miep and Mr. Kraler they created composite characters. The personalities of Miep Gies and Elli Vossen, both of whom worked in the warehouse building and were friends of Anne, merge on stage in Miep; Mr. Kraler and Mr. Koophuis, both business friends of Mr. Frank and both associated with Travis, Inc.,

become the single character Mr. Kraler.

In reality, the people living in the Secret Annex had more freedom to move around than do the characters in the play. In the diary, Anne frequently mentions the trips to the "private office" on the first floor of the building where the inhabitants of the annex listened to news broadcasts, speeches, and concerts on the radio. The playwrights, however, realizing the difficulties in staging different settings, have confined the action and the characters to one set, the Secret Annex itself.

During the two years the Franks and the Van Daans occupied the Secret Annex, there were several burglaries in the office below. None of them occurred during the Hanukkah season. Again, the playwrights have used dramatic license in presenting only one of these burglaries. By having the burglary occur during the Hanukkah celebration, the playwrights have created an extremely dramatic situation; the hope and strength which the inhabitants receive from the religious ceremony contrast sharply with the

ever-present danger of discovery, brought into focus by the intrusion of the unknown thief.

Much of Anne's diary reveals her thoughts about herself, the special problems with which she, as a teen-ager, is faced. The following diary entry reveals an important aspect of Anne's personality:

Saturday, 15 July, 1944. . . . I have one outstanding trait in my character, which must strike anyone who knows me for any length of time and that is my knowledge of myself. I can watch myself and my actions, just like an outsider. The Anne of every day I can face entirely without prejudice, without making excuses for her, and watch what's good and what's bad about her. This "self-consciousness" haunts me, and every time I open my mouth I know as soon as I have spoken whether "that ought to have been different" or "that was right as it was." There are so many things about myself that I condemn; I couldn't begin to name them all. I understand more and more how true Daddy's words were when he said: "All children must look

The Secret Annex was in the back of this building.

A.N.P. Foto, Amsterdam.

after their own upbringing." Parents can only give good advice or put them on the right paths, but the final forming of a person's character lies in their own hands.[1]

This is the type of personal, intimate revelation which Anne made only in her diary. To reveal this aspect of Anne's personality to the audience, the dramatists incorporated the entry into Scene 4 in which Anne, still frightened and overwrought from her nightmare, confesses to her father things that in actuality she revealed to no one.

Frances Goodrich and Albert Hackett, through their careful selections and adaptations of diary entries, have succeeded in presenting vivid portraits of the inhabitants of the Secret Annex. At the same time, they have preserved the spirit of reality found in the historical source from which they had to work, the diary of a young girl.

1. From *Anne Frank: The Diary of a Young Girl.* Copyright 1952 by Otto H. Frank. Reproduced by permission of Doubleday & Company, Inc. and Valentine, Mitchell & Co., Ltd.

DRAMATIC LICENSE   495

ACT TWO

SCENE ONE

In the darkness we hear ANNE'S VOICE, *again reading from the diary.*

ANNE'S VOICE. Saturday, the first of January, nineteen forty-four. Another new year has begun and we find ourselves still in our hiding place. We have been here now for one year, five months and twenty-five days. It seems that our life is at a standstill.

The curtain rises on the scene. It is afternoon. Everyone is bundled up against the cold. In the main room MRS. FRANK *is taking down the laundry, which is hung across the back.* MR. FRANK *sits in the chair down left, reading.* MARGOT *is lying on the couch with a blanket over her and the many-colored knitted scarf around her throat.* ANNE *is seated at the center table, writing in her diary.* PETER, MR. *and* MRS. VAN DANN, *and* DUSSEL *are all in their own rooms, reading or lying down.*

As the lights dim on, ANNE'S VOICE *continues, without a break.*

ANNE'S VOICE. We are all a little thinner. The Van Daans' "discussions" are as violent as ever. Mother still does not understand me. But then I don't understand her either. There is one great change, however. A change in myself. I read somewhere that girls of my age don't feel quite certain of themselves.

(The buzzer of the door below suddenly sounds. Everyone is startled; MR. FRANK *tiptoes cautiously to the top of the steps and listens. Again the buzzer sounds, in* MIEP'S *V-for-Victory signal.[1])*

MR. FRANK. It's Miep! *(He goes quickly down the steps to unbolt the door.* MRS.

FRANK *calls upstairs to the* VAN DAANS *and then to* PETER.)

MRS. FRANK. Wake up, everyone! Miep is here! *(*ANNE *quickly puts her diary away.* MARGOT *sits up, pulling the blanket around her shoulders.* MR. DUSSEL *sits on the edge of his bed, listening, disgruntled.* MIEP *comes up the steps, followed by* MR. KRALER. *They bring flowers, books, newspapers, etc.* ANNE *rushes to* MIEP, *throwing her arms affectionately around her.)* Miep . . . and Mr. Kraler . . . What a delightful surprise!

MR. KRALER. We came to bring you New Year's greetings.

MRS. FRANK. You shouldn't . . . you should have at least one day to yourselves. *(She goes quickly to the stove and brings down teacups and tea for all of them.)*

ANNE. Don't say that, it's so wonderful to see them! *(Sniffing at* MIEP'S *coat)* I can smell the wind and the cold on your clothes.

MIEP *(giving her the flowers)*. There you are. *(Then to* MARGOT, *feeling her forehead)* How are you, Margot? . . . Feeling any better?

MARGOT. I'm all right.

ANNE. We filled her full of every kind of pill so she won't cough and make a noise.

(She runs into her room to put the flowers in water. MR. *and* MRS. VAN DAAN *come from upstairs. Outside there is the sound of a band playing.)*

MRS. VAN DAAN. Well, hello, Miep. Mr. Kraler.

MR. KRALER *(giving a bouquet of flowers to* MRS. VAN DAAN). With my hope for peace in the New Year.

PETER *(anxiously)*. Miep, have you seen

---

1. *V-for-Victory signal,* three short buzzes followed by a long one. In the Morse Code the letter V is transmitted by three dots and a dash. It was widely used as a victory symbol during World War II.

Mouschi? Have you seen him anywhere around?

MIEP. I'm sorry, Peter. I asked everyone in the neighborhood had they seen a gray cat. But they said no.

(MRS. FRANK *gives* MIEP *a cup of tea.* MR. FRANK *comes up the steps, carrying a small cake on a plate.*)

MR. FRANK. Look what Miep's brought for us!

MRS. FRANK *(taking it).* A cake!

MR. VAN DAAN. A cake! *(He pinches* MIEP's *cheeks gaily and hurries up to the cupboard.)* I'll get some plates.

(DUSSEL, *in his room, hastily puts a coat on and starts out to join the others.*)

MRS. FRANK. Thank you, Miepia.[2] You shouldn't have done it. You must have used all of your sugar ration for weeks. *(Giving it to* MRS. VAN DAAN*)* It's beautiful, isn't it?

MRS. VAN DAAN. It's been ages since I even saw a cake. Not since you brought us one last year. *(Without looking at the cake, to* MIEP*)* Remember? Don't you remember, you gave us one on New Year's Day? Just this time last year? I'll never forget it because you had "Peace in nineteen forty-three" on it. *(She looks at the cake and reads.)* "Peace in nineteen forty-four!"

MIEP. Well, it has to come sometime, you know. *(As* DUSSEL *comes from his room)* Hello, Mr. Dussel.

MR. KRALER. How are you?

MR. VAN DAAN *(bringing plates and a knife).* Here's the knife, *liefje.* Now, how many of us are there?

MIEP. None for me, thank you.

MR. FRANK. Oh, please. You must.

MIEP. I couldn't.

MR. VAN DAAN. Good! That leaves one . . . two . . . three . . . seven of us.

DUSSEL. Eight! Eight! It's the same number as it always is!

MR. VAN DAAN. I left Margot out. I take it for granted Margot won't eat any.

ANNE. Why wouldn't she!

MRS. FRANK. I think it won't harm her.

MR. VAN DAAN. All right! All right! I just didn't want her to start coughing again, that's all.

DUSSEL. And please, Mrs. Frank should cut the cake.

MR. VAN DAAN. What's the difference?

MRS. VAN DAAN. It's not Mrs. Frank's cake, is it, Miep? It's for all of us.

} *(Together)*

DUSSEL. Mrs. Frank divides things better.

MRS. VAN DAAN *(going to* DUSSEL*).* What are you trying to say?

MR. VAN DAAN. Oh, come on! Stop wasting time!

} *(Together)*

MRS. VAN DAAN *(to* DUSSEL*).* Don't I always give everybody exactly the same? Don't I?

MR. VAN DAAN. Forget it, Kerli.

MRS. VAN DAAN. No. I want an answer! Don't I?

DUSSEL. Yes. Yes. Everybody gets exactly the same . . . except Mr. Van Daan always gets a little bit more.

(VAN DAAN *advances on* DUSSEL, *the knife still in his hand.*)

MR. VAN DAAN. That's a lie!

(DUSSEL *retreats before the onslaught of the* VAN DAANS.)

MR. FRANK. Please, please! *(Then to* MIEP*)* You see what a little sugar cake does to us? It goes right to our heads!

MR. VAN DAAN *(handing* MRS. FRANK *the knife).* Here you are, Mrs. Frank.

---

2. *Miepia* (mēp′Hyə)

MRS. FRANK. Thank you. (*Then to* MIEP *as she goes to the table to cut the cake*) Are you sure you won't have some?

MIEP (*drinking her tea*). No, really, I have to go in a minute.

(*The sound of the band fades out in the distance.*)

PETER (*to* MIEP). Maybe Mouschi went back to our house . . . they say that cats . . . Do you ever get over there . . . ? I mean . . . do you suppose you could . . . ?

MIEP. I'll try, Peter. The first minute I get I'll try. But I'm afraid, with him gone a week . . .

DUSSEL. Make up your mind, already someone has had a nice big dinner from that cat!

(PETER *is furious, inarticulate. He starts toward* DUSSEL *as if to hit him.* MR. FRANK *stops him.* MRS. FRANK *speaks quickly to ease the situation.*)

MRS. FRANK (*to* MIEP). This is delicious, Miep!

MRS. VAN DAAN (*eating hers*). Delicious!

MR. VAN DAAN (*finishing it in one gulp*). Dirk's in luck to get a girl who can bake like this!

MIEP (*putting down her empty teacup*). I have to run. Dirk's taking me to a party tonight.

ANNE. How heavenly! Remember now what everyone is wearing, and what you have to eat and everything, so you can tell us tomorrow.

MIEP. I'll give you a full report! Good-by, everyone!

MR. VAN DAAN (*to* MIEP). Just a minute. There's something I'd like you to do for me.

(*He hurries off up the stairs to his room.*)

MRS. VAN DAAN (*sharply*). Putti, where are you going? (*She rushes up the stairs after him, calling hysterically.*) What do you want? Putti, what are you going to do?

MIEP (*to* PETER). What's wrong?

PETER. (*His sympathy is with his mother.*) Father says he's going to sell her fur coat. She's crazy about that old fur coat.

DUSSEL. Is it possible? Is it possible that anyone is so silly as to worry about a fur coat in times like this?

PETER. It's none of your darn business . . . and if you say one more thing . . . I'll, I'll take you and I'll . . . I mean it . . . I'll . . .

(*There is a piercing scream from* MRS. VAN DAAN *above. She grabs at the fur coat as* MR. VAN DAAN *is starting downstairs with it.*)

MRS. VAN DAAN. No! No! No! Don't you dare take that! You hear? It's mine! *(Downstairs* PETER *turns away, embarrassed, miserable.)* My father gave me that! You didn't give it to me. You have no right. Let go of it . . . you hear?

*(*MR. VAN DAAN *pulls the coat from her hands and hurries downstairs.* MRS. VAN DAAN *sinks to the floor, sobbing. As* MR. VAN DAAN *comes into the main room the others look away, embarrassed for him.)*

MR. VAN DAAN *(to* MR. KRALER*).* Just a little—discussion over the advisability of selling this coat. As I have often reminded Mrs. Van Daan, it's very selfish of her to keep it when people outside are in such desperate need of clothing . . . *(He gives the coat to* MIEP.*)* So if you will please to sell it for us? It should fetch a good price. And by the way, will you get me cigarettes. I don't care what kind they are . . . get all you can.

MIEP. It's terribly difficult to get them, Mr. Van Daan. But I'll try. Good-by.

(She goes. MR. FRANK *follows her down the steps to bolt the door after her.* MRS. FRANK *gives* MR. KRALER *a cup of tea.)*

MRS. FRANK. Are you sure you won't have some cake, Mr. Kraler?

MR. KRALER. I'd better not.

MR. VAN DAAN. You're still feeling badly? What does your doctor say?

MR. KRALER. I haven't been to him.

MRS. FRANK. Now, Mr. Kraler! . . .

MR. KRALER *(sitting at the table).* Oh, I tried. But you can't get near a doctor these days . . . they're so busy. After weeks I finally managed to get one on the telephone. I told him I'd like an appointment . . . I wasn't feeling very well. You know what he answers . . . over the telephone . . . Stick out your tongue! *(They laugh. He turns to* MR. FRANK *as* MR. FRANK *comes back.)* I have some contracts here . . . I wonder if you'd look over them with me . . .

MR. FRANK *(putting out his hand).* Of course.

MR. KRALER. *(He rises.)* If we could go downstairs . . . *(*MR. FRANK *starts ahead,* MR. KRALER *speaks to the others.)* Will you forgive us? I won't keep him but a minute. *(He starts to follow* MR. FRANK *down the steps.)*

MARGOT *(with sudden foreboding).* What's happened? Something's happened! Hasn't it, Mr. Kraler?

*(*MR. KRALER *stops and comes back, trying to reassure* MARGOT *with a pretense of casualness.)*

MR. KRALER. No, really. I want your father's advice . . .

MARGOT. Something's gone wrong! I know it!

MR. FRANK *(coming back, to* MR. KRALER*).* If it's something that concerns us here, it's better that we all hear it.

MR. KRALER *(turning to him, quietly).* But . . . the children . . . ?

MR. FRANK. What they'd imagine would be worse than any reality.

(As MR. KRALER *speaks, they all listen with intense apprehension.* MRS. VAN DAAN *comes down the stairs and sits on the bottom step.)*

MR. KRALER. It's a man in the storeroom . . . I don't know whether or not you remember him . . . Carl, about fifty, heavy-set, near-sighted . . . He came with us just before you left.

MR. FRANK. He was from Utrecht?

MR. KRALER. That's the man. A couple of weeks ago, when I was in the storeroom, he closed the door and asked me . . . how's Mr. Frank? What do you hear from Mr. Frank? I told him I only knew there was a rumor that you were in Switzerland.

He said he'd heard that rumor too, but he thought I might know something more. I didn't pay any attention to it . . . but then a thing happened yesterday . . . He'd brought some invoices to the office for me to sign. As I was going through them, I looked up. He was standing staring at the bookcase . . . your bookcase. He said he thought he remembered a door there . . . Wasn't there a door there that used to go up to the loft? Then he told me he wanted more money. Twenty guilders[3] more a week.

MR. VAN DAAN. Blackmail!

MR. FRANK. Twenty guilders? Very modest blackmail.

MR. VAN DAAN. That's just the beginning.

DUSSEL (*coming to* MR. FRANK). You know what I think? He was the thief who was down there that night. That's how he knows we're here.

MR. FRANK (*to* MR. KRALER). How was it left? What did you tell him?

MR. KRALER. I said I had to think about it. What shall I do? Pay him the money? . . . Take a chance on firing him . . . or what? I don't know.

DUSSEL (*frantic*). For God's sake don't fire him! Pay him what he asks . . . keep him here where you can have your eye on him.

MR. FRANK. Is it so much that he's asking? What are they paying nowadays?

MR. KRALER. He could get it in a war plant. But this isn't a war plant. Mind you, I don't know if he really knows . . . or if he doesn't know.

MR. FRANK. Offer him half. Then we'll soon find out if it's blackmail or not.

DUSSEL. And if it is? We've got to pay it, haven't we? Anything he asks we've got to pay!

MR. FRANK. Let's decide that when the time comes.

MR. KRALER. This may be all imagination. You get to a point, these days, where you suspect everyone and everything. Again and again . . . on some simple look or word, I've found myself . . .

(*The telephone rings in the office below.*)

MRS. VAN DAAN (*hurrying to* MR. KRALER). There's the telephone! What does that mean, the telephone ringing on a holiday?

MR. KRALER. That's my wife. I told her I had to go over some papers in my office . . . to call me there when she got out of church. (*He starts out.*) I'll offer him half then. Good-by . . . we'll hope for the best!

(*The group call their good-bys halfheartedly.* MR. FRANK *follows* MR. KRALER, *to bolt the door below. During the following scene,* MR. FRANK *comes back up and stands listening, disturbed.*)

DUSSEL (*to* MR. VAN DAAN). You can thank your son for this . . . smashing the light! I tell you, it's just a question of time now. (*He goes to the window at the back and stands looking out.*)

MARGOT. Sometimes I wish the end would come . . . whatever it is.

MRS. FRANK (*shocked*). Margot!

(ANNE *goes to* MARGOT, *sitting beside her on the couch with her arms around her.*)

MARGOT. Then at least we'd know where we were.

MRS. FRANK. You should be ashamed of yourself! Talking that way! Think how lucky we are! Think of the thousands dying in the war, every day. Think of the people in concentration camps.

ANNE (*interrupting*). What's the good of that? What's the good of thinking of misery when you're already miserable? That's stupid!

---

3. *Twenty guilders,* a little over $5.00 in American money. The guilder is the monetary unit of the Netherlands.

MRS. FRANK. Anne!

(As ANNE goes on raging at her mother, MRS. FRANK tries to break in, in an effort to quiet her.)

ANNE. We're young. Margot and Peter and I! You grownups have had your chance! But look at us . . . If we begin thinking of all the horror in the world, we're lost! We're trying to hold onto some kind of ideals . . . when everything . . . ideals, hopes . . . everything, are being destroyed! It isn't our fault that the world is in such a mess! We weren't around when all this started! So don't try to take it out on us! (She rushes off to her room, slamming the door after her. She picks up a brush from the chest and hurls it to the floor. Then she sits on the settee, trying to control her anger.)

MR. VAN DAAN. She talks as if we started the war! Did we start the war?

(He spots ANNE'S cake. As he starts to take it, PETER anticipates him.)

PETER. She left her cake. (He starts for ANNE'S room with the cake. There is silence in the main room. MRS. VAN DAAN goes up to her room, followed by MR. VAN DAAN. DUSSEL stays looking out the window. MR. FRANK brings MRS. FRANK her cake. She eats it slowly, without relish. MR. FRANK takes his cake to MARGOT and sits quietly on the sofa beside her. PETER stands in the doorway of ANNE'S darkened room, looking at her, then makes a little movement to let her know he is there. ANNE sits up, quickly, trying to hide the signs of her tears. PETER holds out the cake to her.) You left this.

ANNE (dully). Thanks.

(PETER starts to go out, then comes back.)

PETER. I thought you were fine just now. You know just how to talk to them. You know just how to say it. I'm no good . . . I

never can think . . . especially when I'm mad . . . That Dussel . . . when he said that about Mouschi . . . someone eating him . . . all I could think is . . . I wanted to hit him. I wanted to give him such a . . . a . . . that he'd . . . That's what I used to do when there was an argument at school . . . That's the way I . . . but here . . . And an old man like that . . . it wouldn't be so good.

ANNE. You're making a big mistake about me. I do it all wrong. I say too much. I go too far. I hurt people's feelings . . .

(DUSSEL leaves the window, going to his room.)

PETER. I think you're just fine . . . What I want to say . . . if it wasn't for you around here, I don't know. What I mean . . .

(PETER is interrupted by DUSSEL'S turning on the light. DUSSEL stands in the doorway, startled to see PETER. PETER advances toward him forbiddingly. DUSSEL backs out of the room. PETER closes the door on him.)

ANNE. Do you mean it, Peter? Do you really mean it?

PETER. I said it, didn't I?

ANNE. Thank you, Peter!

(In the main room MR. and MRS. FRANK collect the dishes and take them to the sink, washing them. MARGOT lies down again on the couch. DUSSEL, lost, wanders into PETER'S room and takes up a book, starting to read.)

PETER (looking at the photographs on the wall). You've got quite a collection.

ANNE. Wouldn't you like some in your room? I could give you some. Heaven knows you spend enough time in there . . . doing heaven knows what. . . .

PETER. It's easier. A fight starts, or an argument . . . I duck in there.

ANNE. You're lucky, having a room to go to. His lordship is always here . . . I hardly ever get a minute alone. When they start in on me, I can't duck away. I have to stand there and take it.

PETER. You gave some of it back just now.

ANNE. I get so mad. They've formed their opinions . . . about everything . . . but we . . . we're still trying to find out . . . We have problems here that no other people our age have ever had. And just as you think you've solved them, something comes along and bang! You have to start all over again.

PETER. At least you've got someone you can talk to.

ANNE. Not really. Mother . . . I never discuss anything serious with her. She doesn't understand. Father's all right. We can talk about everything . . . everything but one thing. Mother. He simply won't talk about her. I don't think you can be really intimate with anyone if he holds something back, do you?

PETER. I think your father's fine.

ANNE. Oh, he is, Peter! He is! He's the only one who's ever given me the feeling that I have any sense. But anyway, nothing can take the place of school and play and friends of your own age . . . or near your age . . . can it?

PETER. I suppose you miss your friends and all.

ANNE. It isn't just . . . (She breaks off, staring up at him for a second.) Isn't it funny, you and I? Here we've been seeing each other every minute for almost a year and a half, and this is the first time we've ever really talked. It helps a lot to have someone to talk to, don't you think? It helps you to let off steam.

PETER (going to the door). Well, any time you want to let off steam, you can come into my room.

ANNE (following him). I can get up an awful lot of steam. You'll have to be careful how you say that.

PETER. It's all right with me.

ANNE. Do you really mean it?

PETER. I said it, didn't I?

(He goes out. ANNE stands in her doorway looking after him. As PETER gets to his door he stands for a minute looking back at her. Then he goes into his room. DUSSEL rises as he comes in, and quickly passes him, going out. He starts across for his room. ANNE sees him coming, and pulls her door shut. DUSSEL turns back toward PETER'S room. PETER pulls his door shut. DUSSEL stands there, bewildered, forlorn.

The scene slowly dims out. The curtain falls on the scene. ANNE'S VOICE comes over in the darkness . . . faintly at first, and then with growing strength.)

ANNE'S VOICE. We've had bad news. The people from whom Miep got our ration books have been arrested. So we have had to cut down on our food. Our stomachs are so empty that they rumble and make strange noises, all in different keys. Mr. Van Daan's is deep and low, like a bass fiddle. Mine is high, whistling like a flute. As we all sit around waiting for supper, it's like an orchestra tuning up. It only needs Toscanini[4] to raise his baton and we'd be off in the Ride of the Valkyries.[5] Monday, the sixth of March, nineteen forty-four. Mr. Kraler is in the hospital. It seems he has ulcers. Pim says we are his ulcers. Miep has to run the business and us too. The Americans have landed on the southern tip of Italy. Father looks for a quick finish to the war. Mr. Dussel is waiting every day for the warehouse man to

---

4. *Toscanini* (tos′kə nē′nē), American musical conductor, born in Italy.
5. *Ride of the Valkyries* (val kir′ēz), a vigorous and inspiring musical composition by German composer Richard Wagner.

demand more money. Have I been skipping too much from one subject to another? I can't help it. I feel that spring is coming. I feel it in my whole body and soul. I feel utterly confused. I am longing . . . so longing . . . for everything . . . for friends . . . for someone to talk to . . . someone who understands . . . someone young, who feels as I do . . .

(As these last lines are being said, the curtain rises on the scene. The lights dim on. ANNE'S VOICE *fades out.)*

Discussion

1. (a) Approximately how much time has passed between the end of Act One and the beginning of Act Two? **(b)** For how long have the Franks been in hiding? **(c)** How do the dramatists show the passing of time?

2. Describe incidents in this scene which make evident each of the following: **(a)** Mr. Dussel's disagreeable personality; **(b)** Miep's and Mr. Kraler's generosity; **(c)** Mr. Van Daan's greed; **(d)** Mrs. Van Daan's vanity; **(e)** Mr. Frank's level-headedness.

3. (a) What new problem does Mr. Kraler present to the inhabitants of the annex? **(b)** What solution is decided upon?

4. (a) Explain the situation that causes Anne to flare up at her mother. **(b)** Do you think her behavior is justified? Explain your answer. **(c)** How does Anne's anger lead to greater intimacy between herself and Peter?

5. (a) What does Anne mean when she says to Peter that in all the time in the annex "this is the first time we've ever really talked"? **(b)** In their private conversation what are some of the things they reveal about themselves?

6. (a) How long after the rest of the scene is Anne's diary entry written? **(b)** What do you learn from this entry?

SCENE TWO

It is evening, after supper. From the outside we hear the sound of children playing. The "grownups," with the exception of MR. VAN DAAN, *are all in the main room.* MRS. FRANK *is doing some mending,* MRS. VAN DAAN *is reading a fashion magazine.* MR. FRANK *is going over business accounts.* DUSSEL, *in his dentist's jacket, is pacing up and down, impatient to get into his bedroom.* MR. VAN DAAN *is upstairs working on a piece of embroidery in an embroidery frame.*

In his room PETER *is sitting before the mirror, smoothing his hair. As the scene goes on, he puts on his tie, brushes his coat and puts it on preparing himself meticulously for a visit from* ANNE. *On his wall are now hung some of* ANNE'S *motion picture stars.*

In her room ANNE *too is getting dressed. She stands before the mirror in her slip, trying various ways of dressing her hair.* MARGOT *is seated on the sofa, hemming a skirt for* ANNE *to wear.*

In the main room DUSSEL *can stand it no longer. He comes over, rapping sharply on the door of his and* ANNE'S *bedroom.*

ANNE *(calling to him).* No, no, Mr. Dussel! I

am not dressed yet. (DUSSEL *walks away, furious, sitting down and burying his head in his hands.* ANNE *turns to* MARGOT.) How is that? How does that look?

MARGOT *(glancing at her briefly).* Fine.

ANNE. You didn't even look.

MARGOT. Of course I did. It's fine.

ANNE. Margot, tell me, am I terribly ugly?

MARGOT. Oh, stop fishing.

ANNE. No. No. Tell me.

MARGOT. Of course you're not. You've got nice eyes . . . and a lot of animation, and . . .

ANNE. A little vague, aren't you?

(She reaches over and takes a brassière out of MARGOT's *sewing basket. She holds it up to herself, studying the effect in the mirror. Outside,* MRS. FRANK, *feeling sorry for* DUSSEL, *comes over, knocking at the girls' door.)*

MRS. FRANK *(outside).* May I come in?

MARGOT. Come in, Mother.

MRS. FRANK *(shutting the door behind her).* Mr. Dussel's impatient to get in here.

ANNE *(still with the brassière).* Heavens, he takes the room for himself the entire day.

MRS. FRANK *(gently).* Anne, dear, you're not going in again tonight to see Peter?

ANNE *(dignified).* That is my intention.

MRS. FRANK. But you've already spent a great deal of time in there today.

ANNE. I was in there exactly twice. Once to get the dictionary, and then three-quarters of an hour before supper.

MRS. FRANK. Aren't you afraid you're disturbing him?

ANNE. Mother, I have some intuition.

MRS. FRANK. Then may I ask you this much, Anne. Please don't shut the door when you go in.

ANNE. You sound like Mrs. Van Daan! *(She throws the brassière back in* MARGOT's *sewing basket and picks up her blouse, putting it on.)*

MRS. FRANK. No. No. I don't mean to suggest anything wrong. I only wish that you wouldn't expose yourself to criticism . . . that you wouldn't give Mrs. Van Daan the opportunity to be unpleasant.

ANNE. Mrs. Van Daan doesn't need an opportunity to be unpleasant!

MRS. FRANK. Everyone's on edge, worried about Mr. Kraler. This is one more thing . . .

ANNE. I'm sorry, Mother. I'm going to Peter's room. I'm not going to let Petronella Van Daan spoil our friendship.

*(MRS. FRANK *hesitates for a second, then goes out, closing the door after her. She gets a pack of playing cards and sits at the center table, playing solitaire. In* ANNE's *room* MARGOT *hands the finished skirt to* ANNE. *As* ANNE *is putting it on,* MARGOT *takes off her high-heeled shoes and stuffs paper in the toes so that* ANNE *can wear them.)*

MARGOT *(to* ANNE).* Why don't you two talk in the main room? It'd save a lot of trouble. It's hard on Mother, having to listen to those remarks from Mrs. Van Daan and not say a word.

ANNE. Why doesn't she say a word? I think it's ridiculous to take it and take it.

MARGOT. You don't understand Mother at all, do you? She can't talk back. She's not like you. It's just not in her nature to fight back.

ANNE. Anyway . . . the only one I worry about is you. I feel awfully guilty about you. *(She sits on the stool near* MARGOT, *putting on* MARGOT's *high-heeled shoes.)*

MARGOT. What about?

ANNE. I mean, every time I go into Peter's room, I have a feeling I may be hurting you. (MARGOT *shakes her head.)* I know if it were me, I'd be wild. I'd be desperately jealous, if it were me.

MARGOT. Well, I'm not.

ANNE. You don't feel badly? Really? Truly? You're not jealous?

MARGOT. Of course I'm jealous . . . jealous that you've got something to get up in the morning for . . . But jealous of you and Peter? No.

(ANNE *goes back to the mirror.*)

ANNE. Maybe there's nothing to be jealous of. Maybe he doesn't really like me. Maybe I'm just taking the place of his cat . . . *(She picks up a pair of short, white gloves, putting them on.)* Wouldn't you like to come in with us?

MARGOT. I have a book.

(The sound of the children playing outside fades out. In the main room DUSSEL *can stand it no longer. He jumps up, going to the bedroom door and knocking sharply.)*

DUSSEL. Will you please let me in my room!

ANNE. Just a minute, dear, dear Mr. Dussel. *(She picks up her Mother's pink stole and adjusts it elegantly over her shoulder, then gives a last look in the mirror.)* Well, here I go . . . to run the gauntlet. *(She starts out, followed by* MARGOT.*)*

DUSSEL *(as she appears—sarcastic).* Thank you so much.

*(*DUSSEL *goes into his room.* ANNE *goes toward* PETER'S *room, passing* MRS. VAN DAAN *and her parents at the center table.)*

MRS. VAN DAAN. My God, look at her! *(*ANNE *pays no attention. She knocks at* PETER'S *door.)* I don't know what good it is to have a son. I never see him. He wouldn't care if I killed myself. *(*PETER *opens the door and stands aside for* ANNE *to come in.)* Just a minute, Anne. *(She goes to them at the door.)* I'd like to say a few words to my son. Do you mind? *(*PETER *and* ANNE *stand waiting.)* Peter, I don't want you staying up till all hours tonight. You've got to have your sleep. You're a growing boy. You hear?

MRS. FRANK. Anne won't stay late. She's going to bed promptly at nine. Aren't you, Anne?

ANNE. Yes, Mother . . . *(To* MRS. VAN DAAN*)* May we go now?

MRS. VAN DAAN. Are you asking me? I didn't know I had anything to say about it.

MRS. FRANK. Listen for the chimes, Anne dear.

(The two young people go off into PETER'S *room, shutting the door after them.)*

MRS. VAN DAAN *(to* MRS. FRANK*).* In my day it was the boys who called on the girls. Not the girls on the boys.

MRS. FRANK. You know how young people like to feel that they have secrets. Peter's room is the only place where they can talk.

MRS. VAN DAAN. Talk! That's not what they called it when I was young.

*(*MRS. VAN DAAN *goes off to the bathroom.* MARGOT *settles down to read her book.* MR. FRANK *puts his papers away and brings a chess game to the center table. He and* MRS. FRANK *start to play. In* PETER'S *room,* ANNE *speaks to* PETER, *indignant, humiliated.)*

ANNE. Aren't they awful? Aren't they impossible? Treating us as if we were still in the nursery. *(She sits on the cot.* PETER *gets a bottle of pop and two glasses.)*

PETER. Don't let it bother you. It doesn't bother me.

ANNE. I suppose you can't really blame them . . . *they* think back to what they were like at our age. They don't realize how much more advanced we are . . . When you think what wonderful discussions we've had! . . . Oh, I forgot. I was going to bring you some more pictures.

PETER. Oh, these are fine, thanks.

ANNE. Don't you want some more? Miep just brought me some new ones.

PETER. Maybe later. *(He gives her a glass of*

pop and taking some for himself, sits down facing her.)

ANNE *(looking up at one of the photographs).* I remember when I got that . . . I won it. I bet Jopie that I could eat five ice-cream cones. We'd all been playing ping-pong . . . We used to have heavenly times . . . we'd finish up with ice cream at the Delphi, or the Oasis, where Jews were allowed . . . there'd always be a lot of boys . . . we'd laugh and joke . . . I'd like to go back to it for a few days or a week. But after that I know I'd be bored to death. I think more seriously about life now. I want to be a journalist . . . or something. I love to write. What do you want to do?

PETER. I thought I might go off some place . . . work on a farm or something . . . some job that doesn't take much brains.

ANNE. You shouldn't talk that way. You've got the most awful inferiority complex.

PETER. I know I'm not smart.

ANNE. That isn't true. You're much better than I am in dozens of things . . . arithmetic and algebra and . . . well, you're a million times better than I am in algebra. *(with sudden directness)* You like Margot, don't you? Right from the start you liked her, liked her much better than me.

PETER *(uncomfortably).* Oh, I don't know.
(In the main room MRS. VAN DAAN *comes from the bathroom and goes over to the sink, polishing a coffeepot.)*

ANNE. It's all right. Everyone feels that way. Margot's so good. She's sweet and bright and beautiful and I'm not.

PETER. I wouldn't say that.

ANNE. Oh, no, I'm not. I know that. I know quite well that I'm not a beauty. I never have been and never shall be.

PETER. I don't agree at all. I think you're pretty.

ANNE. That's not true!

PETER. And another thing. You've changed . . . from at first, I mean.

ANNE. I have?

PETER. I used to think you were awful noisy.

ANNE. And what do you think now, Peter? How have I changed?

PETER. Well . . . er . . . you're . . . quieter.
(In his room DUSSEL *takes his pajamas and toilet articles and goes into the bathroom to change.)*

ANNE. I'm glad you don't just hate me.

PETER. I never said that.

ANNE. I bet when you get out of here you'll never think of me again.

PETER. That's crazy.

ANNE. When you get back with all of your friends, you're going to say . . . now what did I ever see in that Mrs. Quack Quack.

PETER. I haven't got any friends.

ANNE. Oh, Peter, of course you have. Everyone has friends.

PETER. Not me. I don't want any. I get along all right without them.

ANNE. Does that mean you can get along without me? I think of myself as your friend.

PETER. No. If they were all like you, it'd be different.
(He takes the glasses and the bottle and puts them away. There is a second's silence and then ANNE *speaks, hesitantly, shyly.)*

ANNE. Peter, did you ever kiss a girl?

PETER. Yes. Once.

ANNE *(to cover her feelings).* That picture's crooked. (PETER *goes over, straightening the photograph.)* Was she pretty?

PETER. Huh?

ANNE. The girl that you kissed.

PETER. I don't know. I was blindfolded.

(He comes back and sits down again.) It was a party. One of those kissing games.

ANNE *(relieved).* Oh, I don't suppose that really counts, does it?

PETER. It didn't with me.

ANNE. I've been kissed twice. Once a man I'd never seen before kissed me on the cheek when he picked me up off the ice and I was crying. And the other was Mr. Koophuis,[1] a friend of Father's who kissed my hand. You wouldn't say those counted, would you?

PETER. I wouldn't say so.

ANNE. I know almost for certain that Margot would never kiss anyone unless she was engaged to them. And I'm sure too that Mother never touched a man before Pim. But I don't know . . . things are so different now. . . . What do you think? Do you think a girl shouldn't kiss anyone except if she's engaged or something? It's so hard to try to think what to do, when here we are with the whole world falling around our ears and you think . . . well . . . you don't know what's going to happen tomorrow and . . . What do you think?

PETER. I suppose it'd depend on the girl. Some girls, anything they do's wrong. But others . . . well . . . it wouldn't necessarily be wrong with them. *(The carillon starts to strike nine o'clock.)* I've always thought that when two people . . .

ANNE. Nine o'clock. I have to go.

PETER. That's right.

ANNE *(without moving).* Good night.

(There is a second's pause, then PETER gets up and moves toward the door.)

PETER. You won't let them stop you coming?

ANNE. No. *(She rises and starts for the door.)* Sometime I might bring my diary. There are so many things in it that I want to talk over with you. There's a lot about you.

PETER. What kind of thing?

ANNE. I wouldn't want you to see some of it. I thought you were a nothing, just the way you thought about me.

PETER. Did you change your mind, the way I changed my mind about you?

ANNE. Well . . . You'll see . . .

(For a second ANNE stands looking up at PETER, longing for him to kiss her. As he makes no move she turns away. Then suddenly PETER grabs her awkwardly in his arms, kissing her on the cheek. ANNE walks out dazed. She stands for a minute, her back to the people in the main room. As she regains her poise she goes to her mother and father and MARGOT, silently kissing them. They murmur their good nights to her. As she is about to open her bedroom door, she catches sight of MRS. VAN DAAN. She goes quickly to her, taking her face in her hands and kissing her first on one cheek and then on the other. Then she hurries off into her room. MRS. VAN DAAN looks after her, and then looks over at PETER's room. Her suspicions are confirmed.)

MRS. VAN DAAN. *(She knows.)* Ah hah!

(The lights dim out. The curtain falls on the scene. In the darkness ANNE'S VOICE comes faintly at first and then with growing strength.)

ANNE'S VOICE. By this time we all know each other so well that if anyone starts to tell a story, the rest can finish it for him. We're having to cut down still further on our meals. What makes it worse, the rats have been at work again. They've carried off some of our precious food. Even Mr. Dussel wishes now that Mouschi was here. Thursday, the twentieth of April,

---

1. *Mr. Koophuis* (kōp′hous)

nineteen forty-four. Invasion fever[2] is mounting every day. Miep tells us that people outside talk of nothing else. For myself, life has become much more pleasant. I often go to Peter's room after supper. Oh, don't think I'm in love, because I'm not. But it does make life more bearable to have someone with whom you can exchange views. No more tonight. P.S. . . . I must be honest. I must confess that I actually live for the next meeting. Is there anything lovelier than to sit under the skylight and feel the sun on your cheeks and have a darling boy in your arms? I admit now that I'm glad the Van Daans had a son and not a daughter. I've outgrown another dress. That's the third. I'm having to wear Margot's clothes after all. I'm working hard on my French and am now reading *La Belle Nivernaise*.[3]

(As she is saying the last lines, the curtain rises on the scene. The lights dim on, as ANNE'S VOICE *fades out.)*

---

2. *Invasion fever,* the expectation that the Allies would invade Europe to free it from German occupation. The invasion actually began on June 6, 1944.
3. *La Belle Nivernaise* (lä bel′ niv′ər nez′), a moral tale for children by Alphonse Daudet, a nineteenth-century French novelist.

Discussion

1. (a) In what ways has Anne changed since the beginning of the previous scene? (b) What has caused this change? (c) Is Mrs. Frank justified in her concern for Anne's behavior? Explain your answer.

2. (a) How do Anne and Margot differ? (b) In what ways does Margot show mature good sense when talking with Anne? (c) Does the relationship between the sisters seem natural? Explain.

3. (a) What feelings exist between the mother and each daughter? (b) What accounts for the closer relationship between Mrs. Frank and Margot?

4. (a) What are some of the things Peter and Anne are concerned about? (b) Discuss whether or not you think these concerns are typical for people their age.

5. (a) How and why does Anne dramatically alter her behavior to Mrs. Van Daan? (b) How does Mrs. Van Daan respond?

Vocabulary • Context

Use the context clues provided to figure out the meaning of the italicized word in each sentence below. Write the letter of the correct answer.

1. As I made my way through the poorly lighted streets, I had the sudden *foreboding* that I would soon be hopelessly lost. (a) memory; (b) hope; (c) feeling that something good will happen; (d) feeling that something bad will happen.

2. The senator would neither *confirm* nor deny the rumor that she was resigning. (a) ask questions about; (b) state the truth of; (c) argue; (d) understand.

3. Just when the Union troops thought they had won the battle, the Confederate forces defeated them with one last fierce *onslaught*. (a) agreement; (b) shot; (c) attack; (d) threat.

4. Her *animation* when she spoke about the project convinced us that she was truly enthusiastic about it. (a) sarcastic smile; (b) liveliness of manner; (c) angry tone; (d) organized discussion.

5. When the reporter disagreed with his views, Professor Turner seemed to be *disgruntled* and refused to continue with the interview. (a) in a bad mood; (b) in a good mood; (c) lazy; (d) amused.

SCENE THREE

It is night, a few weeks later. Everyone is in bed. There is complete quiet. In the VAN DAANS' *room a match flares up for a moment and then is quickly put out.* MR. VAN DAAN, *in bare feet, dressed in underwear and trousers, is dimly seen coming stealthily down the stairs and into the main room, where* MR. *and* MRS. FRANK *and* MARGOT *are sleeping. He goes to the food safe and again lights a match. Then he cautiously opens the safe, taking out a half-loaf of bread. As he closes the safe, it creaks. He stands rigid.* MRS. FRANK *sits up in bed. She sees him.*

MRS. FRANK *(screaming).* Otto! Otto! *Komme schnell!*[1]

(The rest of the people wake, hurriedly getting up.)

MR. FRANK. *Was ist los? Was ist passiert?*[2]

*(*DUSSEL, *followed by* ANNE, *comes from his room.)*

MRS. FRANK *(as she rushes over to* MR. VAN DAAN*). Er stiehlt das Essen!*[3]

DUSSEL *(grabbing* MR. VAN DAAN*).* You! You! Give me that.

MRS. VAN DAAN *(coming down the stairs).* Putti . . . Putti . . . what is it?

DUSSEL *(his hands on* VAN DAAN'S *neck).* You dirty thief . . . stealing food . . . you good-for-nothing . . .

MR. FRANK. Mr. Dussel! For God's sake! Help me, Peter!

*(*PETER *comes over, trying, with* MR. FRANK, *to separate the two struggling men.)*

PETER. Let him go! Let go!

*(*DUSSEL *drops* MR. VAN DAAN, *pushing him away. He shows them the end of a loaf of bread that he has taken from* VAN DAAN.*)*

DUSSEL. You greedy, selfish . . . !

*(*MARGOT *turns on the lights.)*

MRS. VAN DAAN. Putti . . . what is it?

(All of MRS. FRANK'S *gentleness, her self-control, is gone. She is outraged, in a frenzy of indignation.)*

MRS. FRANK. The bread! He was stealing the bread!

DUSSEL. It was you, and all the time we thought it was the rats!

MR. FRANK. Mr. Van Daan, how could you!

MR. VAN DAAN. I'm hungry.

MRS. FRANK. We're all of us hungry! I see the children getting thinner and thinner. Your own son Peter . . . I've heard him moan in his sleep, he's so hungry. And you come in the night and steal food that should go to them . . . to the children!

MRS. VAN DAAN *(going to* MR. VAN DAAN *protectively).* He needs more food than the rest of us. He's used to more. He's a big man.

*(*MR. VAN DAAN *breaks away, going over and sitting on the couch.)*

MRS. FRANK *(turning on* MRS. VAN DAAN*).* And you . . . you're worse than he is! You're a mother, and yet you sacrifice your child to this man . . . this . . . this . . .

MR. FRANK. Edith! Edith!

*(*MARGOT *picks up the pink woolen stole, putting it over her mother's shoulders.)*

---

1. *Komme schnell!* Hurry!
2. *Was ist los? Was ist passiert?* What's the matter? What happened?
3. *Er stiehlt das Essen!* He is stealing food.

MRS. FRANK *(paying no attention, going on to* MRS. VAN DAAN*)*. Don't think I haven't seen you! Always saving the choicest bits for him! I've watched you day after day and I've held my tongue. But not any longer! Not after this! Now I want him to go! I want him to get out of here!

MR. FRANK. Edith!

MR. VAN DAAN. Get out of here? } *(Together)*

MRS. VAN DAAN. What do you mean?

MRS. FRANK. Just that! Take your things and get out!

MR. FRANK *(to* MRS. FRANK*)*. You're speaking in anger. You cannot mean what you are saying.

MRS. FRANK. I mean exactly that!

*(*MRS. VAN DAAN *takes a cover from the* FRANKS' *bed, pulling it about her.)*

MR. FRANK. For two long years we have lived here, side by side. We have respected each other's rights . . . we have managed to live in peace. Are we now going to throw it all away? I know this will never happen again, will it, Mr. Van Daan?

MR. VAN DAAN. No. No.

MRS. FRANK. He steals once! He'll steal again!

*(*MR. VAN DAAN, *holding his stomach, starts for the bathroom.* ANNE *puts her arms around him, helping him up the step.)*

MR. FRANK. Edith, please. Let us be calm. We'll all go to our rooms . . . and afterwards we'll sit down quietly and talk this out . . . we'll find some way . . .

MRS. FRANK. No! No! No more talk! I want them to leave!

MRS. VAN DAAN. You'd put us out, on the streets?

MRS. FRANK. There are other hiding places.

MRS. VAN DAAN. A cellar . . . a closet. I

know. And we have no money left even to pay for that.

MRS. FRANK. I'll give you money. Out of my own pocket I'll give it gladly.

(She gets her purse from a shelf and comes back with it.)

MRS. VAN DAAN. Mr. Frank, you told Putti you'd never forget what he'd done for you when you came to Amsterdam. You said you could never repay him, that you . . .

MRS. FRANK *(counting out money)*. If my husband had any obligation to you, he's paid it, over and over.

MR. FRANK. Edith, I've never seen you like this before. I don't know you.

MRS. FRANK. I should have spoken out long ago.

DUSSEL. You can't be nice to some people.

MRS. VAN DAAN *(turning on* DUSSEL*)*. There would have been plenty for all of us, if *you* hadn't come in here!

MR. FRANK. We don't need the Nazis to destroy us. We're destroying ourselves.

(He sits down, with his head in his hands. MRS. FRANK *goes to* MRS. VAN DAAN.*)*

MRS. FRANK *(giving* MRS. VAN DAAN *some money)*. Give this to Miep. She'll find you a place.

ANNE. Mother, you're not putting *Peter* out. Peter hasn't done anything.

MRS. FRANK. He'll stay, of course. When I say I must protect the children, I mean Peter too.

*(*PETER *rises from the steps where he has been sitting.)*

PETER. I'd have to go if Father goes.

*(*MR. VAN DAAN *comes from the bathroom.* MRS. VAN DAAN *hurries to him and takes him to the couch. Then she gets water from the sink to bathe his face.)*

MRS. FRANK *(while this is going on)*. He's no father to you . . . that man! He doesn't know what it is to be a father!

PETER (starting for his room). I wouldn't feel right. I couldn't stay.

MRS. FRANK. Very well, then. I'm sorry.

ANNE (rushing over to PETER). No, Peter! No! (PETER goes into his room, closing the door after him. ANNE turns back to her mother, crying.) I don't care about the food. They can have mine! I don't want it! Only don't send them away. It'll be daylight soon. They'll be caught . . .

MARGOT (putting her arms comfortingly around ANNE). Please, Mother!

MRS. FRANK. They're not going now. They'll stay here until Miep finds them a place. (To MRS. VAN DAAN) But one thing I insist on! He must never come down here again! He must never come to this room where the food is stored! We'll divide what we have . . . an equal share for each! (DUSSEL hurries over to get a sack of potatoes from the food safe. MRS. FRANK goes on, to MRS. VAN DAAN.) You can cook it here and take it up to him.

(DUSSEL brings the sack of potatoes back to the center table.)

MARGOT. Oh, no. No. We haven't sunk so far that we're going to fight over a handful of rotten potatoes.

DUSSEL (dividing the potatoes into piles). Mrs. Frank, Mr. Frank, Margot, Anne, Peter, Mrs. Van Daan, Mr. Van Daan, myself . . . Mrs. Frank . . .

(The buzzer sounds in MIEP's signal.)

MR. FRANK. It's Miep! (He hurries over, getting his overcoat and putting it on.)

MARGOT. At this hour?

MRS. FRANK. It is trouble.

MR. FRANK (as he starts down to unbolt the door). I beg you, don't let her see a thing like this!

MR. DUSSEL (counting without stopping). . . . Anne, Peter, Mrs. Van Daan, Mr. Van Daan, myself . . .

MARGOT (to DUSSEL). Stop it! Stop it!

DUSSEL. . . . Mr. Frank, Margot, Anne, Peter, Mrs. Van Daan, Mr. Van Daan, myself, Mrs. Frank . . .

MRS. VAN DAAN. You're keeping the big ones for yourself! All the big ones . . . Look at the size of that! . . . And that!

(DUSSEL continues on with his dividing. PETER, with his shirt and trousers on, comes from his room.)

MARGOT. Stop it! Stop it!

(We hear MIEP's excited voice speaking to MR. FRANK below.)

MIEP. Mr. Frank . . . the most wonderful news! . . . The invasion has begun!

MR. FRANK. Go on, tell them! Tell them!

(MIEP comes running up the steps, ahead of MR. FRANK. She has a man's raincoat on over her nightclothes and a bunch of orange-colored flowers in her hand.)

MIEP. Did you hear that, everybody? Did you hear what I said? The invasion has begun! The invasion!

(They all stare at MIEP, unable to grasp what she is telling them. PETER is the first to recover his wits.)

PETER. Where?

MRS. VAN DAAN. When? When, Miep?

MIEP. It began early this morning . . .

(As she talks on, the realization of what she has said begins to dawn on them. Everyone goes crazy. A wild demonstration takes place. MRS. FRANK hugs MR. VAN DAAN.)

MRS. FRANK. Oh, Mr. Van Daan, did you hear that?

(DUSSEL embraces MRS. VAN DAAN. PETER grabs a frying pan and parades around the room, beating on it, singing the Dutch National Anthem. ANNE and MARGOT follow him, singing, weaving in and out among the excited grownups. MARGOT breaks away to take the flowers from MIEP and distribute them to everyone. While this pandemonium *is going on* MRS. FRANK *tries to make herself heard above the excitement.*)

MRS. FRANK *(to* MIEP*).* How do you know?

MIEP. The radio . . . The B.B.C.![4] They said they landed on the coast of Normandy!

PETER. The British?

MIEP. British, Americans, French, Dutch, Poles, Norwegians . . . all of them! More than four thousand ships! Churchill spoke, and General Eisenhower![5] D-Day they call it!

MR. FRANK. Thank God, it's come!

MRS. VAN DAAN. At last!

MIEP *(starting out).* I'm going to tell Mr. Kraler. This'll be better than any blood transfusion.

MR. FRANK *(stopping her).* What part of Normandy did they land, did they say?

MIEP. Normandy . . . that's all I know now . . . I'll be up the minute I hear some more! *(She goes hurriedly out.)*

MR. FRANK *(to* MRS. FRANK*).* What did I tell you? What did I tell you?

(MRS. FRANK *indicates that he has forgotten to bolt the door after* MIEP. *He hurries down the steps.* MR. VAN DAAN, *sitting on the couch, suddenly breaks into a convulsive sob. Everybody looks at him, bewildered.*)

MRS. VAN DAAN *(hurrying to him).* Putti! Putti! What is it? What happened?

MR. VAN DAAN. Please. I'm so ashamed.

(MR. FRANK *comes back up the steps.*)

DUSSEL. Oh, for God's sake!

MRS. VAN DAAN. Don't, Putti.

MARGOT. It doesn't matter now!

MR. FRANK *(going to* MR. VAN DAAN*).* Didn't you hear what Miep said? The invasion has come! We're going to be liberated! This is a time to celebrate! *(He embraces* MRS. FRANK *and then hurries to the cupboard and gets the cognac and a glass.)*

MR. VAN DAAN. To steal bread from children!

MRS. FRANK. We've all done things that we're ashamed of.

ANNE. Look at me, the way I've treated Mother . . . so mean and horrid to her.

MRS. FRANK. No, Anneke, no.

(ANNE *runs to her mother, putting her arms around her.*)

ANNE. Oh, Mother, I was. I was awful.

MR. VAN DAAN. Not like me. No one is as bad as me!

---

4. **B.B.C.,** the British Broadcasting Corporation.
5. **Churchill . . . Eisenhower.** Churchill was prime minister of England. Eisenhower was supreme commander of the Allied forces. He later became President of the U.S.

DUSSEL *(to* MR. VAN DAAN*)*. Stop it now! Let's be happy!

MR. FRANK *(giving* MR. VAN DAAN *a glass of cognac).* Here! Here! *Schnapps! Locheim!*[6]

*(*VAN DAAN *takes the cognac. They all watch him. He gives them a feeble smile.* ANNE *puts up her fingers in a V-for-Victory sign. As* VAN DAAN *gives an answering V-sign, they are startled to hear a loud sob from behind them. It is* MRS. FRANK, *stricken with remorse. She is sitting on the other side of the room.)*

MRS. FRANK *(through her sobs).* When I think of the terrible things I said . . .

*(*MR. FRANK, ANNE, *and* MARGOT *hurry to her, trying to comfort her.* MR. VAN DAAN *brings her his glass of cognac.)*

MR. VAN DAAN. No! No! You were right!

MRS. FRANK. That I should speak that way to you! . . . Our friends! . . . Our guests! *(She starts to cry again.)*

DUSSEL. Stop it, you're spoiling the whole invasion!

(As they are comforting her, the lights dim out. The curtain falls.)

ANNE'S VOICE *(faintly at first and then with growing strength).* We're all in much better spirits these days. There's still excellent news of the invasion. The best part about it is that I have a feeling that friends are coming. Who knows? Maybe I'll be back in school by fall. Ha, ha! The joke is on us! The warehouse man doesn't know a thing and we are paying him all that money! . . . Wednesday, the second of July, nineteen forty-four. The invasion seems temporarily to be bogged down. Mr. Kraler has to have an operation, which looks bad. The Gestapo have found the radio that was stolen. Mr. Dussel says they'll trace it back and back to the thief, and then, it's just a matter of time till they get to us. Everyone is low. Even poor Pim can't raise their spirits. I have often been downcast myself . . . but never in despair. I can shake off everything if I write. But . . . and that is the great question . . . will I ever be able to write well? I want to so much. I want to go on living even after my death. Another birthday has gone by, so now I am fifteen. Already I know what I want. I have a goal, an opinion.

(As this is being said—the curtain rises on the scene, the lights dim on, and ANNE'S VOICE *fades out.)*

---

6. *Schnapps!* (shnäps) ***Locheim!*** (lə Hī′əm). Mr. Frank is proposing a toast to life.

Discussion

1. **(a)** Why does Mrs. Frank become enraged for the first time? **(b)** Is her anger justified? Explain. **(c)** How have the playwrights foreshadowed this episode?

2. **(a)** What reason does Mrs. Van Daan give for her husband's behavior? **(b)** Is this an adequate defense for what he has done? Explain your answer.

3. **(a)** How does Peter display loyalty to his father? **(b)** Does this loyalty seem reasonable or unreasonable to you in the light of Peter's previous attitude toward his father? Why?

4. During this scene Mr. Frank says, "We don't need the Nazis to destroy us. We're destroying ourselves." **(a)** Point out the attitudes and actions of various characters that might lead Mr. Frank to make such a remark. **(b)** Explain why you think each of these characters behaves as he or she does.

5. **(a)** What news does Miep bring? **(b)** Why does this news lead to a general reconciliation?

6. By the end of this scene what are your feelings toward Mr. Van Daan? toward Mrs. Frank?

7. **(a)** With what mixture of good and bad news does Anne conclude the scene? **(b)** Why do you think the joyous news of the invasion is mingled with a feeling of foreboding?

SCENE FOUR

It is an afternoon a few weeks later . . . Everyone but MARGOT *is in the main room. There is a sense of great tension.*

Both MRS. FRANK *and* MR. VAN DAAN *are nervously pacing back and forth,* DUSSEL *is standing at the window, looking down fixedly at the street below.* PETER *is at the center table, trying to do his lessons.* ANNE *sits opposite him, writing in her diary.* MRS. VAN DAAN *is seated on the couch, her eyes on* MR. FRANK *as he sits reading.*

The sound of a telephone ringing comes from the office below. They all are rigid, listening tensely. MR. DUSSEL *rushes down to* MR. FRANK.

DUSSEL. There it goes again, the telephone! Mr. Frank, do you hear?

MR. FRANK *(quietly).* Yes. I hear.

DUSSEL *(pleading, insistent).* But this is the third time, Mr. Frank! The third time in quick succession! It's a signal! I tell you it's Miep, trying to get us! For some reason she can't come to us and she's trying to warn us of something!

MR. FRANK. Please. Please.

MR. VAN DAAN *(to* DUSSEL*).* You're wasting your breath.

DUSSEL. Something has happened, Mr. Frank. For three days now Miep hasn't been to see us! And today not a man has come to work. There hasn't been a sound in the building!

MRS. FRANK. Perhaps it's Sunday. We may have lost track of the days.

MR. VAN DAAN *(to* ANNE*).* You with the diary there. What day is it?

DUSSEL *(going to* MRS. FRANK*).* I don't lose track of the days! I know exactly what day it is! It's Friday, the fourth of August. Friday, and not a man at work. *(He rushes back to* MR. FRANK, *pleading with him, almost in tears.)* I tell you Mr. Kraler's dead. That's the only explanation. He's dead and they've closed down the building, and Miep's trying to tell us!

MR. FRANK. She'd never telephone us.

DUSSEL *(frantic).* Mr. Frank, answer that! I beg you, answer it!

MR. FRANK. No.

MR. VAN DAAN. Just pick it up and listen. You don't have to speak. Just listen and see if it's Miep.

DUSSEL (speaking at the same time). For God's sake . . . I ask you.

MR. FRANK. No. I've told you, no. I'll do nothing that might let anyone know we're in the building.

PETER. Mr. Frank's right.

MR. VAN DAAN. There's no need to tell us what side you're on.

MR. FRANK. If we wait patiently, quietly, I believe that help will come.

(There is silence for a minute as they all listen to the telephone ringing.)

DUSSEL. I'm going down. (He rushes down the steps. MR. FRANK tries ineffectually to hold him. DUSSEL runs to the lower door, unbolting it. The telephone stops ringing. DUSSEL bolts the door and comes slowly back up the steps.) Too late. (MR. FRANK goes to MARGOT in ANNE's bedroom.)

MR. VAN DAAN. So we just wait here until we die.

MRS. VAN DAAN (hysterically). I can't stand it! I'll kill myself! I'll kill myself!

MR. VAN DAAN. For God's sake, stop it!

(In the distance, a German military band is heard playing a Viennese waltz.)

MRS. VAN DAAN. I think you'd be glad if I did! I think you want me to die!

MR. VAN DAAN. Whose fault is it we're here? (MRS. VAN DAAN starts for her room. He follows, talking at her.) We could've been safe somewhere . . . in America or Switzerland. But no! No! You wouldn't leave when I wanted to. You couldn't leave your things. You couldn't leave your precious furniture.

MRS. VAN DAAN. Don't touch me!

(She hurries up the stairs, followed by MR. VAN DAAN. PETER, unable to bear it, goes to his room. ANNE looks after him, deeply concerned. DUSSEL returns to his post at the window. MR. FRANK comes back into the main room and takes a book, trying to read.

MRS. FRANK sits near the sink, starting to peel some potatoes. ANNE quietly goes to PETER's room, closing the door after her. PETER is lying face down on the cot. ANNE leans over him, holding him in her arms, trying to bring him out of his despair.)

ANNE. Look, Peter, the sky. (She looks up through the skylight.) What a lovely, lovely day! Aren't the clouds beautiful? You know what I do when it seems as if I couldn't stand being cooped up for one more minute? I think myself out. I think myself on a walk in the park where I used to go with Pim. Where the jonquils and the crocus and violets grow down the slopes. You know the most wonderful part about thinking yourself out? You can have it any way you like. You can have roses and violets and chrysanthemums all blooming at the same time . . . It's funny . . . I used to take it all for granted . . . and now I've gone crazy about everything to do with nature. Haven't you?

PETER. I've just gone crazy. I think if something doesn't happen soon . . . if we don't get out of here . . . I can't stand much more of it!

ANNE (softly). I wish you had a religion, Peter.

PETER. No thanks! Not me!

ANNE. Oh, I don't mean you have to be Orthodox[1] . . . or believe in heaven and hell and purgatory and things . . . I just mean some religion . . . it doesn't matter what. Just to believe in something! When I think of all that's out there . . . the trees . . . and flowers . . . and sea gulls . . . when I think of the dearness of you, Peter, . . . and the goodness of the people we know . . . Mr. Kraler, Miep, Dirk, the

---

1. *Orthodox,* a follower of the branch of Judaism that keeps most closely to ancient ritual, customs, and traditions.

vegetable man, all risking their lives for us every day . . . When I think of these good things, I'm not afraid any more . . . I find myself, and God, and I . . .

(PETER *interrupts, getting up and walking away.*)

PETER. That's fine! But when I begin to think, I get mad! Look at us, hiding out for two years. Not able to move! Caught here like . . . waiting for them to come and get us . . . and all for what?

ANNE. We're not the only people that've had to suffer. There've always been people that've had to . . . sometimes one race . . . sometimes another . . . and yet . . .

PETER. That doesn't make me feel any better!

ANNE (*going to him*). I know it's terrible, trying to have any faith . . . when people are doing such horrible . . . But you know what I sometimes think? I think the world may be going through a phase, the way I was with Mother. It'll pass, maybe not for hundreds of years, but some day . . . I still believe, in spite of everything, that people are really good at heart.

PETER. I want to see something now . . . Not a thousand years from now!

(*He goes over, sitting down again on the cot.*)

ANNE. But, Peter, if you'd only look at it as part of a great pattern . . . that we're just a little minute in the life . . . (*She breaks off.*) Listen to us, going at each other like a couple of stupid grownups! Look at the sky now. Isn't it lovely? (*She holds out her*

hand to him. PETER *takes it and rises, standing with her at the window looking out, his arms around her.)* Some day, when we're outside again, I'm going to . . .

(She breaks off as she hears the sound of a car, its brakes squealing as it comes to a sudden stop. The people in the other rooms also become aware of the sound. They listen tensely. Another car roars up to a screeching stop. ANNE *and* PETER *come from* PETER'S *room.* MR. *and* MRS. VAN DAAN *creep down the stairs.* DUSSEL *comes out from his room. Everyone is listening, hardly breathing. A doorbell clangs again and again in the building below.* MR. FRANK *starts quietly down the steps to the door.* DUSSEL *and* PETER *follow him. The others stand rigid, waiting, terrified.*

In a few seconds DUSSEL *comes stumbling back up the steps. He shakes off* PETER'S *help and goes to his room.* MR. FRANK *bolts the door below, and comes slowly back up the steps. Their eyes are all on him as he stands there for a minute. They realize that what they feared has happened.* MRS. VAN DAAN *starts to whimper.* MR. VAN DAAN *puts her gently in a chair, and then hurries off up the stairs to their room to collect their things.* PETER *goes to comfort his mother. There is a sound of violent pounding on a door below.)*

MR. FRANK *(quietly).* For the past two years we have lived in fear. Now we can live in hope.

(The pounding below becomes more insistent. There are muffled sounds of voices, shouting commands.)

MEN'S VOICES. *Auf machen! Da drinnen! Auf machen! Schnell! Schnell! Schnell!*[2] *etc., etc.*

(*The street door below is forced open. We hear the heavy tread of footsteps coming up.* MR. FRANK *gets two school-bags from the shelves, and gives one to* ANNE *and the other to* MARGOT. *He goes to get a bag for* MRS. FRANK. *The sound of feet coming up grows louder.* PETER *comes to* ANNE, *kissing her good-by, then he goes to his room to collect his things. The buzzer of their door starts to ring.* MR. FRANK *brings* MRS. FRANK *a bag. They stand together, waiting. We hear the thud of gun butts on the door, trying to break it down.*

ANNE *stands, holding her school satchel, looking over at her father and mother with a soft, reassuring smile. She is no longer a child, but a woman with courage to meet whatever lies ahead.*

The lights dim out. The curtain falls on the scene. We hear a mighty crash as the door is shattered. After a second ANNE'S VOICE *is heard.*)

ANNE'S VOICE. And so it seems our stay is over. They are waiting for us now. They've allowed us five minutes to get our things. We can each take a bag and whatever it will hold of clothing. Nothing else. So, dear Diary, that means I must leave you behind. Good-by for a while. P.S. Please, please, Miep, or Mr. Kraler, or anyone else. If you should find this diary, will you please keep it safe for me, because some day I hope . . .

(*Her voice stops abruptly. There is silence. After a second the curtain rises.*)

---

2. *Auf machen . . . Schnell!* Open up in there! Hurry up!

Discussion

1. (a) Why does Mr. Dussel want Mr. Frank to answer the phone? (b) Why does Mr. Frank refuse to answer it? (c) Suppose you were in the theater audience watching this scene. What effect do you think the ringing telephone would have on you? Why?

2. How is tension between the Van Daans revealed?

3. (a) How does Anne attempt to cheer Peter up? (b) What does she say gives her faith? (c) How does Peter respond to Anne's ideas?

4. Mr. Frank says, "For the past two years we have lived in fear. Now we can live in hope." What does this statement show about him?

5. (a) How do the inhabitants behave upon the arrival of the police? (b) Do they behave as you would expect them to?

6. Anne's actual diary ends three days before her arrest. What, then, is the purpose of the diary entry in this scene?

SCENE FIVE

It is again the afternoon in November, 1945. The rooms are as we saw them in the first scene. MR. KRALER *has joined* MIEP *and* MR. FRANK. *There are coffee cups on the table. We see a great change in* MR. FRANK. *He is calm now. His bitterness is gone. He slowly turns a few pages of the diary. They are blank.*

MR. FRANK. No more. (*He closes the diary and puts it down on the couch beside him.*)

MIEP. I'd gone to the country to find food.

When I got back the block was surrounded by police . . .

MR. KRALER. We made it our business to learn how they knew. It was the thief . . . the thief who told them.

(MIEP *goes up to the gas burner, bringing back a pot of coffee.*)

MR. FRANK *(after a pause).* It seems strange to say this, that anyone could be happy in a concentration camp. But Anne was happy in the camp in Holland where they first took us. After two years of being shut up in these rooms, she could be out . . . out in the sunshine and the fresh air that she loved.

MIEP *(offering the coffee to* MR. FRANK*).* A little more?

MR. FRANK *(holding out his cup to her).* The news of the war was good. The British and Americans were sweeping through France. We felt sure that they would get to us in time. In September we were told that we were to be shipped to Poland . . . The men to one camp. The women to another. I was sent to Auschwitz. They went to Belsen.[1] In January we were freed, the few of us who were left. The war wasn't yet over, so it took us a long time to get home. We'd be sent here and there behind the lines where we'd be safe. Each time our train would stop . . . at a siding, or a crossing . . . we'd all get out and go from group to group . . . Where were you? Were you at Belsen? At Buchenwald? At Mauthausen? Is it possible that you knew my wife? Did you ever see my husband? My son? My daughter? That's how I found out about my wife's death . . . of Margot, the Van Daans . . . Dussel. But Anne . . . I still hoped. . . . Yesterday I went to Rotterdam. I'd heard of a woman there. . . . She'd been in Belsen with Anne . . . I know now.

(*He picks up the diary again, and turns the pages back to find a certain passage. As he finds it we hear* ANNE'S VOICE.)

ANNE'S VOICE. In spite of everything, I still believe that people are really good at heart.

(MR. FRANK *slowly closes the diary.*)

MR. FRANK. She puts me to shame.

(*They are silent.*)

The CURTAIN *falls.*

1. *Auschwitz* (oush′vits) . . . *Belsen,* the sites of Nazi concentration camps. Auschwitz is in Poland, Belsen in Germany. Buchenwald (bü′khən vält), mentioned later, is also a concentration camp.

Discussion

1. What is implied by Mr. Frank's reading Anne's diary entry, then saying, "She puts me to shame"?

2. (a) What is the time relationship between the first scene and the last scene of the play? (b) How does Act One, Scene 1 end? (c) Reread the stage directions for Act Two, Scene 5. What has Mr. Frank supposedly been doing for the entire time in between these scenes? (d) What device have the playwrights used to build up this illusion?

The Aftermath

Loomis Dean, Courtesy Otto Frank.
LIFE Magazine © Time Inc.

After the inhabitants of the annex were captured on August 4, 1944, they were first sent to Westerbork, a concentration camp in Holland, about eighty miles from Amsterdam. On the morning of September 3, they began the long journey to Auschwitz, the infamous camp in Poland where 4,000,000 Jews died in the gas chambers. For three days they traveled, packed into freight cars. At the camp the men were separated from the women. Mrs. Frank died in the women's camp on January 6, 1945, after her daughters had been sent on to Bergen-Belsen.

It was October 30 when Anne and Margot began the journey to Bergen-Belsen in a cattle car. This camp, where 30,000 prisoners died, was located in Germany. In late 1944 it was in a disorganized state. The Allies were approaching. Food was scarce, and typhus was raging. Here Margot died at the end of February or the beginning of March, 1945, probably of a combination of typhus and starvation. Anne, already ill of typhus, died peacefully soon after. Three weeks later British troops liberated the camp.

Mrs. Van Daan also died of the typhus epidemic at Bergen-Belsen. Mr. Van Daan died in the gas chambers at Auschwitz. When the Nazis left Auschwitz in January, 1945, they took Peter Van Daan with them. Among other prisoners forced to march in freezing weather, he was not heard from again. Mr. Dussel was sent back to Germany and died in Neuengamme. Only Mr. Frank, who remained at Auschwitz until its liberation, survived.

A fuller record of the aftermath of the capture of Anne Frank can be found in Ernst Schnabel's book, *Anne Frank: A Portrait in Courage.*

8: The Diary of Anne Frank

CONTENT REVIEW

1. In a true-to-life play such as this, it is especially important that the reader see the characters clearly and in depth. **(a)** Which of Anne's feelings and concerns appear to you to be completely normal for a girl her age? **(b)** In what ways does she seem to be unusual? **(c)** Had she lived, what kind of person do you believe she would have become as an adult? Support your answer with evidence from within the play.

2. Since Anne's diary supplied the source material for the play, you see people and incidents from her point of view. What different picture of the various inhabitants of the annex, including Anne, might you have if the diary had been written by: **(a)** Mr. Dussel? **(b)** Mrs. Frank? **(c)** Mrs. Van Daan?

3. Consider the following statement: "*The Diary of Anne Frank* is not dramatic enough. The last scene should have shown Anne's death in a concentration camp. Then we could really have *felt* the tragedy." Explain why you agree or disagree with the viewpoint expressed in this statement.

4. The introduction to the unit speaks of the diary of Anne Frank as "a living tribute to the dignity, courage, and perseverance of the human spirit." Do these words seem an accurate description of the play you have just read? Defend your answer by referring to specific scenes and passages.

5. Do you believe that works such as Anne's diary and the play and motion picture based upon it can be influential in preventing future persecution of innocent people? Discuss.

Unit 8, Test 1
INTERPRETATION: NEW MATERIAL

from The Pen of My Aunt
Gordon Daviot

The setting is a French country house; the time is a day during World War II. France, like Holland and several other European countries, has been invaded and occupied by German troops. As the scene opens, Madame and her servant Simone have been watching out their window as two German soldiers escort a young stranger up to their door. Read this excerpt carefully and then answer the questions that follow it.

STRANGER (*in a bright, confident, casual tone*). Ah, there you are, my dear aunt. I am so glad. Come in, my friend, come in. My dear aunt, this gentleman wants you to identify me.

MADAME. Identify you?

CORPORAL. We found this man wandering in the woods—

STRANGER. The corporal found it inexplicable that anyone should wander in a wood.

CORPORAL. And he had no papers on him—

STRANGER. And I rightly pointed out that if I carry all the papers one is supposed to these days, I am no good to God or man. If I put them in a hip pocket, I can't bend forward; if I put them in a front pocket, I can't bend at all.

CORPORAL. He said that he was your nephew, madame, but that did not seem to us very likely, so we brought him here.

(There is the slightest pause; just one moment of silence.)

MADAME. But of course this is my nephew.

CORPORAL. He is?

MADAME. Certainly.

CORPORAL. He lives here?

MADAME *(assenting).* My nephew lives here.

CORPORAL. So! *(Recovering.)* My apologies, madame. But you will admit that appearances were against the young gentleman.

MADAME. Alas, Corporal, my nephew belongs to a generation who delight in flouting appearances. It is what they call 'expressing their personality,' I understand.

CORPORAL *(with contempt).* No doubt, madame.

MADAME. Convention is anathema[1] to them, and there is no sin like conformity. Even a collar is an offense against their liberty, and a discipline not to be borne by free necks.

CORPORAL. Ah yes, madame. A little more discipline among your nephew's generation, and we might not be occupying your country today.

STRANGER. You think it was that collar of yours that conquered my country? You flatter yourself, Corporal. The only result of wearing a collar like that is varicose veins in the head.

MADAME *(repressive).* Please! My dear boy. Let us not descend to personalities.

STRANGER. The matter is not personal, my good aunt, but scientific. Wearing a collar like that retards the flow of fresh blood to the head, with the most disastrous consequences to the grey matter of the brain. The hypothetical grey matter. In fact, I have a theory—

CORPORAL. Monsieur, your theories do not interest me.

STRANGER. No? You do not find speculation interesting? . . .

CORPORAL. I have only one desire, monsieur, and that is to see your papers.

STRANGER *(taken off-guard and filling in time).* My papers?

---

1. *anathema* (ə nath′ə mə), something that is completely detested.

MADAME. But is that necessary, Corporal? I have already told you that—

CORPORAL. I know that Madame is a very good collaborator and in good standing—

MADAME. In that case—

CORPORAL. But when we begin an affair we like to finish it. I have asked to see Monsieur's papers, and the matter will not be finished until I have seen them.

MADAME. You acknowledge that I am in 'good standing,' Corporal?

CORPORAL. So I have heard, madame.

MADAME. Then I must consider it a discourtesy on your part to demand my nephew's credentials.

CORPORAL. It is no reflection on Madame. It is a matter of routine, nothing more.

STRANGER *(murmuring).* The great god Routine.

MADAME. To ask for his papers was routine; to insist on their production is discourtesy. I shall say so to your commanding officer.

CORPORAL. Very good, madame. In the meantime, I shall inspect your nephew's papers.

MADAME. And what if I—

STRANGER *(quietly).* You may as well give it up, my dear. You could as easily turn a steamroller. They have only one idea at a time. If the Corporal's heart is set on seeing my papers, he shall see them. *(Moving towards the door.)* I left them in the pocket of my coat.

SIMONE *(unexpectedly, from the background).* Not in your *linen* coat?

STRANGER *(pausing).* Yes. Why?

SIMONE *(with apparently growing anxiety).* Your *cream* linen coat? The one you were wearing yesterday?

STRANGER. Certainly.

SIMONE. Merciful Heaven! I sent it to the laundry!

STRANGER. To the laundry!

SIMONE. Yes, monsieur; this morning; in the basket.

STRANGER *(in incredulous anger).* You sent my coat, *with my papers in the pocket,* to the laundry!

SIMONE *(defensive and combatant).* I didn't know Monsieur's papers were in the pocket.

STRANGER. You didn't know! You didn't know that a packet of documents weighing half a ton were in the pocket. An identity card, a *laisser passer,* a food card, a drink card, an army discharge, a permission to wear civilian clothes, a permission to go farther than ten miles to the east, a permission to go more than ten miles to the west, a permission to—

SIMONE *(breaking in with spirit)*. How was I to know the coat was heavy! I picked it up with the rest of the bundle that was lying on the floor.

STRANGER *(snapping her head off)*. My coat was on the back of the chair.

SIMONE. It was on the floor.

STRANGER. On the back of the chair!

SIMONE. It was on the floor with your dirty shirt and your pajamas, and a towel and what not. I put my arms round the whole thing and then—woof! into the basket with them.

STRANGER. I tell you that coat was on the back of the chair. It was quite clean and was not going to the laundry for two weeks yet—if then. I hung it there myself, and—

MADAME. My dear boy, what does it matter? The damage is done now. In any case, they will find the papers when they unpack the basket, and return them tomorrow.

STRANGER. If someone doesn't steal them. There are a lot of people who would like to lay hold of a complete set of papers, believe me.

MADAME *(reassuring)*. Oh, no. Old Fleureau is the soul of honesty. You have no need to worry about them. They will be back first thing tomorrow, you shall see; and then we shall have much pleasure in sending them to the Administration Office for the Corporal's inspection. Unless, of course, the Corporal insists on your personal appearance at the office.

CORPORAL *(cold and indignant)*. I have seen Monsieur. All that I want now is to see his papers.

STRANGER. You shall see them, Corporal, you shall see them. The whole half-ton of them. You may inspect them at your leisure. Provided, that is, that they come back from the laundry to which this idiot has consigned them.

MADAME *(again reassuring)*. They will come back, never fear. And you must not blame Simone. She is a good child and does her best.

SIMONE *(with an air of belated virtue)*. I am not one to pry into pockets.

MADAME. Simone, show the Corporal out, if you please.

SIMONE *(natural feeling overcoming her for a moment)*. He knows the way out. *(Recovering.)* Yes, madame.

MADAME. And Corporal, try to take your duties a little less literally in future. My countrymen appreciate the spirit rather than the letter.

CORPORAL. I have my instructions, madame, and I obey them. Good day, madame. Monsieur.

(He goes, followed by Simone—door closes. There is a moment of silence.)

STRANGER. For a good collaborator, that was a remarkably quick adoption.

MADAME. Sit down, young man. I will give you something to drink. I expect your knees are none too well.

STRANGER. My knees, madame, are pure gelatine. As for my stomach, it seems to have disappeared.

MADAME *(offering him the drink she has poured out).* This will recall it, I hope.

STRANGER. You are not drinking, madame.

MADAME. Thank you, no.

STRANGER. Not with strangers. It is certainly no time to drink with strangers. Nevertheless, I drink the health of a collaborator. *(He drinks.)* Tell me, madame, what will happen tomorrow when they find that you have no nephew?

MADAME *(surprised).* But of course I have a nephew. I tell lies, my friend; but not *silly* lies. My charming nephew has gone to Bonneval for the day. He finds country life dull.

STRANGER. Dull? This—this heaven?

MADAME *(dryly).* He likes to talk and here there is no audience. At Headquarters in Bonneval he finds the audience sympathetic.

STRANGER *(understanding the implication).* Ah.

MADAME. He believes in the Brotherhood of Man—if you can credit it.

STRANGER. After the last six months?

MADAME. His mother was American, so he has half the Balkans in his blood. To say nothing of Italy, Russia, and the Levant.[2]

STRANGER *(half-amused).* I see.

MADAME. A silly and worthless creature, but useful.

STRANGER. Useful?

MADAME. I—borrow his cloak.

STRANGER. I see.

MADAME. Tonight I shall borrow his identity papers, and tomorrow they will go to the office in St. Estephe.

STRANGER. But—he will have to know.

MADAME *(placidly).* Oh, yes, he will know, of course.

STRANGER. And how will you persuade such an enthusiastic collaborator to deceive his friends?

MADAME. Oh, that is easy. He is my heir.

---

2. *His mother . . . the Levant,* Madame is referring to the fact that many Americans have ancestors of several different nationalities.

1. The Germans have brought the stranger to Madame's house because the stranger had told them that Madame is his **(a)** aunt; **(b)** sister; **(c)** wife; **(d)** mother.

2. What was the stranger doing when the soldiers first spotted him?

3. The soldiers took the stranger into custody because **(a)** he had a gun; **(b)** he was not carrying identification papers; **(c)** he tried to ambush them; **(d)** he looked like an American.

4. When the soldiers ask Madame to identify the stranger, she **(a)** says he is her son; **(b)** becomes very flustered; **(c)** hesitates very briefly; **(d)** becomes very serious.

5. By identifying the stranger as her relative, Madame indicates to him that she will **(a)** protect him from the soldiers; **(b)** let Simone wash his clothes; **(c)** take him on as a servant; **(d)** betray him.

6. When the Corporal asks to see the stranger's identity papers, Madame responds by acting **(a)** kind and helpful; **(b)** confused and slow-witted; **(c)** frightened and nervous; **(d)** haughty and insulted.

7. Who invented the story about the coat being sent to the laundry?

8. The story about the coat was told in order to **(a)** make the Corporal angry; **(b)** prove that Madame was loyal to the Germans; **(c)** explain why the stranger could not produce his identity papers; **(d)** all of the above.

9. Madame says that the identity papers will be **(a)** destroyed at the laundry; **(b)** sent to the Corporal at the Administration Office; **(c)** delivered to

Headquarters by Simone; **(d)** taken better care of in the future.

10. After the Corporal leaves, the stranger says, "My knees . . . are pure gelatine" (526, line 5). He means that he is very **(a)** nervous; **(b)** sad; **(c)** happy; **(d)** angry.

11. The "Headquarters at Bonneval" that Madame's nephew likes to visit (526, line 20) is a **(a)** church; **(b)** social club; **(c)** theater; **(d)** German military headquarters.

12. The stranger's *main* concern about borrowing the nephew's identity papers is that Madame's nephew **(a)** is too young; **(b)** is out of town for the day; **(c)** does not look like him; **(d)** might report him to the Germans.

13. What message is Madame trying to communicate when she says that her nephew is her heir (526, line 38)? **(a)** that she values family relationships; **(b)** that his mother was her sister; **(c)** that if he doesn't let her use the identity papers, she will not leave him her money; **(d)** that anyone she leaves her money to must be a worthwhile person.

14. When the Corporal calls Madame a "good collaborator" (523, line 3), he is indicating that he thinks **(a)** she goes along with what the Germans want; **(b)** she is a hard worker; **(c)** her only loyalty is to France; **(d)** she is a very good liar.

15. When the stranger calls Madame a "good collaborator"

(526, line 1), he is speaking **(a)** seriously; **(b)** ironically; **(c)** angrily; **(d)** kindly.

Unit 8, Test II
COMPOSITION

Choose one of the following assignments to write about. Assume you are writing for your classmates.

1. If the stranger in *The Pen of My Aunt* is going to avoid being held by the Germans, he must have more than his share of good luck. Discuss why each of the following things that happened in the excerpt was lucky for the stranger: that he chose to be taken to Madame's house in the first place; that Madame had a nephew; that Madame's nephew was not around.

2. Although *The Diary of Anne Frank* focuses primarily on Anne herself, it presents clear pictures of several other characters as well. Which of these other characters did you find most admirable? In a brief character sketch, describe specific qualities that caused you to have particular respect for this individual.

3. One of the most significant statements made by Anne Frank is "In spite of everything, I still believe that people are really good at heart." Discuss how the actions of (1) Miep and Mr. Kraler and (2) Madame and Simone help to prove the truth of this statement.

Handbook
of
Literary
Terms

alliteration

She sells seashells by the seashore.
Peter Piper picked a peck of pickled peppers.
Better buy better baby-buggy bumpers.

These old tongue twisters have always been enjoyed because people like to play with the sounds of language. We use repeated letter sounds in such everyday expressions as: "busy as a bee," "down the drain," and "smooth as silk." Advertisers use them in slogans; poets use them in their writing.

The use of repeated consonant sounds is called *alliteration.* Usually, the alliterative sounds occur at the beginnings of words as in these lines by nineteenth-century English poet Percy Bysshe Shelley:

> When the *l*amp is shattered
> The *l*ight in the *d*ust *l*ies *d*ead—

But sometimes they are found within words as well. Note the repetition of *b* and *l* in this line:

> *L*ie *l*ight*l*ess, a*ll* the spark*l*es *bl*eared and *bl*ack and *bl*ind.

Repeated sound, or alliteration, in poetry helps create melody, which is pleasant to the ear. However, as Alexander Pope, an eighteenth-century English poet, said, "The sound must be an echo to the sense," and capable poets follow Pope's rule. How sound can echo sense is demonstrated clearly below:

from Scythe Song

> *Hush, ah hush, the Scythes are saying,*
> *Hush, and heed not, and fall asleep;*
> *Hush, they say to the grasses swaying,*
> *Hush, they sing to the clover deep!*
> 5 *Hush—'tis the lullaby Time is singing—*
> *Hush, and heed not, for all things pass,*
> *Hush, ah hush! and the Scythes are swinging*
> *Over the clover, over the grass!*

Andrew Lang

Notice how the repeated *h, s,* and *sh* sounds echo the noise made by scythes, or long-handled mowers, that are being swung through tall grass.

The emphasis produced by alliteration can also be used to call attention to certain important words in a poem:

> . . . *d*readful was the *d*in of *h*issing through the *H*all.

Alliteration can point out contrasts:

> Depth of *p*ain and height of *p*assion.

Alliteration can link words that are similar in image, thought, and feeling:

> . . . *sp*ikes of *l*ight
> *Sp*eared open *l*ustrous gashes . . .

Finally, the sounds produced by alliteration can affect the mood of a poem. Read the following examples and answer the questions that follow each.

> She sent the gentle sleep from Heaven,
> That slid into my soul.

1. In these lines, does the repeated *s* sound help create a calm, uneasy, or frightened effect?

> Down sunk the broad-beamed boat beneath the briny deep.

2. Do the repeated *b* and *d* sounds help make this line seem dull and heavy or light and carefree? In what ways are the sounds an "echo to the sense"?

---

alliteration (ə lit′ə rā′shən)

Repeated consonant sounds occurring at the beginning of words or within words. Alliteration is used to create melody, establish mood, call attention to important words, and point out similarities and contrasts.

characterization

In order to create a fictitious character, the author may simply describe the character.

Karen was small for her age and inclined to plumpness. Her blue eyes viewed the people and events around her with a mixture of curiosity and amusement. She was not a woman, but she was past being a child; too sophisticated for toys, she might still, on impulse, turn a somersault on the living room rug.

1. Approximately how old is Karen?
2. What details help you visualize her?
3. What details reveal something about Karen's personality?

An author may reveal a character through his or her speech and actions.

"But why can't I go?" Karen wailed. "Everyone else is going. You never let me go anywhere! You just don't want me to grow up and have fun!" Karen wheeled around and stormed out of the house, slamming the door behind her.

4. What does Karen reveal about her personality in this speech?
5. What do her actions contribute to your picture of her?

An author may give the reactions and opinions of other characters.

"I've known Karen a long time, ever since first grade. We've been best friends since last year. I like her because . . . well, I guess it's because she's always so happy and sure of herself and she's good at things like baseball and swimming and painting and stuff." Joanie paused, then added, "Everybody at school likes her."

6. What is Joanie's relationship to Karen?
7. What do you learn about Karen from Joanie's comments?

An author may show the character's inner thoughts and feelings.

The sunlight trickled between the slates of the bamboo blinds. Karen stretched luxuriously, pleasantly aware of the tingling sensation in her muscles.

She really ought to get up, she thought. Sally was coming over at eleven. Maybe she should make some sandwiches so they could eat out in the backyard. Mrs. Henley was taking them to the beach in the afternoon. She should also finish that letter to Peggy . . . maybe she would tonight . . . if she remembered . . . and if she had the time.

8. What is Karen thinking about?
9. What do her thoughts tell you about her personality?

Authors may use any one of the four methods of characterization illustrated above to bring to life the fictional people they create: **(1)** describing the character's appearance, **(2)** reporting the character's speech and behavior, **(3)** describing the reactions of other characters to the individual, and **(4)** revealing the character's thoughts and feelings. Most authors, however, use a combination of methods.

In the following excerpt from the novel *The Mill on the Floss*, George Eliot uses all four methods to characterize Tom Tulliver, a boy who is arriving home from boarding school. Tom and Maggie are Mrs. Tulliver's children; Yap is the family dog.

Tom was to arrive early in the afternoon, and there was another fluttering heart besides Maggie's when it was late enough for the sound of the gig[1] wheels to be expected; for if Mrs. Tulliver had a strong feeling, it was fondness for her boy. At last the sound came—the quick, light bowling of the gig wheels—and in spite of the wind, which was blowing the clouds about, and was not likely to respect Mrs. Tulliver's curls and cap strings, she came outside the door, and even held her hands on Maggie's offending head, forgetting all the griefs of the morning.

"There he is, my sweet lad! But Lord ha' mercy! he's got never a collar on; it's been lost on the road, I'll be bound, and spoilt the set."

---

1. *gig* (gig), a light, open, two-wheeled carriage drawn by one horse.

Mrs. Tulliver stood with her arms open; Maggie jumped first on one leg and then on the other; while Tom descended from the gig, and said, with masculine reticence as to the tender emotions, "Hullo! Yap—what, are you there?"

Nevertheless, he submitted to be kissed willingly enough, though Maggie hung on his neck in rather a strangling fashion, while his blue gray eyes wandered toward the croft,[2] and the lambs, and the river, where he promised himself that he would begin to fish the first thing tomorrow morning. He was one of those lads that grow everywhere in England, and, at twelve or thirteen years of age, look as much alike as goslings—a lad with light-brown hair, cheeks of cream and roses, full lips, indeterminate nose and eyebrows. . . .

Each of the following is a true statement about Tom. For each one (1) point out the lines from the excerpt which prove the statement and (2) name the method or methods of characterization used.

2. *croft* (krôft), BRITISH, a small, rented farm.

A. Tom is somewhat careless about his clothes.

B. Tom does not like to display emotion to his mother and sister.

C. Tom is glad to be home.

D. Tom is an ordinary-looking boy.

E. Tom is happy to see his family.

characterization

The method an author uses to acquaint the reader with his or her characters. Any or all of four different methods of *characterization* may be used. An author may:

1. describe the character's physical traits and personality.

2. report the character's speech and behavior.

3. give the opinions and reactions of other characters toward this individual.

4. reveal the character's thoughts and feelings.

connotation/denotation

You may live in a *house,* but we live in a *home.*

If you were to look up the words *house* and *home* in a dictionary, you would find that both words have approximately the same meaning—"a dwelling place." However, the speaker in the sentence above suggests that *home* has an additional meaning. Aside from the strict dictionary definition, or *denotation,* many people associate such things as comfort, love, security, or privacy with a home but do not necessarily make the same associations with a house. What is the first thing that comes to your mind when you think of a home? of a house? Why do you think that real-estate advertisers use the word *home* more frequently than *house?*

The various feelings, images, and memories that surround a word make up its *connotation.* Although both house and home have the same denotation, or dictionary meaning, *home* also has many connotations.

Read the following sentences and answer the questions that follow.

Annette was surprised.
Annette was amazed.
Annette was astonished.

1. What is the general meaning of each of the three sentences about Annette? Do the words *surprised, amazed,* and *astonished* have approximately the same denotation?

2. What additional meanings are suggested by *astonish?* Would one be more likely to be *surprised* or *astonished* at seeing a ghost?

3. Which word in each pair below has the more favorable connotation to you?

> thrifty—penny-pinching
> pushy—aggressive
> politician—statesman
> chef—cook
> slender—skinny

Since everyone reacts emotionally to certain words, writers often deliberately select words that they think will influence your reactions and appeal to your emotions. Read the dictionary definition below.

cock roach (kok′rōch′), *n.* any of an order of nocturnal insects, usually brown with flattened oval bodies, some species of which are household pests inhabiting kitchens, areas around water pipes, etc. [Spanish *cucaracha*]

What does the word *cockroach* mean to you? Is a cockroach merely an insect or is it also a household nuisance and a disgusting creature? See what meanings poets Wild and Morley find in roaches in the following poems.

Roaches

Last night when I got up
to let the dog out I spied
a cockroach in the bathroom
crouched flat on the cool
5   porcelain,
             delicate
antennae probing the toothpaste cap
and feasting himself on a gob
of it in the bowl:
10 I killed him with one unprofessional
             blow,
scattering arms and legs
and half his body in the sink . . .

I would have no truck with roaches,
15 crouched like lions in the ledges of sewers
their black eyes in the darkness
             alert for tasty slime,
breeding quickly and without design,
laboring up drainpipes through filth
20   to the light;
I read once they are among
the most antediluvian[1] of creatures,

"Roaches" by Peter Wild from *Poetry of the Desert Southwest* published by The Baleen Press, 1973. Reprinted by permission of the author.
1. *antediluvian* (an′ti də lü′vē ən), very old.

surviving everything,
    and in more primitive times
25 thrived to the size of your hand . . .

    yet when sinking asleep
        or craning at the stars,
    I can feel their light feet
        probing in my veins,
30 their whiskers nibbling
        the insides of my toes;
    and neck arched,
        feel their patient scrambling
up the dark tubes of my throat.

                        Peter Wild

from **Nursery Rhymes for the Tender-hearted**

      (dedicated to Don Marquis)

Scuttle, scuttle, little roach—
How you run when I approach:
Up above the pantry shelf
Hastening to secrete yourself.

5 Most adventurous of vermin,
How I wish I could determine
How you spend your hours of ease,
Perhaps reclining on the cheese.

  Cook has gone, and all is dark—
10 Then the kitchen is your park;
In the garbage heap that she leaves
Do you browse among the tea leaves?

How delightful to suspect
All the places you have trekked:
15 Does your long antenna whisk its
Gentle tip across the biscuits?

Do you linger, little soul,
Drowsing in our sugar bowl?
Or, abandonment most utter,
20 Shake a shimmy on the butter?

Do you chant your simple tunes
Swimming in the baby's prunes?
Then, when dawn comes, do you slink
Homeward to the kitchen sink?

25 Timid roach, why be so shy?
We are brothers, thou and I.
In the midnight, like yourself,
I explore the pantry shelf!

            Christopher Morley

Reread the dictionary definition. Which of the denotative characteristics of a cockroach do both poets include in their poems? What characteristics does Wild give his roaches that are not in the dictionary definition? What additional characteristics does Morley give to roaches?

In each poem, the insect acquires meanings beyond its dictionary definition. Both poets lead us away from a literal view of roaches to a nonliteral one. Which poet succeeds in giving roaches favorable connotations? Which poet comes closer to expressing your own feelings about roaches?

connotation (kon′ə tā′shən)

The emotional, imaginative, cultural, or traditional associations surrounding a word, as opposed to its strict, literal dictionary meaning.

denotation (dē′nō tā′shən)

The strict dictionary meaning of a word, presented objectively and without emotional associations.

figurative language

The Eagle

He clasps the crag with crooked hands;
Close to the sun in lonely lands,
Ringed with the azure world, he stands.

The wrinkled sea beneath him crawls;
He watches from his mountain walls,
And like a thunderbolt he falls.

Alfred, Lord Tennyson

1. Explain the meaning of each of the following phrases in the context of the poem:
   a. crooked hands
   b. close to the sun in lonely lands
   c. wrinkled sea beneath him crawls
   d. his mountain walls
   e. like a thunderbolt he falls

2. This poem is a description of an eagle, yet it differs greatly from the ordinary dictionary definition of *eagle:* "a large, strong bird of prey that has keen eyes and powerful wings." How does the above poem suggest the eagle's strength? Which lines emphasize his keen vision? Which presents a more colorful description of the eagle, the poem or the dictionary? Explain your answer.

To make his description of the eagle especially clear and appealing, Tennyson used *figurative language* instead of literal language. In literal language words are used in their ordinary meaning, without exaggeration or inventiveness. (The dictionary definition of *eagle* is written in literal terms.) Figurative language goes beyond the ordinary meanings of words in order to emphasize ideas or emotions. Whenever we use a *figure of speech* such as "you're eating like a pig" or "he runs like the wind" you are comparing two different things in order to emphasize a similarity. Some of the most common figures of speech are SIMILE, METAPHOR, and HYPERBOLE.

Read the poem below and answer the questions about it on page 536.

The Succession of the Four Sweet Months

First, April, she with mellow showers
Opens the way for early flowers;
Then after her comes smiling May,
In a more rich and sweet array;
5 Next enters June, and brings us more
Gems than those two, that went before:
Then, lastly, July comes, and she
More wealth brings in than all those three.

Robert Herrick

What is the poem about? To what do the "gems" and "wealth" refer? How has the poet made the months seem like people?

Effective figurative language has several characteristics: it makes its point by being both forceful and brief; it has a quality of freshness about it; it fits the situation; the things being compared must be alike in some recognizable way so that the general effect of the comparison is consistent and appropriate:

> And their revenge is as the tiger's spring,
> Deadly, and quick, and crushing;

Look at the cartoon below. Has the cartoonist illustrated the literal or the figurative meaning of the expression "work for peanuts"?

Reprinted by permission of Lawrence Lariar.

"I'm awful tired of working for peanuts!"

figurative language

Any language that goes beyond the literal meaning of words in order to furnish new effects or fresh insights into an idea or a subject. The most common figures of speech are *simile, metaphor,* and *hyperbole.*

It was a perfect day for a picnic. The morning was bright and clear with a few scattered clouds of the white, fluffy variety that kids find pictures in. Roses were in bloom, and birds sang outside my window. Nothing could go wrong on such a perfect day. Or so I, in my childlike innocence, thought.

1. Where does the author first suggest that something is going to spoil the narrator's perfect day?

2. At this point, do you have any definite idea of what may go wrong?

Sometimes an author gives the reader clues or suggestions about events that will happen later. This technique is called *foreshadowing.* In the paragraph above, you know that something will happen to mar the "perfect day," but you don't know whether it will be a humorous incident, such as a cow eating the picnic lunch, or a tragic event, such as a drowning or an automobile accident.

Not all foreshadowing is as obvious as that in the example above. Frequently, future events are merely hinted at through dialogue, description, or the attitudes and reactions of the characters.

In the following excerpt from Charles Dickens's novel *David Copperfield,* David recounts an event from his childhood. His mother, a young, attractive woman, had been widowed shortly before David was born. Peggotty is a trusted and devoted servant of the Copperfield family. As you read, notice clues which might foreshadow future events.

from **David Copperfield**

Peggotty and I were sitting one night by the parlor fire, alone. I had been reading to Peggotty about crocodiles. I remember she had a cloudy impression, after I had done, that they were a sort of vegetable. I was tired of reading, and dead sleepy; but having leave, as a high treat, to sit up until my mother came home from spending the evening at a neighbor's, I would rather have died upon my post (of course) than have gone off to bed. . . .

"Peggotty," says I suddenly, "were you ever married?"

"Lord, Master Davy," replied Peggotty, "what's put marriage in your head?"

She answered with such a start that it quite woke me. And then she stopped in her work, and looked at me, with her needle drawn out to its thread's length.

"But were you ever married, Peggotty?" says I. "You are a very handsome woman, an't you?"

"Me handsome, Davy!" said Peggotty. "Lawk no, my dear! But what put marriage in your head?"

"I don't know! You mustn't marry more than one person at a time, may you, Peggotty?"

"Certainly not," says Peggotty, with the promptest decision.

"But if you marry a person, and the person dies, why then you may marry another person, mayn't you, Peggotty?"

"You may," says Peggotty, "if you choose."

"You an't cross, I suppose, Peggotty, are you?" said I, after sitting quiet for a minute.

I really thought she was, she had been so short with me. But I was quite mistaken; for she laid aside her work (which was a stocking of her own), and opening her arms wide, took my curly head within them, and gave it a good squeeze. I know it was a good squeeze, because, being very plump, whenever she made any little exertion after she was dressed, some of the buttons on the back of her gown flew off. And I recollect two bursting while she was hugging me.

"Now let me hear some more about the crorkindills," said Peggotty, "for I an't heard half enough."

I couldn't quite understand why Peggotty looked so queer, or why she was so ready to go back to the crocodiles. However, we returned to those monsters, with fresh interest on my part; but I had my doubts of Peggotty, who was thoughtfully sticking her needle into various parts of her face and arms all the time.

We had exhausted the crocodiles, and begun with the alligators, when the garden bell rang. We went to the door, and there was my mother, looking unusually pretty, I thought, and with her a gentleman with beautiful black hair and whiskers, who had walked home with us from church last Sunday.

As my mother stepped down on the threshold to take me in her arms and kiss me, the gentleman said I was a more highly privileged little fellow than a monarch.

"What does that mean?" I asked him.

He patted me on the head; but somehow I didn't like him or his deep voice, and I was jealous that his hand should touch my mother's in touching me—which it did. I put it away as well as I could.

"Oh, Davy!" remonstrated my mother.

"Dear boy!" said the gentleman. "I cannot wonder at his devotion. Come, let us shake hands!"

My right hand was in my mother's left, so I gave him the other.

"Why, that's the wrong hand, Davy!" laughed the gentleman.

My mother drew my right hand forward; but I resolved, for my former reason, not to give it to him, and I did not. I gave him the other, and he shook it heartily, and said I was a brave fellow, and went away.

At this minute I see him turn around in the garden, and give us a last look with his ill-omened black eyes, before the door was shut.

Peggotty, who had not said a word or moved a finger, secured the fastenings instantly, and we all went into the parlor. My mother, contrary to her usual habit, instead of coming to the elbow-chair by the fire, remained at the other end of the room, and sat singing to herself.

"Hope you have had a pleasant evening, ma'am," said Peggotty, standing as stiff as a barrel in the center of the room, with a candlestick in her hand.

"Much obliged to you, Peggotty," returned my mother in a cheerful voice, "I have had a very pleasant evening."

"A stranger or so makes an agreeable change," suggested Peggotty.

"A very agreeable change, indeed," returned my mother.

Peggotty continuing to stand motionless in the

middle of the room, and my mother resuming her singing, I fell asleep. . . .

Charles Dickens

1. How does Peggotty's attitude suggest that David's mother is about to remarry? When do you learn whom she will probably marry?

2. Which of Mrs. Copperfield's actions lead you to expect the marriage?

3. What hints are there in the man's attitude that foreshadow the marriage?

4. Find the clues in this passage that suggest that the man is not as kind and generous as he tries to be.

Foreshadowing frequently serves two purposes. It builds suspense by raising questions that encourage the reader to go on and find out more about the event that is being foreshadowed. The preceding passage, for example, foretells Mrs. Copperfield's marriage to the black-haired gentleman. It does not, however, explain how David will fit into this marriage, or what will happen to Peggotty, who obviously does not approve of the marriage.

Foreshadowing is also a means of adding plausibility to a narrative by partially preparing the reader for events which are to follow. In the preceding passage, the gentleman appears to like David even though the boy seems to dislike him immediately. David's statement that the gentleman gave them a "last look with his ill-omened black eyes" also suggests that the man is not so kind and generous as he appears to be and that he may be the cause of much future unhappiness for the Copperfields.

foreshadowing

An author's use of hints or clues to suggest events that will occur later in a narrative.

So fair art thou, my bonnie lass,
    So deep in love am I:
And I will love thee still, my dear,
    Till all the seas go dry.

According to the last line, how long will the speaker's love last? Do you think the last line is intended to be taken literally? What is the effect of the last line?

Hyperbole is an exaggerated statement used to increase or heighten effect. When you say, "I could eat a horse," you are deliberately exaggerating in order to let your listener know that you are extremely hungry.

Read the poem below and answer the questions that follow.

For a Hopi Silversmith

he has gathered the windstrength
from the third mesa
into his hand
and cast it into silver

5 i have wanted to see
the motion of wind
for a long time

thank you
for showing me

Joy Harjo

"For a Hopi Silversmith" from *The First Skin Around Me* published by Territorial Press. Copyright © 1976 by Joy Harjo. Reprinted by permission.

1. Has the silversmith actually captured the motion of the wind in his work? Is such a feat possible? What has he done?

2. What is the purpose of the hyperbole?

hyperbole (hī pėr′bə lē)

An exaggerated statement used to heighten effect.

imagery

The hot July sun beat relentlessly down, casting an orange glare over the farm buildings, the fields, the pond. Even the usually cool green willows bordering the pond hung wilting and dry. Our sun-baked backs ached for relief. We quickly pulled off our sweaty clothes and plunged into the pond, but the tepid water only stifled us and we soon climbed back onto the brown, dusty bank. Our parched throats longed for something cool—a strawberry ice, a tall frosted glass of lemonade.

We pulled on our clothes and headed through the dense, crackling underbrush, the sharp briars pulling at our damp jeans, until we reached the watermelon patch. As we began to cut open the nearest melon, we could smell the pungent skin mingling with the dusty odor of dry earth. Suddenly the melon gave way with a crack, revealing the deep, pink sweetness inside.

1. From the paragraph above pick out words and phrases that appeal to your sense of **(a)** sight; **(b)** sound; **(c)** smell; **(d)** taste; **(e)** touch and feeling.

2. Which sense impression is strongest?

To make an imaginary world seem real, an author often makes use of words and phrases that appeal to the senses. These words and phrases, called *images*, help a reader mentally experience what the characters in the literary selection are actually experiencing.

A well-written description should arouse a particular response or emotion in the reader's imagination.

from **The Lotos-Eaters**

> There is sweet music here that softer
>   falls
> Than petals from blown roses on the
>   grass,
> Or night-dews on still waters between
>   walls
> Of shadowy granite, in a gleaming pass;
> 5 Music that gentlier on the spirit lies
> Than tired eyelids upon tired eyes;
> Music that brings sweet sleep from
>   the blissful skies.
> Here are cool mosses deep,
> And through the moss the ivies creep,
> 10 And in the stream the long-leaved
>   flowers weep,
> And from the craggy ledge the poppy
>   hangs in sleep.

Alfred, Lord Tennyson

1. To what senses does the poet appeal in this passage? Pick out the sensory images which seem most vivid to you.

2. What sensations is the author trying to produce in the reader?

imagery

Concrete details that appeal to the senses. By using specific images, authors establish mood and arouse emotion in their readers.

inference

Help Wanted:
Young person to work at Sox ballpark. Some sales experience helpful but not necessary. Uniform provided. Apply at concession stand, corner Addison and 14th.

1. The person who takes this job will probably be **(a)** a major-league baseball player; **(b)** an usher; **(c)** a hot-dog vendor.

2. What details tell you what kind of job this is?

Reprinted by permission of Lawrence Lariar.

"Miss Feiner. Yoo-hoo."

1. Why is the skier calling to Miss Feiner?

2. What do you think happened to Miss Feiner?

Drawing correct conclusions from a few hints is called *making inferences.*

Many writers do not tell a reader everything outright. Instead they rely on a reader's ability to "read between the lines" and make reasonable inferences from the information presented.

A reader can make inferences from an author's description of a scene or character, from a character's conversation and actions, from the way in which other characters react to a particular individual, and even from an author's choice of words. In the following passage the author describes a school owned and run by a Mr. Wackford Squeers. What inferences can you make about the characters and the school?

from **Nicholas Nickleby**

Obedient to this summons there ranged themselves in front of the schoolmaster's desk half a dozen scarecrows, out at knees and elbows, one of whom placed a torn and filthy book beneath his learned eye.

"This is the first class in English spelling and philosophy, Nickleby," said Squeers, beckoning Nicholas to stand beside him. "We'll get up a Latin one and hand that over to you. Now then, where's the first boy?"

"Please, sir, he's cleaning the back-parlor window," said the temporary head of the philosophical class.

"So he is, to be sure," rejoined Squeers. "We go upon the practical mode of teaching, Nickleby, the regular education system. C-l-e-a-n, clean, verb active, to make bright, to scour. W-i-n, win, d-e-r, der, winder, a casement. When the boy knows out of book, he goes and does it. Where's the second boy?"

"Please, sir, he's weeding the garden," replied a small voice.

"To be sure," said Squeers, by no means disconcerted. "So he is. B-o-t, bot, t-i-n, tin, bottin, n-e-y, ney, bottinney, noun substantive, a knowledge of plants. When he has learned that bottinney means a knowledge of plants, he goes and knows 'em. That's our system, Nickleby; what do you think of it?"

"It's a useful one, at any rate," answered Nicholas.

"I believe you," rejoined Squeers, not remarking the emphasis of his usher.[1] "Third boy, what's a horse?"

---

1. *remarking . . . usher.* Squeers has not taken any notice of Nickleby's tone of voice.

inversion

SUBJECT VERB COMPLEMENT
↓   ↓   ↓
The February sky   is   pale.

The sentence above illustrates the normal pattern of an English sentence: subject, followed by verb, followed by complement. Poet William Cullen Bryant alters the normal order in the verse below.

> Pale is the February sky,
>   And brief the midday's sunny hours;
> The wind-swept forest seems to sigh
>   For the sweet time of leaves and flowers

The parts of the sentences in lines 1 and 2 of the verse are not in normal order—the complement comes before the verb. Are the parts of the third line in normal order? Would this verse rhyme if Bryant had written the first line in normal order?

> 1. Very old are the woods.
>   de la Mare, "All That's Past"

The parts of this line are not in normal order either. They are *inverted.* When the sentence is rewritten in normal order, it reads:

> 2. The woods are very old.

What main idea does sentence one seem to stress? What idea is emphasized in the rewritten sentence?

Writers often use *inversion* for emphasis or to achieve a certain poetic effect. Sometimes only the normal order of noun and modifier is reversed as in "It came upon a midnight clear" instead of "It came upon a clear midnight." At

horse (hôrs), *n., pl.* **hors es** or **horse**

"A beast, sir," replied the boy.

"So it is," said Squeers. "Ain't it, Nickleby?"

"I believe there is no doubt of that, sir," answered Nicholas.

"Of course there isn't," said Squeers. "A horse is a quadruped, and *quadruped's* Latin for beast, as everybody that's gone through the grammar knows, or else where's the use of having grammars at all?"

"Where indeed!" said Nicholas, abstractedly.

Charles Dickens

1. Who are the scarecrows?

2. Is Squeers a well-educated man? How do you know?

3. What is Nicholas's attitude toward Squeers? (Note especially his final statement.)

inference

A reasonable and intelligent conclusion drawn from hints provided by the author.

From "All That's Past" in *Collected Poems, 1901–1918* by Walter de la Mare. Reprinted by permission of The Literary Trustees of Walter de la Mare and The Society of Authors as their representative.

INVERSION 541

other times the normal order of noun, verb, and modifiers may be reversed as in these lines:

Daily the fishers' sails drift out
Upon the ocean's breast . . .

An inverted line may seem difficult at first, but it should not cause you problems if you concentrate on the meaning instead of the form.

A Fine Day

Clear had the day been from the dawn,
All checkered was the sky,
Thin clouds like scarfs of cobweb lawn
Veil'd heaven's most glorious eye.
5 The wind had no more strength than this,
That leisurely it blew,
To make one leaf the next to kiss
That closely by it grew.

Michael Drayton

Read the poem aloud. What idea is emphasized in the first two lines? Now put these two lines in normal order, beginning with the subjects, "the day" and "the sky." Then read the rest of the poem as it is written. Was the meaning of the first two lines altered when you changed the order? Was the effect of the poem changed? How did rewriting the first two lines affect the rhyme scheme of the poem? Explain.

inversion

The reversal of the usual order of words in a sentence to create a special effect or for emphasis.

Verbal irony

It was one of those days! The alarm clock failed to go off, John ripped the sleeve of his new T-shirt, spilled orange juice on his math paper, and missed his ride to school. When he finally climbed on a city bus after a thirty-minute wait in the rain, he told the driver, "This is certainly going to be a great day!"

1. What does John mean by his statement?
2. Does he actually believe it *is* going to be a great day? That is, does he want his statement to be taken literally?

John is using *verbal irony* when he says the opposite of what he really means or feels. Can you recall a situation in which you used verbal irony? Describe it.

Irony of situation

Read the following synopsis of a short story by O. Henry entitled "The Cop and the Anthem."

It is late autumn in New York, and Soapy, a bum, decides that it is time for him to make his usual arrangements for the winter months: he will get himself arrested and sentenced to prison. There he will have food and lodging, at least. To achieve this goal, Soapy plans to eat a large and expensive meal, and then leave without paying for it. However, when he goes into a fashionable restaurant, he is turned away because of his shabby clothes. Next he smashes a store window and immediately confesses his deed to a policeman. But the policeman refuses to believe him. He does get his meal in a not-so-fashionable restaurant, but instead of being arrested when he can't pay, he is merely thrown out onto the street.

Soapy makes several more attempts to be arrested, including stealing an umbrella. But it turns out that the man with the umbrella had himself stolen it earlier. Soapy gives up in despair and heads for the park and his accustomed bench, but on the way he stops before a church. As he stands there listening to the music from within, he is reminded of his happy childhood and the depths to which he has now fallen. He resolves to reform his life, find a job, and to become successful. But as he stands there lost in thought, he is finally arrested—for vagrancy!

1. What does Soapy at first hope will happen to him?

2. Why doesn't it happen?

3. When does the result he hoped for actually occur?

4. Why is the outcome a surprise?

This story, in which things turn out contrary to what is expected, is an example of *irony of situation*. The ironic situation occurs because Soapy does not get arrested when he actually commits crimes but does get arrested when he loiters in front of a church making the decision to alter his life for the better.

Dramatic irony

Below is part of a synopsis for a detective mystery. Read it and answer the questions that follow.

Scene One: The play begins in the dimly lighted library of a huge, old house. A tall man wearing gloves enters and crosses to a painting which hangs above a sofa. He removes the painting, revealing a wall safe behind it. With the skill of a professional burglar, he carefully begins twirling the lock until after a few moments he succeeds in opening the safe. Greedily he grabs the jewels he finds within and makes a speedy exit.

Scene Two: The library is now ablaze with light. The wall safe is open as we left it at the close of the last scene. A famous detective has just arrived and has assembled in the library the owners of the house, guests, and various servants. Among those seated on the sofa beneath the safe is the tall man. He appears to be completely calm and collected. One by one, the detective questions each of the servants. The tall man is next. . . .

1. At this point in the action, what do you know that none of the characters in the play (except the tall man) know?

2. Why might the tall man's answers to the detective's questions take on an added meaning for you that may not be necessarily significant to the other characters in the play?

Dramatic irony occurs in fiction or drama when the reader or spectator knows more about the true state of affairs than the characters do. Authors often employ dramatic irony to create suspense. For example, dramatic irony is used in *The Diary of Anne Frank*. You were probably aware of the story's tragic outcome before you read the play. Even if you were not, once you read the Introduction and first scene, you could not help but infer that Mr. Frank was the only inhabitant of the Secret Annex to survive. By allowing you to know more about what was to happen than the characters themselves did, the authors heightened your feelings of suspense.

irony

The contrast between what is expected, or what appears to be, and what actually is.
Verbal irony is the contrast between what is said and what is actually meant.
Irony of situation refers to a happening that is the opposite of what is expected or intended.
Dramatic irony occurs when the audience or reader knows more than the characters do.

metaphor

Night

Night is a cavalier dauntless and bold;
Riding through clouds on a steed strapped
   with gold,
Sapphires flash from his cloak's sable folds
And each silken pocket a star-baby holds.

Christine Wood Bullwinkle

Christine Wood Bullwinkle. "Night" from *Poems for the Children's Hour* by Josephine Bouton, ed. (Springfield, Mass.: Milton Bradley Co.), 1927.

1. The speaker in the poem above makes a comparison between two essentially different things, night and a cavalier. What does this comparison suggest about night?

2. In line 3 what are the sapphires being compared to? In what ways are the two things the same? What is the sable cloak being compared to? What similarities exist between them?

3. Consider each of the following literal descriptions of night: "the time between evening and morning," "dark," "evening." Which is a more vivid description of night—the poem, or any of the literal descriptions?

In literature and, particularly, in poetry, a writer often expresses one thing in terms of another (night as a cavalier). This use of FIGURATIVE LANGUAGE helps the reader see unexpected, but valid, connections between things that are basically different. When things that are basically unlike are related through implied comparison, they are called *metaphors*.

In a metaphor there is never a connective such as *like* or *as* to signal that a comparison is being made. (See SIMILE.) As a result, metaphors are not always easy to spot. Is this sentence a metaphor: "The tumbleweeds are the children of the desert"? Why or why not?

Explain the metaphor in this line:

> The road was a ribbon of moonlight . . .

---

metaphor

A figure of speech which involves an implied comparison between two relatively unlike things.

mood

Franklin Avenue Bridge

the river is dying
near the universities

every morning
new carp yawn four times
5 then wash ashore

pollution storms
frothing down the sewers

poison rains
disfiguring familiar faces
10 fine umbrellas

patterns of recognition
changing with the faces in a crowd

children of plastic flowers
gather under the bridge
15 retouching old photographs

                              Gerald Vizenor

1. Describe the setting of the poem in your own words. Is the environment described pleasant?

2. At the end of the poem, why do you think the children are "retouching old photographs" rather than taking new photographs of the scene?

3. What is the effect of the poet's use of words such as *dying, pollution, poison, disfiguring,* and *plastic?* What feelings do these words create?

4. How would the effect or mood of the poem differ **(a)** if the scene took place on a sunny day in the country; **(b)** if instead of dead carp on the shore there were fishermen and sunbathers; **(c)** if it rained clean water instead of poison?

As you answered the questions, you probably could not help noticing that the selection of setting, specific details, and certain words and images combine to convey the desired mood—an atmosphere of ugliness, contamination, or decay. Another author might wish to create a different mood such as one that is joyful or quiet or sad or optimistic. In any case, specific words, details, and setting communicate that mood.

Read the poem below and tell what mood you think is indicated. Be sure to give the details that support your answer.

Running

What were we playing? Was it prisoner's base?
I ran with whacking keds
Down the cart-road past Rickard's place,
And where it dropped beside the tractor-sheds

5 Leapt out into the air above a blurred
Terrain, through jolted light,
Took two hard lopes, and at the third
Spanked off a hummock-side exactly right,

And made the turn, and with delighted strain
10 Sprinted across the flat
By the bull-pen, and up the lane.
Thinking of happiness, I think of that.

                              Richard Wilbur

mood

The climate of feeling in a literary work. The choice of setting, objects, details, images, and words all contribute in creating a specific mood.

plot

The material following the story "If Cornered, Scream" deals with *conflict, details, pattern of events, climax,* and *conclusion.* These are all important elements of *plot.*

If Cornered, Scream

On the night it happened she hurried across the hospital parking lot, unlocked her car door, and got in. She started the car, waved to her co-workers, honked to the security guard, and drove the half block to the freeway entrance. The late hour meant light traffic, and though she was a good driver, she was always relieved whenever she had negotiated an entrance ramp. That done, she settled back, driving easily.

Then in the dim dashboard light she saw the gas gauge indicating empty and remembered with annoyance that she hadn't had time to stop for gas. Working a late shift at the hospital was not an ideal situation, but it meant more money and allowed her to attend graduate classes during the days.

As she drove, she found herself gripping the steering wheel and made a conscious effort to relax and think pleasant thoughts. Each night during the drive home, she relived the safety lectures given to the nurses—make sure someone on the ward knows where you are at all times; leave the grounds in groups; avoid isolated places in the hospital; if cornered, scream.

Again she deliberately relaxed her grip on the wheel and took a deep breath.

Funny, she thought, she didn't know why, but she was even more uptight tonight than usual. She was tired and looked forward to a long soak in the tub and her new magazine which had lain unread the last three days.

The gas gauge again caught her attention. She could probably make it home on what was still left in the tank, but she would have to fill up before class in the morning. If she stopped tonight at the station that Gabriel ran on Imperial Highway, she'd have a few extra minutes in the morning and wouldn't have to rush.

She approached Imperial Highway, flicked on the right blinker, headed down the off-ramp, waited at the stoplight, and then made a left turn. She pulled into

From "If Cornered Scream" by Patricia J. Thurmond. First published in *Ellery Queen's* Mystery Magazine, January 1978. Copyright © 1977 by Patricia J. Thurmond. Reprinted by permission.

the station at a pump and rolled down the window as Gabriel walked to the car.

Since he always spoke pleasantly on the nights she stopped for gas, she had automatically discounted the few disturbing rumors that accompanied his sudden appearance in the area.

"Hi, Florence Nightingale. Fill 'er up?"

"Hi, Gabriel. Yes, fill it up, please."

As she handed him the gas-tank key, he asked, "Any more ping-pong playing under the hood?"

"No, no more noise. It stopped when you did whatever you did."

Gabriel filled the tank, cleaned the windows and mirrors, and gave her the change from a twenty. When he finished he said offhandedly, "By the way, my birthday was Sunday. Why don't you step inside the office and see what my sister gave me? You won't believe your eyes!"

"Oh, Gabriel, I'm in a really big hurry. I just can't stop tonight. But I will next time. I promise."

"Aw, come on. It won't be new any more by then. Besides, this is something extra-special. Come on. Only take a second."

As she and Gabriel talked back and forth, she realized she was wasting more time than if she went in and saw the silly gift.

Looking more agreeable than she felt, she said, "Okay, you win, Gabriel. Remember, this better be good!"

"It is. You'll see. Oh, before you get out, angle the car over this way—just in case anyone wants to pull in." Watching his gestures, she parked the car and followed him to the station office.

Once inside, Gabriel locked the door and quickly took a gun out of the drawer. Through the roar of her heartbeat in her ears she heard him say that there was no birthday and no present. Her fingers tingled. Nausea pitched and rolled through her body like seasickness. Each time the nausea crested, her legs felt like loosened moorings.

Her nose and toes were cold and she knew clinically, almost like an observer, that she was experiencing the symptoms of shock. She was unable to make a self-protective move, or even to scream. She tried to prepare to die, but didn't know how. Crazily, in the midst of her silent hysteria, the absurdity of it struck her, and she had a demented desire to laugh. Gabriel's lips were moving but she still couldn't hear above the roar in her ears.

Finally she heard sounds coming from his mouth. The sounds became words as her head cleared, and the words began to make sense.

". . . sorry I had to scare you by telling you that. But don't feel bad, I was scared myself when I saw that dude on the floor in the back of your car. I had you angle the car that way so that I can see both doors from here. And if he tries to get out, he belongs to me. I'll call the cops now. It's okay. Good thing you stopped for gas tonight."

In a few minutes she was aware of the sirens, the flashing lights of the squad cars, and the bellow of the bullhorn.

Patricia J. Thurmond

Conflict

1. When does the main character first think that her life is in danger? Is she able to make any move to prevent this danger? Is her conflict with Gabriel real or imagined?

2. Has this "danger" been foreshadowed earlier in the story? If so, where?

Every story, novel, or play develops around a struggle or conflict. Sometimes there may be only one main conflict. Sometimes, characters may be involved with several conflicts.

Conflicts in literature are of two general types: 1. *external conflict*, in which the character or main figure (sometimes an animal or group) struggles against another character, nature, or society; and 2. *internal conflict*, in which the character struggles against some element of his or her own feelings or personality (conscience or code of values, for example). What is the internal conflict in this story? Is there an external conflict? Explain.

Details

Why is each of the following details important to the story?

1. the late hour

2. the empty gas gauge

3. the main character's early-morning class

An author usually includes only those details that are important to a story. In this story, for example, you are not told what the main charac-

ter looks like or what kind of car she is driving because those details are not important.

Pattern of Events

1. What purpose does each of the following incidents serve?

    a. The main character drives out of a hospital parking lot.

    b. She looks at her gas gauge.

    c. She turns off the freeway.

    d. Gabriel cleans all the windows and mirrors.

    e. Gabriel asks her to look at his birthday present.

    f. The main character decides to get out of the car.

    g. Gabriel tells her to angle the car out of the way of the gas pumps.

    h. He takes a gun out of a drawer.

    i. He tells her there's a man on the floor in the back of her car.

2. Could any of these incidents be eliminated without damaging the story? Explain.

3. Could the order of these incidents be rearranged without lessening the impact of the story?

4. What is the outcome of the story?

An author writes a story with a specific outcome in mind. Therefore, those incidents that are important to the ending are arranged in a cause-effect relationship. Each incident should logically follow the preceding ones since each is a necessary link to the outcome. In a well-planned story no one incident can be moved or eliminated without damaging or even ruining the effect the writer is trying to achieve.

Climax and Conclusion

In your opinion, where in the story is the highest point of interest or emotional intensity? Does the course of events or the main character's course of action change at this point? Explain.

point of view

The *climax* of a story takes place when the reader experiences the greatest emotional response to a character's problem, when the situation is such that the conflict must be resolved one way or another, or when the main character starts to take a decisive action to end the conflict.

The climax of "If Cornered, Scream" begins when the main character suffers numbing shock as she realizes that Gabriel has a gun and continues until she starts listening to what he is telling her and realizes that the gun is only meant to protect her. Not every story contains a climax in this sense; sometimes the problem is left unresolved.

The *conclusion* of a story includes the resolution of the conflict and any events following it. Sometimes the conclusion contains a direct or implied comment on the significance of the conflict.

What events follow the resolution of the conflict or the climax in this story?

plot

A series of related events selected by the author to present and bring about the resolution of some internal or external conflict. In a carefully constructed plot, each detail is important. The incidents are selected and arranged in a cause-effect relationship so that each is a necessary link leading to the outcome of the story. The events usually follow a pattern: the conflict or problem is established; complications arise from the conflict; the situation itself brings about a climax, or a character takes a decisive action; the conflict is resolved.

On Friday, September 13, 1965, I was born to JoAnn and Bob Cheever.

Robert H. Cheever, Jr., was born to JoAnn and Bob Cheever on Friday, September 13, 1965.

What is the only important difference between the two sentences above?

Before beginning to write, an author must decide whether the story will be told by one of the characters, as in the first sentence, or by an outsider, as in the second sentence. The relationship between the narrator and the story he or she tells is called *point of view*.

The four passages that follow tell the same incident from different points of view. Notice how the amount of information given about each character depends upon the point of view used.

1. As I placed the carefully wrapped package on the park bench, I looked up and saw Molly walking across the street. I hoped that she hadn't seen me.

   a. Is the narrator a character in the incident or an outsider?
   b. Do you know what the narrator was doing?
   c. Do you know what Molly was doing? what she was thinking?

2. As George placed the carefully wrapped package on the park bench, he looked up and saw Molly walking across the street.

   a. Is the narrator a character in the incident or an outsider?
   b. Do you know what George was doing? what he was thinking?
   c. Do you know what Molly was doing? what she was thinking?

3. George, anxiously hoping that no one was watching him, placed a carefully wrapped package on an empty park bench. But when he looked around, he saw Molly watching him from across the street.

a. Is the narrator a character in the incident or an outsider?

b. Do you know what George was doing? what he was thinking?

c. Do you know what Molly was doing? what she was thinking?

4. George, anxiously hoping that no one was watching him, placed a carefully wrapped package on an empty park bench. But Molly, who was walking home, saw him and couldn't help thinking that he was acting strangely.

a. Is the narrator a character in the incident or an outsider?

b. Do you know what George was doing? what he was thinking?

c. Do you know what Molly was doing? what she was thinking?

An author uses a narrator much as a movie director uses a camera. Through choice of point of view (who the narrator is), the author can focus sharply on some details and characters while showing others less clearly.

First-Person Point of View

In example number 1, the narrator is a character in the story. In telling the story from his personal point of view, the narrator ("I," or first person) can tell us his own thoughts, but he cannot tell us the thoughts of other characters. Just as you can report what you see others doing, the narrator can tell us only what he sees other characters doing or what he is told by other characters; and just as you cannot enter the minds of other people, the narrator cannot enter the minds of characters other than himself. (For examples of the first-person point of view see "Top Man" and "A Christmas Memory.")

Third-Person-Objective Point of View

In example number 2 the narrator is not a character in the story but is an outsider, or third person. This narrator can tell us what is happening, but he does not tell us the thoughts of any of the characters. He is like a newspaper reporter who can give only the facts as they occur; he cannot enter into the characters' minds. Example 2 is written from the third-person-objective point of view.

rhyme

This point of view is also called the third-person-dramatic point of view because it is the point of view a playwright uses. (Since this point of view greatly limits the amount of information an author can give, it is seldom used except in plays and in mystery or detective stories.)

Third-Person-Limited Point of View

In the third example the narrator sees into the mind of only one character, George. This is known as the third-person-limited point of view.

Omniscient (om nish′ənt)

In the fourth example, the narrator again is an outsider, a third person. But here the narrator has the ability to see into the minds and record the thoughts of both characters. Like a superhuman being, this narrator is omniscient (all-knowing). (For another example of the use of the omniscient point of view see "The Lady, or the Tiger?" and "To Build a Fire.")

point of view

The relationship between the narrator and the story he or she tells. The author's choice of narrator for a story determines the amount of information a reader will be given. The four major points of view are:

1. *First Person:* The narrator ("I") is a character in the story who can reveal only personal thoughts and feelings and what he or she sees and is told by other characters.

2. *Third-Person Objective:* The narrator is an outsider who can report only what he or she sees and hears.

3. *Third-Person Limited:* The narrator is an outsider who sees into the mind of one of the characters.

4. *Omniscient:* The narrator is an all-knowing outsider who can enter the minds of more than one of the characters.

Lone Dog

I'm a lean dog, a keen dog, a wild dog
   and lone;
I'm a rough dog, a tough dog, hunting on
   my own;
I'm a bad dog, a mad dog, teasing silly
   sheep;
I love to sit and bay the moon, to keep
   fat souls from sleep.

5 I'll never be a lap dog, licking dirty
   feet,
A sleek dog, a meek dog, cringing for
   my meat;
Not for me the fireside, the well-filled
   plate,
But shut door, and sharp stone, and cuff
   and kick and hate.

Not for me the other dogs, running by
   my side,
10 Some have run a short while, but none of
   them would bide.
Oh, mine is still the lone trail, the hard
   trail, the best,
Wide wind and wild stars, and hunger of
   the quest.

Irene Rutherford McLeod

In the first stanza of "Lone Dog," which words at the ends of lines rhyme? Which words rhyme in the second stanza? the third?

In poetry, this device of ending two or more lines with words that sound alike is called *end rhyming;* end words that share a particular sound are *end rhymes.*

When used in a poem, end rhymes set up a definite pattern of sounds, or a *rhyme scheme.* You can chart a rhyme scheme with letters of the alphabet by using the same letter for end words that rhyme. Consider, for example, the limerick on the following page.

There was an old man from Flint   *a*
Who peered at the sky with a squint; *a*
    He announced that the moon   *b*
    Was a sweet macaroon,   *b*
Surrounded by dark chocolate mint. *a*

The rhyme scheme for this limerick is *a* (the sound ending line 1); *a* (a sound rhyming with line 1); *b* (a new, or second rhyming sound); *b* (a sound rhyming with the second sound); *a* (a rhyme for the first sound).

If the limerick had a third rhyming sound, it would be designated by the letter *c*. A fourth rhyme would be labeled *d*, and so on. By using this method, you can chart the rhyme scheme of any poem that uses end rhymes.

1. Make a chart of the rhyme scheme for a stanza of McLeod's "Lone Dog."

2. Reread the first line of "Lone Dog." Which words *within* the line rhyme?

Rhyming words within a line are called *internal rhymes*. Find at least three examples of internal rhyme in "Lone Dog."

A second type of internal rhyme rhymes a word within a line with the end word. For example:

> The splendor *falls* on castle *walls*.

Can you find any internal rhymes of this type in "Lone Dog"?

I never saw a purple cow,
I never hope to see one.
But I can tell you anyhow,
I'd rather see than be one.

           Gelett Burgess

Read the above verse aloud. Did you notice that its author has arranged words in a way that automatically causes you to place greater stress on some words or syllables than on others? This combination of stressed and unstressed words or syllables creates a pattern that gives the line a definite flow, or *rhythm*. In the case of this nonsense rhyme, the rhythm is very regular (capital letters indicate stressed words or syllables):

> i NEVer SAW a PURple COW,
> i NEVer HOPE to SEE one.
> but I can TELL you ANyHOW,
> i'd RATHer SEE than BE one.

The *ti TUM ti TUM ti TUM* rhythm gives the verse a singsong effect. Also, each line of the verse is *end-stopped;* that is, the words are so arranged that a pause, designated by a punctuation mark, is necessary at the end of each line. These pauses, which call attention to the verse's rhymes, strengthen its singsong effect.

Because "Purple Cow" is a nonsense verse, its regular rhythm is suitable; its regularity heightens its feeling of nonsense. But in more serious poetry, poets try to avoid the monotony caused by such absolute regularity. To a skilled poet, the regular beat is a foundation from which to depart and return.

rhyme

The repetition of syllable sounds. End words that share a particular sound are called end rhymes. Rhyming words within a line of poetry are called internal rhymes.

The splendor falls on castle walls
   And snowy summits old in story;
The long light shakes across the lakes,
   And the wild cataract leaps in glory.
5 Blow, bugle, blow, set the wild echoes
     flying,
  Blow, bugle; answer, echoes, dying,
     dying, dying.

Tennyson, from The Princess

1. Which words or syllables in the first line should be accented? in the second? the third? the fourth? (Notice how the rhythm changes in the last two lines.)

2. Where is the first pause in the stanza? the second pause?

Line 1 of this stanza overflows into the second line; it is a *run-on* line. Because you do not pause at the end of a run-on line, you do not emphasize the rhyme, thus increasing the poem's rhythmical variety. The variety of the rhythm causes the reader to stress the poem's meaning rather than its rhythm.

Rhythm is everywhere; it is inescapable. Even the most CASual EVeryday SPEECH FALLS into RHYTHmic PHRASes. But poets do not use rhythm simply because it exists. In poetry—as in well-written prose—rhythm has definite purposes.

First of all, rhythm is used because it is enjoyable for its own sake. This is evidenced by the pleasure young children derive from nursery rhymes. And on all the sidewalks of America children jump rope to chants such as the one below:

> aLONG CAME the DOCtor!
> aLONG CAME the NURSE!
> aLONG CAME the LAdy
> with the BIG, FAT PURSE!

Second, rhythm allows the poet to fit the movement of the poem to the mood he or she is trying to create.

"O WHERE ha you BEEN, Lord RANdal, my SON?
And WHERE ha you BEEN, my HANDsome young
    MAN?"
"I ha BEEN at the GREENwood; Mother, MAK my
    bed SOON,
For I'm WEARied wi HUNTin, and FAIN wad lie
    DOWN."

Is the rhythm in keeping with the mood of the poem? Before answering this question, re-read the complete poem (pages 155–156).

Third, the poet can use rhythm to emphasize important words:

> Most WEAry SEEMED the SEA,
>   WEAry the AIR,
> WEAry the WANdering FIELDS of
>   BARren FOAM.

The first syllable of *weary* is naturally accented each time the word appears. The second and third *weary* follow pauses, thus giving them extra emphasis. By stressing this word so strongly, the poet suggests a feeling of great tiredness.

Imagine that the poet who wrote the above lines had said this instead:

> Weariness was here.
> Weariness was there.
> Weariness was round me
> Everywhere.

Is the rhythm used in the second version suitable to a serious poem? Why or why not?

rhythm

A series of stressed and unstressed sounds in a group of words. Rhythm may be regular or it may be varied.

satire

Rodrigues,
The Late Look Magazine.

"I remember when you could crawl through this desert and feel safe even at three o'clock in the morning. . . ."

1. According to the cartoon, why is it no longer safe to crawl through the desert?

2. Do you think the cartoonist intended this cartoon to be taken literally? Why or why not?

3. What social problem is the cartoonist commenting on?

The Ingredients of Expedience

There's a new recipe for water
That's caught on to such a degree
I now pass it on to others
The way it was passed on to me:
5   Into an ocean of fluids
    Add a roentgen of fallout or two,
    Aluminum cans, detergents
    (With the phosphates most pleasing to you).
    Stir in ground glass, melted plastics,
10   Any leftovers, sewage, rough waste.
    Thicken with chemical acids
    And mix to a pliable paste:
    Mercury, mustard or nerve gas
    Well blended with plenty of oil,
15   Insecticides, powdered or liquid,
    Then slowly bring all to a boil.
That's it. Oh, yes, one remainder——
And forgive me for throwing a curve——
Fish die, but children prefer it
20 If you cool before you serve.

Henry Gibson

1. According to the poem, what is the "new recipe for water"?

2. What is the poet's attitude toward this new kind of water?

3. *Expedience* means "personal advantage" or "self-interest." Who might benefit by having water like that described in the poem?

A literary work in which the author makes fun of the vices or follies of society is called a *satire*. A satire can deal with almost any subject, from minor human absurdity (the existence of a particular clothing fad, for example) to major social and political problems (crime, pollution, the futility of war). But all satire has one thing in common: it uses humor, which may range from light-hearted to bitter, to comment on the weakness of people and society.

The purpose of much satire is to eliminate serious social problems by encouraging people to think or act in a certain way. What is the author of "The Ingredients of Expedience" satirizing? How is he trying to influence readers' ideas about the state of our water supply?

Sometimes the language, style, or ideas of a literary work are mimicked for satiric or comic effect. This is called *parody* (par′ə dē).

Read the parody of a Greek myth below and answer the questions that follow.

Endremia and Liason
(From the Greek Mythology)

Endremia was the daughter of Polygaminous, the God of Ensilage, and Reba, the Goddess of Licorice. She was the child of a most unhappy union, it later turned out, for when she was a tiny child her father struck her mother with an anvil and turned himself into a lily pad to avoid the vengeance of Jove. But

Jove was too sly for Polygaminous and struck him with a bolt of lightning the size of the Merchants Bank Building which threw him completely off his balance so that he toppled over into a chasm and was dashed to death.

In the meantime, Little Endremia found herself alone in the world with nobody but Endrocine, the Goddess of Lettuce, and her son Bilax, the God of Gum Arabic, to look after her. But, as Polygaminous (her father; have you forgotten so soon, you dope?) had turned Endremia into a mushroom before he turned himself into a lily pad, neither of her guardians knew who she was, so their protection did her no good.

But Jove had not so soon forgotten the daughter of his favorite (Reba), and appeared to her one night in the shape of a mushroom gatherer. He asked her how she would like to get off that tree (she was one of those mushrooms which grow on trees) and get into his basket. Endremia, not knowing that it was Jove who was asking her, said not much. Whereupon Jove unloosed his mighty wrath and struck down the whole tree with a bolt of lightning which he had brought with him in case Endremia wouldn't listen to reason.

This is why it is never safe to eat the mushrooms which grow on trees, or to refuse to get into Jove's basket.

Robert Benchley

1. Compare "Endremia and Liason" to other Greek myths you have read. Is the style similar? the characters? the plot? How is it different?

2. In your opinion, what purpose did the author have in mind in writing "Endremia and Liason"?

satire

A literary work in which the author ridicules the vices or follies of people and society, usually for the purpose of producing some change in attitude or action. In *parody,* the language, style, or ideas of another literary work are mimicked for comic or satiric effect.

Below is the first paragraph of a short story by Ambrose Bierce. Read it and answer the questions that follow.

One sunny afternoon in the autumn of the year 1861 a soldier lay in a clump of laurel by the side of a road in western Virginia. He lay at full length upon his stomach, his feet resting upon the toes, his head upon the left forearm. His extended right hand loosely grasped his rifle. But for . . . a slight rhythmic movement of the cartridge box at the back of his belt he might have been thought to be dead. He was asleep at his post of duty . . . if detected he would be dead shortly afterward, death being the just and legal penalty of his crime.

1. Where does the story take place? What details tell you this?

2. When do the events of this story take place?

The time and place in which the events of a narrative occur form what is called the *setting.* The place may be a region, a city or town, or even a house or room. The time may be a period in history, a particular time of year, or a certain time of day. In some narratives, the setting is specific and detailed, as in the paragraph reprinted above, but in others, it may be intentionally obscure.

The stranger rode slowly into the dusty town. His wide-brimmed Stetson was pulled forward on his head, casting a shadow over his gaunt face. The sunlight sparkled on his spurs and on the handle of his gun which hung casually by his right side. He headed straight for the stagecoach office and reined his horse.

1. Where does this event take place? What details tell you this?

2. In approximately what period of history does this event occur? How do you know?

Soon after the successful lift-off, Mission Control received its first communication from the spacecraft *Encounter.* "All systems are GO," reported Astronaut

Jake Lewis, whose voice came in loud and clear. "Next stop—the planet Mars!"

1. Where does this take place? How do you know?

2. In approximately what period does it take place? What details tell you this?

"Land ho!" shouted the lookout. "To the starboard beam, about three miles off!"

1. Where does this take place? How do you know?

2. Is there any indication of time of day? of time in history? Explain.

In some narratives the description of setting is either brief or merely suggested through the use of details scattered throughout the story. An author can suggest the setting by references to articles of clothing, famous historical figures, well-known landmarks, or through the dialect and speech patterns of the characters that have been created. Not all stories have a setting in which both the time and place are identifiable.

Frequently a setting which is presented in detail forms an important part of the narrative. It may have an effect on the events of the plot, it may reveal character, or, as in the next example from "Padre Ignacio" by Owen Wister, it may create a certain mood or atmosphere.

At Santa Ysabel del Mar the season was at one of those moments when the air rests quiet over land and sea. The old breezes were gone; the new ones were not yet risen. The flowers in the mission garden opened wide; no wind came by day or night to shake the loose petals from their stems. Along the basking, silent, many-colored shore gathered and lingered the crisp odors of the mountains. The dust hung golden and motionless long after the rider was behind the hill, and the Pacific lay like a floor of sapphire, whereon to walk beyond the setting sun into the East.[1] One white sail shone there. Instead of an hour, it had been from

dawn till afternoon in sight between the short headlands; and the Padre had hoped that it might be the ship his homesick heart awaited. But it had slowly passed. From an arch in his garden cloisters he was now watching the last of it. Presently it was gone, and the great ocean lay empty.

1. What is the setting?

2. How does part of the setting affect the Padre?

3. What effect does the author create in this paragraph?

4. What specific words and phrases help to create this effect?

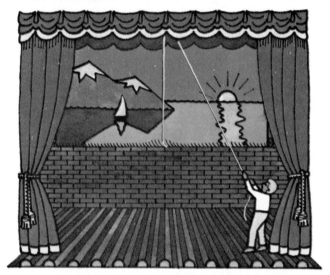

setting

The time and place in which the events of a narrative occur. The setting may be specific and detailed, and introduced at the very beginning of the story, or it may be merely suggested through the use of details scattered throughout the story. In some stories the setting is vital to the narrative: it may have an effect on the events of the plot; reveal character; or create a certain atmosphere. In other stories the setting is relatively unimportant: the story could have happened almost anywhere or at any time.

---

1. *East,* here, the Orient.

My heart is like an apple-tree
    Whose boughs are bent with thick-set fruit . . .
                  Rossetti, "A Birthday"

And the muscles of his brawny arms
    Are strong as iron bands.
              Longfellow, "The Village Blacksmith"

In both examples above, comparisons are made. What is being compared in each? What word in each example tells you that a comparison is being made?

A *simile* is a stated comparison between two things that are really very different but that share some common quality. To create a vivid picture, a writer points out the quality they share. Similes are introduced by the use of *like* or *as*. If you were to say "Jason runs *like* the wind and is *as* strong as an ox," you would be using similes. You would be indicating comparisons between Jason's speed and the speed of the wind, and Jason's strength and the strength of an ox.

One important thing to remember is that statements comparing things that are essentially alike are not similes. Ordinary statements such as "She looks like her mother" or "She skates as well as I do" are not similes. A simile reveals a similar quality in two elements that are otherwise different. Is "They came dressed like their favorite literary characters" a simile? Why or why not?

simile (sim′ə lē)

A figure of speech which involves a direct comparison between two unlike things, usually with the words *like* or *as*.

Imagine a person whom you think of as a typical truck driver. What does this person look like? act like?

Does your mental picture of a truck driver in any way resemble the truck driver above?

You may have a fixed idea, or *stereotype,* in your mind of what a typical truck driver looks and acts like. If you find the cartoon funny, it is probably because you are aware that the artist took the stereotypical idea of a truck driver hounding motorists on the highway and made the truck driver a woman, whom, traditionally, we do not expect to see in *this* stereotypical role.

Stereotypes are helpful to the cartoonist who wants to make us laugh through a simple sketch, to the author who wishes to create a character in as few words as possible, and to the television or film writer who has only a limited time to spend on characterization. Each relies upon commonly held generalizations to characterize a person, group, issue, etc. Always remember, however, that stereotyped characters lack individuality and that they have no distinguishing traits except those expected of the larger group to which they belong. For example, in fairy tales, the courageous, handsome, and charming prince is a stereotype. You have probably been exposed so often to this stereotype that every time you encounter a prince in your reading you may still *expect* him to be handsome, courageous, and charming, unless the author specifically tells you differently.

Read the following descriptions of stereotyped characters. Then from the choices listed below each, pick the one that fits the stereotype.

1. wears large white hat; is happiest riding the range; seldom talks; best friend is horse. **(a)** rancher; **(b)** cowboy; **(c)** gambler; **(d)** rancher's daughter.

2. young and attractive; wears frilly clothes; reacts to a mouse or crawling insect by screaming or fainting. **(a)** mother-in-law; **(b)** gangster's girlfriend; **(c)** actor; **(d)** maiden in distress.

3. loud; pushy; wears flashy clothes; smokes a cigar. **(a)** used-car dealer; **(b)** airline pilot; **(c)** judge; **(d)** actress.

PLOTS or situations may also be stereotyped. While watching television you may have had the feeling at some time that you have seen a program before, although the names and characters have been changed. Stereotyped situations or plots include those that have become trite or uninteresting from overuse, such as the disabled airplane with at least one ill passenger or the widow who fights to save the ranch. Can you name other stereotyped plots?

Stereotypes can be misleading and potentially damaging if they lead a reader to accept certain highly generalized views about *real* people and situations. In real life, people and situations are much more complicated.

---

stereotype (ster′ē ə tīp′)

A fixed, generalized idea about a character or situation. An example of a stereotyped character might be the wicked stepmother in fairy tales; a stereotyped situation might be a plot about a small boy and his brave dog.

Uphill

Does the road wind uphill all the way?
    Yes, to the very end.
Will the day's journey take the whole long
    day?
    From morn to night, my friend.

But is there for the night a resting
5   place?
    A roof for when the slow dark hours
    begin.
May not the darkness hide it from my
    face?
    You cannot miss that inn.

Shall I meet other wayfarers at night?
10   Those who have gone before.
Then must I knock, or call when just
    in sight?
    They will not keep you standing at
    that door.

Shall I find comfort, travel-sore and
    weak?
    Of labor you shall find the sum.
15 Will there be beds for me and all who
    seek?
    Yea, beds for all who come.

                Christina Rossetti

1. What kind of "journey" do you think is being discussed?

2. What does each of the following elements represent: **(a)** the road; **(b)** the uphill climb; **(c)** the day; **(d)** the night; **(e)** the journey's end; **(f)** the inn; **(g)** the other wayfarers; **(h)** the first speaker; **(i)** the second speaker?

At first "Uphill" may seem to be a conversation about the lodgings to be found at the end of a difficult trip. But if the poem is read carefully, it takes on a different meaning. The road is more than a link between two places; it is the path all people take toward death. The road, as well as the other items noted in question 2, is a *symbol*. A symbol may be an object, a person, an action, a situation—anything that suggests a meaning beyond its obvious meaning.

While some symbols suggest the same thing to most people (the heart is a universal symbol of love), other symbols have different meanings for different people. What might a gun symbolize to a hunter? a thief? a soldier?

Characters in literature often have personal symbols. You can recognize them by noting the objects, persons, or situations for which a character shows strong feelings. Watch for the repetition of an object or an action.

Look for the symbols in this poem.

I Saw a Man Pursuing the Horizon

I saw a man pursuing the horizon;
Round and round they sped.
I was disturbed at this;
I accosted the man.
5 "It is futile," I said.
"You can never——"
"You lie," he cried,
And ran on.

Stephen Crane

1. To the speaker, does the horizon symbolize an impossible goal or a goal difficult to achieve? Explain.

2. To the speaker, does the man's pursuit symbolize industriousness or ridiculous activity? Explain.

symbol

A person, place, event, or object which has a meaning in itself but suggests other meanings as well.

About Crows

The old crow is getting slow.
  The young crow is not.
Of what the young crow does not know
  The old crow knows a lot.

5 At knowing things the old crow
  Is still the young crow's master.
What does the slow old crow not know?
  How to go faster.

The young crow flies above, below,
10 And rings around the slow old crow.
What does the fast young crow not know?
  Where to go.

John Ciardi

1. What is the chief characteristic of the young crow in this poem? What is the chief characteristic of the old crow?

2. What accounts for the differences between the two crows?

3. Is this poem only about birds? Could the comment the speaker makes about youth and age be applied to people as well? Explain.

4. Which of the following statements best expresses the main idea of the poem? **(a)** Youthful enthusiasm is often a poor substitute for the wisdom of experience. **(b)** Don't expend too much energy without having a destination in mind. **(c)** Although the young crow can fly much faster than the old crow, the young crow does not know in which direction to go.

The main idea of a literary work is called the *theme*. The theme, or main idea, of the poem reprinted above is best expressed in statement **(a)**.

Statement **(b)** presents a moral: it tells the reader how to act. It is not the theme because the poem does not tell the reader how to act or behave.

tone

Statement **(c)** gives the plot of the poem, not the theme. A plot is the pattern of events—the "what specifically happens"—in a poem or narrative. For example, the plot of a story might concern a young soldier during his first battle. The events of the plot might include the man's thoughts before the battle, the battle itself and what the young man thinks, feels, and does during the battle, and the outcome of the battle and the young man's new impressions of war.

The theme of such a story might be the idea that fighting solves nothing. This theme might not be stated anywhere in the story but it will be suggested through the events of the plot and the attitudes of the characters.

It is important also to recognize the difference between the *theme* of a literary work and the *subject* of a literary work. The subject is the topic on which an author has chosen to write. The theme, however, makes some statement about or expresses some opinion on that topic. For instance, in the above example the subject of the story might be war while the theme of the story might be the idea that war is futile.

Not every literary work has a theme. Some are written purely to entertain the reader. A mystery story, for example, written primarily to keep the reader in suspense, may not have a theme.

theme

The main idea or underlying meaning of a literary work. A theme may be stated or implied. Theme differs from the subject, or topic, of a literary work in that it involves a statement or opinion about the topic. Not every literary work has a theme.

Afoot and light-hearted I take to the open road,
Healthy, free, the world before me,
The long, brown path before me leading wherever I choose.
Henceforth I ask not good-fortune, I myself am good-fortune.
5 Henceforth I whimper no more, postpone no more, need nothing,
Done with indoor complaints, libraries, querulous criticisms.
Strong and content I travel the open road.

Whitman, "Song of the Open Road"

1. What is this poem about? What might the "open road" represent?
2. Does the speaker regret leaving the indoors? Explain.
3. What is the speaker's attitude as he sets forth? What words and phrases convey his attitude?

To achieve a complete understanding of most literary works, you must determine how the author feels about the subject. An author's attitude toward the subject is called *tone.* The tone of a literary work serves the same basic purpose as a tone of voice; it helps to indicate the speaker's attitude, whether it is one of anger, sadness, amusement, joy, defiance, or some other emotion. The tone may, in fact, reflect a combination of several different emotions.

Sometimes an author will state directly how he feels about a character, a situation, or an idea. The speaker in the poem, for example, states that he feels "light-hearted," "healthy," "free," "strong," and "content." The attitude, or tone, of Whitman's poem is one of enthusiasm and joyful optimism. Read the following excerpt from *David Copperfield* to see whether you can determine the author's attitude toward his subject.

It was Miss Murdstone who was arrived, and a gloomy-looking lady she was; dark, like her brother,

whom she greatly resembled in face and voice, and with very heavy eyebrows, nearly meeting over her large nose. She brought with her two uncompromising hard black boxes, with her initials on the lids in hard brass nails. When she paid the coachman she took her money out of a hard steel purse, and she kept the purse in a very jail of a bag which hung upon her arm by a heavy chain, and shut up like a bite. It seemed that there had never been such a metallic lady altogether as Miss Murdstone was.

    1. **(a)** What sort of woman is being described in this paragraph? Cite specific words that the author uses to describe her. **(b)** How do the things she is carrying contribute to the picture of this woman?
    2. **(a)** What is the author's attitude toward the woman? How do you know? **(b)** Is his attitude stated or implied?
    In most literary works the author's attitude will not be stated directly, as it is in the excerpt from Whitman's "Song of the Open Road," but will be suggested through the author's choice of words and details. In the paragraph above, for

example, Charles Dickens never states that this character is not likable. However, by describing her as "gloomy-looking," "dark," "uncompromising," and "metallic," he implies his opinion of her and draws the reader into sharing his attitude.

tone

The author's attitude, stated or implied, toward a subject. Some possible attitudes are earnestness, seriousness, bitterness, humor, sympathy, indignation, whimsicality, joy, mockery, cynicism, and irony. An author's tone can be revealed through choice of words and details. (Remember, however, that the author's tone, as reflected in a literary work, may differ from the *narrator's* attitude toward the events described.) Tone should not be confused with *mood*, which is the climate of feeling within a literary work. For example, an author may create a mood of mystery around a character or setting but may treat that character or setting in an ironic, serious, or humorous tone.

Glossary

The pronunciation of each word is shown just after the word, in this way: **ab bre vi ate** (ə brē′vē āt). The letters and signs used are pronounced as in the words below. The mark ′ is placed after a syllable with primary or heavy accent, as in the example above. The mark ′ after a syllable shows a secondary or lighter accent, as in **ab bre vi a tion** (ə brē′vē ā′shən).

Some words, taken from foreign languages, are spoken with sounds that do not otherwise occur in English. Symbols for these sounds are given in the key as "foreign sounds."

Full pronunciation key

a	hat, cap	j	jam, enjoy	u	cup, butter
ā	age, face	k	kind, seek	u̇	full, put
ä	father, far	l	land, coal	ü	rule, move
		m	me, am		
b	bad, rob	n	no, in	v	very, save
ch	child, much	ng	long, bring	w	will, woman
d	did, red			y	young, yet
		o	hot, rock	z	zero, breeze
e	let, best	ō	open, go	zh	measure, seizure
ē	equal, be	ô	order, all		
ėr	term, learn	oi	oil, voice	ə	represents:
		ou	house, out		a in about
f	fat, if				e in taken
g	go, bag	p	paper, cup		i in pencil
h	he, how	r	run, try		o in lemon
		s	say, yes		u in circus
i	it, pin	sh	she, rush		
ī	ice, five	t	tell, it		
		th	thin, both		
		₮H	then, smooth		

foreign sounds

Y as in French *du*. Pronounce (ē) with the lips rounded as for (ü).

a as in French *ami*. Pronounce (ä) with the lips spread and held tense.

œ as in French *peu*. Pronounce (ā) with the lips rounded as for (ō).

N as in French *bon*. The N is not pronounced, but shows that the vowel before it is nasal.

H as in German *ach*. Pronounce (k) without closing the breath passage.

Grammatical key

adj.	adjective	*prep.*	preposition
adv.	adverb	*pron.*	pronoun
conj.	conjunction	*v.*	verb
interj.	interjection	*v.i.*	intransitive verb
n.	noun	*v.t.*	transitive verb
sing.	singular	*pl.*	plural

From *Thorndike-Barnhart Advanced Dictionary*, Second Edition. Copyright © 1974 by Scott, Foresman and Company. Reprinted by permission.

ab-

ab-¹, *prefix.* from; away; away from; off: *Abnormal = away from normal.* [< Latin < *ab* off, away from]

ab-², *prefix.* form of **ad-** before *b*, as in *abbreviate.*

-able, *suffix forming adjectives from verbs and nouns.* **1** that can be ___ed: *Enjoyable = that can be enjoyed.* **2** giving ___; suitable for ___: *Comfortable = giving comfort.* **3** inclined to ___: *Peaceable = inclined to peace.* **4** deserving to be ___ed: *Lovable = deserving to be loved.* **5** liable to be ___: *Breakable = liable to be broken.* [< Old French < Latin *-abilem*]

a bode (ə bōd′), *n.* place of residence; dwelling; house or home.

a brupt (ə brupt′), *adj.* **1** characterized by sudden change; unexpected: *an abrupt turn.* **2** very steep. **3** short or sudden in speech or manner; blunt. **4** disconnected: *an abrupt style of writing.* —**a brupt′ly**, *adv.* —**a brupt′ness**, *n.*

ab scond (ab skond′), *v.i.* go away hurriedly and secretly, especially to avoid punishment; go off and hide. [< Latin *abscondere* < *abs-* away + *condere* store up]

ab sorbed (ab sôrbd′, ab zôrbd′), *adj.* very much interested; completely occupied.

ab surd (ab sėrd′, ab zėrd′), *adj.* plainly not true, logical, or sensible; ridiculous. [< Latin *absurdus* out of tune, senseless] —**ab surd′ly**, *adv.* —**ab surd′ness**, *n.*

a bun dance (ə bun′dəns), *n.* **1** an overflowing quantity or amount; great plenty; profusion. **2** plentiful supply of money and possessions; affluence; wealth.

a bys mal (ə biz′məl), *adj.* **1** too deep or great to be measured; bottomless: *abysmal ignorance.* **2** of the lowest depths of the ocean. **3** INFORMAL. extremely bad; of very low quality. —**a bys′mal ly**, *adv.*

a byss (ə bis′), *n.* **1 a** a bottomless or very great depth; chasm. **2** anything too deep or great to be measured; lowest depth. **3** the chaos before the Creation. [< Greek *abyssos* < *a-* without + *byssos* bottom]

ac cede (ak sēd′), *v.i.,* **-ced ed, -ced ing.** **1** give in; agree; consent *(to)*: *Please accede to my request.* **2** become a party *(to)*: *Our government acceded to the treaty.* [< Latin *accedere* < *ad-* to + *cedere* move, go]

ac cel e ra tion (ak sel′ə rā′shən), *n.* **1** act or process of accelerating. **2** condition of being accelerated; increased speed. **3** change in velocity, either a gradual increase (**positive acceleration**) or a gradual decrease (**negative acceleration**). **4** rate of change in the velocity of a moving body.

ac claim (ə klām′), *v.t.* **1** welcome with shouts or other signs of approval; praise highly; applaud: *The crowd acclaimed the winning team.* **2** proclaim or announce with approval: *The newspapers acclaimed the results of the election.* —*n.* a shout or show of approval; approval; applause. [< Latin *acclamare* < *ad-* to + *clamare* cry out] —**ac claim′er**, *n.*

ac cli mate (ə klī′mit, ak′lə māt), *v.t., v.i.,* **-mat ed, -mat ing.** accustom or become accustomed to a new climate, surroundings, or conditions. —**ac cli ma tion** (ak′lə mā′shən), *n.*

ac quire (ə kwīr′), *v.t.,* **-quired, -quir ing.** **1** get by one's own efforts or actions: *acquire an education.* **2** come into the possession of: *acquire land.* [< Latin *acquirere* < *ad-* to + *quaerere* seek] —**ac quir′a ble**, *adj.* —**ac quir′er**, *n.*

a cute (ə kyüt′), *adj.* **1** acting keenly on the senses; sharp; intense: *acute pain.* **2** coming quickly to a crisis; brief and severe: *an acute disease.* **3** crucial; critical: *an acute shortage of water.* **4** quick in perceiving and responding to impressions; keen: *Dogs have an acute sense of smell.* **5** quick in discernment; sharp-witted; clever: *an acute thinker.* [< Latin *acutum* sharpened < *acuere* sharpen] —**a cute′ly**, *adv.* —**a cute′ness**, *n.*

ad min is ter (ad min′ə stər), *v.t.* **1** manage the affairs of (a business, a city, etc.); control in behalf of others; supervise or direct: *administer a department of the government, administer a household.* **2** give out, apply, or dispense: *administer first aid, administer justice.* **3** deliver or bestow (a blow, rebuke, advice, etc., to a person, animal, etc.). **4** tender (an oath): *The witness could not testify until the judge administered an oath to him to tell the truth.* —*v.i.* give aid; contribute beneficially; minister *(to)*: *administer to the needs of flood victims.* [< Latin *administrare* < *ad-* to + *minister* servant]

ad vis a bil i ty (ad vī′zə bil′ə tē), *n.* quality of being advisable; fitness.

aes thet ic (es thet′ik), *adj.* **1** having to do with the beautiful, as distinguished from the useful, scientific, etc. **2** (of persons) sensitive to beauty. **3** (of things) pleasing; artistic. Also, **esthetic.**

af firm (ə fėrm′), *v.t.* **1** declare positively to be true; maintain firmly; assert: *I affirmed the report to be true.* **2** confirm or ratify: *The higher court affirmed the lower court's decision.* —*v.i.* declare solemnly, but without taking an oath. [< Latin *affirmare* < *ad-* to + *firmus* strong]

a fore men tioned (ə fôr′men′shənd, ə-fōr′men′shənd), *adj.* spoken of before; mentioned earlier.

a gen da (ə jen′də), *n.* **1** list of items of business to be brought before a meeting of a committee, council, board, etc., as things to be dealt with or done: *The agenda has already been settled.* **2** routine of things to be done. [< Latin, things to be done < *agere* do]

ag gres sive (ə gres′iv), *adj.* **1** taking the first step in a quarrel or war; attacking; quarrelsome: *an aggressive country.* **2** characterized by aggression; offensive: *an aggressive war.* **3** very active; energetic: *an aggressive campaign against crime.* **4** too confident and certain; assertive: *an insultingly aggressive manner.* —**ag gres′sive ly**, *adv.* —**ag gres′sive ness**, *n.*

ag ile (aj′əl), *adj.* **1** moving with speed, ease, and elegance; lively; nimble: *as agile as a kitten.* **2** mentally alert; quick-witted. [< Latin *agilis* < *agere* to move] —**ag′ile ly**, *adv.* —**ag′ile ness**, *n.*

ag i ta tion (aj′ə tā′shən), *n.* **1** a violent moving or shaking. **2** a disturbed, upset, or troubled state. **3** vigorous argument, discussion, etc., to arouse public interest and feeling.

aim less (ām′lis), *adj.* without purpose; pointless: *engage in friendly but aimless talk.* —**aim′less ly**, *adv.* —**aim′less ness**, *n.*

a jar (ə jär′), *adj.* slightly open: *Please leave the door ajar.* [Middle English *on char* on the turn; Old English *cerr* turn]

a li as (ā′lē əs), *n.* name used by a person instead of his real name to hide who he is; assumed name; other name. —*adv.* otherwise called; with the assumed name of: *The spy's name was Harrison, alias Johnson.* [< Latin, otherwise < *alius* other]

al ien (ā′lyən, ā′lē ən), *n.* **1** person who is not a citizen of the country in which he lives; a resident foreigner whose allegiance is owed to a foreign state. **2** person belonging to a different ethnic or social group; stranger; foreigner. —*adj.* **1** of or by another country; foreign: *an alien language, alien domination.* **2** having the legal status of an alien: *an alien resident.* **3** entirely different from one's own; strange: *alien customs.* **4** not in agreement; opposed, adverse, or repugnant: *Unkindness is alien to her nature.* [< Latin *alienus* < *alius* other]

al ien ate (ā′lyə nāt, ā′lē ə nāt), *v.t.,* **-at ed, -at ing.** **1** turn away the normal feelings, fondness, or devotion of anyone; make unfriendly; estrange: *The colonies were alienated from England by disputes over trade and taxation.* **2** transfer (property, a property right, etc.) to the ownership of another: *Enemy property was alienated during the war.* **3** turn away; transfer. —**al′ien a′tor**, *n.*

a light (ə līt′), *adj.* **1** on fire; lighted. **2** lighted up; aglow. [Old English *ālīht*]

al le giance (ə lē′jəns), *n.* **1** the loyalty owed by a citizen to his country; obligation of a subject to his ruler or government. **2** faithfulness to a person, cause, etc.; loyalty; fidelity. [Middle English *alegeaunce* < Old French *ligeance* < *lige* liege]

al li ance (ə lī′əns), *n.* **1** union formed by mutual agreement, especially to protect or further mutual interests. **2** a joining of independent nations by treaty. **3** a joining of family interests through marriage. **4** the nations, persons, etc., who are allied. **5** any joining of efforts or interests by persons, families, states, or organizations: *an alliance between church and state.* [< Old French *aliance* < *alier* unite.]

al lure (ə lür′), *v.,* **-lured, -lur ing,** *n.* —*v.t.* tempt or attract very strongly; fascinate; charm: *City life allured her with its action and excitement.* —*n.* great charm; fascination.

a loof (ə lüf′), *adv.* **1** away at some distance but within view; apart. **2** without community of feeling: *stand aloof from family joys and sorrows.* —*adj.* unsympathetic; not interested; reserved: *an aloof manner.* —**a loof′ly**, *adv.* —**a loof′ness**, *n.*

al ter (ôl′tər), *v.t.* **1** make different; change the appearance of; modify. **2** adjust the measurements of (a garment) to obtain a better fit. —*v.i.* become different. —**al′ter a ble**, *adj.* —**al′ter a ble ness**, *n.* —**al′ter a bly**, *adv.*

al ter nate ly (ôl′tər nit lē, al′tər nit lē), *adv.* **1** one after the other by turns. **2** on each side in turn.

a lum ni (ə lum′nī), *n.* pl. of **alumnus.**

a lum nus (ə lum′nəs), *n., pl.* **-ni.** graduate or former student of a school, college, or university. [Am.E; < L *alumnus* foster child < *alere* nourish]

am ber (am′bər), *n.* **1** a hard, translucent, yellow or yellowish-brown fossil resin, easily polished and used for jewelry, in making pipe stems, etc. **2** the color of amber; yellow or yellowish brown. —*adj.* **1** made of amber. **2** yellow or yellowish-brown.

am ne sia (am nē′zhə), *n.* partial or entire loss of memory caused by injury to the brain, or by disease, shock, etc.

am or ous (am′ər əs), *adj.* **1** inclined to love: *an amorous disposition.* **2** in love; enamored. **3** showing love; loving: *an amorous letter.* **4** having to do with love or

562

courtship. [< Old French < *amour* love < Latin *amor*] —**am′or ous ly,** *adv.* —**am′-or ous ness,** *n.*

am phib i an (am fib′ē ən), *n.* 1 animal that lives on land and in water. 2 plant that grows on land or in water. 3 aircraft that can take off from and alight on either land or water. 4 in military use, a tank for use on land and in water.

am ple (am′pəl), *adj.,* **-pler, -plest.** 1 more than enough to satisfy all demands; abundant: *an ample supply of food.* 2 as much as is needed; enough: *an allowance ample for carfare and lunches.* 3 large in capacity or volume: *a house with ample closets.* 4 large in extent or amount; extensive: *ample praise.* [< Latin *amplus*] —**am′ple ness,** *n.*

-an, *suffix forming adjectives and nouns, especially from proper nouns.* 1 of or having to do with ___: *Mohammedan = of or having to do with Mohammed.* 2 of or having to do with ___ or its people: *Asian = of or having to do with Asia or its people.* 3 native or inhabitant of ___: *American = native or inhabitant of America.* 4 person who knows much about or is skilled in ___: *Magician = person skilled in magic. Historian = person who knows much about history.* Also, **-ian, -ean.** [< Latin *-anus*]

-ance, *suffix forming nouns chiefly from verbs.* 1 act or fact of ___ing: *Avoidance = act or fact of avoiding.* 2 quality or state of being ___ed: *Annoyance = quality or state of being annoyed.* 3 thing that ___s: *Conveyance = thing that conveys.* 4 what is ___ed: *Contrivance = what is contrived.* 5 quality or state of being ___ant: *Importance = quality or state of being important.* [< Old French < Latin *-antia, -entia*]

an ec dote (an′ik dōt), *n.* a short account of some interesting incident or single event, especially one in the life of a person. [< Greek *anekdota* (things) unpublished < *an-* not + *ek-* out + *didonai* give]

an es thet ic (an′əs thet′ik), *n.* substance that causes anesthesia, as chloroform, ether, procaine, etc. —*adj.* 1 causing anesthesia. 2 of or with anesthesia. Also, **anaesthetic.** —**an′es thet′i cal ly,** *adv.*

an i ma tion (an′ə mā′shən), *n.* 1 liveliness of manner; spirit; vivacity: *She talks with great animation.* 2 an animating. 3 a being animated: *a case of suspended animation.* 4 the production of an animated cartoon.

an tag o nist (an tag′ə nist), *n.* person who fights, struggles, or contends against another; adversary; opponent.

anti-, *prefix.* 1 against ___; opposed to ___: *Antiaircraft = against aircraft.* 2 not ___; the opposite of ___: *Antisocial = the opposite of social.* 3 rival ___: *Antipope = rival pope.* 4 reducing or counteracting ___: *Antifriction = reducing or counteracting friction.* 5 preventing, curing, or alleviating ___: *Antiscorbutic = preventing or curing scurvy.* Also, **ant-** before vowels and *h.* [< Greek]

➔ **Anti-** is usually pronounced (an′ti) before consonants and (an′tē) before vowels, although (an′tī) is often used for emphasis.

ap a thet ic (ap′ə thet′ik), *adj.* 1 lacking interest or desire for action; indifferent. 2 lacking in feeling; unemotional. —**ap′-a thet′i cal ly,** *adv.*

ap pall or **ap pal** (ə pôl′), *v.t.,* **-palled, -pall ing.** fill with consternation and horror; dismay; terrify: *The thought of another war appalled us.* [< Old French *apallir* make pale < *a-* to + *pale* pale]

ap pease (ə pēz′), *v.t.,* **-peased, -peas ing.** 1 put an end to by satisfying (an appetite or desire): *A good dinner will appease your hunger.* 2 make calm or quiet; pacify. 3 give in to the demands of (especially those of a potential enemy): *Chamberlain appeased Hitler at Munich.* —**ap peas′er,** *n.* —**ap-peas′ing ly,** *adv.*

ap pend age (ə pen′dij), *n.* 1 thing attached to something larger or more important; addition. 2 (in biology) any of various external or subordinate parts. Arms, tails, fins, legs, etc., are appendages.

ap pli ca bil i ty (ap′lə kə bil′ə tē), *n.* quality of being applicable, useful, or appropriate.

ap pre hen sion (ap′ri hen′shən), *n.* 1 expectation of misfortune; dread of impending danger; fear. 2 arrest.

a rach nid (ə rak′nid), *n.* any of a class of arthropods closely allied to the insects and crustaceans, but distinguished by the possession of eight legs, the absence of wings and antennae, having the body divided into two regions, and breathing by means of tracheal tubes or pulmonary sacs. Spiders, scorpions, mites, ticks, and daddy-longlegs belong to this class. —*adj.* arachnidan. [< Greek *arachnē* spider, web]

ar bor (är′bər), *n.* a shady place formed by trees, shrubs, or by vines growing on a lattice.

ar cha ic (är kā′ik), *adj.* 1 no longer used in ordinary language, but surviving in certain special contexts, as that of law or older translations of the Bible. The words *forsooth* and *methinks* are archaic. 2 of earlier times; out-of-date; antiquated.

ar dent (ärd′nt), *adj.* 1 glowing with passion; passionate; impassioned: *ardent love.* 2 eager; keen. 3 burning; fiery; hot: *an ardent fever.* 4 glowing. [< Latin *ardentem* burning] —**ar′dent ly,** *adv.*

ar dor (är′dər), *n.* 1 warmth of emotion; passion. 2 great enthusiasm; eagerness; zeal: *patriotic ardor.* [< Latin < *ardere* to burn]

ar du ous (är′jü əs), *adj.* 1 hard to do; requiring much effort; difficult: *an arduous lesson.* 2 using up much energy; strenuous: *an arduous climb.* [< Latin *arduus* steep] —**ar′du ous ly,** *adv.* —**ar′du ous ness,** *n.*

ar ma da (är mä′də), *n.* 1 a large fleet of warships. 2 **the Armada,** the Spanish fleet that was sent to attack England in 1588 but was defeated in the English Channel. [< Spanish < Medieval Latin *armata* armed force]

ar mor y (är′mər ē), *n., pl.* **-mor ies.** 1 place where weapons are kept; arsenal. 2 place where weapons are manufactured. 3 a building with a drill hall, offices, etc., for militia.

ar mour y (är′mər ē), *n.* armory.

ar o mat ic (ar′ə mat′ik), *adj.* sweet-smelling; fragrant; spicy. —*n.* a fragrant plant or substance. —**ar′o mat′i cal ly,** *adv.*

ar rang er (ə rān′jər), *n.* one who adapts (a piece of music) to voices or instruments for which it was not written or to the style of a particular performer or group.

art ful (ärt′fəl), *adj.* 1 slyly clever; crafty; deceitful: *a swindler's artful tricks.* 2 skillful; clever. 3 artificial. —**art′ful ly,** *adv.* —**art′ful ness,** *n.*

ar til ler y (är til′ər ē), *n.* 1 mounted guns or rocket launchers manned by a crew; guns of larger caliber than machine guns; cannon; ordnance. 2 the part of an army that uses and manages such guns. 3 science or practice of firing and coordinating the firing of guns of

hat, āge, fär; let, ēqual, tėrm;
it, īce; hot, ōpen, ôrder;
oil, out; cup, pút, rüle;
ch, child; ng, long; sh, she;
th, thin; ₸H, then; zh, measure;

ə represents *a* in about, *e* in taken,
i in pencil, *o* in lemon, *u* in circus.

< = from, derived from, taken from.

larger caliber than machine guns. [< Old French *artillerie* < *artiller* equip]

as cend (ə send′), *v.i.* go up; rise; move upward: *He watched the airplane ascend.* —*v.t.* go to or toward the top of: *A small party is planning to ascend Mount Everest.*

as cent (ə sent′), *n.* 1 act of going up; upward movement; rising: *early balloon ascents.* 2 improvement in position, rank, etc.; advancement; promotion. 3 act of climbing a ladder, mountain, etc. 4 way of ascending; upward route: *a very steep ascent.* 5 degree of upward slope: *an ascent of ten degrees.*

as cot (as′kət, as′kot), *n.* necktie with broad ends, resembling a scarf, tied so that the ends may be laid flat, one across the other.

a skew (ə skyü′), *adv., adj.* out of the proper position; turned or twisted the wrong way; awry.

as pen (as′pən), *n.* any of several poplar trees of North America and Europe whose leaves tremble and rustle in the slightest breeze.

as pi ra tion (as′pə rā′shən), *n.* earnest desire; longing; ambition: *She had aspirations to be a doctor.*

as pire (ə spir′), *v.i.,* **-pired, -pir ing.** 1 have an ambition for something; desire earnestly; seek: *I aspired to be captain of the team.* 2 rise high.

as sent (ə sent′), *v.i.* express agreement; agree; consent: *Everyone assented to the plans for the dance.* —*n.* acceptance of a proposal, statement, etc.; agreement.

as sert (ə sert′), *v.t.* 1 state positively; declare firmly; affirm: *She asserts that she will go whether we do or not.* 2 maintain (a right, a claim, etc.); insist upon: *Assert your independence.* 3 **assert oneself,** put oneself forward; make demands: *A leader must assert himself sometimes in order to be followed.*

asth ma (az′mə), *n.* a chronic disease of respiration, characterized by intermittent paroxysms of breathing with a wheezing sound, a sense of constriction in the chest, and coughing. —**asth mat ic,** *adj.*

a sun der (ə sun′dər), *adv.* in pieces; into separate parts: *Lightning split the tree asunder.* —*adj.* apart or separate from each other.

-ate¹, *suffix forming adjectives, verbs, and nouns.* 1 of or having to do with ___: *Collegiate = having to do with college.* 2 having or containing ___: *Compassionate = having compassion.* 3 having the form of ___; like ___: *Stellate = having the form of a star.* 4 become ___: *Maturate = become mature.* 5 cause to be ___: *Alienate = cause to be alien.* 6 produce ___: *Ulcerate = produce ulcers.* 7 supply or treat with ___: *Aerate = treat with air.* 8 combine with ___: *Oxygenate = combine with oxygen.* [< Latin *-atus, -atum,* past participle endings]

-ate², *suffix forming nouns.* office, rule, or condition of ___: *Caliphate = rule of a caliph.* [< Latin *-atus*]

-ate³, *suffix forming nouns.* salt or ester of ____ic acid: *Sulfate = salt or ester of sulfuric acid.* [special use of *-ate¹*]

at tain (ə tān′), *v.t.* 1 reach (a state or condition) by living, growing, or developing: *attain the age of 80.* 2 win, gain, or acquire by effort; accomplish: *attain freedom, attain a goal.* 3 reach (a place); arrive at; gain: *attain the top of a hill.* —*v.i.* 1 succeed in coming or getting (*to*): *attain to a position of great influence.* 2 reach by living, growing, or developing (*to*): *This tree attains to a great height.*

at trib ute (*v.* ə trib′yüt; *n.* at′rə byüt), *v.*, **-ut ed, -ut ing,** *n.* —*v.t.* 1 regard as an effect or product of; think of as caused by: *She attributes her great age to a carefully planned diet.* 2 think of as belonging to or appropriate to: *We attribute courage to the lion and cunning to the fox.* —*n.* 1 an object considered appropriate to a person, rank, or office; symbol: *The eagle was the attribute of Jupiter.* 2 a quality considered as belonging to a person or thing; characteristic: *Patience is an attribute of a good teacher.* —**at trib′ut a ble,** *adj.* —**at trib′ut er,** *n.*

au da cious (ô dā′shəs), *adj.* 1 having the courage to take risks; recklessly daring; bold: *an audacious pilot.* 2 rudely bold; impudent. —**au da′cious ly,** *adv.* —**au da′cious ness,** *n.*

au dac i ty (ô das′ə tē), *n.* 1 reckless daring; boldness. 2 rude boldness; impudence; presumption. [< Latin *audacia* < *audax* bold < *audere* to dare]

au di ble (ô′də bəl), *adj.* that can be heard; loud enough to be heard. [< Latin *audire* hear] —**au′di bly,** *adv.*

aus tere (ô stir′), *adj.* 1 stern in manner or appearance; harsh: *a silent, austere man.* 2 severe in self-discipline; strict in morals: *The Puritans were austere.* 3 severely simple: *The tall, plain columns stood against the sky in austere beauty.* 4 grave; somber; serious. [< Greek *austēros* < *auos* dry] —**aus tere′ly,** *adv.* —**aus tere′ness,** *n.*

au thor i ta tive (ə thôr′ə tā′tiv, ə thor′ə tā′tiv), *adj.* 1 proceeding from a recognized authority; official: *The president issued an authoritative declaration of policy.* 2 of or characterized by authority; commanding: *In authoritative tones the policeman shouted, "Keep back."* 3 entitled to obedience and respect; having the authority of expert knowledge: *We have long desired an authoritative edition of this author's works.* —**au thor′i ta′tive ly,** *adv.* —**au thor′i ta′tive ness,** *n.*

a vail (ə vāl′), *v.t.* 1 be of use or value to; help: *Money will not avail you after you are dead.* 2 **avail oneself of,** take advantage of; profit by; make use of. —*v.i.* be of use or value; help: *Talk will not avail without work.* —*n.* **of no avail** or **to no avail,** of no use or value.

a venge (ə venj′), *v.,* **a venged, a veng ing.** —*v.t.* take revenge for or on behalf of: *avenge an insult. Hamlet avenged his father's murder.* —*v.i.* get revenge. —**a veng′er,** *n.*

awe (ô), *n., v.,* **awed, aw ing.** —*n.* 1 a feeling of wonder and reverence inspired by anything of great beauty, sublimity, majesty, or power: *The sight of the great waterfall filled us with awe. The young girl stood in awe before the queen.* 2 dread mingled with reverence. —*v.t.* 1 cause to feel awe; fill with awe: *The majesty of the mountains awed us.* 2 influence or restrain by awe.

ban tam (ban′təm), *n.* 1 Often, **Bantam.** a small variety of domestic fowl. The roosters are often spirited fighters. 2 a small person who is fond of fighting. —*adj.* 1 light in weight; small. 2 laughably aggressive. [< *Bantam,* town in Java, where the fowl are imported from]

ba rom e ter (bə rom′ə tər), *n.* instrument for measuring the pressure of air, used in determining height above sea level and in predicting probable changes in the weather.

bar rage (bə räzh′), *n., v.,* **-raged, -rag ing.** —*n.* 1 barrier of artillery fire to check the enemy or to protect one's own soldiers when advancing or retreating. 2 a large number of words, blows, etc., coming quickly one after the other: *The reporters kept up a barrage of questions for an hour.* —*v.t., v.i.* fire at with artillery; subject to a barrage. [< French < *barrer* to bar]

barrel organ, hand organ.

bar ren (bar′ən), *adj.* 1 not producing anything; unproductive: *A sandy desert is barren.* 2 not able to produce offspring or yield fruit; not fertile; sterile. 3 without interest; unattractive; dull. 4 of no advantage; fruitless; unprofitable. —**bar′ren ly,** *adv.* —**bar′ren ness,** *n.*

bask (bask), *v.i.* 1 expose oneself to the warmth of sunshine, the heat of a fire, etc.; warm oneself pleasantly. 2 feel great pleasure: *bask in the love of one's family.* —*v.t.* warm pleasantly. [Middle English]

bas-re lief (bä′ri lēf′, bas′ri lēf′), *n.* carving or sculpture in which the figures stand out only slightly from the background. [< French, literally, low relief]

baste (bāst), *v.t.,* **bast ed, bast ing.** moisten (meat, fowl, etc.) while roasting by dripping or pouring melted fat, butter, etc., on it. [origin unknown] —**bast′er,** *n.*

bat tal ion (bə tal′yən), *n.* 1 a military unit of infantry, etc., consisting of at least two companies, batteries, etc., and a headquarters company, usually forming part of a regiment, and commanded by a major or a lieutenant colonel. 2 a large division of an army in battle array. 3 **battalions,** *pl.* armies; military forces. 4 any large group of people thought of as having a common purpose.

bat ter y (bat′ər ē), *n., pl.* **-ter ies.** 1 a single electric cell: *a flashlight battery.* 2 set of two or more electric cells connected together for the production of electric current: *a car battery.* 3 set of similar pieces of equipment, such as mounted guns, searchlights, mortars, etc., used as a unit. 4 any set of similar or connected things: *a battery of tests.* 5 a military unit of artillery, usually commanded by a captain. A battery corresponds to a company or troop in other branches of the army. 6 the armament, or one part of it, of a warship. 7 (in baseball) the pitcher and catcher together. 8 (in law) the unlawful beating of another person or any threatening touch to his clothes or body.

bat tle ment (bat′l mənt), *n.* 1 a low wall for defense at the top of a tower or wall, with indentations and loopholes through which soldiers could shoot. 2 wall built like this for ornament.

bea con (bē′kən), *n.* 1 fire or light used as a signal to guide or warn. 2 an apparatus that sends out radio beams or light to guide aircraft, ships, etc., through fogs, storms, etc. 3 a tall tower for a signal; lighthouse. 4 anything or person that is a guiding or warning signal.

beck on (bek′ən), *v.i., v.t.* to signal by a motion of the head or hand: *He beckoned me to follow him. The tall man beckoned to her.* [Old English *bēcnan* < *bēacen* sign, beacon]

bed lam (bed′ləm), *n.* 1 noisy confusion; uproar. 2 ARCHAIC. insane asylum; madhouse. [< *Bedlam,* old name for the Hospital of St. Mary of *Bethlehem,* an insane asylum in London]

be get (bi get′), *v.t.,* **be got** or (ARCHAIC) **be gat, be got ten** or **be got, be get ting.** 1 become the father of. 2 cause to be; produce. [Old English *begitan*] —**be get′ter,** *n.*

be lat ed (bi lā′tid), *adj.* happening or coming late or too late; delayed: *The belated letter arrived at last.* —**be lat′ed ly,** *adv.* —**be lat′ed ness,** *n.*

be lea guer (bi lē′gər), *v.t.* 1 surround with troops; besiege. 2 surround; beset. [< Dutch *belegeren*]

bel fry (bel′frē), *n., pl.* **-fries.** 1 tower for a bell or bells, usually attached to a church or other building. 2 room, cupola, or turret in which a bell or bells may be hung.

ben e dic tion (ben′ə dik′shən), *n.* 1 the asking of God's blessing, as at the end of a church service or a marriage ceremony. 2 the form or ritual of this invocation. 3 blessing.

be reft (bi reft′), *adj.* 1 bereaved; deprived. 2 left desolate.

be set ting (bi set′ing), *adj.* habitually attacking: *a besetting sin.*

bes tial (bes′chəl), *adj.* 1 like a beast; beastly. 2 sensual; obscene. 3 of beasts. [< Latin *bestialis* < *bestia* beast] —**bes′tial ly,** *adv.*

bes tial ize (bes′chə līz), *v.t.,* to make bestial or beastlike: *War bestializes its participants.*

be troth al (bi trō′ᴛʜəl, bi trô′thəl), *n.* a promise in marriage; engagement.

bid dy (bid′ē), *n., pl.* **-dies.** DIALECT. hen. [origin uncertain]

black out (blak′out′), *n.* 1 a turning out or concealing of all the lights of a city, district, etc., as a protection against an air raid. 2 temporary blindness or unconsciousness experienced by a pilot, resulting from rapid changes in velocity or direction. 3 a turning off of all the lights on the stage of a theater.

blanch (blanch), *v.* 1 make white; bleach. Almonds are blanched by soaking off their skins in boiling water. 2 turn white or pale: *blanch with fear.*

bland (bland), *adj.* 1 gentle or soothing; balmy: *a bland summer breeze.* 2 smoothly agreeable and polite: *a bland smile.* [< Latin *blandus* soft] —**bland′ly,** *adv.* —**bland′ness,** *n.*

bla tant (blāt′nt), *adj.* 1 offensively loud or noisy; loud-mouthed. 2 showy in dress, manner, etc. 3 obvious; flagrant: *blatant hypocrisy, blatant lies.* —**bla′tant ly,** *adv.*

board ing house (bôr′ding hous′, bōr′ding hous′), *n., pl.* **-hous es** (-hou′ziz). house where meals, or room and meals, are provided for pay.

booby trap, 1 bomb or mine arranged to explode when a harmless-looking object to which it is attached is touched or moved by an unsuspecting person. 2 trick arranged to annoy some unsuspecting person.

brake (brāk), *n.* thicket.

brand (brand), *n.* 1 the quality or kind (of goods) as indicated by a mark, stamp, or label; a certain kind, grade, or make: *a brand* *of coffee.* **2** trademark. **3** an iron stamp for branding. **4** mark made by burning the hide (of cattle, horses, etc.) with a brand to identify them. **5** mark of disgrace; stigma. —*v.t.* **1** mark by burning the skin or hide with a hot iron. In former times criminals were often branded. **2** put a mark of disgrace on; stigmatize: *branded as a traitor.*

bran dish (bran′dish), *v.t.* wave or shake threateningly; flourish.

bridge head (brij′hed′), *n.* **1** position obtained and held by advance troops within enemy territory, used as a starting point for further attack. **2** any position taken as a foothold from which to make further advances. **3** fortification protecting the end of a bridge nearer to the enemy.

brig and (brig′ənd), *n.* person who robs travelers on the road, especially one of a gang of robbers in mountain or forest regions; robber; bandit.

buck skin (buk′skin′), *n.* a strong, soft leather, yellowish or grayish in color, made from the skins of deer or sheep.

buf fet (buf′it), *n.* **1** a blow of the hand or fist. **2** a knock, stroke, or hurt. —*v.t.* **1** strike with the hand or fist. **2** knock about; strike repeatedly; beat back: *The waves buffeted me.* **3** fight or struggle against: *The boat buffeted the heavy waves caused by the storm.* —*v.i.* deal blows; struggle; contend.

bunk house (bungk′hous′), *n., pl.* **-hous es** (-hou′ziz). a rough building with sleeping quarters or bunks, especially one provided for workers on a ranch, at a construction camp, etc.

buoy an cy (boi′ən sē, bü′yən sē), *n.* **1** power to float. **2** power to keep things afloat. **3** a body's loss in weight when immersed in a fluid. **4** tendency to rise. **5** tendency to be hopeful and cheerful; lightheartedness: *Her buoyancy kept us from being downhearted.*

buoy ant (boi′ənt, bü′yənt), *adj.* **1** able to float. **2** able to keep things afloat. **3** tending to rise. **4** cheerful and hopeful; light-hearted: *Children are usually more buoyant than adults.* —**bouy′ant ly,** *adv.*

bur eau (byùr′ō), *n, pl.* **bur eaus, bureaux** (byùr′ōz). chest of drawers for clothes, often having a mirror; dresser.

bur nish (bėr′nish), *v.t.* **1** make (metal) smooth and bright; polish (a surface) by rubbing until shiny; *burnish brass.* **2** make bright and glossy. —*n.* polish; luster.

buz zard (buz′ərd), *n.* **1** any of various large, heavy, slow-moving hawks. **2** turkey buzzard.

cache (kash), *n., v.,* **cached, cach ing.** —*n.* **1** a hiding place, especially of goods, treasure, food, etc. **2** the store of food or supplies hidden. —*v.t.* put or store in a cache; hide.

ca coph o ny (kə kof′ə nē), *n., pl.* **-nies.** a harsh, clashing sound; dissonance; discord. [< **Greek** *kakophōnia* < *kakos* bad + *phōnē* sound]

ca jole (kə jōl′), *v.t.,* **-joled, -jol ing.** persuade by pleasant words, flattery, or false promises; coax.

cal li o pe (kə lī′ə pē; *for 1, also* kal′ē ōp), *n.* **1** a musical instrument having a series of steam whistles played by pushing keys.

cam e o (kam′ē ō), *n., pl.* **cam e os.** **1** a precious or semiprecious stone carved so that there is a raised design on a background usually of a different color. Agates, other stones having a layered structure, and sometimes shells, are used for cameos.

can dor (kan′dər), *n.* **1** a saying openly what one really thinks; honesty in giving one's view or opinion; frankness and sincerity. **2** fairness; impartiality.

ca pit u late (kə pich′ə lāt), *v.i.,* **-lat ed, -lat ing.** surrender on certain terms or conditions: *The men in the fort capitulated on condition that they be allowed to go away unharmed.* [< Medieval Latin *capitulatum* arranged under headings or chapters < Latin *capitulum* small head < *caput* head] —**ca pit′u la′tor,** *n.*

ca pit u la tion (kə pich′ə lā′shən), *n.* a surrender on certain terms or conditions.

ca price (kə prēs′), *n.* **1** a sudden change of mind without reason; unreasonable notion or desire; whim. **2** tendency to change suddenly and without reason.

car a van (kar′ə van), *n.* **1** group of merchants, pilgrims, etc., traveling together for safety through difficult or dangerous country. **2** the vehicles or beasts of burden used by such a group. **3** a closed truck or, formerly, a large, covered wagon, for moving goods; van.

car il lon (kar′ə lon, kar′ə lən, kə ril′yən), *n.* **1** set of bells arranged for playing melodies. **2** melody played on such bells. **3** part of an organ imitating the sound of bells.

car nage (kär′nij), *n.* slaughter of a great number of people. [< Middle French < Italian *carnaggio,* ultimately < Latin *carnem* flesh]

cas cade (ka skād′), *n., v.,* **-cad ed, -cad ing.** —*n.* **1** a small waterfall. **2** anything like this: *Her dress had a cascade of ruffles down the front.* —*v.i.* fall, pour, or flow in a cascade.

case ment (kās′mənt), *n.* **1** window or part of a window which opens on hinges like a door. **2** any window.

Cau ca sian (kô kā′zhən, kô kā′shən; kô-kazh′ən, kô kash′ən), *n.* member of the so-called white race, including the chief peoples of Europe, southwestern Asia, northern Africa, the Western Hemisphere, Australia, and New Zealand. —*adj.* of or having to do with the so-called white race.

cau ter ize (kô′tə rīz′), *v.t.,* **-ized, -iz ing.** burn with a hot iron or a caustic substance. Doctors sometimes cauterize wounds to prevent bleeding or infection.

ca vort (kə vôrt′), *v.* U.S. prance about; jump around: *The children cavorted about the field, racing and tumbling.*

ceil ing (sē′ling), *n.* **1** the greatest height to which an aircraft can go under certain conditions. **2** distance from the earth to the lowest clouds.

chafe (chāf), *v.,* **chafed, chaf ing,** *n.* —*v.t.* **1** rub so as to wear away, scrape, or make sore: *The stiff collar chafed my neck.* **2** rub to make warm: *She chafed her cold hands.* **3** wear away by rubbing. **4** make angry: *Their teasing chafed me.* —*v.i.* **1** become worn away by rubbing. **2** become irritated by rubbing. **3** become angry: *I chafed under their teasing.* —*n.* a chafing; irritation.

chaff (chaf), *n.* **1** husks of wheat, oats, rye, etc., especially when separated from grain by threshing. **2** hay or straw cut fine for feeding cattle. **3** worthless stuff; rubbish.

chasm (kaz′əm), *n.* a deep opening or crack in the earth; gap.

chas tise (cha stīz′), *v.t.,* **-tised, -tis ing.** **1** inflict punishment or suffering on to improve; punish. **2** criticize severely; rebuke.

chic o ry (chik′ər ē), *n., pl.* **-ries.** **1** plant with bright-blue flowers whose leaves are used for salad. **2** its root, roasted and used as a substitute for coffee.

chid den (chid′n), *v.* a pp. of **chide.**

chide (chīd), *v.,* **chid ed** or **chid, chid ed, chid,** or **chid den, chid ing.** reproach; blame; scold.

cho ris ter (kôr′ə stər, kor′ə stər), *n.* **1** singer in a choir. **2** choirboy. **3** leader of a choir.

chro mi um (krō′mē əm), *n.* a grayish, hard, brittle metallic element that does not rust or become dull easily; chrome. Chromium is used to electroplate other metals, as part of stainless steel and other alloys, for making dyes and paints, in photography, etc.

chron ic (kron′ik), *adj.* **1** lasting a long time: *Rheumatism is often a chronic disease.* **2** suffering long from an illness: *a chronic invalid.* **3** never stopping; constant; habitual: *a chronic liar.* [< Greek *chronikos* of time < *chronos* time] —**chron′i cal ly,** *adv.*

chron o log i cal (kron′ə loj′ə kəl), *adj.* of or in accordance with chronology; arranged in the order in which the events happened: *In telling a story a person usually follows chronological order.* —**chron′o log′i cal ly,** *adv.*

chro nom e ter (krə nom′ə tər), *n.* clock or watch that keeps very accurate time.

cit ron (sit′rən), *n.* **1** a pale-yellow citrus fruit somewhat like a lemon but larger, with less acid and a thicker rind. **2** its rind, candied and used in fruit cakes, plum pudding, candies, etc.

clam ber (klam′bər), *v.i., v.t.* climb, using both hands and feet; climb awkwardly or with difficulty; scramble. —*n.* an awkward or difficult climb.

clar et (klar′ət), *n.* **1** kind of red wine. **2** a dark purplish red. —*adj.* dark purplish-red.

cleave (klēv), *v.,* **cleft** or **cleaved** or **clove, cleft** or **cleaved** or **clo ven, cleav ing.** —*v.t.* **1** cut, divide, or split open. **2** pass through; pierce; penetrate: *The airplane cleft the clouds.* **3** make by cutting: *They cleft a path through the wilderness.* —*v.i.* **1** split, especially into layers. **2** pass; penetrate.

cleft (kleft), *v.* a pt. and a pp. of **cleave.** —*adj.* split; divided: *a cleft stick.* —*n.* space or opening made by splitting; crack; fissure.

clutch¹ (kluch), *n.* **1** a tight grasp; hold: *I lost my clutch on the rope and fell.* **2** Often, **clutches,** *pl.* **a** a grasping claw, paw, hand, etc.: *The fish escaped from the bear's clutch.* **b** control; power: *a country in the clutches of a dictator.* **3** device in a machine for transmitting motion from one shaft to another or for disconnecting related moving parts. The clutch in an automobile is used to connect the engine with the transmission or to disconnect it from the transmission.

clutch² (kluch), *n.* **1** nest of eggs. **2** brood of chickens. **3** group of people or things. [< Scandinavian (Old Icelandic) *klekja*]

co-, *prefix.* **1** with; together: *Coexist = exist*

hat, āge, fär; let, ēqual, tėrm;
it, īce; hot, ōpen, ôrder;
oil, out; cup, pùt, rüle;
ch, child; ng, long; sh, she;
th, thin; ₮H, then; zh, measure;

ə represents *a* in about, *e* in taken,
i in pencil, *o* in lemon, *u* in circus.

< = from, derived from, taken from.

together or with. **2** joint: *Coauthor = joint author.* **3** equally: *Coextensive = equally extensive.* [< Latin, variant of *com-*]

cock sure (kok′shur′), *adj.* **1** too sure; overly confident. **2** perfectly sure; absolutely certain.

co ed u ca tion al (kō′ej ə kā′shə nəl), *adj.* **1** educating boys and girls or men and women together in the same school or classes. **2** having to do with coeducation.

co gnac (kō′nyak, kon′yak), *n.* a French brandy of superior quality.

coif (koif), *n.* a cap or hood that fits closely around the head. —*v.t.* to cover with a coif or something like a coif.

col lab o rate (kə lab′ə rāt′), *v.i.*, **-rat ed, -rat ing.** **1** work together: *Two authors collaborated on that book.* **2** aid or cooperate traitorously.

com-, *prefix.* with; together; altogether: *Commingle = mingle with one another. Compress = press together.* [< Latin]

com mem o rate (kə mem′ə rāt′), *v.,* **-rat ed, -rat ing.** **1** preserve the memory of: *Roman emperors built arches to commemorate their victories.* **2** honor the memory of: *Christmas commemorates Christ's birth.* [< Latin *commemoratum* remembered < *com-* + *memorare* bring to mind] —**com mem′o ra′tor,** *n.*

com mence (kə mens′), *v.,* **-menced, -menc ing.** —*v.i.* make a start; begin. —*v.t.* begin (an action); enter upon: *commence legal action.*

com mend (kə mend′), *v.t.* **1** speak well of; praise. **2** recommend. **3** hand over for safekeeping; entrust: *She commended the child to her aunt's care.*

com mon wealth (kom′ən welth′), *n.* **1** the people who make up a nation; citizens of a state. **2** a democratic state; republic. **3** any state of the United States, especially Kentucky, Massachusetts, Pennsylvania, and Virginia.

com mune (*v.* kə myün′; *n.* kom′yün), *v.,* **-muned, -mun ing,** *n.* —*v.i.* **1** talk intimately. **2** receive Holy Communion. —*n.* intimate talk; communion.

community chest, fund of money contributed voluntarily by people to support charity and welfare in their community.

com pas sion ate (kəm pash′ə nit), *adj.* desiring to relieve another's suffering; sympathetic; pitying.

com pel (kəm pel′), *v.t.,* **-pelled, -pel ling.** **1** drive or urge with force; force: *Rain compelled them to stop.* **2** cause or get by force: *A policeman can compel obedience to the law.* [< Latin *compellere* < *com-* + *pellere* to drive] —**com pel′ling ly,** *adv.*

com pen sate (kom′pən sāt), *v.,* **-sat ed, -sat ing.** —*v.t.* **1** make an equal return to; give an equivalent to: *The hunters gave the farmer $100 to compensate him for their damage to his field.* **2** pay: *The company compensated her for extra work.* —*v.i.* **1** balance by equal weight, power, etc.; make up (*for*): *Skill sometimes compensates for lack of strength.* **2** make amends.

com pe tent (kom′pə tənt), *adj.* **1** properly qualified; able; fit: *a competent bookkeeper, competent to decide.* **2** legally qualified: *Two competent witnesses testified.* —**com′- pe tent ly,** *adv.*

com plect ed (kəm plek′tid), *adj.* complexioned.

➤ **Complected** (as in *dark-complected* and *light-complected*), though commonly used, especially in the United States, is not regarded as standard. The standard term is *complexioned.*

com pli men tar y (kom′plə men′tər ē), *adj.* **1** like or containing a compliment; praising. **2** U.S. given free: *a complimentary ticket to a concert.* —**com′pli men tar′i ly,** *adv.*

com ply (kəm plī′), *v.i.,* **-plied, -ply ing.** act in agreement with a request or command: *I will comply with the doctor's request.*

com pound (kom pound′, kəm pound′), —*v.t.* **1** mix; combine: *The druggist compounds medicines.* **2** settle (a quarrel or a debt) by a yielding on both sides. **3** charge, pay, or increase by compound interest. **4** add to; increase; multiply: *I compounded my troubles by arguing with the teacher.*

com press (kəm pres′), *v.t.* squeeze together; make smaller by pressure.

com pro mise (kom′prə mīz), *v.,* **-mised, -mis ing,** —*v.t.* **1** settle (a dispute) by agreeing that each will give up a part of what he demands. **2** expose to suspicion, danger, etc.: *compromise one's reputation.* —*v.i.* make a compromise. —*n.* **1** settlement of a dispute by a partial yielding on both sides. **2** result of such a settlement. **3** anything halfway between two different things. **4** an exposing to suspicion, danger, etc.; endangering.

con-, *prefix.* form of **com-** before *n,* as in *connote,* and before consonants except *b, h, l, m, p, r, w,* as in *concern.*

con ceive (kən sēv′), *v.,* **-ceived, -ceiv ing.** —*v.t.* **1** form in the mind; think up: *The Wright brothers conceived the design of the first successful motor-driven airplane.* **2** have (an idea or feeling). **3** put in words; express: *The warning was conceived in the plainest language.* **4** become pregnant with. —*v.i.* **1** have an idea or feeling; think; imagine: *We cannot conceive of such a thing happening.* **2** become pregnant.

con cus sion (kən kush′ən), *n.* **1** a sudden, violent shaking; shock: *The concussion caused by the explosion broke many windows.* **2** injury to a soft part of the body, especially the brain, caused by a blow, fall, or other physical shock.

con de scend ing (kon′di sen′ding), *adj.* **1** stooping to the level of one's inferiors. **2** patronizing. —**con′de scend′ing ly,** *adv.*

con firm (kən fèrm′), *v.t.* **1** prove to be true or correct; make certain: *confirm a rumor.* **2** approve by formal consent; approve; consent to: *The Senate confirmed the treaty.* **3** make firmer; strengthen: *A sudden storm confirmed my decision not to leave.* **4** admit to full membership in a church or synagogue after required study and preparation. [< Latin *confirmare* < *com-* + *firmus* firm] —**con firm′a ble,** *adj.*

con fla gra tion (kon′flə grā′shən), *n.* a great and destructive fire: *A conflagration destroyed most of the city.*

con flict (*n.* kon′flikt; *v.* kən flikt′), *n.* **1** fight or struggle. **2** direct opposition; disagreement; clash: *A conflict of opinions divided the members into two groups.* —*v.i.* be directly opposed; disagree; clash.

con found (kon found′, kən found′ for 1,2, 4,5; kon′found′ for 3), *v.t.* **1** confuse; mix up: *The shock confounded me.* **2** surprise and puzzle. **3** damn: *Confound your impudence.* **4** ARCHAIC. make uneasy and ashamed. **5** ARCHAIC. defeat; overthrow.

con jec tur al (kən jek′chər əl), *adj.*

1 involving conjecture. **2** inclined to conjecture. —**con jec′tur al ly,** *adv.*

con jec ture (kən jek′chər), *n., v.,* **-tured, -tur ing.** —*n.* **1** formation of an opinion with some evidence for proof; guessing. **2** a guess. —*v.t., v.i.* guess.

con ju gate (*v.* kon′jə gāt; *adj., n.* kon′jə git, kon′jə gāt), *v.,* **-gat ed, -gat ing,** *adj., n.* —*v.t.* **1** give the forms of (a verb) according to a systematic arrangement. **2** join together; couple. —*v.i.* **1** give the conjugation of a verb. **2** (in biology) unite or fuse in conjugation. —*adj.* **1** joined together; coupled. **2** (in grammar) derived from the same root. —*n.* word derived from the same root as another.

con sign (kən sīn′), *v.t.* **1** hand over; deliver: *The dog was consigned to the pound.* **2** send; transmit: *We will consign the goods to you by express.* **3** set apart; assign.

con spic u ous (kən spik′yü əs), *adj.* **1** easily seen; clearly visible: *A traffic sign should be conspicuous.* **2** worthy of notice; remarkable: *Lincoln is a conspicuous example of a poor boy who succeeded.* —**con spic′u ous ly,** *adv.*

con sta ble (kon′stə bəl, kun′stə bəl), *n.* **1** a police officer, especially in a township, district, or rural area of the United States. **2** BRITISH. policeman. **3** a chief officer of a household, court, army, etc., especially in the Middle Ages.

con strue (kən strü′), *v.t.,* **-strued, -stru ing.** **1** show the meaning of; explain; interpret: *Different judges may construe the same law differently.* **2** analyze the arrangement and connection of words in (a sentence, clause, phrase, etc.).

con tig u ous (kən tig′yü əs), *adj.* **1** in actual contact; touching: *A fence showed where the two farms were contiguous.* **2** adjoining; near. [< Latin *contiguus* < *contingere* touch closely.] —**con tig′u ous ly,** *adv.* —**con tig′u ous ness,** *n.*

con va les cence (kon′və les′ns), *n.* **1** the gradual recovery of health and strength after illness. **2** time during which one is convalescing.

con ven tion (kən ven′shən), *n.* **1** a meeting for some purpose; gathering; assembly. A political party holds a convention to choose candidates for public offices. **2** delegates to a meeting or assembly. **3** general agreement; common consent; custom: *Convention governs how most people dress and wear their hair.* **4** custom or practice approved by general agreement; rule based on common consent: *Using the right hand to shake hands is a convention.* **5** agreement signed by two or more countries about matters less important than those in a treaty.

con ven tion al (kən ven′shə nəl), *adj.* **1** depending on conventions; customary: *"Good morning" is a conventional greeting.* **2** acting or behaving according to commonly accepted and approved ways. **3** of the usual type or design; commonly used or seen: *conventional furniture.* **4** (in the arts) following custom and traditional models; formal: *The ode and the sonnet are conventional forms of English poetry.* —**con ven′- tion al ly,** *adv.*

con vic tion (kən vik′shən), *n.* **1** act of convincing (a person). **2** a being convinced. **3** firm belief; certainty.

con vulse (kən vuls′), *v.t.,* **-vulsed, -vuls ing.** **1** shake violently: *An earthquake convulsed the island.* **2** cause violent disturbance in; disturb violently: *His face was convulsed with rage.* **3** throw into convulsions; shake with muscular spasms: *The sick child was convulsed before the doctor came.* 4 throw into fits of laughter; cause to shake with laughter: *The clown convulsed the audience with his funny acts.*

con vul sive (kən vul′siv), *adj.* 1 violently disturbing. 2 having convulsions. 3 producing convulsions. —**con vul′sive ly**, *adv.* —**con vul′sive ness**, *n.*

cor net (kôr net′), *n.* a musical wind instrument somewhat like a trumpet, usually made of brass. It has three valves that control the pitch.

cor nice (kôr′nis), *n., v.,* **-niced, -nic ing.** —*n.* 1 an ornamental, horizontal molding along the top of a wall, pillar, building, etc. 2 a molding around the walls of a room just below the ceiling or over the top of a window.

coun te nance (koun′tə nəns), *n., v.,* **-nanced, -nac ing.** —*n.* 1 expression of the face: *an angry countenance.* 2 face; features: *a noble countenance.* 3 approval; encouragement: *They gave countenance to our plan, but no active help.* 4 calmness; composure: *lose countenance.* —*v.t.* approve or encourage; sanction: *I will not countenance such a plan.*

coun ter plot (koun′tər plot′), *n., v.,* **-plotted, -plot ting.** —*n.* a plot to defeat another plot. —*v.i.* plot in opposition. —*v.t.* plot against (another plot or plotter).

coup (kü), *n., pl.* **coups** (küz). 1 a sudden, brilliant action; unexpected, clever move; master stroke. 2 coup d'état. [< French, literally, a blow, stroke < Late Latin *colpus* < Greek *kolaphos*]

cour i er (kėr′ē ər, kùr′ē ər), *n.* 1 messenger sent in haste: *Government dispatches were sent by couriers.* 2 a secret agent who transfers information to and from other agents.

cour ti er (kôr′tē ər, kōr′tē ər), *n.* 1 person often present at the court of a king, emperor, etc.; court attendant. 2 person who tries to win the favor of another by flattering and pleasing him.

cow er (kou′ər), *v.i.* 1 crouch in fear or shame. 2 draw back tremblingly from another's threats, blows, etc. [apparently < Scandinavian (Old Icelandic) *kūra* doze, lie quiet]

crag gy (krag′ē), *adj.,* **-gi er, -gi est.** 1 having many crags; steep and rugged. 2 rough; uneven: *a craggy, weathered face.* —**crag′gi ness**, *n.*

cre mate (krē′māt, kri māt′), *v.t.,* **-mat ed, -mat ing.** 1 burn (a dead body) to ashes instead of burying it. 2 burn.

cre scen do (krə shen′dō), *adj., adv., n., pl.* **-dos.** —*adj., adv.* (in music) with a gradual increase in force or loudness. —*n.* 1 a gradual increase in force or loudness, especially in music. 2 (in music) a crescendo passage. [< Italian, literally, increasing]

crest (krest), *n.* 1 comb, tuft, etc., on the head of a bird or other animal. 2 decoration of plumes or feathers worn on the top of a helmet. 3 decoration at the top of a coat of arms. A family crest is sometimes put on silverware, dishes, or stationery. 4 the top part; high point; peak; summit: *the crest of a wave, the crest of the hill, the crest of a career.*

cre vasse (krə vas′), *n.* 1 a deep crack or crevice in the ice of a glacier, or in the ground after an earthquake. 2 break in the levee of a river, dike, or dam.

crev ice (krev′is), *n.* a narrow split or crack; fissure.

crone (krōn), *n.* a withered old woman.

croon (krün), *v.i., v.t.* 1 hum, sing, or murmur in a low tone: *I crooned to the baby.* 2 sing in a low, sentimental voice.

crouch (krouch), *v.i.* 1 stoop low with bent legs like an animal ready to spring. 2 shrink down in fear. 3 bow down in a timid or slavish manner; cower. —*v.t.* bend low. —*n.* 1 act or state of crouching. 2 a crouching position. [perhaps blend of *couch* and *crook*]

crypt (kript), *n.* an underground room or vault. *The crypt beneath the main floor of a church was formerly often used as a burial place.*

cryp tic (krip′tik), *adj.* having a hidden meaning; secret; mysterious: *a cryptic message.* —**cryp′ti cal ly**, *adv.*

cu bi cle (kyü′bə kəl), *n.* a very small room or compartment.

cudg el (kuj′əl), *n., v.,* **-eled, -el ing** or **-elled, -el ling.** —*n.* 1 a short, thick stick used as a weapon; club. 2 **take up the cudgels for,** defend strongly. —*v.t.* beat with a cudgel. [Old English *cycgel*]

cun ning (kun′ing), *adj.* 1 clever in deceiving; sly: *a cunning fox, a cunning thief.* 2 skillful; clever: *The old watch was a fine example of cunning workmanship.* 3 INFORMAL. pretty and dear; cute: *a cunning baby.* —*n.* 1 slyness in getting what one wants; cleverness in deceiving one's enemies: *The fox has a great deal of cunning.* 2 skill; cleverness. [Related to CAN.] —**cun′ning ly**, *adv.*

cur (kėr), *n.* 1 a dog of mixed breed; mongrel. 2 a surly, contemptible person. [Middle English *curre*, probably < Scandinavian (Old Icelandic) *kurra* snarl]

curt (kėrt), *adj.* rudely brief; short; abrupt: *a curt way of talking.* [< Latin *curtus* cut short] —**curt′ly**, *adv.*

cy clone (sī′klōn), *n.* 1 storm moving around and toward a calm center of low pressure, which also moves. 2 a very violent windstorm; tornado.

cyn i cal (sin′ə kəl), *adj.* 1 doubting the sincerity and goodness of others. 2 sneering; sarcastic. —**cyn′i cal ly**, *adv.* —**cyn′i cal ness**, *n.*

das tard ly (das′tərd lē), *adj.* like a dastard; mean and cowardly; sneaking. —**das′tard li ness**, *n.*

da tive (dā′tiv), *adj.* showing the indirect object of a verb or the object of a preposition. Latin and some other languages have a dative case. In English, the dative function is expressed by word order or by a prepositional phrase: "Give *him* the book." "Give the book *to him.*" —*n.* 1 the dative case. 2 word in this case.

daub (dôb), *v.t.* 1 coat or cover with plaster, clay, mud, or any greasy or sticky substance. 2 apply (greasy or sticky substance) to a surface. 3 make dirty; soil; stain. 4 paint (something) unskillfully. —*v.i.* daub something. 2 paint unskillfully. —*n.* 1 anything daubed on. 2 a badly painted picture. 3 act of daubing. 4 material for daubing, such as rough plaster or mortar.

daze (dāz), *v.,* **dazed, daz ing,** *n.* —*v.t.* 1 make unable to think clearly; confuse; bewilder; stun: *The blow on my head dazed me.* 2 hurt (one's eyes) with light; dazzle: *The child was dazed by the bright sun.* —*n.* a dazed condition; bewilderment.

deb o nair or **deb o naire** (deb′ə ner′, deb′ə när′), *adj.* pleasant, courteous, and gay. [< Old French *debonaire* < *de bon aire* of good disposition] —**deb′o nair′ly**, *adv.* —**deb′o nair′ness**, *n.*

hat, āge, fär; let, ēqual, tėrm;
it, īce; hot, ōpen, ôrder;
oil, out; cup, pùt, rüle;
ch, child; ng, long; sh, she;
th, thin; ₮H, then; zh, measure;

ə represents *a* in about, *e* in taken,
i in pencil, *o* in lemon, *u* in circus.

< = from, derived from, taken from.

de cease (di sēs′), *n., v.,* **-ceased, -ceasing.** —*n.* act or fact of dying; death. —*v.i.* die.

de ceive (di sēv′), *v.,* **-ceived, -ceiv ing.** —*v.t.* make (a person) believe as true something that is false; mislead. —*v.i.* use deceit; lie. —**de ceiv′er**, *n.* —**de ceiv′ing ly**, *adv.*

de ci sive (di sī′siv), *adj.* 1 having or giving a clear result; settling something beyond question or doubt: *The Battle of Saratoga was a decisive victory for the Americans.* 2 having or showing decision; resolute: *a decisive answer.* —**de ci′sive ly**, *adv.* —**de ci′sive ness**, *n.*

de code (dē kōd′), *v.t.,* **-cod ed, -cod ing.** translate (secret writing) from code into ordinary language. —**de cod′er**, *n.*

de co rum (di kôr′əm, di kōr′əm), *n.* 1 proper behavior; good taste in conduct, speech, dress, etc.: *act with decorum, observe decorum at church.* 2 observance or requirement of polite society: *a meeting completely lacking in decorum.* [< Latin, (that which is) seemly < *decor* seemliness]

de cree (di krē′), *n., v.,* **-creed, -cree ing.** —*n.* 1 something ordered or settled by authority; official decision. 2 a decision or order of a court or judge. 3 law of a church council, especially one settling a disputed point of doctrine. —*v.t.* 1 order or settle by authority: *Fate decreed that Ulysses should travel long and far.* 2 decide; determine. —*v.i.* decide; determine.

de cry (di krī′), *v.t.,* **-cried, -cry ing.** 1 express strong disapproval of; condemn; denounce: *The pacifist decried all forms of violence.* 2 make little of; try to lower the value of by slighting statements; disparage: *The lumber dealer decried the use of concrete for houses.*

deem (dēm), *v.t., v.i.* form or have an opinion; think, believe, or consider.

deft (deft), *adj.* quick and skillful in action; nimble: *the deft fingers of a surgeon.* [variant of *daft*] —**deft′ly**, *adv.* —**deft′ness**, *n.*

de fy (di fī′), *v.t.,* **-fied, -fy ing.** 1 resist boldly or openly: *defy the law.* 2 be beyond the power of; withstand: *Granite defies weathering more than sandstone.* 3 challenge (a person) to do or prove something; dare.

de grade (di grād′), *v.t.,* **-grad ed, -grading.** 1 reduce in rank, especially as a punishment. 2 bring into dishonor or contempt. 3 lower in character or quality; debase. 4 wear down by erosion.

de lib e ra tion (di lib′ə rā′shən), *n.* 1 careful thought: *After long deliberation, I decided not to go.* 2 discussion of reasons for and against something; debate: *the deliberations of Congress.* 3 slowness and care: *The hunter aimed his gun with great deliberation.*

de lir i ous (di lir′ē əs), *adj.* 1 temporarily out of one's senses; wandering in mind; raving. 2 wildly enthusiastic. 3 caused by delirium. —**de lir′i ous ly**, *adv.* —**de lir′-**

i ous ness, *n.* [< Latin < *delirare* rave, be crazy < *de lira (ire)* (go) out of the furrow (in plowing)]

de mer it (dē mer′it), *n.* 1 fault or defect. 2 a mark against a person's record for unsatisfactory behavior or poor work.

de mure (di myür′), *adj.,* **-mur er, -mur est.** 1 artificially proper; assuming an air of modesty; coy: *the demure smile of a flirt.* 2 reserved or composed in demeanor; serious and sober. [< *de-* + Old French *meür* discreet, mature < Latin *maturus*] **—de mure′ly,** *adv.* **—de mure′ness,** *n.*

de plete (di plēt′), *v.t.,* **-plet ed, -plet ing.** empty or exhaust by drawing away or using up resources, strength, vitality, etc. [< Latin *depletum* emptied out < *de-* + *-plere* fill]

de ploy (di ploi′), *v.t., v.i.* 1 spread out (troops, military units, etc.) from a column into a long battle line. 2 spread out or extend (anything). **—de ploy′ment,** *n.*

de port (di pôrt′, di pōrt′), *v.t.* 1 force to leave a country; banish; expel. An alien whose presence is undesirable or illegal is often deported and sent back to his native land. 2 behave or conduct (oneself) in a particular manner: *The children deported themselves well.*

de pose (di pōz′), *v.,* **-posed, -pos ing.** **—v.t.** 1 put out of office or a position of authority, especially a high one like that of king. 2 declare under oath; testify: *The witness deposed that she had seen the accused on the day of the murder.*

dep re da tion (dep′rə dā′shən), *n.* act of plundering; robbery; ravaging.

de prive (di prīv′), *v.t.,* **-prived, -priv ing.** 1 take away from by force; divest: *deprive a dictator of his power.* 2 keep from having or doing: *Worrying deprived me of sleep.*

de pute (di pyüt′), *v.t.,* **-put ed, -put ing.** 1 appoint to act on one's behalf; appoint as one's substitute or agent; delegate. 2 give (one's work, authority, etc.) to another; transfer.

de ri sion (di rizh′ən), *n.* 1 scornful laughter; ridicule. 2 object of ridicule.

de scend (di send′), *v.i.* 1 go or come down from a higher to a lower place: *The river descends from the mountains to the sea.* 2 go or come down from an earlier to a later time: *a superstition descended from the Middle Ages.* 3 go from greater to less numbers; go from higher to lower on any scale: *75-50-25 form a series that descends.* 4 slope downward. 5 make a sudden attack: *The wolves descended on the sheep.* 6 be handed down from parent to child; pass by inheritance: *This land has been in our family for 150 years, descending from father to son.* 7 come down or spring from: *He is descended from pioneers.*

des o la tion (des′ə lā′shən), *n.* 1 act of making desolate; devastation. 2 a ruined, lonely, or deserted condition. 3 a desolate place. 4 lonely sorrow; sadness.

des pi ca ble (des′pi kə bəl, des pik′ə bəl), *adj.* to be despised; contemptible: *a despicable liar.* **—des′pi ca bly,** *adv.*

de tect (di tekt′), *v.t.* 1 discover (a person) in the performance of some act: *The child was detected stealing cookies in the pantry.* 2 discover the presence, existence, or fact of: *detect any odor in the room, detect an error in the account.* 3 demodulate.

de te ri o rate (di tir′ē ə rāt′), *v.,* **-rat ed,**

-rat ing. **—v.i.** become worse; lessen in value; depreciate: *Machinery deteriorates rapidly if it is not taken care of.* **—v.t.** make worse. **—de ter′i o ra′tion,** *n.*

de ter mi nate (di tèr′mə nit), *adj.* 1 with exact limits; fixed; definite. 2 settled; positive. 3 determined; resolute. **—de ter′mi nate ly,** *adv.*

de throne (di thrōn′), *v.t.,* **-throned, -thron ing.** put off a throne or a high position; remove from ruling power; depose.

de vi ous (dē′vē əs), *adj.* 1 out of the direct way; winding; roundabout: *We took a devious route through side streets and alleys to avoid the crowded main street.* 2 straying from the right course; not straightforward: *His devious nature was shown in little lies and other dishonesties.* **—de′vi ous ly,** *adv.* **—de′vi ous ness,** *n.*

de vise (di vīz′), *v.,* **-vised, -vis ing,** *n.* **—v.t.** 1 think out; plan or contrive; invent: *I devised a way of raising boards up to my tree house by using a pulley.* 2 give or leave (land, buildings, etc.) by a will.

di a tribe (dī′ə trīb), *n.* speech or discussion bitterly and violently directed against some person or thing; denunciation.

dic ta to ri al (dik′tə tôr′ē əl, dik′tə tōr′ē əl), *adj.* 1 of or like that of a dictator; absolute: *dictatorial government.* 2 domineering; overbearing: *a dictatorial manner.* **—dic′ta to′ri al ly,** *adv.*

dic ta tor ship (dik′tā tər ship, dik tā′tər ship), *n.* 1 position or rank of a dictator. 2 term of a dictator; period of time a dictator rules. 3 absolute authority; power to give orders that must be obeyed. 4 country under the rule of a dictator.

di e tar y (dī′ə ter′ē), *adj., n., pl.* **-tar ies.** **—adj.** having to do with diet: *Dietary rules tell what foods to eat for healthy living and how to prepare them.*

dig ni fied (dig′nə fīd), *adj.* having dignity of manner, style, or appearance; noble; stately. **—dig′ni fied′ly,** *adv.*

di lap i dat ed (də lap′ə dā′tid), *adj.* fallen into ruin or disrepair; decayed through neglect.

di min ish (də min′ish), *v.t.* 1 make smaller; lessen; reduce. 2 lessen the importance, power, or reputation of; degrade. 3 (in architecture) to cause to taper. **—v.i.** 1 become smaller; lessen; decrease. 2 (in architecture) to taper. [ultimately < Latin *dis-* apart + *minus* less] **—di min′ish a ble,** *adj.*

din (din), *n., v.,* **dinned, din ning.** **—n.** a continuing loud, confused noise. **—v.i.** make a din. **—v.t.** 1 strike with a din. 2 say over and over again; repeat in a tiresome way.

dire (dīr), *adj.,* **dir er, dir est.** causing great fear or suffering; dreadful. [< Latin *dirus*] **—dire′ly,** *adv.* **—dire′ness,** *n.*

dis-, *prefix.* 1 opposite of; lack of; not: *Dishonest = not honest; opposite of honest. Discomfort = lack of comfort.* 2 do the opposite of: *Disentangle = do the opposite of entangle.* 3 apart; away, as in *dispel.* [< Latin]

dis ap prove (dis′ə prüv′), *v.,* **-proved, -prov ing.** **—v.t.** 1 have or express an opinion against. 2 refuse consent to; reject: *The judge disapproved the verdict.* **—v.i.** show dislike (*of*): *Most children disapprove of going to school in the summer.* **—dis′ap prov′ing ly,** *adv.*

dis be lief (dis′bi lēf′), *n.* lack of belief; refusal to believe.

dis card (*v.* dis kärd′; *n.* dis′kärd), *v.t.* 1 give up as useless or not wanted; throw

aside. 2 get rid of (unwanted playing cards) by throwing them aside or playing them. **—v.i.** throw out an unwanted card. **—n.** 1 act of throwing aside as useless or not wanted. 2 thing or things thrown aside as useless or not wanted. 3 cards thrown aside or played as not wanted.

dis cre tion (dis kresh′ən), *n.* 1 quality of being discreet; great carefulness in speech or action; good judgment; wise caution: *Use your own discretion.* 2 freedom to decide or choose: *It is within the principal's discretion to punish a pupil.*

dis dain (dis dān′), *v.t.* think unworthy of oneself or one's notice; regard or treat with contempt; scorn. **—n.** a disdaining; feeling of scorn.

dis dain ful (dis dān′fəl), *adj.* feeling or showing disdain; scornful. **—dis dain′ful ly,** *adv.* **—dis dain′ful ness,** *n.*

dis em bark (dis′em bärk′), *v.i., v.t.* go or put ashore from a ship; land from a ship.

dis en gage (dis′en gāj′), *v.t.,* **-gaged, -gag ing.** 1 free or release from anything that holds; detach; loosen: *disengage the clutch. He disengaged his hand from that of the sleeping child.* 2 free from an engagement, pledge, or obligation. 3 (in military use) withdraw from combat or contact with (an enemy). **—dis′en gage′ment,** *n.*

dis en tan gle (dis′en tang′gəl), *v.t., v.i.* **-gled, -gling.** free from tangles or complications; untangle. **—dis′en tan′gle ment,** *n.*

dis grun tled (dis grun′tld), *adj.* in bad humor; discontented.

dis heart en (dis härt′n), *v.t.* cause to lose hope; discourage; depress. **—dis heart′en ing ly,** *adv.*

dis in ter est ed (dis in′tər ə stid, dis in′tər es′tid), *adj.* 1 free from selfish motives; impartial; fair. 2 uninterested. **—dis in′ter est ed ly,** *adv.*

dis mem ber (dis mem′bər), *v.t.* 1 separate or divide into parts: *After the war the defeated country was dismembered.* 2 cut or tear the limbs from; divide limb from limb. **—dis mem′ber ment,** *n.*

dis qui et (dis kwī′ət), *v.t.* make uneasy or anxious; disturb. **—n.** uneasy feelings; anxiety. **—dis qui′et ing ly,** *adv.*

dis re gard (dis′ri gärd′), *v.t.* 1 pay no attention to; take no notice of: *Disregarding the child's screams, the doctor cleaned and bandaged the cut.* 2 treat without proper regard or respect; slight. **—n.** 1 lack of attention; neglect: *disregard of the traffic laws.* 2 lack of proper regard or respect: *disregard for tradition.*

dis sec tion (dis sek′shən, dī sek′shən), *n.* 1 act of cutting apart an animal, plant, etc., in order to examine or study the structure. 2 examination of something part by part; criticism in detail; analysis.

dis sem ble (di sem′bəl), *v.,* **-bled, -bling.** **—v.t.** 1 hide (one's real feelings, thoughts, plans, etc.); disguise: *She dissembled her anger with a smile.* 2 pretend; feign: *The bored listener dissembled an interest he didn't feel.* **—v.i.** conceal one's opinions, motives, etc.

dis sim i lar (di sim′ə lər), *adj.* not similar; unlike; different. **—dis sim′i lar ly,** *adv.*

dis sim u la tion (di sim′yə lā′shən), *n.* act of dissembling; hypocrisy; pretense; deceit.

dis suade (di swād′), *v.t.,* **-suad ed, -suad ing.** 1 persuade not to do something. 2 advise against.

dis tem per (dis tem′pər), *n.* 1 an infectious

viral disease of dogs and other animals, accompanied by fever, a short, dry cough, and a loss of strength. 2 any sickness of the mind or body; disorder; disease. 3 disturbance.

dis tort (dis tôrt´), *v.t.* 1 pull or twist out of shape; change the normal appearance of: *Rage distorted his face.* 2 give a twist or turn to (the mind, thoughts, views); misrepresent: *The driver distorted the facts of the accident to escape blame.*

dis tri bu tion (dis´trə byü´shən), *n.* 1 act of distributing: *After the contest the distribution of prizes to the winners took place.* 2 way of being distributed: *If some get more than others, there is an uneven distribution.* 3 thing distributed. 4 a distributing to consumers of goods grown or made by producers. 5 the area over which a particular thing is spread: *the distribution of a species of animal.*

di ver si ty (də vėr´sə tē, dī vėr´sə tē), *n., pl.* **-ties.** 1 complete difference; unlikeness. 2 point of unlikeness. 3 variety: *a diversity of food on the table.*

di vert (də vėrt´, dī vėrt´), *v.t.* 1 turn aside: *A ditch diverted water from the stream into the fields.* 2 amuse; entertain: *Listening to music diverted me after a hard day's work.*

dog ged (dô´gid, dog´id), *adj.* not giving up; stubborn; persistent: *dogged determination.* [< *dog*] **—dog´ged ly,** *adv.* **—dog´ged ness,** *n.*

dole ful (dōl´fəl), *adj.* very sad or dreary; mournful; dismal. **—dole´ful ly,** *adv.*

do main (dō mān´), *n.* 1 territory under the control of one ruler or government. 2 land owned by one person; estate. 3 (in law) the absolute ownership of land. 4 field of thought, action, etc.; sphere of activity: *the domain of science, the domain of religion.*

do mes tic (də mes´tik), *adj.* 1 of the home, household, or family affairs: *domestic problems, a domestic scene.* 2 attached to home; devoted to family life. 3 living with or under the care of man or in or near his habitations; not wild; tame. Cats, dogs, cows, horses, pigs, and sheep are domestic animals. 4 of one's own country; not foreign: *domestic news.* 5 made in one's own country; native: *domestic woolens.* **—n.** servant in a household. [< Latin *domesticus* < *domus* house] **—do mes´ti cal ly,** *adv.*

do min ion (də min´yən), *n.* 1 power or right of governing and controlling; rule; control. 2 territory under the control of one ruler or government. 3 a self-governing territory.

dote (dōt), *v.i.,* **dot ed, dot ing.** 1 be weak-minded and childish because of old age. 2 **dote on** or **dote upon,** be foolishly fond of; be too fond of.

du bi ous (dü´bē əs, dyü´bē əs), *adj.* 1 filled with or being in doubt; doubtful; uncertain: *a dubious compliment.* 2 feeling doubt; wavering or hesitating. 3 of questionable character; probably bad: *a dubious scheme for making money.* **—du´bi ous ly,** *adv.*

duffel bag, a large canvas sack used by soldiers, campers, etc., for carrying clothing and other belongings.

dun (dun), *adj.* dull, grayish-brown. **—n.** 1 a dull, grayish brown. 2 horse of a dun color. [Old English *dunn*]

dusk (dusk), *n.* 1 the darker stage of twilight; time just before dark. 2 shade; gloom. **—adj.** dark-colored; dusky. **—v.t., v.i.** make or become dusky. [Old English *dox* dark]

dwin dle (dwin´dl), *v.t., v.i.,* **-dled, -dling.** make or become smaller and smaller; shrink; diminish.

ebb (eb), *n.* 1 a flowing of the tide away from the shore; fall of the tide. 2 a growing less or weaker; decline; decay. 3 point of decline: *His fortunes were at an ebb.* **—v.i.** 1 flow out; fall: *The tide ebbed.* 2 grow less or weaker; decline: *My courage ebbed as I neared the haunted house.* [Old English *ebba*]

ed i ble (ed´ə bəl), *adj.* fit to eat; eatable. **—n. edibles,** *pl.* things fit to eat; food.

ed i fy (ed´ə fī), *v.t.,* **-fied, -fy ing.** improve morally; benefit spiritually; instruct and uplift. [< Old French *edifier* < Latin *aedificare* build. **—ed´i fi´er,** *n.*

ef fi cient (ə fish´ənt), *adj.* 1 able to produce the effect wanted without waste of time, energy, etc.; capable; competent. 2 actually producing an effect: *Heat is the efficient cause in changing water to steam.* **—ef fi´cient ly,** *adv.*

ef fort less (ef´ərt lis), *adj.* requiring or showing little or no effort; easy. **—ef´fort less ly,** *adv.*

e go tism (ē´gə tiz´əm, eg´ə tiz´əm), *n.* 1 habit of thinking, talking, or writing too much of oneself; conceit. 2 selfishness.

eke (ēk), *v.t., v.i.,* **eked, ek ing.** 1 **eke out,** a add to; increase: *The clerk eked out her regular wages by working evenings and Sundays.* b barely manage to make (a living).

e lab or ate (*adj.* i lab´ər it, i lab´rit; *v.* i lab´ə rāt´), *adj., v.,* **-at ed, -at ing.** **—adj.** worked out with great care; having many details; complicated. **—v.t.** 1 work out with great care; add details to: *She is elaborating her plans for the new addition to the house.* 2 make with labor; produce. **—v.i.** talk, write, etc., in great detail; give added details: *The witness was asked to elaborate upon one of his statements.* **—e lab´or ate ly,** *adv.*

e lic it (i lis´it), *v.t.* draw forth; bring out: *elicit the truth by discussion.* [< Latin *elicitum* lured out < *ex-* out + *lacere* entice]

e lude (i lüd´), *v.t.,* **e lud ed, e lud ing.** 1 avoid or escape by cleverness, quickness, etc.; slip away from; evade: *The sly fox eluded the dogs.* 2 baffle: *The cause of cancer has eluded scientists.*

e lu sive (i lü´siv), *adj.* 1 hard to describe or understand; baffling: *an elusive idea.* 2 tending to elude or escape; evasive: *an elusive enemy.*

em a nate (em´ə nāt), *v.,* **-nat ed, -nat ing.** **—v.i.** originate from a person or thing as a source; come forth; spread out: *The rumor emanated from Chicago.* **—v.t.** send out; emit. [< Latin *emanatum* flowed out < *ex-* out + *manare* to flow]

em bed (em bed´), *v.t.,* **-bed ded, -bedding.** 1 fix or enclose in a surrounding mass; fasten firmly: *Precious stones are often found embedded in rock.* 2 plant in a bed: *He embedded the bulbs in a box of sand.* Also, **imbed.**

em boss (em bôs´, em bos´), *v.t.* 1 decorate with a design, pattern, etc., that stands out from the surface: *Our coins are embossed with letters and figures.* 2 cause to stand out from the surface: *The letters on the book's cover had been embossed.*

em i grate (em´ə grāt), *v.i.,* **-grat ed, -grating.** leave one's own country or region to settle in another. [< Latin *emigratum* moved out < *ex-* out + *migrare* to move]

➤ **emigrate, immigrate.** *Emigrate* means to move out of a country or region, *immigrate* to move into a country. One who *emigrates* from Norway might *immigrate* to the United States.

e mit (i mit´), *v.t.,* **e mit ted, e mit ting.**

hat, āge, fär; let, ēqual, tėrm;
it, īce; hot, ōpen, ôrder;
oil, out; cup, pùt, rüle;
ch, child; ng, long; sh, she;
th, thin; ₮H, then; zh, measure;

ə represents *a* in about, *e* in taken,
i in pencil, *o* in lemon, *u* in circus.

< = from, derived from, taken from.

1 give off; send out; discharge: *The sun emits light and heat.* 2 put into circulation; issue. 3 utter; express.

en-, *prefix.* 1 cause to be ____; make ____: *Enfeeble* = make feeble. 2 put in ____; put on ____: *Enthrone* = put on a throne. 3 other meanings, as in *enact, encourage, entwine.* The addition of *en-* rarely changes the meaning of a verb except to make it more emphatic. [< Old French < Latin *in-*]

-en¹, *suffix forming verbs from adjectives and nouns.* 1 cause to be ____; make ____: *Blacken* = make black. 2 cause to have ____: *Heighten* = cause to have height. 3 become ____: *Sicken* = become sick. 4 come to have ____; gain ____: *Lengthen* = come to have length.* [Old English *-nian*]

-en², *suffix added to nouns to form adjectives.* made of ____: *Silken* = made of silk. [Old English]

-en³, *suffix.* *-en* (or *-n*) ends the past participles of many strong verbs, as in *fallen, shaken, written, sworn.* [Old English]

-en⁴, *suffix.* *-en* is used to form the plural of a few nouns, as in *children, oxen.* [Old English *-an*]

en camp (en kamp´), *v.i.* 1 make a camp. 2 live in a camp for a time. **—v.t.** put in a camp: *They were encamped in tents.* **—en camp´ment,** *n.*

en deav or (en dev´ər), *v.i., v.t.* make an effort; try hard; attempt earnestly; strive: *A runner endeavors to win a race.* **—n.** an earnest attempt; hard try; effort.

en graft (en graft´), *v.t.* 1 graft (a shoot, etc.) from one tree or plant into another. 2 fix in; implant. Also, **ingraft.**

en grave (en grāv´), *v.t.,* **-graved, -graving.** 1 cut deeply in; carve in; carve artistically on a surface: *engrave initials on a ring.* 2 cut (a picture, design, map, etc.) in lines on a metal plate, block of wood, etc., for printing. 3 print from such a plate, block, etc. 4 fix firmly: *a face engraved in one's mind.*

en sue (en sü´), *v.i.,* **-sued, -su ing.** 1 come after; follow. The ensuing year means the year following this. 2 happen as a result: *I spent my allowance the first day, and a lean week ensued.*

-ent, *suffix added to verbs.* 1 (to form adjectives) that ____s; ____ing: *Absorbent* = that *absorbs* or *absorbing.* 2 (to form nouns) one that ____s: *Correspondent* = one that *corresponds.* 3 (to form adjectives) other meanings, as in *competent, confident.* [< Latin *-entem*]

en ter prise (en´tər prīz), *n.* 1 an important, difficult, or dangerous plan to be tried; great or bold undertaking. 2 any undertaking; project; venture: *a business enterprise.* 3 readiness to try important, difficult, or dangerous plans; willingness to undertake great or bold projects. 4 the carrying on of enterprises; taking part in enterprises.

en treat y (en trē´tē), *n., pl.* **-treat ies.** an

569

earnest request; prayer or appeal: *I gave in to the children's entreaties.* [< Old French *entraitier* < *en-* in + *traitier* to treat]

ep i logue or **ep i log** (ep/ə lôg, ep/ə log), *n.* 1 a concluding section added to a novel, poem, etc., that rounds out or interprets the work. 2 speech or poem, addressed to the audience by one of the actors at the end of a play. 3 any concluding act or event.

ep i taph (ep/ə taf), *n.* a short statement in memory of a dead person, usually put on a gravestone or tombstone.

ep i tha la mic (ep/ə thə lā/mik), *adj.* of marriage.

-er¹, *suffix forming nouns.* 1 *(added to verbs)* person or thing that ___s: *Admirer = a person who admires. Burner = thing that burns.* 2 *(added to nouns)* person living in ___: *New Yorker = a person living in New York. Villager = a person living in a village.* 3 *(added to nouns)* person who makes or works with ___: *Hatter = a person who makes hats.* 4 person or thing that is or has ___: *Six-footer = a person who is six feet tall.* [Old English *-ere*, ultimately < Latin *-arium* -ary]

-er², *suffix forming nouns from other nouns.* person or thing connected with ___: *Officer = person connected with an office.* [< Old French < Latin *-arium*]

-er³, *suffix forming the comparative degree of adjectives and adverbs.* more: *Softer = more soft. Slower = more slow.* [Old English, *-or, -ra, -re*]

er mine (ėr/mən), *n., pl.* **-mines** or **-mine.** 1 any of several kinds of weasel of northern regions which are brown in summer but white with a black-tipped tail in winter. 2 the soft, white fur of the winter phase, used for women's coats, trimming, etc.

etch (ech), *v.t.* 1 engrave (a drawing or design) on a metal plate, glass, etc., by means of acid that eats away the lines. When filled with ink, the lines of the design will reproduce a copy on paper. 2 engrave a drawing or design on by means of acid: *The artist etched only a few copper plates.* 3 impress deeply; fix firmly: *Her face was etched in my memory.* —*v.i.* make etchings.

e vac u ate (i vak/yü āt), *v.t.,* **-at ed, -at ing.** 1 leave empty; withdraw from: *The tenants evacuated the building.* 2 withdraw; remove: *evacuate civilians from a war zone.* 3 clear out the contents of; empty (a container). 4 make empty: *evacuate the stomach.*

e ven tu al ly (i ven/chü ə lē), *adv.* in the end; finally.

ewe (yü), *n.* a female sheep. [Old English *ēowu*]

ex-¹, *prefix.* 1 former; formerly: *Ex-president = former president.* 2 out of; from; out: *Express = press out.* 3 thoroughly; utterly: *Exterminate = terminate (finish or destroy) thoroughly.* [< Latin < *ex* out of, without]

ex-², *prefix.* from; out of, as in *exodus.* Also, **ec-** before consonants. [< Greek]

ex cru ci at ing (ek skrü/shē ā/ting), *adj.* 1 causing great suffering; very painful; torturing. 2 excessively elaborate; extreme: *excruciating politeness.* —**ex cru/ci at/ing ly,** *adv.*

ex e cute (ek/sə kyüt), *v.t.,* **-cut ed, -cut ing.** 1 carry out; do: *The nurse executed the doctor's orders.* 2 put into effect; enforce: *Congress makes the laws; the President executes them.* 3 put to death according to a legal sentence or decree: *The murderer was executed.* 4 make according to a plan or design: *The same artist executed that painting and that statue.* 5 perform or play (a piece of music).

ex hil a rate (eg zil/ə rāt/), *v.t.,* **-rat ed, -rat ing.** make merry or lively; put into high spirits; cheer: *The joy of the holiday season exhilarates us all.*

ex pul sion (ek spul/shən), *n.* 1 an expelling; forcing out: *expulsion of air from the lungs.* 2 a being expelled; being forced out: *Expulsion from school is a punishment for bad behavior.*

ex tin guish (ek sting/gwish), *v.t.* 1 put out; quench: *Water extinguished the fire.* 2 bring to an end; snuff out; destroy: *A government may extinguish liberty but not the love of liberty.* 3 eclipse or obscure by superior brilliancy; outshine.

extra-, *prefix.* outside ___; beyond ___: *Extraordinary = outside the ordinary.* [< Latin < *extra* outside]

ex trem i ty (ek strem/ə tē), *n., pl.* **-ties.** 1 the very end; farthest possible place; last part or point. 2 **extremities,** *pl.* the hands and feet. 3 very great danger or need: *In their extremity the people on the sinking ship bore themselves bravely.* 4 an extreme degree: *Joy is the extremity of happiness.* 5 an extreme action or measure: *The soldiers were forced to the extremity of firing their rifles to scatter the angry mob.*

ex u ber ant (eg zü/bər ənt), *adj.* 1 very abundant; overflowing; lavish: *exuberant joy, an exuberant welcome.* 2 profuse in growth; luxuriant: *the exuberant vegetation of the jungle.* 3 abounding in health and spirits; overflowing with good cheer: *an exuberant young man.* [< Latin *exuberantem* growing luxuriantly < *ex-* thoroughly + *uber* fertile] —**ex u/ber ant ly,** *adv.*

fal ter (fôl/tər), *v.i.* 1 hesitate in action from lack of courage; draw back; waver: *The soldiers faltered for a moment as their captain fell.* 2 move unsteadily; stumble; totter. 3 come forth in hesitating, broken sounds: *Her voice faltered as she described her fall from the bicycle.* —*v.t.* speak in hesitating or broken words; stammer; stutter: *Greatly embarrassed, he faltered out his thanks.* —*n.* 1 act of faltering. 2 a faltering sound. [Middle English *faltren*] —**fal/ter er,** *n.*

fa nat ic (fə nat/ik), *n.* person who is carried away beyond reason by his feelings or beliefs, especially in religion or politics. —*adj.* unreasonably enthusiastic or zealous, especially in religion or politics. [< Latin *fanaticus* inspired by divinity < *fanum* temple]

fa nat i cal (fə nat/ə kəl), *adj.* fanatic. —**fa nat/i cal ly,** *adv.*

fan ci er (fan/sē ər), *n.* person who has a liking for or is especially interested in something: *a dog fancier.*

fa tal ism (fā/tl iz/əm), *n.* 1 belief that fate controls everything that happens. 2 acceptance of everything that happens because of this belief.

fa tal ist (fā/tl ist), *n.* believer in fatalism.

fa tu i ty (fə tü/ə tē, fə tyü/ə tē), *n., pl.* **-ties.** self-satisfied stupidity; idiotic folly; silliness.

fe do ra (fi dôr/ə, fi dōr/ə), *n.* a man's low, soft felt hat with a curved brim, having the crown creased lengthwise. [< *Fédora*, a play by Victorien Sardou, 1831-1908, French playwright]

fe ro cious (fə rō/shəs), *adj.* 1 savagely cruel or destructive; fierce. 2 INFORMAL. extremely intense: *a ferocious headache.* [< Latin *ferocem* fierce] —**fe ro/cious ly,** *adv.*

fer vent (fėr/vənt), *adj.* 1 showing great warmth of feeling; very earnest; ardent: *fervent devotion.* 2 hot; glowing; intense. —**fer/vent ly,** *adv.*

fer vid (fėr/vid), *adj.* 1 full of strong feeling; intensely emotional; ardent; spirited. 2 intensely hot. —**fer/vid ly,** *adv.* —**fer/vid ness,** *n.*

fes toon (fe stün/), *n.* 1 a string or chain of flowers, leaves, ribbons, etc., hanging in a curve between two points: *The bunting was draped on the wall in colorful festoons.* 2 a carved or molded ornament like this on furniture, pottery, architectural work, etc. —*v.t.* 1 decorate with festoons. 2 form into festoons; hang in curves.

fi as co (fē as/kō), *n., pl.* **-cos** or **-coes.** a complete or ridiculous failure; humiliating breakdown. [< Italian, literally, flask]

fiend ish (fēn/dish), *adj.* very cruel or wicked; devilish: *fiendish tortures, a fiendish yell.* —**fiend/ish ly,** *adv.* —**fiend/ish ness,** *n.*

fi na le (fə nä/lē, fi nal/ē), *n.* 1 the concluding part of a piece of music or a play. 2 the last part; end. [< Italian]

fir kin (fėr/kən), *n.* 1 quarter of a barrel, used in Great Britain as a measure of capacity. 2 a small wooden cask for liquids, fish, butter, etc. [Middle English *ferdekyn*]

flank (flangk), *n.* 1 the fleshy or muscular part of the side of an animal or person between the ribs and the hip. 2 piece of beef cut from this part. 3 side of a mountain, building, etc. 4 the far right or the far left side of an army, fleet, or fort. —*v.t.* 1 be at the side of: *A garage flanked the house.* 2 get around the far right or the far left side of. 3 attack from or on the side. —*v.i.* 1 occupy a position on a flank or side. 2 present the flank or side. [< Old French *flanc* < Germanic]

flaw (flô), *n.* 1 a defective place; crack: *A flaw in the dish caused it to break.* 2 a slight defect; fault; blemish.

fledg ling or **fledge ling** (flej/ling), *n.* 1 a young bird that has just grown feathers needed for flying. 2 a young, inexperienced person.

fleet ing (flē/ting), *adj.* passing swiftly; soon gone; transitory: *a fleeting smile.*

flip pant (flip/ənt), *adj.* smart or pert in speech or manner; not respectful; impertinent; saucy: *a flippant answer.* —**flip/pant ly,** *adv.*

flirt (flėrt), *v.i.* 1 play at making love; make love without meaning it. 2 trifle; toy: *He flirted with the idea of going to Europe, even though he couldn't afford it.* 3 move quickly to and fro; flutter: *The bird flirted from one branch to another.* —*v.t.* 1 give a brisk, sudden motion to; flutter: *She flirted her fan impatiently.* 2 toss; jerk.

flo rid (flôr/id, flor/id), *adj.* 1 highly colored with red; ruddy: *a florid complexion.* 2 elaborately ornamented; showy; ornate: *florid language, florid architecture.*

flot sam (flot/səm), *n.* 1 wreckage of a ship or its cargo found floating on the sea. [< Anglo-French *floteson* < Old French *floter* to float]

floun der (floun/dər), *v.i.* 1 struggle awkwardly without making much progress; plunge about: *The horses were floundering in the deep snowdrifts.* 2 be clumsy or confused and make mistakes: *The frightened girl could only flounder through her song.*

flout (flout), *v.t.* treat with contempt or scorn; scoff at; mock: *The foolish boy flouted his mother's advice.* —*v.i.* show contempt or scorn; scoff. —*n.* a contemptuous speech or act; mockery; scoffing. [variant of *flute,* verb] —**flout'er,** *n.* —**flout'ing ly,** *adv.*

flu ent (flü'ənt), *adj.* 1 flowing smoothly or easily: *speak fluent French.* 2 speaking or writing easily and rapidly. 3 not fixed or stable; fluid. [< Latin *fluentem* < *fluere* to flow] —**flu'ent ly,** *adv.*

flu o res cent (flü'ə res'nt), *adj.* that gives off light by fluorescence. Fluorescent substances glow in the dark when exposed to X rays.

foal (fōl), *n.* a young horse, donkey, etc.; colt or filly. —*v.t., v.i.* give birth to (a foal).

foil (foil), *v.t.* 1 prevent from carrying out plans, attempts, etc.; get the better of; outwit or defeat: *The hero foiled the villain.* 2 prevent (a scheme, plan, etc.) from being carried out or from succeeding.

fold (fōld), *n.* 1 pen to keep sheep in. 2 sheep kept in a pen. 3 group sharing a common belief or cause, especially a church or congregation. —*v.t.* put or keep (sheep) in a pen. [Old English *fALod*]

fol ly (fol'ē), *n., pl.* **-lies.** 1 a being foolish; lack of sense; unwise conduct. 2 a foolish act, practice, or idea; something silly. 3 a costly but foolish undertaking.

foot lock er (fut'lok'ər), *n.* a small chest for personal belongings, usually kept at the foot of one's bed, as in a barracks.

fore bod ing (fôr bō'ding, fōr bō'ding), *n.* 1 prediction; warning. 2 a feeling that something bad is going to happen; presentiment.

fore close (fôr klōz', fōr klōz'), *v.,* **-closed, -clos ing.** —*v.t.* 1 shut out; prevent; exclude: *foreclose objections.* 2 take away the right to redeem (a mortgage). When the conditions of a mortgage are not met, the holder can foreclose and have the property sold to satisfy his claim. —*v.i.* take away the right to redeem a mortgage.

fore sight (fôr'sīt', fōr'sīt'), *n.* 1 power to see or know beforehand what is likely to happen. 2 careful thought for the future; prudence.

for get-me-not (fər get'mē not'), *n.* 1 any of a genus of small plants of the same family as the borage, with hairy stems and curving spikes of small blue, pink, or white flowers. 2 the flower of any of these plants.

for ti fy (fôr'tə fī), *v.,* **-fied, -fy ing.** —*v.t.* 1 strengthen against attack; provide with forts, walls, etc. 2 give support to; strengthen. 3 enrich with vitamins and minerals: *fortify bread.* —*v.i.* build forts, walls, etc.; protect a place against attack.

fraud u lent (frô'jə lənt, frô'dyə lənt), *adj.* 1 guilty of fraud; cheating; dishonest. 2 intended to deceive: *a fraudulent offer.* 3 done by fraud; obtained by trickery. —**fraud'u lent ly,** *adv.*

fray (frā), *v.t.* 1 cause to separate into threads; make ragged or worn along the edge. 2 wear away; rub. —*v.i.* become frayed; ravel out or wear through.

free throw, (in basketball) an unhindered shot from about 15 feet away from the basket, awarded to a player fouled by a member of the opposing team, and worth one point; foul shot.

freight (frāt), *—v.t.* 1 load with freight. 2 carry as freight. 3 send as freight. 4 load; burden; oppress.

fren zy (fren'zē), *n., pl.* **-zies,** *v.,* **-zied, -zy ing.** —*n.* 1 state of near madness; frantic condition. 2 condition of very great excitement. —*v.t.* drive (a person) to frenzy.

fret (fret), *v.,* **fret ted, fret ting.** —*v.t.* 1 make peevish, unhappy, discontented, or worried; harass; vex; provoke. 2 eat or wear away. 3 make or form by wearing away. 4 agitate or ruffle.

fric tion (frik'shən), *n.* 1 a rubbing of one object against another; rubbing: *Matches are lighted by friction.* 2 resistance to motion of surfaces that touch; resistance of a body in motion to the air, water, etc., through which it travels or to the surface on which it travels: *Oil reduces friction.* 3 conflict of differing ideas, opinions, etc.; disagreement; clash: *Constant friction between the two nations brought them dangerously close to war.*

fruit ful (früt'fəl), *adj.* 1 producing much fruit. 2 producing much of anything; prolific: *a fruitful mind.* 3 having good results; bringing benefit or profit: *a fruitful plan.* —**fruit'ful ly,** *adv.* —**fruit'ful ness,** *n.*

fugue (fyüg), *n.* a contrapuntal musical composition based on one or more short themes in which different voices or instruments repeat the same melody with slight variations.

-ful, *suffix added to nouns to form adjectives or other nouns.* 1 full of ___: *Cheerful = full of cheer.* 2 showing ___: *Careful = showing care.* 3 having a tendency to ___: *Harmful = having a tendency to harm.* 4 enough to fill a ___: *Cupful = enough to fill a cup.* 5 that can be of ___: *Useful = that can be of use.* 6 having the qualities of ___: *Masterful = having the qualities of a master.* [Old English < adjective *full* full]

fur row (fėr'ō), *n.* 1 a long, narrow groove or track cut in the earth by a plow. 2 any long, narrow groove or track: *Heavy trucks made deep furrows in the muddy road.* 3 wrinkle: *a furrow in one's brow.* —*v.t.* 1 plow. 2 make furrows in. 3 make wrinkles in; wrinkle: *The old man's face was furrowed with age.* —*v.i.* make a furrow or furrows. [Old English *furh*]

fu til i ty (fyü til'ə tē), *n., pl.* **-ties.** 1 uselessness; ineffectiveness. 2 unimportance. 3 futile action, event, etc.

fu tur i ty (fyü tùr'ə tē, fyü tyůr'ə tē), *n., pl.* **-ties.** 1 future. 2 a future state or event. 3 quality, condition, or fact of being future.

-fy, *suffix forming verbs chiefly from adjectives.* 1 make ___; cause to be ___: *Simplify = make simple.* 2 become ___: *Solidify = become solid.* [< Old French *-fier* < Latin *-ficare* < *facere* do, make]

gait (gāt), *n.* 1 the manner of walking or running: *He has a lame gait because of an injured foot.* 2 (of horses) any one of various manners of stepping or running, as the gallop, trot, pace, etc.

gal le on (gal'ē ən, gal'yən), *n.* a large, high ship with three or four decks, used especially in the 1400's and 1500's.

gal ley (gal'ē), *n., pl.* **-leys.** 1 a long, narrow ship propelled by both oars and sails, used in medieval times in the Mediterranean. 2 a large warship of the ancient Greeks and Romans with one or more banks of oars.

gan gling (gang'gling), *adj.* awkwardly tall and slender; lank and loosely built.

gang way (gang'wā'), *n.* 1 passageway. 2 passageway on a ship. 3 gangplank.

hat, āge, fär; let, ēqual, tėrm;
it, īce; hot, ōpen, ôrder;
oil, out; cup, pút, rüle;
ch, child; ng, long; sh, she;
th, thin; ₮H, then; zh, measure;

ə represents *a* in about, *e* in taken,
i in pencil, *o* in lemon, *u* in circus.

< = from, derived from, taken from.

gar ish (ger'ish, gar'ish), *adj.* 1 excessively bright; glaring: *a garish yellow.* 2 obtrusively bright in color; gaudy: *a garish suit.* 3 adorned to excess.

gar ru lous (gar'ə ləs, gar'yə ləs), *adj.* 1 talking too much; talkative. 2 using too many words; wordy. [< Latin *garrulus* < *garrire* to chatter] —**gar'ru lous ly,** *adv.*

gaunt let (gônt'lit, gänt'lit), *n.* 1 a former punishment or torture in which the offender had to run between two rows of men who struck him with clubs or other weapons as he passed. 2 **run the gauntlet,** a pass between two rows of men each of whom strikes the runner as he passes. b be exposed to unfriendly attacks or severe criticism. Also, **gantlet.**

gel a tin or **gel a tine** (jel'ə tən), *n.* 1 an odorless, tasteless protein substance like glue or jelly, obtained by boiling animal tendons, bones, hoofs, etc. It dissolves easily in hot water and is used in making jellied desserts and salads, glue, camera film, etc. 2 any of various vegetable substances having similar properties. 3 preparation or product in which gelatin is the essential constituent.

gen ial (jē'nyəl), *adj.* 1 smiling and pleasant; cheerful and friendly; kindly: *a genial welcome.* 2 helping growth; pleasantly warming; comforting: *a genial climate.* —**gen'ial ly,** *adv.*

ge ol o gist (jē ol'ə jist), *n.* an expert in geology.

ge ol o gy (jē ol'ə jē), *n., pl.* **-gies.** 1 science that deals with the earth's crust, the layers of which it is composed, and their history. 2 features of the earth's crust in a place or region; rocks, rock formation, etc., of a particular area: *the geology of North America.*

ges tic u late (je stik'yə lāt), *v.i.,* **-lat ed, -lat ing.** make or use gestures to show ideas or feelings.

ges tic u la tion (je stik'yə lā'shən), *n.* 1 a making lively or excited gestures. 2 a lively or excited gesture: *His wild gesticulations showed that he was losing his temper rapidly.*

gid dy (gid'ē), *adj.,* **-di er, -di est.** 1 having a whirling feeling in one's head; dizzy. 2 likely to make dizzy; causing dizziness: *a giddy dance.* 3 never or rarely serious; frivolous; fickle: *a giddy person.* —**gid'di ly,** *adv.* —**gid'di ness,** *n.*

Gi la monster (hē'lə), a large, poisonous lizard of the southwestern United States and northern Mexico, which has a thick tail, a heavy, clumsy body, and is covered with beadlike, orange-and-black scales.

gild (gild), *v.t.,* **gild ed** or **gilt, gild ing.** 1 cover with a thin layer of gold or similar material; make golden. 2 make (something) look bright and pleasing. 3 make (something) seem better than it is.

gin ger ly (jin'jər lē), *adv.* with extreme care or caution. —*adj.* extremely cautious or wary. —**gin'ger li ness,** *n.*

571

gir dle (gèr′dl), *n., v.,* **-dled, -dling.** —*n.*
1 belt, sash, cord, etc., worn around the
waist. 2 anything that surrounds or encloses:
a girdle of trees around the pond. 3 a light
corset worn about the hips or waist.

glad i a tor (glad′ē ā′tər), *n.* 1 slave, captive, or paid fighter who fought at the public
shows in the arenas in ancient Rome. 2 a
skilled contender in any fight or struggle.

glan du lar (glan′jə lər, glan′dyə lər), *adj.*
1 of or like a gland. 2 having glands. 3 made
up of glands. —**glan′du lar ly,** *adv.*

glow er (glou′ər), *v.i.* stare angrily; scowl
fiercely: *The rivals glowered at each other.*
—*n.* an angry stare; fierce scowl.

gnash (nash), *v.t.* 1 strike or grind together:
gnash one's teeth. 2 bite by gnashing the
teeth; bite upon. [Middle English *gnasten*]

gnat (nat), *n.* any of various small, two-
winged flies. Most gnats are bloodsucking
and give bites that itch. [Old English *gnætt*]

gnaw (nô), *v.,* **gnawed, gnawed** or **gnawn,
gnaw ing.** —*v.t.* 1 bite at and wear away: *A
mouse has gnawed the cover of this box.*
2 make by biting: *A rat can gnaw a hole
through wood.* 3 wear away; consume; cor-
rode. 4 trouble; harass; torment. —*v.i.* 1 to
bite: *gnaw at a bone.* 2 torment as if by
biting: *The feeling of guilt gnawed at my
conscience day and night.*

goad (gōd), *n.* 1 a sharp-pointed stick for
driving cattle; gad. 2 anything which drives
or urges one on. —*v.t.* drive or urge on; act
as a goad to: *Hunger goaded him to steal a
loaf of bread.* [Old English *gād*]

gore (gôr, gōr), *v.t.,* **gored, gor ing.** wound
with a horn or tusk: *The angry bull gored the
farmer in the leg.* [Middle English *goren* <
Old English *gār* spear]

gorge (gôrj), *n., v.,* **gorged, gorg ing.** —*n.*
a deep, narrow valley, usually steep and
rocky, especially one with a stream.

grace (grās), *n., v.,* **graced, grac ing.** —*n.*
1 beauty of form, movement, or manner;
pleasing or agreeable quality; charm, ease, or
elegance. 2 good will; favor. 3 mercy or
pardon. 4 Graces, *pl.* (in Greek myths) three
sister goddesses who give beauty, charm, and
joy to people and nature.

graft (graft), *n.* 1 dishonest gains or unlawful
profits made by a person in and through his
official position, especially in connection with
politics or government business. 2 money
dishonestly and improperly taken. —*v.i.*
make money by dishonest or unlawful
means. —**graft′er,** *n.*

gran deur (gran′jər, gran′jùr), *n.* 1 mag-
nificence or splendor of appearance, style of
living, etc. 2 quality of being grand or imposing; majesty; nobility.

gran dil o quent (gran dil′ə kwənt), *adj.*
using lofty or pompous words. —**gran-
dil′o quent ly,** *adv.*

grap ple (grap′əl), *v.,* **-pled, -pling,** *n.*
—*v.t.* 1 seize and hold fast; grip or hold firmly.
—*v.i.* 1 struggle by seizing one another; fight
closely: *The wrestlers grappled in the center
of the ring.* 2 try to overcome, solve, or deal
(with a problem, question, etc.). [< Old
French *grapil* a hook] —**grap′pler,** *n.*

grate (grāt), *n., v.,* **grat ed, grat ing.** —*n.*
1 framework of iron bars to hold burning fuel
in a furnace, fireplace, etc. 2 fireplace.
3 framework of bars over a window or opening; grating.

graze (grāz), *v.,* **grazed, graz ing,** *n.* —*v.t.*

1 touch lightly in passing; rub lightly against:
The car grazed the garage door. 2 scrape the
skin from: *The bullet grazed his shoulder.*
—*n.* 1 a grazing. 2 a slight wound or abra-
sion made by grazing. [origin uncertain]

grim (grim), *adj.,* **grim mer, grim mest.**
1 without mercy; stern, harsh, or fierce: *grim,
stormy weather.* 2 not yielding; not relenting:
a grim resolve. 3 looking stern, fierce, or
harsh. 4 horrible; frightful; ghastly: *grim
jokes about death.* [Old English *grimm* fierce]
—**grim′ly,** *adv.* —**grim′ness,** *n.*

grim y (grī′mē), *adj.,* **grim i er, grim i est.**
covered with grime; very dirty. —**grim′i ly,**
adv. —**grim′i ness,** *n.*

gro tesque (grō tesk′), *adj.* 1 odd or unnatural in shape, appearance, manner, etc.; fantastic; queer: *pictures of dragons and other
grotesque monsters.* 2 ridiculous; absurd:
*The monkey's grotesque antics made the chil-
dren laugh.* 3 (of painting or sculpture) in or
resembling the grotesque. —*n.* painting,
sculpture, etc., combining designs, orna-
ments, figures of persons or animals, etc., in a
fantastic or unnatural way, much used in the
Renaissance. [< French < Italian *grottesco,*
literally, of caves, cavelike < *grotta.*]
—**gro tesque ly,** *adv.* —**gro tesque′ness,**
n.

gru el ing or **gru el ling** (grü′ə ling), *adj.*
very tiring; exhausting: *The marathon is a
grueling contest.* —*n.* an exhausting or very
tiring experience.

grue some (grü′səm), *adj.* causing fear or
horror; horrible; revolting. Also, **grewsome.**
[Middle English *gruen* to shudder] —**grue′-
some ly,** *adv.* —**grue′some ness,** *n.*

guer ril la (gə ril′ə), *n.* member of a band of
fighters who harass the enemy by sudden
raids, ambushes, the plundering of supply
trains, etc. Guerrillas are not part of a regular
army. —*adj.* of or by guerrillas: *a guerrilla
attack.* Also, **guerilla.**

guise (gīz), *n.* 1 style of dress; garb: *The spy
went in the guise of a monk and was not
recognized by the enemy.* 2 outward appearance; aspect; semblance: *Her theory is nothing but an old idea in a new guise.* 3 assumed
appearance; pretense: *Under the guise of
friendship he plotted treachery.*

gul ly (gul′ē), *n., pl.* **-lies,** *v.,* **-lied, -ly ing.**
—*n.* a narrow gorge; small ravine; ditch made
by heavy rains or running water. —*v.t.* make
gullies in. [probably variant of *gullet*]

haft (haft), *n.* handle, especially that of a
knife, sword, dagger, etc.

hag gard (hag′ərd), *adj.* looking worn from
pain, fatigue, worry, hunger, etc.; careworn;
gaunt. [perhaps < Old French *hagard*]

half nelson, (in wrestling) a hold applied
by hooking one arm under an opponent's
armpit and putting a hand on the back of his
neck.

ha lo (hā′lō), *n., pl.* **-los** or **-loes,** *v.* —*n.*
1 ring of light around the sun, moon, a star, or
other luminous body, caused by the refraction of light through ice crystals suspended in
the air. 2 a golden circle or disk of light
represented about the head of a saint or angel
in pictures or statues; nimbus. 3 glory or
glamour that surrounds an idealized person
or thing: *A halo of romantic adventure surrounds King Arthur and his knights.*

hand i work (han′dē wèrk′), *n.* 1 work
done by a person's hands. 2 work which a
person has done himself.

har ry (har′ē), *v.,* **-ried, -ry ing.** —*v.t.*
1 raid and rob with violence; lay waste; pillage. 2 keep troubling; worry; torment. —*v.i.*
make predatory raids.

haugh ty (hô′tē), *adj.,* **-ti er, -ti est.** too
proud and scornful of others: *a haughty
glance, haughty words.* [Middle English *haute*
< Middle French *haut* < Latin *altus* high]
—**haugh′ti ly,** *adv.* —**haugh′ti ness,** *n.*

haunt (hônt, hänt), *v.t.* 1 go often to; visit
frequently. 2 be often with; come often to:
Memories of his youth haunted the old man.
3 visit frequently and habitually with mani-
festations of influence and presence: *People
say ghosts haunt that old house.* —*v.i.* stay
or remain usually (in a place). —*n.* place
often gone to or visited: *The swimming pool
was the children's favorite haunt on hot summer days.*

heft (heft), INFORMAL. —*v.t.* 1 lift; heave.
2 judge the weight of by lifting. [< *heave;*
patterned on *weft* < *weave*]

he red i tar y (hə red′ə ter′ē), *adj.* 1 passing by inheritance from generation to generation: *"Prince" and "princess" are hereditary titles.* 2 holding a position, title, etc., by
inheritance: *The queen of England is a hereditary ruler.* 3 transmitted or capable of being
transmitted by means of genes from parents
to offspring: *Color blindness is hereditary.*
4 derived from one's parents or ancestors: *a
hereditary custom, a hereditary enemy to a
country.* 5 of or having to do with inheritance
or heredity: *hereditary descent.*

here to fore (hir′tə fôr′, hir′tə fōr′), *adv.*
before this time; until now.

her on (her′ən), *n.* any of a family of wading
birds with long necks, bills, and legs but short
tails. Herons feed on fish, frogs, etc.

her ring (her′ing), *n., pl.* **-rings** or **-ring.**
any of a family of fishes, especially a small,
bony food fish of the northern Atlantic. The
grown fish are eaten fresh, salted, or smoked,
and the young are canned as sardines.

hilt (hilt), *n.* 1 handle of a sword, dagger, or
tool. **2 to the hilt,** thoroughly; completely.
—*v.t.* furnish with a hilt. [Old English]

hin der (hin′dər), *v.t.* keep back; hold back;
get in the way of; make difficult; hamper.
—*v.i.* get in the way; be a hindrance.

hith er to (hiᴛʜ′ər tü′), *adv.* until now: *a
fact hitherto unknown.*

hoard (hôrd, hōrd), *v.t., v.i.* save and store
away (money, goods, etc.) for preservation or
future use: *A squirrel hoards nuts for the
winter.* —*n.* what is saved and stored away
for preservation or future use; things stored.
[Old English *hordian*] —**hoard′er,** *n.*

ho bo (hō′bō), *n., pl.* **-bos** or **-boes.** U.S.
1 person who wanders about and lives by
begging or doing odd jobs; tramp. 2 a migra-
tory workman. [origin uncertain]

hoist (hoist), *v.t.* raise on high; lift up, often
with ropes and pulleys: *hoist a flag, hoist
sails.* —*n.* 1 a hoisting; lift; boost. 2 elevator
or other apparatus for hoisting heavy loads.

hom age (hom′ij, om′ij), *n.* 1 dutiful respect; reverence: *Everyone paid homage to
the great leader.* 2 (in the Middle Ages) a
formal acknowledgment by a vassal that he
owed loyalty and service to his lord. 3 thing
done or given to show such acknowledgment.

hom i ny (hom′ə nē), *n.* whole or coarsely
ground hulled corn, usually eaten boiled.
[short for *rockahominy* < Algonquian *rokeha-
men* parched corn]

horde (hôrd, hōrd), *n.* 1 a great company or
number; multitude; swarm: *hordes of grasshoppers.* 2 a wandering tribe or troop.

hos tler (os′lər, hos′lər), *n.* person who takes care of horses at an inn or stable. Also, **ostler.**

hov el (huv′əl, hov′əl), *n.* 1 house that is small, crude, and unpleasant to live in. 2 an open shed for sheltering cattle, tools, etc.

hov er (huv′ər, hov′ər), *v.i.* 1 hang fluttering or suspended in air: *The two birds hovered over their nest.* 2 stay in or near one place; wait nearby: *The dogs hovered around the kitchen door at mealtime.* 3 be in an uncertain condition: *The patient hovered between life and death.*

hu mil i ate (hyü mil′ē āt), *v.t.,* **-at ed, -at ing.** lower the pride, dignity, or selfrespect of; make ashamed: *Do not humiliate him by referring to his failures.*

hum mock (hum′ək), *n.* 1 a very small, rounded hill; knoll; hillock. 2 a bump or ridge in a field of ice. [origin unknown]

hur tle (hėr′tl), *v.,* **-tled, -tling,** *n.* —*v.i.* 1 dash or drive violently; rush violently; come with a crash: *The car hurtled across the road into a fence.* 2 move with a clatter; rush noisily: *The old subway train hurtled past.* —*v.t.* dash or drive violently; fling: *The impact of the crash hurtled the driver against the windshield of the car.* —*n.* act or fact of hurtling; clash. [Middle English *hurtelen* < *hurten* to hurt, in early sense "dash against"]

hy giene (hī′jēn′), *n.* science that deals with the maintenance of health; system of principles or rules for preserving or promoting health.

hyp o crite (hip′ə krit), *n.* 1 person who pretends to be very good or religious. 2 person who pretends to be what he is not; pretender. [< Greek *hypokritēs* actor < *hypo-* under + *kritēs* a judge]

hyp o crit i cal (hip′ə krit′ə kəl), *adj.* of or like a hypocrite; insincere. —**hyp′o crit′-i cal ly,** *adv.*

hy poth e sis (hī poth′ə sis), *n., pl.* **-ses** (-sēz′). 1 something assumed because it seems likely to be a true explanation. 2 proposition assumed as a basis for reasoning. [< Greek < *hypo-* under + *thesis* a placing]

hys ter i cal (hi ster′ə kəl), *adj.* 1 excited or emotional. 2 showing an unnatural lack of self-control; unable to stop laughing, crying, etc. 3 of, having to do with, or affected by hysteria. 4 INFORMAL. very funny: *Isn't that picture hysterical!* —**hys ter′i cal ly,** *adv.*

-ible, *suffix* added to verbs to form adjectives. that can be ____ed: *Reducible = that can be reduced.* [< Old French < Latin *-ibilis*]

-ical, *suffix.* 1 *-ic,* as in *geometrical, parasitical, hysterical.* 2 *-ic + -al* or *-ics + -al,* as in *critical, musical, ethical, statistical.* [< Latin *-icalem < -icus -ic + -alem* -al[1]]

i de al ism (ī dē′ə liz′əm), *n.* 1 an acting according to one's ideals of what ought to be, regardless of circumstances or of the approval or disapproval of others; a cherishing of fine ideals. 2 a neglecting practical matters in following ideals; not being practical. 3 (in philosophy) the belief that all our knowledge is a knowledge of ideas and that it is impossible to know whether or not there really is a world of objects on which our ideas are based. Idealism is opposed to materialism. 4 (in art or literature) the representation of imagined types rather than of exact likenesses of people, instances, or situations.

il lit er a cy (i lit′ər ə sē), *n., pl.* **-cies.**

1 inability to read and write. 2 lack of education; lack of cultural knowledge. 3 error in speaking or writing, caused by a lack of education or knowledge.

il lu sion (i lü′zhən), *n.* 1 appearance or feeling that misleads because it is not real; thing that deceives by giving a false idea. 2 a false impression or perception: *an optical illusion.* 3 a false notion or belief: *Many people have the illusion that wealth is the chief cause of happiness.*

im mac u late (i mak′yə lit), *adj.* 1 without a spot or stain; absolutely clean. 2 without fault or errors. 3 without sin; pure. [< Latin *immaculatus* < *in-* not + *macula* spot] —**im mac′u late ly,** *adv.* —**im mac′-u late ness,** *n.*

im meas ur a ble (i mezh′ər ə bəl, i mā′-zhər ə bəl), *adj.* too vast to be measured; very great; boundless. —**im meas′ur a-ble ness,** *n.* —**im meas′ur a bly,** *adv.*

im mi nent (im′ə nənt), *adj.* likely to happen soon; about to occur: *The black clouds showed that a storm was imminent.* [< Latin *imminentem* overhanging, threatening] —**im′-mi nent ly,** *adv.*

im mor tal (i môr′tl), *adj.* 1 living forever; never dying; everlasting. 2 of or having to do with immortal beings or immortality; divine. 3 remembered or famous forever. —*n.* 1 an immortal being. 2 **immortals,** *pl.* the gods of ancient Greece and Rome. 3 person remembered or famous forever. —**im mor′tal ly,** *adv.*

im mor tal i ty (im′ôr tal′ə tē), *n.* 1 life without death; a living forever. 2 fame that lasts forever.

imp (imp), *n.* 1 a young or small devil; little demon. 2 a mischievous child.

im pair (im per′, im par′), *v.t.* make worse; damage; harm; weaken: *Poor food impaired her health.* [< Old French *empeirer,* ultimately < Latin *in- + pejor* worse] —**im pair′er,** *n.* —**im pair′ment,** *n.*

im par tial (im pär′shəl), *adj.* showing no more favor to one side than to the other; fair; just. —**im par′tial ly,** *adv.*

im per a tive (im per′ə tiv), *adj.* 1 not to be avoided; that must be done; urgent: *It is imperative that this very sick child should stay in bed.* 2 expressing a command or request: *an imperative statement.* 3 (in grammar) having to do with a verb form which expresses a command, request, or advice. "Go!" and "Stop, look, listen!" are in the imperative mood. —*n.* 1 something imperative; command: *The great imperative is "Love thy neighbor as thyself."* 2 a verb form in the imperative mood. 3 the imperative mood. [< Latin *imperativus* < *imperare* to command] —**im per′a tive ly,** *adv.* —**im per′a tive ness,** *n.*

im per cep ti ble (im′pər sep′tə bəl), *adj.* that cannot be perceived or felt; very slight, gradual, subtle, or indistinct. —**im′per-cep′ti bly,** *adv.*

im per i ous (im pir′ē əs), *adj.* 1 haughty or arrogant; domineering; overbearing. 2 not to be avoided; necessary; urgent. —**im per′-i ous ly,** *adv.* —**im per′i ous ness,** *n.*

im pli ca tion (im′plə kā′shən), *n.* 1 an implying. 2 a being implied. 3 something implied; indirect suggestion; hint: *There was no implication of dishonesty in his failure in business.* 4 an implicating. 5 a being implicated.

im preg nate (im preg′nāt), *v.t.,* **-nat ed, -nat ing.** 1 make pregnant. 2 spread through the whole of; fill; saturate: *Sea water is*

hat, āge, fär; let, ēqual, tėrm;
it, īce; hot, ōpen, ôrder;
oil, out; cup, půt, rüle;
ch, child; ng, long; sh, she;
th, thin; ŦH, then; zh, measure;

ə represents *a* in about, *e* in taken,
i in pencil, *o* in lemon, *u* in circus.

< = from, derived from, taken from.

impregnated with salt. 3 fill the mind of; inspire: *The captain impregnated the crew with his own courage.* [< Late Latin *impraegnatum* made pregnant < Latin *in- + praegnas* pregnant] **im′preg na′tion,** *n.*

im pro vise (im′prə vīz), *v.,* **-vised, -vis ing.** —*v.t.* 1 make up (music, poetry, etc.) on the spur of the moment; sing, recite, speak, etc., without preparation. 2 provide offhand; make for the occasion: *The stranded motorists improvised a tent out of two blankets and some long poles.* —*v.i.* compose, utter, or do anything without preparation or on the spur of the moment.

im pul sive (im pul′siv), *adj.* 1 acting or done upon impulse; with a sudden inclination or tendency to act: *The impulsive child gave all his money to the beggar.* 2 driving with sudden force; able to impel; impelling. —**im pul′sive ly,** *adv.* —**im pul′sive-ness,** *n.*

in-[1], *prefix.* not; the opposite of; the absence of: *Inexpensive = not expensive. Inattention = the absence of attention.* [< Latin]

in-[2], *prefix.* in; into; on; upon: *Incase = (put) into a case. Intrust = (give) in trust.* [< Latin < *in,* preposition]

in-[3], *prefix.* in; within; into; toward: *Indoors = within doors. Inland = toward land.* [Old English]

in ap pro pri ate (in′ə prō′prē it), *adj.* not appropriate; not fitting; unsuitable. —**in′-ap pro′pri ate ly,** *adv.* —**in′ap pro′-pri ate ness,** *n.*

in ar tic u late (in′är tik′yə lit), *adj.* 1 not uttered in distinct syllables or words: *an inarticulate mutter.* 2 unable to speak in words; dumb: *Cats and dogs are inarticulate.* 3 not able to put one's thoughts or feelings into words easily and clearly. 4 not jointed: *A jellyfish's body is inarticulate.* —**in′ar-tic′u late ly,** *adv.*

in au gu rate (in ô′gyə rāt′), *v.t.,* **-rat ed, -rat ing.** 1 install in office with formal ceremonies: *A President of the United States is inaugurated every four years.* 2 make a formal beginning of; begin: *The invention of the airplane inaugurated a new era in transportation.* 3 open for public use with a formal ceremony or celebration.

in cal cu la ble (in kal′kyə lə bəl), *adj.* 1 too great in number to be counted; innumerable. 2 impossible to foretell or reckon beforehand. 3 that cannot be relied on; uncertain. —**in cal′cu la bly,** *adv.*

in car cer ate (in kär′sə rāt′), *v.t.,* **-rat ed, -rat ing.** imprison. [< Late Latin *incarceratum* imprisoned < Latin *in- + carcer* prison]

in cli na tion (in′klə nā′shən), *n.* 1 a tending toward a certain character or condition; natural bent; tendency: *an inclination toward fatness.* 2 preference; liking: *have a strong inclination for sports.* 3 an inclining toward something; leaning, bending, or bowing: *an* *inclination* of the head. 4 deviation from a normal position; slope; slant: *roof with a sharp inclination.* 5 an inclined surface; incline.

in cline (*v.* in klīn′; *n.* in′klīn, in klīn′), *v.,* **-clined, -clin ing,** *n.* —*v.i.* be favorable or willing; tend: *Dogs incline to eat meat as a food.* 2 slope; slant. 3 lean, bend, or bow. —*v.t.* 1 make favorable or willing; influence. 2 lean, bend, or bow: *incline one's head in prayer.* 3 cause to slope or slant; tilt. —*n.* 1 a slope; slant. 2 an inclined plane or surface.

in con ti nent (in kon′tə nənt), *adj.* 1 without self-control. 2 not chaste; licentious. —**in con′ti nent ly,** *adv.*

in cor rupt i ble (in′kə rup′tə bəl), *adj.* 1 not to be corrupted; honest: *The incorruptible judge could not be bribed.* 2 not subject to decay; lasting forever: *Diamonds are incorruptible.* —**in′cor rupt′i bly,** *adv.*

in cred u lous (in krej′ə ləs), *adj.* 1 not ready to believe; doubting; skeptical: *If they look incredulous show them the evidence.* 2 showing a lack of belief: *an incredulous smile.* —**in cred′u lous ly,** *adv.*

in dent[1] (*v.* in dent′; *n.* in′dent, in dent′), *v.t.* 1 make notches or jags in (an edge, line, border, etc.): *an indented coastline.* 2 begin (a line) farther from the left margin than the other lines: *The first line of a paragraph is usually indented.* —*v.i.* form a notch or recess. —*n.* a notch; indentation. [< Old French *endenter* < Late Latin *indentare* to crunch on < Latin *in-* in + *dentem* tooth]

in dent[2] (in dent′), *v.t.* 1 make a dent in; mark with a dent. 2 press in; stamp. [< *in-* + *dent*]

in den ta tion (in′den tā′shən), *n.* 1 an indenting. 2 a being indented. 3 a dent, notch, or cut.

in dig nant (in dig′nənt), *adj.* angry at something unworthy, unjust, unfair, or mean. —**in dig′nant ly,** *adv.*

in dig na tion (in′dig nā′shən), *n.* anger at something unworthy, unjust, unfair, or mean; anger mixed with scorn; righteous anger: *Cruelty to animals aroused his indignation.*

in dom i ta ble (in dom′ə tə bəl), *adj.* that cannot be conquered; unyielding. [< Late Latin *indomitabilis* < Latin *indomitus* untamed < *in-* not + *domare* to tame] —**in dom′i ta bly,** *adv.*

in duce (in düs′, in dyüs′), *v.t.,* **-duced, -duc ing.** 1 lead on; influence; persuade: *Advertisements induce people to buy.* 2 bring about; cause: *Some drugs induce sleep.* 3 produce (an electric current, electric charge, or magnetic change) by induction. 4 infer by reasoning from particular facts to general truths or principles. [< Latin *inducere* < *in-* in + *ducere* to lead] —**in duc′er,** *n.*

in dulge (in dulj′), *v.,* **-dulged, -dulg ing.** —*v.i.* give in to one's pleasure; let oneself have, use, or do what one wants: *A smoker indulges in tobacco.* —*v.t.* 1 give in to; let oneself have, use, or do: *She indulged her fondness for candy by eating a whole box.* 2 give in to the wishes or whims of; humor: *We often indulge a sick person.*

in ef fa ble (in ef′ə bəl), *adj.* not to be expressed in words; too great to be described in words. [< Latin *ineffabilis* < *in-* not + *effari* express in words < *ex-* out + *fari* speak] —**in ef′fa ble ness,** *n.* —**in ef′fa bly,** *adv.*

in ef fec tu al (in′ə fek′chü əl), *adj.* 1 with-

out effect; useless. 2 not able to produce the effect wanted; powerless. —**in ef fec′-tu al ly,** *adv.*

in ert (in ėrt′), *adj.* 1 having no power to move or act; lifeless: *A stone is an inert mass of matter.* 2 inactive; slow; sluggish. 3 with few or no active chemical, physiological, or other properties: *Helium and neon are inert gases.* [< Latin *inertem* idle, unskilled < *in-* without + *artem* art, skill] —**in ert′ly,** *adv.* —**in ert′ness,** *n.*

in ev i ta bil i ty (in ev′ə tə bil′ə tē), *n.* a being inevitable.

in ev i ta ble (in ev′ə tə bəl), *adj.* not to be avoided; sure to happen; certain to come: *Death is inevitable.* [< Latin *inevitabilis* < *in-* not + *evitare* avoid < *ex-* out + *vitare* shun] —**in ev′i ta ble ness,** *n.* —**in ev′i ta bly,** *adv.*

in ex haust i ble (in′ig zô′stə bəl), *adj.* 1 that cannot be exhausted; very abundant. 2 that cannot be wearied; tireless. —**in′-ex haust′i bly,** *adv.*

in fan try (in′fən trē), *n., pl.* **-tries.** 1 troops trained, equipped, and organized to fight on foot. 2 branch of an army consisting of such troops.

in fer i or (in fir′ē ər), *adj.* 1 below most others; low in quality; below the average: *an inferior mind, an inferior grade of coffee.* 2 not so good or so great; lower in quality; worse: *This cloth is inferior to real silk.* 3 lower in position, rank, importance, etc.; lesser; subordinate: *A lieutenant is inferior to a captain.* —*n.* 1 person who is lower in rank or station. 2 something that is below average.

inferiority complex, an abnormal feeling of being inferior to other people, sometimes compensated for by overly aggressive behavior.

in fest (in fest′), *v.t.* trouble or disturb frequently or in large numbers: *a swamp infested with mosquitoes. The national park was infested with tourists.*

in fi nite (in′fə nit), *adj.* 1 without limits or bounds; endless: *the infinite reaches of outer space.* 2 extremely great; vast: *Teaching little children sometimes takes infinite patience.* 3 (in mathematics) greater than any assignable quantity or magnitude of the sort in question. —*n.* 1 that which is infinite. 2 **the Infinite,** God. —**in′fi nite ly,** *adv.*

in fin i ty (in fin′ə tē), *n., pl.* **-ties.** 1 condition of being infinite. 2 an infinite distance, space, time, or quantity. 3 an infinite extent, amount, or number: *the infinity of God's mercy.* 4 (in mathematics) an infinite quantity.

in fla tion (in flā′shən), *n.* 1 a swelling (with air, gas, pride, etc.). 2 a puffing up with pride, self-importance, etc.; elation. 3 a sharp increase in prices resulting from too great an expansion in paper money or bank credit.

in frac tion (in frak′shən), *n.* a breaking of a law or obligation; violation: *Reckless driving is an infraction of the law.* [< Latin *infractionem* < *infringere.*]

in fur i ate (in fyùr′ē āt), *v.t.,* **-at ed, -at ing.** fill with wild, fierce anger; make furious; enrage. —**in fur′i at′ing ly,** *adv.* —**in fur′i a′tion,** *n.*

in gen ious (in jē′nyəs), *adj.* 1 skillful in making; good at inventing. 2 cleverly planned or made: *This mousetrap is an ingenious device.* —**in gen′ious ly,** *adv.* —**in gen′ious ness,** *n.*

in graft (in graft′), *v.t.* engraft.

in gra ti ate (in grā′shē āt), *v.t.,* **-at ed, -at ing.** bring (oneself) into favor; make (one-

self) acceptable: *He tried to ingratiate himself with the teacher by giving her presents.* [ultimately < Latin *in gratiam* into favor] —**in gra′ti at′ing ly,** *adv.*

in ject (in jekt′), *v.t.* 1 force (liquid, medicine, etc.) into a chamber, passage, cavity, or tissue: *inject penicillin into a muscle, inject fuel into an engine.* 2 fill (a cavity, etc.) with liquid forced in: *The dentist injected the boy's gums with Novocaine.* 3 throw in; insert; interject: *inject a remark into a conversation.* [< Latin *injectum* thrown in < *in-* in + *jacere* to throw] —**in jec′tor,** *n.*

in jec tion (in jek′shən), *n.* 1 act or process of injecting: *Drugs are often given by injection.* 2 liquid injected: *an injection of penicillin.*

in nu mer a ble (i nü′mər ə bəl, i nyü′mər-ə bəl), *adj.* too many to count; very many; countless.

in sist ence (in sis′təns), *n.* 1 act of insisting. 2 quality of being insistent.

in sist ent (in sis′tənt), *adj.* 1 continuing to make a strong, firm demand or statement; insisting: *In spite of the rain she was insistent on going out.* 2 compelling attention or notice; pressing; urgent: *an insistent knocking on the door.* —**in sist′ent ly,** *adv.*

in so lent (in′sə lənt), *adj.* boldly rude; intentionally disregarding the feelings of others; insulting. [< Latin *insolentem* < *in-* not + *solere* be accustomed] —**in′so lent ly,** *adv.*

in sol u ble (in sol′yə bəl), *adj.* 1 that cannot be dissolved; not soluble: *Fats are insoluble in water.* 2 that cannot be solved; unsolvable. —**in sol′u ble ness,** *n.* —**in sol′-u bly,** *adv.*

in still or **in stil** (in stil′), *v.t.,* **-stilled, -still ing.** 1 put in little by little; cause to enter the mind, heart, etc., gradually: *Reading good books instills a love for really fine literature.* 2 put in drop by drop. [< Latin *instillare* < *in-* + *stilla* a drop]

in sub stan tial (in′səb stan′shəl), *adj.* 1 frail; flimsy: *A cobweb is very insubstantial.* 2 unreal; not actual; imaginary: *Dreams and ghosts are insubstantial.* —**in′sub stan′-tial ly,** *adv.*

in suf fer a ble (in suf′ər ə bəl), *adj.* intolerable; unbearable: *insufferable rudeness.* —**in suf′fer a ble ness,** *n.* —**in suf′fer-a bly,** *adv.*

in su per a ble (in sü′pər ə bəl), *adj.* that cannot be passed over or overcome; insurmountable: *an insuperable barrier.* —**in-su′per a bly,** *adv.*

in tan gi ble (in tan′jə bəl), *adj.* 1 not capable of being touched or felt: *Sound and light are intangible.* 2 not easily grasped by the mind; vague: *The very popular girl had that intangible quality called charm.* —*n.* something intangible. —**in tan′gi ble ness,** *n.* —**in tan′gi bly,** *adv.*

in te gral (in′tə grəl), *adj.* 1 necessary to make something complete; essential: *Steel is an integral part of a modern skyscraper.* 2 entire; complete. 3 formed of parts that together constitute a whole. —**in′te gral ly,** *adv.*

in tent (in tent′), *n.* 1 that which is intended; purpose; intention: *I'm sorry I hurt you; that wasn't my intent.* 2 meaning; significance: *What is the intent of that remark?* —*adj.* 1 very attentive; having the eyes or thoughts earnestly fixed on something; earnest: *an intent look.* 2 earnestly engaged; much interested: *intent on making money.* —**in tent′ly,** *adv.* —**in tent′ness,** *n.*

inter-, *prefix.* 1 one with the other; together: *Intercommunicate = communicate with each other.* 2 between: *Interpose = put between.* 3 between or among a group: *International = between or among nations.* [< Latin < *inter* among, between, during.]

in ter cept (in′tər sept′), *v.t.* 1 take or seize on the way from one place to another: *intercept a letter, intercept a messenger.* 2 cut off (light, water, etc.). 3 check; stop: *intercept the flight of an escaped criminal.* —**in′ter cep′tion**, *n.*

in ter im (in′tər im), *n.* time between; the meantime. —*adj.* for the meantime; temporary. [< Latin, in the meantime < *inter* between]

in tern (in tėrn′), *v.t.* confine within a country or place; force to stay in a certain place, especially during wartime. [< French *interner* < *interne* inner, internal < Latin *internus* < *in* in]

in ter ro gate (in ter′ə gāt), *v.*, **-gat ed, -gat ing.** —*v.t.* ask questions of; examine or get information from by asking questions; question thoroughly or in a formal manner: *The lawyer took two hours to interrogate the witness.* —*v.i.* ask a series of questions. —**in ter′ro ga′tor**, *n.*

in ter val (in′tər vəl), *n.* 1 period of time between; pause: *an interval of a week, intervals of freedom from worry.* 2 space between things; intervening space: *an interval of ten feet between trees.* 3 **at intervals, a** now and then. **b** here and there.

in ter vene (in′tər vēn′), *v.i.*, **-vened, -ven ing.** 1 come between; be between: *A week intervenes between Christmas and New Year's Day.* 2 come between persons or groups to help settle a dispute; act as an intermediary: *The President was asked to intervene in the coal strike.* [< Latin *intervenire* < *inter-* between + *venire* come] —**in′ter ven′er**, *n.*

in ti mate (in′tə mit), *adj.* 1 very familiar; known very well; closely acquainted: *intimate friends.* 2 resulting from close familiarity; close: *an intimate connection, intimate knowledge of a matter.* 3 personal; private: *A diary is a very intimate book.*

in tol er a ble (in tol′ər ə bəl), *adj.* too much to be endured; unbearable: *intolerable pain.* —**in tol′er a ble ness**, *n.* —**in tol′er a bly**, *adv.*

in tol er ance (in tol′ər əns), *n.* 1 lack of tolerance for difference of opinion or practice, especially in religious matters; denial of the right of others to differ. 2 inability to tolerate or endure some particular thing: *an intolerance to penicillin.*

intra-, *prefix.* within; inside; on the inside, as in *intramural, intrastate.* [< Latin < *intra* inside of]

in trigue (*n.* in trēg′, in′trēg′; *v.* in trēg′), *n.*, *v.*, **-trigued, -tri guing.** —*n.* 1 secret scheming; underhand planning to accomplish some purpose; plotting. 2 a crafty plot; secret scheme. —*v.i.* form and carry out plots; plan in a secret or underhand way. —*v.t.* excite the curiosity and interest of.

in tro spec tive (in′trə spek′tiv), *adj.* inclined to examine one's own thoughts and feelings.

in tu i tion (in′tü ish′ən, in′tyü ish′ən), *n.* 1 immediate perception or understanding of truths, facts, etc., without reasoning: *By experience with many kinds of people the doctor had developed great powers of intuition.* 2 truth, fact, etc., so perceived or understood.

in var i a ble (in ver′ē ə bəl, in var′ē ə bəl), *adj.* always the same; unchanging; unchangeable; constant: *an invariable habit.* —*n.* something invariable; a constant. —**in var′i a ble ness**, *n.* —**in var′i a bly**, *adv.*

in vec tive (in vek′tiv), *n.* a violent attack in words; railing speech, writing, or expression; abusive language. [< Late Latin *invectivus* abusive < Latin *invehi.*]

in voice (in′vois), *n.*, *v.*, **-voiced, -voic ing.** —*n.* 1 list of goods sent to a purchaser showing prices, amounts, shipping charges, etc. 2 shipment of invoiced goods. —*v.t.* make an invoice of; enter on an invoice.

-ion, *suffix forming nouns chiefly from verbs.* 1 act of ____ing: *Attraction = act of attracting.* 2 condition of being ____ed: *Adoption = condition of being adopted.* 3 result of ____ing: *Abbreviation = result of abbreviating.* [< Old French < Latin *-ionem*, or directly < Latin]

irk (ėrk), *v.t.* cause to feel disgusted, annoyed, or troubled; weary by being tedious or disagreeable: *It irks us to wait for people who are late.* [< Middle English *irken*]

ir re place a ble (ir′i plā′sə bəl), *adj.* not replaceable; impossible to replace with another.

ir re sist i ble (ir′i zis′tə bəl), *adj.* that cannot be resisted; too great to be withstood; overwhelming: *an irresistible desire to succeed.* —**ir′re sist′i ble ness**, *n.* —**ir′re sist′i bly**, *adv.*

-ish, *suffix forming adjectives from other adjectives and from nouns.* 1 somewhat ____: *Sweetish = somewhat sweet.* 2 like a ____: *Childish = like a child.* 3 like that of a ____: *Girlish = like that of a girl.* 4 of or having to do with ____: *English = of or having to do with England.* 5 inclined to be a ____: *Thievish = inclined to be a thief.* 6 near, but usually somewhat past ____: *Fortyish = near forty.* [< Old English *-isc*]

-ity, *suffix forming nouns from adjectives.* quality, condition, or fact of being ____: *Sincerity = quality or condition of being sincere.* Also, **-ty.** [< Old French *-ité* < Latin *-itatem*]

-ive, *suffix forming adjectives from nouns.* 1 of or having to do with, as in *interrogative, inductive.* 2 tending to; likely to, as in *active, appreciative.* [< French *-ive* (feminine of *-if* < Latin *-ivus*) or directly < Latin]

-ize, *suffix forming verbs from adjectives and nouns.* 1 make ____: *Legalize = make legal.* 2 become ____: *Crystallize = become crystal.* 3 engage in or use ____: *Criticize = engage in criticism.* 4 treat or combine with ____: *Oxidize = combine with oxygen.* 5 other meanings, as in *alphabetize, colonize, memorize.* Also, **-ise.** [< French *-iser* or Latin *-izare* < Greek *-izein*, or directly < Greek]
➤ **-ize, -ise.** American usage favors the spelling *-ize* for the suffix in words like *apologize, characterize, realize, revolutionize, visualize*, where British usage calls for *-ise.* A number of words which end in the sound of (-īz), however, do not include the suffix and do not have variant spellings. For instance, *chastise, devise, exercise, supervise,* and *surmise* are spelled only one way in American and British spelling.

jad ed (jā′did), *adj.* 1 worn out; tired; weary. 2 dulled from continual use; surfeited; satiated: *a jaded appetite.* —**jad′ed ly**, *adv.* —**jad′ed ness**, *n.*

---

hat, āge, fär; let, ēqual, tėrm;
it, īce; hot, ōpen, ôrder;
oil, out; cup, pùt, rüle;
ch, child; ng, long; sh, she;
th, thin; ₮H, then; zh, measure;

ə represents *a* in about, *e* in taken,
i in pencil, *o* in lemon, *u* in circus.

< = from, derived from, taken from.

---

ja pon i ca (jə pon′ə kə), *n.* 1 camellia. 2 an Asiatic shrub of the rose family, with showy red, pink, or white flowers; Japanese quince.

jaun ty (jôn′tē, jän′tē), *adj.*, **-ti er, -ti est.** 1 easy and lively; sprightly; carefree: *The happy children walked with jaunty steps.* 2 smart; stylish: *She wore a jaunty little hat.* —**jaun′ti ly**, *adv.* —**jaun′ti ness**, *n.*

jave lin (jav′lən), *n.* 1 a light spear thrown by hand. 2 a wooden or metal spear, thrown for distance in athletic contests.

jeer (jir), *v.i.* make fun rudely or unkindly; mock; scoff. —*v.t.* speak to or treat with scornful derision. —*n.* a mocking or insulting remark; rude, sarcastic comment. [origin uncertain] —**jeer′ing ly**, *adv.*

jest (jest), *n.* 1 something said to cause laughter; joke. 2 act of poking fun at; mockery. 3 thing to be mocked or laughed at. 4 **in jest**, in fun; not seriously. —*v.i.* 1 to joke. 2 poke fun; make fun. —**jest′ing ly**, *adv.*

jock ey (jok′ē), *n., pl.* **-eys**, *v.* —*n.* person whose occupation is riding horses in races. —*v.t.* 1 ride (a horse) in a race. 2 trick; cheat: *Swindlers jockeyed them into buying some worthless land.* 3 maneuver so as to get advantage: *The crews were jockeying their boats to get into the best position for the race.* —*v.i.* 1 ride as a jockey. 2 aim at an advantage by skillful maneuvering. 3 act in a tricky way; trick; cheat. [originally proper name, diminutive of *Jock*, Scottish variant of *Jack*]

jowl[1] (joul, jōl), *n.* 1 jaw, especially the part under the jaw. 2 cheek. [Old English *ceafl*]

jowl[2] (joul, jōl), *n.* fold of flesh hanging from the jaw. [perhaps related to Old English *ceole* throat]

ju bi lant (jü′bə lənt), *adj.* expressing or showing joy; rejoicing. [< Latin *jubilantem* < *jubilum* wild shout] —**ju′bi lant ly**, *adv.*

ju bi la tion (jü′bə lā′shən), *n.* 1 a rejoicing. 2 a joyful celebration.

---

keel (kēl), *n.* 1 the main timber or steel piece that extends the whole length of the bottom of a ship or boat. The whole ship is built up on the keel. 2 ARCHAIC. ship. 3 something that resembles a ship's keel in any way, such as the bottom of an airship or airplane. 4 **on an even keel, a** horizontal. **b** calm; steady. —*v.t.* turn upside down; upset. —*v.i.* 1 turn over. 2 **keel over, a** turn over or upside down; upset. **b** fall over suddenly.

khak i (kak′ē, kä′kē), *n.* 1 a dull yellowish brown. 2 a heavy twilled wool or cotton cloth of this color, much used for soldiers' uniforms. 3 **khakis**, *pl.* uniform made of this cloth. —*adj.* dull yellowish-brown. [< Hindi *khākī*, originally, dusty < Persian *khāk* dust]

kin dle (kin′dl), *v.*, **-dled, -dling.** —*v.t.* 1 set on fire; light. 2 stir up; arouse: *kindle enthusiasm. His cruelty kindled our anger.* 3 light up; brighten: *Pleasure kindled the* boy's face. —*v.i.* **1** catch fire; begin to burn: *This damp wood will never kindle.* **2** become stirred up or aroused. **3** light up; brighten: *The girl's face kindled as she told about the airplane ride.*

knap sack (nap′sak′), *n.* a canvas or leather bag with two shoulder straps, used by soldiers, hikers, etc., for carrying clothes, equipment, and other articles on the back; rucksack.

knoll (nōl), *n.* a small, rounded hill; mound. [Old English *cnoll*]

lab y rinth (lab′ə rinth′), *n.* **1** number of connecting passages so arranged that it is hard to find one's way from point to point; maze. **2 Labyrinth** (in Greek legends) the maze built by Daedalus for King Minos of Crete to imprison the Minotaur. **3** any confusing, complicated arrangement: *a labyrinth of dark and narrow streets.* **4** a confusing, complicated state of affairs. **5** the inner ear. [< Greek *labyrinthos*]

lack a dai si cal (lak′ə dā′zə kəl), *adj.* lacking interest or enthusiasm; languid; listless; dreamy. [< *lackaday* alas, variant of *alack a day!*] —**lack′a dai′si cal ly,** *adv.*

la ment (lə ment′), *v.t.* **1** express grief for; mourn for: *lament the dead.* **2** regret: *We lamented his absence.* —*v.i.* express grief; mourn; weep: *Why does she lament?* —*n.* **1** expression of grief or sorrow; wail. **2** poem, song, or tune that expresses grief.

lam en ta tion (lam′ən tā′shən), *n.* **1** loud grief; cries of sorrow; mourning; wailing.

lan guid (lang′gwid), *adj.* **1** without energy; drooping; weak; weary: *A hot, sticky day makes a person feel languid.* **2** without interest or enthusiasm; indifferent; listless. **3** not brisk or lively; sluggish; dull. [< Latin *languidus* < *languere* be faint] —**lan′guid ly,** *adv.* —**lan′guid ness,** *n.*

lank y (lang′kē), *adj.,* **lank i er, lank i est.** awkwardly long and thin; tall and ungraceful: *a lanky boy.* —**lank′i ly,** *adv.* —**lank′-i ness,** *n.*

lapse (laps), *n., v.,* **lapsed, laps ing.** —*n.* **1** a slight mistake or error. A slip of the tongue, pen, or memory is a lapse. **2** a slipping or falling away from what is right: *a moral lapse.* **3** the ending of a right or privilege because it was not renewed, not used, or otherwise neglected. **4** a falling into disuse: *the lapse of a custom.* —*v.i.* **1** make a slight mistake or error. A slip or fall away from what is right. **3** (of a privilege) end because it was not renewed, not used, etc. If a legal claim is not enforced, it lapses after a certain number of years. **4** fall into disuse. [< Latin *lapsus* fall < *labi* to slip] —**laps′er,** *n.*

lax (laks), *adj.* **1** not firm or tight; loose; slack. **2** not strict; careless; remiss. **3** loose in morals. **4** not exact; vague. **5** (of tissue, soils, etc.) loose in texture; loosely cohering. —**lax′ness,** *n.*

lean (lēn), *adj.* **1** not plump or fat; thin; spare: *a lean face, lean cattle.* **2** containing little or no fat: *lean meat.* **3** producing little; scant; meager: *a lean harvest, a lean year for business.* —*n.* meat having little fat. [Old English *hlǣne*] —**lean′ness,** *n.*

ledg er (lej′ər), *n.* book of accounts in which a business keeps a final record of all

transactions, showing the debits and credits of the various accounts.

leech (lēch), *n.* **1** any of a class of bloodsucking or carnivorous annelid worms usually having a sucker at each end of the body and living chiefly in freshwater ponds and streams. Doctors formerly used leeches to draw blood from sick people. **2** person who tries persistently to get what he can from others, without doing anything to earn it; parasite.

len ient (lē′nyənt, lē′nē ənt), *adj.* mild or gentle; not harsh or stern; merciful: *a lenient judge, a lenient punishment.* [< Latin *lenientem* < *lenis* mild] —**len′ient ly,** *adv.*

-less, *suffix forming adjectives from verbs and nouns.* **1** without a ___; that has no ___: *Homeless = without a home.* **2** that does not ___: *Ceaseless = that does not cease.* **3** that cannot be ___ed: *Countless = that cannot be counted.* [Old English *-lēas* < *lēas* without]

leth ar gy (leth′ər jē), *n., pl.* **-gies.** **1** drowsy dullness; lack of energy; sluggish inactivity. **2** (in medicine) a state of prolonged unconsciousness resembling deep sleep, from which the person can be roused but immediately loses consciousness again.

lib e rate (lib′ə rāt′), *v.t.,* **-rat ed, -rat ing.** set free; free or release from slavery, prison, confinement, etc. [< Latin *liberatum* freed < *liber* free] —**lib′e ra′tor,** *n.*

lib e ra tion (lib′ə rā′shən), *n.* **1** a setting free. **2** a being set free.

lim bo (lim′bō), *n.* **1** Often, **Limbo.** (in Roman Catholic theology) a place for those who have not received the grace of Christ while living, and yet have not deserved the punishment of willful and impenitent sinners. **2** place for persons and things forgotten, cast aside, or out of date: *The belief that the earth is flat belongs to the limbo of outworn ideas.* **3** prison; jail; confinement. [< Latin *(in) limbo* (on) the edge]

limp (limp), *adj.* **1** lacking stiffness; ready to bend or droop: *limp flowers, a limp body.* **2** lacking firmness, force, energy, etc. [perhaps related to *limp*] —**limp′ly,** *adv.* —**limp′ness,** *n.*

lin tel (lin′tl), *n.* a horizontal beam or stone over a door, window, etc., to support the structure above it.

lit er al ly (lit′ər ə lē), *adv.* **1** word for word; without exaggeration or imagination: *translate literally.* **2** actually: *He is literally without fear.* **3** INFORMAL. in effect, though not actually; virtually: *The champion runner literally flew around the track.*

lithe (līᴛʜ), *adj.* bending easily; supple: *lithe of body, a lithe willow.* [Old English *lithe* mild] —**lithe′ly,** *adv.* —**lithe′ness,** *n.*

loathe (lōᴛʜ), *v.t.,* **loathed, loath ing.** feel strong dislike and disgust for; abhor; hate; detest: *loathe cockroaches.* [Old English *lāthian* to hate < *lāth* hostile]

loath some (lōᴛʜ′səm), *adj.* making one feel sick; disgusting. —**loath′some ly,** *adv.* —**loath′some ness,** *n.*

loon (lün), *n.* any of a genus of large, fish-eating, web-footed diving birds that have a loud, wild cry and live in northern regions.

lo qua cious (lō kwā′shəs), *adj.* talking much; fond of talking. —**lo qua′cious ly,** *adv.* —**lo qua′cious ness,** *n.*

love knot, an ornamental knot or bow of ribbons as a symbol or token of love.

lull (lul), *v.t.* **1** soothe with sounds or caresses; hush to sleep: *The mother lulled the crying baby.* **2** make peaceful or tranquil; quiet: *lull*

one's suspicions. —*v.i.* become calm or more nearly calm. —*n.* **1** period of less noise or violence; brief calm: *a lull in a storm.* **2** period of reduced activity: *a lull in trade.* [Middle English *lullen*]

lu mi nous (lü′mə nəs), *adj.* **1** shining by its own light: *The sun and stars are luminous bodies.* **2** full of light; shining; bright. **3** easily understood; clear; enlightening. —**lu′mi nous ly,** *adv.* —**lu′mi nous ness,** *n.*

lu nar (lü′nər), *adj.* **1** of the moon. **2** like the moon. **3** measured by the moon's revolutions: *a lunar year.* [< Latin *luna* moon]

lunge (lunj), *n., v.,* **lunged, lung ing.** —*n.* any sudden forward movement, such as a thrust with a sword or other weapon. —*v.i.* move with a lunge; make a sudden forward movement; thrust.

lurk (lėrk), *v.i.* **1** stay about without arousing attention; wait out of sight. **2** be hidden; be unsuspected or latent. **3** move about in a secret and sly manner.

lyr ic (lir′ik), *n.* **1** a short poem expressing personal emotion. A love poem, a patriotic song, a lament, and a hymn might all be lyrics. **2** Usually, **lyrics,** *pl.* the words for a song, especially a popular song. —*adj.* **1** having to do with lyric poems: *a lyric poet.* **2** characterized by a spontaneous expression of feeling. **3** of or suitable for singing.

mack i naw (mak′ə nô), *n.* **1** kind of short coat made of heavy woolen cloth, often in a plaid pattern. **2** kind of thick woolen blanket, often with bars of color, used in the northern and western United States by Indians, lumbermen, etc. **3** a large, heavy, flat-bottomed boat with a sharp prow and square stern, formerly used on the Great Lakes. [< *Mackinaw* City, town in northern Michigan]

ma hog a ny (mə hog′ə nē), *n., pl.* **-nies,** *adj.* —*n.* **1** any of a genus of large tropical American trees which yield a hard, durable, reddish-brown wood. **2** its wood, used in making furniture. **3** any of various related or similar trees of the same family or their woods. **4** a dark reddish brown. —*adj.* **1** made of mahogany. **2** dark reddish-brown.

maize (māz), *n.* **1** corn; Indian corn. **2** the color of ripe corn; yellow.

ma lar i a (mə ler′ē ə, mə lar′ē ə), *n.* disease characterized by periodic chills, fever, and sweating. [< Italian < *mala aria* bad air]

mal ice (mal′is), *n.* **1** active ill will; wish to hurt or make suffer; rancor. **2** (in law) intent to commit an act which will result in harm to another person without justification.

ma lig nant (mə lig′nənt), *adj.* **1** very evil, hateful, or malicious. **2** having an evil influence; very harmful. **3** very dangerous; causing or threatening to cause death: *A cancer is a malignant growth.* **4** ARCHAIC. disaffected; malcontent. —**ma lig′nant ly,** *adv.*

ma neu ver (mə nü′vər), *n.* **1** a planned movement of troops, ships, etc., especially for tactical purposes. **2 maneuvers,** *pl.* a training exercise between two or more military or naval units, simulating combat situations. **3** a skillful plan; clever trick: *a series of political maneuvers to get votes.* **4** an agile or skillful movement made to elude or deceive. —*v.i.* **1** perform maneuvers. **2** plan skillfully; use clever tricks; scheme: *maneuver for some advantage.* —*v.t.* **1** cause to perform maneuvers. **2** force by skillful plans; get by clever tricks: *She maneuvered* *her lazy brother out of bed.* 3 move or manipulate skillfully: *maneuver scenery on a stage.*

ma ni a (mā′nē ə), *n.* 1 kind of mental disorder characterized by great excitement, elation, and uncontrolled, often violent, activity. It is a recurring state in manic-depressive psychosis. 2 unusual or unreasonable fondness; craze. [< Latin < Greek < *mainesthai* to rage]

man i fest (man′ə fest), *adj.* apparent to the eye or to the mind; plain; clear: *a manifest error.* —*v.t.* 1 show plainly; reveal; display. 2 put beyond doubt; prove. —*n.* list of cargo of a ship or aircraft.

ma nip u la tion (mə nip′yə lā′shən), *n.* 1 skillful handling or treatment. 2 clever use of influence. 3 change made for one's own purpose or advantage.

mar row (mar′ō), *n.* 1 the soft, vascular tissue that fills the cavities of most bones and is the source of red blood cells and many white blood cells. 2 the inmost or essential part. [< Old English *mearg*]

mar shal (mär′shəl), *n., v.,* **-shaled, -shaling** or **-shalled, -shal ling.** —*n.* 1 officer of various kinds, especially a police officer. 2 chief of police or head of the fire department in some cities. 3 officer of the highest rank in certain foreign armies. 4 person who arranges the order of march in a parade. —*v.t.* 1 arrange in proper order: *He marshaled his facts well.* 2 conduct with ceremony: *We were marshaled before the queen.*

martial law, rule by the army or militia with special military courts instead of the usual civil authorities. Martial law is declared during a time of trouble or war.

mas tiff (mas′tif), *n.* any of a breed of large, powerful dogs having a short, thick coat, drooping ears, and hanging lips. [< Old French *mastin;* influenced by Old French *mestif* mongrel]

ma tron (mā′trən), *n.* 1 wife or widow, especially one who is mature in age, character, or bearing. 2 woman who manages the household affairs of a school, hospital, dormitory, or other institution. A police matron has charge of the women in a jail.

ma tron ly (mā′trən lē), *adj.* like a matron; suitable for a matron; dignified.

maze (māz), *n.* 1 network of paths through which it is hard to find one's way; labyrinth. 2 state of confusion; muddled condition.

mea ger or **mea gre** (mē′gər), *adj.* 1 lacking fullness or richness; poor or scanty; sparse: *a meager meal.* 2 thin; lean: *a meager face.* —**mea′ger ly, mea′gre ly,** *adv.*

me di ate (*v.* mē′dē āt; *adj.* mē′dē it), *v.,* **-at ed, -at ing,** *adj.* —*v.i.* come in to help settle a dispute; be a go-between; act in order to bring about an agreement between persons or sides. —*v.t.* 1 effect by intervening; settle by intervening: *mediate an agreement, mediate a strike.* 2 be a connecting link between. 3 be the medium for effecting (a result), for conveying (a gift), or for communicating (knowledge). —*adj.* 1 connected, but not directly; involving or dependent on some intermediate agency. 2 intermediate.

med i ta tion (med′ə tā′shən), *n.* quiet thought; reflection, especially on sacred or solemn subjects; contemplation.

men ace (men′is), *n., v.,* **-aced, -ac ing.** —*n.* something that threatens; threat: *In dry weather forest fires are a menace.* —*v.t.* offer a menace to; threaten: *Floods menaced the valley with destruction.* —*v.i.* be threatening.

-ment, *suffix added to verbs to form nouns.* 1 act, process, or fact of ____ing: *Enjoyment = act of enjoying.* 2 condition of being ____ed: *Amazement = condition of being amazed.* 3 product or result of ____ing: *Pavement = product of paving.* 4 means of or instrument for ____ing: *Inducement = means of inducing.* [< French < Latin *-mentum* result of]

mer cur i al (mər kyùr′ē əl), *adj.* 1 sprightly and animated; quick. 2 changeable; fickle. 3 caused by the use of mercury: *mercurial poisoning.* 4 containing mercury. —*n.* drug containing mercury. —**mercur′i al ly,** *adv.* —**mer cur′i al ness,** *n.*

me sa (mā′sə), *n.* a small, isolated, high plateau with a flat top and steep sides, common in dry regions of the western and southwestern United States. [< Spanish < Latin *mensa* table]

mes cal (mes kal′), *n.* 1 an alcoholic drink of Mexico made from the fermented juice of certain agaves, especially the maguey. 2 any of the plants yielding this. 3 a small cactus of northern Mexico and the southwestern United States, whose buttonlike tops are dried and chewed as a stimulant and hallucinogen, especially by some tribes of Indians during religious ceremonies.

me te or ol o gist (mē′tē ə rol′ə jist), *n.* an expert in meteorology.

me te or ol o gy (mē′tē ə rol′ə jē), *n.* science dealing with the atmosphere and atmospheric conditions or phenomena, especially as they relate to weather.

me tic u lous (mə tik′yə ləs), *adj.* extremely or excessively careful about small details. [< Latin *meticulosus* fearful, timid < *metus* fear] —**me tic′u lous ly,** *adv.*

met tle (met′l), *n.* 1 quality of disposition or temperament. 2 spirit; courage. 3 **on one's mettle,** ready to do one's best. [variant of *metal*]

mi ca (mī′kə), *n.* any of a group of minerals containing silicon that divide readily into thin, partly transparent, and usually flexible layers; isinglass. Mica is highly resistant to heat and is used in electric fuses, lanterns, etc. [< Latin, grain, crumb]

minc ing (min′sing), *adj.* 1 putting on a dainty and refined manner: *a mincing voice.* 2 walking with short steps. —**minc′ing ly,** *adv.*

min i mum (min′ə məm), *n., pl.* **-mums, -ma** (-mə), *adj.* —*n.* 1 the least possible amount; lowest amount: *Eight hours' sleep is the minimum I need a night.* 2 the lowest amount of variation attained or recorded. —*adj.* least possible; lowest: *Eighteen is the minimum age for voting.*

mi rage (mə räzh′), *n.* 1 an optical illusion, usually in the desert, at sea, or over a hot paved road, in which some distant scene appears to be much closer than it actually is. It is caused by the refraction of light rays from the distant scene by air layers of different temperatures. Often what is reflected is seen inverted or as something other than it is. Travelers on the desert may see a mirage of palm trees and water. 2 anything that does not exist; illusion. [< French < *mirer* look at]

mis-, *prefix.* 1 bad: *Misgovernment = bad government.* 2 badly: *Misbehave = behave badly.* 3 wrong: *Mispronunciation = wrong pronunciation.* 4 wrongly: *Misapply = apply wrongly.* [Old English < Old French *mes-*]

mi ser (mī′zər), *n.* person who loves money for its own sake; one who lives poorly in order to save money and keep it.

hat, āge, fär; let, ēqual, tėrm;
it, īce; hot, ōpen, ôrder;
oil, out; cup, pùt, rüle;
ch, child; ng, long; sh, she;
th, thin; ₮н, then; zh, measure;

ə represents *a* in about, *e* in taken, *i* in pencil, *o* in lemon, *u* in circus.

< = from, derived from, taken from.

moat (mōt), *n.* a deep, wide ditch dug around a castle, town, etc., as a protection against enemies. Moats were usually kept filled with water. [< Old French *mote* mound]

mod er ate (*adj., n.* mod′ər it; *v.* mod′ə rāt′), *adj., n., v.,* **-at ed, -at ing.** —*adj.* 1 kept or keeping within proper bounds; not extreme: *moderate expenses, moderate styles.* 2 not violent, severe, or intense; calm: *moderate in speech.* 3 not very large or good; fair; medium: *a moderate profit.* —*n.* person who holds moderate opinions, especially in politics. —*v.t.* 1 make less violent, severe, or intense. 2 act as moderator; preside over. —*v.i.* 1 become less extreme or violent. 2 act as moderator; preside. [< Latin *moderatum* regulated < *modus* measure] —**mod′er ate ly,** *adv.*

moi e ty (moi′ə tē), *n., pl.* **-ties.** 1 half. 2 part: *Only a small moiety of college students win scholarships.*

mon arch (mon′ərk), *n.* 1 king, queen, emperor, empress, etc.; ruler. 2 person or thing like a monarch: *A tall, solitary pine was monarch of the forest.*

mon i tor (mon′ə tər), *n.* 1 pupil in school with special duties, such as helping to keep order and taking attendance. 2 person who gives advice or warning. 3 something that reminds or gives warning. —*v.t., v.i.* 1 check the quality, wave frequency, of (radio or television transmissions, telephone messages, etc.) by means of a monitor. 2 check in order to control something.

mo not o nous (mə not′n əs), *adj.* 1 continuing in the same tone or pitch: *a monotonous voice.* 2 not varying; without change; uniform. 3 wearying because of its sameness; tedious: *monotonous work.* —**mo not′o nous ly,** *adv.* —**mo not′o nous ness,** *n.*

moor (mùr), *n.* open, waste land, especially if heather grows on it. [Old English *mōr*]

mo rose (mə rōs′), *adj.* gloomy; sullen; ill-humored: *a morose scowl, a morose person.* [< Latin *morosus,* originally, set in one's ways < *morem* custom, habit] —**morose′ly,** *adv.* —**mo rose′ness,** *n.*

mote (mōt), *n.* 1 speck of dust. 2 any very small thing. [Old English *mot*]

mo ti va tion (mō′tə vā′shən), *n.* act or process of furnishing with an incentive or inducement to action.

muse (myüz), *v.,* **mused, mus ing.** —*v.i.* 1 be completely absorbed in thought; ponder; meditate. 2 look thoughtfully. —*v.t.* say thoughtfully.

mute (myüt), *adj., n., v.,* **mut ed, mut ing.** —*adj.* 1 not making any sound; silent: *The little girl stood mute with embarrassment.* 2 unable to speak; dumb. 3 not pronounced; silent: *The "e" in "mute" is mute.* 4 without speech or sound: *a mute refusal of an offer, mute astonishment.* —*n.* person who cannot speak, usually because of deafness, loss of or

damage to the tongue, etc. —**mute′ly,** *adv.*
—**mute′ness,** *n.*

mu tu al (myü′chü əl), *adj.* 1 done, said, felt, etc., by each toward the other; given and received: *mutual promises, mutual dislike.* 2 each to the other: *mutual enemies.* 3 belonging to each of several: *our mutual friend.* [< Latin *mutuus* reciprocal] —**mu′- tu al ly,** *adv.*

muz zle (muz′əl), *n., v.,* **-zled, -zling.** —*n.* 1 the projecting part of the head of an animal, including the nose, mouth, and jaws; snout. 2 cover or cage of straps or wires to put over an animal's head or mouth to keep it from biting or eating. 3 the open front end of the barrel of a gun, pistol, etc. —*v.t.* 1 put a muzzle on. 2 compel to keep silent about something; prevent from expressing views: *The government muzzled the newspapers during the rebellion.* [< Old French *musel* < *muse* muzzle] —**muz′zler,** *n.*

na ï ve té or **na i ve te** (nä ē′və tā′), *n.* 1 quality of being naïve; unspoiled freshness; artlessness. 2 a naïve action, remark, etc.
nap py (nap′ē), *adj.,* **-pi er, -pi est.** having a nap; downy; shaggy.
nec tar (nek′tər), *n.* 1 (in Greek and Roman myths) the drink of the gods. 2 any delicious drink. 3 a sweet liquid found in many flowers. Bees gather nectar and make it into honey.
ne go ti ate (ni gō′shē āt), *v.,* **-at ed, -at ing.** —*v.i.* talk over and arrange terms; confer; consult: *The colonists negotiated for peace with the Indians.* —*v.t.* 1 arrange for: *They finally negotiated a peace treaty.* 2 INFORMAL. get past or over: *The car negotiated the sharp curve by slowing down.*
-ness, *suffix added to adjectives to form nouns.* 1 quality or condition of being____: *Preparedness = condition of being prepared.* 2 ____ action; ____ behavior: *Carefulness = careful action; careful behavior.* [Old English *-ness, -niss*]
neu ro sur geon (nú rō′sėr′jən), *n.* a doctor who specializes in neurosurgery.
neu ro sur ger y (nú rō′sėr′jər ē), *n.* surgery of the nervous system, especially of the brain.
no mad ic (nō mad′ik), *adj.* of nomads or their life; wandering; roving. —**no mad′i- cal ly,** *adv.*
non-, *prefix.* not; not a; opposite of; lack of; failure of: *Nonessential = not essential. Nonresident = not a resident. Nonconformity = lack of conformity.* [< Latin < *non* not]
non cha lant (non′shə lənt, non′shə länt′), *adj.* without enthusiasm; coolly unconcerned; indifferent: *It was hard to remain nonchalant during all the excitement.* [< French < *non-* not + *chaloir* care about] —**non′cha lant ly,** *adv.*
non com mit tal (non′kə mit′l), *adj.* not committing oneself; not saying yes or no: *"I will think it over" is a noncommittal answer.*
no ta ble (nō′tə bəl), *adj.* worthy of notice; striking; remarkable: *a notable event, a notable book.* —*n.* person who is notable.
no to ri ous (nō tôr′ē əs, nō tōr′ē əs), *adj.* 1 well-known, especially because of something bad; having a bad reputation: *a notorious gambler.* 2 well-known; celebrated: *a notorious court case.*

nov el (nov′əl), *adj.* of a new kind or nature; strange; new; unfamiliar: *a novel idea, a novel sensation.*
nu cle us (nü′klē əs, nyü′klē əs), *n., pl.* **-cle i** or **-cle us es.** 1 a central part or thing around which other parts or things are collected. 2 a beginning to which additions are to be made. 3 the central part of an atom, consisting of a proton or protons, neutrons, and other particles.
nug get (nug′it), *n.* 1 a valuable lump; lump: *nuggets of gold.* 2 anything valuable: *nuggets of wisdom.* [origin uncertain]
nymph (nimf), *n.* 1 (in Greek and Roman myths) one of the lesser goddesses of nature, who lived in seas, rivers, fountains, springs, hills, woods, or trees. 2 a beautiful or graceful young woman. 3 any of certain insects in the stage of development between the egg and the adult form.

o blique (ə blēk′; *military* ə blīk′), *adj., v.,* **o bliqued, o bliqu ing.** —*adj.* 1 neither perpendicular to nor parallel with a given line or surface; not straight up and down or straight across; slanting. 2 not straightforward; indirect: *She made an oblique reference to her illness, but did not mention it directly.* —*v.i., v.t.* have or take an oblique direction; slant. —**o blique′ly,** *adv.*
ob scure (əb skyúr′), *adj.,* **-scur er, -scur est,** *v.,* **-scured, -scur ing.** —*adj.* 1 not clearly expressed; hard to understand: *an obscure passage in a book.* 2 not expressing meaning clearly: *an obscure style of writing.* 3 not well known; attracting no notice: *an obscure little village, an obscure poet, an obscure position in the government.*
ob se qui ous (əb sē′kwē əs), *adj.* polite or obedient from hope of gain or from fear; servile; fawning: *Obsequious courtiers greeted the king.* —**ob se′qui ous ly,** *adv.*
ob sti na cy (ob′stə nə sē), *n., pl.* **-cies.** 1 a being obstinate; stubbornness. 2 an obstinate act.
ob struct (əb strukt′), *v.t.* 1 make hard to pass through; block or close up: *Fallen trees obstruct the road.* 2 be in the way of; block or close off: *Trees obstruct our view of the ocean.* 3 oppose the course of; hinder; impede: *obstruct justice.*
o gre (ō′gər), *n.* 1 (in folklore and fairy tales) a man-eating giant or monster. 2 man like such a monster in appearance or character.
oint ment (oint′mənt), *n.* substance made from oil or fat, often containing medicine, used on the skin to heal, soothe, or beautify.
o men (ō′mən), *n.* 1 sign of what is to happen; object or event that is believed to mean good or bad fortune; augury; presage: *Spilling salt is said to be an omen of misfortune.* 2 prophetic meaning; foreboding: *Some people consider a black cat a creature of ill omen.* —*v.t.* be a sign of; presage; forebode.
om i nous (om′ə nəs), *adj.* of bad omen; unfavorable; threatening: *ominous clouds.* —**om′i nous ly,** *adv.* —**om′i nous ness,** *n.*
on slaught (ôn′slôt′, on′slôt′), *n.* a vigorous attack: *The pirates made an onslaught on the ship.*
op por tun ist (op′ər tü′nist, op′ər tyü′nist), *n.* person who uses every opportunity to his advantage, regardless of right or wrong.
op pres sive (ə pres′iv), *adj.* 1 hard to bear; burdensome: *The intense heat was oppressive.* 2 harsh; unjust; tyrannical: *Oppres-*

sive measures were taken to crush the rebellion. —**op pres′sive ly,** *adv.*
o ra tor i cal (ôr′ə tôr′ə kəl, or′ə tor′ə kəl), *adj.* 1 of oratory; having to do with orators or oratory: *an oratorical contest.* 2 characteristic of orators or oratory: *He has an oratorical manner even in conversation.* —**or′a tor′i cal ly,** *adv.*
orb (ôrb), *n.* 1 anything round like a ball; sphere; globe. 2 sun, moon, planet, or star. 3 the eyeball or eye. 4 Also, **Orb.** globe surmounted by a cross, symbolizing royal sovereignty.
or bit (ôr′bit), *n.* the curved, usually elliptical path of a heavenly body, planet, or satellite about another body in space: *the earth's orbit about the sun, the moon's orbit about the earth, the orbit of a weather satellite about the earth.*
or ches trate (ôr′kə strāt), *v.t.,* **-trat ed, -trat ing.** compose or arrange (music) for performance by an orchestra. —**or′ches tra′tion,** *n.* —**or′ches tra′tor,** *n.* [< French < Latin < Greek *orchēstra* the place where the chorus of dancers performed < *orcheisthai* to dance]
or dain (ôr dān′), *v.t.* 1 establish as a law; order; fix; decide; appoint. 2 appoint or consecrate officially as a clergyman. 3 appoint as part of the order of the universe or of nature; destine.
or nate (ôr nāt′), *adj.* 1 much adorned; much ornamented. 2 characterized by the use of elaborate figures of speech, flowery language, etc. —**or nate′ly,** *adv.*
os ten ta tious (os′ten tā′shəs), *adj.* 1 done for display; intended to attract notice. 2 showing off; liking to attract notice. —**os′- ten ta′tious ly,** *adv.*
ost ler (os′lər), *n.* hostler.
-ous, *suffix forming adjectives from nouns.* 1 full of; having much; having: *Joyous = full of joy.* 2 characterized by: *Zealous = characterized by zeal.* 3 having the nature of: *Idolatrous = having the nature of an idolater.* 4 of or having to do with: *Monogamous = having to do with monogamy.* 5 like: *Thunderous = like thunder.* 6 committing or practicing: *Bigamous = practicing bigamy.* 7 inclined to: *Blasphemous = inclined to blasphemy.* 8 (in chemistry) indicating the presence in a compound of the designated element in a lower valence than indicated by the suffix *-ic,* as in *stannous, ferrous, sulfurous.* [< Old French *-os, -us* < Latin *-osum*]
out skirts (out′skėrts′), *n.pl.* the outer parts or edges of a town, district, etc., or of a subject of discussion; outlying parts.
o va tion (ō vā′shən), *n.* an enthusiastic public welcome; burst of loud clapping or cheering: *The President received a great ovation.*
o ver lap (v. ō′vər lap′; n. ō′vər lap′), *v.,* **-lapped, -lap ping,** *n.* —*v.t.* 1 lap over; cover and extend beyond: *Shingles are laid to overlap each other.* 2 coincide partly with. —*v.i.* overlap another thing or each other.

pag eant (paj′ənt), *n.* 1 an elaborate spectacle; procession in costume; pomp; display; show: *The coronation of a new ruler is always a splendid pageant.* 2 a public entertainment that represents scenes from history, legend, or the like.
pal at a ble (pal′ə tə bəl), *adj.* 1 agreeable to the taste; pleasing. 2 agreeable to the mind or feelings; acceptable.

pall (pôl), *n.* **1** a heavy, dark cloth, often made of velvet, spread over a coffin, a hearse, or a tomb. **2** a dark, gloomy covering: *A pall of smoke shut out the sun from the city.*

pal let (pal′it), *n.* bed of straw; small or poor bed. [< Old French *paillet* < *paille* straw < Latin *palea*]

pal pa ble (pal′pə bəl), *adj.* **1** readily seen or heard and recognized; obvious: *a palpable error.* **2** that can be touched or felt; tangible. [< Late Latin *palpabilis* < Latin *palpare* to feel, pat]

pal try (pôl′trē), *adj.*, **-tri er, -tri est.** **1** almost worthless; trifling; petty; mean. **2** of no worth; despicable; contemptible.

pan de mo ni um (pan′də mō′nē əm), *n.* **1** place of wild disorder or lawless confusion. **2** wild uproar or lawlessness. **3 Pandemonium, a** abode of all the demons; hell. **b** hell's capital. [< Greek *pan-* + *daimōn* demon]

par a pet (par′ə pet, par′ə pit), *n.* **1** a low wall or mound of stone, earth, etc., in front of a walk or platform at the top of a fort, trench, etc., to protect soldiers; rampart. **2** a low wall or barrier at the edge of a balcony, roof, bridge, etc.

par a pher nal ia (par′ə fər nā′lyə), *n., pl.* or *sing.* **1** personal belongings. **2** equipment; outfit.

par ent age (per′ən tij, par′ən tij), *n.* **1** descent from parents; family; ancestry. **2** parenthood.

par ox ysm (par′ək siz′əm), *n.* **1** a sudden, severe attack of the symptoms of a disease, usually recurring periodically: *a paroxysm of coughing.* **2** a sudden outburst of emotion or activity: *a paroxysm of rage.*

par ry (par′ē), *v.*, **-ried, -ry ing,** *n., pl.* **-ries.** —*v.t.* **1** ward off or block (a thrust, stroke, weapon, etc.) in fencing, boxing, etc. **2** meet and turn aside (an awkward question, a threat, etc.); avoid; evade.

par tridge (pär′trij), *n., pl.* **-tridg es** or **-tridge.** **1** any of several game birds of Europe, Asia, and Africa belonging to the same family as the quail and pheasant. **2** any of several similar birds of the United States, such as the ruffed grouse and the quail or bobwhite.

pas sive (pas′iv), *adj.* **1** being acted on without itself acting; not acting in return: *a passive mind, a passive disposition.* **2** not resisting; yielding or submitting to the will of another; submissive: *the passive obedience of a slave.* —**pas′sive ly,** *adv.*

pa ter nal (pə tèr′nl), *adj.* **1** of or like a father; fatherly. **2** related on the father's side of the family: *a paternal aunt, paternal grandparents.* [< Latin *paternus* < *pater* father] —**pa ter′nal ly,** *adv.*

pa tri arch (pā′trē ärk), *n.* **1** father and ruler of a family or tribe, especially one of the ancestral figures in the Bible, such as Abraham, Isaac, or Jacob. **2** person thought of as the father or founder of something. **3** a venerable old man, especially the elder of a village, community, etc. **4** bishop of the highest rank in the early Christian church, especially the bishop of Antioch, Alexandria, Rome, Constantinople, or Jerusalem. **5** bishop of the highest rank in the Eastern Church or the Roman Catholic Church. [< Latin *patriarcha* < Greek *patriarchēs* < *patria* family, clan + *archos* leader]

peak ed (pē′kid), *adj.* sickly in appearance; wan; thin. [< earlier *peak* look sick; origin uncertain]

ped i ment (ped′ə mənt), *n.* **1** the low trian-

gular part on the front of buildings in the Greek style. A pediment is like a gable. **2** any similar decorative part on a building, door, bookcase, etc.

peer less (pir′lis), *adj.* without an equal; matchless.

pend ing (pen′ding), *adj.* **1** waiting to be decided or settled: *while the agreement was pending.* **2** likely to happen soon; about to occur; threatening. —*prep.* **1** while waiting for; until: *Pending your return, we'll get everything ready.* **2** during.

pen non (pen′ən), *n.* **1** a long, narrow flag, triangular or swallow-tailed, originally carried on the lance of a knight. **2** any flag or banner. **3** pennant.

pent (pent), *adj.* closely confined; penned; shut: *pent in the house all winter.*

pent-up (pent′up′), *adj.* shut up; closely confined: *pent-up feelings.*

per ceive (pər sēv′), *v.t.,* **-ceived, -ceiving.** **1** be aware of through the senses; see, hear, taste, smell, or feel. **2** take in with the mind; observe; understand: *I soon perceived that I could not make him change his mind.*

per cep tion (pər sep′shən), *n.* **1** act of perceiving: *His perception of the change came in a flash.* **2** power of perceiving: *a keen perception.* **3** understanding that is the result of perceiving: *I now have a clear perception of what went wrong.*

pe remp tor y (pə remp′tər ē, per′əmp tôr′ē, per′əmp tōr′ē), *adj.* **1** leaving no choice; decisive; final; absolute: *a peremptory decree.* **2** allowing no denial or refusal: *a peremptory command.* **3** imperious; dictatorial: *a peremptory teacher.* [< Latin *peremptorius* that puts an end to, ultimately < *per-* to the end + *emere* to take] —**pe remp′tor i ly,** *adv.* —**pe remp′tor i ness,** *n.*

pe ren ni al (pə ren′ē əl), *adj.* **1** lasting through the whole year: *a perennial stream.* **2** lasting for a very long time; enduring: *the perennial beauty of the hills.* **3** (of a plant) lasting more than two years. —*n.* a perennial plant. [< Latin *perennis* < *per-* through + *annus* year] —**pe ren′ni al ly,** *adv.*

per me ate (pèr′mē āt), *v.t.,* **-at ed, -at ing.** **1** spread through the whole of; pass through; pervade: *Smoke permeated the house.* **2** penetrate through pores or openings; soak through: *Water will easily permeate a cotton dress.* [< Latin *permeatum* passed through < *per-* through + *meare* to pass] —**per′me a′tion,** *n.*

pe rox ide (pə rok′sīd), *v.,* **-id ed, -id ing.** —*v.t.* bleach (hair) by applying hydrogen peroxide.

per pen dic u lar (pèr′pən dik′yə lər), *adj.* **1** standing straight up; vertical; upright. **2** very steep; precipitous. **3** at right angles to a given line, plane, or surface. —**per′pen dic′u lar ly,** *adv.*

per pet u al (pər pech′ü əl), *adj.* **1** lasting forever; eternal: *the perpetual hills.* **2** lasting throughout life: *a perpetual income.* **3** never ceasing; continuous; constant: *a perpetual stream of visitors.* —**per pet′u al ly,** *adv.*

per sist ent (pər sis′tənt, pər zis′tənt), *adj.* **1** not giving up, especially in the face of dislike, disapproval, or difficulties; persisting; persevering: *a persistent worker, a persistent beggar.* **2** going on; continuing; lasting: *a persistent headache that lasted for three days.* —**per sist′ent ly,** *adv.*

per vade (pər vād′), *v.t.,* **-vad ed, -vad ing.** go or spread throughout; be throughout: *The odor of pines pervades the air.*

hat, āge, fär; let, ēqual, tèrm; it, īce; hot, ōpen, ôrder; oil, out; cup, pùt, rüle; ch, child; ng, long; sh, she; th, thin; ŦH, then; zh, measure;

ə represents *a* in about, *e* in taken, *i* in pencil, *o* in lemon, *u* in circus.

< = from, derived from, taken from.

pe so (pā′sō), *n., pl.* **-sos.** **1** the monetary unit in various countries of Latin America and in the Philippines, a coin or note usually equal to 100 centavos, its value varying from 8¹/₃ cents in Bolivia to one dollar in Cuba. **2** coin or piece of paper money worth one peso. **3** a former gold or silver coin used in Spain and in the Spanish colonies, worth eight reals.

pet ri fy (pet′rə fī), *v.,* **-fied, -fy ing.** —*v.t.* **1** turn into stone; change (plant or animal matter) into a substance like stone. **2** make hard as stone; stiffen; deaden. **3** paralyze with fear, horror, or surprise: *The bird was petrified as the snake came near.* —*v.i.* **1** become stone or a substance like stone. **2** become rigid like stone; harden.

pet u lant (pech′ə lənt), *adj.* likely to have little fits of bad temper; irritable over trifles; peevish. —**pet′u lant ly,** *adv.*

phan tom (fan′təm), *n.* **1** image of the mind which seems to be real: *phantoms of a dream.* **2** thought or apprehension of anything that haunts the imagination. **3** a vague, dim, or shadowy appearance; ghost; apparition. —*adj.* like a ghost; unreal: *a phantom ship.*

phase (fāz), *n., v.,* **phased, phas ing.** —*n.* **1** one of the changing states or stages of development of a person or thing. **2** one side, part, or view (of a subject): *What phase of mathematics are you studying now?*

phi los o phy (fə los′ə fē), *n., pl.* **-phies.** **1** study of the truth or principles underlying all real knowledge; study of the most general causes and principles of the universe. **2** explanation or theory of the universe, especially the particular explanation or system of a philosopher: *the philosophy of Plato.* **3** system for guiding life.

pho to stat (fō′tə stat), *n.* photograph made with a special camera for making photocopies directly on specially prepared paper. —*v.t.* make a photostat of.

pig ment (pig′mənt), *n.* **1** a coloring matter, especially a powder or some easily pulverized dry substance that constitutes a paint or dye when mixed with oil, water, or some other liquid. **2** the natural substance occurring in and coloring the tissues of an animal or plant. —*v.t.* color with or as if with pigment. [< Latin *pigmentum* < *pingere* to paint.]

pig nut (pig′nut′), *n.* **1** the thin-shelled, oily, somewhat bitter nut of any of several species of hickory grown in North America. **2** any of the trees that bear these nuts.

Pima (pē′mə), *n., pl.* **-mas.** a member of an Indian people living in the Gila and Salt river valleys of southern Arizona and northern Mexico.

pin na cle (pin′ə kəl), *n.* **1** a high peak or point of rock. **2** the highest point: *at the pinnacle of one's fame.* **3** a slender turret or spire.

579

pique (pēk), *n., v.,* **piqued, pi quing.** —*n.* a feeling of anger at being slighted; wounded pride: *In a pique, she left the party.* —*v.t.* 1 cause a feeling of anger in; wound the pride of: *It piqued her that they should have a secret she did not share.* 2 arouse; stir up: *Our curiosity was piqued by the locked trunk.* 3 **pique oneself on,** feel proud about. [< French < *piquer* to prick, sting]

pis ton (pis′tən), *n.* a short cylinder, or a flat, round piece of wood or metal, fitting closely inside a tube or hollow cylinder in which it is moved back and forth by the force of vapor combustion or steam. Pistons are used in pumps, engines, compressors, etc. [< French < Italian *pistone* < *pistare* to pound]

plac id (plas′id), *adj.* pleasantly calm or peaceful; quiet: *a placid lake, a placid temper.* [< Latin *placidus* < *placere* to please] —**plac′id ly,** *adv.*

plait (plāt, plat *for 1;* plāt, plēt *for 2*), *n., v.t.* 1 braid. 2 pleat.

plume (plüm), *n.* 1 a large, long feather; feather. 2 a feather, bunch of feathers, or tuft of hair worn as an ornament on a hat, helmet, etc. 3 something resembling a plume. 4 the hollow cylinder of spray thrown up by an underwater atomic explosion.

poetic justice, ideal justice, with virtue being suitably rewarded and vice properly punished, as shown often in poetry, drama, and fiction.

poign ant (poi′nyənt), *adj.* 1 very painful; piercing: *poignant suffering.* 2 stimulating to the mind, feelings, or passions; keen; intense: *a subject of poignant interest.* 3 sharp, pungent, or piquant to the taste or smell: *poignant sauces.* [< Old French, present participle of *poindre* to prick < Latin *pungere*] —**poign′ant ly,** *adv.*

poise (poiz), *n., v.,* **poised, pois ing.** —*n.* 1 mental balance, composure, or self-possession: *She has perfect poise and never seems embarrassed.* 2 the way in which the body, head, etc., are held; carriage. 3 state of balance; equilibrium. —*v.t.* 1 balance: *poise yourself on your toes.* 2 hold or carry evenly or steadily: *The waiter poised the tray on his hand.* —*v.i.* 1 be balanced or held in equilibrium. 2 hang supported or suspended.

pome gran ate (pom′gran′it, pom gran′it, pum′gran′it), *n.* a reddish-yellow fruit with a thick skin and many seeds, each enveloped in a juicy red pulp which has a pleasant, slightly sour taste.

pon der (pon′dər), *v.t.* consider carefully; think over.

pon toon (pon tün′), *n.* 1 a low, flat-bottomed boat. 2 such a boat, or some other floating structure, used as one of the supports of a temporary bridge.

po rous (pôr′əs, pōr′əs), *adj.* full of pores; permeable by water, air, etc.: *Cloth, blotting paper, and earthenware are porous.*

por tal (pôr′tl, pōr′tl), *n.* door, gate, or entrance, usually an imposing one.

por ter (pôr′tər, pōr′tər), *n.* 1 person employed to carry loads or baggage, especially at a hotel, railroad station, airport, etc. 2 attendant in a parlor car or sleeping car of a railroad train.

port ly (pôrt′lē, pōrt′lē), *adj.,* **-li er, -li est.** 1 having a large body; stout; corpulent. See synonym study below. 2 stately; dignified. [< *port*] —**port′li ness,** *n.*

Syn. *adj.* 1 **Fat, stout, portly** mean having too much flesh. **Fat** commonly applies to any degree from healthy, well-fed plumpness to ugly, unhealthy excess of weight: *The fat man had difficulty walking up the flight of stairs.* **Stout** emphasizes thickness and bulkiness, suggesting firm rather than flabby flesh, but is often used as a euphemism for "too fat": *She calls herself stylishly stout.* **Portly** suggests stately stoutness: *The retired admiral is a portly old gentleman.*

pos se (pos′ē), *n.* 1 group of men summoned by a sheriff to help him: *The posse pursued the thief.* 2 band, company, or assemblage: *a posse of spectators.*

post-, *prefix.* 1 after in time; later: *Postwar = after a war.* 2 after in space; behind: *Postnasal = behind the nasal cavity.*

pos ter i ty (po ster′ə tē), *n.* 1 generations of the future: *Posterity may travel to distant planets.* 2 all of a person's descendants.

po tent (pōt′nt), *adj.* having great power; powerful; strong: *a potent ruler, potent reasons, a potent remedy for a disease.*

pre-, *prefix.* 1 before in time, rank, etc.: *Precambrian = before the Cambrian.* 2 before in position, space, etc.; in front of: *Premolar = in front of the molars.* [< Latin *prae-, pre-*]

pre am ble (prē′am′bəl), *n.* 1 a preliminary statement; introduction to a speech or a writing. 2 a preliminary or introductory fact or circumstance, especially one showing what is to follow.

pre cau tion (pri kô′shən), *n.* 1 care taken beforehand; thing done beforehand to ward off evil or secure good results: *Locking doors is a precaution against thieves.* 2 a taking care beforehand; prudent foresight.

pre cau tion ar y (pri kô′shə ner′ē), *adj.* of or using precaution.

prec i pice (pres′ə pis), *n.* 1 a very steep or almost vertical face of a rock, etc.; cliff, crag, or steep mountainside. 2 situation of great peril; critical position.

pre cip i tate (*v.* pri sip′ə tāt; *adj., n.* pri sip′ə tit, pri sip′ə tāt), *v.,* **-tat ed, -tat ing,** *adj., n.* —*v.t.* 1 hasten the beginning of; bring about suddenly: *precipitate an argument.* 2 throw headlong; hurl: *precipitate a rock down a cliff, precipitate oneself into a struggle.* —*adj.* 1 very hurried; sudden: *A cool breeze caused a precipitate drop in the temperature.* 2 with great haste and force; plunging or rushing headlong; hasty; rash. —**pre cip′i tate ly,** *adv.*

pre cip i tous (pri sip′ə təs), *adj.* 1 like a precipice; very steep: *precipitous cliffs.* 2 hasty; rash. 3 rushing headlong; very rapid. —**pre cip′i tous ly,** *adv.* —**pre cip′i tous ness,** *n.*

pred e ces sor (pred′ə ses′ər), *n.* 1 person holding a position or office before another: *John Adams was Jefferson's predecessor as President.* 2 thing that came before another.

pre dom i nance (pri dom′ə nəns), *n.* a being predominant; prevalence.

pre em i nent or **pre-em i nent** (prē-em′ə nənt), *adj.* standing out above all others; superior to others. —**pre em′i nent ly, pre-em′i nent ly,** *adv.*

pre lim i nar y (pri lim′ə ner′ē), *adj., n., pl.* **-nar ies.** —*adj.* coming before the main business; leading to something more important: *After the preliminary exercises of prayer and song, the speaker of the day gave an address.* —*n.* 1 a preliminary step; something preparatory. 2 a preliminary examination.

pre ma ture (prē′mə chůr′, prē′mə tůr′, prē′mə tyůr′), *adj.* before the proper time; too soon. —**pre′ma ture′ly,** *adv.*

pre mo ni tion (prē′mə nish′ən, prem′ə-nish′ən), *n.* notification or warning of what is to come; forewarning: *a vague premonition of disaster.* [< Latin *praemonitionem < praemonere* warn beforehand < *prae-* pre- + *monere* warn]

pre par a to ry (pri par′ə tôr′ē, pri par′ə-tōr′ē), *adj.* 1 of or for preparation; making ready; preparing. 2 as an introduction; preliminary.

pre tense (prē′tens, pri tens′), *n.* 1 make-believe; pretending. 2 a false appearance: *Under pretense of picking up the handkerchief, she took the money.* 3 a false claim: *She made a pretense of being surprised but knew about the party all along.* 4 claim: *He makes no pretense to knowledge of electronics.* 5 a showing off; display; ostentation: *Her manner is free from pretense.* 6 anything done to show off. Also, **pretence.**

prim (prim), *adj.,* **prim mer, prim mest.** stiffly precise, neat, proper, or formal. [origin uncertain] —**prim′ly,** *adv.*

prim er (pri′mər), *n.* a first coat of paint or oil applied on a surface so that the finishing coat of paint will not soak in.

pro-¹, *prefix.* 1 forward, as in *project.* 2 forth; out, as in *prolong, prolapse.* 3 on the side of; in favor of, as in *pro-British.* 4 in place of; acting as, as in *pronoun, proconsul.* [< Latin, forward, forth, for]

pro-², *prefix.* 1 before; preceding; prior to, as in *prologue.* 2 in front of; anterior, as in *prothorax, proscenium.* [< Greek]

pro cliv i ty (prō kliv′ə tē), *n., pl.* **-ties.** tendency; inclination. [< Latin *proclivitatem < proclivis* sloping forward < *pro-* forward + *clivus* slope]

proc tor (prok′tər), *n.* official in a university or school designated to supervise students, especially during an examination.

pro cure (prə kyůr′), *v.t.,* **-cured, -cur ing.** 1 obtain by care or effort; secure: *procure a job.* 2 bring about; cause: *procure a person's death.*

pro duce (*n.* prod′üs, prod′yüs, prō′düs, prō′dyüs), —*n.* farm products, especially fruits and vegetables. [< Latin *producere < pro-* forth + *ducere* bring]

pro found (prə found′), *adj.* 1 very deep: *a profound sigh, a profound sleep.* 2 deeply felt; very great: *profound despair, profound sympathy.*

pro gres sive (prə gres′iv), *adj.* 1 making progress; advancing to something better; improving: *a progressive nation.* 2 favoring progress; wanting improvement or reform in government, business, etc. 3 moving forward; developing: *a progressive disease.* —**pro gres′sive ness,** *n.*

pro jec tion (prə jek′shən), *n.* 1 part that projects or sticks out: *rocky projections on the face of a cliff.* 2 a sticking out. 3 a throwing or casting forward: *the projection of a shell from a cannon.*

pro jec tive (prə jek′tiv), *adj.* 1 of, having to do with, or produced by projection. 2 projecting. [< Latin *projectum* thrown forward < *pro-* forward + *jacere* to throw] —**pro jec′tive ly,** *adv.*

prom i nent (prom′ə nənt), *adj.* 1 well-known or important; distinguished: *a prominent citizen.* 2 that catches the eye; easy to see: *A single tree in a field is prominent.* 3 standing out; projecting: *Some insects have prominent eyes.* [< Latin *prominentem* pro-

jecting < *pro-* forward + *minere* to jut]
—**prom′i nent ly,** *adv.*

proph e cy (prof′ə sē), *n., pl.* **-cies.** 1 a telling what will happen; foretelling future events. 2 thing told about the future. 3 a divinely inspired utterance, revelation, writing, etc.

proph e sy (prof′ə sī), *v.,* **-sied, -sy ing.** —*v.i.* 1 tell what will happen. 2 speak when or as if divinely inspired. —*v.t.* 1 foretell; predict: *The sailor prophesied a severe storm.* 2 utter in prophecy. —**proph′e si′er,** *n.*

pro por tion (prə pôr′shən, prə pōr′shən), *n.* 1 relation in magnitude; size, number, amount, or degree of one thing compared to another: *Each girl's pay will be in proportion to her work.* 2 a proper relation between parts: *His short legs were not in proportion to his long body.* 3 **proportions,** *pl.* **a** size; extent. **b** dimensions. 4 part; share: *A large proportion of Nevada is desert.*

prop o si tion (prop′ə zish′ən), *n.* 1 what is offered to be considered; proposal: *The tailor made a proposition to buy out his rival's business.* 2 statement. EXAMPLE: "All men are created equal." 3 statement that is to be proved true. EXAMPLE: Resolved: that our school should have a bank. 4 problem to be solved: *a proposition in geometry.* 5 INFORMAL. a business enterprise; an undertaking: *a paying proposition.*

pro pound (prə pound′), *v.t.* put forward; propose: *propound a theory, propound a riddle.*

pro sa ic (prō zā′ik), *adj.* like prose; matter-of-fact; ordinary; not exciting.

pros e cute (pros′ə kyüt), *v.,* **-cut ed, -cut ing.** —*v.t.* 1 bring before a court of law: *Reckless drivers will be prosecuted.* 2 carry out; follow up: *prosecute an inquiry into reasons for a company's failure.* —*v.i.* 1 bring a case before a court of law. 2 carry on (a business or occupation).

pro trude (prō trüd′), *v.,* **-trud ed, -trud-ing.** —*v.t.* thrust forth; stick out: *The saucy child protruded her tongue.* —*v.i.* be thrust forth; project: *Her teeth protrude too far.*

prov erb (prov′erb′), *n.* a short, wise saying used for a long time by many people; adage. EXAMPLE: "Haste makes waste."

prov i den tial (prov′ə den′shəl), *adj.* 1 happening by or as if by God's intervention; fortunate: *Our delay seemed providential, for the train we had planned to take was wrecked.* 2 of or proceeding from divine power or influence. —**prov′i den′tial ly,** *adv.*

prow (prou), *n.* 1 the front part of a ship or boat; bow. 2 the projecting front of anything: *the prow of an aircraft.*

psy cho ex per i men tal ist (sī′kō eks-per′ə men′tl ist), *n.* one who conducts tests or experiments which have to do with the mind or behavior.

psy chol o gy (sī kol′ə jē), *n., pl.* **-gies.** 1 science or study of the mind; branch of science dealing with the actions, feelings, thoughts, and other mental or behavioral processes of people and animals. 2 the mental states and processes of a person or persons; mental nature and behavior.

pueb lo (pweb′lō), *n., pl.* **-los.** 1 an Indian village consisting of houses built of adobe and stone, usually with flat roofs and often several stories high. 2 **Pueblo,** member of any of a group of Indian tribes in the southwestern United States and northern Mexico living in such villages. [< Spanish, people, community]

pul sate (pul′sāt), *v.t.,* **-sat ed, -sat ing.** 1 expand and contract rhythmically, as the heart or an artery; beat; throb. 2 vibrate; quiver.

pul sa tion (pul sā′shən), *n.* 1 a beating; throbbing. 2 a beat; throb. 3 vibration; quiver.

pum mel (pum′əl), *v.t., v.i.,* **-meled, -mel-ing** or **-melled, -mel ling.** strike or beat; beat with the fists. Also, **pommel.**

pun gent (pun′jənt), *adj.* 1 sharply affecting the organs of taste and smell: *a pungent pickle, the pungent smell of burning leaves.* 2 sharp; biting: *pungent criticism.* 3 stimulating to the mind; keen; lively: *a pungent wit.* [< Latin *pungentem* piercing, pricking < *punctum* point] —**pun′gent ly,** *adv.*

pur ga to ry (pèr′gə tôr′ē, pèr′gə tōr′ē), *n., pl.* **-ries.** 1 (in Roman Catholic belief) a temporary condition or place in which the souls of those who have died penitent are purified from venial sin or the effects of sin by punishment. 2 any condition or place of temporary suffering or punishment.

pyg my (pig′mē), *n., pl.* **-mies,** *adj.* —*n.* 1 **Pygmy,** one of a group of Negroid people of equatorial Africa who are less than five feet tall. 2 a very small person; dwarf. 3 any very small animal or thing. —*adj.* 1 of or having to do with the Pygmies. 2 very small: *a pygmy marmoset.* Also, **pigmy.**

quad rant (kwod′rənt), *n.* 1 quarter of the circumference of a circle; arc of 90 degrees. 2 the area contained by such an arc and two radii drawn perpendicular to each other. 3 thing or part shaped like a quarter circle. 4 instrument with a scale of 90 degrees, used in astronomy, surveying, and navigation for measuring altitudes. 5 (in geometry) one of the four parts into which a plane is divided by two straight lines crossing at right angles. The upper right-hand section is the first quadrant, and, in a counterclockwise direction, the others are the second, third, and fourth quadrants respectively. [< Latin *quadrantem* a fourth]

quay (kē), *n.* a solid landing place where ships load and unload, often built of stone.

queue (kyü), *n., v.,* **queued, queu ing.** —*n.* 1 braid of hair hanging down from the back of the head. 2 a line of people, automobiles, etc.: *There was a long queue in front of the theater.* —*v.i.* 1 form or stand in a long line. 2 **queue up,** line up. —*v.t.* arrange (persons) in a queue. Also, **cue.** —**queu′er,** *n.* [< French < Latin *coda, cauda* tail]

quick sand (kwik′sand′), *n.* a very deep, soft, wet sand, that will not support a person's weight. A quicksand may engulf people and animals.

quiv er (kwiv′ər), *n.* 1 case to hold arrows. 2 supply of arrows in such a case.

rab id (rab′id), *adj.* 1 unreasonably extreme; fanatical; violent: *The rebels are rabid idealists.* 2 furious; raging: *rabid with anger.* 3 having rabies; mad: *a rabid dog.* [< Latin *rabidus* < *rabere* be mad] —**rab′id ly,** *adv.*

ra di ant (rā′dē ənt), *adj.* 1 shining; bright; beaming: *a radiant smile.* 2 sending out rays of light or heat: *The sun is a radiant body.* 3 sent off in rays from some source; radiated: *radiant heat.* —**ra′di ant ly,** *adv.*

hat, āge, fär; let, ēqual, tèrm;
it, īce; hot, ōpen, ôrder;
oil, out; cup, pùt, rüle;
ch, child; ng, long; sh, she;
th, thin; ŦH, then; zh, measure;

ə represents *a* in about, *e* in taken,
i in pencil, *o* in lemon, *u* in circus.

< = from, derived from, taken from.

rad i cal (rad′ə kəl), *adj.* 1 going to the root; fundamental: *If she wants to reduce, she must make a radical change in her diet.* 2 favoring extreme changes or reforms; extreme.

ra di us (rā′dē əs), *n., pl.* **-di i** or **-di us es.** 1 any line segment going straight from the center to the outside of a circle or a sphere. Any spoke in a wheel is a radius. 2 a circular area measured by the length of its radius: *The explosion could be heard within a radius of ten miles.*

railroad bull, *n.* SLANG. a railroad policeman.

ral ly (ral′ē), *v.,* **-lied, -ly ing,** *n., pl.* **-lies.** —*v.t.* 1 bring together, especially to get in order again: *The commander was able to rally the fleeing troops.* 2 pull together; revive: *We rallied all our energy for one last effort.* —*v.i.* 1 come together in a body for a common purpose or action. 2 come to help a person, party, or cause: *She rallied to the side of her injured friend.*

ram bler (ram′blər), *n.* 1 person or thing that rambles. 2 any of various climbing roses having clusters of small red, yellow, or white flowers.

ram rod (ram′rod′), *n.* 1 rod for ramming down the charge in a gun that is loaded from the muzzle. 2 rod for cleaning the barrel of a gun. —*adj.* stiff; rigid; unbending.

ran dom (ran′dəm), *adj.* without a definite aim, plan, method, or purpose; by chance: *a random guess, random questions, pick a random number.* —*n.* 1 **at random,** by chance; with no aim, plan, or purpose. 2 a random course or movement. [< Old French *randon* impetuosity, rush] —**ran′dom ly,** *adv.*

rank (rangk), *adj.* 1 large and coarse: *rank grass.* 2 growing thickly in a coarse way: *a rank growth of weeds.* 3 producing a dense but coarse growth: *rank swampland.* 4 having a strong, bad smell or taste: *rank meat, rank tobacco.* 5 strongly marked; extreme: *rank ingratitude, rank nonsense.* 6 not decent; coarse; obscene. [Old English *ranc* proud] —**rank′ly,** *adv.* —**rank′ness,** *n.*

ra pi er (rā′pē ər), *n.* a long and light sword used for thrusting.

rapt (rapt), *adj.* 1 lost in delight. 2 so busy thinking of or enjoying one thing that one does not know what else is happening. 3 showing a rapt condition; caused by a rapt condition: *a rapt smile.*

rap ture (rap′chər), *n.* a strong feeling that absorbs the mind; ecstasy, especially of delight or joy.

rap tur ous (rap′chər əs), *adj.* full of rapture; expressing or feeling rapture. —**rap′tur ous ly,** *adv.*

rar e fy (rer′ə fī, rar′ə fī), *v.,* **-fied, -fy ing.** —*v.t.* 1 make less dense: *The air on high mountains is rarefied.* 2 refine; purify. —*v.i.* become less dense. Also, **rarify.**

rash (rash), *adj.* 1 too hasty and careless; impetuous. 2 characterized by undue haste:

raucous

a rash promise. [Middle English *rasch* quick] —**rash′ly,** *adv.* —**rash′ness,** *n.*

rau cous (rô′kəs), *adj.* hoarse; harsh-sounding: *the raucous caw of a crow.* [< Latin *raucus*] —**rau′cous ly,** *adv.*

ra vine (rə vēn′), *n.* a long, deep, narrow gorge eroded by running water.

rav ish (rav′ish), *v.t.* 1 fill with delight. 2 carry off by force.

razz (raz), SLANG. —*v.t.* 1 laugh at; tease. 2 express disapproval of; boo: *The angry crowd razzed the umpire.* —*n.* derision. [< *raspberry*]

re-, *prefix.* 1 again; anew; once more: *Reappear = appear again.* 2 back: *Repay = pay back.* Also, sometimes before vowels, **red-.** [< Latin]

➤ **re-.** Words formed with the prefix *re-* are sometimes hyphenated (1) when the word to which it is joined begins with *e*: *re-echo,* (2) when the form with hyphen can have a different meaning from the form without: *reform,* to make better—*re-form,* to shape again, and (3) (rarely) for emphasis, as in "now *re-seated* in fair comfort," or in informal or humorous compounds: *re-remarried.*

realm (relm), *n.* 1 kingdom. 2 region or sphere in which something rules or prevails.

re as sure (rē′ə shur′), *v.t.,* **-sured, -suring.** 1 restore to confidence: *The captain's confidence during the storm reassured the passengers.* 2 assure again or anew. 3 insure again. —**re′as sur′ing ly,** *adv.*

re coil (*v.* ri koil′; *n.* ri koil′, rē′koil), *v.i.* 1 draw back; shrink back: *Most people would recoil at seeing a snake in the path.* 2 spring back: *The gun recoiled after I fired.* 3 react: *Revenge often recoils on the avenger.*

re con nais sance (ri kon′ə səns), *n.* examination or survey, especially for military purposes. [< French]

rec on noi ter (rek′ə noi′tər, rē′kə noi′tər), *v.t.* approach and examine or observe in order to learn something; make a first survey of (the enemy, the enemy's strength or position, a region, etc.) in order to gain information for military purposes. —*v.i.* approach a place and make a first survey of it. [< French *reconnoître* < Old French *reconoistre* recognize. Doublet of RECOGNIZE.] —**rec′on noi′ter er,** *n.*

red o lent (red′l ənt), *adj.* 1 having a pleasant smell; fragrant; aromatic. 2 smelling strongly; giving off an odor: *a house redolent of fresh paint.* 3 suggesting thoughts or feelings; reminiscent: *"Ivanhoe" is a name redolent of romance.* [< Latin *redolentem* emitting scent < *re-* back + *olere* to smell] —**red′o lent ly,** *adv.*

reek (rēk), *n.* a strong, unpleasant smell; disagreeable fumes or odor. —*v.i.* 1 send out a strong, unpleasant smell. 2 be wet with sweat or blood. 3 be filled with something unpleasant or offensive: *a government reeking with corruption.* [Old English *rēc*]

reel (rēl), *v.i.* 1 sway, swing, or rock under a blow, shock, etc. 2 sway in standing or walking. 3 be in a whirl; be dizzy. 4 go with swaying or staggering movements. 5 become unsteady; give way; waver: *The regiment reeled under the sudden enemy attack.*

ref or ma tion (ref′ər mā′shən), *n.* 1 a reforming or a being reformed; change for the better; improvement.

re frain (ri frān′), *v.i.* hold oneself back, especially from satisfying a momentary impulse; abstain: *Refrain from talking in the library.*

ref uge (ref′yüj), *n.* 1 shelter or protection from danger, trouble, etc.; safety; security. 2 place of safety or security.

re gal (rē′gəl), *adj.* 1 belonging to a king; royal. 2 fit for a king; kinglike; stately; splendid; magnificent.

re gion al (rē′jə nəl), *adj.* 1 of or in a particular region: *a regional storm.* 2 of a particular part of the body: *a regional disorder.*

re gres sion (ri gresh′ən), *n.* 1 act of regressing. 2 (in psychology) reversion to an earlier stage or way of thinking, feeling, acting, etc. 3 (in biology) reversion to a less developed state or form or to an average type.

re it e rate (rē it′ə rāt′), *v.t.,* **-rat ed, -rating.** say or do several times; repeat (an action, demand, etc.) again and again: *The teacher reiterated her command.*

re lent less (ri lent′lis), *adj.* without pity; not relenting; unyielding. —**re lent′less ly,** *adv.*

rel ic (rel′ik), *n.* 1 thing, custom, etc., that remains from the past: *This ruined bridge is a relic of the Civil War.* 2 something belonging to a holy person, kept as a sacred memorial. 3 object having interest because of its age or its associations with the past; keepsake; souvenir. 4 **relics,** *pl.* remains; ruins.

re lief (ri lēf′), *n.* 1 help given to poor people, especially money or food. 2 **on relief,** receiving money to live on from public funds.

re luc tant (ri luk′tənt), *adj.* 1 showing unwillingness; unwilling. 2 slow to act because unwilling: *be reluctant to leave.* [< Latin *reluctantem* struggling against < *re-* back + *luctari* to struggle] —**re luc′tant ly,** *adv.*

re morse (ri môrs′), *n.* deep, painful regret for having done wrong; compunction; contrition: *The thief felt remorse for his crime and confessed.*

rend (rend), *v.t.,* **rent, rend ing.** 1 pull apart violently; tear: *Wolves will rend a lamb.* 2 split: *Lightning rent the tree.* 3 disturb violently: *a mind rent by doubt.* 4 remove with force or violence. [Old English *rendan*]

ren e gade (ren′ə gād), *n., adj., v.,* **-gad ed, -gad ing.** —*n.* deserter from a religious faith, a political party, etc.; traitor. —*adj.* like a traitor; deserting; disloyal. —*v.i.* turn renegade. [< Spanish *renegado* < *renegar* deny one's faith < Medieval Latin *renegare*.]

re nounce (ri nouns′), *v.t.,* **-nounced, -nounc ing.** 1 declare that one gives up; give up entirely; give up: *He renounces his claim to the money.* 2 cast off; refuse to recognize as one's own; repudiate; disown. [< Middle French *renoncer* < Latin *renuntiare* < *re-* back + *nuntius* message] —**re nounce′ment,** *n.*

re pose (ri pōz′), *n., v.,* **-posed, -pos ing.** —*n.* 1 rest or sleep: *Do not disturb her repose.* 2 quietness; ease: *She has repose of manner.* 3 peace; calmness. —*v.i.* 1 lie at rest: *The cat reposed upon the cushion.* 2 lie in a grave. 3 rest from work or toil; take a rest. 4 be supported. 5 depend; rely (on). —*v.t.* lay to rest.

rep re sent a tive (rep′ri zen′tə tiv), —*adj.* 1 having its citizens represented by chosen persons: *a representative government.* 2 representing: *Images representative of animals were made by the children.* 3 serving as an example of; typical: *Oak, birch, and maple are representative American hardwoods.*

rep ri mand (rep′rə mand), *n.* a severe or formal reproof. —*v.t.* reprove severely or formally; censure. [< French *réprimande* < Latin *reprimenda* to be repressed < *reprimere* < *re-* back + *premere* to press]

re served (ri zėrvd′), *adj.* 1 kept in reserve; kept by special arrangement: *a reserved seat.* 2 set apart: *a reserved section at the stadium.* 3 self-restrained in action or speech. 4 disposed to keep to oneself. —**re serv′ed ly,** *adv.*

res i dent (rez′ə dənt), *n.* 1 person living in a place permanently; dweller. 2 an official sent to live in a foreign land to represent his country.

res o lute (rez′ə lüt), *adj.* 1 having a fixed resolve; determined; firm. 2 constant in pursuing a purpose; bold.

re sort (ri zôrt′), *v.i.* 1 go or repair *(to),* especially habitually; go often: *Many people resort to the beaches in hot weather.* 2 have recourse *(to);* turn for help: *resort to violence.*

res pite (res′pit), *n., v.,* **-pit ed, -pit ing.** —*n.* 1 time of relief and rest; lull: *a respite from the heat.* 2 a putting off; delay, especially in carrying out a sentence of death; reprieve. —*v.t.* 1 give a respite to. 2 put off; postpone. [< Old French *respit* < Late Latin *respectus* expectation < Latin, regard.]

re sume (ri züm′), *v.,* **-sumed, -sum ing.** —*v.t.* 1 begin again; go on: *Resume reading where we left off.* 2 get or take again: *Those standing may resume their seats.* —*v.i.* begin again; continue.

re trac tive (ri trak′tiv), *adj.* tending to draw back or in.

re treat (ri trēt′), *v.i.* go back; move or draw back; withdraw: *The enemy retreated before the advance of our troops.* —*n.* 1 act of going back or withdrawing; withdrawal: *an orderly retreat.* 2 signal for retreat: *The drums beat a retreat.* 3 signal on a bugle or drum, given at sunset during the lowering of the flag. 4 a safe, quiet place; place of rest or refuge. 5 a retirement, or period of retirement, by a group of people for religious exercises, meditation, etc. 6 **beat a retreat,** run away; retreat.

ret ri bu tion (ret′rə byü′shən), *n.* a deserved punishment; return for evil done. [< Latin *retributionem,* ultimately < *re-* back + *tribuere* assign]

rev eil le (rev′ə lē), *n.* a signal on a bugle or drum to waken soldiers or sailors in the morning. [< French *réveillez(-vous)* awaken!]

rev el ry (rev′əl rē), *n., pl.* **-ries.** boisterous reveling or festivity.

re vere (ri vir′), *v.t.,* **-vered, -ver ing.** love and respect deeply; honor greatly; show reverence for.

rev er ie (rev′ər ē), *n.* 1 dreamy thoughts; dreamy thinking of pleasant things. 2 condition of being lost in dreamy thoughts. Also, **revery.** [< French *rêverie* < *rêver* to dream]

re viv al (ri vī′vəl), *n.* 1 a bringing or coming back to life or consciousness. 2 restoration to vigor or health. 3 a bringing or coming back to style, use, activity, etc.: *the revival of an old play.* 4 an awakening or increase of interest in religion. 5 special services or efforts made to awaken or increase interest in religion.

re voke (ri vōk′), *v.,* **-voked, -vok ing,** *n.* —*v.t.* take back; repeal; cancel; withdraw: *revoke a driver's license.*

rhap so dy (rap′sə dē), *n., pl.* **-dies.** 1 utterance or writing marked by extravagant enthusiasm: *go into rhapsodies over a gift.* 2 (in music) an instrumental composition, irregular in form, resembling an improvisation:

Liszt's Hungarian rhapsodies. 3 an epic poem, or a part of such a poem, suitable for recitation at one time.

rheu mat ic (ru mat′ik), *adj.* 1 of or having to do with rheumatism. 2 having or liable to have rheumatism. 3 causing rheumatism. 4 caused by rheumatism. —*n.* person who has rheumatism. —**rheu mat′i cal ly,** *adv.*

rime (rīm), *n., v.,* **rimed, rim ing.** —*n.* white frost; hoarfrost, especially from the freezing of vapor in drifting fog.

ring mas ter (ring′mas′tər), *n.* person in charge of the performances in the ring of a circus.

riv et (riv′it), *n.* a metal bolt having a head at one end, the other end being passed through holes in the things to be joined together and then hammered into another head. Rivets fasten heavy steel beams together. —*v.t.* 1 fasten with a rivet or rivets. 2 flatten (the end of a bolt) so as to form a head. 3 fasten firmly; fix firmly: *Their eyes were riveted on the speaker.* 4 command and hold (one's attention, interest, etc.)

ruck sack (ruk′sak′, rük′sak′), *n.* knapsack. [< German *Rucksack*]

ru in a tion (rü′ə nā′shən), *n.* ruin; destruction; downfall.

rur al (rür′əl), *adj.* in or of the country, as opposed to the city; belonging to or characteristic of the country or country life.

ruse (rüz, rüs), *n.* scheme or device to mislead others; trick.

sac ri le gious (sak′rə lij′əs, sak′rə lē′jəs), *adj.* injurious or insulting to sacred persons or things. —**sac′ri le′gious ly,** *adv.* —**sac′ri le′gious ness,** *n.*

sa dist (sā′dist, sad′ist), *n.* person who has an unnatural love of cruelty. [< French *sadisme* < Marquis de *Sade,* 1740-1814, who wrote about it]

safe ty (sāf′tē), *n.* a defensive back who usually lines up closest to his team's goal line.

sa gac i ty (sə gas′ə tē), *n.* keen, sound judgment; mental acuteness; shrewdness.

sa hib (sä′ib, sä′hib), *n.* sir; master. Natives in colonial India called a European "sahib" when speaking to or of him.

sal u tar y (sal′yə ter′ē), *adj.* 1 beneficial: *give someone salutary advice.* 2 good for the health; wholesome: *Walking is a salutary exercise.*

sal vage (sal′vij), *v.t.* save from fire, flood, shipwreck, etc. [< French, ultimately < Latin *salvus* safe] —**sal′vag er,** *n.*

sar cas tic (sär kas′tik), *adj.* using sarcasm; sneering; cutting: *"Don't hurry!" was his sarcastic comment as I began to dress at my usual slow rate.* —**sar cas′ti cal ly,** *adv.*

sat u rate (sach′ə rāt′), *v.t.,* **-rat ed, -rat ing.** 1 soak thoroughly; fill full: *During the fog, the air was saturated with moisture.* 2 cause (a substance) to unite with the greatest possible amount of another substance. A saturated solution of sugar or salt is one that cannot dissolve any more sugar or salt.

sa tyr (sā′tər, sat′ər), *n.* 1 (in Greek myths) a deity of the woods, part man and part goat or horse. The satyrs were merry, riotous followers of Bacchus, the god of wine. 2 man who is beastly in thought and action; lecherous man. 3 any of a family of brown or grayish butterflies having eyespots on the wings.

saun ter (sôn′tər, sän′tər), *v.i.* walk along slowly and happily; stroll: *saunter in the park.*

scab bard (skab′ərd), *n.* sheath or case for the blade of a sword, dagger, etc.

scan (skan), *v.t.* 1 look at closely; examine with care: *His mother scanned his face to see if he was telling the truth.* 2 glance at; look over hastily.

scant ling (skant′ling), *n.* 1 a small beam or piece of timber, often used as an upright piece in the frame of a building. 2 small beams or timbers collectively.

scoff (skôf, skof), *v.i.* make fun to show one does not believe something; mock. —*v.t.* jeer at; deride. —*n.* 1 mocking words or acts. 2 something ridiculed or mocked. [< Scandinavian (Danish) *skuffe* deceive] —**scoff′er,** *n.* —**scoff′ing ly,** *adv.*

score (skôr, skōr), *n., v.,* **scored, scor ing.** —*n.* 1 the record of points made in a game, contest, test, etc.: *keep score. The score was 9 to 2.* 2 amount owed; debt; account: *He paid his score at the inn.* 3 ARCHAIC. record of this kept by notches or marks. 4 twenty: *A score or more were present at the party.* 5 **scores,** *pl.* a large number; great numbers: *Scores died in the epidemic.* 6 a written or printed piece of music arranged for different instruments or voices: *the score of an opera.* 7 cut; scratch; stroke; mark; line: *The carpenter used a nail to make a score on the board.* 8 reason; ground: *Don't worry on that score.*

scorn ful (skôrn′fəl), *adj.* showing contempt; full of scorn; mocking. —**scorn′ful ly,** *adv.* —**scorn′ful ness,** *n.*

scru ti ny (skrüt′n ē), *n., pl.* **-nies.** 1 close examination; careful inspection: *His work looks all right, but it will not bear scrutiny.* 2 a looking searchingly at something; searching gaze.

scut tle (skut′l), *n., v.,* **-tled, -tling.** —*n.* 1 an opening in the deck or side of a ship, with a lid or cover. 2 an opening in a wall or roof, with a lid or cover. 3 the lid or cover for any such opening. —*v.t.* 1 cut a hole or holes through the bottom or sides of (a ship) to sink it. 2 cut a hole or holes in the deck of (a ship) to salvage the cargo.

scythe (sīᴛн), *n., v.,* **scythed, scyth ing.** —*n.* a long, thin, slightly curved blade on a long handle, for cutting grass, etc. —*v.t.* cut or mow with a scythe. [Old English *sithe;* spelling influenced by Latin *scindere* to cut]

sed i men tar y (sed′ə men′tər ē), *adj.* 1 of or having to do with sediment. 2 (in geology) formed by the depositing of sediment. Shale is a sedimentary rock.

seethe (sēᴛн), *v.,* **seethed, seeth ing.** —*v.i.* 1 be excited; be disturbed: *seethe with discontent.* 2 bubble and foam: *Water seethed under the falls.* 3 ARCHAIC. boil. —*v.t.* 1 soak; steep. 2 boil. [Old English *sēothan*]

se man tic (sə man′tik), *adj.* 1 having to do with the meaning of words. 2 having to do with semantics.

sem blance (sem′bləns), *n.* 1 outward appearance: *Their story had the semblance of truth, but was really false.* 2 likeness: *These clouds have the semblance of a huge head.* [< Old French < *sembler* seem < Latin *similare* make similar < *similis* similar]

semi-, *prefix.* 1 half: *Semicircle = half circle.* 2 partly; incompletely: *Semicivilized = partly civilized.* 3 twice. Semi____ly means in each half of a ____, or twice in a ____: *Semiannually = every half year, or twice a year.* [< Latin]

➤ Words starting with **semi-** are not usually hyphenated except before proper names *(semi-Christian)* or words beginning with *i (semi-invalid).*

hat, āge, fär; let, ēqual, tèrm;
it, īce; hot, ōpen, ôrder;
oil, out; cup, pùt, rüle;
ch, child; ng, long; sh, she;
th, thin; ᴛн, then; zh, measure;

ə represents *a* in about, *e* in taken,
i in pencil, *o* in lemon, *u* in circus.

< = from, derived from, taken from.

semi bar bar ic (sem′i bär bar′ik), *adj.* not completely barbaric; partly civilized.

se nil i ty (sə nil′ə tē), *n.* 1 old age. 2 the mental and physical deterioration often characteristic of old age.

sen ti nel (sen′tə nəl), *n.* person stationed to keep watch and guard against surprise attacks.

se rene (sə rēn′), *adj.* 1 peaceful; calm: *a serene smile.* 2 not cloudy; clear; bright: *a serene sky.*

set tee (se tē′), *n.* sofa or long bench with a back and, usually, arms.

sev er (sev′ər), *v.t.* 1 cut apart; cut off: *sever a rope.* 2 break off: *The two countries severed friendly relations.* —*v.i.* part; divide; separate: *The rope severed and the swing fell down.* [< Old French *sevrer,* ultimately < Latin *separare* to separate]

se ver i ty (sə ver′ə tē), *n., pl.* **-ties.** 1 strictness; sternness; harshness. 2 sharpness or violence: *the severity of a storm, the severity of grief.* 3 simplicity of style or taste; plainness. 4 seriousness. 5 accuracy; exactness.

sheaf (shēf), *n., pl.* **sheaves.** 1 one of the bundles in which grain is bound after reaping. 2 bundle of things of the same sort bound together or so arranged that they can be bound together: *a sheaf of arrows, a sheaf of papers.* [Old English *scēaf*]

shear (shir), *v.,* **sheared, sheared** or **shorn, shear ing.** —*v.t.* 1 cut with shears or scissors: *shear wool from sheep.* 2 cut the wool or fleece from: *The farmer sheared his sheep.* 3 cut close; cut off; cut. 4 break by a force causing two parts or pieces to slide on each other in opposite directions: *Too much pressure on the handles of the scissors sheared off the rivet holding the blades together.* 5 strip or deprive as if by cutting: *The assembly had been shorn of its legislative powers.* —*v.i.* break by shearing force: *Several bolts sheared, causing the floor to sag dangerously.*

sheath (shēth), *n., pl.* **sheaths** (shēᴛнz, shēths). 1 case or covering for the blade of a sword, knife, etc. 2 any similar covering, especially on an animal or plant. 3 a narrow, tight-fitting dress with straight lines.

sheath ing (shē′ᴛнing, shē′thing), *n.* casing; covering. The first covering of boards on a house is sheathing.

shin gle (shing′gəl), *n., v.,* **-gled, -gling.** —*n.* a woman's short haircut in which the hair is made to taper from the back of the head to the nape of the neck. —*v.t.* cut (the hair) in a shingle.

shorn (shôrn, shōrn), *v.* a pp. of **shear.**

shrew (shrü), *n.* a bad-tempered, quarrelsome woman.

shrewd (shrüd), *adj.* 1 having a sharp mind; showing a keen wit; clever. 2 keen; sharp. 3 mean; mischievous: *a shrewd turn.* [earlier *shrewed* bad-tempered, shrewish; wicked <

583

shroud

shrew] —**shrewd′ly**, *adv.* —**shrewd′-
ness**, *n.*
shroud (shroud), *v.t.* 1 wrap or dress for
burial. 2 cover; conceal; veil: *Their plans are
shrouded in secrecy.* [Old English *scrūd*]
shut tle (shut′l), *n., v.,* **-tled, -tling.** —*n.*
1 device that carries the thread from one side
of the web to the other in weaving. 2 a
similar device on which thread is wound,
used in knitting, tatting, and embroidery.
—*v.i., v.t.* move quickly to and fro.
shy (shī), *v. i.* **shied, shy ing.** 1 start back
or aside suddenly: *The horse shied at the
newspaper blowing along the ground.* 2 draw
back; shrink.
si dle (sī′dl), *v.,* **-dled, -dling,** *n.* —*v.i.*
1 move sideways. 2 move sideways slowly
so as not to attract attention: *The little boy
shyly sidled up to the visitor.* —*n.* movement
sideways. [< *sideling,* variant of *sidelong*]
sig ni fy (sig′nə fī), *v.,* **-fied, -fy ing.** —*v.t.*
1 be a sign of; mean: *"Oh!" signifies surprise.*
2 make known by signs, words, or actions:
signify consent with a nod. —*v.i.* have importance; be of consequence; matter.
sil hou ette (sil′ü et′), *n., v.,* **-et ted, -et
ting.** —*n.* 1 an outline portrait, especially in
profile, cut out of a black paper or drawn and
filled in with some single color. 2 a dark
image outlined against a lighter background.
3 contour of a garment, figure, etc. —*v.t.*
show in outline: *The mountain was silhouetted against the sky.*
si mon ize (sī′mə nīz), *v.t.* polish to a high
shine, especially with wax. [< Simoniz (originally a trademark)]
si mul ta ne ous (sī′məl tā′nē əs, sim′əl-
tā′nē əs), *adj.* 1 existing, done, or happening
at the same time: *The two simultaneous shots
sounded like one.* 2 indicating two or more
equations or inequalities, with two or more
unknowns, for which a set of values of the
unknowns is sought that is a solution of all
the equations or inequalities. [< Medieval
Latin *simultaneus* simulated < Latin *similis*
like; confused in sense with Latin *simul* at
the same time] —**si′mul ta′ne ous ly,** *adv.*
—**si′mul ta′ne ous ness,** *n.*
sin is ter (sin′ə stər), *adj.* 1 showing ill will;
threatening: *a sinister rumor, a sinister look.*
2 bad; evil; dishonest. 3 disastrous; unfortunate. 4 on the left; left. 5 (in heraldry)
situated on that part of an escutcheon to the
left of the bearer. [< Latin, left; the left side
being considered unlucky] —**sin′is ter ly,**
adv. —**sin′is ter ness,** *n.*
sire (sīr), *n., v.,* **sired, sir ing.** —*n.* 1 a male
ancestor. 2 male parent; father: *Lightning
was the sire of the racehorse Danger.* 3 title
of respect used formerly to a great noble and
now to a king. —*v.t.* be the father of.
skein (skān), *n.* 1 a small, coiled bundle of
yarn or thread. There are 120 yards in a skein
of cotton yarn. 2 a confused tangle.
skull cap (skul′kap′), *n.* a close-fitting cap
without a brim.
sky light (skī′līt′), *n.* window in a roof or
ceiling.
slan der (slan′dər), *n.* 1 a false statement
spoken with intent to harm the reputation of
another. 2 the spreading of false reports.
—*v.t.* talk falsely about. —*v.i.* speak or
spread slander.
slath er (slaᴛH′ər), INFORMAL. —*n.* **slath-
ers,** *pl.* a large amount. —*v.t.* spread or pour
lavishly. [origin unknown]

slav er (slav′ər), *v.i.* let saliva run from the
mouth; drool. —*v.t.* wet with saliva; slobber.
—*n.* saliva running from the mouth.
smirk (smėrk), *v.i.* smile in an affected, silly,
or self-satisfied way; simper. —*n.* an affected, silly, or self-satisfied smile.
smite (smīt), *v.,* **smote, smit ten** or **smit,
smit ing.** —*v.t.* 1 give a hard blow to (a
person, etc.) with the hand, a stick, or the
like; strike. 2 give or strike (a blow, stroke,
etc.). 3 strike with a weapon, etc., so as to
cause serious injury or death. 4 attack with a
sudden pain, disease, etc.: *a city smitten with
pestilence. His conscience smote him.*
5 impress suddenly with a strong feeling,
sentiment, etc.: *smitten with curiosity.*
6 punish severely; chasten. —*v.i.* 1 deliver a
blow or blows, a stroke, etc., with or as with a
stick, weapon, etc.; strike. 2 come with force
(upon): *The sound of a blacksmith's hammer
smote upon their ears.*
snick er (snik′ər), *n.* a half-suppressed and
usually disrespectful laugh; sly or silly laugh;
giggle. —*v.i.* laugh in this way. Also, **snig-
ger.** [imitative]
snig ger (snig′ər), *n., v.i.* snicker.
snip er (snī′pər), *n.* a hidden sharpshooter.
snuff (snuf), *v.t.* 1 draw in through the nose;
draw up into the nose. 2 smell at; examine by
smelling: *The dog snuffed the track of the fox.*
—*v.i.* 1 draw air, etc., up or in through the
nose. 2 sniff, especially curiously as a dog
would. 3 take powdered tobacco into the
nose by snuffing; use snuff. —*n.* 1 powdered
tobacco, often scented, taken into the nose.
2 act of snuffing.
so ber (sō′bər), *adj.* 1 not drunk.
2 temperate; moderate: *The Puritans led sober, hard-working lives.* 3 quiet; serious;
solemn: *a sober expression.* 4 calm; sensible:
*a sober opinion not influenced by prejudice or
strong feeling.* 5 free from exaggeration or
distortion: *sober facts.* 6 quiet in color:
dressed in sober gray. —*v.t., v.i.* make or
become sober.
so cial ism (sō′shə liz′əm), *n.* 1 theory or
system of social organization by which the
major means of production and distribution
are owned, managed, or controlled by the
government, by associations of workers, or
by the community as a whole. 2 a political
movement advocating or associated with this
system.
so ci ol o gy (sō′sē ol′ə jē), *n.* study of the
nature, origin, and development of human
society and community life; science of social
facts. Sociology deals with the facts of crime,
poverty, marriage, the church, etc.
sod (sod), *n., v.,* **sod ded, sod ding.** —*n.*
1 ground covered with grass. 2 piece or layer
of this containing the grass and its roots.
—*v.t.* cover with sods.
sol emn (sol′əm), *adj.* 1 of a serious, grave,
or earnest character: *a solemn face.*
2 causing serious or grave thoughts: *The
organ played solemn music.* 3 done with
form and ceremony: *a solemn procession.*
4 connected with religion; sacred. 5 gloomy;
dark; somber in color. —**sol′emn ly,** *adv.*
sol em nize (sol′əm nīz), *v.t.,* **-nized, -niz
ing.** 1 observe with ceremonies: *Christian
churches solemnize the resurrection of Christ
at Easter.* 2 hold or perform (a ceremony or
service): *The marriage was solemnized in the
cathedral.*
so lic it (sə lis′it), *v.t.* 1 ask earnestly; try to
get: *The tailor sent around cards soliciting
trade.* 2 influence to do wrong; tempt; entice:
To solicit a judge means to offer him bribes.

—*v.i.* 1 make appeals or requests: *solicit for
contributions to the Red Cross.* 2 accost a
person with immoral offers.
sol i tar y (sol′ə ter′ē), *adj., n., pl.* **-tar ies.**
1 alone or single; only: *A solitary rider
was seen in the distance.* 2 without companions; away from people; lonely: *lead a solitary life. The house is in a solitary spot miles
from a town.* 3 (in zoology) living alone,
rather than in colonies: *a solitary bee.* 4 (in
botany) growing separately; not forming
clusters. —*n.* person living alone, away from
people. —**sol′i tar′i ly,** *adv.*
som ber or **som bre** (som′bər), *adj.*
1 having deep shadows; dark; gloomy: *A
cloudy winter day is somber.* 2 melancholy;
dismal: *His losses made him very somber.*
som no lent (som′nə lənt), *adj.* 1 sleepy;
drowsy. 2 tending to produce sleep.
[< Latin *somnolentus* < *somnus* sleep]
—**som′no lent ly,** *adv.*
sor cer er (sôr′sər ər), *n.* person who practices magic with the supposed aid of evil
spirits.
sour dough (sour′dō′), *n.* INFORMAL.
1 prospector or pioneer in Alaska or northwestern Canada. 2 any old resident, experienced hand, etc.
spar (spär), *v.,* **sparred, spar ring,** *n.* —*v.i.*
1 make motions of attack and defense with
the arms and fists; box. 2 dispute. 3 (of
roosters) fight with the feet or spurs. —*n.* 1 a
boxing match. 2 a sparring motion.
sparse (spärs), *adj.,* **spars er, spars est.**
1 occurring here and there; thinly scattered:
a sparse population, sparse hair. 2 scanty;
meager. [< Latin *sparsum* scattered]
—**sparse′ly,** *adv.* —**sparse′ness,** *n.*
spasm (spaz′əm), *n.* 1 a sudden, abnormal,
involuntary contraction of a muscle or muscles. 2 any sudden, brief fit or spell of
unusual energy or activity.
spas mod ic (spaz mod′ik), *adj.* 1 having to
do with, like, or characterized by a spasm or
spasms: *a spasmodic cough.* 2 occurring
very irregularly; intermittent: *a spasmodic
interest in reading.* 3 having or showing
bursts of excitement. —**spas mod′i cal ly,**
adv.
spec ter (spek′tər), *n.* 1 phantom or ghost,
especially one of a terrifying nature or appearance. 2 thing causing terror or dread.
Also, **spectre.**
spec tre (spek′tər), *n.* specter.
spec u la tion (spek′yə lā′shən), *n.*
1 careful thought; reflection. 2 a guessing;
conjecture. 3 a buying or selling when there
is a large risk, with the hope of making a
profit from future price changes.
spec u la tive (spek′yə lā′tiv, spek′yə lə-
tiv), *adj.* 1 carefully thoughtful; reflective.
2 theoretical rather than practical. 3 risky.
4 of or involving buying or selling at a large
risk. —**spec′u la′tive ly,** *adv.*
spit tle (spit′l), *n.* saliva; spit.
splat (splat), *n.* a splash or spot of something
spattered: *His face was freckled with splats of
yellow paint.*
spright ly (sprīt′lē), *adj.,* **-li er, -li est,** *adv.*
—*adj.* lively; gay. —*adv.* in a sprightly
manner. Also, **spritely.**
sprint (sprint), *v.i.* run at full speed, especially for a short distance. —*n.* a race or any
short spell of running, rowing, etc., at top
speed. —**sprint′er,** *n.*
spur (spėr), *n., v.,* **spurred, spur ring.** —*n.*
a pricking instrument consisting of a small
spike or spiked wheel, worn on a horseman's
heel for urging a horse on. —*v.t.* 1 prick with

584

spurs: *The rider spurred his horse on.* 2 urge on; incite: *Pride spurred the boy to fight.* —*v.i.* ride quickly.

spurn (spėrn), *v.t.* 1 refuse with scorn; scorn: *spurn a bribe, spurn an offer of friendship.* 2 strike with the foot; kick away. —*v.i.* oppose with scorn: *spurn at restraint.*

squan der (skwon′dər), *v.t.* spend foolishly; waste: *squander one's money in gambling.*

sta ple (stā′pəl), *adj.* 1 most important; principal: *The weather was their staple subject of conversation.* 2 established in commerce: *a staple trade.* 3 regularly produced in large quantities for the market. —*v.t.* sort according to fiber: *staple wool.*

stat ic (stat′ik), *adj.* 1 in a fixed or stable condition; not in a state of progress or change; at rest; standing still: *Civilization does not remain static, but changes constantly.* 2 having to do with stationary electrical charges. Static electricity can be produced by rubbing a glass rod with a silk cloth. —*n.* 1 electrical disturbances in the air, caused by electrical storms, etc. 2 interference, especially with radio signals, caused by such disturbances. [< Greek *statikos* causing to stand, ultimately < *histanai* cause to stand]

sta tus (stā′təs, stat′əs), *n.* 1 social or professional standing; position; rank: *lose status. What is her status in the government?* 2 state; condition: *Diplomats are interested in the status of world affairs.*

stealth y (stel′thē), *adj.,* **stealth i er, stealth i est.** done in a secret manner; secret; sly: *The cat crept in a stealthy way toward the bird.*

ster e op ti con (ster′ē op′tə kən, stir′ē-op′tə kən), *n.* projector arranged to combine two images on a screen so that they gradually become one image with three-dimensional effect.

sti fle (stī′fəl), *v.,* **-fled, -fling.** —*v.t.* 1 stop the breath of; smother: *The smoke stifled the firemen.* 2 keep back; suppress; stop: *stifle a cry, stifle a yawn, stifle business activity, stifle a rebellion.* —*v.i.* 1 be unable to breathe freely: *I am stifling in this hot room.* 2 die or become unconscious by being unable to breathe.

stoke (stōk), *v.,* **stoked, stok ing.** —*v.t.* 1 poke, stir up, and feed (a fire). 2 tend the fire of (a furnace or boiler). —*v.i.* tend a fire.

stout ly (stout′lē), *adv.* bravely, stubbornly.

stran gu la tion (strang′gyə lā′shən), *n.* 1 a strangling or strangulating. 2 a being strangled or strangulated.

strat e gy (strat′ə jē), *n., pl.* **-gies.** 1 science or art of war; the planning and directing of military movements and operations. 2 the skillful planning and management of anything. 3 plan based on strategy.

stren u ous (stren′yü əs), *adj.* 1 very active: *We had a strenuous day moving into our new house.* 2 full of energy: *a strenuous worker.* 3 requiring much energy: *strenuous exercise.*

stu di ous (stü′dē əs, styü′dē əs), *adj.* 1 fond of study. 2 showing careful consideration; careful; thoughtful; zealous: *The clerk made a studious effort to please customers.* —**stu′di ous ly,** *adv.* —**stu′di ous ness,** *n.*

stul ti fy (stul′tə fī), *v.t.,* **-fied, -fy ing.** 1 make futile; frustrate: *stultify a person's efforts.* 2 cause to appear foolish or absurd; reduce to foolishness or absurdity.

stun (stun), *v.,* **stunned, stun ning,** *n.* —*v.t.* 1 make senseless; knock unconscious: *I was stunned by the fall.* 2 daze; bewilder; shock; overwhelm: *She was stunned by the*

news *of her friend's death.* —*n.* 1 act of stunning. 2 condition of being stunned.

stunt (stunt), *v.t.* check in growth or development: *Lack of proper food stunts a child.* —*n.* 1 a stunting. 2 a stunted animal or plant. [earlier sense "to confound" < Middle English and Old English *stunt* foolish]

stu pe fy (stü′pə fī, styü′pə fī), *v.t.,* **-fied, -fy ing.** 1 make stupid, dull, or senseless. 2 overwhelm with shock or amazement; astound: *They were stupefied by the calamity.*

stu por (stü′pər, styü′pər), *n.* 1 a dazed condition; loss or lessening of the power to feel: *He lay in a stupor, unable to tell what had happened to him.* 2 intellectual or moral numbness. [< Latin < *stupere* be dazed]

suave (swäv), *adj.* smoothly agreeable or polite. —**suave′ly,** *adv.*

sub-, *prefix.* 1 under; below: *Subnormal = below normal.* 2 down; further; again: *Subdivide = divide again.* 3 near; nearly: *Subtropical = nearly tropical.* 4 lower; subordinate: *Subcommittee = a lower or subordinate committee.* 5 resulting from further division: *Subsection = section resulting from further division of something.* 6 slightly; somewhat: *Subacid = slightly acid.* [< Latin *sub* under, beneath]

sub con scious (sub kon′shəs), *adj.* not wholly conscious; existing in the mind but not fully perceived or recognized: *a subconscious fear.* —*n.* thoughts, feelings, etc., that are present in the mind but not fully perceived or recognized. —**sub con′scious ly,** *adv.*

sub due (səb dü′, səb dyü′), *v.t.,* **-dued, -du ing.** 1 overcome by superior force; conquer: *The Spaniards subdued the Indian tribes in Mexico.* 2 keep down; hold back; suppress: *We subdued a desire to laugh.* 3 tone down; soften: *Pulling down the shades subdued the light in the room.*

sub ju gate (sub′jə gāt), *v.t.,* **-gat ed, -gat ing.** 1 subdue; conquer. 2 bring under complete control; make subservient or submissive. [< Latin *subjugatum* brought under the yoke < *sub-* under + *jugum* yoke] —**sub′ju ga′tion,** *n.* —**sub′ju ga′tor,** *n.*

sub mis sion (səb mish′ən), *n.* 1 a yielding to the power, control, or authority of another; submitting: *The defeated general showed his submission by giving up his sword.* 2 obedience; humbleness: *They bowed in submission to the queen's order.* 3 a referring or a being referred to the consideration or judgment of some person or group. [< Latin *submissionem* < *submittere.*]

sub or di nate (*adj., n.* sə bôrd′n it; *v.* sə-bôrd′n āt), *adj., n., v.,* **-nat ed, -nat ing.** —*adj.* 1 lower in rank: *In the army, lieutenants are subordinate to captains.* 2 lower in importance; secondary. 3 under the control or influence of something else; dependent. 4 (in grammar) subordinating. *Because, since, if, as,* and *whether* are subordinate conjunctions. —*n.* a subordinate person or thing. —*v.t.* make subordinate: *A polite host subordinates his wishes to those of his guests.* —**sub or′di nate ly,** *adv.* —**sub or′di nate ness,** *n.*

sub side (səb sīd′), *v.i.,* **-sid ed, -sid ing.** 1 grow less; die down; become less active; abate: *The storm finally subsided.* 2 sink to a lower level: *After the rain stopped, the flood waters subsided.* 3 sink or fall to the bottom.

suf fuse (sə fyüz′), *v.t.,* **-fused, -fus ing.** overspread (with a liquid, dye, etc.): *eyes suffused with tears. At twilight the sky was suffused with color.*

hat, āge, fär; let, ēqual, tėrm;
it, īce; hot, ōpen, ôrder;
oil, out; cup, pụt, rüle;
ch, child; ng, long; sh, she;
th, thin; ᴛʜ, then; zh, measure;

ə represents *a* in about, *e* in taken,
i in pencil, *o* in lemon, *u* in circus.

< = from, derived from, taken from.

sul phur (sul′fər), *n.* 1 sulfur. 2 any of several kinds of yellow or orange butterflies. 3 a greenish yellow. —*adj.* greenish-yellow.

sump tu ous (sump′chü əs), *adj.* lavish and costly; magnificent; rich: *a sumptuous banquet.*

super-, *prefix.* 1 over; above: *Superimpose = impose over or above.* 2 besides; further: *Superadd = add besides or further.* 3 in high proportion; to excess; exceedingly: *Superabundant = abundant to excess.* 4 surpassing: *Supernatural = surpassing the natural.* [< Latin *super* over, above]

su perb (sụ pėrb′), *adj.* 1 grand and stately; majestic: *Mountain scenery is superb.* 2 rich; elegant: *a superb dinner.* 3 very fine; first-rate; excellent: *a superb performance.* —**su perb′ly,** *adv.* —**su perb′ness,** *n.*

su per cil i ous (sü′pər sil′ē əs), *adj.* haughty, proud, and contemptuous; disdainful; showing scorn or indifference because of a feeling of superiority: *a supercilious stare.* [< Latin *superciliosus* < *supercilium* eyebrow, pride < *super-* above + *-cilium* (< *celare* to cover, conceal)] —**su′per cil′i ous ly,** *adv.* —**su′per cil′i ous ness,** *n.*

su per fi cial (sü′pər fish′əl), *adj.* 1 of the surface: *superficial measurement.* 2 on the surface; at the surface: *His burns were superficial and soon healed.* 3 concerned with or understanding only what is on the surface; not thorough; shallow: *superficial education, superficial knowledge.* 4 not real or genuine: *superficial friendship.* [< Latin *superficialis* < *superficies* surface < *super-* above + *facies* form] —**su′per fi′cial ly,** *adv.*

su per hu man (sü′pər hyü′mən), *adj.* 1 above or beyond what is human: *Angels are superhuman beings.* 2 above or beyond ordinary human power, experience, etc.: *With a superhuman effort, the high jumper soared to a new Olympic record.*

su per nat ur al (sü′pər nach′ər əl), *adj.* above or beyond what is natural: *Angels and devils are supernatural beings.* —**su′per nat′ur al ly,** *adv.*

su per phos phate (sü′pər fos′fāt), *n.* any of various fertilizing materials composed chiefly of soluble phosphates.

su per sede (sü′pər sēd′), *v.t.,* **-sed ed, -sed ing.** 1 take the place of; cause to be set aside; displace: *Electric lights have superseded gaslights in most homes.* 2 succeed and supplant; replace: *A new governor superseded the old one.* [< Latin *supersedere* be superior to, refrain from < *super-* above + *sedere* sit] —**su′per sed′er,** *n.*

su per son ic (sü′pər son′ik), *adj.* 1 of or having to do with sound waves beyond the limit of human audibility (above frequencies of 20,000 cycles per second); ultrasonic. 2 greater than the speed of sound in air (1087 feet per second). 3 capable of moving at a speed greater than the speed of sound: *super-*

supplement

sonic aircraft. —su′per son′i cal ly, adv.

sup ple ment (n. sup′lə mənt; v. sup′lə ment), n. 1 something added to complete a thing, or to make it larger or better, especially a part added to a literary work or any written account or document. 2 something added to supply a deficiency: a diet supplement. 3 amount needed to make an angle or arc equal 180 degrees. —v.t. supply something additional to.

sup po si tion (sup′ə zish′ən), n. 1 act of supposing. 2 thing supposed; belief; opinion.

surge (sėrj), v., **surged, surg ing,** n. —v.i. 1 rise and fall; move like waves: A great wave surged over us. The crowd surged through the streets. 2 rise or swell (up) violently or excitedly, as feelings, thoughts, etc. —n. 1 a swelling wave; sweep or rush of waves. 2 something like a wave: A surge of anger swept over him.

sur mise (v. sər mīz′; n. sər mīz′, sėr′mīz), v., **-mised, -mis ing,** n. —v.t., v.i. infer or guess: We surmised that the delay was caused by some accident. —n. formation of an idea with little or no evidence; a guessing: His guilt was a matter of surmise; there was no proof.

sur pass (sər pas′), v.t. 1 do better than; be greater than; excel: Her work surpassed expectations. 2 be too much or too great for; go beyond; exceed: The horrors of the battlefield surpassed description. —sur pass′a ble, adj. —sur pass′ing ly, adv.

sur plus (sėr′pləs, sėr′plus), n. 1 amount over and above what is needed; extra quantity left over; excess. 2 excess of assets over liabilities. —adj. more than is needed; extra; excess: Surplus wheat and cotton are shipped abroad. [< Old French surplus < sur- over + plus more]

sur rep ti tious (sėr′əp tish′əs), adj. 1 stealthy; secret: a surreptitious glance. 2 secret and unauthorized; clandestine: surreptitious meetings. —sur′rep ti′tious ly, adv. —sur′rep ti′tious ness, n.

sur vey (sər vā′), v.t. 1 look over; view; examine: survey the situation. 2 measure for size, shape, position, boundaries, etc.: Men are surveying the land before it is divided into house lots. —v.i. survey land.

sus pend (sə spend′), v.t. 1 hang down by attaching to something above: The lamp was suspended from the ceiling. 2 hold in place as if by hanging: We saw the smoke suspended in the still air. 3 stop for a while: suspend work. 4 remove or exclude for a while from some privilege or job: suspend a student for infraction of rules. 5 defer temporarily (a law, punishment, etc.). 6 keep undecided; put off: The court suspended judgment till next Monday. —v.i. 1 come to a stop for a time. 2 stop payment; be unable to pay debts or claims.

sus te nance (sus′tə nəns), n. 1 food or provisions; nourishment: The lost campers went without sustenance for two days. 2 means of living; support: give money for the sustenance of the poor.

swaddling clothes, 1 long, narrow strips of cloth for wrapping a newborn infant. 2 long clothes for an infant.

swag ger (swag′ər), v.i. 1 walk with a bold, rude, or superior air; strut about or show off in a vain or insolent way: The bully swaggered into the schoolyard. 2 talk boastfully and loudly; brag noisily. 3 bluster; bluff.

—v.t. affect by bluster. —n. act of swaggering; a swaggering way of walking, acting, speaking, etc. —swag′ger ing ly, adv.

swiv el (swiv′əl), n., v., **-eled, -el ing** or **-elled, -el ling.** —n. 1 a fastening that allows the thing fastened to turn round freely upon it. 2 a chain link having two parts, one of which turns freely in the other. 3 support on which a gun, chair, etc., can turn round. —v.i., v.t. 1 turn on a swivel. 2 swing around; rotate.

swoon (swün), v.i. 1 faint: swoon at the sight of blood. 2 fade or die away gradually. —n. a faint.

syl van (sil′vən), adj. of, in, or having woods: They lived in a sylvan retreat. Also, **silvan.**

sym met ri cal (si met′rə kəl), adj. having a regular, balanced arrangement on opposite sides of a line or plane, or around a center or axis.

syn drome (sin′drōm), n. group of signs and symptoms considered together as characteristic of a particular disease.

tab u late (tab′yə lāt), v.t., v.i. arrange (facts, figures, etc.) in tables or lists.

tac i turn (tas′ə tėrn′), adj. speaking very little; not fond of talking. [< Latin taciturnus < tacitum unspoken, tacit]

tact ful (takt′fəl), adj. 1 having tact; diplomatic. 2 showing tact. —tact′ful ly, adv. —tact′ful ness, n.

taint (tānt), n. 1 a stain or spot; trace of decay, corruption, or disgrace. 2 a cause of any such condition; contaminating or corrupting influence. —v.t. give a taint to; spoil, corrupt, or contaminate. —v.i. become tainted; decay.

tam a rack (tam′ə rak′), n. 1 a North American larch tree which yields strong, heavy timber; hackmatack. 2 its wood.

tan gi ble (tan′jə bəl), adj. 1 that can be touched or felt by touch: A chair is a tangible object. 2 real; actual; definite: a tangible improvement, tangible evidence. 3 whose value can be accurately appraised: Real estate is tangible property.

tar nish (tär′nish), v.t. 1 dull the luster or brightness of: The salt tarnished the silver saltcellar. 2 bring disgrace upon (a reputation, one's honor, etc.); sully; taint. —v.i. lose luster or brightness: The brass doorknobs tarnished.

taut (tôt), adj. 1 tightly drawn; tense: a taut rope. 2 in neat condition; tidy: a taut ship. —taut′ly, adv.

taw ny (tô′nē), adj., **-ni er, -ni est,** n., pl. **-nies.** —adj. brownish-yellow: A lion has a tawny coat. —n. a brownish yellow. —taw′ni ness, n.

tem per a men tal (tem′pər ə men′tl), adj. 1 subject to moods and whims; easily irritated; sensitive: a temperamental actor. 2 showing a strongly marked individual temperament. —tem′per a men′tal ly, adv.

tend er (ten′dər), n. 1 person or thing that tends another. 2 boat or small ship used for carrying supplies and passengers to and from larger ships. 3 a small boat carried on or towed behind a larger boat or a ship for similar use. 4 the car that carries coal and water, attached behind a steam locomotive.

ten der foot (ten′dər füt′), n., pl. **-foots** or **-feet.** INFORMAL. 1 newcomer to the pioneer life of the western United States. 2 person not used to rough living and hard-

ships. 3 an inexperienced person; beginner.

ten dril (ten′drəl), n. 1 a threadlike part of a climbing plant that attaches itself to something and helps support the plant. 2 something similar: curly tendrils of hair.

Ter ti ar y (tėr′shē er′ē, tėr′shər ē), n., pl. **-ar ies,** adj. —n. 1 the earlier of the two periods making up the Cenozoic era. During this period the great mountain systems, such as the Alps, Himalayas, Rocky Mountains, and Andes, appeared, and rapid development of mammals occurred. 2 rocks formed in this period. —adj. 1 of or having to do with the Tertiary or its rocks.

tête-à-tête (tāt′ə tāt′), adv. two together in private: They dined tête-à-tête. —adj. of or for two people in private. —n. 1 a private conversation between two people. 2 an S-shaped seat built so that two people can sit facing one another. [< French, head to head]

thatch (thach), n. 1 straw, rushes, palm leaves, etc., used as a roof or covering. 2 roof or covering of thatch. —v.t. roof or cover with or as with thatch. [Old English thæc]

this tle (this′əl), n. any of various composite plants with prickly stalks and leaves and usually with purple flowers.

thresh old (thresh′ōld, thresh′hōld), n. 1 piece of wood or stone across the bottom of a door frame; doorsill. 2 doorway. 3 point of entering; beginning point: The scientist was on the threshold of an important discovery.

throng (thrông, throng), v.t. crowd; fill with a crowd: The people thronged the theater to see the new movie. —v.i. come together in a crowd; go or press in large numbers.

throt tle (throt′l), —v.t. 1 stop the breath of by pressure on the throat; choke; strangle. 2 check or stop the flow of; suppress: High tariffs throttle trade. 3 check, stop, or regulate the flow of (fuel) to an engine. —v.i. be choked; strangle. [Middle English throtel < throte throat]

ti tan ic (tī tan′ik), adj. 1 having great size, strength, or power; gigantic; colossal; huge: titanic energy. 2 **Titanic,** of or like the Titans.

to ken (tō′kən), n. 1 mark or sign: Black dress is a token of mourning. His actions are a token of his sincerity. 2 sign of friendship; keepsake: a parting token, birthday tokens. 3 piece of metal, somewhat like a coin, stamped for a higher value than the metal is worth and used for some special purpose, as bus or subway fares.

top o graph i cal (top′ə graf′ə kəl), adj. of or having to do with the surface features of a place or region, including hills, valleys, streams, lakes, bridges, tunnels, roads, etc.

tor rent (tôr′ənt, tor′ənt), n. 1 a violent, rushing stream of water. 2 a heavy downpour: The rain came down in torrents. 3 any violent, rushing stream; flood.

tor til la (tôr tē′yə), n. a thin, flat, round cake made of corn meal, commonly eaten in Spanish America.

tran quil li ty or **tran quil i ty** (trang-kwil′ə tē), n. tranquil condition; calmness; peacefulness; quiet.

trans-, prefix. 1 across; over; through, as in transcontinental, transmit. 2 on the other side of; beyond, as in transatlantic. 3 to a different place, condition, etc., as in transmigration, transform. 4 (in chemistry) having certain atoms on the opposite side of a plane: a trans-isomeric compound. [< Latin trans across]

trans fix (tran sfiks′), v.t. 1 pierce through:

586

The hunter transfixed the lion with a spear.
2 fasten or fix by piercing through with something pointed; impale. 3 make motionless or helpless (with amazement, terror, grief, etc.).

trans fu sion (tran sfyü′zhən), *n.* transfer of blood from one person or animal to another.

trans port (tran spôrt′, tran spōrt′), *n.* 1 a carrying from one place to another: *Trucks are much used for transport.* 2 ship used to carry soldiers, supplies, equipment, etc. 3 aircraft that transports passengers, mail, freight, etc. [< Latin *transportare* < *trans-* across + *portare* carry]

trans pose (tran spōz′), *v.t.*, **-posed, -posing.** 1 change the position or order of; interchange: *Transpose the two colors to get a better design.* 2 change the usual order of (letters, words, or numbers): *I transposed the numbers and mistakenly wrote 19 for 91.* 3 (in music) change the key of.

trav erse (trav′ərs, trə vèrs′), *v.* 1 pass across, over, or through: *We traversed the desert.* 2 walk or move in a crosswise direction; move back and forth: *That horse traverses.* 3 go to and fro over or along (a place, etc.). 4 move sideways; turn from side to side.

treach er ous (trech′ər əs), *adj.* not to be trusted; not faithful; disloyal: *The treacherous soldier carried reports to the enemy.* **—treach′er ous ly,** *adv.*

treach er y (trech′ər ē), *n., pl.* **-er ies.** a breaking of faith; treacherous behavior; deceit.

trem or (trem′ər), *n.* 1 an involuntary shaking or trembling: *a nervous tremor in the voice.* 2 a shaking or vibrating movement. An earthquake is sometimes called an earth tremor.

tress (tres), *n.* 1 a lock, curl, or braid of hair. 2 **tresses,** *pl.* long, flowing hair of a woman.

tri bu nal (tri byü′nl, trī byü′nl), *n.* 1 court of justice; place of judgment. 2 place where judges sit in a court of law.

trib ute (trib′yüt), *n.* 1 money paid by one nation or ruler to another for peace or protection, in acknowledgment of submission, or because of some agreement. 2 any forced payment.

tri dent (trīd′nt), *n.* a three-pronged spear. **—adj.** three-pronged. [< Latin *tridentem* < *tri-* three + *dentem* tooth]

tri fle (trī′fəl), *n., v.,* **-fled, -fling.** **—n.** 1 thing having little value or importance. 2 a small amount; little bit: *I was a trifle late.* 3 a small amount of money: *buy something for a trifle.* **—v.i.** 1 talk or act lightly, not seriously: *Don't trifle with serious matters.*

trill (tril), *v.t., v.i.* sing, play, sound, or speak with a tremulous, vibrating sound. **—n.** act or sound of trilling.

tri reme (trī′rēm′), *n.* (in ancient Greece and Rome) a warship, usually a warship, with three rows of oars on each side, one above the other. [< Latin *triremis* < *tri-* three + *remus* oar]

trite (trīt), *adj.,* **trit er, trit est.** worn out by use; no longer new or interesting; commonplace; hackneyed: *"Cheeks like roses" is a trite expression.*

truce (trüs), *n.* 1 a stop in fighting; temporary peace: *A truce was declared between the two armies.*

tu mult (tü′mult, tyü′mult), *n.* 1 noise or uproar; commotion: *the tumult of the storm.* 2 a violent disturbance or disorder: *The cry of "Fire!" caused a tumult in the theater.*

ul cer (ul′sər), *n.* 1 an open sore on the skin, or within the body, on a mucous membrane. It sometimes discharges pus. 2 a moral sore spot; corrupting influence. [< Latin *ulceris*]

um ber (um′bər), *n.* 1 any of various mixtures of clay and iron oxide. In its natural state it is a brown pigment called **raw umber.** After heating it becomes dark reddish brown and is called **burnt umber.** 2 a brown or dark reddish brown. **—adj.** brown or dark reddish-brown.

un-1, *prefix.* not ___; the opposite of ___: *Unequal = not equal; the opposite of equal. Unchanged = not changed. Unjust = not just.* [Old English]

un-2, *prefix.* do the opposite of ___; do what will reverse the act: *Unfasten = do the opposite of fasten. Uncover = do the opposite of cover.* [Old English *un-, on-*]

un a bashed (un′ə basht′), *adj.* not embarrassed, ashamed, or awed. **—un′a bash′ed ly,** *adv.*

un au thor ized (un ô′thə rizd), *adj.* not authorized; done without permission.

un bri dled (un brī′dld), *adj.* 1 not having a bridle on. 2 not controlled; not restrained.

un com pro mis ing (un kom′prə mī′zing), *adj.* unyielding; firm.

un der class man (un′dər klas′mən), *n., pl.* **-men.** freshman or sophomore.

un der priv i leged (un′dər priv′ə lijd), *adj.* having fewer advantages than most people have, especially because of poor economic or social status.

un der state ment (un′dər stāt′mənt), *n.* statement that expresses a fact too weakly or less emphatically than it should. Understatement is often used for humorous effect.

un doubt ed ly (un dou′tid lē), *adv.* beyond doubt; certainly.

un du la tion (un′jə lā′shən, un′dyə lā′shən), *n.* 1 a waving motion. 2 wavy form. 3 one of a series of wavelike bends, curves, swellings, etc. 4 a sound wave. 5 vibration.

un hewn (un hyün′), *adj.* uncut.

u ni son (yü′nə sən, yü′nə zən), *n.* harmonious combination or union; agreement: *The feet of marching soldiers move in unison. They spoke in unison.*

un nerve (un nèrv′), *v.t.,* **-nerved, -nerving.** deprive of firmness or self-control.

un rul y (un rü′lē), *adj.* hard to rule or control; not manageable; disorderly: *an unruly horse, an unruly child.* **—un rul′i ness,** *n.*

un shack le (un shak′əl), *v.t.,* **-led, -ling.** remove shackles from; set free.

un sur passed (un′sər past′), *adj.* not surpassed or exceeded, particularly in excellence.

un tram meled or **un tram melled** (un tram′əld), *adj.* not hindered; not restrained; free.

un wont ed (un wun′tid, un wōn′tid), *adj.* 1 not customary; not usual: *unwonted anger.* 2 not accustomed; not used.

up right (up′rīt′, up rīt′), *adj.* good; honest; righteous. **—up′right′ly,** *adv.* **—up′right′ness,** *n.*

va cate (vā′kāt), *v.* go away from and leave empty or unoccupied; make vacant: *They will vacate the house at the end of the month.*

vac u ous (vak′yü əs), *adj.* 1 showing no thought or intelligence; foolish; stupid: *a vacuous smile.* 2 having no meaning or direction; idle; indolent: *a vacuous life.* 3 empty.

hat, āge, fär; let, ēqual, tèrm;
it, īce; hot, ōpen, ôrder;
oil, out; cup, pút, rüle;
ch, child; ng, long; sh, she;
th, thin; ŦH, then; zh, measure;

ə represents *a* in about, *e* in taken,
i in pencil, *o* in lemon, *u* in circus.

< = from, derived from, taken from.

[< Latin *vacuus*] **—vac′u ous ly,** *adv.* **—vac′u ous ness,** *n.*

vague (vāg), *adj.,* **va guer, va guest.** 1 not definitely or precisely expressed: *a vague statement.* 2 indefinite; indistinct: *a vague feeling.* 3 indistinctly seen or perceived; obscure; hazy: *In a fog everything looks vague.* 4 lacking clarity or precision: *a vague personality.* **—vague′ly,** *adv.* **—vague′ness,** *n.*

var i cose (var′ə kōs), *adj.* 1 abnormally swollen or enlarged: *legs covered with varicose veins.* 2 having to do with, afflicted with, or designed to remedy varicose veins.

vault (vôlt), *n.* an underground cellar or storehouse.

veer (vir), *v.i.* change in direction; shift; turn: *The wind veered to the south. The talk veered to ghosts.* **—v.t.** change the direction of: *We veered our boat.*

ve he ment (vē′ə mənt), *adj.* 1 having or showing strong feeling; caused by strong feeling; eager; passionate. 2 forceful; violent. [< Latin *vehementem* being carried away < *vehere* carry] **—ve′he ment ly,** *adv.*

ven er a ble (ven′ər ə bəl), *adj.* worthy of reverence; deserving respect because of age, character, or importance: *a venerable priest, venerable customs.* **—ven′er a bly,** *adv.*

ven i son (ven′ə sən, ven′ə zən), *n.* the flesh of a deer, used for food; deer meat.

verge (vèrj), *n., v.,* **verged, verg ing.** **—n.** 1 the point at which something begins or happens; brink: *business on the verge of ruin.* 2 a limiting edge, margin, or bound of something; border: *the verge of a cliff.* **—v.i.** be on the verge; border: *Their silly talk verged on nonsense.*

ver i fy (ver′ə fī), *v.t.,* **-fied, -fy ing.** 1 prove to be true; confirm: *The driver's report of the accident was verified by eyewitnesses.* 2 test the correctness of; check for accuracy: *You can verify the spelling of a word by looking in a dictionary.* [< Old French *verifier* < Medieval Latin *verificare* < Latin *verus* true + *facere* to make] **—ver′i fi′er,** *n.*

ver mil ion (vər mil′yən), *n.* 1 a bright red. 2 a bright-red coloring matter. **—adj.** bright-red. [< Old French *vermillon* < *vermeil.*]

ver ti cal (vèr′tə kəl), *adj.* straight up and down; perpendicular to a level surface; upright. A person standing up straight is in a vertical position.

vex (veks), *v.t.* 1 anger by trifles; annoy; provoke. 2 worry; trouble; harass. 3 disturb by commotion; agitate: *The island was much vexed by storms.* [< Latin *vexare*]

vir ile (vir′əl), *adj.* 1 of, belonging to, or characteristic of a man; manly; masculine. 2 full of manly strength or masculine vigor. 3 vigorous; forceful.

vise (vīs), *n.* tool having two jaws opened and closed by a screw, used to hold an object firmly while work is being done on it. Also, **vice.** [< Old French *vis* screw < Latin *vitis* tendril of a vine]

587

vol un tar i ly (vol′ən ter′ə lē, vol′ən ter′ə lē), *adv.* of one's own free will; without force or compulsion.

vo lup tu ous (və lup′chü əs), *adj.* 1 caring much for the pleasures of the senses. 2 giving pleasure to the senses: *voluptuous music, voluptuous beauty.* —**vo lup′ tu ous ly,** *adv.* —**vo lup′tu ous ness,** *n.*

voo doo (vü′dü), *n., pl.* **-doos.** religion that came from Africa, made up of mysterious rites and practices that include the use of sorcery, magic, and conjuration. Belief in voodoo still prevails in many parts of the West Indies and some parts of the southern United States. [< Creole; of African origin]

vouch safe (vouch sāf′), *v.t.,* **-safed, -saf ing.** be willing to grant or give; deign (to do or give): *The proud man vouchsafed no reply when we spoke to him.*

vul ner a ble (vul′nər ə bəl), *adj.* 1 that can be wounded or injured; open to attack: *Achilles was vulnerable only in his heel.* 2 sensitive to criticism, temptations, influences, etc.: *Most people are vulnerable to ridicule.* [< Late Latin *vulnerabilis* < Latin *vulnerare* to wound < *vulnus* wound]

wab ble (wôb′əl), *v.i., v.t.,* **-bled, -bling,** *n.* wobble. —**wab′bler,** *n.*

waft (waft), *v.t.* carry over water or through air: *The waves wafted the boat to shore.* —*v.i.* float. —*n.* 1 a breath or puff of air, wind, scent, etc. 2 a waving movement; wave. 3 act of wafting. [< earlier *wafter* convoy ship < Dutch and Low German *wachter* guard] —**waft′er,** *n.*

wane (wān), *v.,* **waned, wan ing,** *n.* —*v.i.* 1 lose size; become smaller gradually: *The moon wanes after it has become full.* 2 decline in power, influence, or importance: *Many great empires have waned.* 3 decline in strength or intensity: *The light of day wanes in the evening.* 4 draw to a close: *Summer wanes as autumn approaches.* —*n.* 1 act or process of waning. 2 **on the wane,** growing less; waning. [Old English *wanian*]

war i ly (wer′ə lē, war′ə lē), *adv.* in a wary manner; cautiously; carefully.

wast rel (wā′strəl), *n.* 1 waster; spendthrift. 2 an idle, disreputable person; good-for-nothing.

wa ver (wā′vər), *v.i.* 1 move to and fro; flutter: *a wavering voice.* 2 vary in intensity; flicker: *a wavering light.* 3 be undecided; hesitate: *My choice wavered between the blue sweater and the green one.* 4 become unsteady; begin to give way: *The battle line wavered and broke.* —*n.* act of wavering. —**wa′ver er,** *n.* —**wa′ver ing ly,** *adv.*

wel ter (wel′tər), *n.* 1 a rolling or tumbling about. 2 a surging or confused mass. 3 confusion; commotion. [< Middle Dutch and Middle Low German *welteren*]

wel ter weight (wel′tər wāt′), *n.* boxer who weighs more than 135 pounds and less than 147 pounds.

wend (wend), *v.,* **wend ed** or **went, wending.** —*v.t.* 1 direct (one's way): *We wended our way home.* —*v.i.* go.

white wash (hwīt′wosh′, hwīt′wôsh′), *n.* 1 liquid for whitening walls, woodwork, etc., usually made of lime and water. 2 a covering up of faults or mistakes. —*v.t.* 1 whiten with whitewash. 2 cover up the faults or mistakes of. —**white′wash′er,** *n.*

wick et (wik′it), *n.* 1 a small door or gate: *The big door has a wicket in it.* 2 a small window or opening, often having a grate or grill over it: *Buy your tickets at this wicket.* [< Anglo-French *wiket,* ultimately < Scandinavian (Old Icelandic) *vikja* a move, turn]

wick i up (wik′ē up′), *n.* an Indian hut made of brushwood or covered with mats, formerly used by nomadic tribes in the western and southwestern United States. [of Algonquian origin]

wield (wēld), *v.t.* hold and use; manage; control: *wield a hammer. A writer wields the pen. The people wield the power in a democracy.* [Old English *wieldan*] —**wield′er,** *n.*

wil ful (wil′fəl), *adj.* willful. —**wil′ful ly,** *adv.* —**wil′ful ness,** *n.*

will ful (wil′fəl), *adj.* 1 wanting or taking one's own way; stubborn. 2 done on purpose; intended: *willful murder, willful waste.* —**will′ful ly,** *adv.* —**will′ful ness,** *n.*

wince (wins), *v.,* **winced, winc ing,** *n.* —*v.i.* draw back suddenly; flinch slightly: *I winced when the dentist's drill touched my tooth.* —*n.* act of wincing. [< variant of Old French *guencir;* of Germanic origin]

wind fall (wind′fôl′), *n.* 1 fruit, tree, etc., blown down by the wind. 2 an unexpected advantage, piece of good luck, etc.

wi no (wī′nō), *n., pl.* **-nos.** SLANG. an alcoholic addicted to wine.

wist ful (wist′fəl), *adj.* longing; yearning: *A child stood looking with wistful eyes at the toys in the window.* —**wist′ful ly,** *adv.* —**wist′ful ness,** *n.*

with al (wi ฿ôl′, wi thôl′), *adv.* with it all; as well; besides; also: *The lady is rich and fair and wise withal.*

with stand (with stand′, wi฿ stand′), *v.t.,* **-stood, -stand ing.** stand against; hold out against; oppose, especially successfully; resist: *withstand hardships. These shoes will withstand much hard wear.*

woe (wō), *n.* great grief, trouble, or distress: *Sickness and poverty are common woes.*

woe ful (wō′fəl), *adj.* 1 full of woe; sad; sorrowful; wretched. 2 of wretched quality. —**woe′ful ly,** *adv.* —**woe′ful ness,** *n.*

wraith (rāth), *n.* 1 ghost of a person seen before or soon after his death. 2 specter; ghost. [origin uncertain]

wrath ful (rath′fəl), *adj.* feeling or showing wrath; very angry. —**wrath′ful ly,** *adv.* —**wrath′ful ness,** *n.*

wretch ed (rech′id), *adj.* 1 very unfortunate or unhappy. 2 very unsatisfactory; miserable: *a wretched hut.* —**wretch′ed ly,** *adv.* —**wretch′ed ness,** *n.* [Old English *wrecca* exile]

writhe (rī฿), *v.,* **writhed, writh ing.** —*v.i.* 1 twist and turn; twist about: *writhe with pain. The snake writhed along the branch.* 2 suffer mentally; be very uncomfortable. —*v.t.* twist or bend (something). [Old English *wrīthan*]

yeo man ry (yō′mən rē), *n.* class of people who own land, but not a large amount, and who farm it themselves.

zeal (zēl), *n.* eager desire or effort; earnest enthusiasm; fervor: *religious zeal, work with zeal for pollution control.*

ze nith (zē′nith), *n.* 1 the point in the heavens directly overhead; point opposite the nadir. 2 the highest point; apex: *At the zenith of its power Rome ruled all of civilized Europe.*

Index of Extensions:

Index of Vocabulary Exercises:

Index of Authors and Titles